Pages of Perfection

Pages of Perfection

Islamic Paintings and Calligraphy from the Russian Academy of Sciences, St. Petersburg

written by
Yuri A. Petrosyan, Oleg F. Akimushkin,
Anas B. Khalidov, Efim A. Rezvan

with essays by
Marie Lukens Swietochowski
and Stefano Carboni

ARCH Foundation
Electa

Front Cover:
Cat. no. 39: Abū al-Qāsim
Firdausī al-Ṭūsī,
Shāhnāma ("The Book of Kings")
Folio 388r: *Iskandar Leaves in Search of the Water of Life*,
24.5 × 21.7 cm., Tabriz, 1524.
Accession no. D 184
The St. Petersburg Branch of the Institute of Oriental Studies, Russian Academy of Sciences

Pages of Perfection

Islamic Paintings and Calligraphy
from the Russian Academy of Sciences,
St. Petersburg

Musée du Petit Palais, Paris
14 October 1994 - 8 January 1995

Villa Favorita, Lugano
2 June 1995 - 12 August 1995

The Metropolitan Museum of Art, New York
15 September - 10 December 1995

An exhibition organized by the
ARCH Foundation
(Art Restoration for Cultural Heritage),
Villa Favorita, Lugano,
and the St. Petersburg Branch of the
Institute of Oriental Studies,
Russian Academy of Sciences

Catalogue

Editor
Professor Yuri A. Petrosyan

Associate Editors
Professor Oleg F. Akimushkin, Professor Anas B. Khalidov and Dr. Efim A. Rezvan

in collaboration with
Dr. Edward N. Tyomkin and Dr. Margarita J. Vorobyova-Desyatovskaya

with essays by
Marie Lukens Swietochowski and Dr. Stefano Carboni

Photography
Svetlana Shevelchinskaya
George Skachkov

Cartography
John Callanan

Translation
Christopher Freeland

Scientific consultants
Dr. Stefano Carboni
Dr. Muhammad Isa Waley

Coordination
Maria Yakimov

Exhibition

Exhibition Coordinator
Elisabeth Storm Nagy

Curators
Marie Lukens Swietochowski
Dr. Stefano Carboni

Restoration
Mark Barnard, Nadya Brovenko, Anna Skliarskaia and Olga Grigorieva

Installation design
Michael Batista
Jeffrey Daly

Technical Assistance
Katherine Daniels

Professor Doctor Yuri A. Petrosyan, Director of the St. Petersburg Branch of the Institute of Oriental Studies, Russian Academy of Sciences. Specialized in the political and cultural history of Turkey. Author of the series of monographs on the history of the Ottoman Empire as well as of the publication of the unique Turkish historical chronicle from the manuscript collection of the St. Petersburg Branch of the Institute of Oriental Studies. For many years he has supervised studies in the history of the Oriental manuscript heritage and its role in the culture of the Orient.

Professor Doctor Oleg F. Akimushkin, Head of Middle Eastern Studies Department of the St. Petersburg Branch of the Institute of Oriental Studies, Russian Academy of Sciences; Chairman of the Kurdish Studies Group of the same Branch. One of the most prominent specialists in Persian and Islamic studies. His main research fields are: the arts of the Islamic manuscript book (especially Persian, Indo-Persian, Kashmiri, Turkish and Tajiki manuscripts); Islamic codicology and textology; history of Iran, Central Asia (Maweramnahr) and Eastern Turkestan (including the sources studies) of the Mediaeval period (till the end of the 18th century) and studies on Brotherhood Persian mysticism. He is the author of more than 200 works in the above mentioned fields. All of his work is based on original sources.

Professor Doctor Anas B. Khalidov, Head of the Near Eastern Department of the St. Petersburg Branch of the Institute of Oriental Studies, Russian Academy of Sciences. One of the most prominent specialists in the Arabic manuscript heritage and Islamic culture, author of the series of research works on Arabic manuscripts from the collection of manuscripts at the St. Petersburg Branch of the Institute of Oriental Studies. For many years he has supervised the research program on the Arabic manuscript collection of the Institute. He is the General Editor and one of the main authors of the catalogue of the Arabic manuscript collection at the Institute.

Doctor Efim A. Rezvan, Executive Director of Independent Research Projects and Head of the Group of Multi-lingual Computing of the St. Petersburg Branch of the Institute of Oriental Studies, Russian Academy of Sciences. He specialized in Qur'anic studies and is the author of the series of publications connected with the history of Islam and Arab-Russian relations. He is the Head of the "Asiatic Museum Project" with the aim of establishing the computer data-base on the manuscript collection at the St. Petersburg Branch of the Institute of Oriental Studies.

Marie Lukens Swietochowski, Associate Curator, Department of Islamic Art, The Metropolitan Museum of Art, New York; Adjunct Associate Professor of Art History and Archaeology, Columbia University, 1970–1991. Studied Islamic art with Richard Ettinghausen at the Institute of Fine Arts of New York University. Her specialization is in miniature painting and drawings in manuscripts and albums, as well as other aspects of the art of the book, particularly in Iran, Turkey, and India. She has authored many scholarly publications, lectured widely, taught a variety of courses, and arranged a number of exhibitions on these subjects. As a curator of Islamic art in The Metropolitan Museum of Art, she is responsible for the later galleries, containing art from ca. 1400 on, and miniature paintings of all periods.

Doctor Stefano Carboni, Assistant Curator, Department of Islamic Art, The Metropolitan Museum of Art, New York. Graduated in Arabic language and Islamic art at the University of Venice, he completed his doctoral dissertation in Islamic art at the School of Oriental and African Studies, University of London, in 1992. In the same year, he joined the staff of the Metropolitan Museum of Art. Specialized in miniature painting and in glass, he is the author of numerous scholarly publications in the field and has lectured broadly. As a curator in the Department of Islamic Art, he is responsible for the collection of the early period, ranging from the beginning of Islam to ca. 1400, and of the Qur'an manuscripts.

The authors of the catalogue would like to express their sincere thanks to Maria Yakimov, Anne Serkova and Victoria Melentzevitch for the great help in preparations for the catalogue. Thanks also to the conservators of this project, Mark Barnard and Nadya Brovenko for their mastery and enthusiasm.

Contents

I am delighted that this exhibition offers for the first time, to all of those interested in the cultures of the Orient, an opportunity to draw closer to the treasury of Islamic manuscripts preserved in St. Petersburg and previously unknown to the general public. St. Petersburg possesses an overwhelming array of cultural treasures which represent some of the most diverse countries and civilizations and has earned the status of being one of the most respected centers for the study of Oriental cultures.

Conceived by its founder, Tsar Peter the Great, to be a city with a window to the West and open to the influences of Western European cultures, St. Petersburg prized itself on its worldly outlook on other civilizations. As the capital of the Russian empire whose land embraced the gigantic expanse of both Asia and Europe, St. Petersburg turned to the majestic East with all of the splendors of its ancient and unique cultures.

The present-day St. Petersburg could not have preserved its foremost characteristics as a culturally open-minded city for all cultures if it were not for the coming of a new political age which now lends an opening to these treasures and, again, St. Petersburg calls to its attention peoples from the most diverse cultures.

I am pleased that St. Petersburg is able to offer its Oriental treasures for display to dedicated collectors, diplomats, academics and lovers of antiquity. This exhibition is a spiritual tribute to our times, appealing to people from different cultures to aim for greater mutual understanding of themes common to all mankind and belonging to all humanity.

Professor Anatoli A. Sobchak
Mayor of St. Petersburg

More than a commitment to a friend writing this foreword is a true pleasure, for reasons which I shall try to summarize.

The ARCH Foundation is a meritorious venture per se, considering the background of its founder, Francesca von Habsburg, Archduchess of Austria. The goal of this foundation is in its name. Whereas collecting or sponsoring art are both noble and commendable, I feel that restoration, i.e. saving a cultural heritage, has a very special connotation.

In East and Central Europe countless wonderful pieces of art, often masterpieces, are left to decay, either through negligence or for lack of funds and this is why restoration is so important for coming generations.

To me this exhibition "Pages of Perfection" is especially important because it is truly unique, artistically as well as culturally and thus historically. Showing the public treasures of a world civilization, helping the institute in which these treasures are kept to conserve them, are all important tasks.

Having lived in a Muslim country in my youth, I have a particularly deep attachment to the world of Islam and hence am doubly pleased when this faith, so close to Judaism and Christianity, is shown in its rightful light. Much nonsense has been spread in the past, and more so lately, about Islam supposedly being a conquering religion, a warring one, a threat, that when one sees the exquisite beauty and the superb craftsmanship of the Islamic artist, the viewer will judge for himself.

Those who know that Islam means prostration, a surrender to God's will and hence peace and serenity, will be all the more proud of Francesca von Habsburg's exhibition, laboriously put together and presented by the ARCH Foundation.

Culture being one of the best sources of understanding among human beings, a lot can be achieved just by participating in ventures such as this one. By participating, I mean visiting the exhibition and supporting the Islamic Manuscript Conservation Project, so more projects can materialize and other forgotten masterpieces can be restored.

The quality and beauty of "Pages of Perfection" carries a message: that at some point in history there were people who thought more in terms of intellectual and spiritual achievements and aesthetics than war and destruction. Let us try hard — in this day and age — to increase their ranks!

H.R.H. King Simeon of Bulgaria
Patron of the exhibition

Honorary Committee

St. Petersburg

Professor Anatoli A. Sobchak
Mayor of St. Petersburg

Professor Vladimir Yakovlev
Vice-Mayor of St. Petersburg, Department of Cultural Affairs

Professor Djores I. Alfyorov
Chairman, The St. Petersburg Center of Science, Russian Academy of Sciences

Professor Alexander A. Fursenko
Vice-Chairman, The St. Petersburg Center of Science, Russian Academy of Sciences

Lugano

H.R.H. King Simeon of Bulgaria

Baron H.H. Thyssen-Bornemisza

Organizing Committee

St. Petersburg

Professor Dr. Yuri A. Petrosyan
Director, The St. Petersburg Branch of the Institute of Oriental Studies, Russian Academy of Sciences

Lugano

Francesca von Habsburg, Archduchess of Austria

Professor J. Michael Rogers
Khalili Professor of Islamic Art, School of Oriental and African Studies, University of London

Dr. Muhammad Isa Waley
Curator for Persian and Turkish Section, Oriental and India Office Collections, The British Library, London

New York

Dr. Mahrukh Tarapor
Associate Director for Exhibitions, The Metropolitan Museum of Art, New York

Daniel Walker
Curator in Charge, Department of Islamic Art, The Metropolitan Museum of Art, New York

Curatorial Committee

St. Petersburg

Professor Dr. Oleg F. Akimushkin
Head of Middle Eastern Studies Department and Chairman of the Kurdish Studies Group, the St. Petersburg Branch of the Institute of Oriental Studies, Russian Academy of Sciences

Professor Dr. Anas B. Khalidov
Head of the Near Eastern Department, the St. Petersburg Branch of the Institute of Oriental Studies, Russian Academy of Sciences

Dr. Efim A. Rezvan
Research Director, the St. Petersburg Branch of the Institute of Oriental Studies, Russian Academy of Sciences

Dr. Edward N. Tyomkin
Head of the Oriental Manuscript Department, the St. Petersburg Branch of the Institute of Oriental Studies, Russian Academy of Sciences

Dr. Margarita I. Vorobyova-Desyatovskaya
Curator of the Oriental Manuscript Department, the St. Petersburg Branch of the Institute of Oriental Studies, Russian Academy of Sciences

Nadya I. Brovenko
Chief Conservator, the St. Petersburg Branch of the Institute of Oriental Studies, Russian Academy of Sciences

Lugano

Elisabeth Storm Nagy
Director of Exhibitions and Chief Curator, ARCH Foundation

Gilles Chazal
Chief Curator, Musée du Petit Palais, Paris

Mark Barnard
Senior Conservator, Oriental Conservation Studio, The British Library, London

Maria Yakimov
Project Coordinator, ARCH Foundation

New York

Marie Lukens Swietochowski
Associate Curator, Department of Islamic Art, The Metropolitan Museum of Art, New York

Dr. Stefano Carboni
Assistant Curator, Department of Islamic Art, The Metropolitan Museum of Art, New York

ARCH

ART **R**ESTORATION FOR **C**ULTURAL **H**ERITAGE

The ARCH Foundation (Art Restoration for Cultural Heritage) was created in 1991 by Francesca von Habsburg, Archduchess of Austria, in response to the rapid changes that have taken place in the Greater European landscape which have presented the world community concerned with the arts with new opportunities as well as responsibilities to assist emerging democracies with all the help we can afford.

The ARCH Foundation is a non-profit organization, which actively contributes to the conservation, promotion and exhibition of the little known but unique masterpieces from the numerous and immensely rich art collections from former Eastern and Central European countries which have suffered tremendously in the last seventy years due to neglect, lack of funds and acts of war.

The ARCH Foundation is committed to helping others to help themselves, by providing them with means and expertise as well as hope and inspiration. This in turn inspires a sense of self-esteem and responsibility towards their own cultural legacy as well as that of others.

Supporting Members of the ARCH Foundation

Francesca von Habsburg, Archduchess of Austria
Baron and Baroness Hans Heinrich Thyssen-Bornemisza
Baron Georg Heinrich Thyssen-Bornemisza
Baron Lorne Thyssen-Bornemisza

Internet - World Wide Web
With over thirty million users, Internet is the largest computer network in the world.
The ARCH Foundation is taking advantage of this unique opportunity to create an awareness of its concerns and projects, especially among a broader, younger audience.
Regularly updated information about the activities and projects of the ARCH Foundation can be viewed on our World Wide Web page:
http://www.enigmacom.com/~arch/

Without invaluable support and generous donations of time, advice, services and funds, it would not have been possible to organize this international exhibition tour. The ARCH Foundation wishes to extend a heartfelt thanks to those who have sustained the foundation and its mission and contributed to the realization of this event.

Consultants

Elisabeth Storm Nagy, Lugano
Madeleine Livingston Hammond Alatas, London
Marie Lukens Swietochowski, New York
Dr. Stefano Carboni, New York
Martine Chazal, Paris
Gilles Chazal, Paris
Volkmar Enderlein, Berlin
Prof. Maurizio Pistoso, University of Bologna
Dr. Muhammad Isa Waley, London
Fidinam Fiduciaria SA, Lugano
Spiess-Brunoni & Associati, Lugano
Phase, Bologna, Florence
Swissair

Within the ARCH Foundation Islamic Manuscript Conservation Project the manuscripts listed below have been restored thanks to donations from the following benefactors:

Baron and Baroness H.H. Thyssen-Bornemisza: *The Assemblies* (cat. no. 18)

Peter Istvan Nagy: *Khusrau and Shīrīn* (cat. no. 28)

Prince Sadruddin Aga Khan: *The Book of Kings* (cat. no. 31)

David Sulzberger: *The Book of Sciences* (cat. no. 34)

Ina Piattini Pelloni: *Collected Poems* (cat. no. 36)

Ira Spanierman: *Jung* (cat. no. 40)

Foundation Max von Berchem: *Quintet* (cat. no. 44)

Nan Kempner: *The Book of Herbs* (cat. no. 49)

Samuel H. Kress Foundation: *Muraqqaʿ* (cat. no. 51)

Banco di Lugano and Unione di Banche Svizzere: *Muraqqaʿ* (cat. no. 52)

Baron Lorne Thyssen-Bornemisza: *Lailā and Majnūn* (cat. no. 59)

I am very proud to present this particular catalogue, because it is one of the first publications which clearly reflects the commitment that the ARCH Foundation has undertaken in the scope of its mission for the preservation and promotion of Central and Eastern European cultural heritage. I founded ARCH in 1991 in response to a challenging sphere of cultural interaction brought on by the rapid changes taking place within the Greater European geo-political landscape. These have opened the door to unique opportunities, which in turn have increased the responsibility of the world community concerned with the arts. It is within this framework that I feel that it is imperative to not only preserve and restore but also to exhibit this extraordinary collection of Islamic manuscripts from the St. Petersburg Branch of the Institute of Oriental Studies. They form an important link in the comparative study of Islamic manuscripts from around the world. The unique calligraphy which many of these manuscripts abound in is as rich a contribution to scholarly research as it is to reverential admiration, not to mention the unique insight we are offered into the artistic excellence and refined beauty of the magnificent miniatures which accompany many of the texts.

One of the things that has struck me most profoundly over the last few years is the honorable and vigilant approach that Professor Petrosyan has taken towards the heavy responsibility of ensuring not only the survival of the Institute of Oriental Studies in St. Petersburg during the post-Communist era, since which the Academy of Sciences institutions have lost a substantial share in the massive government subsidies they previously enjoyed, but also its outreach. He began by broadening the horizons of the Institute by exploring new opportunities that could benefit the Institute in a variety of ways, which have recently presented themselves to them due to the new relaxed political regime. It was Professor Petrosyan himself that initiated this wonderful project. I feel particularly privileged to have been invited to develop our relationship with the Institute, and to actively participate in their renaissance as one of the world's leading research libraries for Oriental studies.

To this end, ARCH is working in cooperation with the Institute on an important preservation/restoration/and exhibition project that has led us towards a triple tier result. We have determined that the natural step that follows the conservation of works of art, since the limited physical process of restoring an object to its former glory is only part of the more complete action of restoring it to its correct place and proper context, is to build around it a major international touring exhibition. Thus together we are presenting this magnificent and quite unique collection of Islamic manuscripts in prestigious locations around the world. In addition to actively fund-raising on behalf of the Institute's urgently needed restoration and modernization of its storage and reading room facilities, we are presently studying how best to digitalize the collection of Islamic manuscripts of the Institute (of which only a small part is included in this exhibition), so that researchers from around the world will not need to handle the originals on a continual basis, thereby preserving the original documents. The Institute would also benefit enormously by being plugged into the Internet system, thus putting them in direct contact with museums, research centers and universities from around the world, whilst making their own collection far more accessible. This all calls for an important investment, which is most necessary for the long-term preservation of these extremely important Islamic treasures for the future.

Such an exhibition also gives our mission a platform, and enhances our goal of introducing to the prosperous West, Middle East, and Far East an unexpected but extremely important section of the extraordinary variety and wealth of cultures that is concentrated in St. Petersburg. Nearly 300 years of voracious collecting have contributed enormously to the broad variety and richness of the cultural heritage of St. Petersburg due to the immense respect and importance given to art and science by the city's founder, Tsar Peter the Great. He built the great libraries and founded several of the museums which still flourish today. The tradition of collecting continued feverishly up until the last Tsar Nicholas II.

I cannot stress often enough the importance of appreciating and preserving the great libraries whose contents span several continents, and many centuries, going back in time to when the written word was first invented. In cultural and artistic terms the Russian Academy of Sciences, of which the St. Petersburg Branch of the Institute of Oriental Studies forms an integral part, compares in quality and in importance to the great eclectic collections around the world. Most of this huge collection is unknown to the outside world and has certainly never been exhibited to date. The ARCH Foundation is planning several other projects with the Russian Academy of Sciences of St. Petersburg in the future, in the hope of generating not only interest but also funding towards the preservation of this unique legacy.

It is also tragic that the museums in St. Petersburg are only able to exhibit only between 1 and 10 % of their holdings to the public, due to lack of appropriate space. However if one spends an energetic week in St. Petersburg, one would have difficulties to find the time to visit even a fraction of what is actually exhibited. The Mayor of St. Petersburg, Mr. Sobchack, is the protagonist of many cultural initiatives in a near impossible task of restoring the city to its former glory, and justifying its title of the cultural capital of Europe. His charisma and determination have led him to successfully turn the situation around, although it was not without pain. His task is enormous, and I sincerely hope that this project will play a modest but significant role in this process. He was so kind as to give us his full support towards its completion.

During the long years of the cold war we have learned that the promotion of cultural activities is an important step toward fostering cultural identity, freedom of expression and pa-

triotic sentiments as opposed to the dangerous impulses driven by nationalism. It is an important step to take, and a welcome one in this unstable environment of the new democracies to engage in cultural first-aid.

When I think that more than half of the world's cultural heritage has been destroyed and lost forever during this century alone, due to neglect, greed, ignorance, war and cultural holocausts, I marvel at how the immense legacy of the Russian Empire has been preserved, and partially restored, throughout the period of the Communist yoke. On occasion, other than having accumulated a substantial coat of dust, it languishes quietly, protected fervently by its keepers, waiting to be kissed back to life. What more noble mission could we dream of than extending that kiss?

Predictably, the problems run much broader and deeper than just blowing off the layer of dust. There is much to do and our work has just begun. I sincerely hope that this exhibition brings you as much joy as it did us in the preparation, but at the same time instilled a sense of responsibility in your consciousness, which appropriately inspires you to participate, in your own way, in our mission. Our efforts will be most effective as part of a common goal. A vision of Europe united in acceptance of cultural diversity, by spiritual and intellectual integrity, and by dedicated adherence to moral principles. On their part the Institute of Oriental Studies of St. Petersburg responded to our call with refreshing enthusiasm, which has led to their willingness to share with us some of their greatest treasures, their experience and their knowledge with tremendous generosity. It is now our turn to respond with mutual generosity.

Francesca von Habsburg,
Archduchess of Austria

Acknowledgments

This exhibition would simply not have taken place hadn't it been for a massive effort combined with an inspired vision by a small group of really dedicated collaborators, and I wish to mention those of particular merit.
First of all my great friend and colleague Elisabeth Storm Nagy who was with me when the Institute first showed me the bulk of the material which makes up this beautiful exhibition. Her probing mind and professional application in establishing this project, and seeing it through until its fulfillment impressed me enormously, and was much appreciated at the Institute. She has held the torch of the Foundation single-handedly on occasion, and not even the fiercest gust of wind could ever hope to blow it out. To her the ARCH Foundation owes a great deal, and I want to thank her from all my heart to have given so much, in so many different ways, to see us through our darkest hour, and into the light.
To this end I have to say that she had the enthusiastic and dedicated support of the staff of the ARCH Foundation, which include Massimo D'Onofrio, Simona Mazzuchelli, Benito Magana-Rangel, Judith Clark and especially Maria Yakimov, whose excellent professional approach to her work, coupled with an extremely pleasant and friendly disposition make her a valuable member of our staff, and I would like to take this opportunity of thanking her for her special enthusiasm towards our work at the ARCH Foundation.
I must thank Gilles Chazal, Chief Curator from the Petit Palais in Paris and Martine Chazal, who took a personal interest in the work of the ARCH Foundation.
We met a few years ago in St. Petersburg and discovered quite fast that we shared certain sensitivities. This project has given us the opportunity to explore them deeper, and it has been a genuine pleasure. It is with enthusiasm that I welcome such a collaboration.
I would like to extend a special welcome to the ARCH team to a childhood friend of mine, Madeleine Alatas. She has injected ARCH with an important business-like approach to our management. She also has been pivotal in bringing structure to our projects which has substantially improved our self-confidence for which I am truly grateful.
It is the Institute of Oriental Studies, its inspired Director, Professor Yuri A. Petrosyan and his entire staff that I thank most of all. Working with the scientists of the Institute of Oriental Studies and authors of this catalogue has left me immensely impressed with their scholarly knowledge and their passion for both their academic work and the institution for which they work. It has been a true inspiration to all of us to see how dedication to the Institute and its future has motivated employees of the Institute across the board to strive for making this exhibition and its catalogue a success. The authors Oleg Akimushkin, Anas Khalidov and Efim Rezvan have poured years of research and in-depth studies into the texts which, for the first time ever, introduces an international public to the richness of the Islamic manuscript collections of the Institute. I am deeply honored to have en-

joyed the opportunity to make the fruits of their knowledge and research available in print, and share with them the intense joy of seeing this unique material published. In the intense preparation of this exhibition we have all relied on the unfailing precision and enthusiasm of Margarita Vorobyova-Desyatovskaya and Edward Tyomkin from the Manuscript Department without whom this enormous task would have been impossible to accomplish in time. Nadya Brovenko, the Conservator at the Institute of Oriental Studies, took her professional responsibilities for the well being of these manuscripts very, very seriously — an attitude which perfectly reflects the concerns of the ARCH Foundation.

I would also like to thank Mark Barnard, from the British Library, for dedicating so much effort to the conservation of these manuscripts as Chief Conservator on this project. He has a long term friendship with the Institute of Oriental Studies, and we are extremely fortunate to be able to have the advantage of his wisdom and experience. His kind and gentle manner were extremely comforting in Russia, where things can get a little rough on the edges on occasion, and the colleagues from the ARCH Foundation always felt safe with him, which is important. We trusted him with more than just our reputation. Mark Barnard directed a one-month intense conservation program at the Villa Favorita attended by Nadya M. Brovenko, Chief Conservator, and Olga Grigorieva, Assistant Conservator at the St. Petersburg Branch of the Institute of Oriental Studies, and Anna Skliarskaia, Chief of Paper Conservation at the Library of the Russian Academy of Sciences, St. Petersburg. During this educational program the four conservators completed conservation on a series of manuscripts included in this exhibition. We are proud and grateful to them as well as to the many donors to our "Adopt a Manuscript" program which will assure the long term preservation of this valuable selection of manuscripts.

Putting the artworks that the Foundation undertakes to conserve and promote into a proper and accessible context is one of the foremost concerns of ARCH, since it is through the correct balance and juxtaposition of these works that I find that the uniqueness of much of the world's unknown treasury reaches the most varied and broad audience. I am particularly grateful to Marie Lukens Swietochowski, Associate Curator of Islamic Art, and Dr. Stefano Carboni, Assistant Curator of Islamic Art, who have successfully done so in their excellent comparative essays. Together with Mahrukh Tarapor, Associate Director for Exhibitions at The Metropolitan Museum of Art, New York, they gave us tremendous confidence with their scholarly support, and I would like to thank them for all their enthusiasm and personal contributions which helped move this project on in very much the right direction.

The catalogue text is logically and nicely complimented with the maps preceding it. To this end I would like to thank John Callanan for his technical brilliance and knowledge in producing, once again, the fine maps illustrated in this catalogue.

Electa can always be counted on for producing a beautiful catalogue, on time with good humor and a smile.

The text was translated into English by Christopher Freeland, while Maria Yakimov, Benito Magana-Rangel and Judith Clark provided invaluable assistance in coordinating editorial matters. That this catalogue is a pleasure to read is also thanks to their highly professional commitment.

I am especially proud to be associated with Leonardo Mondadori, the new owner of Electa, because I can sense in him a man of great culture, whose appreciation of the mission of ARCH is going to become a substantial pillar of support to the Foundation. I can only thank him for all the encouragement I have received from him and the "new" Electa — I genuinely look forward to developing a new and substantial relationship with the Mondadori group under his guidance and leadership.

Field-work is often a thrilling and exciting process, which forms an integral part of research and development of projects such as these. However, some locations are more livable than others, which makes the comfort, safety and friendly efficacy of the Nevskij Palace Hotel, of Marco Polo Hotels and Resorts, in St. Petersburg, an appreciated safe haven from the strains of being on location.

A special thanks goes to Professor Michael Rogers, Khalili Professor of Islamic Art, London, for having generously been available to us with profound insight, constructive criticism and advice. Also, I would like to make a special mention of David Sulzberger who gave me proper insight into the fragile sensitivities one can encounter when dealing with Islamic material, especially its sacred content; he has given me excellent advice and encouragement on more than one occasion. Many thanks go to him as well.

ARCH considers the opportunities for bringing its mission to the whole world through the Internet and integral part of its awareness campaign and has created an interactive media product in collaboration with ROYG-BIV, a new media design company inspired by Marc Brickman. Mark displays a rare combination of genius, imagination and talent, and together with Michael Keeling and Thomas Hollier, he has generously contributed all of the creative direction necessary to take the ARCH Foundation in a very exciting new direction. I am especially grateful to them for having taken this subject so much to heart, and for giving it the vision and the head start that it deserves.

I would like to thank my father Baron H.H. Thyssen-Bornemisza, his wife Tita and my brothers Heini, Alexander and Lorne to whom I would like to dedicate this catalogue as a token of my respect for their tremendous support and encouragement. Having a family that really pulled together to lend a hand when it was badly needed was really a gift from the heart. I also owe a great deal to my daughter Eleonore, to whom I gave birth at the same time as I did this project, and who spent many long hours together with me at the Institute. If what Professor Petrosyan has predicted comes true, she will become a great Orientalist.

Francesca von Habsburg,
Archduchess of Austria

The ballroom in the Palace of the Grand Duke Michael, the son of Tsar Nicholas 1st (1796–1855), now used to preserve manuscripts. Archive photograph.

Introduction

Yuri A. Petrosyan

This exhibition introduces visitors and readers of this catalogue to the fascinating world of Oriental handwritten books, of which role and importance in the history and culture of Oriental nations can never be sufficiently extolled. Among the many factors that go into making up the life of human society, it is books that reveal and transmit the essence of cultural identity. They embody the results of man's material and spiritual endeavor. In this respect, the social and cultural roles of the book among European and Oriental nations are very similar in nature. However, owing to the diversity of geography and religious persuasions in the East, books assume a far more varied form, both from the linguistic and formal viewpoints.

Numerous languages and literary forms contributed to the development of books in the Orient. They became the vehicle of several world religions: Islam, Buddhism and Christianity. Books served to consolidate the doctrine of many religious and ethical persuasions and to transmit antique and mediaeval thought. The role of the book in the cultural life of Oriental nations was so great that one can consider the handwritten book as the principal means of transmitting the cultural values of these peoples. It is in books that one finds the necessary information to build an encyclopedic compendium of Oriental culture, an essential stage in the process of mankind's cultural development. It must be appreciated that the book, originally handwritten, then printed, played a role comparable to that of tools in the complex history of human cultural evolution. The manuscript appeared in the East at different periods and among different races. For centuries it was the main repository of all kinds of knowledge and the most widely used for their dissemination. So, wisdom would have it that the feeling one has when reading and contemplating ancient manuscripts, the source of knowledge and aesthetic pleasure, is much the same as making a scientific discovery. Here, for the first time, the public is offered treasures which are normally hidden, created by people of the Near and Middle East—treasures which leave a powerful impression of the intense intellectual and spiritual life which exists in that part of the world.

The handwritten book of the Muslim East, with its wealth both material and cultural, was the result of the intelligence and artistic taste of people who constructed the civilization of Islam. In the handwritten book a host of ideas and images the roots of which go way back to the very depths of this unique source of human culture, the ancient Orient, were brought into a new social and political context—that of the young Muslim state. From there they spread to Europe, just when the latter was on the point of assimilating its ancient cultural heritage.

The Near and Middle East had a highly developed literary culture, a culture that is little known and often hard to understand now, therefore little appreciated by the vast majority. This is partially due to a lack of information and to ignorance of the fabulous wealth concealed in the scarcely accessible libraries of the world, where the rarest manuscripts—texts of which only one or two copies exist—are kept alongside numerous highly varied copies of the most popular literary works of the time. Many of these manuscripts are made by the most talented masters of calligraphy and miniature art. They are of inestimable value, comparable to works by the most renowned artists admired by modern man in museums and galleries. The destiny of these wonderful manuscripts is something quite different. There is no museum for them where admirers can go to contemplate the fusion of thought and artistic elegance. Primarily, it is the Orientalist in his research who profits from these treasures and experiences immense aesthetic pleasure in fulfilling his scientific duty. He alone can relate to the contact and union with another powerful culture, so present and yet almost nonexistent, because it is locked away in old cupboards of remote and inaccessible archives. This exhibition makes possible what would otherwise have remained impenetrable to the vast majority. It introduces the general public to the masterpieces of a collection of Near and Middle Eastern manuscripts that make up one of the world's main collections: The St. Petersburg Branch of the Institute of Oriental Studies, Russian Academy of Sciences. It took three hundred years to build up this collection, starting with the founding of St. Petersburg by Tsar Peter the Great (1689–1725). The manuscripts began to be collected through the efforts of diplomats and travelers, lovers of antiquity and Oriental culture who frequented the East. Among the many patrons to this enormously important cultural venture were several monarchs, fully aware of what was at stake. Russia shares extensive borders directly with some Oriental neighbors, and so in the nature of things, Russians were obliged to understand the often difficult languages of their magnificent cultures.

Towards the beginning of the 19th century, conditions were just right to found a center for Oriental studies in St. Petersburg. In November 1818, the Asiatic Museum was inaugurated in the St. Petersburg Academy of Sciences. Its purpose was to house Oriental manuscripts and books dealing with Oriental studies. Once it was open, the Arabic manuscripts kept at the St. Petersburg Academy of Sciences were transferred there. In 1819, it acquired a valuable collection of manuscripts in Arabic, Persian, and Turkish from Jean-Louis Rousseau, at the time the Consul General of France in Baghdad, formerly the Consul in Aleppo. There were five hundred manuscripts in the collection, some of which were extremely precious. Rousseau was all set to sell his collection to the French government, but the government had financial problems and the sale fell through. So the manuscripts were acquired by the Russian government for the Asiatic Museum through the intermediary of P.P. Dubrovskii, a famous Russian collector who had lived in Paris for a long time. In 1825, Rousseau, by then Consul General in Tripoli, sold a further two hundred manuscripts to the Asiatic Museum. These two acquisitions not only initiated a lengthy process of expanding the Museum's collection but instantly placed it among the leading museum libraries of Oriental manuscripts in Europe. Assembled by this scholar and connoisseur of rare Oriental books in the main centers of Oriental Arabic science (especially Baghdad and Aleppo), the collections of Rousseau made the Asiatic Museum the owner of a series of valuable monuments of Arabic and Persian literature, and, in many instances, unique copies. Hence, the Rousseau collection has always been the pride of the Asiatic Museum, which, even so, continued growing throughout the 19th century and the beginning of the 20th. By the end of the 19th century, the Asiatic Museum was one of the principal rallying and preservation points for the literary legacy of Oriental peoples, thanks to the contribution, often by donation, of manuscripts from a variety of Russian researchers, travelers, diplomats and philanthropists. These collectors were well aware of the cultural importance of their work, which they carried out with profound respect for the traditional heritage of Oriental peoples. Consequently, the collection expanded in its geographic, historic, cultural and linguistic scope. The largest in size and of greatest scientific value were the manuscripts from Central Asia and China, brought back by the Russian archaeological and archaeographic expeditions led by P.K. Kozlov and S.F. Oldenburg (1909–1910). In the first decades of the 20th century, the collection grew further with the addition of many manuscripts from the Near East, and from North and Central Asia. During the 1930s, a large selection of Tibetan manuscripts and woodcuts was contributed. Although a few acquisitions were made in the 1940s and 1950s, the collection was completed for the most part by the end of the 1930s. It was in 1930 that the Institute of Oriental Studies of the USSR Academy of Sciences was created in place of the Asiatic Museum. In 1951, the Institute was relocated to Moscow, but the collection of manuscripts and books remained in Leningrad. A small group of employees from the Department of Oriental Manuscripts took care of their safe-keeping and their research. In 1956, this department was transformed into the Leningrad Branch of the Institute of Oriental Studies, USSR Academy of Sciences. In 1991, it became the St. Petersburg Branch of the Institute of Oriental Studies, Russian Academy of Sciences. These changes in name had little effect on the collection of Oriental manuscripts and monographs in St. Petersburg. However, in the 1930s and 1940s, the curators of the various departments within the Institute suffered at the hands of Stalin. Many of them were sent to prison or the camps where some lost not only their cherished families and work, but their lives too. The remaining staff at the Institute were not spared either, for war broke out and Leningrad was besieged for months. Many talented Russian scientists died of cold and famine. Despite the deprivation and suffering, a handful of orientalists selflessly protected the works of art. The manuscripts are now housed in the Novo-Mikhailovskii Palace, one of St. Petersburg's celebrated buildings on the banks of the Neva. It belonged to Grand Duke Michael, the son of Tsar Nicholas I (1796–1855), a scion of the imperial Romanov family. In the course of the last forty years, researchers from the Institute of Oriental Studies of the Russian Academy of Sciences have performed an exceptionally important scholarly task, consisting of compiling catalogues and detailed scientific descriptions. To give an idea of this Herculean effort, it must be appreciated that this collection of manuscripts is one of the largest in the world. There are approximately 80,000 manuscripts and woodblock prints or xylographs, in sixty-five Oriental languages. The collection is the equal of that of the Bibliothèque nationale in Paris, or London's British Library. The labor of forty years is almost complete. More than forty catalogue volumes and manuscript descriptions have been printed. The very fact of compiling and printing scholarly catalogues of the entire collection is of capital importance in making its contents known and accessible to researchers throughout the world. This task brought a number of unique texts to light. Some have been studied and printed in the Pamiatniki pis'mennosti Vostoka (Written Monuments of the Orient) series started four decades ago by the

main editorial staff for Oriental literature of the Nauka publishing company. It was while cataloguing the collection, and more specifically the Islamic section, that the specialists accomplished the difficult task of selecting works for this exhibition.
In the category of manuscripts written in Arabic script (Arabic, Persian, Turkic, Afghan and Kurdish) there are now 9,825 items. Among the most interesting manuscripts in this series, already published by our specialists, particular mention should be made of a historical Arabic document from the 11th century by an anonymous author recounting the history of the ʿAbbasid dynasty, a historical document of the 13th century in Arabic by Muḥammad al-Ḥamawī, *Al-Tārākh al-Mansūrī* (both published by P.A. Gryaznevich); the work of an 11th-century Syrian author, Usāma ibn Munqidh, *Kitāb al-manāzil wa al-diyār* ("The Book of Halting Places and Encampments"), published by A.B. Khalidov; a Persian work by Muḥammad Kāẓim entitled *ʿĀlam ārā-i Nādir* ("The World-Adorning [Book] of Nādir"), a unique monument of Persian historiography of the 18th century, published by N.D. Miklukho-Maklai. The Arabic collection numbers almost 8,000 manuscript units which represent almost 4,000 texts. They include some of the most ancient specimens of Arabic literature, some very old copies of the Qur'an, compendiums of hadiths, and works on Islamic dogma and law, philosophy and grammar, poetry and prose, geography and mathematics, astronomy and medicine. All these manuscripts reflect the culture of the Islamic Near East, Central Asia, and the region of the Volga River and the Caucasus, that is to say, regions where the Arabic language was the literary vehicle and as such, ensured the development of the Islamic world. No less important from the historic and cultural viewpoints are the Persian and Tajiki manuscripts. The first volumes were those of the first Rousseau collection, with over one hundred and fifty Persian works. At present, this collection numbers 4,680 manuscripts representing more than 1,700 texts.
There are numerous works on the Qur'an, Islamic law, literary texts in prose and verse by mediaeval authors, treatises on philosophy, lexicography, grammar, geography, history and mathematics. Many other manuscripts illustrate the exceptional art form of the Persian miniature. The exhibition "Pages of Perfection" presents to the general public almost fifty Arabic and Persian manuscripts from the St. Petersburg Branch of the Institute of Oriental Studies, Russian Academy of Sciences. It is no exaggeration that this is an exceptional event in the long history of the collection, as it is for the curators. In choosing the works to be displayed, the curators have tried to give visitors as complete an idea as possible of the immensity of the written culture of Islamic peoples of the Near and Middle East, of the wealth of their cultural values and their artistic taste. Finally, they have attempted to show the role and place of Islam's written culture in the much larger process of human cultural evolution in general.
The Arabic manuscripts exhibited are written on papyrus, leather, parchment or paper. They cover a vast period of history, from the 8th to the 19th centuries, and a vast expanse of territory, from North Africa and Syria to Iran and Central Asia.
In regard to the Persian manuscripts, they represent the principal schools of miniature painting from the 15th to the 19th centuries: Tabriz (first half of the 16th century), Shiraz (second half of the 15th to the first half of the 16th century), Herat (end of the 15th to the beginning of the 16th century) and Isfahan (beginning of the 17th to mid-19th century). Miniatures from other artistic traditions of the 17th to 19th centuries are also presented, especially the Kashmiri school (late 18th and 19th centuries), and the Mughal school (16th to 17th centuries). The

amazing skill and fine artistic taste of the authors of these works cannot leave one indifferent, whether one is a specialist or simply a spectator open to the creativity of the world of Islam. The President of the ARCH Foundation, H.I.R.H. Francesca von Habsburg, Archduchess of Austria, with whom, for the past three years, the St. Petersburg Branch of the Institute of Oriental Studies, Russian Academy of Sciences, has had the honor and pleasure of working, demonstrated great spontaneous appreciation for these manuscripts and was immediately aware of their vital historic and cultural importance. Our close cooperation with Francesca von Habsburg dates back to the inclusion of some of our Hsi Hsia, Tibetan and Sanskrit manuscripts in the highly interesting exhibition "Buddhist Art from Khara-Khoto" (10th–13th centuries), organized by her in Lugano, Vienna and Berlin in 1993–1994, together with the State Hermitage Museum, St. Petersburg. The present exhibition, "Pages of Perfection," is a further demonstration of a relationship which, thanks to her enthusiasm, her organizational ability, and her artistic sensitivity and understanding of the cultural universe of the peoples of the East, brought together specialists from Lugano, Paris, London, New York, and St. Petersburg to accomplish a remarkable project. A major role has also been played by Elisabeth Storm Nagy, Director of Exhibitions at the ARCH Foundation, thanks to her exceptional professional qualities, her faith in the success of the enterprise, and confidence in the abilities of the St. Petersburg orientalists. We are most grateful to the Musée du Petit Palais, Paris, and especially its Chief Curator, Gilles Chazal, for hosting the first venue of this exhibition, and we are grateful for his energy and professional approach in its preparation. The St. Petersburg Branch of the Institute of Oriental Studies was honored and pleased that through the personal engagement of Mr. Chazal our first exhibition ever got its premiere in one of the most celebrated museums in Paris, allowing the inhabitants of the French capital, a remarkable center of world culture, to better appreciate the cultural universe of the Islamic peoples and to admire their originality. The involvement and participation of The Metropolitan Museum of Art, New York, in this exhibition dates back to the very early stages of its preparation. Dr. Mahrukh Tarapor, Associate Director for Exhibitions, accepted to join the exhibition organizing committee and in that capacity was consulted by the organizers. Given the exceptional quality of the material, Marie Lukens Swietochowski and Stefano Carboni, curators in the Department of Islamic Art, were asked to contribute to the catalogue with two essays. They did so by discussing the most important manuscripts in our collection as compared to material found in collections of Islamic manuscripts around the world. These essays were written by Ms. Swietochowski and Dr. Carboni after an examination of our manuscripts in Lugano. They have contributed to this exhibition catalogue in the most admirable and complementary manner. May the works exhibited in Paris, Lugano, New York and further venues, serve as a cultural reconciliation and bond between the peoples of the Orient and the West! If only that could be so, the organizers would know that their aim has been achieved.

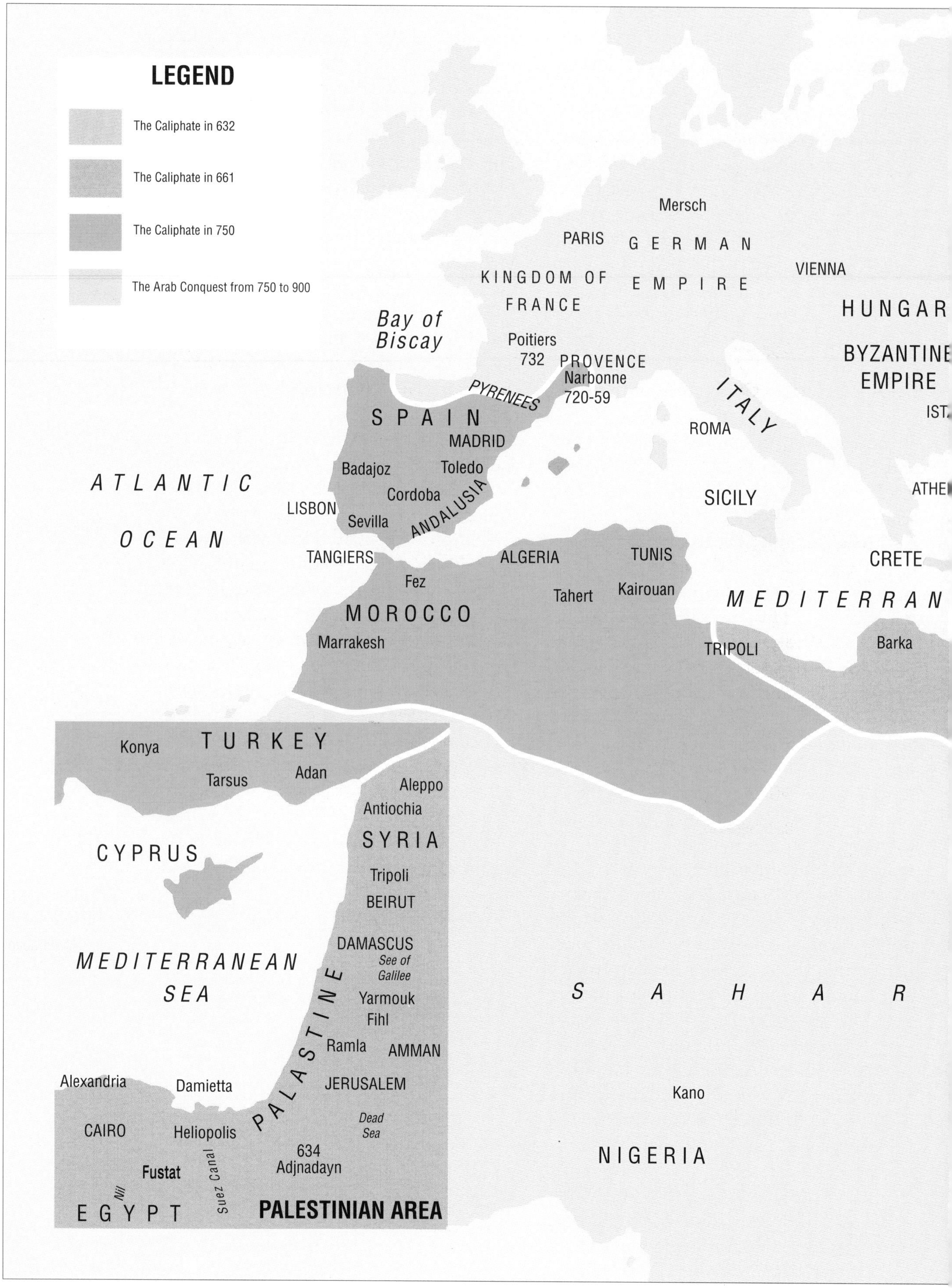
LEGEND
The Caliphate in 632
The Caliphate in 661
The Caliphate in 750
The Arab Conquest from 750 to 900
Mersch
PARIS
GERMAN
EMPIRE
VIENNA
KINGDOM OF
FRANCE
HUNGAR
Bay of
Biscay
Poitiers
732
PROVENCE
Narbonne
720-59
BYZANTINE
EMPIRE
PYRENEES
ITALY
SPAIN
MADRID
ROMA
IST.
Badajoz
Toledo
ATLANTIC
OCEAN
Cordoba
ANDALUSIA
LISBON
Sevilla
SICILY
ATHE
TANGIERS
ALGERIA
TUNIS
CRETE
Fez
Tahert
Kairouan
MEDITERRAN
MOROCCO
Marrakesh
TRIPOLI
Barka
Konya
TURKEY
Tarsus
Adan
Aleppo
Antiochia
CYPRUS
SYRIA
Tripoli
BEIRUT
DAMASCUS
See of
Galilee
MEDITERRANEAN
SEA
PALESTINE
Yarmouk
Fihl
Ramla
AMMAN
S A H A R
Alexandria
Damietta
JERUSALEM
Kano
CAIRO
Heliopolis
Dead
Sea
634
Adjnadayn
NIGERIA
Fustat
Suez Canal
Nil
EGYPT
PALESTINIAN AREA

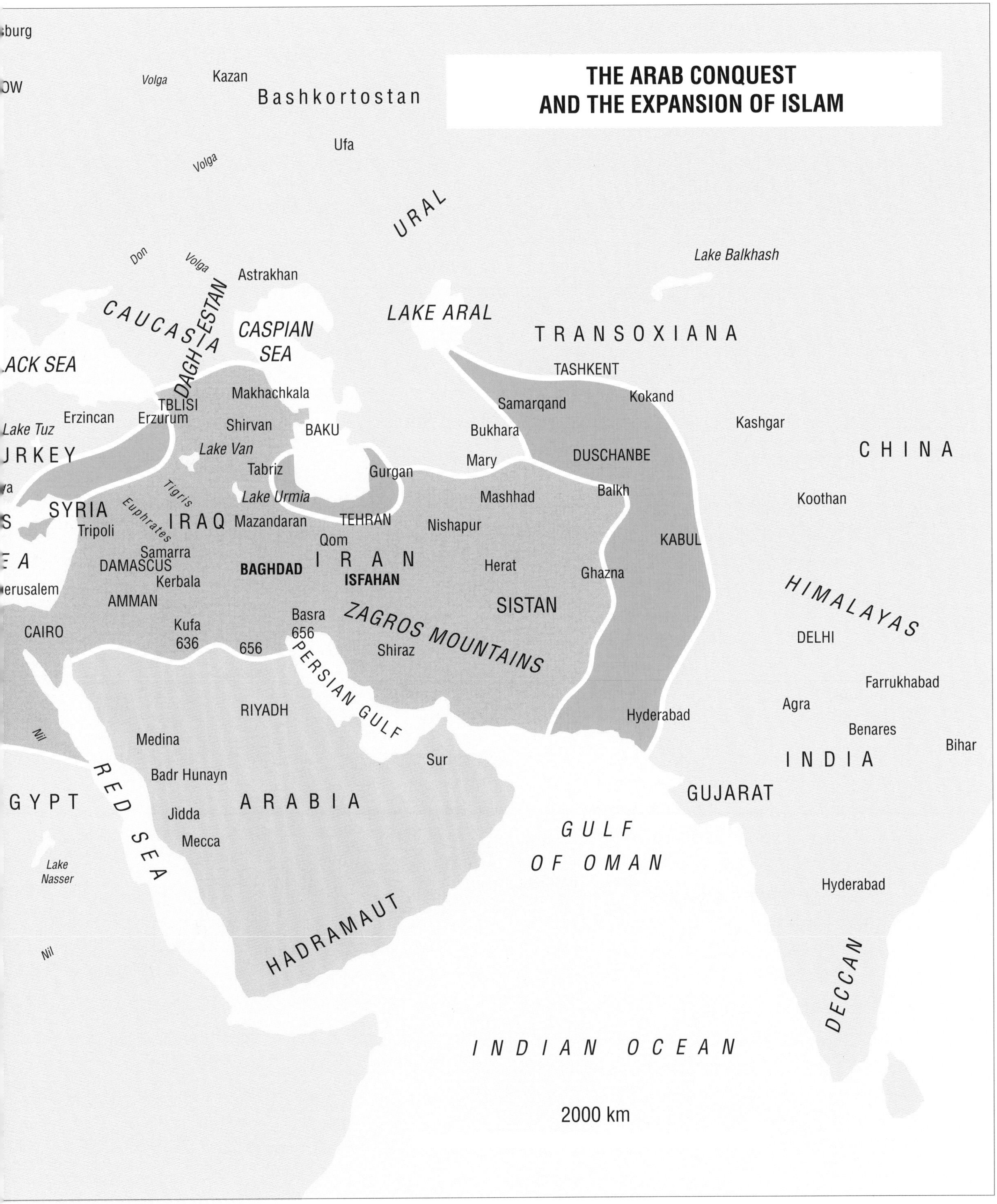
THE ARAB CONQUEST
AND THE EXPANSION OF ISLAM
Volga
Kazan
Bashkortostan
Ufa
Volga
URAL
Don
Volga
Astrakhan
Lake Balkhash
CAUCASIA
DAGHESTAN
CASPIAN SEA
LAKE ARAL
TRANSOXIANA
TASHKENT
Makhachkala
Kokand
Samarqand
TBLISI
Erzincan
Erzurum
Shirvan
BAKU
Bukhara
Kashgar
Lake Tuz
Lake Van
DUSCHANBE
CHINA
Mary
Tabriz
Gurgan
Tigris
Lake Urmia
Mashhad
Balkh
Koothan
SYRIA
Euphrates
IRAQ
Mazandaran
TEHRAN
Nishapur
Tripoli
Qom
KABUL
Samarra
DAMASCUS
BAGHDAD
IRAN
Herat
Ghazna
ISFAHAN
Kerbala
AMMAN
HIMALAYAS
Basra 656
ZAGROS MOUNTAINS
SISTAN
CAIRO
Kufa 636
656
DELHI
Shiraz
PERSIAN GULF
Farrukhabad
RIYADH
Hyderabad
Agra
Nil
Medina
Benares
Sur
Bihar
INDIA
RED SEA
Badr Hunayn
GUJARAT
ARABIA
Jìdda
GULF OF OMAN
Mecca
Lake Nasser
Hyderabad
HADRAMAUT
Nil
DECCAN
INDIAN OCEAN
2000 km

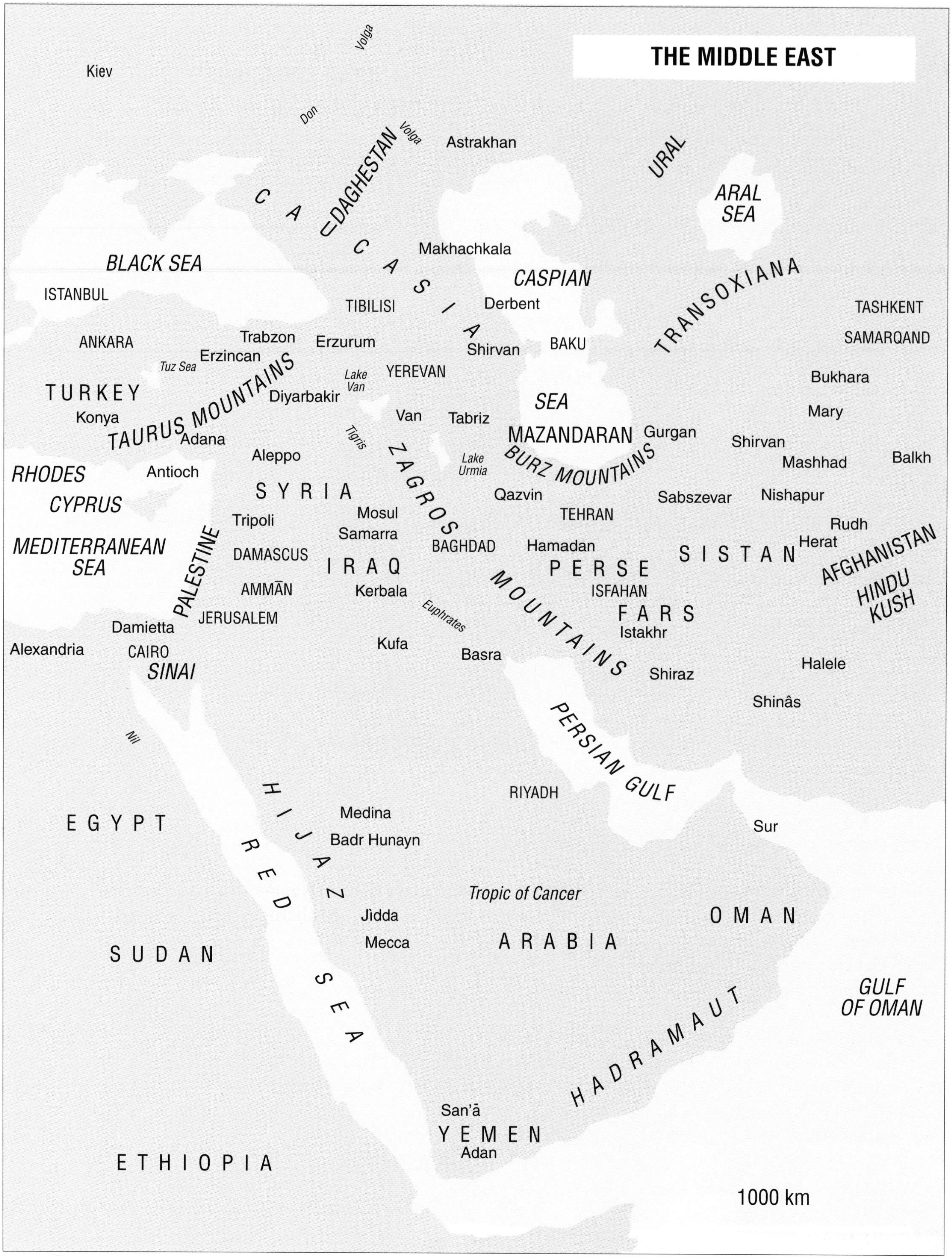
THE MIDDLE EAST
Kiev
Volga
Don
DAGHESTAN
Volga
Astrakhan
URAL
ARAL SEA
C A U C A S I A
BLACK SEA
Makhachkala
CASPIAN
ISTANBUL
TIBILISI
Derbent
TRANSOXIANA
TASHKENT
SAMARQAND
ANKARA
Trabzon
Erzurum
Shirvan
BAKU
Tuz Sea
Erzincan
Lake Van
YEREVAN
Bukhara
TURKEY
TAURUS MOUNTAINS
Diyarbakir
SEA
Konya
Adana
Van
Tabriz
Mary
MAZANDARAN
Gurgan
Tigris
Shirvan
RHODES
Antioch
Aleppo
Lake Urmia
BURZ MOUNTAINS
Mashhad
Balkh
CYPRUS
S Y R I A
ZAGROS MOUNTAINS
Qazvin
Sabszevar
Nishapur
Tripoli
Mosul
TEHRAN
MEDITERRANEAN SEA
PALESTINE
Samarra
Rudh
DAMASCUS
BAGHDAD
Hamadan
S I S T A N
Herat
AFGHANISTAN
I R A Q
P E R S E
HINDU KUSH
AMMĀN
Kerbala
ISFAHAN
Euphrates
F A R S
Damietta
JERUSALEM
Istakhr
Alexandria
CAIRO
Kufa
Basra
SINAI
Shiraz
Halele
Shinâs
PERSIAN GULF
Nil
H I J A Z
RIYADH
Medina
E G Y P T
Badr Hunayn
Sur
RED SEA
Tropic of Cancer
Jidda
O M A N
Mecca
A R A B I A
S U D A N
GULF OF OMAN
HADRAMAUT
San'ā
Y E M E N
Adan
E T H I O P I A
1000 km

The Triumph of the Qalam

Oleg F. Akimushkin, Anas B. Khalidov, Efim A. Rezvan

I am surrounded by precious yellowing parchment inscribed in austere kufic script or in the slow style of the Sinaï monks, dazzling pages of waxed paper in the luxurious editions from the libraries of the Mamluk sultans, the modest but invaluable manuscripts of scholars, the rapid scribble of their pupils and the sure, elegant but cold, soulless *naskh* writing of the professional scribes. Some pages are in perfect condition, as if their original owners have just laid them there, others are burnt or spoilt by water, traces of disasters that spared neither man nor book. Manuscripts deprived of their first and last pages, like terrifying cripples, the bleak reproach of human cruelty, it hurts to see these gaping wounds and ugly scars. They are all there, whispering: "Don't forget us! Will you be back? We have paid you a hundredfold for bringing us back to life."
(I.Y. Krachkovskii, *Concerning Arabic Manuscripts*)

At the beginning of the 7th century, Western Arabia was a land burnt by the sun, scrub desert, with rugged brown mountains, dusty trading towns and cultivated oases, a country of wandering Bedouin and caravan merchants making fortunes from commerce between the Yemen and Syria, on the road that linked Byzantium to Ethiopia and India. It was there, on the edge of the civilized world, where certain events occurred that have profoundly changed the course of history. It was the birthplace of mediaeval Islamic civilization, the link between Hellenism and the Renaissance. Towards the year 610, in Mecca, a major trading and religious center in pagan Arabia, Muḥammad ibn ᶜAbd-Allāh (ca. 570–632), a respected, wealthy merchant, an orphan and former shepherd who had experienced misery and humiliation, called humanity to a new faith acknowledging a single God. In 622, he had to flee his native town and went to Yathrib, subsequently called Medina (the City [of the Prophet]). This event, the Ḥijra, was the starting point of the Islamic era.

At the time, the world's eyes were anxiously on the mortal combat of two giants, Sasanian Persia and Byzantium. The war started in 603; it was intense and unbelievably cruel. The Sasanian success—vast territorial conquests leading to the siege of Constantinople—gave them the advantage. However, a surprise march by the Byzantium troops led by the Emperor Heraclius through Transcaucasia to the Persian capital routed Khusrau II's troops. This was decisive in world history. For many years to follow, nothing could stop the advance of the Christian world after the defeat of its archenemy, Zoroastrian Persia.

Towards 614, as the news of the Byzantine victory reached Arabia, Muḥammad announced the following: "The Greeks have been vanquished in the nearer part of the land; and, in a few years, after they are vanished, they shall be the victors.

As before and after the command belongs to Allāh and on that day the believers shall rejoice in Allāh's help; Allāh gives help to whomever He wishes; and He is the All-mighty, the All-compassionate." Qur'an XXX:2–5. (translated by A.J. Arberry, Oxford University Press, World's Classics).

Indeed, Allāh helped the Prophet consolidate his power over Arabia, and his successors, the Caliphs, created an immense state under the Muslim banner spreading from the Pyrenees to the Indus. For the first time since Alexander the Great, the West was united with the East, the Indo-Iranian universe was joined to the Mediterranean world. Destiny was to have the Arabic language—the original vehicle of the prophecies uttered by the founder of this new world religion—employed for centuries as the cultural means of expression over an immense polyglot and multi-ethnic region.

The History of the Islamic Manuscript Tradition

The love of books is one of the most characteristic traits of Islamic culture. Manuscripts were written in large numbers and the specialists themselves are not always aware of the real magnitude of this production. To stress this point, suffice it to say that in the 12th century, the largest libraries in monasteries and towns of western Europe held anything from several dozen to one hundred and fifty or two hundred volumes. Only wealthy libraries like Durham or Cluny had more than five hundred (the Pope's and the Turkish libraries most probably had more but we do not know the exact figures), whereas in Baghdad, Damascus, Cairo, Cordoba, Shiraz, Bukhara and other cities of the Islamic world, there were a series of libraries and private collections of 10,000 volumes and more in the 10th and 11th centuries. In regard to the contents of the books, Oriental libraries were a lot richer and more varied. By far the most read and recopied book in Islam, the leading Arabic book, the Book par excellence, "the Mother of Books" (*umm al-kitāb*) is the Qur'an. Jorge Luis Borges gave a very fine definition that applies only too well: "A book can be said to be a classic when a nation, or a group of nations decide to read it, over a long period of time, as if everything in it has been pondered over, inevitable, as deep as the cosmos and amenable to endless interpretation."[1] The Qur'an has played an essential role in the life of Islamic society for fourteen centuries. The origin of this book, the story of its interpretation and research, are inseparably bound to the most important stages in the development of social thought and to the most crucial historical effects. Thousands of authorities and religious thinkers, jurists and historians, covering a vast expanse from Africa's Atlantic coast to Indonesia and from the Baltic to Equatorial Africa, attentively read, comment on and analyze the sacred text (see figs. A-536, C-185, D-723). Goethe's *West-östlicher Divan*, Pushkin's *In Imitation of the Qur'an*, and many other works in world literature show that the influence of this exceptionally original monument transcends the Islamic world.

The Qur'an has probably been copied hundreds of thousands of times. Huge, sumptuous copies, tiny pocket versions (cat. no. 4), simple or richly decorated versions (cat. nos. 63, 64, 66) were created. The first copies of the Qur'an (cat. nos. 1–4) are of great interest, because they are a record of the complex process of formulating this text, the first step in the development of Arabic script and the evolution of spelling.

It is difficult to say how fast copies were made, and for how long the Qur'an was the only Arabic book, or when the second book appeared and subsequent works appeared. In the 8th century, there were already quite a few written Arabic works, whose titles and authors are known. Some books were even preserved through later copies. In the next century, authors and books were counted in their hundreds, and later, written literature took off with a wide variety of books, both sacred and profane.

Subsequently, the Arab tradition itself was inclined to trace all branches of written Arabic literature back to the 8th century and in part to the 7th century. How-

[1] J.L. Borges, *Various Years of Prose*, Moscow, 1984.

Fig. A-536. This is one of the most popular tafsīr *(Qur'anic commentaries),* Tafsīr al-Jalālayn, *written in 1465 by one of the most prolific Islamic authors, Jalāl al-Dīn al-Suyūṭī (1445–1405) who completed the work of his teacher, Jalāl al-Dīn al-Maḥallī (1388–1459).*
According to tradition, al-Suyūṭī completed this tafsīr *in forty days and it gained its popularity because of the reputation of the author. The* tafsīr *is in the school of the Islamic exegesis, traditionally known as "the Arabic Translation of the Qur'an." The appearance of works of this type was largely due to the requirements created in the spread of Islam in South and South East Asia and Africa during the later Middle Ages.*
This manuscript was copied in 1519, a few years after the death of one of the authors, al-Suyūṭī. The margins are covered with notes written by various owners and successive readers, a sign of the intense spiritual effort applied. Folios 80v–81r.

ever, very little remains of the original source documents. So, one can logically assume that profane Arabic literature began at the end of the 7th century and the beginning of the 8th century, and developed slowly. But our knowledge of this is greatly limited by the perishing of the earliest works.
The origins of Arabic literature derived from different traditions and schools of scientific thought. The discussion became more lively as material proliferated and research procedures became more refined. The two opposing approaches rely either on complete scepticism towards the data and explanation contained in the Arabic tradition itself, or on the recognition of that tradition with some reservations and modifications. The advocates of the two extremes or moderate compromises differ as to how Arabic literature developed in the intervening period (between 630 and 750). But it would appear that books were created primarily for folklore, developed well before Islam and maintained by verbal tradition (cat. no. 35). In the second instance, they served as translations of foreign works. Thirdly, they emerged as the thought of the early Islamic period.
The historic events of the 7th and 8th centuries were abrupt and profound in their effect on peoples of the Near East. Social structures were reorganized and dissimilar elements began to be integrated. In the resultant society, traditions of different cultures merged into a single entity. In this vast region, involved in the new syncretic trend that was affecting Southern Asia, North Africa and Southern Europe, Arabia played a minor role. Among its founders, Arabs formed a minority, albeit they were initially very active and privileged. But the Arabic language became an essential means of communication and expression.
The expansion of Arab power, the establishment of Arabs in new lands, particularly in towns founded by them or existing long before their arrival, the spread of Islam and the Arabic language among the most active sections of the newly colonized populations, the status of Arabic as a state language, and the completed reform of the spelling system, were all factors that went into forming the basis for the subsequent development of Arabic literature.
At the time of the Arab conquests (the late 7th, early 8th centuries), the centers

of intellectual life among Islamic communities and Arabic literary creation were Arabia, Syria and Iraq.
Poetry burgeoned, an interest in the genealogy of Arabian tribes developed, political and religious debates flared up, traditions concerning the early days of Islam began to be preserved.
Theological and legal questions were of special importance and their solution was closely related to the exegesis and application of a given Qur'anic regulation.
In parallel, attention was given to the small variants of texts between manuscripts and the different ways of reciting them.
All these issues and the linguistic situation throughout the state heightened the importance of philology and, of course, grammar.
In the discussion and solution of numerous problems facing new generations of Muslims, Qur'anic institutions were insufficient.
An additional and major element in solving these difficulties was to be found in the way of behavior, the sayings and the advice of Muḥammad.
Shortly after his death, he became a legendary figure, a model for every believer. The image of the preacher and ideal leader was renewed and modified by subsequent generations. Very early, numerous written texts and folklore dedicated to him appeared. Studies of Muḥammad became a part of the manifestations of faith, of law, of theology, historiography and Islamic literature (cat. no. 26).
Accounts of the declarations or actions of Muḥammad form an independent section of literature (cat. no. 35)—the hadiths, which is particularly precious because of the reference to an uninterrupted chain of people back to the immediate entourage of Muḥammad.
The Qur'an, its commentary (*tafsīr*, fig. A-536) and the hadiths are the basis of the Islamic concept of customs and standards in the individual Muslim's personal and social life.
The study of the law (*sharʿ*, *sharʿia*), inseparable from sunna (customs, habits) of the prophet and the community, go by the name of fiqh (knowledge) which

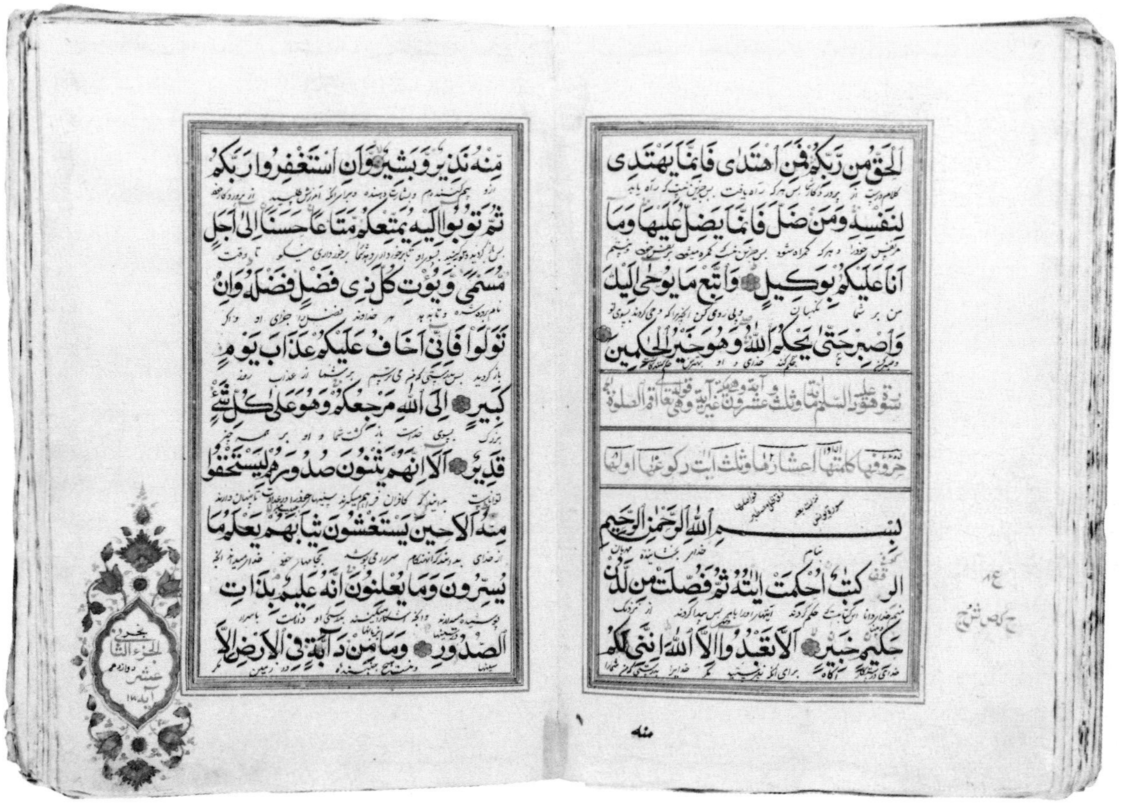

Fig. C-185. This copy of the Qur'an with a parallel Persian translation is decorated with rich, gilded ʿunvān and colored medallions. The originality of the Qur'anic text and the profound pious respect it commanded were the cause of a long-held but not always respected interdiction on translating it. However, the need of thousands of Muslims for whom Arabic was a foreign language gave rise to a tradition of paraphrased or commented translation, where an equivalent term to the Arabic word is provided. The most important thing was to translate individual words and not the entire text, which was held to be untranslatable. In Muslim dogma, this particularity of the Qur'an is manifest in the idea of iʿjāz al-qur'ān, *the miraculous and unique nature of the Qur'an both as regards its content and form. Folios 248v–249r.*

became a legal doctrine, a branch of Arabic literature that blossomed superbly (cat. no. 57, fig. C-2084).
It was forbidden to translate the Qur'an. Translation was replaced by commentary (*tafsīr*) (cat. no. 17, fig. A-536) or the word of another language was placed next to the Qur'anic text (fig. C-185), which gave rise to an original literal translation.
By way of example, there is a curious manuscript dating from the 19th century found among the Lithuanian Tatars, a Belorussian translation written in Arabic script of a Qur'anic text (fig. D-723).
As in all major civilizations of the Middle Ages, mysticism appeared in the Muslim world, on a backdrop of ancient doctrines and popular belief. In Islam, partisans of such tenets were known as sufis (cat. no. 12).
Sufism was to give birth to a distinct written tradition.
Historiography was to become a major component of Arabic literature during the Middle Ages. By origin and ideological proclivity, it tended towards dogma on the one hand and to profane literature on the other. The history of the community, expressed in the light of the acts of the leaders and wise men, is the principle subject matter. Popular Arabic traditions prior to Islam were also added, with legendary stories of ancient prophets and Persian kings. All of this gave the development of Islam an appearance of universal history. The Caliphs of Damascus and their aristocracy maintained the custom of ancient tribal chiefs and Arab kings (*mulūk*) of protecting poetry. The foremost poets of the epoch (Jarīr, al-Farazdaq, al-Akhṭal, Dhū al-Rumma) produced numerous qasidas in the ancient tradition, particularly of an eulogistic or denigrating style (cat. no. 9, fig. D-164).
Iraqi philologists and theologians translated a series of Pahlavi works into Arabic. It was for ᶜAbd-Allāh ibn al-Muqaffaᶜ (died in 759) to translate the celebrated *Kalīla wa Dimna* and several other edifying works (cat. no. 53). There is rumor that well before that texts on alchemy, medicine, astronomy and music were translated from Greek in Damascus, but it was obviously a legend cre-

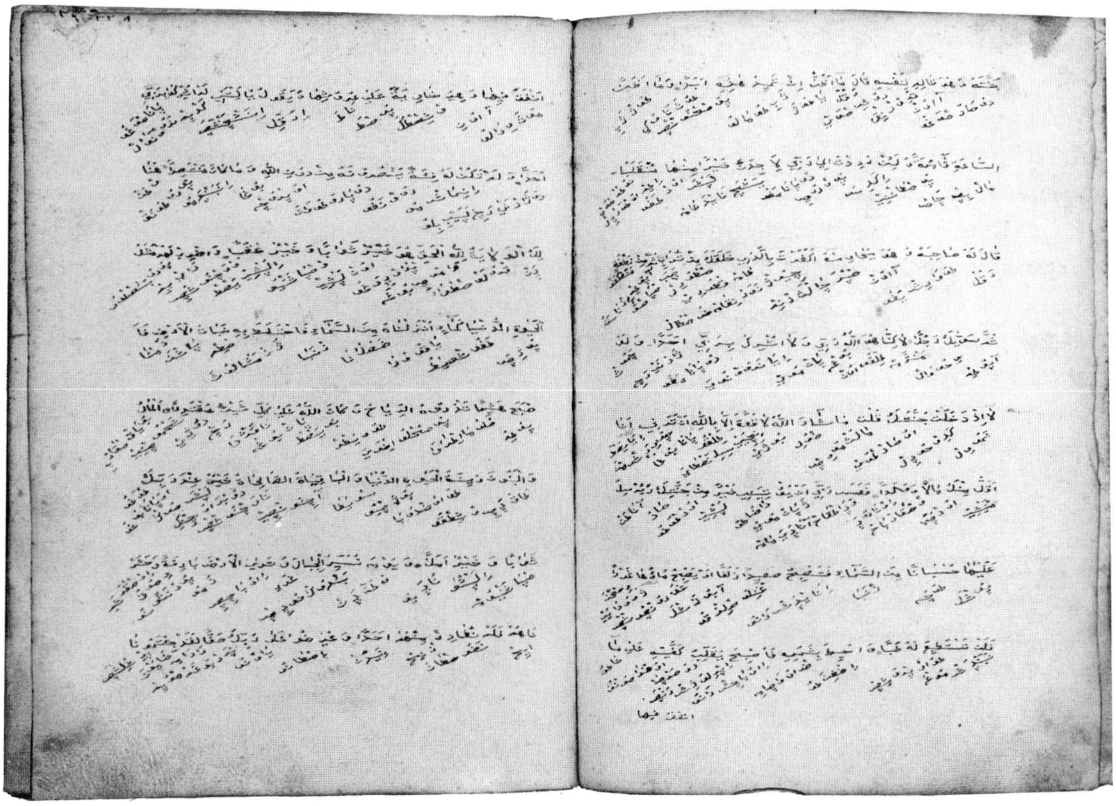

Fig. D-723. This copy of the Qur'an with its Belorussian translation in Arabic script below the text is rare proof of an original tradition that developed in the 18th and 19th centuries among the Tatars of Belorussia and the Baltic states. Folios 240v–241r.

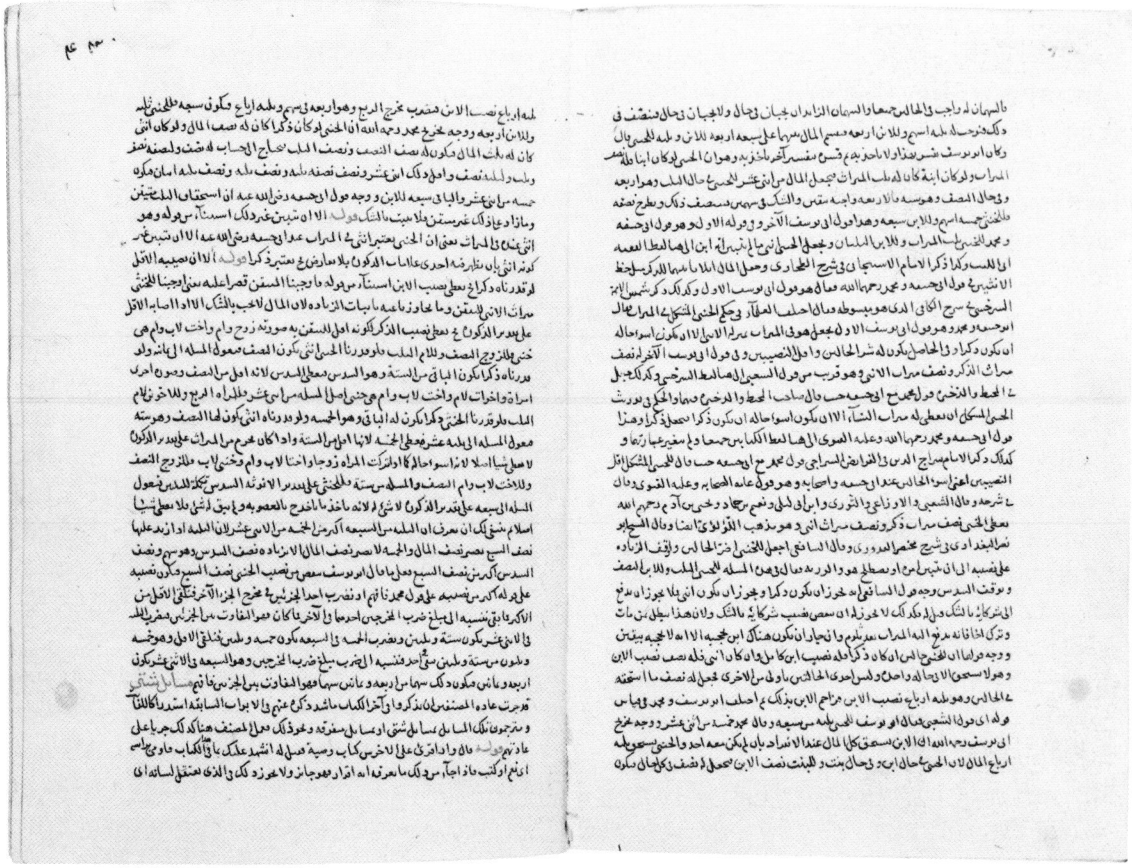

Fig. C-2084. This manuscript, dated 1444, relates to religious law (fiqh): it is the commentary of Amīr Kātib al-Ikānī on al-Hidāya ("The Direction") *of Burhān al-Dīn al-Marghīnānī, one of the main authorities of Central Asia in the 12th century. The calligraphy is mediocre. Folios 429v–430r.*

ated later. Such was the first stage in Arabic literature. It covers a period of a little more than one hundred years (610–750): the era of Muḥammad, the reign of the four Caliphs in Medina and the Umayyad Caliphs of Damascus—in short, the formative period of Arab power. However, it is extremely difficult to estimate the quantity of this initial written output, as it has almost entirely been absorbed by subsequent literature (except for poetry, the Qur'an and a few translations), leaving behind only names, titles, citations and memoirs.

Arabic literature really came into its own during the time of the ᶜAbbasid dynasty (750–1258) in Baghdad. The mid-8th century was an extremely important time in the development of the Muslim state and society. The advance made by Arab troops was halted for a hundred years. While conquering campaigns were replaced by internal fighting, the frontiers of the Caliphate were calm.

Given that, in principle, all Muslims enjoyed equal rights, conversion to Islam and the arabization of extensive stretches of territory soon started. In less than one hundred years, the local population no longer distinguished itself from the Arabs. A new cultural identity based on Islam and the Arabic language took over from the Hellenistic tradition.

Right from the beginning, the role of knowledge was emphasized as one of the conditions of faith in Islamic teaching. This contributed to the early and intense development of philological and theological disciplines. Men originating from different ethnic and religious communities, converted to Islam and speaking the Arabic language, sat beside Arabs in their studies. In the initial stages of the ᶜAbbasid dynasty, the intellectual influence of men who were neither Arab nor Muslim again rose abruptly. They were often better trained. The traditional branches of knowledge were not only extended but modified.

Another characteristic of this initial ᶜAbbasid period at its beginning was the intensity of translation activity. To begin

Fig. D-164. This manuscript contains the divan (collected poems) of the Arab poet Ghiyāth ibn Ghawth al-Akhṭal (died in 710), of the Taghlib tribe that had long since settled in Iraq and converted to Christianity under the Sasanians. From a very early age, he became a professional poet, earning his living by composing complimentary verse in honor of influential dignitaries of the Muslim aristocracy in Basra and Kufa. It was no doubt in search of better pay that he went to Damascus, the capital city at the time. He managed to win the confidence of representatives of the ruling Umayyad dynasty. A Christian, he did not hesitate to lambast Muslim adversaries who took the Umayyads to task for their secular approach to governing, and he accused his opponents of betraying the ideals of Arabic Islam. Renowned as the "Poet of the Umayyads," al-Akhṭal especially glorified Yazīd ibn Muʿāwiya and ʿAbd al-Malik ibn Marwān. He boasted of being a Christian, wearing the cross, drinking wine and disparaging Islam, its institutions and ritual, etc. The text of this manuscript, backed by the authority of Arab philologists spanning several generations between the 9th and 11th centuries, is masterfully copied. It is an example of two styles of writing: large thuluth *for the poems of al-Akhṭal, and a stylish medium-size* naskh *for the explanatory notes. There are diacritical marks and the vocalization is meticulously and correctly traced. There is no doubt that it dates from the 13th century. Folios 28v–29r.*

Fig. A-1517. This manuscript of the 14th century from Lebanon (Ṭarābulus, 1347) is a work on psychology entitled Mafraḥ al-nafs *("Spiritual Joy"), written by Badr al-Dīn Muẓaffar, the son of the qadi of the city of Baalbek (13th century). It demonstrates the interest that the intellectual Muslim of the 13th century had in ancient studies of the nature of the soul. Folios 28v–29r.*

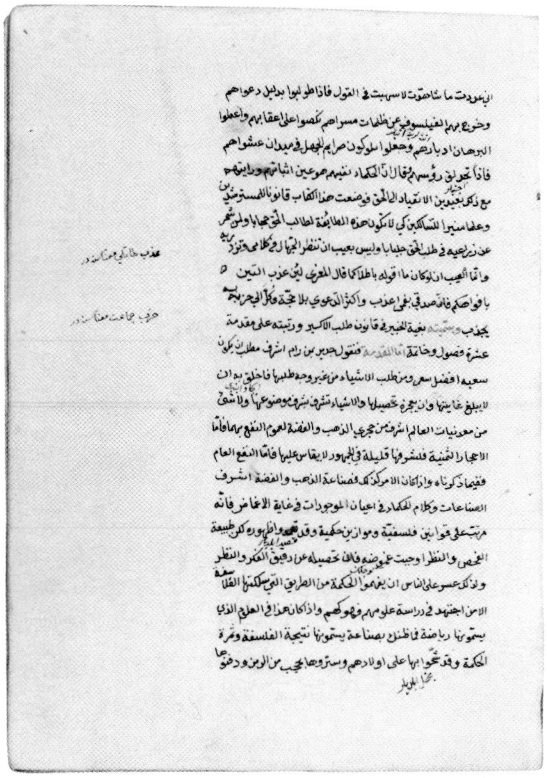

Fig. B-1066. This manuscript of mediocre quality, dating from 1675, contains a collection of magical and cabbalistic treatises by Aydamīr al-Jildakī (died in 1342 or in 1360–1361). Folio 24r.

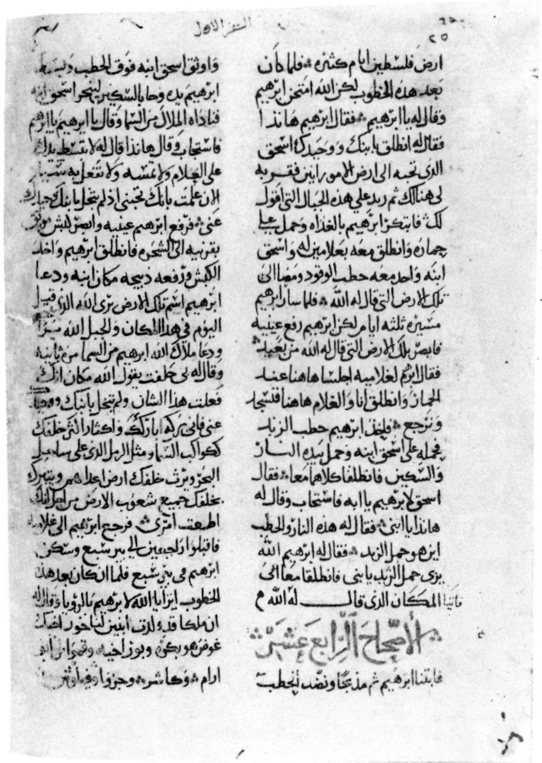

Fig. D-226. This manuscript, copied in Damascus in 1235–1238, contains one of the first drafts of the Bible in Arabic, written in Antioch in 1022. It is the famous original manuscript of the Arabic translation of the Bible belonging to the Vatican, which served as the basis for the Roman edition of 1671. It is decorated with figures of the Evangelists and written in ink. Folio 16v.

with, there was a predominance of manuscripts that had been available to the Persian elite before the Arab conquest, which needed to be translated: edifying works, scientific and general philosophic treatises, most of which had been translated in turn from Sanskrit, Syriac and Greek to Pahlavi. Thanks to the work of the translators, there was a linguistic transformation of immense scope covering knowledge inherited from former civilizations. Arabic philosophy, psychology (fig. A-1517), geography, mathematics, astronomy, musical theory, alchemy and other occult sciences (fig. B-1066), medicine, veterinary art, pharmacopoeia, botany, zoology, mineralogy and several other sciences find their sources in the translated works of Aristotle, Euclid, Galen, Hippocrates, Dioscorides, Ptolemy, etc. The Arabs had the opportunity to fill the role that the Greeks had formerly filled in many domains (cat. nos. 14, 49, 50). For the most part, the translations were subject to a little reworking with a mixture of a specific Islamic content, and then incorporated into new works of Arab authors.

From the 8th century on, the holy servants and monks of Christian communities from the West started to translate the Bible, the Gospels, the Psalms and works of the Church Fathers into Arabic (cat. nos. 8, 48; fig. D-226).

Little by little, the number of authors who wrote in Arabic increased along with their commentaries on the Bible, works defending Christian doctrine and its foundations, polemic treatises countering heresies and arguing against Islam, spiritual, and historical works on the Church.

The Jewish communities in the Caliphate came under the sway of the Arabic language and literature. A large number of Hebrew authors started writing in Arabic, and later in Persian; however, they often used their own alphabet, citing Arab works in transcriptions and translations. This tradition lasted for several

centuries (cat. nos. 27, 55).
Over a period of three centuries, the main themes of Arabic works were determined, the catalogue of works was established and contained a substantial number of books. To begin with, production was concentrated in the ancient Arab centers (Medina, Basra, Kufa, Damascus and Baghdad). Later, the cities of Iran, Afghanistan and Central Asia gained in importance (Nishapur, Merv [Mary], Bukhara, Samarqand, Balkh, Bayhaq, Herat, Ghazna, Rayy, Shiraz, Hamadan, Isfahan, etc.). The most important centers were Mosul, Wasit, Homs, Aleppo, Jerusalem, Cairo, the towns of the Maghrib (Kairouan, Tiaret, Fez) and Andalusia (Cordoba, Sevilla, Toledo, etc.). Without a shadow of a doubt, Baghdad remained the main center.
It is important to stress the unity of the written tradition that developed. It was not just a matter of linguistic hegemony and the structure of the state. On the contrary, the unity of the state started unravelling in the 9th century, and in the hundred years that followed became wholly illusory. Nevertheless, the written tradition continued and manuscript production was unaffected by the ill-defined and unstable frontiers created by the feudal states.
Baghdad remained the cultural and literary capital of the Islamic world from the second half of the 11th century to the middle of the 13th century, at the very time when its own political status was at stake. With the march of political history, cultural centers multiplied. Some cities flourished, whilst others declined. The Crusades, the reconquest of Spain and the Norman victories in the Mediterranean reduced the territory of nations dependent on the Muslims, and the Islamic culture in Sicily, Syria-Palestine and Northern Spain also began to decline. To the east, the Ghūrids (about 1000–1215) perpetuated a policy, initiated by their predecessors, of moving into India. They converted the Indian population to Islam, and in doing so extended the field for Arabic language and its literature. The same phenomena occurred in certain areas of Central Asia, the Caucasus and Asia Minor.

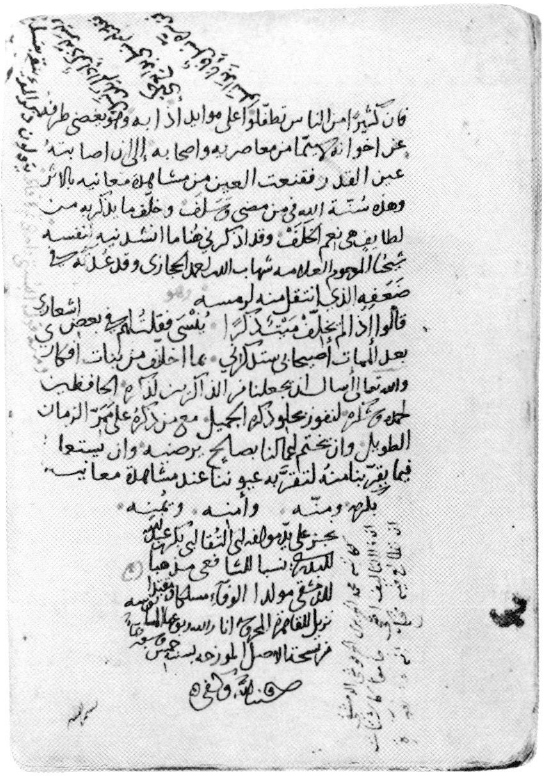

Fig. A-327. The manuscript contains a kind of anthology assembled by Abū al-Tuqā Abū Bakr ibn ʿAbd-Allāh al-Badrī al-Dimashqī between 1470 and 1471. He gathered together all sorts of observations and opinions, from the anatomical to the poetic, concerning the human eye. The example shown here is a copy the author made himself. It is interesting for two reasons: first, as a rare copy of a rare work and secondly, as an example of reworking by the author himself. Further special studies of and comparisons with analogous works would be necessary to better evaluate the contents.

Given its extensive range of subject-matter, the fiqh played a great role in literary production. This production, in no uncertain measure, was instrumental in the establishment of various academic institutions and gave rise to a particular form of fiqh.
The work of the law schools, *madhhab*, was considered to be fundamental and became very widespread. Anthologies also achieved a substantial importance (figs. A-327, B-99, C-371), along with the biographic dictionaries that provided a vast amount of information concerning religious leaders, poets, scholars, and others who were to play a role in the history of Islamic culture in the West (fig. C-2387).
At that time, translations into Arabic were very rare. Interest in the literary and scientific works of countries and peoples outside of the Muslim world was diminishing. On the other hand, Arabic books were the richest in infor-

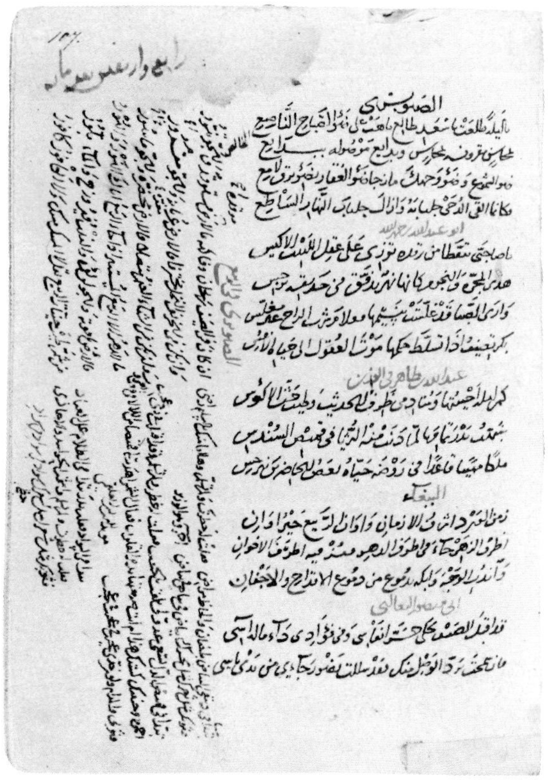

Fig. C-2387. Dozens of biographic dictionaries have provided us details on several thousands of personalities through the history of the Muslim East. This is a biographic dictionary compiled in the 12th century in Khwarazm, Central Asia. The name of the author, Abū al-Karam ʿAbd al-Salām ibn Muḥammad al-Khwārazmī al-Andarashānī was revealed when analyzing the text. This copy is of great interest because of its date and provenance and because it is unique. The mediocre calligraphy is probably by the hand of the author. Folios 20v–21r.

Fig. B-99. An anthology of prose and poetry, dated 769/1367–1368, collected and transcribed personally by Manṣūr ibn Muḥammad al-Shanbakī al-Asadī. No further copies are known. Only further textual investigation will reveal whether the contents have rarity value or constitute an example of literary trivia.

mation, and were being translated in substantial quantities: into Persian and Turkish for use within the Islamic community, and into Hebrew and Latin for use outside the community. The European Renaissance would have been inconceivable if it were not for the great epoch of translation which was to give European scholars and scientists access to the discoveries of Islamic civilizations.

Many events in the period from the second half of the 13th century to the 15th century further restricted the area where Arabic was used, limiting the scope of literary and scientific activity in Arabic. Arabic books disappeared in vast quantities. Elsewhere, the Muslim victories over the crusaders and Mongols conferred greater importance to Egypt and Syria as cultural centers. Many scholars from the Western regions of the old Caliphate, from Andalusia to the Maghrib, migrated there. Several generations later, however, when the Mongol leaders in Iran and the Golden Horde converted to Islam, the traditional branches of theology, science and Arabic literature rekindled. The advances in the exact sciences and medicine were remarkable. But this led to a further breakdown in spheres of influence between Arabic, Persian and Turkish. Arabic remained the language of the Qur'an and its related disciplines, hadith, fiqh, dogma, exact and natural sciences, Arabic philology and didactic material for the madrasa, as well as all compilations based on early texts. General topics in the field of social thinking, literature and historiography were written in languages other than Arabic in those Muslim countries where the population was not Arab. Even scientific and theological works were frequently drafted in Persian and Turkish, or accompanied by a translation or commentary in those languages. However, most educated people spoke Arabic and were able to read it.

In the 16th and 17th centuries, the Near East and North Africa were absorbed by the Ottoman Empire. Only the sultans of Morocco, the Sharif of Mecca, and, at certain periods, the dynasties in the south of Arabia remained relatively independent. In the remaining sections of the Islamic world, the Iranian Safavids and the empire of the Great Mughals exercised their domination. There were semi-independent dynasties in the region of the Caspian Sea, the Black Sea, Central Asia, Afghanistan, India, and Equatorial Africa. The pressure of European states gradually pushed Muslim lands into becoming colonies or semi-colonies.

In this environment, Arabic literary activity flourished with the same impetus as before, at least in regards to the copying of texts. The geographical spread of Arabic manuscripts expanded, thanks to the Turkish conquests in Europe (in the Balkans), the spread of Islam in India, the commercial and missionary activity of the Ottomans and the Maghribians in Africa, and that of the inhabitants of the Hadramawt in the Indian Ocean basin and especially in Indonesia.

Copying of manuscripts and their use in teaching continued, even in countries which fell under the colonial domination of European powers.

It is best to discuss separately the culture in the Arabic language which existed in the northern Caucasus. There, as I.Y. Krachkovskii writes, "for several centuries, Arabic was the only language, not just for science but also in business. An original tradition developed in this language, producing jurists, historians and local poets. A living literature arose from a dead language, and resounded among the races, a vibrant means of communication."[2]

In our collection, there is an interesting series of about 328 manuscripts from Daghestan. One of them relates to the memories of the comrade in arms of Imām Shāmil (1797–1871), for many years the leader of the Muslim resistance against the Russians in the Caucasus (fig. A-710).

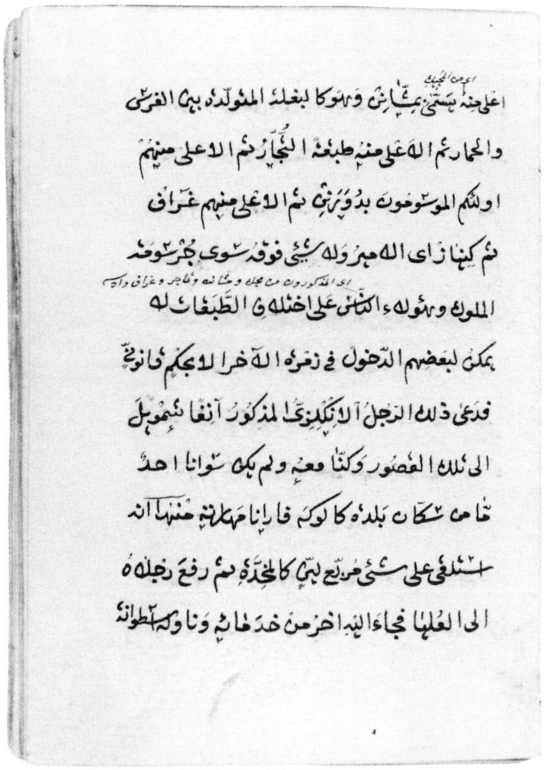

Fig. A-710. This manuscript contains the memoirs concerning Shāmil and the Caucasian War of 1830–1859, when the peoples of Daghestan and the Chechens tried to defend their independence. It was written by ʿAbd al-Raḥmān ibn Jamāl al-Dīn ol Ghāzīqumukh, the comrade in arms and the son-in-law of Shāmil whom he accompanied into captivity at Kaluga in 1864–1865. Additions in the margin were made in 1882–1883. It is a fine example of the Daghestan style of writing. Folio 74r.

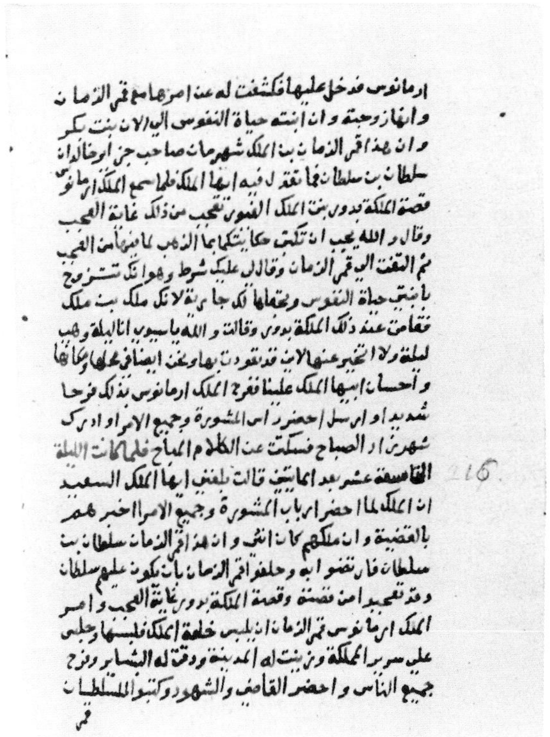

Fig. B-1114. The Thousand and One Nights *is the most common and most faithful symbol of popular Arabic literature. This late and voluminous manuscript is one of the versions of the work, dated 1804, from Egypt; it is witness to a living and original cultural tradition, hundreds of years old and now a symbol of Oriental Islam. Folio 493v.*

[2] I.Y. Krachkovskii, *Concerning Arabic Manuscripts. Memories of Libraries and People.* t. I, Moscow-Leningrad, 1955, p. 119.

Fig. B-876. This manuscript contains a manual on medicine by a court physician of the Caliphs in Baghdad in the 11th century, Ibn Jazla (died in 1100), entitled Minhaj al-bayān fī mā yastaᶜmiluhu al-insān *("Methodical Exposition of What Should be Used by Man"). Dated 587/1191, it most probably comes from Baghdad and is a good example of archaic calligraphy. Folios 195v–196r.*

Generally speaking, judging by its content, the production by hand in the later period, 16th–18th centuries, slowed considerably compared to previous times in the Islamic world. In the best of circumstances, previous levels were achieved and production maintained. In comparison to Europe at the time, there was a decline. The development of the Islamic manuscript ended in the 19th century. It was replaced by the printed book and a new form of literature. However, the printing press did not spring into instant life. To begin with, there was lithographic printing, a stage in the transition to the typographic process. One can imagine that the masters of manuscript writing who executed the orders of lithographic press owners played a major role in slowing this evolution.

How many manuscripts were produced in the Muslim East? Research indicates that in each of the vast regions of Iraq, Egypt, Syria, Spain, Iran, Afghanistan, Turkey, and the southern ex-USSR, almost half a million manuscripts were created up to the beginning of the 20th century. For North Africa, Arabia and the Indian sub-continent, the figure may be about 200,000 for each region. The total number of manuscripts that have existed is thus close to five million. Today, however, only 630,000 manuscripts[3] survive and it is unlikely that research will substantially modify that figure.[4]

Two-thirds of these manuscripts are copies—in some cases by the authors—dating from the 17th to the beginning of the 20th centuries when the production of printed books in Arabic script (fig. B-1114) finally took over. As a result, only two hundred thousand[5] manuscripts have come down to us from the Islamic Middle Ages.

Authors and Pupils

Of the many specialists of hadith, jurists, theologians, historians and philologists whose works survive, most were wealthy Muslim citizens. Doctors and philosophers, specialists of exact and natural sciences were mainly rich citizens of Christian or Jewish belief, whilst others were Muslim. The poets formed the most mixed social structure, hence the art of amateur verse writing became

3 The following items are examples in the collection of the Institute of which only one copy exists today: the collection of Ibn Quzmān's poems (died in 1160) (cat. no. 19), the anonymous history of the Caliphs to the beginning of the 11th century (cat. no. 16), *The Book of Halting Places and Encampments* by Usāma ibn Munqidh (died in 1188), made while the author was alive (cat. no. 13), attached are more than 40 unique texts, including some late versions. Sometimes, the unique copy is the author's own manuscript. In our collection, among several dozen of such Arabic manuscripts, mention should be made of a work on rhetoric by al-Muẓaffar ibn Muḥammad ibn al-Muẓaffar al-Manbijī, handwritten in 1240; *The Delights of the Eyes* by Abū al-Tuqā Abū Bakr ibn ᶜAbd-Allāh al-Badrī al- Dimashqī (fig. A-327), written in Baghdad, 1367–1368; and a treatise on fiqh, *The Key to Happiness* by Kamāl al-Dīn ibn Asā'ish ibn Yūsuf al-Shirvanī (1510–1511) (Accession no. C-1436).

4 A.B. Khalidov, *Arabic Manuscripts and the Arab Manuscript Tradition*, Moscow, 1985, pp. 254–255.

5 O.F. Akimushkin, *An Appraisal of the Persian Manuscript and its Creators. A Study of the Cultural History of Medieval Iran. Writing and Literature*, Moscow, 1984, p. 10.

widespread. The professional poets were also from varied backgrounds, from aristocrats to unconventional individuals.
In the court of nearly every Caliph, sultan or emir, there was a group of poets, biographers (cat. no. 22), doctors (fig. B-876), astrologers and soothsayers. The relations of lay rulers was more complex with theologians, authors of works on fiqh, hadith and sufism, who never tired of proclaiming their refusal to participate in the processes of secular power and their opposition thereto. The quantity and quality of writers at the courts were an indication of the relative power of the Islamic world sovereigns, who frequently enticed specialists away from the other courts.
Men of letters were always prepared to seek more generous protectors (fig. C-306). Viziers, generals, governor generals and other elevated dignitaries imitated their overlords. It was reported that at the court of the ᶜAbbasids in the 11th century translators enjoyed exceptionally favorable conditions. It is said that the Caliph al-Ma'mūn gave Ḥunayn ibn Isḥāq the equivalent weight in gold of the works he had translated. Under the next Caliph, al-Muᶜtaṣim (833–842), Ḥunayn ibn Isḥāq was appointed head translator and was given three rooms in the Caliph's palace at Samarra, where he was provided with everything he needed.
However, authors and men of letters did not always, and far from it, achieve prosperity and well paid positions in the bureaucratic hierarchy. Under the influence of ascetic tendencies in the early days of Islam, and later with sufi doctrines, a modest and morally strict lifestyle was expected of such specialists. They could maintain their independence from powerful patrons, working in solitude, and a form of pious opposition. Many works were written free of charge and without dedication by experts in hadith, jurists and theologians. Most books on medicine, exact and natural sciences, military art, other applied disciplines, and official historiography were, however, created with the direct support of the powerful patrons and dedicated to their protectors.
The sheer volume of literary works by certain authors is noteworthy. It was not uncommon to find several dozen works by one author. There are even some who produced far more.
Before Islam and at the beginning of the Islamic period, oral transmission was the only way to guarantee the conservation of information and to pass it on.
It seems quite probable that, at that time, conservation and correct transmission of information became the business of a special category of persons entrusted and esteemed by society. The system of documenting information provided by the story-teller strengthened with the advent and subsequent development of writing. The recording of texts gained recognition slowly, overcoming distrust. From a certain moment the expert was authorized to recite information from a written text and not have to rely solely on his memory.
When a pupil was studying the works of

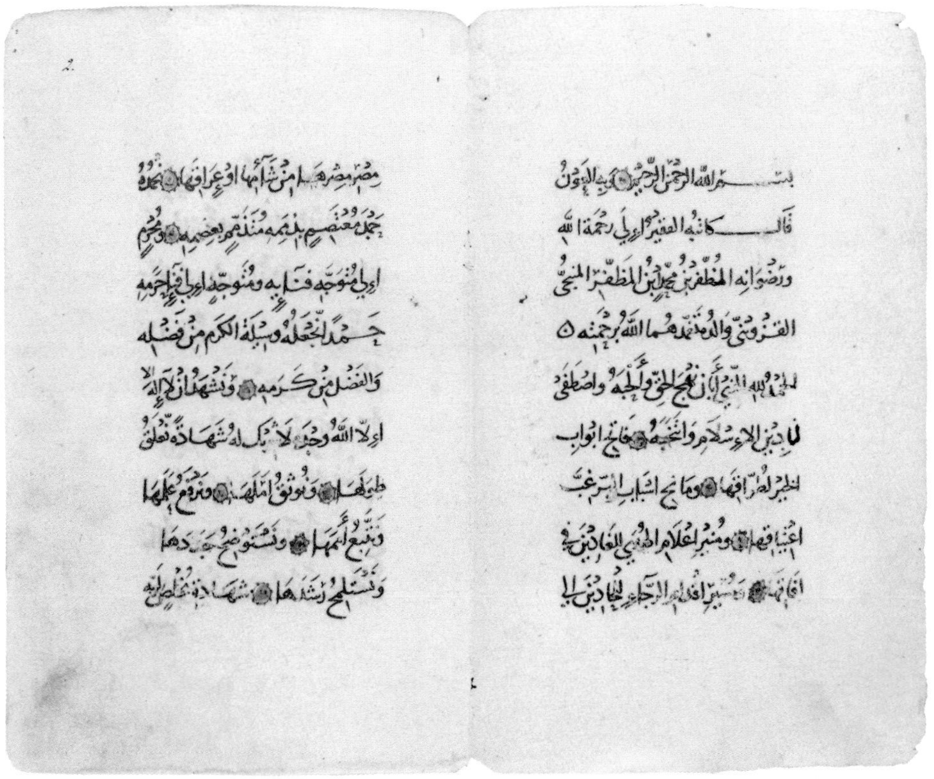

Fig. C-306. This manuscript, written in the 13th century, contains the work entitled Tabyīn al-manāqib ("*The Explanation of Merits*"), *dealing with principles of rhetoric and poetry. The author and copyist, al-Muẓaffar ibn Muḥammad al-Manbijī al-Qazvīnī, dedicated it to one of the dignitaries in the service of the Ayyubid dynasty (founded by Saladin). Folios 1v–2r.*

famous authors he normally made a new, but exact copy of an original text and then requested and received permission (*ijāza*) from his teacher to transmit the text himself (*riwāya*). With this permission, he could legally cite this work orally and copy it in writing, as well as teach it to others. The process of copying and reading with the teacher was referred to as "reading," "listening," "authorization" or simply "coming from." In any case the "right to transmit" (*ḥaqq al-riwāya* or *al-riwāya*) from the teacher was essential.

There were numerous rules to be observed by "the one dictating" (*mumlī*), as well as by "the one requesting the dictation" (*mustamlī*). "The one dictating" must be carefully prepared, in his apparel and his affairs, first brushing his teeth, cutting his nails, then his mustache, smoothing his hair, putting on white clothing, tying his turban carefully, brushing his beard, using perfume, then checking himself in the mirror before going soberly to the meeting (*majlis*). He should prevent those already seated from rising to greet him, address those listening gently, invite everyone to be quiet, speak in an audible voice, mention the name of the person at whose feet he studied and go back along the line of transmitters to the original preceptor. He should only pronounce the hadith in the presence of reliable people, preferably a celebrated hadith, easy for simple people to understand, useful for the fiqh, encouraging goodness, prayer and moderation. He must explain difficult words and obscure expressions, not speak of what he does not understand, avoid tiring those listening. He should close the meeting with stories or anecdotes, then with songs and poems.[6] The number of books studied and the reputation of his pupils served as a yardstick to judge the quality of instruction and authority of a particular scholar.

Teaching and studying were not subject to any legal formula and there was no diploma. But it is amusing to note that the origin of the term "baccalauréat" (*bi-ḥaqq al-riwāya*), used in Western European universities,[7] came from "the right to transmit."

Copyists and Merchants

Copyists can be divided into two groups: professionals, and amateurs who copy on their own initiative, either by necessity or out of personal interest. "The work of a copyist is a miserable, cursed profession; my life has been ruined by it. While alive, I starve, and when dead, I will have no shroud." So wrote Abū Ḥātim, who worked as a copyist in Nishapur[8] for fifty years. Despite that, we have reason to believe that the work of a copyist was considered one highly qualified and remunerative in line with the artistic professions.

For centuries in the Muslim East, the demand for books was high. This calling employed a host of professionals capable of copying rapidly and carefully. This army of copyists was recruited by diverse means. However, to become a professional copyist, it was not sufficient merely to be educated. One had to copy fast, in a legible and elegant hand, comprehensible to the reader. Unfortunately, we cannot say with certitude today how the average copyist was trained, but we do know how the elite, the masters of the art of writing, studied. It must be stressed, however, that the vast majority of books was produced by average copyists and not by the elite master calligraphers.

In the state chancelleries another professional group was working alongside the copyists—the secretaries. Legends abound of their ingenuity, their finesse and degree of knowledge. Although we are not concerned with them here, it is interesting to note that despite there being one hundred and fifty manuals devoted to the profession (fig. B-522), there is not one now known that mentions their training.

The variety and quantity of books circu-

[6] *Die Methodik des Diktatkollegs (Adab al-imlāʿ wa al-istimlāʿ)* by ʿAbd al-Karīm ibn Muḥammad al-Samʿānī, edited by M. Weisweiller, pp. 25–174.

[7] Manuscript of the Institute of Oriental Studies, St. Petersburg, Accession no. C–2077, folios 1v–43r.

[8] *Yatīmat al-dahr fī maḥāsin ahl al-aʿṣr li-abī manṣūr* by ʿAbd al-Malik ibn Muḥammad ibn Ismāʿīl al-Thaʿālibī al-Nīshāpūrī. Ed. Muḥammad M. ʿAbd al-Ḥamīd, IV, Cairo, 1958, pp. 442–443.

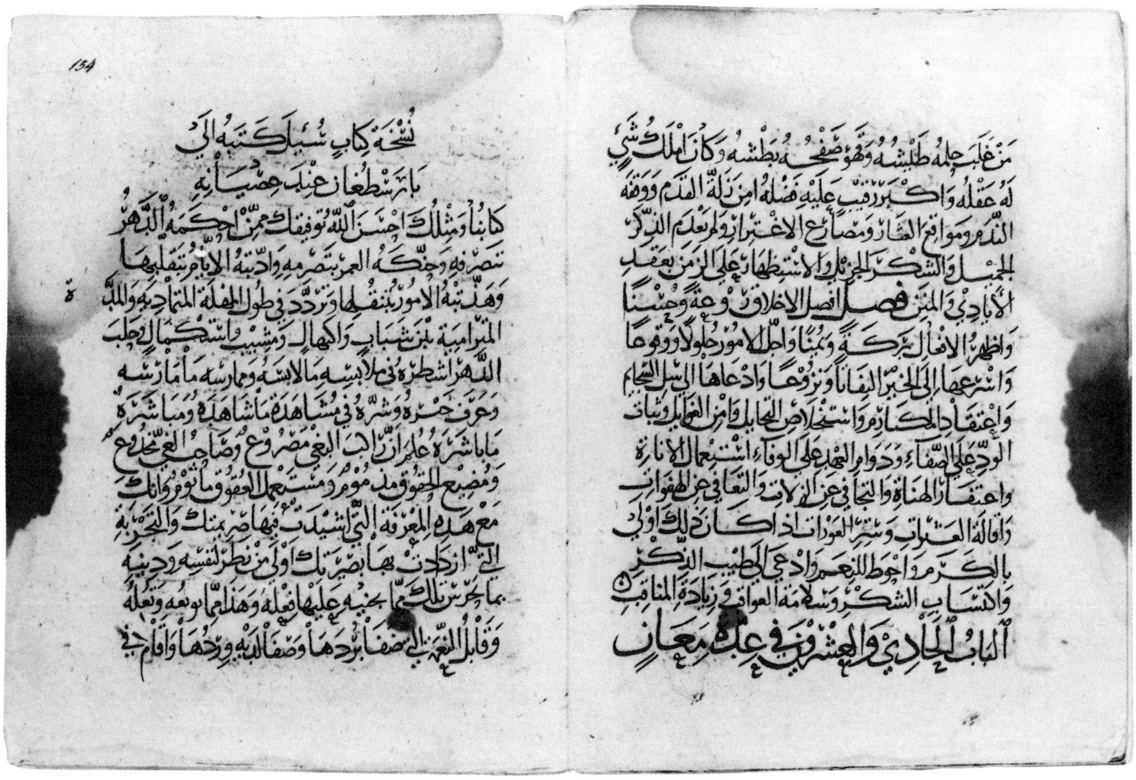

Fig. B-522. This manuscript is of a work by Hilāl al-Ṣābīl (died in 1056) entitled Ghurar al-balāgha *("Models of Eloquence"). It is a compilation of letters whose authors or receivers were famous civil servants, writers and men of letters in the 10th and 11th centuries. The question as to whether they are originals or compositions of the author has yet to be studied. This copy apparently dates from the 12th or 13th century and is an excellent example of calligraphy. Folios 152v–153r.*

lating freely on the market reveal the interests of the various groups in Muslim society. Although the copyists rarely wrote except by commission, they nevertheless created a fashion. Every citizen knew where he could buy or order a book. In Baghdad alone, there were no fewer than one hundred copyist-merchants, and their stalls were to be found in a specific street known as *sūq al-warrāqīn*. At the end of the 19th century and beginning of the 20th century, there were galleries reserved for copyist-merchants (*rasta-i kitābfurūshān*) in Central Asian towns. The experts who worked permanently in the palaces and state libraries were normally employed by their patron to perform tasks that were generally secular, apart from copying the Qur'an. The mosques and the madrasas did not necessarily have special copying centers like the monasteries of Europe and Russia. Furthermore, in the libraries that were attached to many mosques and madrasas, there was a tradition that allowed individuals to copy any work they desired for free. There were also cases of owners of private collections who donated their collections to such libraries, and included sums specially deducted from the revenues of the *waqf* to pay for paper and accessories needed for writing. They were to be given freely to whoever wished to make a copy of a donated book.

The copyists working in a stable job were few. However, they also were entitled to take orders from other clients, according to accepted standards. Manifestly, the condition of the copyist was quite free; he depended neither on the state nor on religion, but only on consumer demand.

Private workshops of high artistic quality were established at the courts of local leaders, governors general, feudal lords, and others, at Shiraz, Herat, Tabriz, Mashhad, Isfahan, Bukhara, Samarqand, Yazd, etc. Costly manuscripts produced in small quantities in such workshops never went outside the palace walls. It follows that most manuscripts which were made for sale were not created in these workshops.

We cannot say today whether there were guilds or corporations among the copyists. But in the years between 1520 and 1560, a substantial number of well-made manuscripts with a consistent quality of writing, decoration, style and color used in the miniatures, were produced at Shiraz. This led to the belief that, at the time, there were one or more independent workshops where experts in different specialties were gathered.

That theory was vividly confirmed by Budaq Qazvīnī (1576), author of *Javāhir al-akhbār* ("Pearls of News"): "In Shiraz, there are many who write the *nastaᶜlīq*; they all imitate each other. It is quite impossible to distinguish their individual hands. Even the women of Shiraz are impromptu copyists. Although they do not know how to read nor write, they write and draw according to a model. The author [of these lines] went to Shiraz to check on this report, and indeed, in every home in town, the wife is a copyist, the husband a miniaturist, the daughter decorates the manuscripts and the son binds them. No matter what book you want, it is made in the same family. If one suddenly wanted one thousand decorated books, within a year, you can be sure that in Shiraz one's desire will be satisfied. They all work in the same manner, to the extent that it is impossible to differentiate their work. Bahrām Mīrzā has a joke which goes like this: 'In Shiraz, the calligraphers are unemployed: some because they are too numerous, others because you cannot tell who did what'."[9]

In all available sources, the tendency to regard the speed of the work of the calligrapher from one extreme to the other is consistent. Either it is mentioned as being very slow work, or it is executed very rapidly. The normal pace of copying is of no interest to them; only whatever is unusual. Budaq Qazvīnī relates in his *Javāhir al-akhbār* that his contemporary Qāsim-i Shādishāh "normally writes five verses a day, correcting them and presenting them perfectly."[10]

The historian from Bukhara, Muḥammad Yūsuf al-Munshī, speaks of the court calligrapher, ᶜAbd al-ᶜAzīz Khān Khwāja Yadgar, saying that he spent seven years copying the poems of Ḥāfiẓ,"[11] on the order of the Khan. Examples taken from the life of calligraphers show that it took just as much time to make a perfect manuscript as it did to paint one large picture.

Furthermore, among copyists and calligraphers, a great deal was made of the speed of copying and the indispensable preservation of legible writing. Qāẓī Aḥmad Qumī, who dedicated a short novel to Sīmī Nīshāpūrī, employed at the court of ᶜAlā al-Daula, the son of Bāisunghur (died in 1458–1459) writes that the master composed, in his imagination, two thousand verses in a day and calligraphed them. No other poet or copyist ever managed to beat that record.[12] But the copyists themselves rarely speak of the speed at which they worked. If one does read in the colophon of a given document that it was hastily written, it is more of an excuse for any faults that the copyist did not detect, rather than publicity for his own merits. Calligraphers and copyists who worked in a court workshop producing artistic manuscripts (*kitābkhāna*) had to copy a given number of lines or verses each day, set by a standard. That was the custom in the 15th century under the Timurids and the Āq-Quyūnlū dynasty. Something similar was clearly upheld under the Safavids too (1502–1736). Ẓahīr al-Dīn Bābur (1483–1530) points out in his *Memoirs* that Sulṭān ᶜAlī Mashhadī copied thirty verses each day for Sulṭān Ḥusain Bāiqarā and twenty for ᶜAlī Shīr Navā'ī. It is quite probable that there was a long tradition for such practice, given that Budaq Qazvīnī mentions in his recital on the famous Arab calligrapher Yāqūt al-Mustaᶜṣimī (d. 1298) that he "wrote one hundred Arabic verses every day for the Caliph and seventy for the viziers."[13] Generally, as regards text in verse, the standard daily output was between one hundred and sixty and two hundred and ten couplets, but a recognized master did not write more than one hundred and fifty. As for prose, the standard (depend-

[9]Budaq Qazvīnī, *Javāhir al-akhbār*. Manuscript in the Russian National Library, St. Petersburg, Dorn 288, folio 109r-v.
[10]*Ibid.*, folio 110v.
[11]A. A. Semyenov, *The Art of Manuscript from Herat and its Creators*, by ᶜAlī Shīr Navā'ī, Moscow-Leningrad, 1946, p. 154.
[12]Budaq Qazvīnī, *op. cit.*, folio 107v.
[13]V. Rosen, *Summary Notices of Arabic Manuscripts in the Asiatic Museum*, 1st delivery, St. Petersburg, 1881, pp. 157–158 (on the basis of the buyer's inscription on this copy, today Institute Accession no. B–630).

ing on manuscript format) was between fifty and a hundred lines.
The scribe or calligrapher practically always depended on the client and produced what the client ordered. Cases in which the client, trusting in the good taste of the artist, requested a selection of verses from the artist's favorite poems, were exceptional. The fashion for such compilations developed in Iran during the 14th century. This type of collection was not only compiled by the professional scribe but also by poets and connoisseurs (cat. nos. 40, 58).
As already mentioned, the social position of copyists varied consistently. They sometimes worked individually under contract in the private workshop, in the service of the state, in a private library of a wealthy landowner or in a court workshop. Materially speaking, the best position was that of the scribe working in state chancelleries and at the court because he received a fixed salary, either daily, monthly or annually, normally consisting of a combination of money, food and clothing.
When a patron was particularly pleased with the work, it was customary for him to give an additional recompense.
It is impossible to say, even approximately, how much a copyist earned. We know that in the Caliphate of the 10th century they belonged to a low-paid social class. The evidence provided above by Abū Ḥātim would confirm this idea. However, the sources contain a considerable number of examples of copyists earning handsome wages. The father of the 12th-century Shafiᶜite-tendency jurist al-Juvainī copied a book and, with the money earned, bought a slave and supported him. The manuscript *Tabāqāt al-fuqahā'* by Ibn Qāḍī Shuhba, copied in 1442, while the author was alive, was bought in 1558 for 500 old dirhams.
Attempts to determine the normal price of a book result in approximate figures. According to A. Grohmann, a gold dinar was the average price for a manuscript. Yūsuf al-ᶜUshsh thinks that the price of a simple book was ten dirhams (about half a dinar), and one hundred for a high quality book. E. Ashtor thinks that the average price of a book was half a dinar, and a quarter of a dinar[14] for a scientific book. Taking into account the changing exchange parities, the average price varied between a quarter of a dinar and one dinar (a dinar represented the monthly salary of a qualified artisan).
Seven centuries after Abū Ḥātim, Adam Olearius, on his return from a visit to Iran made in 1637–1639, noted that because of the high price of books "many Persians, especially those with many children, go to great effort to teach their children how to write well." It is more than likely that as more people learnt how to read and write the demand for books increased, thus leading to an improved social status for the copyist and an increase in his revenue.
Most manuscripts, whether made for personal use or for sale, eventually ended up on the market. For example, the son of Ibn Yūnus al-Ṣadafī inherited the books of his father, who was an astronomer, and sold them by weight in the soapmakers' market!
In the early days of the Islamic community, the question of legality in selling books was raised, but this probably only concerned copies of the Qur'an. Bookselling became an accepted practice with the increase of books in circulation and was sanctioned by jurists. From the 8th century on, this trade flourished and contributed to the wide circulation of manuscripts throughout the Caliphate, and then into other countries.
The seller of manuscripts and writing materials was known as *warrāq*. He was both artisan and trader, the combination of these two functions being commonplace. He was to be found at his workshop-counter (*dukkān, ḥānūt*) and on the shelves were displayed the manuscripts for sale. Mention of visits to the *warrāq* are found in practically all biographies of famous poets, historians, philologists, jurists and theologians, particularly the

[14] A. Grohmann, Th.W. Arnold, *Denkmaler Islamischer Buchkunst*, Munich, 1929, p. 37; Y. Eche, *Arabic Public and Semi-Public Libraries in Mesopotamia, Syria and Egypt during the Middle Ages*, Damascus, 1967, p. 65. E. Ashtor, *History of Prices and Wages in the Medieval East*, Paris, 1969, p. 215.

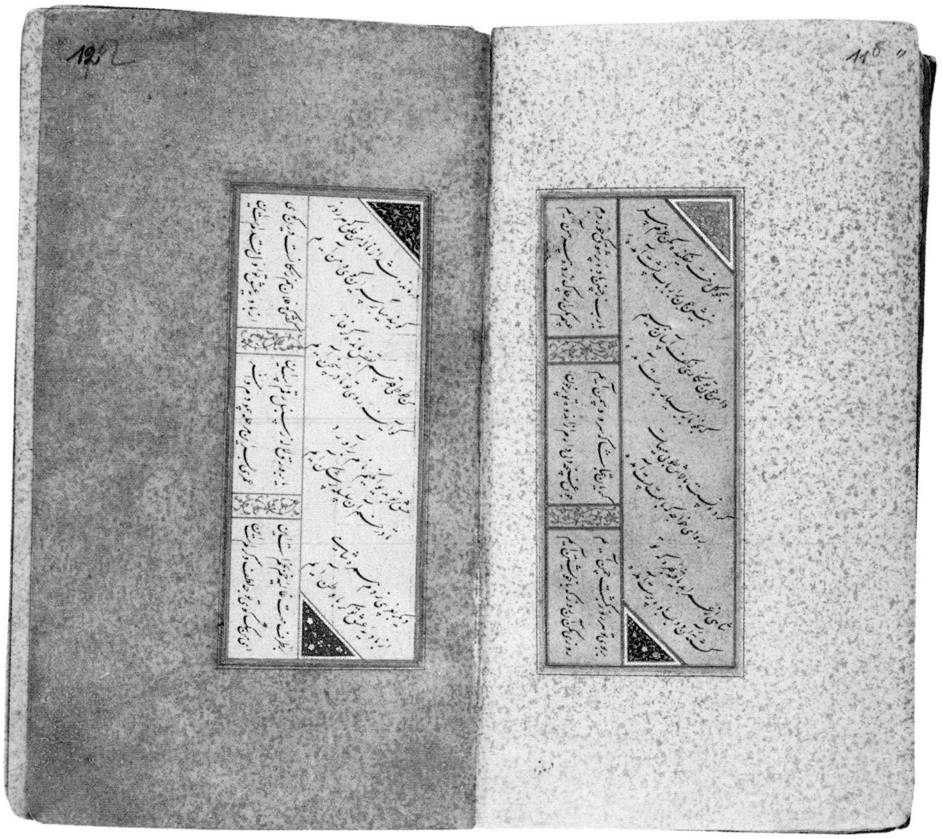

[15]The wife of a *warrāq*, in the heat of an argument, wished upon the unfortunate man "that Allāh gives you a qalam that squeaks, a rusty knife, bad quality paper, a dark day and a sputtering flame" (al-Samʿānī, *Adab al-imʾlā*, p. 162).

[16]*Wafayāt al-aʿyān wa anbā' abnā' al-zamān*, by al-Qāḍī Aḥmad al-shāhir bi-Ibn Khallikān, 1, Cairo, 1310, p. 63. Al-Silafī was a well known faqīh. A substantial proportion of the books in the library of the Fatimid court passed through the hands of Ibn Sawra when the rest of the library was sold after Ṣalāḥ al-Dīn captured Cairo in 1171. He dealt in these books for several years.

[17]As a guide, the collection of Arabic manuscripts in the Institute of Oriental Studies alone (approximately 5,000 volumes, or about 10,700 separate texts) names 1,762 copyists.

inhabitants of Baghdad in the 7th and 8th centuries. Thanks to their select clientele, the *warrāq*'s counter became a meeting place for representatives of the cultivated elite.

The *warrāqs* were the butt of a number of anecdotes.[15] Their business, the quality of their merchandise and their selections were often treated with a certain disdain, as the element of commercial profit was seen to diminish quality. The *warrāqs* also served as intermediaries, but different terms were used for book dealers and traders: *dallāl* or *simsār*, and in later sources the word *kutubī*.

The *dallāl* traveled with his manuscripts and tried to sell them to sovereigns, as well as to amateurs.

Ibn Khallikān relates that a *dallāl*, Ibn Wajīh Ibn Sawra al-Miṣrī, had a magnificent house in Cairo that burnt down. So, a verse was composed along the following lines: "Goods acquired dishonestly disappear and that is only right." He continues: Abū al-Futūḥ Nāṣir ibn ʿAlī ibn Khalaf al-Anṣārī, known as Ibn Sawra, was a very lucky *simsār* in Cairo. He ran his business from the cellar. On Sundays and Wednesdays, the senior civil servants and high-profile dignitaries congregated there. He showed them his manuscripts for sale and they stayed for as long as was necessary to conclude a deal.[16]

These stories mirror the attitude of the cultivated elite in respect of book merchants-intermediaries. Morally they were criticized but their services were appreciated. Although commerce was generally accepted as being a real occupation worthy of a Muslim, socially useful and providing a legal income, the sale of books was regarded with suspicion and considered slightly unethical. These sources mention hundreds and thousands of people entitled al-Warrāq, as having copied specific work.[17]

The Structure of the Manuscript and Terminology

The term *kitāb* implies not just a book of a certain format, volume and use but any written text, be it an invoice, a letter, or any other document. It is used for a whole range of Arabic texts. Often it designates a subdivision or chapter of a work, especially in lexicography, fiqh or hadith, and determines its title. With the definite article (*al-kitāb*), it is used for the Qur'an and the basic work of Sībawayhi on grammar.

For each category of knowledge, the use of terms to designate sections of works and the ways of noting the limits of short sections in the text is quite specific. The Qur'an is divided into suras and *āyāts*, the works on hadith and fiqh into *kitāb*, and so on.

The work invariably opens with "In the Name of God, the Merciful, the Compassionate" (*bism allāh al-raḥmān al-raḥīm*), which goes by the abbreviated form "basmala."

Then there is the glorification of Allāh and of Muḥammad, his prophet. This essential component of the work also has an abridged form, using the first words: *ḥamdala*. Each author modified the *ḥam-*

dala according to his wont, sometimes including praise of Islam and the Muslim community, the Arabic language, and the branch of knowledge to which the work in question was devoted. Then follows the formula *wa baʿd*, with which the work is introduced. Sometimes, the *ḥamdala* phrase was very short or even omitted.

Supports and Writing Materials

Depending on the place and time, different materials were used to write Arabic texts, but for those of substantial length, the main elements were papyrus and parchment. These writing materials were used by eastern nations for millennia and were already mastered by the Arabs in the pre-Islamic period or at the very beginning of that time. Parchment was used in the initial stages to write individual sections of the Qur'an (cat. nos. 1, 2, 3, 4). It was prepared using the carefully tanned skin of sheep, goats, calves, and sometimes gazelles or other animals. Despite its relative scarcity and high cost, parchment was widely used in the first centuries after the hijra.

As for Egyptian papyrus, it was known in Arabia before Islam and was used during the first two centuries after the hijra especially for documents and business purposes (cat. nos. 5, 6). It was prepared and sold in rolls up to 14.5 meters in length, which could then be cut into leaves that were sewn or glued into a book.

Paper imported from China was known in Sasanian Iran from the end of the 6th century. In the first centuries after the hijra, it was used in the Caliphate at the same time as parchment and papyrus. Then came Samarqand paper. Al-Thaʿālibī (d. 1038) explains: "Samarqand is known for its paper, *kāghid*, which has replaced the Egyptian papyrus and skins that our ancestors used, because it is more beautiful, more agreeable, more flexible and easier to use. It is only prepared in Samarqand and in China. The man who prepared *kāghid* came from China to Samarqand as a prisoner of Ziyād ibn Ṣāliḥ. Its production increased and became so common that the paper became a trade commodity among the inhabitants of Samarqand. It was so useful and of such profit that it then spread throughout the entire world."[18]

The event mentioned here, the battle of Talas between the governor general of Samarqand and the T'ang Chinese, occurred in July 751. The Arab troops of Ziyād ibn Ṣāliḥ won and captured about 20,000 prisoners, who were taken to Samarqand. Paper experts from eastern Turkestan were in the region of Samarqand earlier, but nothing indicates that they were prisoners.

The assimilation of the new paper manufacturing technique coincided with the beginning of the development of Arabic literature and science. There is a direct link between the two events. Only paper, an easy material to distribute, allowed the flexibility needed to create manuscript works of vast scope and complex structure, in several tomes and in numerous copies.

A composition and fabrication of paper using the Chinese and Samarqand process were described in an 11th-century treatise from North Africa, attributed to the Zīrīd sultan al-Muʿizz al-Bādīs (governor from 1016 to 1061) or his son Tamīm (d. 1108). Raw materials were required: linen or hemp rags, lime and wheat starch, and simple tools: mill or mortar, vessel and mold.

All Arabic-script manuscripts of the 9th to 14th centuries that we know of were written on Samarqand or Eastern paper, except for a few on papyrus or parchment. By the end of the 14th century and especially in the 15th century, Arabic manuscripts employing paper of European manufacture were to be found.

To write, one used the *qalam* (a Greek word), a reed stick with a notch at one end and a sharpened point. It was sometimes called *misbar*, which means "writing instrument." The *qalam* was nick-

[18]*Lata'if al-ma'arif, auctore Abu Mançur Abdomalik ibn Muhammad ibn Isma'il at-Tha'alibi, qemm librum e codd*, Leiden and Gotha, Edid. P. de Jong. Lugduni Batavorum, 1867, p. 126.

Qurra ibn Sharīk, governor of Egypt, an official letter to the administrator of the city of Asuh, cat. no. 5, detail.

named "second tongue," literally "one of two tongues," "the letter doctor," or "the flame of Islam," and was compared to the sword. It was placed with the ink-pot, *dawāh*, in a sort of pencil-box or small oblong container with a cover.
Inks were prepared with great attention to detail, special importance being given to making them deep black and lustrous. There were several types of ink, and their names revealed their origin or composition. Numerous recipes for their preparation have come down to us, but they all fall into two categories: ferrous walnut inks, which through time and interaction on paper change color from blue-black to russet-brown; and inks made with soot, like India ink, that maintain their deep blackness. There are two different words for ink: *ḥibr and midād*. Scribes know how the colored inks (reds, yellows, blues, violets, various shades) were prepared, although they were used less frequently.

Writing

Abū Raiḥān al-Bīrūnī wrote: "Arabic writing has a major defect: the form of the letters and the need to distinguish them by means of points and signs of inflection. If these are removed, the meaning becomes obscure. Add to this a tendency common to our people of lax quality control and a lack of attention to proper corrections with respect to the original text. In this case the existence or disappearance of books and even the very knowledge or ignorance of their content amount to the same thing."[19]
Indeed, the Arabic alphabet with its consonants requires diacritical marks (for thirteen of the twenty-eight letters) to differentiate between letters of similar form, and diacritical and additional juxtalinear signs to note the short vowels, let alone spelling conventions. Arabic writing, with its complete array of points and signs, resembles a voluminous construction with several floors and creates an impression of abundance and superfluity. But it ensures faithful reading of the text, irrespective of whether the meaning is understood. This type of script was employed rarely, mostly for copying the Qur'an, in displays of propositions and citations, scientific manuals, or even isolated words. Normally, a substantial part of vocalization and complementary signs were deliberately omitted, the same applied to diacritical marks, albeit less frequently. The number of homographs increased in proportion to the quantity of signs and points left out, as did the possible ways of reading and interpreting the text. But we will not elaborate the strict laws for maintaining and omitting these signs. Everything depended on the desire and sense of proportion of the writer, and sometimes the fashion and style of writing. Occasionally, a "vague" writing style was the way to boast of erudition and knowledge of an unusual language.
As Islam spread, the Arabic writing system quickly assumed the predominant position in subject countries. In the territory of the old Sasanian empire, already towards the beginning of the 10th century the Arabic alphabet completely ousted Pahlavi, a very complex writing system. That explains why only a few isolated examples of the rich pre-Islamic Persian literary tradition have come down to us.
The Persians adopted the Arabic graphic system without modification, but the change to this system took place over a relatively long time. Of course, we shall never know by whom and when Arabic script was used for the first time to write Persian. This practice probably appeared quite spontaneously in various parts of the conquered country. One can suppose that it was adopted for reasons of administration and management, the Arabic alphabet being simpler, more convenient and easier to write. Later, it came to be considered possible to write lengthy Persian texts in verse or prose in this alphabet.
It seems that one can talk of three stages

[19] Khalidov, *op. cit.*, p. 12.

in the development of the Persian manuscript; all three are directly related to the advent of the Arabic script as the medium for writing Persian. First, in the initial stage of the 9th century, the Arabic alphabet was used to systemize the new written Persian language. But because it was a question of writing in Arabic script—another language with different phonemes—changes immediately occurred.
The second stage was the creation of a series of additional letters, to reproduce in writing the phonemes used in Persian that were not found in the Arabic language. This apparently took place at the beginning of the 10th century. However, the complete system was not finalized until the late 16th century or early 17th century.
Finally, the third stage was linked to the adaptation of the six classical Arabic scripts (*sitta*) to the Persian aesthetic tendencies themselves, and the ensuing creation of specifically Persian writing styles.

Calligraphy

Calligraphy was considered an important ornamental feature in manuscripts. Already in Arabic inscriptions of the 6th century, there is the germ of what was to foster the development of two forms—the monumental and the cursive scripts. In the first, it is straight lines and angles which predominate, while in the second it is rounded lines and sinuous swings. The monumental style is used for Muslim inscriptions, and sometimes in copies of the Qur'an (cat. no. 2); in other documents the cursive style is used (cat. nos. 5, 6).
Monumental calligraphy produced a whole group of writing styles, traditionally known as *kūfī* (kufic, from the town of Kufa), although developed not only in the south of Iraq (Kufa and Basra), but also in the Hijaz (Mecca and Medina).
Curvilinear cursive writing styles, found on papyrus from 643, are classified by function. At the time of the Umayyads (661–750), the scribe and calligrapher Kutba (died in 771) "invented" four important chancellery writing styles: *al-jalīl* "the majestic," *al-ṭūmār al-kabīr* "the large sheet," *al-niṣf al-thaqīl* "the heavy half," and *al-thuluth al-kabīr* "the large third." Twenty other forms of writing developed from these four.
There was a direct relation between the size of the folio and the size and form of the letters; the larger the context or theme, the greater the folio, the wider the point of the *qalam* the bigger the writing. In the largest scripts, strokes of letters and ligatures were broader, their angles and bends more angular. In fine writing, they were thinner and more rounded. The relation between straight lines (verticals) and curved lines served as a basis for naming a given form of writing "one third" and "two thirds" (*thuluth, thuluthayn*). These relationships can not be taken as absolute, but regarded more as general trends.
The Arabic tradition distinguishes a number of independent scripts. It associates innovations and reforms with names of eminent calligraphers, even if

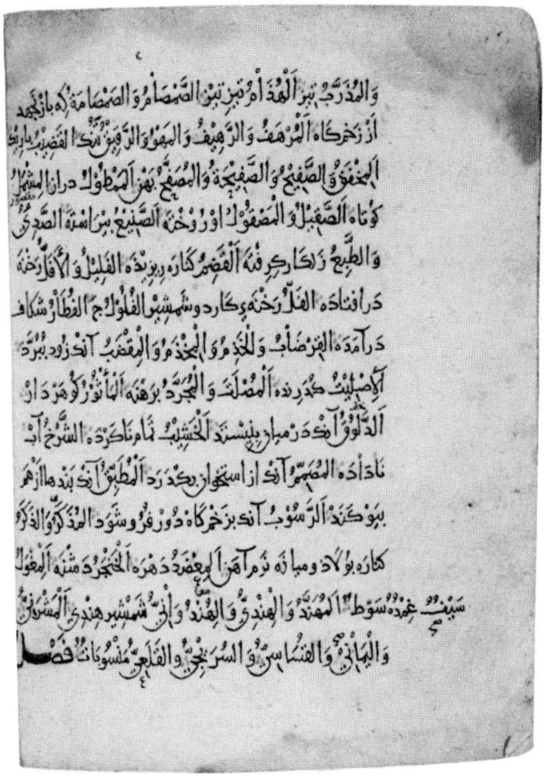

Abū al-Fażl Aḥmad ibn Muḥammad al-Maidānī al Nīshāpūrī, Kitāb al-sāmī fī al-asāmī *("The Excellent Book of Names"), 1104, cat. no. 11.*

they only tried to establish solid groundrules for things that existed before they did.

Abū ᶜAlī Muḥammad ibn ᶜAlī ibn al-Ḥasan ibn Muqla (886–940), vizier to three ᶜAbbasid Caliphs, was a very fine calligrapher. He introduced the "well-proportioned script" (*khaṭṭ mansūb*), thanks to a clearly defined mathematical system. On the basis of kufic, he developed six famous classical scripts: *muḥaqqaq*, *thuluth*, *riqāc*, *naskh*, *tawqīᶜ* and *rayḥān*.

Subsequently, a calligrapher of Persian origin, ᶜAlī ibn Hilāl (died in 1022 or 1031), nicknamed Ibn al-Bawwāb, when working in the famous public library of Shiraz improved the system of Ibn Muqla. The calligrapher of the last ᶜAbbasid Caliph, Yāqūt al-Mustaᶜṣimī (1242–1298) raised it to perfection. Among the scripts developed by the Persians on the basis of those mentioned above, three are of great importance: *taᶜlīq* (sometimes called *dīvānī*, especially in Turkey), *nastaᶜlīq*, and *shikasta* with its varieties: *shikasta-i taᶜlīq* and *shikasta-i nastaᶜlīq*.

In principle, it was normally assumed that a professional copyist could write all six classical scripts of *sitta*, and, from the 15th century onwards, *nastaᶜlīq*. In practice, there were few such scribes; most could write *thuluth* and *naskh*, and subsequently *nastaᶜlīq*.

Naskh is the most popular and widespread script in the Muslim East. Today most publications (newspapers, gazettes, books) are printed in it. It has become universally recognized because of its fluidity, clarity, equilibrium and proportion of its letters and their union in words, but also because of the ease with which it can be taught. Five manuscripts in this exhibition were written in *naskh* by cultivated people (cat. nos. 11, 20), or by professionals (cat. nos. 17, 21, 25), and they well represent the Iraqi *naskh* in the 12th and 13th centuries and the Iranian *naskh* style of writing which replaced it. Calligraphy in a typically Turkish *naskh* can be seen in a document from the mid-17th century (cat. no. 47).

Of the scripts directly created from the Iranian base, into the fabric of which have been carefully woven certain elements from pre-Islamic Arab writing, the *nastaᶜlīq* deservedly occupies a leading position. It is traditionally held that

The St. Petersburg Muraqqaᶜ, folio 19v.

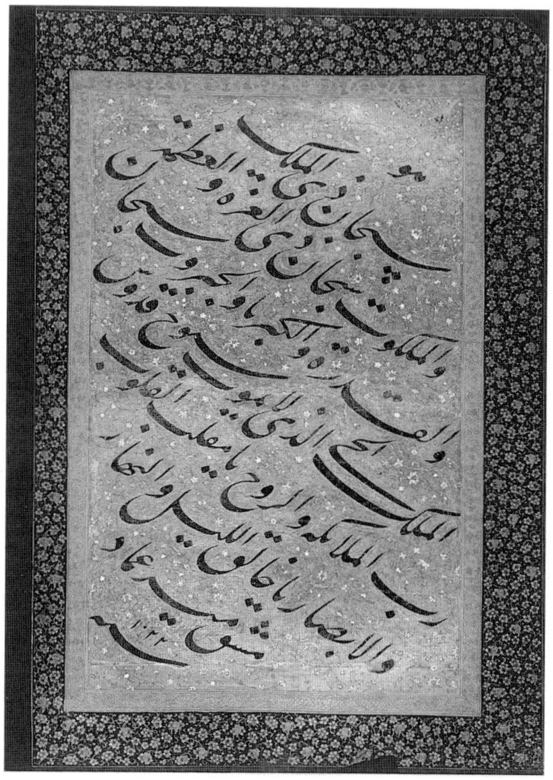

The St. Petersburg Muraqqaᶜ, folio 21v.

this writing is the result of mixing *naskh* and *taᶜlīq*. If most *naskh* is the mathematically proportioned script, precise, clear, and easy to read, *taᶜlīq* is an economical, sinuous and cursive script. The combination of their most characteristic elements gave birth to a new Persian style, known as *nastaᶜlīq* (from *naskh-i taᶜlīq*), which is very common because its elegance and fluidity so appealed to the master calligraphers of Persia. From the first third of the 15th century, manuscripts that have survived clearly illustrate the beginning of a gradual movement in Western Iran of a new style of writing vaguely suggestive of the future *nastaᶜlīq*. Obviously, it was not quite so elegant and well proportioned, but it was quite distinctive from any cursive, rapid writing style. Mīr ᶜAlī ibn Ḥasan Tabrīzī played a leading role in creating this new script. In his treatise, he gave the theoretical basis for its proportions. Furthermore, he introduced a new way of sharpening and cutting the *qalam* to write in this style. By virtue of its particular qualities, the *nastaᶜlīq* appears to have been especially created to write poetry; it is as if its fluidity reflects the rhythm of the verse. Little by little, towards the end of the 15th century, two distinct schools formed: one in Khurasan, the fundamentals of which were laid in Herat by Jaᶜfar ibn ᶜAlī (originally from Tabriz, d. around 1456) and one in the Southwest, founded by masters from the east of Khurasan and Central Asia in Shiraz and Baghdad (especially by ᶜAbd al-Raḥmān al-Khwārazmī and his sons, ᶜAbd al-Raḥīm and ᶜAbd al-Karīm).

Through a host of masters, in the 15th and 16th centuries, a special school of *nastaᶜlīq* was founded in Baghdad and especially Shiraz, quite distinct from the Khurasan school (centers in Herat and Mashhad) and the Western Iranian school in Tabriz, where that script originated. This *nastaᶜlīq* is less ornate, with more compact and rounded elements, greater rationalism and less fantasy. It was obviously created for faster and more legible copying. Indeed, this style of writing deprived students of a certain creative expression.

But as copies in this school of writing were very cheap and of relatively good quality, the *nastaᶜlīq* was much appreciat-

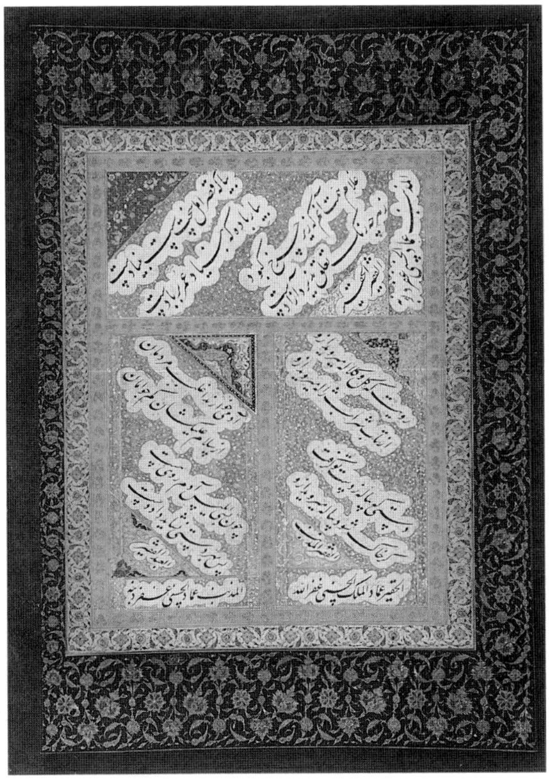

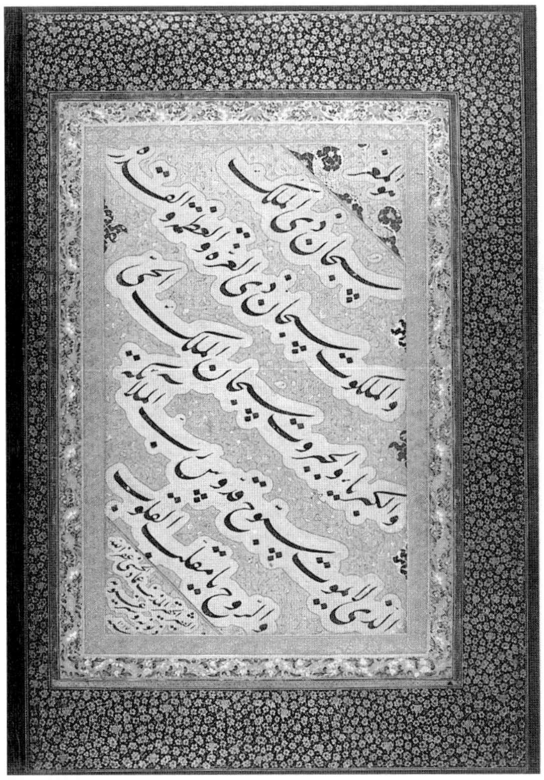

The St. Petersburg Muraqqaᶜ, folio 95v.

The St. Petersburg Muraqqaᶜ, folio 100v.

*Kamāl al-Dīn Bafqī Vaḥshī and Muḥammad-Shafī*ᶜ *al-Shīrāzī Viṣāl,* Farhād u Shīrīn *("Farhād and Shīrīn"), cat. no. 60.*

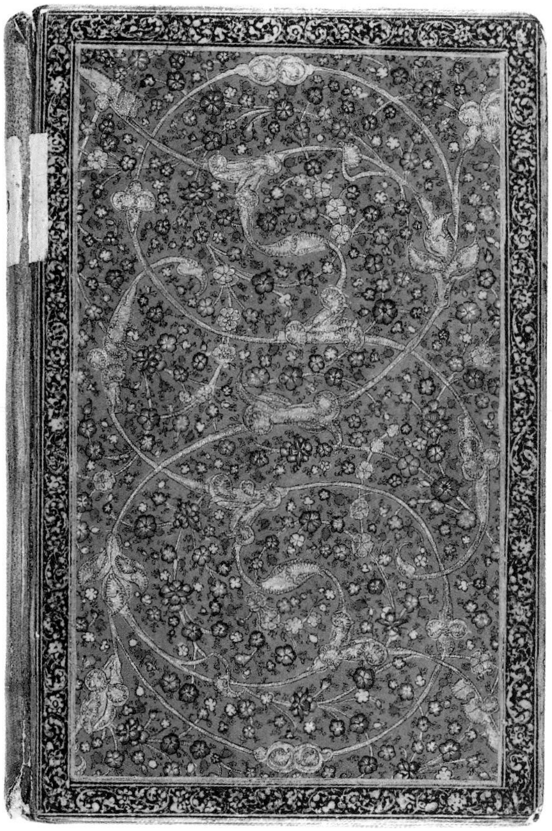

ed by readers and customers.

In this exhibition, calligraphic perfection of the *nastaᶜlīq* style is represented by works by the great masters: Jaᶜfar al-Bāisunghurī (d. towards 1456, cat. no. 28), Mīr ᶜAlī Haravī (d. 1544, cat. no. 40), Mīr Qazvīnī (d. 1615, cat. no. 52), and various masters from the South-western school (Shiraz) of the 16th century (cat. nos. 41, 43, 44).

In the first half of the 17th century another form of writing appeared in Persia that derived from *nastaᶜlīq*: the *shikasta-i nastaᶜlīq*. To begin with, this *nastaᶜlīq* style, specifically Persian, was under the powerful influence of *taᶜlīq*, widely used in private and business calligraphy. The subsequent evolution of writing resulted in the creation of *shikasta-i nastaᶜlīq*, thereafter simply known as *shikasta*. The application of *taᶜlīq* cursive writing principles to this style while at the same time maintaining *nastaᶜlīq* proportions produced a completely cursive script which has been used in Iran ever since, and which has conserved many aesthetic qualities specific to *nastaᶜlīq*. It is traditionally held that Murtaẓā Qulī-Khān ibn Ḥasan-Khān Shamlū (d. 1688–1689), Safavid governor of Herat, created this form of writing. There are two documents in this style of writing in the exhibition (cat. nos. 58, 60).

The peculiarities of writing in the Arabic alphabet, predilection for clarity (proportions of components in rectilinear and curved letters, the proportion of these components one to the other) opened the doors for Persian scribes to an almost unlimited potential of creativity. In mediaeval Persia, spiritual culture was manifest in numerous aspects, especially legible and artistic calligraphy. This art was much appreciated and exalted. In Persia, as in many Islamic countries where Islam prohibited figurative representation, the emotional expression of calligraphy became a basis for ornamental and rhythmic compositions.

The writing styles of North Africa and Spain formed a specifically North African (Maghribi) script style, that is the "Western" (*maghribī*) style. Based on kufic, this style has preserved archaic characteristics. Here also, the tendency towards cursive, rounded writing gradually dominated, without being influenced by Ibn Muqla's reform. As a result, it was not influenced by geometric standardization and the rule of proportionate form (cat. nos. 10, 67).

The requirements for becoming a master in calligraphy were exacting, but they mainly concerned the professional scribes, and particularly the chancellery civil servants. In academic circles there was another viewpoint, which held that an excessive concern to perfect one's handwriting deterred the man of learning from his real aim, the pursuit of knowledge. "If a man has poor handwriting, that means he is fortunate," said a vizier famous for his wisdom, "because he will not waste time on that which could be spent on learning and contemplation."[20] "To have poor handwriting is not a joy in itself," remarked thoughtfully the 11th-century jurist al-Māwardī (11th century).[21]

[20] Abū Ḥasan ᶜAlī al-Māwardī, *Adab al-dunyā wa al-dīn*. Manuscript in the St. Petersburg Branch of the Institute of Oriental Studies, Russian Academy of Sciences, folio 74v.

[21] *Ibid.*

However, in Arabic culture the glorification of writing and the transferral of its aesthetic qualities was, in its own way, influenced by knowledge passed down from one generation to the next, glorifying the Arabic language, Islam, poetry and Arabic sciences. It is sufficient to recall that one compared the beauty of one's beloved, the shape and curves of her body, and her movements to that of individual letters of the alphabet and to poetry. There was a search for the sacred and for harmony in calligraphy. One of the most famous specialists of the Muslim manuscript tradition considers that "in its artistic content, the wealth of its forms, the strength of its aesthetic influence, Arabic writing is as near perfection as the human hand, with its aptitude to write, can achieve... The inspired play of lines, the splendor of their design evoke a blooming flower, their suggestive appearance... compares to no other writing of any other race."[22]

Layout and Illustrations

The ornamental decoration or layout of a manuscript is the primary art of decorating each codex, or parts thereof, and is normally dictated by tradition. The essential elements are geometric ornaments, vegetal or animal (generally stylized) or a combination of both, with paintings in the margin. The entire decoration is of liquid gold (of varying shades), silver and a rich palette of mineral or vegetable colors. At the beginning (towards the middle or late in the 9th century), artistic ornamentation of the codex played a secondary role, the main aim being to decorate and enhance the text, the copyist's work. This period primarily concerned the illumination of the Qur'an. Subsequently, during long impassioned debates, the Islamic jurists considered it a right to decorate other books, and the work of a master decorator was thereafter imbued with the glory of religious effort. Gradually, the artistic aspect of a book became fundamental in the production of Islamic manuscripts, alongside calligraphy, illustration and binding. It was customary to decorate both sides of the first two or three leaves in the book plate, a detailed frontispiece with text, an ordinary title page or an ornamental border framing the introductory text. The integral parts of the text in the manuscript were then laid out, as were the divisions in chapters and colophons. The decoration of the latter deserve special notice. To begin with, colophons may have been modestly decorated with one or two threads of gold framing it like a cone, then a plant element and a thread of color were added, and, as of the end of the 15th century, also miniature paintings.

The *ʿunvān* (frontispiece) assumed a major role in decorating the Arabic manuscript, to begin with painted in color on one half, third or quarter of the page, with a rectangular or domical form.

Abū Muḥammad Ilyās ibn Yūsuf ibn Zakī Mu'ayyad Niẓāmī Ganjavī, Lailā u Majnūn *("Lailā u Majnūn"), cat. no. 59.*

Abū al-Qāsim Firdausī al-Ṭūsī, Shāhnāma *("The Book of Kings"), cat no. 31.*

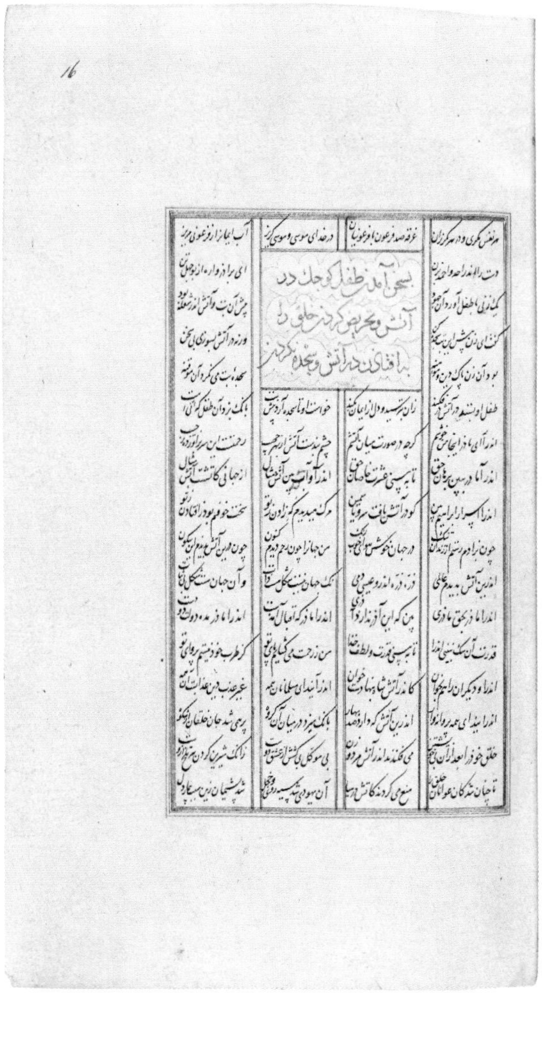

Jalāl al-Dīn Muḥammad ibn Muḥammad al-Balkhī Rūmī, Masnavī-i Maᶜ navī *("The Poem in the Esoteric Sense"), cat. no. 33.*

The range of colors used to decorate the manuscripts of the 11th to 13th centuries was very limited: gold in two shades, silver, blue and white paint, vermilion. Nevertheless, from the first years of the 14th century, there was a trend to further diversify the palette with a quantity of nuances, with richer and brighter colors. The Syro-Egyptian manuscripts (Mamluk) (cat. no. 34) visibly played a determining role in this new tendency. The general current of decoration was towards breaking up parts of the overall composition into small independent sections. In this process, the entire drawing (margin and backdrop) appears as a rich brocade or an inlaid surface.

Certain specific traits of decoration enable us to identify, with certitude, the following schools: the Western school (Baghdad, Shiraz, Asia Minor, 14th century); the Southern school (Shiraz, mid-14th century, 1420–1430, 1470–1590); the Isfahan school (end of the 16th–beginning of the 17th centuries); the Mawaran-nahr school (Transoxiana, Bukhara, 1520–1570, 1590–1670); the Kashmir school (end of the 18th century–1870); the Shiraz school (1830–1870). The exhibition presents manuscripts decorated in Southern Iran dating from the 14th century (cat. no. 25) and the beginning of the 15th century (cat. no. 29), in the east of Iran in the first third of the 15th century (Herat, cat. nos. 28, 31, 33), in Transoxiana towards 1520–1550 (Bukhara, cat. nos. 40, 42), in Isfahan (cat. no. 52). The master who painted these cardboard folios, Muḥammad Hādī, dated them 1169–1172/1755–1759; in Kashmir during 1820–1830 (cat. no. 59).

Manuscripts in Arabic embellished with illustrations are found in very limited quantity, the main reason being, whatever the explanation given by historians, that it was forbidden in the Muslim world to depict living beings. We can, however, cite the *Maqāmāt* by al-Ḥarīrī (cat. no. 18), the *Kitāb al-aghānī* ("The Book of Songs") by Abū al-Faraj al-Iṣfahānī, works of medical botany, collections of stories, fables and parables, like *Kalīla wa Dimna* and *The Fables of Luqmān* (cat. no. 53), works on military science in the Mamluk period in Egypt (cat. no. 34), and descriptions of natural curiosities (cat. no. 24). Drawings of a popular sort appeared in several Arabic works of folklore, recopied in the 17th–19th centuries, especially in Iran, India and Central Asia.

Drawings, diagrams, maps and tables, as abstract representations, were not subject to direct prohibition, which is why they can frequently be found in scientific books. Nevertheless, in theological circles, they were disapproved of and their distribution impeded.

Separate mention is to be made of a surprising artistic phenomenon in the decoration of books: the Persian miniature, which has merited a place of honor in the history of painting. At different stages of its development, Persian miniature painting was subject to influences from paintings of other Oriental nations, but nevertheless maintained its own tradition, and even exercised a considerable influence on the development of miniature painting in regions neighboring Iran.

The first examples of Persian painting in books have been lost. Information provided by the Arab geographer al-Masᶜūdī (died in 956), who in 915 saw a book in Istakhr (Fars) with the portraits of Sasanian rulers, leads us to believe that books with miniatures representing portraits existed in Iran already, at least in that Persian dynasty (3rd–7th centuries). The oldest miniatures now in our possession are from the historic Southern Iranian province of Fars. They were discovered in the copy of ᶜAbd al-Raḥmān al-Ṣūfī's *Kitāb al-ṣuwar al-kawākib al-thābita* ("The Book of Images of the Fixed Stars"), composed on the order of the Buyid sovereign ᶜAḍuḍ al-Daula. The signed manuscript was copied by the author's son, al-Ḥusain, in 1009–1010, from his father's manuscript. He also copied the miniatures[23] (personifications of the stars). Other copies, from the 11th–12th centuries, with miniatures specifically related to Persia,[24] have not as yet been discovered.

A series of manuscripts made in the region of Syria-Iraq at the end of the 12th century and in the second half of the 13th century have survived (cat. no. 18). Specialists differ considerably as regards their precise place of origin (Baghdad, Mosul, Damascus).[25] Whatever the case, there is no doubt that these miniatures had an influence on the subsequent development of Persian painting in the west and south-west of Iran.

All Iranian art came under a strong Chinese influence almost immediately after the Mongol conquest in 1258. First, this influence was simply limited to the copying and borrowing of certain processes. Then, gradually during the 14th century, Persian artists familiarized themselves with and reworked the basics of Chinese painting. As of this period the compositions of Persian miniatures were characterized by specific depiction of clouds and high horizon lines. From then on, the Chinese influence died out slowly. But the Persian miniature again fell under Chinese influence in Herat during the first half of the 15th century, with much greater creativity.

The 14th century was a period of elaboration of the classic style of the miniature.[26] From Shiraz to Baghdad, in the last third of the 14th century, a new style of Persian miniature was developed which scored a brilliant success in Herat during the 15th century. The meticulously detailed landscape, the high horizon, the complexity of composition and the rich palette of colors used are its characteristics.

This style was developed in Iran during the reign of the successors of Tīmūr. This is why Persian miniatures of this century are often referred to as Timurid. It is not a very apt appellation, because it does not explain the origin of the two most important schools of Persian miniatures in the 15th century, Shiraz and

[22]A. Grohmann, *Arabische Paläographie*, t. 1–2, Vienna, 1967.

[23]E. Wellesz, "An Early al-Sufi Manuscript in the Bodleian Library, Oxford," in *Ars Orientalis*, Ann Arbor, vol. 3, 1959, pp. 1–26; R. Ettinghausen, *Arab Painting*, Geneva, 1962, pp. 50–54.

[24]The *Andarznāma (Book of Instruction)*, supposedly dating from 1090, is a perfect fake according to the Iranian specialist, M. Minovi, as are 13-14 other very old copies, put on the antique market in Eastern and Middle Eastern countries in the 1940s and 1950s.

[25]Oleg Grabar, *The Illustrations of the Maqamat*, Chicago-London, 1984, pp. 17–19.

[26]Basil Gray, *The Fourteenth Century*, in B. Gray (ed.), *The Arts of the Book in Central Asia, 14th–16th Centuries*, London, 1979, pp. 93–120.

Herat. During the entire 15th century, the Shiraz miniature school continued to flourish.
B.W. Robinson called it the Turkman school, because of its belonging to two ethnic dynasties, Qarā Quyūnlū and Āq Quyūnlū, that ruled over the south of Iran from the mid-15th to the beginning of the 16th centuries.[27]
It would have been more exact to call it the Shiraz school, to emphasize the continuity in the development of miniature painting, in the south of Iran in any case (cat. nos. 31, 36).
In the 1440s, in Yazd, a series of manuscripts (no less than six) were made, with a substantial number of miniatures of a style that enables one to talk of an independent Yazd school, despite its obvious relation to Shiraz (cat. no. 30).[28]
At the same period, the Herat school was forming in the north-east of Iran. Its creation was closely linked to the patronage of Shāhrukh (1405–1447), and particularly his son, Ghiyāth al-Dīn Bāisunghur Mīrzā (d. 1433).
A great connoisseur of literature, highly appreciative of manuscripts, a good writer himself, Bāisunghur Mīrzā built up a *kitābkhāna* at his court in 1420, where alongside authors, men of letters, and book experts, various representatives of the book trade worked together. At the head of this institute he placed the famous calligrapher, Ja^cfar Tabrīzī, who had just arrived in Herat from Yazd. Twenty-five master craftsmen worked under his direction; calligraphers, decorators, book binders and miniature painters.[29]
The workshop attracted the best artists from all regions of Iran. Craftsmen from Tabriz, Shiraz, Isfahan and Yazd produced real masterpieces there, immensely appreciated by following generations throughout the Muslim East. The tradition of the Herat school, consolidated thanks to the achievements of artists from various regions of Persia, did not diminish with the decline of the *kitābkhāna* in 1448.
In 1502, Ismā^cīl Ṣafavī entered Tabriz and was proclaimed *shāhanshāh* (King of Kings) in Persia. In the east, Muḥammad Shaibānī Khān took Herat in 1507. In the struggle for supreme power, Ismā^cīl won, and towards 1512 the whole of Persia came under the sway of the founder of a new dynasty, the Safavids (1502–1736). Herat was no more the capital of the state. It would stay the center of Khurasan which, as immense as it was, was only a province. Gradually, it lost its role as a cultural center, after being a political hub (cat. no. 37). The fight against the Sunnites, who refused to accept Shi^cism, and the almost annual raids of the Uzbeks of Transoxiana did not help create and maintain a normal cultural activity in the town. The uncertain conditions obliged the "people of the book" to leave Herat for Tabriz or Bukhara.
So, in the period of 1520–1530, a school of painting developed at the court in Bukhara, thanks to the masters from Herat. They painted miniatures in the Herat style, but with local characteristics in the design of form and composition (cat. no. 40). Then, around 1540–1570, the school established the canon of its procedures and artistic choice, which gave it the status of the independent school of Transoxiana (cat. no. 38).
In the capital, Tabriz, workshops were set up in the *kitābkhāna* of the court of the final representatives of the Āq-Quyūnlū dynasty that Ismā^cīl I inherited (died in 1524). The local master, Sulṭān Muḥammad, was to play a major role. In April 1522, the personnel of the *kitābkhāna* increased substantially: artists from Tabriz and Shiraz were joined by those from Herat whose leader was Kamāl al-Dīn Bihzād who was accompanied to Tabriz by Ṭahmāsp, the young heir to the throne. By a decree of Ismā^cīl I, Bihzād was put in charge of the *kitābkhāna* and became principal advisor and preceptor. Initially, one can clearly see in the school of Tabriz a dependence on the rules of miniature composition, on the range of colors and surroundings of the miniatur-

[27]Basil W. Robinson, *The Turkman School to 1503*, in B. Gray (ed.), *The Arts of the Book in Central Asia, 14th–16th Centuries*, pp. 215–247.
[28]I. Stchoukine, "La peinture à Yazd au milieu du XIème siècle," in *Syria*, XI, fasc. 1–2, Paris, 1963, pp. 139–145.
[29]T.W. Lentz, G.D. Lowry, *Timur and the Princely Vision*, Los Angeles, Washington, 1989, pp. 364–365.

es of Herat and Shiraz of the end of the 15th and beginning of the 16th centuries. In fact, each group of masters arrived with his own style that naturally continued to evolve slowly. The *Shāhnāma* by Firdausī created in Tabriz in 1524 (cat. no. 39) is a striking example of a combination of artists working in different styles.

However, in the following period, corresponding to the first quarter of Ṭahmāsp I's reign, the Tabriz school developed its own style, which distinguishes itself by its great technical perfection, by elegance and lightness of drawing, a range of light colors, greater refinement of the figures. There was a great emphasis placed on details in landscapes (background landscapes giving smoothly defined contours to mountains).

Throughout the entire 16th century, the Shiraz school continued, and its production represents a large share of all the miniatures painted in Persia during the 16th century. In the first years following the accession to power of the Safavids (1502) there was little change in style (cat. no. 34). Towards 1515, there came signs of change, under the influence of the style that arose in Tabriz. Around 1530, the new style has developed completely: a softer and more discrete palette of color, a tendency to keep contrasting bright colors to a minimum, and a specific disposition with a vertical layout. This latter particularity is the very rule of the Shiraz school of that period (cat. nos. 43, 44).

In 1598, the Safavid shah, ʿAbbas I (1587–1629), transferred the capital to Isfahan, which was situated in an authentically Iranian region. There, on the basis of the Qazvin school, the new Isfahan school came into being. It was to occupy the leading position among Persian miniature painting schools during the 17th and the beginning of the 18th centuries. The Isfahan school absorbed the local provincial schools and became the school of the empire. The main founder was the eminent Persian artist, Aqā Riẓā ibn ʿAlī Aṣghar Kāshānī (died in 1635), better known by the name of Riẓā-i ʿAbbāsī. His work represents an era of history in Persian painting (cat. no. 51, folio 17r). His pupils and disciples continued his style until the end of the 17th century. His direct pupil, Mu'īn Muṣavvir (died

Above and left:
Abū Muḥammad al-Qāsim ibn ʿAlī al-Ḥarīrī al-Baṣrī, Maqāmāt*("The Assemblies"), cat. no. 18.*

in 1697–1698), who produced a series of Indian ink drawings and miniatures, is to be seen in the exhibition with the *Portrait of Tīmūr-khān Turkmān* (cat. no. 51, folio 1r). It is curious that this portrait was begun by a famous artist, literary personality, poet and soldier, Ṣādiqī beg Afshār (1533–1610), for whose drawings in the artist's own words, "merchants pay three tomans to sell them in Hindustan."[30] Muḥammad Yūsuf Muṣavvir clearly continued in the style of Riżā-i ᶜAbbāsī and in 1658 painted a miniature in Mashhad illustrating a quatrain of the great ᶜUmar Khayyām (cat. no. 51, folio 6r).
In the Isfahan style of the middle and second half of the 17th century are miniatures of the magnificent copy of the *Akhlāq-i Muḥsinī* ("The Ethics of Muḥsin"; cat. no. 46) and the *Kitāb-i ḥashā'ish* ("Book of Plants"), that is sumptuously illustrated (cat. no. 49).
Mu'īn Muṣavvir was the last of the celebrated Persian artists working in the style of Riżā-i ᶜAbbāsī and maintaining the secular traditions of authentically Persian miniatures. As of the second half of the 17th century, a further change appeared under the influence of European painting: the introduction of light and shadow, and perspective. This new style is fully expressed in the work of two masters active during the reign of Shāh Sulaimān (1666–1694): ᶜAlī Qulī Beg Jabbādār (cat. no. 51, folio 1r; cat. no. 52, folio 98r) and Muḥammad Zamān ibn Ḥājjī Yūsuf Qumī (cat. no. 52, folios 82r, 86r, 89r). The works closest in style to Muḥammad Zamān are those of the artist Muḥammad Sulṭānī, who was probably his pupil (cat. no. 51, folio 42r). The internal wars for power in Iran that followed for almost fifty years after the fall of the Safavid dynasty (1736) and the death of Nādir Shāh Afshār (1747) dealt a heavy blow to the country's cultural life. However, when the domestic situation stabilized in Isfahan at the end of the 18th century, the old traditions of miniature painting were taken up again (cat. no.

Opposite and following page: *Musharrif al-Dīn ibn Muṣliḥ al-Dīn Saᶜdī al-Shīrāzī,* Gulistān *("The Rose Garden"), cat. no. 38.*

58). In the middle and the second half of the 16th century, a brilliant school of miniature painting was created at the court of the Great Mughals (Bāburid-Timurid). At its origin were talented Persian masters like Mīr Sayyid ʿAlī Tabrīzī, ʿAbd al-Ṣamad al-Shīrāzī and, somewhat later, Aqā Riżā Haravī Jahāngīrī, and artists from other Persian centers and Transoxiana. But India itself had its pictorial tradition. In fact, the Mughal miniature is the synthesis of the pictorial traditions of Iran, India and Europe. It reached its zenith during the reign of Jahāngīr (1605–1627) (cat. no. 52, folio 21r) and Shāh Jahān (1628–1657) (cat. no. 52, folio 34r).

During the second half of the 18th century, an original school arose in Kashmir from a synthesis of Central Asian Muslim, Indian and Persian traditions, although the extent of its influence and circulation are considerably larger and include the regions of Darvaz and Badakhshan (cat. no. 59).

Exterior Aspect, Dimensions, Binding

The mediaeval Muslim codex had, in most cases, a modest and unpretentious exterior aspect. Only its binding was occasionally luxurious. In regard to its dimensions, it is hardly different from modern-day Arabic books, reproducing a certain form dictated by its function: the format is generally between 18 and 35 cm high, and 13 to 25 cm wide. Nevertheless, there are a small number of tiny or enormous manuscripts. One rarely comes across formats that are wider than the height.

Arabic writing does not use capital letters, paragraphs or division in paragraphs. The title and name of the author are found on the first page by themselves or in front of the text. They are sometimes written by the owner or the library keeper on the binding on the edge. Generally, one only finds the title, without the author's name.

The oldest way of calculating the vol-

Qur'an, cat. no. 64.

ume of an Arabic manuscript is to count by books (*kurrāsa, juz', daftar, mujallad*) of ten, sometimes eight or twelve folios. The ordered number of the book is written at the beginning, in the top right-hand corner of the first page.

In the Muslim world, bookbinding has existed for at least eleven centuries. This art, like the manufacture of a manuscript generally, is the heritage of a tradition that has existed for long in the ancient East and Middle East, among Christians, Jews and Manicheans. The seeds of a new manufacturing technique, found in the Mamluk bindings at the start of the 14th century, were then further developed and perfected at Tabriz towards the beginning of the 15th century and especially at Herat around 1420 and the beginning of the 16th century. The standards created in Herat, perfected by the Tabriz masters and then by local masters, define the parameters of the art of bookbinding in Persia and neighboring countries until the 17th century. They are as follows:

1. A plant pattern replaced geometrical motifs and abstract drawings as the main decorative element on the cover. The central panel gradually turned into a miniature, painted on the skin, depicting gardens, a scene full of plants, birds and exotic beasts, dragons, phoenixes, large-leafed trees and flowers, mountains and "clouds of happiness." These elements were borrowed from Chinese painting and assimilated as decorative ornaments which had lost their traditional symbolic and mythological sense.
2. The technique of gold filigree on the skin, already known from Coptic and Uighur-Manichean bindings of the 8th and 9th centuries, was reused. It involves using colored paper, applying a fine dyed skin and sometimes fabric. It is called *mannabatkārī* (literally: make something stand out, put it in relief by cutting the surrounding material). According to tradition, it was used for the first time by the Tabriz master, Qavām al-Dīn, whom Bāisunghur Mīrzā brought to Herat in 1420.
3. All these ornaments of binding become possible thanks to the use of new instruments and techniques. The lines of the central inset were stamped and angles traced using a cutter or a rounded instrument to cut. To replace certain iron or wooden matrices that were used till then, quadrangular stamping blocks with engraved decorative sets, practically all with decorative elements in the upper section of the binding, were used. For this technique a camel or donkey skin was specially prepared and reinforced (remounted).

Lacquer bindings were introduced at the beginning of the 15th century by the masters of Herat, created under the influence of painted lacquer Chinoiseries that were very much in vogue in Herat then. Towards the end of the century, the monochrome bindings of the first half of the 15th century gave way to bindings painted with polychrome. The best examples of lacquer bindings were produced in Tabriz and Qazvin in the 16th century. In producing these bindings, the painter (expert in miniature or ornamental art) was of great importance. To begin with, the drawing was lacquered directly on to the (slightly reinforced) skin. However, bindings like that did not last long, the lacquer cracked and the paint flaked. Finally, another technique was used: on thick paper, made up of several sheets, well glued and reinforced with chalk (papier mâché), the lacquer was applied in several layers. The support for a watercolor picture was prepared in that way. Over the watercolor, several layers of colorless lacquer were again separately applied as a protection, with gold or silver, and even mother-of-pearl powder was added.

The exhibition presents leather and lacquer bindings produced in various regions of the Islamic world including Southern Persia, Shiraz (cat. nos 25, 29, mid-15th century), Egypt (cat. no. 34; 15th century), Eastern Persia, Herat (cat. nos. 28, 33, 37, 38, 1420–1550), Transox-

Arabic Version of Ancient Popular Stories, cat. no. 53.

iana, Bukhara (cat. no. 40; 1530–1540), Western Persia, Tabriz (cat. no. 39; 1520), Turkey, Constantinople (cat. no. 53; 1530), album binding (cat. no. 51; by master Muḥammad Shafīʿ ibn Muḥammad Masīḥ; 1731–1732), Iraq (cat. no 63; beginning of the 18th century), Isfahan (cat. no. 64; end of the 18th century), Syria (cat. no. 66; mid-19th century). The Gospels in Arabic (cat no. 48), bound in leather with silver inlay, stands apart. Its binding was made in the mid-17th century with the participation of Russian bookbinders. There are even fewer bindings from the early centuries than manuscripts. Designed to embellish and protect, they were the first to suffer. Furthermore, they quickly broke off from the spine which was often not sufficiently solid. In most cases, the bindings were not made at the same time as the manuscripts.

The characteristic feature of the Muslim binding is the extension of the left cover that forms a flap in two parts, the first is quadrangular, the same length and width as the book, the second, pentagonal, fitted beneath the right front flap. The flap protects the outside edges of the folios.

Beside the binding, some manuscripts were provided with a *ṣandūq* (sheath) of cardboard, sometimes covered in leather, all-over or just at the edges.

It is now acknowledged that, technically speaking, European bookbinding was wholly dependent on the Oriental craft (especially as regards Muslim bookbinding techniques).[31]

The History of Collecting and Research of Islamic Manuscripts

Manuscripts were the main subject of research in Oriental studies in Europe during the 16th–18th centuries. At that time, ancient—like contemporary literature, in the Arabic, Persian, Turkic and other Islamic eastern languages—were almost entirely handwritten, as the art of book printing in the Arabic script was practically non-existent. The pioneers of Arabic studies in Europe hunted out and gathered manuscripts that were mainly sold in markets. Given the military, political, commercial and economic superiority of the West, European collectors and specialists had access to the manuscripts. European collections grew steadily and proliferated. But their scientific assimilation was slower because of the scarcity of specialists.

In the 19th century, work took off because of the flow of bibliographic listings and critical editions. A systematic effort at cataloguing works and authors began. From time to time, the accumulated data was synthesized, and so stimulated work devoted to technical and artistic aspects: layout, illumination, binding, writing materials, paleography, and libraries. In the 20th century, all these subjects have been further developed.

In Oriental countries, where most Arabic manuscripts are to be found (despite the export of the most precious items), cataloguing began in an irregular and

[30]Muḥammad Ṭāhir Naṣrābādī, *Tadhkīra*, Tehran, 1937, pp. 39–40.

[31]F. Sarre, *Islamische Bucheinbande*, Berlin, 1923, p. 9. This was a major stimulus in the research of the history of artistic binding in the Arab East among a series of monographs by Western specialists (see bibliography: E. Gratzl, K.A.S. Creswell, R. Ettinghausen, "Bibliographie des Islamischen Einbandkunst, 1871–1956," in *Ars Orientalis*, vol. 2, Ann Arbor, 1956, pp. 519–540; supplements: G. Endress, *Handschriftenkunde, Grundriss des Arabischen Philologie*, vol. 1: *Sprachwissenschaft*, edited by W. Fisher, Wiesbaden, 1982, pp. 277–278, 308–310). Unfortunately, the bindings of the manuscripts in St. Petersburg Arabic collections and elsewhere in the country have not yet been studied by art critics.

sporadic fashion in the last quarter of the 19th century. There has been substantial progress in these countries once political independence was achieved.
In Arab countries, one of the main tasks in the study of humanities is research, interpretation and promotion of "the heritage" (*al-turāth*), "our heritage," "the Arab heritage."

History of the Collection in the Institute of Oriental Studies in St. Petersburg

In Russia, interest into serious research and collecting of Islamic literary works coincided with the founding of the Asiatic Museum of the Academy of Sciences in 1818. At that time, the St. Petersburg Academy of Sciences owned thirty or forty Arabic, Persian and Turkic manuscripts of a theological and grammatical nature.
When the Museum was founded, in accordance with S.S. Uvarov, the President of the Academy of Sciences, the Oriental manuscripts held in the Kunstkamera, the Conference Archives and the Library of the Academy of Sciences were to be handed over to the new Institute, destined to become the center of Oriental studies in Russia. Unfortunately, we no longer have the general inventory of Islamic manuscripts given to the Museum, nor the other Oriental manuscripts.[32] Nevertheless, we can say with relative certainty that there were not many, probably a hundred or so,[33] but enough to launch Arab and Muslim studies in Russia during the 19th century[34].
The Museum has steadily and methodically built up its collection since then. A large number of Islamic manuscripts came into the Museum thanks to orientalists, diplomats, travelers, collectors, civil servants (soldiers and civilians).[35] Assets more than doubled thanks to the acquisition of two collections (in 1819, five hundred manuscripts for the sum of 36,000 francs and in 1825, two hundred for 15,000 francs) from the Consul General of France in Aleppo, then in Tripolitania, Jean-Louis Rousseau (1780–1831), the grandson of the celebrated Jean-Jacques Rousseau.
At the end of the 18th century, Rousseau left Geneva for Syria and grew up in the East. While remaining a representative of French culture, he became a true Levantine. He spoke fluent Arabic, Persian and Turkish. He was not only familiar with Turkey, but also with Persia, where he went on important diplomatic and trade missions for the French government. Following in the steps of his father as a trade and consular official, he surpassed him in knowledge and scientific interest for the countries where he lived. The long stay in Aleppo, that was then a regional cultural center, developed his taste for literature. He gradually built up a major and intelligently selected collection.
Rousseau spent the second part of his somewhat turbulent life in African Tripoli. His financial situation at that time, around 1815, was such that he had to consider selling his collection. He first proposed selling it to the French government but, ruined by the Napoleonic wars, the state could not afford the relatively high price that the owner justifiably was asking. The most eminent Oriental scholar of the time, Silvestre de Sacy (1758–1838), was well aware of the importance of this collection. By way of students invited to St. Petersburg, he informed the Minister of Public Education, Uvarov, a personal friend of his who was the originator of the Asiatic Academy project which had so aroused the interest of Goethe. The collection was purchased in two parts, in 1819 and 1825. France lost a precious asset that was to play a vital role in Russia, as it became the foundation of the Asiatic Museum. By its great attraction, no less than that of the coins in the academic collection, it kept the celebrated Ch.D. Fraehn in Russia, who returned from Kazan to Rostock, his native city, to assume the chair of his deceased teacher.

[32]Furthermore, the material published and archive documents show that Ch.D. Fraehn made a detailed inventory of works from the contributing institutions. Clearly, only one of the three inventories was preserved and published. Compare, for example, the inventory from the Conference Archives. See B. Dorn, *Das Asiatische Museum der Kaiserlichen Akademie de Wissenschaften zu St. Petersburg*, St. Petersburg, 1846, pp. 216–218 (on p. 217 an Arabic manuscript is mentioned).
[33]Such a number of manuscripts gives the following account, so long as all manuscripts were carefully noted in the documents we used (St. Petersburg Archive Department of the Russian Academy of Sciences, fund 152, inventory 1, affair 1061), in 1828, 851 Arabic, Persian and Turkic manuscripts were held (B. Dorn, *Das Asiatische Museum...*, cit., p. 385), from 1819 to 1828, 746 manuscripts were acquired. Subsequently, the basis consisted of 105 manuscripts.
[34]I.Y. Krachkovskii, *Essais sur l'histoire des études arabisantes*, Moscow-Leningrad, 1950, pp. 71–72, 80, 88, 98, 104–105, 106, 112, 120, 123–124, 136, 171, 178.
[35]Three other Islamic manuscript collections were developed in St. Petersburg, at the Public Library (now the Russian National Library), the Library of the Oriental Faculty at the University and the Library of the former Section of Foreign Affairs Studies.
[36]I.Y. Krachkovskii, *Concerning Arabic Manuscripts...*, cit., p. 68, Berlin.

As the first curator of the Asiatic Museum, the founder of research in Arabic sciences in our country, he fully appreciated the worth of the collection, and with the assiduity of a Benedictine monk produced the first inventory, in several tomes.[36] It is most important to note that the Russian collector, P.P. Dubrovskii, who lived for many years in Paris, was very instrumental in the acquisition. "This initial contribution was never equaled, either as regards the remarkable scope of valuable and rare manuscripts collected in a single assembly, or as concerns the impact that the Rousseau collection had on science,"[37] and finally, because the Islamic manuscripts in the Asiatic Museum were instantly raised to the leading position among similar European institutions.

The acquisition of the Rousseau collection may be taken as a fortuitous factor, but the systematic development of the Museum was largely thanks to the driving force of Ch.D. Fraehn (1782–1851), the Asiatic Museum's first curator. He did his utmost to obtain special credits; he used the proceeds from the sale of duplicates; he drew up a list of reference works that had to be found on a priority basis; he demanded from the Ministry of Defense that manuscripts and other objects of cultural interest taken as trophies and spoils of war should be handed over to the Museum.

As director of the Asiatic Museum from 1818–1842, Fraehn endlessly attempted, with the devout enthusiasm of the scientist and as most of his successors, to turn the Asiatic Museum into the reception center for all manuscripts, not just from Russia but from abroad as well,[38] a center where they not only would be kept, but where they would be studied.[39] By way of example, in 1833, he suggested to the Minister of Finance, Count E.F. Kankrin, that the Ministry should instruct consuls appointed to Eastern countries[40] to buy coins and manuscripts for the Museum.[41] Kankrin refused.[42] But Ch.D. Fraehn managed to make his successor, F.P. Vronchenko, issue such a directive in 1844 that remained in force until the outbreak of the First World War. As a result, thanks to the efforts and zeal of Russian consuls in Eastern countries, a series of valuable documents were added to the Museum's collection.

Until about 1875, the number of Islamic manuscripts increased relatively slowly and largely because of foreign sources (sale of collections by Oriental scholars, acquisitions by Russian consuls and diplomats, etc.).[43] These manuscripts were placed at the disposition of foreign specialists, who conducted research or critical studies of the texts.[44] The book by Krachkovskii, *Arabic Manuscripts. Memories of Libraries and People*, was printed in several editions and translated into a series of foreign languages. It made the St. Petersburg collection of manuscripts especially popular.[45]

In the 1870s, Rosen (1849–1908) started his immense work. His father was German, his mother half-Georgian and half-Russian. He founded a new school of Russian Oriental studies, and saw the description of the St. Petersburg manuscripts as his main task. He started by making an excellent catalogue of the Arabic manuscripts in the library of the Foreign Ministry's school, and then a systematic catalogue of the manuscripts in the Asiatic Museum. He hoped to complete the work that Fraehn had started. V. R. Rosen soon published a first catalogue in French (1881), providing details of three hundred manuscripts, and an outline of how to complete the work on all the outstanding texts. "However," wrote Krachkovskii, "he did not finish the second volume... because the Academy of Sciences lost interest."[46] So, for some time, this project came to a halt.

In 1890, K.G. Salemann, a German originally from Tallinn and a specialist in Iranian studies, became director of the Museum until his death in 1916. Right at the beginning of his period in office he wrote a report to the Academy of Sci-

[37]V.I. Belyaev, *Arabic Manuscripts in the Collection of the Oriental Research Institute of the USSR Academy of Sciences*, "Learned notes from the Institute of Oriental Studies." 1953, VI, p. 55.

[38]Obviously, all the manuscripts or several collections were not bought by the Museum. Many had to be relinquished, mainly because of the high price requested by the owners. But when it was due to administrative delay or lack of understanding, that factor always leaves a sense of bitterness and regret. That was the case with the J.Cl. Rich collection, the East India Company representative in Baghdad. When Rich died of cholera in Shiraz in 1824, his widow proposed selling, through the intermediary of Silvestre de Sacy, the collection of Islamic manuscripts carefully gathered by her husband, consisting of over 400 volumes, to the Russian Ministry of Foreign Affairs for 100,000 francs. Negotiations took a very long time not just because it took time to find the necessary financing, but also because of administrative inertia, and uncertainty regarding the utility of such a collection. Finally, Mr. Rich's widow sold the manuscripts to the British Museum in London for £ 7,500 in April 1825. Such unexpected turn of events was quite decisive in the purchase, at the end of 1825, of the second collection offered by J.L. Rousseau, resulting in a rapid and positive conclusion. O.F. Akimushkin, *Kistorii*, p. 11.

[39]Cited from D.E. Berthels, *The Asiatic Museum - The Leningrad Branch of the Institute of Oriental Studies of the USSR Academy of Sciences*, Moscow, 1972, p. 16.

[40]At that time, consuls were appointed by the Ministry of Finance, and as a result, were not granted the same privileges as diplomats.

Opposite:
Facade of the Grand Duke Michael's Palace on the Neva, now the St. Petersburg Branch of the Institute of Oriental Studies, Russian Academy of Sciences.

ences (1891) concerning the "Mahometan" manuscripts accumulated but not catalogued, and expressed his confidence that a complete catalogue would soon be printed. Continuing the work of his predecessors, he paid great attention to curating, research and development of the Museum's collection.

At the end of the 19th and the beginning of the 20th centuries, Russian and foreign orientalists continued to use the Museum's manuscripts for their research and publications. In 1896, Baron David Gintzburg, a student of Rosen's but also of the Frenchman S. Guyard, a specialist in Arabic metrics, subsidized the printing in Berlin of a facsimile edition of the unique manuscript of Ibn Quzmān's poems, a very important source for research into Arabic-Spanish poetry of the 12th century (cat. no. 19). Gintzburg was a collector and book lover. The owner of sugar factories, he "nevertheless found the time to study the poetry of the Arabs and Jews, his posthumous papers contained an almost completed paper on the metrics of Lermontov's poems."[47] Fascinated by Muslim Spain, he had intended to make special research into the manuscript of Ibn Quzmān's collection of poems. "The vast plan that he gave in the subtitle and preface could have been the programme for a man's whole life," wrote Krachkovskii. Gintzburg's publication encouraged many fine specialists to work on this document. "It seems," said Krachkovskii, "that this manuscript held such appeal for all scholars that there are very few who have not spent time, in many cases, years, studying the yellowing pages or their photographs... In fact, the world of international science, united in a single purpose! How touching were the last words of a Finnish specialist, speaking on his death bed in hospital, of his work on Ibn Quzmān: 'Oh, peaceful international effort! May you continue despite all that threatens you today!'"[48]

Material for the History of the Golden Horde by V.G. Tisenhausen, *Turkestan* by V.V. Barthold, *Palestine* by N.A. Mednikov are books that still have impact today, relying as they do on the Museum's manuscripts. The authoritative thesis of Krachkovskii was based on research made on the manuscripts of al-Wā'wā of Damascus' compilation of poems, two of which are in the collection.[49] Barthold and Krachkovskii wrote a series of monograph descriptions of individual Arabic manuscripts belonging to the Museum.

After Russia's annexation of the Caucasus and especially Central Asia, the book markets that were previously abroad were on Russian territory. This had immediate repercussions on developing the Museum's collection. Statistics show that between 1880 and 1917 the number of Arabic, Persian and Turkic manuscripts was practically quadrupled and reached a figure slightly higher than 2,500, largely due to acquisitions in Central Asia.

Information from Russian civil servants in Central Asia[50] indicated that the most valuable manuscripts were being sold abroad, which raised the question of massive purchasing, especially on the Bukhara and Samarqand markets, and of special expeditions. Salemann approached the administrative committee of the Academy of Sciences and asked them to grant the appropriate funds. In 1897, he went on the first expedition which proved to be a great success. The second voyage was not so positive. However, the outcome of V.A. Ivanov's trip to Bukhara in 1915 went way beyond all expectations. This collection, subsequently called the "Bukhara" consisted of 1,057 volumes. Naturally, they were not all of equal quality, because Ivanov followed Salemann's instructions "to buy everything he could find."[51] But they represented a whole, the entire intellectual existence of Bukhara and Transoxiana over several centuries. They are still waiting for a researcher who will develop the historic-cultural

[41]Furthermore, Ch.D. Fraehn compiled a list with B.A. Dorn of the one hundred most important manuscripts. Many scholars of Arabic and of Islamic studies used the document. In 1845, Ch.D. Fraehn enlarged and completed the list at the request of the Minister of Finance, F. P. Vronchenko. That same year the list, with already 244 works, was printed. The issue of developing the Museum's collection was a source for concern among many intellectuals of the time. The well-known Russian writer and Arabic scholar O. I. Senkovskii (1800–1858) drafted a note in the name of Tsar Nicholas I, in which he proposed introducing an article in the peace treaty with Iran whereby Iran would hand over to Russia 500 or so of its most valuable manuscripts. The list was drawn up by O. I. Senkovskii with the help of Ch.D. Fraehn. Nicholas I declined the proposal. See I.E. Borshchevskii, *The Story of the Acquisition of the Ardebil Collection of Manuscripts by Russia*, Proceedings of the IV Conference of the USSR concerning Iranian philology (papers), Tbilisi, 1970, p. 158.

[42]E. F. Krankrin accepted the proposal of the academician, but with a minor modification, that the manuscripts acquired by the consuls should be deposited, not at the Asiatic Museum, but in the Ministry of Finance Board Library.

[43]As an illustration here are some figures from the annual reports of the Asiatic Museum's activities: 1830, 856 manuscripts; 1845, 901 manuscripts; 1861, 1,192 manuscripts; 1870, 1,289 manuscripts; 1878, 1,364 manuscripts.

[44]A few examples: in 1838 already, the manuscript *Kitāb al-aghānī* was sent to I.G.I. Kosegarten in Greifswald. F. Wüstenfeld used the Museum manuscripts for the *History of Mecca* by al-Azraqī (1858) and the *Geographic Dictionary* of Yāqūt (1866–1870), and W. Wright for the publishing of *al-Kāmil* by al-Mubarrad, T.G. Juinboll and B.F. Matthes for the work of Ibn Taghrībirdī on the history of Egypt (1852–1861). The *Cosmography* by al-Gharnāṭī (B 872) was made available to G. Ferrand (Paris); the description of the voyage of Makari of Antioch (B 1230) to that of B. Radu (Bucharest); one of the tomes of the chronicle of Ibn Iyās was wholly edited according to manuscript C–782 (Kahle and Mustafa, Cairo, 1931). The pseudo-Jāḥiz manuscript worked by Rosen was used by Van Vloten and the manuscript *Sources of Tidings* by Ibn Kutayba by C. Brockelmann. M. Amari used the unique manuscript of the *Chronicle of Manṣūr*; H. Derenbourg, the manuscript *Book of Sībawaihi*; H. Hirschfeld, the manuscript of Ḥasan ibn Thābit's collection of poems. Many art historians published reproductions of miniatures from al-Ḥarīrī's 13th-century manuscript *Maqāmāt*. A photocopy of the manuscript C–361 was given to one of the Hyderabad (India) research institutes on the publication of *Kitāb al- ansāb* by al-Samʿānī.

[45]I.Y. Krachkovskii, *Über arabische Handschriften gebeugt, Erinnerungen an Bucher und Menschen, Aus dem Russischen von Dr. Oscar P. Trautmann*, Leipzig, 1949; Ignacy Kraczkowski, *Nad arabskimi rekopisami. Kartki ze wspomnien o ksiegach i ludziach. Przelozyl oraz wstepem i przypisami opatrzyl Ananiasz Zajaczkowski*, Warsaw, 1952; I.Y. Krachkovskii, *Concerning Arabic Manuscripts, Memories of Libraries and People*, translated from Russian by Tatiana Minorskii, Leiden, 1953; I.Y. Krachkovskii, *Concerning Arabic Manuscripts (Memories of Libraries and People)*, translated from Russian by M. Canard, Algiers, 1954, Publications of the Oriental Studies Institute at the Faculty of Letters in Algiers, XIV. Also translated into Arabic by Professor Samic ad-Dakhkhan in Damascus and into Czech by Doctor Hrbek in Prague.

perspective, as did Professor V.I. Belyaev for the Arabic works (40% of the collection).[52]

Certain representatives of the Russian administration in Central Asia or members of the local Russian intelligentsia made a substantial contribution to the Museum's collection by creating contacts with merchants or by starting collections that they then offered to the Museum for sale.[53]

As before, manuscripts continued to arrive from abroad, but they were of considerably less importance. Mention should be made here of the collecting activity of a pupil of the Oriental Faculty, L.F. Bogdanov, an employee of the discount and loan bank in Tehran who, between 1909 and 1914, on written guidance of Salemann, acquired two hundred and forty-six, mostly Persian, manuscripts for the Museum. In 1916–1917, the Museum received another vast collection from the Caucasian front, thanks to the chief curator of the Caucasian Museum, S.V. Ter-Avetissian. Salvaged from devastated regions, abandoned by the population, it comprised the so-called "Van" collection.[54]

At the end of 1916, Salemann suddenly died; "death found him in the middle of identifying and classifying recently acquired Muslim manuscripts." The catalogue that he designed was never completed and his work remained in file form. The problem of his succession arose. Ivanov was invited to research the collection that he had himself gathered in Bukhara. He drew up a list of the Persian section and provided the general characteristics of the collection, but his work did not see the light of day. Krachkovskii was responsible for the groundwork on the Arabic sections of the Bukhara and Van collections and, generally speaking, the preparatory work along the lines of Rosen's catalogue system.

Despite all the hardships that Petrograd suffered at the time, a very special creative atmosphere reigned in the Asiatic Museum. "For me, the period between 1916–1921," wrote Krachkovskii, "was the time of total absorption, not just in individual manuscripts, but collections... For the first time, the picture of literary culture of a section of the Muslim world relating to Arabic culture was displayed before me. There were manuals, erudite academic treatises, in a word, the entire scope of reading material, which had nourished whole generations for several hundreds of years until the 20th century."[55]

The Asiatic museum entered a new phase of its history after the 1917 revolution. The number of Islamic manuscripts has practically been doubled since then, and it now comprises 9,874 volumes (5,184 Arabic, 14 Kurdish, 14 Malay, 28 Pushtu, 3,058 Persian, approximately 1,500 Turkish/Turkic, 3 Urdu).[56]

In the first few years following the revolution, collections from state institutions and private parties were handed over to the Museum by different government organizations: in 1919, for example, the magnificent collection of manuscripts from the Winter Palace library, that of A.A. Polovtsev and the one belonging to the research department of the Asiatic section of the Minister of Foreign Affairs.[57]

The collection of Arabic-Christian manuscripts acquired at that time requires separate treatment. Krachkovskii describes in detail how it came to St. Petersburg and the research that was made: "In 1913, the house of Romanov celebrated its jubilee. The patriarch of Antioch, Grigori al-Haddad, was invited to the feast. The newspapers wrote that he had brought a present to the Romanov family, there were rumors of books, but I paid little attention. After his departure, the rumor became more persistent. Through diverse channels, I managed to find out after the jubilee and the departure of the patriarch that certain Oriental manuscripts had indeed been handed over to His Majesty's personal library in the Winter Palace. It was no easy matter for me, a young assistant professor, to

[46]I.Y. Krachkovskii, *Selected Works*, t. V, p. 100. Also *In Memory of the Academician Rosen*, Moscow-Leningrad, 1947, pp. 133–134.

[47]I.Y. Krachkovskii, *Concerning Arabic Manuscripts...*, cit., p. 69.

[48]*Ibid.*, p. 69.

[49]*Ibid.*, p. 70.

[50]See, for example, letters of V.I. Ignatiev to K.G. Salemann (Archive Department of the St. Petersburg Russian Academy of Sciences, collection 152).

[51]V.A. Ivanov, *Lists of the Bukhara Manuscript Collection* (preface and notes by Y.E. Borshchevskii). *Literary Monuments of the East* (annual reports), 1970, Moscow, 1974, p. 412.

[52]V.I. Belyaev, The Arabic Manuscripts of the Bukhara Collection in the Asiatic Museum, the Institute of Oriental Studies of the USSR Academy of Sciences, *Work of the USSR Academy of Sciences Institute*, II, Leningrad, 1932, pp. I- XVII, 1–52.

[53]For example: D.M. Gramenitskii, 24 manuscripts; A.L. Kuhn, 133; Y.Y. Lioutsh, 28; N.F. Petrovskii, 131; F.F. Pospelov, 22; S.M. Smirnov, 57. Finally, Eastern specialists working in the capital brought manuscripts back from scientific expeditions in Central Asia: V.V. Barthold, 21; A.Z. Validov, 26; S.F. Oldenburg, 89; A.N. Samoilovitch, 42. The collection of N.F. Petrovskii and S.F. Oldenburg aroused special interest as they were gathered in Eastern Turkestan and are a relatively complete image of the literary activity in that region. Similarly, the collection of A.N. Samoilovitch, dating from 1913, of overall interest, contains 34 Turkmen manuscripts.

[54]The initiative of safeguarding manuscripts originated in the Academy of Sciences which, on the suggestion of the Academician N.Y. Marr, took a special turn. In 1926, a substantial section of the Turkish (Ottoman) manuscripts were sent to Moscow. They are now conserved in the Library of the International Relations Institute in Moscow.

[55]I.Y. Krachkovskii, *Concerning Arabic Manuscripts...*, cit., p. 65.

[56]According to the inventories of the Department of Manuscripts in the Branch of the St. Petersburg Institute of Oriental Studies, Russian Academy of Sciences, it was clear that the figure of 12,000 manu-

gain entrance there, but on the persistence of the Academy of Sciences, who were behind me, all the obstacles erected by the court ministry, the police and palace guard were overcome. I received permission to go at certain times and so long as the Tsar's family was not there. Accompanied by a special guard, I was led through an intricate series of subterranean passages to the library building. There was a senior civil servant-chamberlain at the head of the library, who was not there every day; his aide was a general. The purpose of my presence was not clear to them and perhaps for that reason, at the table opposite me, there was always an official, with a French novel in hand, sitting and observing me closely.
Working conditions were not very satisfactory, I was given only one manuscript at a time and it was not possible to see again a document that had already been looked at. It was even forbidden to measure the format of the manuscript. There was no manual in the library, and it was out of the question to bring anything whatsoever with me. All notes were carefully scrutinized and not always returned immediately, for an expert to have the time to see whether my notes in Arabic did not contain some code or other. The patriarch had brought forty or so manuscripts, a complete collection, built with a thorough knowledge of the subject, remarkable examples and frequently unique copies. They admirably characterized the various aspects of Arab Christian literature. I did not have the time to get over one surprise before the next manuscript brought another. It was clear that, with this collection, our country had been given a selection of Christian and Arabic works that compared in quality to those of Paris, the Vatican, Beirut. The Arabic Bible in three volumes, that the Vatican much envies [fig. D-226], gave rise to a plethora of specialist literature and a great controversy, comparing our copy with that of Rome.[58] After the revolution, the Academy of Science's request for the transfer of this collection to the Asiatic Museum was quickly granted, and one frosty winter day, in February 1919, accompanied by a student and an assistant, I personally dragged the forty manuscripts on a sledge, carefully wrapped in sheep skins, through the empty streets of Petrograd, to the old building of the Asiatic Museum."[59]

In the period from 1917 to 1925, the Museum boomed under the directorship of S.F. Oldenburg. The Museum became a hub of scientific Oriental studies in Leningrad. Oldenburg (1853–1934), an eminent scholar in Indian studies, played a special role in the preservation and spreading of the specifically Russian tradition in Oriental research. A single instance from his life speaks volumes for the scientific and cultural ambiance of that period: he was Minister of Instruction in the interim government before it was toppled by the Bolsheviks. Ten to twelve years passed before the appalling wave of Stalinist terror swept through the ranks of even the most modest Oriental scholars, shot or tortured in the camps of Siberia. In 1930, the Asiatic Museum, which had continued to develop its collections during the post-revolutionary period,[60] was reorganized into the Institute of Oriental Studies of the USSR Academy of Sciences. Before, it was a question of increasing the collection, now it was a matter of safeguarding the national heritage, the cultural wealth of the numerous peoples belonging to the USSR, especially the nations of the Caucasus, Transcaucasia, the region of the Volga and Central Asia.
In 1934, an archaeographic expedition was sent by the Academy of Sciences to collect manuscripts in the SSR of Tatar. V.A. Zabinov, the scientific representative of the Institute of Oriental Studies of the USSR Academy of Sciences and S.G. Vahidov, a specialist in Kazan, a book-lover and historian were members. This expedition alone brought back 1,564 manuscripts to the Institute,

scripts quoted by V.I. Belyaev would imply the number of copies rather than the quantity of volumes (V.I. Belyaev, *Arabic Manuscripts*, cit., p. 55).
[57]In fact, these manuscripts only came into the Museum in 1921. Since 1917, they had been in the archives of the former Ministry of Foreign Affairs. By its selection and composition and scientific importance, the collection of the Studies Branch gave way to the collections of J.L. Rousseau. Unfortunately, when transferring the manuscripts to Moscow and on their return, some were lost (about 20). Some time later, K.I. Chaikin, A.A. Starikov, and B.N. Zahkoder bought some of these manuscripts from antique dealers. After the death of Starikov (1962) and Zakhoder (1960), the manuscripts that were in their personal libraries entered the Republican Manuscripts Collection of the Azerbaijan Academy of Sciences (Baku) and the collection of the Institute of Oriental Studies of the Tajik Academy of Sciences (Dushanbe). Cf. the publication of D.E. Berthels and L.V. Dmitrieva, V.A. Zhukovskii, "Description of Manuscripts in the School of Oriental Languages of the Asiatic Department of the Ministry of Foreign Affairs," in *Literary Monuments of the East* (annual reports), 1971, Moscow, 1974, pp. 455–463, 480.
[58]I.Y. Krachkovskii, *Concerning Arabic Manuscripts...*, cit., pp. 42–45.
[59]*Ibid.*, p. 45.
[60]Towards 1930, the collection of Islamic manuscripts was increased with those of V.A. Yakubkovskii (33 manuscripts), A.A. Semyonov (43), the USSR Embassy in Iran (25), V.I. Anuchin (22), N.S. Pashkin, the traveler (171), and others.
[61]On December 17th, 1934, V.A. Zabirov reported to the historians, sociologists, economists and orientalists under the USSR Academy of Sciences' Presidium on the results of the expeditions. The decision was taken to continue the effort of searching for and gathering of manuscripts, extending the area to not only the Tatar SSR, but to the entire Volga region, to Astrakhan, including Bashkir and along the Ural river (V.A. Zabirov, *The Preliminary Report on the Work of the Archeographic Expedition of the Academy of Sciences*, The Collected An-

including 362 unique items offered by Vahidov himself. Manuscripts were sent from the Volga, Astrakhan, Bashkiria, etc.[61]

The specialists of the older generation often spoke of the unique creative atmosphere of the Asiatic Museum, the complete liberty of scientific thought that gradually lost ground as the ideological pressure of new science took root. "We were sad," wrote Krachkovskii in respect of those years, "because the work on the manuscripts and the collections that, after all, was the essence and very life of the Asiatic Museum, took second place and its crucial importance was no longer understood. The restricted circle of specialists, living in the midst of these books and for them only, was becoming lost in an organization of scientific research that was staffed with tens and then hundreds of officials with grandiose ideas. All that was perfectly conforming to the law and clear, but we had memories of the old Asiatic Museum, as one remembers the beauty of hand-made artifacts disappearing under the pressure of contemporary industrial progress. It was inevitable, but for those who had grown up in the former atmosphere, one can understand their regret."[62]

Nevertheless, the collections continued to be assiduously studied. In the 1920s and 1930s, specialists conducted numerous research projects on the manuscripts in the Asiatic Museum, Institute of Oriental Studies.[63] In 1938, the Islamic manuscripts and documents from the Institute of books, documents and writing (formerly, the private collection of N.P. Likhachev) was added to the collection.[64]

There was a general trend at that time for massive acquisitions of manuscripts coming from Central Asian and Caucasian republics. However, with the creation of local state depositories (in Dushanbe, Baku, Erevan, Kazan, Makhachkala, Tashkent and Tbilisi),[65] the need to systematically purchase manuscripts in these areas was no longer felt.[66] The flow of Islamic manuscripts to Leningrad slowly dried up and finally stopped. But even today, the St. Petersburg Branch of the Institute of Oriental Studies, Russian Academy of Sciences has the largest collection of Islamic manuscripts, and is still the most important collection of Oriental manuscripts in the country.

During the Great Patriotic War, the Institute had very little leeway to make new acquisitions, but in 1944, 17 manuscripts belonging to B.D. Yunusov were purchased in Tashkent.

The war, the siege of the city, the death of many specialists, the interruption in training new cadres, repeated relocation of the collections and reorganization of the Institute resulted in a prolonged halt to research. Only in the 1950s did it resume with the need to prepare a catalogue of Persian-Tajik and Turkic manuscripts.[67] The collection continued growing.[68] This important stage in the existence of the collection is linked to the name of the academician I.A. Orbeli who headed the Institute from 1956 to 1961.

Gradually, young specialists, graduates from the Oriental Faculty of the Leningrad State University, joined the Institute of Oriental Studies of the Academy of Sciences (in the Leningrad Branch of Oriental manuscripts, and as of 1956, the Leningrad Branch) and work resumed.[69]

Today, the St. Petersburg Branch of the Institute of Oriental Studies, Russian Academy of Sciences is a leading center for scientific research for the study of the manuscript tradition of Oriental peoples. Many researchers have presented and supported their theses within its premises and are now continuing their work in numerous former Soviet Republics and foreign countries.

The spiritual liberation of the nation enables the Branch's researchers, a refuge for free scientific thought even during the years of ideological pressure, to fulfill numerous projects that were held in abeyance for so long.

We are preparing several sets of manuscripts for publication. Research work

nals, 1935, no. 5, p. 281). Early in 1935, the Presidium of the Academy of Sciences also ratified the decision taken at that meeting to register the most valuable manuscripts held in local depositories, and to hand the manuscripts over to the Institute if such a facility was not locally available. As of 1936, S.A. Alimov was to regularly send manuscripts from Astrakhan, acquired at the Institute's request. In 1941, he was to separately send 472 manuscripts. That same year, I.N. Bikchenteev, a native of Ufa, offered his very precious collection of 66 manuscripts on the history of Bashkir to the Institute.

[62] I.Y. Krachkovskii, *Concerning Arabic Manuscripts...*, cit., p. 66.

[63] They included an article by V.A. Eberman on several Arabic manuscripts from Iran, and a list drawn up by V.I. Belyaev, of Arabic manuscripts from V.A. Ivanov's Bukhara collection. I.Y. Krachkovskii continued his studies and produced further monographic descriptions of manuscripts and publications of texts. M.A. Salie wrote a paper on the manuscripts of the *Thousand and One Nights* and V.I. Belyaev wrote an article on the unique manuscript of the anonymous chronicle of the 11th century. A.I. Borisov published papers on the manuscript of the astrological work of Tankelushi and miniatures of the *Maqāmāt* by al-Ḥarīrī; S.L. Volin wrote a paper on the Arabic manuscripts with Khwarazmian glosses and commentaries (see N 4334–4337, 4493). Some Arabic manuscripts were named in the first tome of *Materials for the History of the Turkmen and Turkmenia*, in the publication of *Ibn Faḍlān's Travels*, by A.P. Kovalevskii; A.M. Barabanov translated and prepared a chronicle on the history of the Shāmil movement.

[64] V.I. Belyaev, *The Arabic Manuscript Book in the Collection of the Institute of Books, Documents and Writing of the USSR Academy of Sciences*, Moscow-Leningrad, 1936.

[65] This produced results. At the end of 1977, the Manuscripts Department of the Institute of Oriental Studies of the Uzbek Academy of Sciences listed 23,687 copies, 6,989 of which were described in the ten tomes of the catalogue. *The collection of Oriental manuscripts of the Uzbekistan Academy of Sciences*, Tashkent, 1952, 1954, 1955, 1957, 1960, 1963, 1964, 1967, 1971, 1975. Cf.

continues on the most valuable documents. A computerized data base is being prepared, gathering the vast amount of information relating to the manuscripts and making it available to colleagues working thousands of kilometers away from St. Petersburg. Many of these projects are only possible because of international cooperation.

Friends of the Institute are to be found the world over and not just among orientalists. The ARCH Foundation is one such, and it is its president, Francesca von Habsburg, who initiated the idea of this exhibition and is constantly attentive to the scientific community in these difficult times, which Russian science, overall, is going through. A short while ago, on the instigation of the German financier, Jan Mayer, the Society of Friends of the St. Petersburg Branch of the Institute of Oriental Studies of the Russian Academy of Sciences was registered in Frankfurt-am-Main. The Society has actively aided us just when state subsidies to science have been drastically cut.

In the conclusion of his book *Concerning Arabic Manuscripts...*, the academician Krachkovskii wrote: "The great Arab philosopher-poet of the Middle Ages, Abū al-ᶜAlā al-Maᶜarrī wrote a collection of poems with the strange title *Luzūm mā lā yalzam* ("The Obligation of the Optional"). Commonly, this is assumed to be an allusion to the double rhyme used in all his poems, although poets occasionally use it to demonstrate their skill in short poems. This is surely the first, explicit meaning of the title, but knowing Abū al-ᶜAlā's works, one can be sure that he had a second, concealed meaning. He wanted to say that his ideas and their implications, as expressed in his poetry, might be optional for others, but were compulsory for him and he could not do without them. Similarly, it is difficult for philologists to give up their habits, that appear superfluous to the eyes of the ordinary reader. These authors are only satisfied when the basic text is accompanied by commentaries and commentaries on the commentaries, when there are notes, indices and glossaries. All such addenda are not necessary for the writer, but for researchers, a strange breed, the need for such 'nonessential' appendices are second nature, and that cannot be changed."[70]

Emulating their teachers, the authors of this catalogue also decided to include additional data which we hope will be useful to the readers. At the end of the book, readers will find an alphabetical list of 286 people and 33 organizations who were instrumental in the creation of this collection, as well as a chronological table indicating the inclusion of manuscripts into the collection. When one considers that behind the names of these people and institutions there were many individuals directly involved in the copying, sale, despatch or transport of manuscripts, this figure can be multiplied several times. Representatives of various walks of life, diplomats and writers, consuls and scholars, statesmen and students, guided by diverse motives, participated one way or another in the development of the collection. One might even say that it was the whole of Russia who put the collection together. We hope that the information herein will be a useful source not only to specialists interested in the history of our collection but also in maintaining the memory of our predecessors and professors, plus the dozens and hundreds of generous and enthusiastic people who have donated their collections or individual manuscripts to the collection. It is largely thanks to them that there is an Oriental treasure trove on the banks of the Neva.

A.O. Urunbaev, *Some Results and the Outlook for the Catalogue "The collection of Oriental Manuscripts of the Uzbekistan Academy of Sciences," Proceedings of the USSR Conference, Guidelines for the Description of Old Written Documents of Oriental Peoples*, Baku, 1977, pp. 84, 86.

[66]The most recent collections gathered by the staff of the Institute in Asia were those of E.E. Berthels (16 manuscripts) in 1933, F.B. Rastopchin in 1934 (17), and A.V. Stanishevskii (10 Ismailite manuscripts).

[67]V.I. Belyaev worked on the Arabic manuscripts. He improved the file system and in 1953, published a major general article on the history of the constitution of the Arabic section of the collection and the characteristics of the most interesting manuscripts as regards history, geography, literature, mathematics and medicine. In the years after the war, some works of Krachkovskii were published, based on the Institute's collection. The Syrian specialist Samic al-Dakhkhan used our manuscripts in some of his text publications.

[68]Mention could be made of the collection of 78 volumes on the history of religions bequeathed to the Museum, almost entirely made up of traditional scholastic literature; 42 very valuable manuscripts from the Moscow Institute of Oriental Studies in 1962; S.M. Shapshal's collection of 22 manuscripts received the same year and 26 volumes from the library of V.F. Minorskii in 1966.

[69]It is essential to mention here the works by O.F. Akimushkin, I.R. Babayants, S.I. Baevskii, K.A. Boïko, Y.E. Borshchevskii, Z.N. Vorozheikina, P.A. Gryaznevitch, A.B. Khalidov, V.V. Kushev, N.D. Miklukho-Maklai, A.I. Mikhailova, I.B. Mikhailova, A.B. Muginov, L.I. Nikolaeva, H.N. Niyazov, S.B. Pevzner, I.E. Petrosyan, Y.A. Petrosyan, T.I. Sultanov, M.A. Salakhetdinova, T.A. Shumovskii, and N.N. Tumanovitch. Later, S.M. Prozorov, M.B. Piotrovskii, Val.V Polosine, V.V. Polosine, E.A. Rezvan, and A.K. Alikberov joined the effort.

[70]I.Y. Krachkovskii *Concerning Arabic Manuscripts...*, cit., p. 139.

We hope that these brief surveys, although inevitably selective, are useful to underline the importance of the collection of Arabic and Persian manuscripts in the Oriental Institute of the Russian Academy of Sciences in St. Petersburg. We have tried in particular to put the St. Petersburg manuscripts in a larger perspective and to compare them with related codices in other collections around the world. The great opportunity to have a close look at the manuscripts in Lugano was instrumental in making us feel more confident about our ideas. We are very grateful to the St. Petersburg Branch of the Institute of Oriental Studies, Russian Academy of Sciences, in particular to Professor Yuri A. Petrosyan and the Authors' Collective which include professor Oleg F. Akimushkin, Professor Anas B. Khalidov, and Dr. Efim A. Rezvan for allowing us to study their manuscripts. We thank warmly all the staff of the ARCH Foundation in Lugano, especially Elisabeth Storm Nagy and Maria Yakimov, for providing great support and for making our contribution to this publication possible. Finally, we are gratified and proud that we were given the opportunity not only to contribute to this publication but also to be the curators of what promises to be an extraordinary exhibition at the Metropolitan Museum of Art.

Stefano Carboni
and Marie Lukens Swietochowski

The Arabic Manuscripts

Stefano Carboni

The expression "Arab miniature painting" is a convention used by scholars in the field of Islamic painting to designate the illustrations included in manuscripts copied in Arabic and produced in Arabic speaking countries, mainly Egypt, Syria, and Iraq. From the material that has come down to us, we can say that Arab painting was at its apogee between the 12th and the 14th centuries, then sadly, it became stereotyped until it virtually disappeared as an artistic expression at the end of the 15th century, just before the defeat of the Mamluk Sultanate of Egypt and Syria by the Ottomans. By that time the production of illustrated manuscripts in the Persian-speaking world had reached new heights and these standards were to be maintained until at least the end of the 17th century. The reasons for these distinct developments of Arab and Persian miniature painting are too many and too complex to be addressed here since they encompass historical facts, different corpora of literature in Arabic and Persian, distinct approaches to religious matters in relation to manuscript production, and dissimilar artistic influences (Arab painting was in debt to the Christian Byzantine classical world while the roots of Persian painting can be found in Central Asia and the Far East). According to the material that has survived, manuscript illustration in the Arab world was strictly limited to secular texts, furthermore it virtually never accompanied poetic works. In stark contrast to this Persian poetry, which is also strongly imbued with religious and mystical meanings, was commonly illustrated. Thus, typical illustrated Arabic manuscripts are scientific—or, in our eyes, pseudo-scientific—works, often translations from the original Greek (or sometimes translated from a Syriac intermediary), and works in prose, or rhymed prose, such as the fables in Ibn al-Muqaffaᶜ's *Kalīla wa Dimna* and the celebrated *Maqāmāt* (see cat. no. 18) by al-Ḥarīrī. The selective nature of book illustration in the Arab world, together with the fact that the majority of illustrated manuscripts were produced in a period of which unfortunately little survives, means that important documents for the study of Arab painting are today rare in both public and private collections.

It is thus a pleasing surprise to learn that the Oriental Branch of the Russian Academy of Sciences in St. Petersburg, a collection undeservedly little-known to the general public, holds, among its many wonders, a number of imporant illustrated and illuminated Arabic manuscripts. Its treasures certainly place this collection on a par with other great public libraries such as the Bibliothèque nationale in Paris, the British Library in London, the Topkapı Sarayi Library in Istanbul, the Bodleian Library in Oxford, and the Chester Beatty Library in

Dublin. The surprise is even greater when one takes into account the many unillustrated Arabic manuscripts that have been selected for the present catalogue. All of these, from the documents on papyrus and the early Qur'ans on parchment through to a number of extremely important later works, many of them unique or amongst the earliest copies of a particular text, are an exceptional testimony to book production in the Arab world. The compilers of the catalogue deserve credit for having included a sizable number of unillustrated Arabic manuscripts in their selection; by doing so they have emphasized the fact that the text itself and its calligraphy were the essence of manuscript production in the Arab world. Illumination was certainly welcomed as a form of abstract decoration to embellish and surround the written words, while illustrations were in most cases a "plus," added essentially to define the text visually when it was needed, but the text itself remained the primary motivation for the copying of the manuscript.

In the present essay only a few of these unillustrated manuscripts will be mentioned when they are of significance to the mainly art-historical purport of this paper. However, it must be stressed that in the eyes of an educated Arab of the period, as well as in the eyes of the majority of Arabs today, these unillustrated manuscripts are in no way less important than those with illustrations.

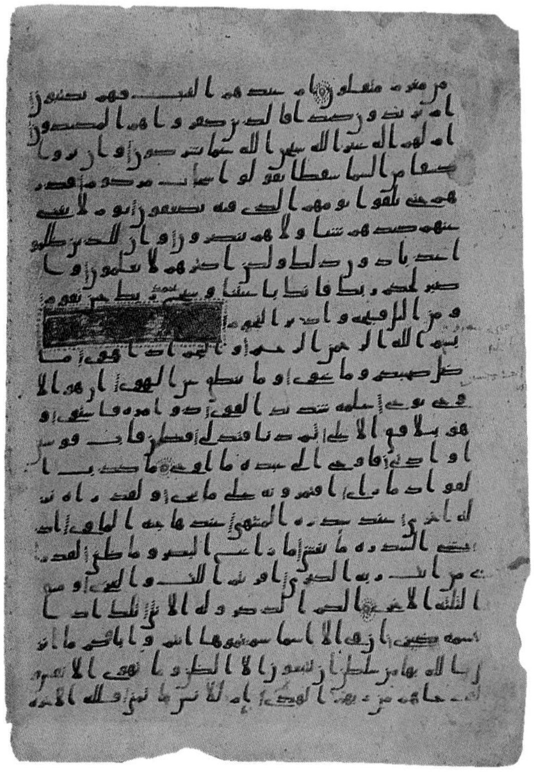

Fig. 1
Page from a Qur'an manuscript, 8th-9th century.
Found under the roof of the Great Mosque at Sanʿa. After Masāḥif Ṣanʿā, *1985, no. 1/, p. 56.*

The Qur'ans

The copying of the Qur'an was in itself an almost sacred act and for this reason all the basic rules of calligraphy were codified in the first centuries of Islam. The most essential illumination was a complement to the written word, colored dots served as vocal markers to facilitate the pronunciation of words during the recitation of the Qur'an, and other markers were employed to separate chapters and verses. We can follow the development of calligraphy, illumination and manuscript format through cat. nos. 1–4 and 61–67: Qur'ans on parchment copied in bold and large angular Kufic script, in black ink or gold, in a horizontal format (cat. nos. 2–3); and Qur'ans on parchment in the vertical format with a greater number of lines to the page and the use of a slender and more cursive calligraphy (cat. nos. 1 and 4). After paper replaced parchment for the writing of Qur'ans around the 10th-11th centuries, many different styles of cursive calligraphy flourished. Parallel to this development in calligraphic style illumination became increasingly prominent until it reached the monumentality of the illuminated opening pages of the Safavid and Qājār Qur'ans (cat. nos. 61–62 and 65). Some styles of calligraphy common in the mediaeval period, such as *maghribī* and *bihārī*, survived into the 19th century (cat. no. 67).

The most interesting among our Qur'ans is without doubt the large fragment of 81 folios, cat. no. 1, executed on parchment of a vertical format. As explained in the catalogue entry, it is a

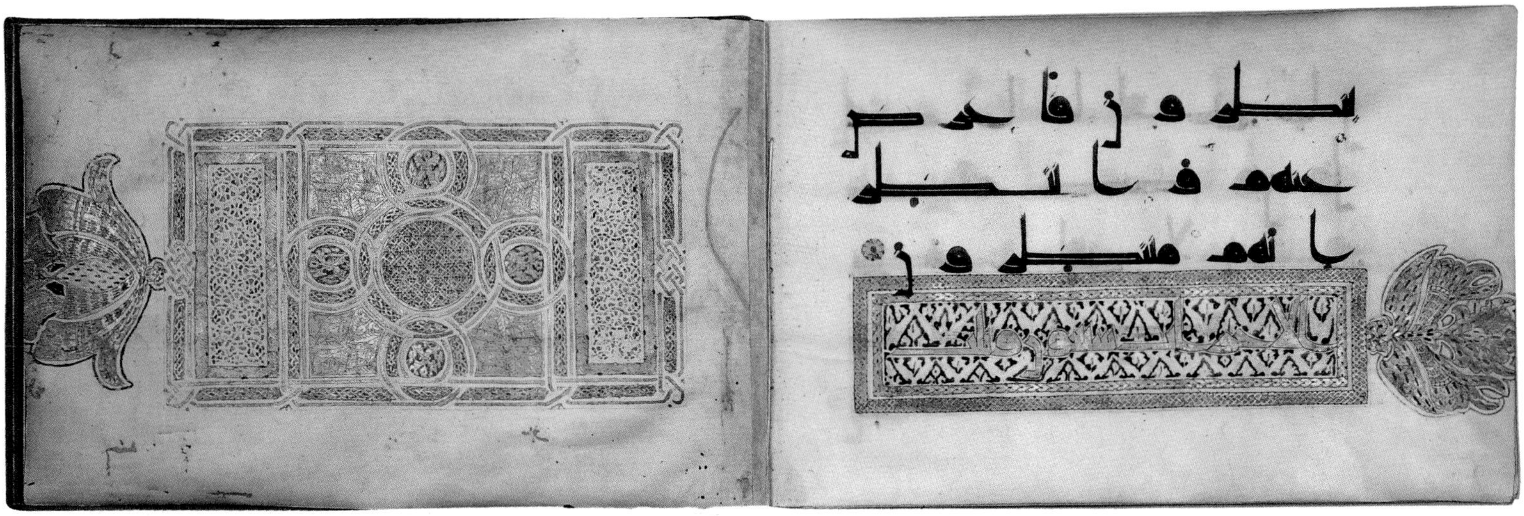

Fig. 2
Page from a Qur'an manuscript, 8th–9th century. Staatliche Museen zu Berlin, Preußischer Kulturbesitz, Museum für Islamische Kunst. I.2211, folio 14r.

good example of the so-called "late Hijazi style," named after the region of the Western Arabian peninsula where the holy cities of Mecca and Medina are also located.

It is interesting to note that fragments of Qur'ans in this style of script were found in 1973, under the roof of the Great Mosque of Ṣanʿā in the Yemen; it is unlikely, however, that they were actually produced there (fig. 1).[1] Another similar example is a large portion of a Qur'an presently in the Chester Beatty Library in Dublin (no. 1404). In her contribution to the ongoing debate on the attribution and dating of these early Qur'ans Estelle Whelan has preferred to define this format more generically as "type 2 script."[2] The conventional term "Hijazi" suggests geographical limitations that do not correspond to what we know of the production of early Qur'ans in this style, therefore Whelan's system seems more appropriate.

In contrast to the above, cat. no. 2 is a very good example of Qur'ans of the classical, horizontal format, written in bold Kufic script, and classified by Whelan as "type 1 script."

With only six or seven lines to the page unevenly spaced, the thick reed-strokes give a very "condensed" aspect to the letters, and reduce the un-inked parchment-white center of the round letters almost to a pinprick.

This type of script, as far as we can tell, was more widespread in the very first centuries of Islam than the "type 2," and single pages and fragments of Qur'an manuscripts in this style are preserved today in many collections. The related example published here is in the Museum für Islamische Kunst in Berlin (fig. 2).[3]

The use of Kufic script and a horizontal format for the production of Qur'ans declined in the Central Islamic lands and Iran from the early 11th century onwards, overtaken by the use of cursive scripts and a vertical page format. North Africa and Islamic Spain were, in contrast, far more conservative and retained the horizontal or squarish format and their own particular version of Kufic (known as the *maghribī* script) well into the 14th century. But the *maghribī* calligraphy survived in Muslim Africa as late as the 19th century (called "African" or *ifrīqī*): a good example of this style is provided by the Qur'an cat. no. 67.

The interest of this manuscript lies also in the fact that it belongs to a group of manuscripts copied on European watermarked paper that was traded in East and West Africa, particularly during the 18th and 19th centuries.

In this case, the watermark showing "three moons with a human profile" points decisively to the paper-factory of Galvani located in Pordenone, in North-Eastern Italy and active until the middle of the 19th century.[4]

[1]See Maṣāḥif Ṣanʿā, 1985, cat. no. 17, p. 56 (IN:00-28.1).
[2]Whelan E., 1990, esp. pp. 119–121.
[3]Published also in Whelan E., 1990, fig. 7.
[4]The group will be discussed by Dr. Anna Contadini in volume IV, part 2 of the Nasser D. Khalili Collection of Islamic Art (forthcoming).

Fig. 3
Abū Zayd in the Encampment,
from a manuscript of the Maqāmāt
dated 634/1237.
Paris, Bibliothèque nationale
de France.
Arabe 5847, folio 38r.

Fig. 6
The Physician's Shop,
from a manuscript of the Maqāmāt
dated 634/1237.
Paris, Bibliothèque nationale
de France.
Arabe 5847, folio 154v.

The Maqāmāt

The most important illustrated Arabic manuscript for which the Oriental Branch of the Russian Academy of Sciences is known is the 13th-century copy of al-Ḥarīrī's *Maqāmāt* (cat. no. 18). The contents and the structure of its text exemplify the very essence of Arabic rhymed prose, and its miniatures symbolize classical Arab painting at its apogee in the few decades that preceded the Mongol invasion of Iraq and the capitulation of Baghdad in 1258. The text was composed by al-Ḥarīrī in 504/1111 and we are fortunate that one unillustrated copy has been preserved, dated to the very same year 1111 and with a certificate stating that it was read in front of an audience in Baghdad.[5]
The importance of the St. Petersburg manuscript for the study of Arab painting was first emphasized by Richard Ettinghausen in his fundamental work on Arab painting written in 1962.[6] This codex ranks as one of the very best copies among the thirteen known illustrated manuscripts of the *Maqāmāt* studied by Oleg Grabar in 1984.[7] Its fame is indeed well deserved as it can be compared in terms of quality to the most celebrated of all copies, the so-called Schefer Ḥarīrī of the Bibliothèque nationale in Paris (arabe 5847), dated 634/1237 and copied and illustrated by Yaḥyā ibn Maḥmūd al-Wāsiṭī (see figs. 3 and 6). Unfortunately, the St. Petersburg manuscript is neither dated nor signed but scholars are inclined to agree that it represents the earliest kind of illustrated *Maqāmāt* along with a very damaged copy in Istanbul (Süleymaniye Library, Esad Efendi 2961) datable between 1242 and 1258. Whether the St. Petersburg codex should be considered as slightly earlier or roughly contemporary to the Paris and Istanbul manuscripts is only a matter of speculation that cannot be resolved at the moment.
A few comparisons with paintings illustrating identical stories will suffice to underline the artistic personality of the painter of the St. Petersburg manuscript and his particular choices in the general composition of the miniatures. The 14th *Maqāma* ("of Mecca"; pl. p. 147), for example, represents a good occasion for the artist to show off his compositional

[5] See Mackay P., 1971.
[6] Ettinghausen R., 1962, pp. 104–124.
[7] Grabar O., 1984.

skills: the scene is set on two separate planes and the main subject (the larger tent on the upper plane) is seized upon as an opportunity to show a complex and crowded open-air scene of an encampment. In illustrating the very same section of the text, the artist of the Paris manuscript, al-Wāsiṭī, is more restrained and prefers to depict only the tent and its temporary dwellers (fig. 3). A similar but much more stereotyped and less lively approach than the Paris scene is seen in a painting in a manuscript of the *Maqāmāt* produced a century later in Syria under Mamluk rule, the best codex of a small group which confirms the popularity of this text in the Arab countries that escaped the Mongol invasion (fig. 4).[8]

Another interesting copy of the *Maqāmāt* produced in the same years as the St. Petersburg manuscript is also in Paris (Bibliothèque nationale, arabe 3929). Although its miniatures appear more archaic and less imaginative than their contemporaries, it has been dated to the 1240s.[9] The unpainted backgrounds of its miniatures, together with their basic compositions, and the captions written in gold set this manuscript apart from all the others. A typical example is from the 34th *Maqāma* ("of Zabīd"; pl. p. 152) illustrating the sale of a slave and the weighing of the money: the St. Petersburg scene is set in an architectural frame on two planes that suggests an interior space in which all figures, including those not directly related to the main action, move freely. In the Paris illustration, on the other hand, only the three characters involved in the transaction are depicted without distracting additions (fig. 5).

Another example of the originality of the St. Petersburg painter is the circular composition employed for the 47th *Maqāma* (of "Ḥajr al-Yamāma"; pl. p. 155). The focus of the scene is the physician's shop represented in its slender architectural frame in the center. Whereas the text indicates that the shop is meant to be

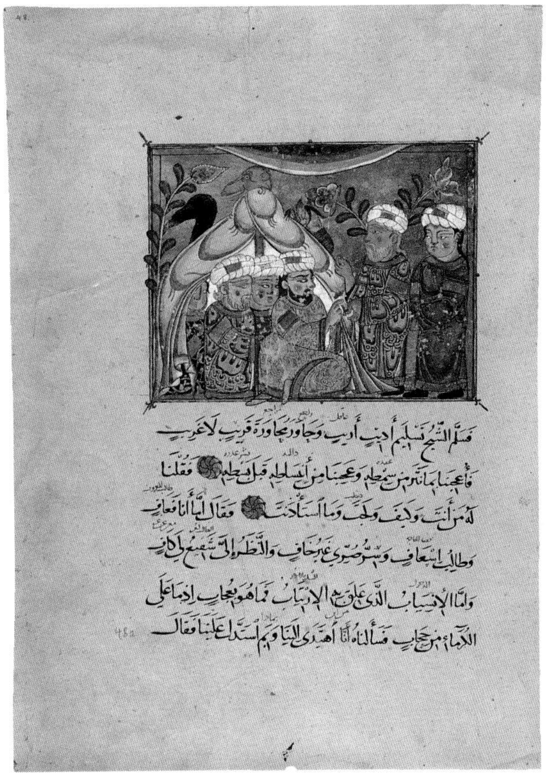

Fig. 4
Abū Zayd in the Encampment,
from a manuscript of the Maqāmāt
dated 734/1334.
Vienna, Nationalbibliothek.
A.F. 9, folio 48r.

Fig. 5
The Weighing of the Money
to Purchase the Slave,
from a manuscript of the Maqāmāt,
c. 1240.
Paris, Bibliothèque nationale
de France.
Arabe 3929, folio 79r.

[8]Vienna, Nationalbibliothek, A.F. 9, dated 734/1334.
[9]Rice D.S., 1959.

located in a covered market or *sūq*, and that it is situated amidst many other shops in narrow alleys, the painter's solution is to draw attention to the main scene by assembling people all around the shop, and to avoid depicting a series of buildings. A circular composition is used to organize the mingling crowd and the almost perfect circle is nearly completed by the domical profile of the shop's roof. Al-Wāsiṭī devised the very same idea in his codex, the Paris Schefer manuscript (fig. 6), but in this case he was more conservative and created a squarish composition with a stationary horizontal bottom line.

Egyptian or Syrian Mamluk Manuscripts

Our understanding of Mamluk painting is still defective, principally because we are as yet unable to make a proper distinction between the illustrated and illuminated manuscripts produced in the Egyptian capital, Cairo, and those made in Syria (especially in Damascus), a country with an equally strong artistic tradition. Much progress has been made recently in assigning a place of production to a number of 14th-century illustrated manuscripts and illuminated Qur'ans, mainly on the basis of style. Definitive evidence, however, provided by colophons which would indicate where the codices were produced is exceptionally scarce. Thus, three copies of the *Maqāmāt* (including the Vienna manuscript mentioned in note 8), three copies of a book on horsemanship (see below, the discussion on the *furūsiyya* codex cat. no. 34), a bestiary, and a book containing moralizing stories are presently regarded as Syrian based on the detailed analyses of three scholars.[10] The first of these three scholars has also succeeded in distinguishing between Syrian and Egyptian artistic trends in Qur'an illumination.[11]
The Oriental Branch of the Academy of Sciences in St. Petersburg possesses two illuminated manuscripts that fit well into this debate and help to clarify this interesting issue. The first is cat. no. 23, a copy of the *Epistles and Acts of the Apostles* in its Arabic translation written by the monk Thomas (known also as Ibn al-Ṣafī) in Damascus in 742/1341 and commissioned by an Italian (?) consul to Syria for his personal library. This manuscript has several complete colophons at the end of the various epistles, something rather exceptional in itself for the 14th century, furthermore it includes three full illuminated pages each decorated with a central rosette and two cartouches lavishly decorated in gold and ultramarine blue. Used together this enables us to tie specific decorative motifs to Syria. Most of the decorative elements in these pages are standard to the Mamluk decorative vocabulary, both in Egypt and Syria, for example, the "tooth-and-dash" pattern bordering the cartouches or the ever-present peony flower. However, the general composition of the pages and the thin blue line with its projecting decorative corners used to surround both rosette and cartouches appear to be "hallmarks" of Syrian-produced manuscripts as opposed to those of Egyptian making. The St. Petersburg codex is therefore essential to this debate because it helps support the argument for a Syrian provenance for most of the manuscripts mentioned above (see note 10).
In addition, it is interesting to notice that at least two other Christian Arabic codices produced in Damascus bear similar illumination: one, in the Coptic Museum in Cairo (Ms. 90), is dated 1340 and is dedicated to a Damascene cleric, the other is in the Topkapı Sarayi in Istanbul (Ahmet III, 3519) and was copied around the same date.[12] A number of Qur'ans have also been identified as coming from Syria on the basis of one in particular whose colophon informs us that it was copied in the Umayyad Mosque in Damascus. The colophon does not mention when the manuscript was finished but it can safely be assumed that this was in the years 1330–1340 (fig. 7).[13]

[10]The most important studies are: James D., 1974; Melikian Chirvani A.S., 1985; Contadini A., 1988–1989.
[11]James D., 1988; James D., 1992.
[12]See respectively James D., 1992, p. 173; Leroy J., 1967.
[13]James D., 1992, no. 43.

The group discussed above, which now includes the important addition of the *Epistles* cat. no. 23, is of great interest because it shows how the same decorative patterns used in the illumination of Mamluk manuscripts are found in Islamic and Christian religious books as well as in secular Arabic texts. Since we know that the copyists of the Qur'an were Muslims and that monks copied the Christian texts in Arabic translations, but that both groups carry identical illumination, we can postulate that the illuminators of these texts were above religious distinctions and were called to decorate a manuscript on the basis of their skill rather than of their faith (it is more logical, however, to assume that the majority of illuminators were Muslim). In short, they were trained professionals who offered their services to a wide range of patrons. A similar phenomenon is noticeable in the illumination of Arabic manuscripts of Northern Mesopotamia and South-Eastern Anatolia in the 13th century because of the widespread artistic influence of the Christian monasteries where illustrated and illuminated manuscripts were also produced.

The second manuscript which contributes to this debate is cat. no. 22. This codex is significant both for its text and its illuminated frontispiece; it is a unique copy of a panegyric for the celebrated Mamluk Sultan al-Malik al-Nāṣir ibn Qalā'ūn, who reigned between 1293 and 1341 with brief interruptions. From its patron's name (written below the illuminated title: see pl. p. 160) we are informed that it was copied for the library of one of the sultan's nephews, a certain Mūsā ibn al-Sulṭān al-Malik al-Ṣāliḥ. We know from the sources that Mūsā was the son of a brother of al-Malik al-Nāṣir, namely al-Malik al-Ṣāliḥ ʿAlī (d. 1287) who never was a true sultan but was briefly put on the throne as regent by his father Qalā'ūn while the latter was campaigning in Syria, hence Mūsā's use of such a hyperbolic title.[14] Mūsā was made

Fig. 7
Colophon page from a Qur'an manuscript; copied in Damascus, c. 1330–1340.
The Nasser D. Khalili Collection of Islamic Art.
QUR. 807, folio 296v.

[14] Al-ʿAsqalānī, s.d., vol. V, p. 148; al-Maqrīzī, 1958, vol. II, pp. 91 and 189; Mayer L.A., 1993, pp. 169–170, and pl. XIV. I am grateful to Abdallah Kahil for his help in this matter.

amīr by his uncle, and married the daughter of another powerful *amīr* of al-Nāṣir, Salār, in 1302. In 1310 Mūsā and Salār grew hostile to the Sultan, and as a result Mūsā was exiled by his uncle to Qūṣ in Upper Egypt where he died in 1318.

The St. Petersburg manuscript was evidently compiled in Egypt and its most likely date is around the time of Mūsā's marriage to Salār's daughter in 1302, but in any case not later than his exile in 1310. The title of the book is itself a parody of another, better known panegyric dedicated some thirty years earlier to the first great Mamluk sultan, Baybars I (r. 1260–1277).[15] Its illuminated opening page shows the features of the Qur'ans produced in Cairo at the beginning of the 14th century which were strongly influenced by contemporary Īlkhānid (Mongols of Iran) illumination. The most prominent of these features is the star-and-polygon composition. The festooned gold border crowning the main pattern is also typical of the period: it seems to have been inaugurated by the illuminator Muḥammad ibn Mubādir on a Qur'an dated 1304–1306 presently in the British Library,[16] although the St. Petersburg manuscript could be earlier than this date.

Unique in the Mamluk repertoire is the crowned eagle in the central polygon, probably intended as Mūsā's armorial emblem. But it must be noticed that the drawing of the eagle is distinctly sketchier than the rest of the illumination and that it is colored in black pigment unlike the remainder of the decoration. It is possible that the eagle is a later addition, however, in this case the presence of a central polygon with an empty gold background is difficult to explain.

The Furūsiyya *Manuscript*

Late Mamluk painting is represented in the St. Petersburg collection by the *furūsiyya* manuscript, cat. no. 34. Manuscripts on horsemanship can be regarded as the most popular illustrated texts in Egypt and Syria after the mid-14th century and throughout the 15th. The extensive entry in the catalogue helps to suggest the importance of this document for the study of this genre in late Mamluk painting. However, it must be added here that, as to my knowledge, this manuscript has escaped the attention of all scholars of Islamic miniature painting so far![17] It represents just another example of how little the St. Petersburg collection was known until the present exhibition.

The earliest illustrated books on horses belong to the classical period of Arab painting, i.e. the 13th century. Two manuscripts presently in Cairo and Istanbul, dated 1209 (produced in Baghdad) and 1210 respectively, deal with veterinary matters pertaining to horses (fig. 8).[18] These two manuscripts are good examples of the tradition of scientific illustrated codices ultimately harking back to Greek-Byzantine models.

The Mamluk *furūsiyya* manuscripts, on the other hand, are more in debt to the Turkic origins of the Mamluks and to the importance of war tactics, cavalry deployment on the battlefield, weapons to be used while riding, jousts, polo games, and so on. It is likely that the Mamluk army commanders found themselves in need of texts of this kind and that these Arabic manuals were also complemented with explanatory paintings. In general, these works tend to be rather monotonous and strictly two-dimensional without indication of background. In some cases, however, as in the St. Petersburg codex the wide range of colors and the quality of the drawing raise the standard and give a much more appealing aspect to the whole book.

At present, there seem to be two distinct groups of Mamluk *furūsiyya* manuscripts copied around the third quarter of the 14th and of the 15th centuries. Each group, copied within the space of a few years, might well have been prompted by specific commissions such as that of

[15]The two titles differ only in the last word containing the name of the sultan, in the first case al-Ẓāhir (Rukn al-Dīn Baybars) and in the case of the St. Petersburg manuscript al-Nāṣir. However, the original is wittier because it plays on the homonymy of the word *al-zāhir* ("radiant") and the name of the sultan, al-Ẓāhir.

[16]London, British Library, Add. 22406-13: see James D. 1988, pp. 34–72. The Qur'an is dedicated to Baybars al-Jāshnagīr (r. 1308–1309).

[17]For example, it is not mentioned neither in Grube E.J., 1976 nor in Haldane D., 1978.

[18]Respectively in Cairo, Dār al-Kutub, no. 8f. Khalil Agha, and Istanbul, Topkapı Sarayi, Ahmet III, 2115.

[19]See James D., 1974. The manuscripts are in Dublin, Chester Beatty Library, uncatalogued; London, British Library, Add. 18866; Istanbul, Topkapı Sarayi, A. 2651.

[20]Paris, Bibliothèque nationale, Arabe 2824: Keir Collection, Richmond, Surrey, II.7–37.

the *silāḥdār* ("sword-bearer") Jarbāsh al-Ashrafī in the case of our manuscript cat. no. 34.

In the 14th century, we have three manuscripts dated 1366, 1371, and 1373, now located in Dublin, London, and Istanbul, respectively: all three are illustrated copies of al-Aqsarāyi's text titled *Nihāyat al-su'l wa al-umniyya fī taʿlīm aʿmāl al-furūsiyya* ("All You Want to Know About Horsemanship") and they were most probably ordered as part of the Mamluk reaction to the sack of Alexandria by the Lusignan Crusaders in 1365,[19] or as part of the bitter struggle between the *Baḥrī* Mamluks and the Circassian Mamluks who would shortly replace them. The Dublin manuscript (fig. 9) is the earliest and the best of the small group.

The *furūsiyya* manuscript in the St. Petersburg collection, *al-Kitāb al-makhzūn fī jāmiʿ al-funūn* ("The Treasured Book on Scientific Disciplines") by Ibn Khazzām (cat. no. 34), belongs to the second group of manuscripts—those copied in the third quarter of the 15th century—together with two other codices with the same text in Paris and in a private collection in England.[20] Although the date provided in the last page was added later and is not part of the original manuscript, it is so precise (19th Ramadan 878/8th February 1474) that it was probably copied from the now lost original colophon. In any case its patron, Jarbāsh, was certainly an emir of the Mamluk sultan al-Malik al-Ashraf Qāitbāy (r. 1467–1494) given his court name of al-Ashrafī.

The Paris manuscript is dated 1470, thus it was supposedly produced four years earlier than the copy now in Russia while the fragmentary Keir copy is undated.

The latter manuscript, for which dates in the second half of the 14th century and in the early 16th century have been proposed, can now be compared to the St. Petersburg manuscript. It can be assigned a comparable date (ca. 1470), particularly on the basis of the obvious similarities between their illustrations (com-

Fig. 9
Four Horsemen Jousting Around a Pool, *from a manuscript of the* Nihāyat al-su'l wa al-umniyya *dated 767/1366.*
By kind permission of the Trustees of the Chester Beatty Library, Dublin. Add. 21 (1), folio 118v.

Fig. 8
Two Horsemen, *from a manuscript of the* Kitāb al-bayṭara *dated 606/1210.*
Istanbul, Topkapı Sarayi Müsezi. A. 2115, folio 57r.

Fig. 10
The Use of Greek Fire,
from a manuscript of the Kitāb al-makhzūn fījāmiᶜ al-funūn,
c. 1470
Richmond, Surrey,
The Keir Collection.
II.12.

pare fig. 10 and pl. p. 204). A hippiatric treatise that can be added to this 15th-century group of books on horses is a text on veterinary science entitled *Kitāb al-zardaqa*, now in the University Library in Istanbul (Yildiz 17, dated 1467), where the horses viewed in profile are drawn and colored in a manner very similar to those in the St. Petersburg manuscript.

A Provincial Ottoman Manuscript

After the Ottomans took control of the lands once governed by the Mamluks at the beginning of the 16th century, Syria and Egypt became provincial regions and all the best artistic styles remained focused in the new capital Istanbul and in Turkey more generally. As a matter of fact, we know almost nothing about illustrated manuscripts in the former Mamluk sultanate after the 16th century, therefore the *Book of Fables* cat. no. 53 is of some importance in this respect.
Copied on European paper and very likely produced in the 17th century because of an ownership note dated 1055/1645–1646, it is no doubt a provincial Ottoman work as can be seen from the facial features and the costumes of the characters portrayed in some of its illustrations. But it does not seem to fit into the best provincial Ottoman production, located in Baghdad.[21] Rather, it is possible to suggest that it was produced either in Egypt or Syria since both its calligraphic style and the iconography of some of its illustrations indicate that this text could be a copy of an earlier, Mamluk manuscript (see, for example, folios 61v–62r, pl. p. 285 [above] which seem directly derived from illustrated *Kalīla wa Dimna* codices).
A detailed study of the text of this manuscript would probably reveal it to be a late survivor of much earlier books of fables, moralizing bestiaries, and similar genres. For example, the story mentioned in the entry on the deer (pl. p. 284, called *ayyil* in the text) which recounts how the deer, very proud of its huge branching horns, gets entangled amongst the trees and is killed by the hunters is already present in 13th-century books on the usefulness of animals and also in al-Qazvīnī's *ᶜAja'ib al-makhlūqāt* (fig. 11); in these texts, it is called *yāmūr, yaḥhmūr*, or *tāmūr* and can be identified either as a roe-deer, a stag, or a steinbock. The story told in the bestiaries and by al-Qazvīnī, which is itself ultimately derived from the Greek and Latin *Physiologus*, does not include the fact that the deer loves its horns but dislikes its legs, as in the St. Petersburg manuscript.[22]

The Qazvīnī Manuscript

One of the most popular Arabic texts ever copied and illustrated is al-Qazvīnī's *ᶜAjā'ib al-makhlūqāt wa gharā'ib al-mawjūdāt* ("The Wonders of Creation and the Peculiarities of Existing Things"; cat. no. 24). Originally written in Arabic around 1270, the text was later translated

[21]Milstein R., 1990.
[22]I am grateful to Anna Contadini for her help in this matter.
[23]Munich, Bayerische Staatsbibliothek, cod. ar. 464.
[24]London, British Library, Or. 14140; Gotha, Forschungsbibliothek, A. 1506. See respectively Carboni S., 1988–1989, and Rührdanz K., 1973.
[25]Carboni S. and Contadini A., 1990.

into Persian and Turkish and a very large number of copies were executed until the 19th century. However, the number of surviving illustrated manuscripts in Arabic that follow the original large format and cycle of illustrations as we know them from the celebrated copy dated 678/1280 presently in Munich (finished when its author was still alive; fig. 12)[23] is scarce and can be easily identified.

Three copies in Arabic can be assigned with confidence to the 14th century: the earliest two, copied towards the beginning of the century, are fragmentary manuscripts in London and in Gotha:[24] the former was probably produced in Northern Iraq while the latter's format is so close to the copy in Munich, which was completed at Wāsiṭ near Baghdad, to suggest a similar Iraqi provenance. The third manuscript is another fragment sold at auction in 1990 and now in a private collection in Jordan: the style of its illustrations places it in Mamluk Syria around the middle of the 14th century.[25]

The St. Petersburg Qazvīnī (cat. no. 24) belongs to a well identified group of manuscripts produced with the same format, number of lines to the page, and iconography ultimately derived from the Munich codex (cfr. fig. 12 and folio 72r, pl. p. 168 [left]). For example, the double-headed heraldic beast illustrating the fabulous bird *ʿanqā* (fig. 13 and folio 199v, pl. p. 169) is peculiar to this group of manuscripts. We know from the colophons of two of these works that they were copied and illustrated in 979/1572 in the Deccan in India for one of the army commanders of the ʿĀdil-shāhīs, Kamāl al-Dīn Ḥusain.[26] A number of other codices, as well as many single pages coming from dispersed works belonging to this Deccani group, are found today in the British Library in London, the Raza Library in Rampur, the Chester Beatty Library in Dublin (fig. 14; see folio 26v, pl. p. 165), the Nationalbibliothek in Vienna, the Ashmolean Museum in Oxford, and other institutions.[27]

These Deccani manuscripts were obviously copied from earlier, possibly 14th-century, illustrated copies of al-Qazvīnī's text which scholars have identified in a manuscript presently shared by the Freer Gallery in Washington (fig. 13) and by the Public Library in New York (so-called "Sarre Qazvīnī" after its previous owner),[28] and in the St. Petersburg Qazvīnī. Scholars have devoted a good deal of attention to the Sarre manuscript and its 14th-century attribution has been challenged: not only was it thought to be an early 15th-century copy but a 17th-century dating has recently been sug-

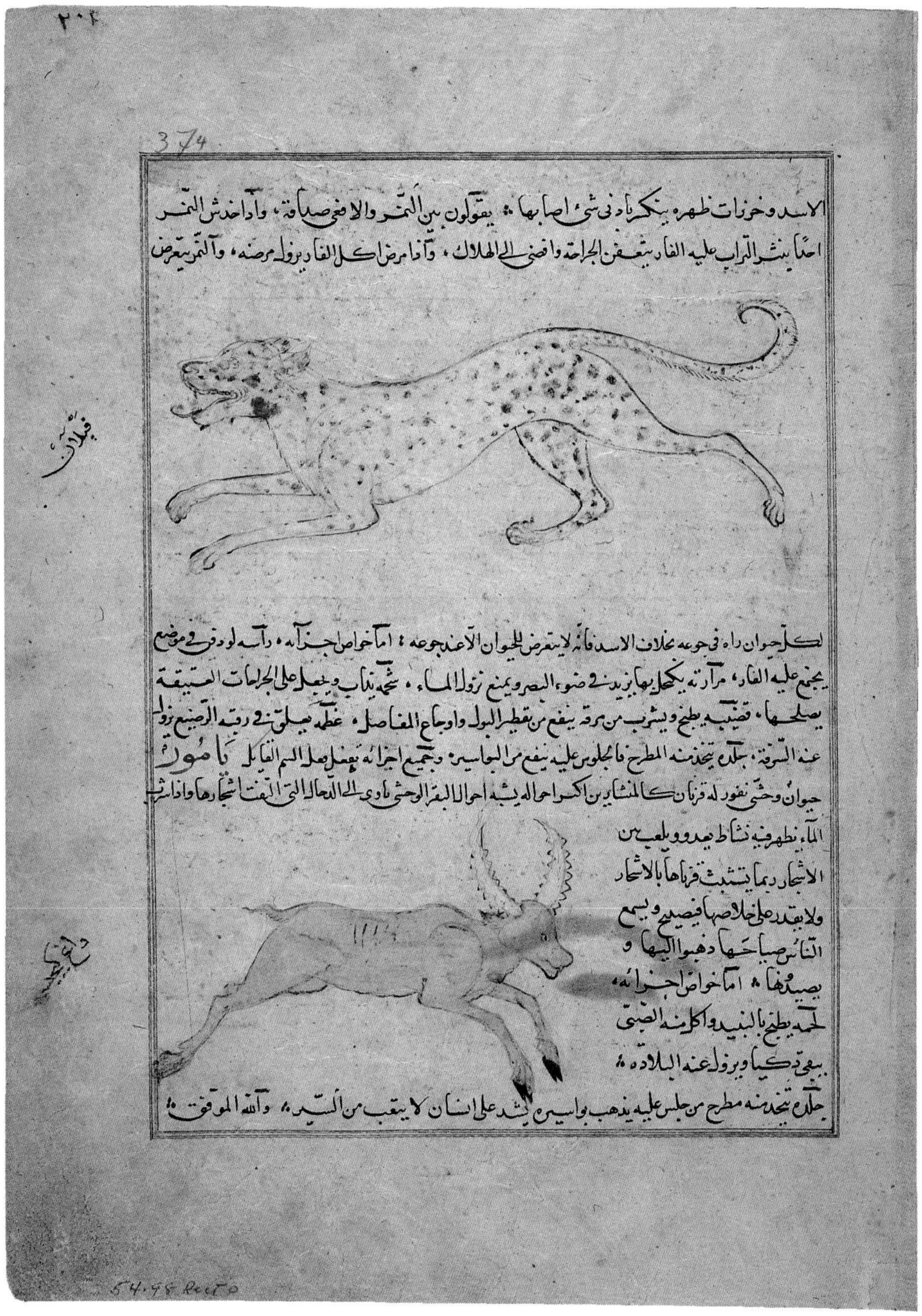

Fig. 11
The Leopard and the Yāmūr, *page from a manuscript of the* ʿAja'ib al-makhlūqāt, *probably Deccan, c. 1570–1600.*
Courtesy of the Freer Gallery of Art, Smithsonian Institution, Washington, D.C.
Folio 54.98r.

نفتر عن ضرب الدهل البتة فقلت انا افعل ذلك فاعطوني من الماء والزاد ما يكفيني اياما فوقفت على الجزيرة
وشرعت في دق الدهل فرايت المياه تحركت والمركب جرت وانا انظر اليه حتى غاب عن بصري فلما فرغت من المركب
جعلت اتردد في الجزيرة فاذا انا بشجرة عظيمة لم ار اعظم منها عليها شبه سطح عريض فلما كان آخر النهار
احسست بهدة شديدة فاذا طائر عظيم ابيض اللون لم ار حيوانا اعظم منه جاء ووقع على ذلك السطح
فاختفيت منه خوفا من ان يصطادني الى ان بدا ضوء الصباح فنفض جناحيه وطار فلما كانت الليلة الثانية
جاء الطير ووقع على عشه وكنت آيسا من حياتي فعرضت نفسي عليه حتى وقفت بين يديه فلم يتعرض لي بشيء
وطار مصبحا فلما كانت الليلة الثالثة قعدت عنده من غير دهشة الى ان نفض جناحيه عند
الفجر فتمسكت برجله فحملني وطار في اسرع طيران الى ان ارتفع النهار

فنظرت نحو الارض فما رايت غير لجة البحر وكدت اترك رجله لشدة ما نالني من الوجع ثم حملت نفسي على الصبر
الى ان نظرت نحو الارض فرايت الشجر والقرى والعمارات فدنا من الارض وتركني على صبرة تبن في بيدر وينظر
الناس الي ثم طار نحو الهواء وغاب عنا فاجتمع الناس علي وحملوني الى ملكهم فاحضر رجلا يفهم
كلامي وقال لي من انت فاخبرته بخبري كله فتعجب منه وتبرك بي وامر لي بمال وسالني ان اقيم عنده فما
مر الا ايام حتى مشيت الى طرف البحر المفرج فاذا مركب اصحابي قد وصل والقوم لما راوني اسرعوا الي سائلين عن حالي
فقلت لهم يا قوم اني بذلت نفسي الله تعالى لنجاني بطريق عجيبة وجعلني آية للناس ورزقني المال واوصلني
الى المقصد قبلكم وهذه حكاية عجيبة وان كانت عن بعد عن لطف الله وعنايته والله ولي الاعانة

gested that implies its derivation from the Deccani manuscripts rather than the contrary.[29]

The 14th-century dating of the St. Petersburg Qazvīnī must also be taken carefully because, at a closer inspection, it seems indeed to belong to the late, Deccani group of manuscripts. Its general layout, its calligraphy, the cartouche of its opening page, the features of both human and animal figures, its use of the palette, all this points to a much closer relation to the dated copies of 1572 than it was thought before. In my opinion, there is little doubt that also the St. Petersburg Qazvīnī should be included in the Deccani group of manuscripts. However, only a chemical analysis of some of the pigments and of the paper of the manuscripts in St. Petersburg, Washington/New York, and of one of the two codices dated 1572 in London could provide definitive evidence one way or the other.

Dioscorides' Translation into Persian

Finally, I wish to include in this discussion on Arabic codices a Persian manuscript (cat. no. 49) because it is, in fact, a translation from another celebrated text in the panorama of Arabic miniature painting of the 13th century. The most common Arabic title for this work, changed in the Persian translation into *Kitāb-i ḥashā'ish* ("Herbarium"), is *Hayūlā al-ṭibb* ("Medical Matters"); the book is, in its turn, a translation from the Greek of the famous *De Materia Medica* by Pedanius Dioscorides (1st century A.D.).[30]

The two most famous illustrated Dioscorides' manuscripts produced in the 13th century (dated 621/1224 and 626/1229) are today for the most part in Istanbul (Süleymaniyye Library, ex Aya Sofia 3703: Topkapı Sarayi, Ahmet III, 2127, respectively), however, a number of pages of the former have been dispersed in several collections around the world.

Fig. 12
The Giant Bird Carrying the Man from Isfahan, *from a manuscript of the* ᶜAja'ib al-makhlūqāt *dated 678/1280.*
Munich, Bayerische Staatsbibliothek. Cod. ar. 464, folio 65v.

Fig. 13
The Magpie and the ᶜAnqā Bird, *page from a manuscript of the* ᶜAja'ib al-makhlūqāt, *probably Deccan, c. 1570–1600.*
Courtesy of the Freer Gallery of Art, Smithsonian Institution, Washington, D.C.
Folio 54.104v.

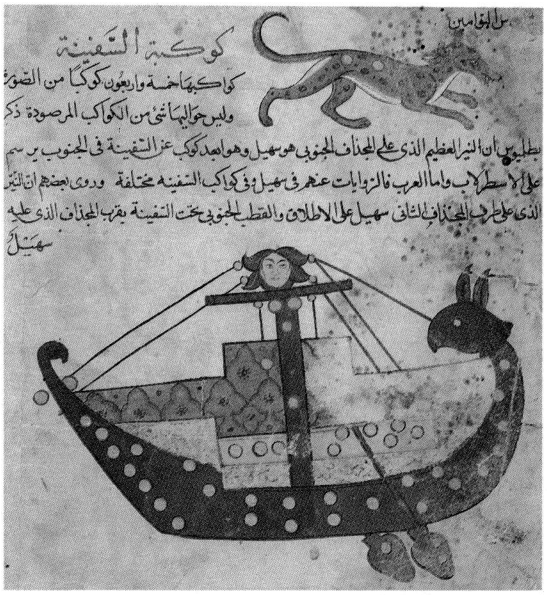

Fig. 14
The Constellations of Canis Minor and Argo Navis, *from a manuscript of the* ᶜAja'ib al-makhlūqāt, *Deccan, c. 1570–1600*
By kind permission of the Trustees of the Chester Beatty Library, Dublin. CBP. 128, folio 28r.

Fig. 15 shows how this medical treatise was indebted to the Greek Byzantine illustrated manuscripts which inspired the Arabic copies.

Another, earlier copy of the *Materia Medica* is even more interesting to our discussion: it is presently in the library of the shrine of the Imām Riẓā in Mashhad and is believed to have been produced between 1152 and 1176 for the Urtuqid ruler of the city of Mayyāfāriqīn in South-Eastern Anatolia (fig. 16). This

[26] The two manuscripts are in the British Library, London, Oriental and India Office Collections, Loth 723 and 724.

[27] See the discussion on this group in my forthcoming article "Constellations, giants and angels from al-Qazwīnī manuscripts" in the next issue of *Oxford Studies in Islamic Art*.

[28] Washington, Freer Gallery of Art, 54-33-114; New York, Public Library, Spencer Collection, no. 45.

[29] A South-Anatolian 15th-century provenance is suggested in Badiee J., 1984; the most recent 17th-century attribution is in Schmitz B., 1992, pp. 7–8.

[30] The basic bibliographic reference for the illustrated copies in Arabic is Grube E.J., 1959.

Fig. 17
Page from a manuscript of the Kitāb al-ḫashā'ish *dated 1054/1645.*
By kind permission of the Trustees of the Chester Beatty Library, Dublin. CBP. 273.

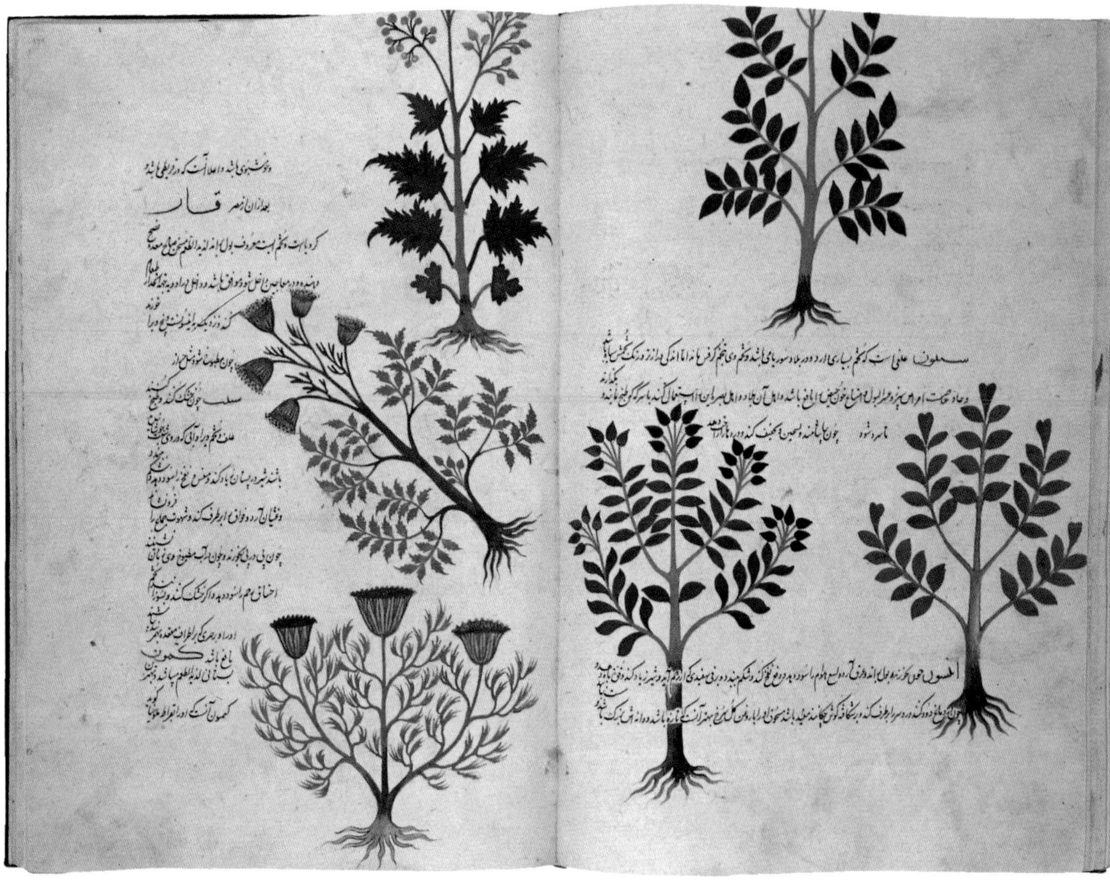

Fig. 15
Page from a manuscript of the Kitāb al-ḫashā'ish *dated 626/1229.*
Istanbul, Topkapı Sarayi Müsezi. A. 2127, folio 80r.

very manuscript belonged to the Safavid Shāh ʿAbbās I (r. 1588–1629) who ordered its translation into Persian: this new version of the work was entitled *Kitāb-iḫashā'ish*.

Barbara Schmitz lists three 17th-century copies of this new Persian translation in Dublin (fig. 17), in a private collection in London (now in Jersey), and in Istanbul.[31]

At present, it seems possible to add this St. Petersburg manuscript of Dioscorides (dated 1068/1658; it represents another manuscript of the collection which is virtually unknown to scholars) to this group of manuscripts copied after the original translation made for Shāh ʿAbbās I. Only a detailed analysis of its text would reveal whether it is another exact copy or a slightly different Persian version.

From the art-historical point of view it is a stunning manuscript for the range of its palette and for its mixture of 12th–13th-century Arabic influences and of nearly contemporary Safavid Persian as well as Indian styles of painting. Although its attribution to Isfahan given in the catalogue entry is sensible especially because the human figures have obvious Safavid features. I would not discount a possible Deccani origin for this manuscript. Some details such as the gold tufts of grass and the flowers that fill the background of many illustrations are typical of the Deccani group of al-Qazvīnī codices mentioned above (in the discussion on cat. no. 24). The fact that faithful copies of an earlier Arabic Qazvīnī manuscript were produced for the ᶜĀdil-shāhīs would support the theory that they were also interested in having identical copies produced of another scientific text, the *Kitāb-i ḥashā'ish*, albeit in its recent Persian version.[32]

Bibliography

Al-Asqalānī, *al-Durar al-kāmina fī aᶜyān al-mā'ah al-thāmina*. Cairo, s.d.

Julie Badiee, "The Sarre Qazwīnī: An Early Aq Qoyunlu Manuscript?," *Ars Orientalis*, XIV, 1984, pp. 97–113.

Stefano Carboni, "The London Qazwīnī: An Early Fourteenth Century Copy of the *ᶜAjā'ib al-makhlūqāt*," *Islamic Art*, III, 1988–1989, pp. 15–31.

Stefano Carboni and Anna Contadini, "An Illustrated Copy of al-Qazwīnī's *The Wonders of Creation*"; *Sotheby's Art at Auction 1989–1990*," London, 1990, pp. 228–233.

Anna Contadini, "The *Kitāb manāfiᶜ al-ḥayawān* in the Escorial Library," *Islamic Art*, III, 1988–1989, pp. 33–57.

Richard Ettinghausen, *Arab Painting*, Geneva, 1962.

Oleg Grabar, *The Illustrations of the Maqāmāt*, Chicago and London, 1984.

Ernst J. Grube, "Materialen zum Dioskurides Arabicus," in R. Ettinghausen (ed.), *Aus der Welt der Islamischen Kunst. Festschrift für Ernst Kühnel*, Berlin, 1959, pp. 163–194.

Ernst J. Grube, "Pre-Mongol and Mamluk Period," in AA.VV., *Islamic Painting and the Arts of the Book*, London, 1976, pp. 69–81.

Duncan Haldane, *Mamluk Painting*, Warminster, 1978.

David James, "Mamluke painting at the time of the 'Lusignan Crusade', 1365–70," *Humaniora Islamica*, 2, 1974, pp. 73–87.

David James, *Arab Painting*, Marg Publications, New Delhi, 1977.

David James, *Qur'ans of the Mamluks*, New York, 1988.

David James, *The Master Scribes. Qur'ans of the 10th to 14th Centuries AD. The Nasser D. Khalili Collection of Islamic Art*, vol. II, U.K., 1992.

J. Leroy, "Une Evangeliaire arabe de la Bibliothèque de Topqapi Sarai a décor byzantin et islamique," *Syria*, XLIV, 1967, pp. 119–130.

Pierre Mackay, *Certificates of Transmission on a Manuscript of the Maqāmāt of Ḥarīrī (ms. Cairo, Adab 105), Transactions of the American Philosophical Society*, n.s., vol. 61, part 4, Philadelphia, 1971.

Terence Macinerney, Indian Painting 1525–1825 (exhibition catalogue), London, 1982.

Al-Maqrīzī, *Kitāb al-sulūk li-ma'rifat duwal al-mulūk*, Cairo, 1958.

Maṣāḥif Ṣan'ā, catalogue of the exhibition held at the Kuwait National Museum, Kuwait, 1985.

Assadullah Souren Melikian Chirvani, *Sulwān al-muṭāᶜ fīᶜudwān al-ittibāᶜ. A Rediscovered Masterpiece of Arab Literature and Painting*, Kuwait, 1985.

Rachel Milstein, *Miniature Painting in Ottoman Baghdad*, Costa Mesa, Cal., 1990.

David S. Rice. "The Oldest Illustrated Arab Manuscript," *Bulletin of the School of Oriental and African Studies*, 22, 1959, pp. 207–220.

Karin Rührdanz, "Islamische Miniaturhandschriften aus den Beständen der DDR. Qazwīnī Illustrationen des 14 Jahrhunderts," *Wissenschaftliche Zeitschrift Martin-Luther Universität Halle-Wittenberg*, XXII, 6, 1973, pp. 123–125.

Barbara Schmitz, *Islamic Manuscripts in the New York Public Library*, New York-Oxford, 1992.

Estelle Whelan, "Writing the Word of God: Some Early Qur'an Manuscripts and Their Milieu. Part I," *Ars Orientalis*, 20, 1990, pp. 113–147.

Fig. 16
Page from a manuscript of the Kitāb al-ḥashā'ish, *c. 1152–1176. Mashhad, Shrine of the Imām Riżā. Photo: The Metropolitan Museum of Art, New York.*

31 Schmitz B., 1992, p. 14. The copies are in Dublin, Chester Beatty Library, Pers, ms. 273; Istanbul, Topkapı Sarayi, Ahmet III, 2147.

32 A Deccani origin for the manuscript now in Jersey has already been suggested, although no mention is made of the copy completed for Shāh 'Abbās: Macinerney T., 1982, pp. 47–48.

The Persian Manuscripts

Marie Lukens Swietochowski

Persian painting developed as early as the Seljuq period, mainly in the form of illustrations for literary works. The first great flowering, however, took place during the course of the 14th century. The classical stage of Persian painting is associated with the Tīmūrīd dynasty in the 15th century with further developments and maturation during the subsequent Safavid period. It is from these two periods that the Oriental Branch of the Academy of Sciences in St. Petersburg possesses a rich and varied collection from the main artistic centers of painting—Shiraz, Herat, Bukhara, Tabriz, and Isfahan.

Shiraz

Shiraz from its first flowering as a center of painting under the Īnjū'īds in the 14th century, had its own distinctive and identifiable style. It is an oversimplification to say, as some scholars have done, that the Īnjū'īd style died out without a trace, because the Tīmūrīd style of Shiraz, developed under Ibrāhīm Sulṭān ibn Shāh Rukh, is indebted to it, particularly in its monumentality and dynamic energy, in addition to its reduction of inessential detail and relative disregard for spatial reality. Shiraz painting in the later 14th century under the Muẓaffarīd dynasty may be considered a provincial manifestation of the Jalāyirīd court-style which was practiced in Baghdad and Tabriz and which further ripened under Iskandar Sulṭān ibn ʿUmar Shaikh as Tīmūrīd governor of Shiraz and Yazd. About the time that Ibrāhīm Sultān ibn Shāh Rukh replaced his rebellious cousin as governor of the Shiraz region his brother Bāisunghur was establishing the court atelier at the Tīmūrīd capital of Herat, and there the former Jalāyirīd court artists from Baghdad, Tabriz, and Shiraz were recruited or sought patronage.

Ibrāhīm was left to build on an earlier tradition in Shiraz and such was its dynamic force that it lasted a few decades after his death in 1435. It is this style that is manifested in several manuscripts of the 1440s and 1450s including the *Shāhnāma* of 1445 from the collection of the Oriental Institute attributed in the catalogue to a Yazd provenance, no doubt based on the publications of Ivan Stchoukine.[1] However, all of these manuscripts seem directly descended from the style of Ibrāhīm Sulṭān, and therefore fall in the Shiraz cultural sphere of influence whether or not actually produced in Yazd. A late flowering of this Shiraz style is exemplified by the Teignmouth *Shāhnāma* of 1457 now in the collection of Prince Sadruddin Aga Khan.[2] After this, Shiraz painting evolved into the so-called Turkman style, either commercial Turkman or court Turkman—terms coined by B.W.Robinson and readily adopted by others in the field.

[1] Stchoukine I., 1963 and Stchoukine I., 1965.
[2] Welch A. and Welch S.C., 1982, cat. no. 16.

Fig. 1
The Fire Ordeal of Siyāvush,
from a Shāhnāma *manuscript dated*
841 A.H./A.D. 1444.
Paris, Bibliothèque nationale
de France.
Suppl. pers. 493, folio 98.

Fig. 2
The Fire Ordeal of Siyāvush,
from a Shāhnāma *manuscript*
of the mid-15th century.
Reproduced by courtesy of the
Director and University Librarian,
the John Rylands University Library
of Manchester; Rylands.
Persian Ms. 9, folio 115v.

This parallelism of the prodigious production of Shiraz manuscripts for local consumption and for export, with the more lavish works produced under a patron's quality control, continued throughout the 16th century. Of the Shirazi manuscripts included in the catalogue the earliest is the *Kulliyyāt* of Saᶜdī dated A.H. Muharram 30, 829/ A.D. December 12, 1425 (cat. no. 29). While the manuscript is unillustrated, the quality of its title and illuminated pages as well as its calligraphy suggest a royal commission. While the style of painting in Shiraz during the governorship of Ibrāhīm Sultān, compared with that produced at Herat under the patronage of his brother Bāisunghur seems provincial, calligraphy and illumination remained of the highest quality. Ibrāhīm Sultān shared the extravagant Tīmūrīd enthusiasm for the arts of the book and was himself proficient in calligraphy, as witnessed by a Qur'an attributed to his hand in the Metropolitan Museum of Art.[3] As a patron, he is best known for an *Anthology* commissioned as a gift for his brother Bāisunghur, completed in A.H. 823 / A.D. 1420 and now in Berlin (Museum für Islamische Kunst) and the *Ẓafarnāma* manuscript, a history of his grandfather Tīmūr, completed in 1436 after Ibrāhīm's death and now dispersed. The St. Petersburg *Shāhnāma* manuscript dated A.H. 849 (cat. no. 30) is, as mentioned above, one of a number of manuscripts of the 1440s and 1450s in a style directly descended from that of Ibrāhīm Sulṭān. Certain compositions in these manuscripts tend to become standardized without, however, being sterile copies of each other. An example of this is the scene of *The fire ordeal of Siyāvush* (folio 70r). Siyāvush, clothed in white, is depicted galloping right on his black horse through the flames in the foreground. The palace, along the left margin, is imaginatively conceived in its elaboration of planes and spaces from which both Kāikavūs and the trouble-making Sūdāba observe the action. The

Fig. 3
Shīrīn Visiting Farhād at Mount Bisūtūn, *from a Khamsa of Niẓāmī dated 951 A.H./A.D. 1544. Istanbul, Topkapı Sarayi Müsezi. Hazine 756, folio 80r.*

Fig. 4
Iskandar Voyaging in a Barque, *from a Khamsa of Niẓāmī dated 951 A.H./A.D. 1544. Istanbul, Topkapı Sarayi Müsezi. Hazine 756, folio 358r.*

tower of the palace appears in the upper margin where ladies are looking down. The curly cloud-pattern presages the standard Turkman type of the later 15th century. Virtually the same composition has been used in an illustration in a *Shāhnāma* manuscript in the Bibliothèque nationale in Paris (suppl. persan 493, folio 98) dated 844/1441, although here the palace hangs awkwardly in the air and has the additional awkwardness of a tree trunk protruding below (fig. 1).[4] A *Shāhnāma* illustrating the fire ordeal in the John Rylands Library in Manchester (ms. Pers. 9, fig. 2) also employs the same layout. It is dated by Stchoukine to ca. 1460 and called "style of Shiraz" while it is attributed by Robinson to Sultanate India.[5] However, whether made in Shiraz or in India it shows the persistence of the legacy of the style of Ibrāhīm Sultān. A totally different subject, a miniature of Khusrau before the castle of Shīrīn, from a *Khamsa* of Niẓāmī copied by a Shiraz calligrapher in 1543, no. 44 in this catalogue (illustration p. 242), uses the same basic composition, demonstrating the persistence of Shiraz traditions even a hundred years later.

The *Khamsa* of Niẓāmī just mentioned is a fine example of Shiraz work of the mid–16th century. It was copied by the prolific calligrapher Muḥammad ibn Qavām al-Shīrāzī, known as Ḥammāmī, completed in 950 A.H./A.D. 1543 and containing 24 miniatures. Muḥammad ibn Qavām was active as a calligrapher in Shiraz between 1537 and 1552 as pointed out by Grace Guest in her book on 16th-century Shiraz painting,[6] where she lists 13 illustrated manuscripts calligraphed by this artist between the dates mentioned. The closest to the St. Petersburg manuscript in subject matter and date is a *Khamsa* in Istanbul in the Topkapi Sarayi, dated 951 A.H./A.D. 1544 and containing 27 miniatures.[7] The most recent study of 16th-century Shiraz illustrated manuscripts has been undertaken by Lalé Uluç, a doctoral candidate at the Institute of Fine Arts at New York University, hopefully to be completed in the near future. Among the more lively illustrations in the St. Petersburg manuscript is that of *Shīrīn arriving at Mount Bisutūn* (folio 79v) where, in addition to Farhād's milk channel, is a rendition of the stone-carving of Tāq-i Bustān, always of interest in miniature paintings for its varying treatment and interpretation. This illustration is also found in the Istanbul *Khamsa* just men-

[3]Lentz T. and Lowry G., 1989, cat. no. 22, color ill. p. 84 (The Metropolitan Museum of Art, 13.228.1–2, dated 830 A.H./A.D. 1427).
[4]Stchoukine I., 1954, ms. no. XXVI.
[5]Stchoukine I., 1954 and Robinson B.W., 1980.
[6]Guest G., 1949, p. 64, note 2.
[7]Stchoukine I., 1977, ms. XLV, H. 756, pp. 125–126.

tioned (fig. 3) as are the many "Bahrām Gūr and the princesses" in their separate pavilions. In both manuscripts the compositions are very characteristic of Shiraz painting in the mid-16th century. The final picture illustrated in the catalogue is *The Voyage of Iskandar in the Sea of China*; it is a highly effective illustration in the boldness and crispness of its presentation; the scene is again found in the Istanbul *Khamsa* (fig. 4).

Herat

Shāh Rukh ibn Tīmūr established the Tīmūrīd capital at Herat in the Eastern province of Khurasan, and that is where the classical canons of Persian art, particularly the arts of the book, were established under the zealous eye of the great prince and patron Bāisunghur ibn Shāh Rukh. Because of its power and prestige the royal *kitābkhāna* at Herat attracted the most illustrious artists from the courts of his predecessors, namely the Jalāyirīds of Baghdad and Tabriz, and the Tīmūrīd Iskandar Sulṭān, governor of Shiraz and Yazd in the early 15th century and son-in-law of the last Jalāyirīd Sulṭān, Aḥmad. The polished and perfected style of Bāisunghur's atelier established in about 1420, did not come to an end with his untimely death in 1433, but continued in Herat until the occupation of that city by the Black Sheep Turkman confederation in mid-century. From then on Bāisunghur-style painting and compositions began to appear in Turkman manuscripts along with those of the Shiraz tradition.

The rule of Sulṭān Ḥusain Bāiqara from 1469 to 1506 saw the last great flowering of Tīmūrīd culture in an Eastern Iranian milieu. The shrinkage of political power could not diminish the brilliant luminaries of this cultural center, such as the painter Bihzād, the calligrapher Sulṭān ᶜAlī al-Mashhadī, the poet Jāmī, and the mycenaeas of the age Mīr ᶜAlī Shīr Navā'ī, to name but a few from a long roster. The contribution of Bihzād and his school was to humanize and render more immediate the remote hierarchical traditions of the art. Never diminishing the rare achievement of harmony of line, color, form, and composition, a more intimate world was now glimpsed, and figures related to each other as humans and to the natural world or architectural environments as participants.

One of the treasures of the collection of the Oriental Institute, apparently hitherto unknown by most scholars of Islamic art, is a manuscript of Niẓāmī's *Khusrau u Shīrīn*, copied at Herat in 824 A.H./A.D. 1421 by Jaᶜfar ibn ᶜAlī al-Bāisunghurī (cat. no. 28, B-132). Jaᶜfar, a pupil of Mīr ᶜAlī al-Tabrīzī, the inventor of the *nastaᶜlīq* script, was head of Prince Bāisunghur's *kitābkhāna*. The early date of 824/1421 of the St. Petersburg manuscript coincides with Bāisunghur's return to Herat following his 1420 governorship of Tabriz, during which time he must have engaged Jaᶜfar, a native of that city, to become head of the *kitābkhāna* the prince was establishing in Herat.

The *Khusrau u Shīrīn* appears to be the earliest known surviving manuscript made for Prince Bāisunghur in Herat after the formation of his *kitābkhāna* and the maturation of the classical Tīmūrīd canons of the arts of the book. An earlier manuscript, a short history, dated 814/1411, when Bāisunghur was a teenager, contains a dedication to him, as does the *Anthology* made in Shiraz in 823/1420, at the time Ibrāhīm Sulṭān, who must have commissioned it as a present for his brother, was governor of Fars Province. Other manuscripts and fragmentary works with dedications to Prince Bāisunghur during the prime of his patronage at Herat fit in the years from 830/1426–1427 to 835/1432.[8] Documented works by the hand of the calligrapher Jaᶜfar, in addition to the *Khusrau u Shīrīn*, are as follows: *Naṣā'iḥ-i Iskandar* dated 828 A.H./A.D. 1425, copied by Jaᶜfar al-Bāisunghurī, a *Gulistān* of Saᶜdī, dated 830 A.H./A.D. 1426–1427, copied by Jaᶜfar al-Bāisunghurī at Herat, in the Ches-

[8]For a list of works of art associated with Bāisunghur, see Lentz T. and Lowry G., 1989, appendix II, pp. 368–369, an expansion of a list compiled by Robinson B.W., 1959.

ter Beatty Library, Dublin, P. 119; a *Shāhnāma* of Firdausī, dated Jumada I 1, 833 A.H./A.D. January 26, 1430, in the Gulistān Library, no. 61, Tehran; a *Kalīla u Dimna* of Abū al-Maᶜālī Naṣr Allāh, dated 834 A.H./A.D. 1431, copied by Jaᶜfar al-Bāisunghurī, Topkapı Sarayi Library, Istanbul, H. 834; a *Ta'rīkh-ī Iṣfahānī* of Ḥamza al-Iṣfahānī, dated 834 A.H./A.D. 1431, copied by Jaᶜfar al-Bāisunghurī, British Library, Or. 1773, London; a *Lamaᶜāt* ofᶜIrāqī and an *Anthology*, dated 835/1431–1432, copied by Jaᶜfar al-Tabrīzī, Chester Beatty Library, P. 122, Dublin. In addition to the manuscripts listed above, single leaves with Jaᶜfar's name have been found in albums in the Topkapi Sarayi Library, Istanbul, such as: a folio of poetry, dated 826 A.H./A.D. 1422–1423, copied by Jaᶜfar al-Bāisunghurī, H. 2153, folio 12v; a text page, dated 829 A.H./A.D. 1425, copied by Jaᶜfar al-Bāisunghurī, H. 2160, folio 12v; a text page, undated, copied by Jaᶜfar al-Tabrīzī, H. 2160, folio 15r.

In June 1994, The Metropolitan Museum of Art in New York was fortunate enough to acquire a manuscript of the *Laila u Majnūn* of Niẓāmī copied by Jaᶜfar "at Herat" in 835/1431–1432, with a dedication to Prince Bāisunghur. The manuscript contains an illuminated rosette bearing the title of the work, as well as double-page illuminated opening pages and an illuminated heading, all of the finest workmanship in typical Herat style. The manuscript also contains a superb miniature painting of *Laila and Majnūn at school* (fig. 5). Two miniatures originally from this manuscript are now in the Keir Collection in London.[9] A probable fourth miniature is missing. The *Laila u Majnūn* manuscript would appear to be part of a set of the *Khamsa*, but one apparently unrelated to the *Khusrau u Shīrīn* because it is somewhat larger (page size 30.5 × 22.2 cm as opposed to 23.7 × 18.5 cm) and illustrated. The small number of surviving dated manuscripts copied by the renowned calligrapher who was in charge of Prince

Fig. 5
Lailā and Majnūn at School, *from a* Lailā ū Majnūn *of Niẓamī, calligraphed by Ja'far in Herat in 835 A.H./A.D. 1432. New York, The Metropolitan Museum of Art. Purchase, Lila Acheson Wallace Gift, 1994 (1994. 232).*

Bāisunghur ibn Shāh Rukh's *kitābkhāna* now stands at seven. Jaᶜfar was clearly at the center of the intense artistic activity that took place in Herat between Bāisunghur's return from Tabriz in 1420 and, it would seem, his appointment to the governorship of Astarabad in Safar 835/October 1431. After 835 until his untimely death at Herat on Jumada I 7, 837 A.H./A.D. December 19, 1433, at the age of thirty-six, no works produced under his patronage have come to light.

It is difficult to know where to place manuscript C-822 (cat. no. 31), a *Shāhnāma* of Firdausī which in the catalogue entry has been tentatively given a Herat provenance of the mid-15th century. The illuminated opening page of the manuscript is certainly very striking and the white bands surrounding panels and cartouches could perhaps serve as a forerunner to the illumination of Herat manuscripts under Sultan Ḥusain Bāiqarā during the last quarter of the 15th century, although these later compositions are generally more complex in conception and controlled in execution.[10] The double page frontispiece does indeed seem to belong to the Turkman school of the

[9]See Robinson B.W., 1976: "Laila, Majnūn, and the Old Man," "Laila and Majnūn Fainting," III, 74, 75, color plates 8 and 9.
[10]Lentz T. and Lowry G., 1989, nos. 146 and 148.

Fig. 6
Khusrau Enthroned,
from a Khamsa *of Niẓāmī dated 931 A.H./A.D. 1524-1525.*
Probably by Shaikh Zāda, in Herat.
New York, The Metropolitan Museum of Art.
Gift of Alexander Smith Cochran, 1913 (13.228.7, folio 64r).

1460s or 1470s, as stated in the catalogue, but it must be remembered that Pīr Būdāq was a keen patron of the arts during his governorship of Baghdad under his father Jahanshāh, the Black Sheep Turkman ruler headquartered in Tabriz where fine manuscripts were also produced. It might also be suggested that wrestling matches, like the one illustrated in the frontispiece court scene, were a popular form of royal entertainment and therefore do not always refer to the famous wrestling episode found in Saᶜdī's *Gulistān*. For example, in the *Shāhnāma* itself, there is the episode in which Bahrām Gūr, while being entertained by the king of Hind, cannot resist showing off his own prowess in the sport.[11] The miniatures of this *Shāhnāma*, in spite of a suggestion of provinciality and even archaism in their largely horizontal format, are extremely lively and dynamic, often pouring into the margins from what appears to be sheer energy. It is difficult to associate them with a particular school but there seems to be a certain relationship to the more mainstream style paintings of the late 15th-century Gilan manuscript most of which is in Istanbul.[12] Another problem that is not addressed in the catalogue entry is reconciling the different provenances suggested for the calligraphy and illumination (Herat), the double page frontispiece (Shiraz), and the remainder of the illustrations (Transoxiana). Until this attractive manuscript is further studied there remain many unanswered questions.

An extremely beautiful manuscript (cat. no. 37) is a *Dīvān* or *Collected Poems* of Sulṭān Ḥusain Bāiqarā with four Safavid-period miniatures. In the catalogue it has been given a probable Herat provenance with a ca. 1540 date. Possibly its contents, poems in Eastern Turkī by the last Tīmūrīd ruler of Herat (r. 1469–1506), have understandably had some influence in its being assigned to this artistic center. Influences from the Tabriz court have been noted in the catalogue,[13] particularly for the fourth miniature on folio 50v. Another influence from Tabriz would appear to be the gold sprinkling of the borders in a manner identical to those of the *Shāhnāma* of Shāh Ṭahmāsp (the Houghton *Shāhnāma*). However, compositionally and in decorative detail the miniatures' closest parallel would appear to be those in a *Dīvān* of Amīr Khusrau Dihlavī in the Nationalbibliothek in Vienna dated 943/1536–1537. Compare, for example, the miniature of the prince hawking in that manuscript with the one here (folio 50v, p. 189).[14] The position of the prince and his mount and the disposition of the other figures are remarkably close. The two throne scenes in the *Dīvān* of Ḥusain Mīrza, particularly that on folio 33v, also have a strong resemblance to a throne scene in the Vienna manuscript. Compare the thrones with their diminutive domes, the niche-shaped design on the panel behind the prince, and the low elevation of the hexagonal footed throne, as well as the rectangular courtyard tiles and the cypresses and fruit tree at the upper left.[15]

Ivan Stchoukine places the manuscript of Amīr Khusrau's *Dīvān* of 1536–1537 in Isfahan, seemingly on the basis of a combination of older stylistic elements with obvious stylistic influences from the royal ateliers of Tabriz, as well as Isfahan's status as a large provincial center. This reasoning could equally apply to Herat, except perhaps for the lingering heritage there of the style associated with Shaikh Zāda, the pupil of Bihzād, which is absent from these paintings. For example, a *Khamsa* of Niẓāmī in the Metropolitan Museum (13.228.7, fig. 6) which is dated 931 A.H./A.D. 1524–1525 and was copied by the calligrapher Sulṭān Muḥammad Nūr has illustrations in a style more directly descended from the late Tīmūrīd Herat school than those in the St. Petersburg manuscript.

The few other known manuscripts of the *Dīvān* of Sulṭān Ḥusain were made in Herat at the end of the 15th century and are not illustrated.

The frontispiece of one is published in *Timur and the Princely Vision*:[16] it is dated there to about 1490.

Two other manuscripts of the *Dīvān* are mentioned, one in the Bibliothèque nationale in Paris (suppl. persan 993), dated 1485, and the other in the Topkapı Sarayi Library (E.H. 1636), dated 897/1492.

There is also a *Dīvān* of Sulṭān Ḥusain's in the Metropolitan Museum of Art dated A.H. 905/A.D. 1500–1501 with very beautiful marginal decoration, a practice that is later a characteristic of Bukharan manuscripts.

Bukhara

The Herat heritage was prolonged in the court painting of the Uzbek dynasty with their capital at Bukhara. The style gradually became more simplified, flatter, and more angular with illumination and decoration growing more dense and wiry.

A very fine manuscript of the *Gulistān* of Saᶜdī (cat. no. 42) appears in the catalogue which states that it was made in Transoxiana, probably Bukhara. It has no miniatures but has very fine illuminated opening pages that are directly descended from those found in manuscripts of the late 15th century in Herat such as that of the Cairo *Bustān* of 1488 and the *Dīvān* of Sulṭān Ḥusain Mīrzā of about 1490 (fig. 7).[17] Also characteristic of Bukharan manuscripts are the varying colored margins with floral and other decoration, usually in gold with superimposed cartouches of different colors. The paper is often unusually thick.

An album in the St. Petersburg collection (cat. no. 40) containing two quintessentially Bukharan miniatures was copied by Mīr ᶜAlī al-Ḥusainī al-Kātib al-Harāvī at Bukhara in 935/1529 for his Shaibānīd patron ᶜUbaid-Allāh Khān. Mīr ᶜAlī, as mentioned in the catalogue entry, was a most revered Herat calligrapher. He was taken from his beloved city of birth to work for the Uzbek rulers of Bukhara, where in his own verses he laments his exile and the long hours of working at his profession of calligrapher. His calligraphy was much coveted by the Mughals, as witnesses the album in the Metropolitan Museum with all of the calligraphy samples mounted in it by the pen of Mīrᶜ Alī, or his pupils, who borrowed his name, sometimes with his permission and sometimes not.[18] The two miniatures, one depicting a young man and a young woman in an idyllic garden, and the other two young men in a similar setting, seem to have set the stage for a whole genre of loving couples popular in Bukharan painting. There are

[11]This episode is illustrated in the "First Small *Shāhnāma*" page of ca. 1300, now in the Metropolitan Museum of Art (34.24.6), unpublished.

[12]For two of these paintings in the collection of Prince Sadruddin Aga Khan see Welch A. and Welch S.C., 1982, cat. nos. 18–19, pp. 62–65.

[13]For Tabriz miniatures that may be suggested as comparisons see, for example, Welch S.C., 1979, cat. nos. 32, 41, and 56–57.

[14]Holter K., Vienna, 1951, cod. mixt. 353, folio 84a, pl. V (color).

[15]Stchoukine I., *Les Peintures des Manuscrits Safavi*, Paris, 1959, ms. no. 173, p. 130 and pl. XVIII.

[16]Lentz T. and Lowry G., 1989, no. 148.

[17]Lentz T. and Lowry G., 1989, nos. 146 and 148.

[18]Welch S.C. et al., 1987, pp. 32 ffolio

Fig. 7
Right hand side of a double page illumination from a Dīvān *of Sulṭān Ḥusain Mīrzā.*
Herat, c. 1490.
Istanbul, Türk ve Islam Eserleri Müsezi (no. 1926).

Fig. 8
A Maiden and her Persistent Lover.
Bukhara, c. 1530.
Collection Abolala Soudavar, Art and History Trust, Liechtenstein (Soudavar Cat. no. 75).

two paintings by Shaikh Zāda similar in style and composition to these in a *Haft Manzar* of Hātifī, also copied by Mīr ᶜAlī, in 1537–1538, now in the Freer Gallery of Art in Washington, D.C.[19] A. Soudavar believes that his painting of *A Maiden and her Persistent Lover* is also by Shaikh Zāda and illustrates as a comparison folio 41v in the album of the Oriental Institute, which is dated 1529, about the time that Shaikh Zāda emigrated from his native Herat to Bukhara (fig. 8).[20] Bukhara later became a transition zone between Herat and Mughal India.

Another *Gulistān* of Saᶜdī (cat. no. 38) was, according to the catalogue entry, copied in Herat in the 1520s with four miniatures added in Bukhara in the 1540s. The only subject of a painting mentioned in the catalogue entry is folio 27r (p. 219), *The old wrestler vanquishes his pupil.* As mentioned earlier, wrestling matches were one of the regular princely entertainments, so this particular episode could easily be adapted by an artist from such generic illustrations, with attention to such details as the appropriate ages of the wrestlers. An example is an illustration in a *Gulistān* of Saᶜdī dated 891/1486, in the Herat style established at the court of Ḥusain Bāiqarā by the painter Bihzād.[21] In the present manuscript, however, the artists have taken the scene outdoors and generally simplified it.[22]

Tabriz

At the beginning of the 16th century the militantly shīᶜite Safavid dynasty came to power in Western Iran with its capital at Tabriz and soon dominated all the former Turkman and Tīmūrīd territories. Painting under the Safavids, as so graphically presented by Stuart Cary Welch in his publications centered on the so-called Houghton *Shāhnāma*, at first was subject to the dual influences of the Turkman court style of Tabriz and the Tīmūrīd court style of Herat, that is, a style exuberant, dynamic, even mystical, und unconcerned with such matters as the logic of spacial relationships on the one hand, and on the other, a style excelling in the controlled mastery of line, color, decorative detail, spatial harmony, and subtly balanced composition. In the maturing of the Safavid style these qualities blended into a rich, sophisticated court mode, increasingly lending itself to single figure studies and drawings as well as paintings for albums. Later in the century, when the court had moved to Qazvin (1550s through 1580s) a more mannered, attenuated, artificial style became fashionable, spreading to Eastern Iran with the retinues of Safavid princes established as governors there. The style of painting produced in Herat in the second half of the 16th century is influenced by this modified Eastern offshoot of the Safavid court style. Certainly one of the most important illustrated manuscripts from the St. Petersburg collection is a *Shāhnāma* copied by Muḥammad al-Harāvī dated Muharram 5, 931 A.H./A.D. November 2, 1524. As clearly stated in the colophon it was made at the Safavid capital of Tabriz in the Dār-i Sulṭāna (cat. no. 39). Of the 27 miniatures, five have been chosen for illustration in this catalogue and would seem to be a good, representative selection. What is intriguing about these illustrations is that they certainly relate to other Tabriz paintings of the early Shāh Ṭahmāsp period, such as the celebrated *Shāhnāma* of Shāh Ṭahmāsp, otherwise known as the Houghton *Shāhnāma*, but exhibit a less even integration into the mature Safavid court style from the various styles of pre-Ṭahmāsp Persian painting. In discussing the background of the Shāh Ṭahmāsp *Shāhnāma*, in the book written with Martin Dickson, the *Houghton Shāhnāmeh*, Stuart Cary Welch mentions a "smaller, humbler *Shāhnāmeh*, now in Leningrad...," copied in Tabriz in 1524. He goes on to say "Painted on pages similar to those of the Houghton manuscript, with identical gold flecking, they can be attributed to Sultan Muḥammad and his workshop."[23] Here there is a little confusion because these leaves do not appear from the illustrations in the catalogue to be gold flecked, so he must have confused them with those of catalogue number 37, B 282, which are gold flecked. Welch considers the manuscript old fashioned in that he sees no trace of Bihzād's influence and states that, although painted by artists of the royal atelier, it is not a royal manuscript. He suggests that it was either a royal present to someone undeserving of the court artists' best efforts, or a non royal commission. For all its splendor, one has to agree that there are unmistakable archaizing elements in the miniatures and one yearns for more concrete information on its patron and production. Neither Welch nor Akimushkin, however, mention that this *Shāhnāma* was made in Dār-i Sulṭāna, the royal workshop. This information only adds to the puzzling aspects of the manuscript. More historical research may well shed more light on the subject.

The first painting illustrated on folio 5v (p. 221), of Firdausī presenting his poem to Sultan Maḥmūd of Ghazna (identified by Welch as Painter D/ᶜAbd al-Azīz?), is not without parallels to *Firdausī and the court poets of Ghazna* from the Shāh Ṭahmāsp *Shāhnāma* now in the collection of Prince Sadruddin Aga Khan (fig. 9). The figure of Firdausī, including his stance, the set of his turban, and the position of his hands, is very close in both pictures, while the graceful pose of the courtier presenting the poet in the St. Petersburg picture is not unlike that of the elegant figure to the right in the other manuscript, theoretically the young Ṭahmāsp himself.[24] Yet the overall composition of the leaf now in Geneva is far more sophisticated and subtle without any of the awkwardness, such as the shape of the hill accommodating itself to the curve of a Turkman-style tree at the upper left, of the picture in this catalogue.

The next illustration in the catalogue, *Siyāvush plays polo before Afrāsiyāb* (folio 140r, p. 222), has been attributed by

[19]Dickson M.B. and Welch S.C., 1981, vol. I, p. 39, ill. p. 40; see also note 25.

[20]Soudavar A., 1992, cat. no. 75, p. 197, and fig. 34.

[21]Stchoukine I., 1954, pl. LXXV, from ms. LXXVIII.

[22]For a stylistic comparison, see Soudavar 1992, no. 76b and c. ill. on p. 207.

[23]Dickson M.B. and Welch S.C., 1981, vol. I, p. 35. See also note 19 for his attributions to individual painters.

[24]Welch S.C., 1972, folio 7r, pp. 81–82.

Welch and Soudavar to the hand of Sultān Muḥammad himself (see Soudevar reference in the catalogue entry). Still, a certain static balance in the polo players and a lack of integration between them and the figures in the background could lead to the surmise that some of these paintings were attempts to provide illustrations, which were ultimately rejected, for the great royal manuscript for Ṭahmāsp. Compare, for example, this composition to the same illustration in the latter manuscript now in the Metropolitan Museum (fig. 10) where the swirling movement of the game is fully realized. The third miniature to be illustrated here, *Gudarz slays Pirān in the mountains* (folio 251r, p. 223), attributed by Welch to Painter D/ᶜAbd al-Azīz?), while archaic, as mentioned in the catalogue entry, is at the same time wonderfully vibrant and dramatic, reminiscent of the Turkman court style before the sobering influence of Herat painting spread out its calming hand. It is certainly very different from the same scene in the Shāh Ṭahmāsp *Shāhnāma* where the ineluctable fate of Gudarz is quietly played out.[25]

Folio 370v (p. 224), *The death of Dārā*, seems to have a deliberately static quality and an archaic bilateral symmetry the better to set off and dramatize the central event. This compositional device has been used with effect since the classical style of Persian painting reached maturity in the Bāisunghur period in the 15th century.

The last painting from this manuscript to be illustrated, *Iskandar departs to search for the water of life* (folio 388 r, p. 225) attributed by Welch to Painter E/Bashdān Qarā?), is an extraordinary work of art, whether by Sulṭān-Muḥammad or Painter E (if by the latter, certainly his best work). The 1530s date suggested in the catalogue seems late, since there are enough archaisms in the painting to place it in time somewhat prior to the more fully integrated style of Shāh Ṭahmāsp's atelier. The St. Petersburg manuscript is a fascinating work that deserves further study.

Isfahan

With the accession of Shāh ᶜAbbās the Great in the late 16th century and the influence of his most prominent court painter, Riżā-i ᶜAbbāsī, the style of drawing and painting took a new course and became associated with the city of Isfahan, fully established as the Safavid

[25]Welch S.C., 1981, folio 346r, no. 183.

[26]See, for example, a portrait of a Russian ambassador in the Davis album in The Metropolitan Museum of Art (30.95.174, no. 4), signed by ᶜAlī Qulī Jabbādār, of which there is another version illustrated in black and white in Welch A., 1973, p. 120.

capital by the turn of the 17th century. Album paintings and drawings of single figures or small groups now completely overshadowed manuscript illustration. The domination of line, flowing, swelling, diminishing, and all-encompassing in the definition of form in paintings as well as drawings became the accepted norm, which was then followed by the successors of Rizā well into mid-century. Rizā's prolific pupil Mu'in Muṣavvir dominated Persian painting in the second half of the 17th century. An artist of prodigious talent, his work is easy to recognize but difficult to study because of consistency of style over a long period. Equally challenging are the works of Muḥammad Zamān, an artist intrigued by European subject matter as well as style. His oeuvre is difficult to sort out because among the many inscriptions in his name the quality of the actual works is very uneven. Those in the *Muraqqa*ᶜ (cat. no. 52, ills. pp. 276–282) are among the very finest and as such could thus function as a yardstick. His name is often associated with that of ᶜAlī Qulī Jabbādār, a less talented artist—allegedly a European converted to Islam—who was also intrigued by European subject matter. This *Muraqqa*ᶜ has a separate publication and therefore its art and artists will not be discussed in this essay.

In regard to the second *Muraqqa*ᶜ in St. Petersburg (cat. no. 51) a few comments are worth making on the small number of its fifteen Persian paintings and drawings produced in Isfahan in the 17th century which are illustrated in the catalogue. Within the very handsome 18th-century lacquer binding the first illustration is, according to its inscription, a portrait of Mīrzā Jalālā by ᶜAlī Qulī (folio 1r, p. 268), that is, ᶜAlī Qulī Jabbādār, a contemporary of Muḥammad Zamān working in the latter decades of the 17th century. The picture shows a gaunt featured middle-aged man to below the waist wearing a bright yellow robe, a color to which this artist seems to have been particularly drawn,[26] holding a hawk on his right wrist. The architectural backdrop behind the figure, topped by swathed curtains of a rich blue, seems more suited to a European painting of a Madonna and Child from which it was probably borrowed. It has been suggested in the catalogue that ᶜAlī Qulī was a European converted to Islam but if so it seems likely that he had a different profession, perhaps a weaver or designer of tapestries as some of his works seem influenced by such European prototypes. Folio 6r is a drawing of a young woman standing before a kneeling shaikh or dervish (folio 6r, p. 270). The drawing is of particular interest for two reasons: one is the signature of the artist, given as "Muḥammad Yūsuf Muṣavvir" which states that it was drawn in A.H. 1068/A.D. 1658) in the "sublime, pure, saintly" city of Mashhad. Here Muḥammad Yūsuf, no doubt while on pilgrimage, has followed in the footsteps of his illustrious predecessor Rizā-i ᶜAbbāsī who was himself inspired to produce a drawing while in that same pilgrimage city during the month of Muharram some sixty years earlier.[27] The second point of particular interest as regards the subject of

Opposite:
Fig. 9
Firdausī and the Court Poets of Ghazna, *from the* Shāhnāma *of Shāh Ṭahmāsp.*
Attributed to Aqā Mīrak, c. 1532.
Collection Prince Sadruddin Aga Khan, M. 185.

Fig. 10
Siyāvush Plays Polo before Afrāsiyāb, *from the* Shāhnāma *of Shāh Ṭahmāsp.*
Probably by Qāsim ibn ᶜAlī supervised by Mīr Muṣavvir, c. 1525-1530.
New York, The Metropolitan Museum of Art.
Gift of Arthur A. Houghton, Jr., 1970 (1970. 301.26, folio 180v).

Fig. 11
The Final "Joust of the Rooks": Gūdarz against Pīrān, *from the* Shāhnāma *of Shāh Ṭahmāsp. Probably by Qāsim ᶜAlī supervised by Aqā Mīrak, 2nd quarter of the 16th century. New York, The Metropolitan Museum of Art. Gift of Arthur A. Houghton, Jr., 1970 (1970.301.46, folio 346r).*

Fig. 12
Man with Prayer Beads. *Signed by Muḥammad Alī. Isfahan, mid-17th century. New York, The Metropolitan Museum of Art. Gift of Alexander Smith Cochran, 1913 (13.228.34).*

the drawing is the quatrain of ᶜUmar Khayyām that surrounds it. The catalogue entry states that the drawing illustrates this poetry which basically consists of a repartee between a loose young woman and a shaikh who admonishes her. But if, as seems likely, the verse was added to the existing drawing when mounted in the album, then, rather than being a specific illustration to the quatrain, the drawing fits into a long tradition illustrating the dichotomy between the earthy and the spiritual, temptation and yearning, or youth and old age. This seems a more likely explanation.[28] The three most prominent artists working in the post-Riẓā era and in closely related versions of the master's style were Muḥammad Qāsim, Muḥammad ᶜAlī, and Muḥammad Yūsuf, the artist whose work is seen here.[29] The kneeling dervish or shaikh figure was popular with all three artists as borne out by the figure of the dervish with a rosary by Muḥammad ᶜAlī in the Metropolitan Museum in an almost identical pose to Muḥammad Yūsuf's shaikh (fig. 11). The reinterpretation of Muḥammad Yūsuf's drawing by the addition of the quatrain is not a unique concept. For example, there are two separate drawings in the Metropolitan Museum, each signed by Riẓā-i ᶜAbbāsī: a youth holding a wine bottle looking back over his shoulder and an elderly shaikh leaning on a staff (fig. 12). These two have been mounted together on an album page and are juxtaposed in such a way as to suggest a pursuit of the beautiful but elusive youth by the elderly but ever yearning dervish. Folio 17r (p. 271) in the album is a drawing of the head and shoulders of a middle aged holy man with an inscription by Riẓā stating that it was made in August 1634 (Rabi I 6, 1044 A.H.), less than a year before Riẓā's death in 1635. It is a very fine and sensitive drawing of someone both acutely observing the world and contemplating its more profound truths that will add still further to our appreciation of this master. On folio 16r (p. 269) of the *Muraqqa*ᶜ is a portrait of Tīmūr Khān Turkmān drawn by Ṣādiqī Beg Afshār in 1002/1593–1594 and finished by Mu'in Muṣavvir in 1095/1683–1684. Again, the incomparable Riẓā is the link between the older artist Ṣādiqī, made head of the *kitābkhāna* of Shāh ᶜAbbās I in the late

16th century, before the move of the capital from Qazvin to Isfahan, and Mu'in. Ṣādiqī, in spite of himself, was obviously influenced by the innovative younger man in his use of the calligraphic line.[30] Mu'in, of course, was the greatest pupil of Riẓā with a long and distinguished career spanning much of the 17th century. The combined work of both these artists adds to the interest of this particularly accomplished drawing.
Folio 36r (p. 272) of the album is a wash drawing of a group of dervishes in a landscape preparing some sort of intoxicant or, perhaps, drug. There are many versions of this subject beginning in the late 16th century and continuing into the 17th as well as spreading to the Indian subcontinent where it became equally popular.[31]
Folio 42r (p. 273), the last picture of the *Muraqqa*^{c} illustrated in the catalogue, shows a courtier seated on the balcony with a land- and seascape behind him. It is by Muḥammad Sulṭāni and was painted at the end of the 17th century. As pointed out in the catalogue the style has its roots in the works of Muḥammad Zamān (although with the publication of the *Muraqqa*^{c} E 14 it would seem that more study is needed for a better understanding of the works and style of this artist). In any case this is a style that continues well into the 18th century as witness the picture of a young woman in the Metropolitan Museum seated on a similar balcony but wearing a costume of the Zand or early Qājār period.[32] This *Muraqqa*^{c} is evidently a treasure chest worthy of further study and appreciation.

Fig. 13
The Old Man and the Youth.
Signed by Riẓa-i ʿAbbāsī.
Isfahan, 2nd quarter of the 17th century.
New York, The Metropolitan Museum of Art.
Gift of Fletcher Fund, 1925 (25.58.5).

Bibliography

Esin Atil, *The Brush of the Masters: Drawings from Iran and India*, Washington, D.C., 1978.
Martin Bernard Dickson and Stuart Cary Welch, *The Houghton Shahnameh*, 2 vols., Cambridge and London, 1981.
Richard Ettinghausen and Marie Lukens Swietochowski, *Islamic Painting, The Metropolitan Museum of Art Bulletin*, Fall 1978.
Massumeh Farhad, *Safavid Single Page Painting 1629 to 1666*, microfilmed and printed Ph. D. dissertation, Ann Arbor, 1988.
Grace Guest, *Shiraz Painting in the 16th Century*, Washington, D.C., 1949.
Kurt Holter, *Persische Miniaturen*, Vienna, 1951, cod. mixt. 353.
Thomas W. Lentz and Glenn D. Lowry, *Timur and the Princely Vision, Persian Art and Culture in the Fifteenth Century*, Los Angeles, 1989.
Basil W. Robinson, "Prince Bāisunghur's Niẓāmī: A Speculation", *Ars Orientalis*, II, 1957, pp. 384–385.
B.W. Robinson (ed.), *Islamic Painting and the Arts of the Book*, London, 1976.
Basil W. Robinson, *Persian Paintings in the John Rylands Library*, London, 1980.
Abolala Soudavar, *Art of the Persian Courts*, New York, 1992.
Ivan Stchoukine, *Les peintures des manuscrits timurides*, Paris, 1954.
Ivan Stchoukine, *Les peintures des manuscrits Safavi de 1502 à 1587*, Paris, 1959.
Ivan Stchoukine, "La peinture à Yazd au milieu du XVe siècle", *Syria*, XL, 1963, pp. 139–145.
Ivan Stchoukine, "Une Khamseh de Nīẓāmī illustrée à Yazd entre 1442 et 1444", *Ars Asiatique*, XII, 1965, pp. 3–20.
Ivan Stchoukine, *Les peintures des manuscrits de la "Khamseh" de Niẓāmī au Topkapı Sarayi Müzesi d'Istanbul, Paris, 1977.*
Marie Lukens Swietochowski and Sussan Babaie, *Persian Drawings in the Metropolitan Museum of Art*, New York, 1989.
Wheeler Thackston, *A Century of Princes: Sources in Timurid History and Art*, Cambridge, Mass., 1989.
Anthony Welch, *Shah ʿAbbas and the Arts of Isfahan*, New York, 1973.
Anthony Welch, *Artists for the Shah*, New Haven and London, 1976.
Anthony Welch and Stuart Cary Welch, *Arts of the Islamic Book. The Collection of Prince Sadruddin Aga Khan*, Ithaca and London, 1982.
Stuart Cary Welch, *A King's Book of Kings. The Shah-Nameh of Shah Tahmasp*, New York, 1972.
Stuart Cary Welch, *Wonders of the Age. Masterpieces of Early Safavid Painting, 1501–1576*, Cambridge, Mass., 1979.
Stuart Cary Welch, et al. *The Emperors' Album. Images of Mughal India*, New York, 1987.

[27]Atil E., 1978, fig. 27.
[28]See for example a discussion of this subject in Swietochowski M.L. and Babaie S., 1989, no. 32, p. 74.
[29]Farhad M., 1988.
[30]Welch A., 1976, fig. 24, p. 95 for a superb calligraphic drawing of a Turkman; see also fig. 11, p. 63 for a reproduction of this drawing of Tīmūr Khān.
[31]Swietochowski M.L. and Babaie S., 1989, no. 35, figs. 32–33. Fig. 33 is a drawing in the Museum of Fine Arts, Boston, mentioned in the present catalogue as the one most similar to the St. Petersburg drawing.
[32]Ettinghausen R. and Swietochowski M.L. 1978, p. 31, inv. no. 30.95.174.31.

Transliteration

The system of transliteration used for Arabic and Persian is largely based on that of the Journal for Middle East Studies *and adapted for the Department of Islamic Art, The Metropolitan Museum of Art. As a rule, Arabic and Persian words and personal names are rigorously transliterated. Place names found on the atlas are rendered in their common English form (ex.: Harāt = Herat). Some words of Arabic or Persian origin that are found in* Webster's Dictionary *are given in their English form (ex.:* amīr *= emir). The spelling Qur'an is preferred to Koran. The transliteration from Russian is taken from the system used in the Library of Congress.*
The dates in this catalogue are given in the following order: the Hijra date is shown first if quoted in a manuscript proceeded by the Christian date.

Arabic script	*Arabic trans.*	*Persian trans.*
أ ؤ ئ	'	'
آ ى	ā	ā
ب	b	b
پ	-	p
ت	t	t
ث	th	s̱
ج	j	j
چ	-	ch
ح	ḥ	ḥ
خ	kh	kh
د	d	d
ذ	dh	ẕ
ر	r	r
ز	z	z
ژ	-	zh
س	s	s
ش	sh	sh
ص	ṣ	ṣ
ض	ḍ	ż
ط	ṭ	ṭ
ظ	ẓ	ẓ
ع	ʿ	ʿ
غ	gh	gh
ف	f	f
ق	q	q
ك	k	k
گ	-	g
ل	l	l
م	m	m
ن	n	n
ه	h	h
و	w, ū	v, ū
ي	y, ī	y, ī
َو	aw	au
َي	ay	ai

Cyrillic script	*Russian trans.*
а	a
б	b
в	v
г	g
д	d
е	e, ye
ж	zh
з	z
и	i
й	j
к	k
л	l
м	m
н	n
о	o
п	p
р	r
с	s
т	t
у	u
ф	f
х	kh
ц	ts
ч	ch
ш	sh
щ	shch
ы	y
'	'
э	e
ю	yu
я	ya

Catalogue

Measurements are in centimeters, height by width.

Written by:

Professor Dr. O. F. Akimushkin	[O.A.]
Professor Dr. A. B. Khalidov	[A.Kh.]
Dr. E. A. Rezvan	[E.R.]

The First Qur'ans

Efim A. Rezvan

Al-Qur'ān (which means reading aloud or reciting) is the main holy book of the Muslims, the record of prophetic revelations pronounced by Muḥammad between 610 and 632, mostly in Mecca and Medina. In Muḥammad's lifetime, the text of the Qur'an was generally transmitted orally. The texts were produced in Medina by the order of Muḥammad although initially only a few revelations existed elsewhere independent of him. On the basis of the most rational hypothesis, the first complete records of the Qur'an appeared among the close circle of Muḥammad's companions after his death in 632. These records differed somewhat in the quantity and order of revelations, by the names of certain suras and by the spelling of certain words. The decision to draft a general text of the Qur'an was taken at a critical time for Islam, just when the community of Medina was attempting to consolidate its power over Arabia. The prevailing viewpoint relies on an Islamic tradition according to which a special body of experts headed by Zayd ibn Thābit prepared a version of the Qur'an on the order of Caliph ʿUthmān between 650 and 656. That text gradually replaced other versions which were based on previous ones, taking into account other records with evidence provided by people who knew Muḥammad's preaching by heart.

This second stage of the text was related to the circumstances that resulted after the Muslim armies' conquest of Iraq, Syria, and Egypt in the middle of the 7th century.

The oldest surviving copies of the Qur'an apparently date from the turn of the 8th century.

As Arabic writing developed, and this process was largely due to the need to

Folio 2r (detail). Cat. no. 22.

precisely interpret Qur'anic texts, its form changed. The entire effort at improving the script was more or less completed by the end of the 9th century, when diacritical marks were used in the Qur'an. However, even then there was still room for variants. The appearance and the final setting of vocalization in the Qur'an (that is to say, the establishment of a totally unequivocal text) were inseparable from the heated ideological discussions that roused Muslim society throughout the 8th and 9th centuries. With the writing of Ibn Mujāhid's work (859–936), seven different ways of reading the Qur'an (*al-qirā'a*) were legally recognized. However, spelling, structure of the text and rules for reading were finally canonized with the publication of the Qur'an in Cairo (1919, 1923, 1928).

This follows one of the seven manners of reading, that of the *rāwī* (transmitter) Ḥafṣ (died in 805), which comes from the *qārī'* (reciter) ʿĀṣim of Kufa (died in 744). Here again, work on the text of the Qur'an was related to the processes and changes that took place in the Islamic world. It was during this time that Muslim reformists attempted to give fresh impetus to Islam by reviving the main traditions. In such a context, the creation of a canonical Qur'anic text was of utmost importance, especially in developing unity in the Muslim world. In fact, it was just when the Turkish sultanate was abolished (1922) that the Caliphate was separated from secular authority before being removed (1924), regarded by many Muslims as a real catastrophe. Furthermore, the critical work on the Qur'anic text was meant to demonstrate the primacy of Muslim sages over Western orientalists in respect of this vital aspect of the Islamic world.

In its present form, the Qur'an has 114 suras of varying length (from 3 to 286 *āyāt*). After the first short sura Fatiha, there are longer suras that tend to become shorter as one approaches the end of the Qur'an. Depending when they

Folio 104v (detail). Cat. no. 17.

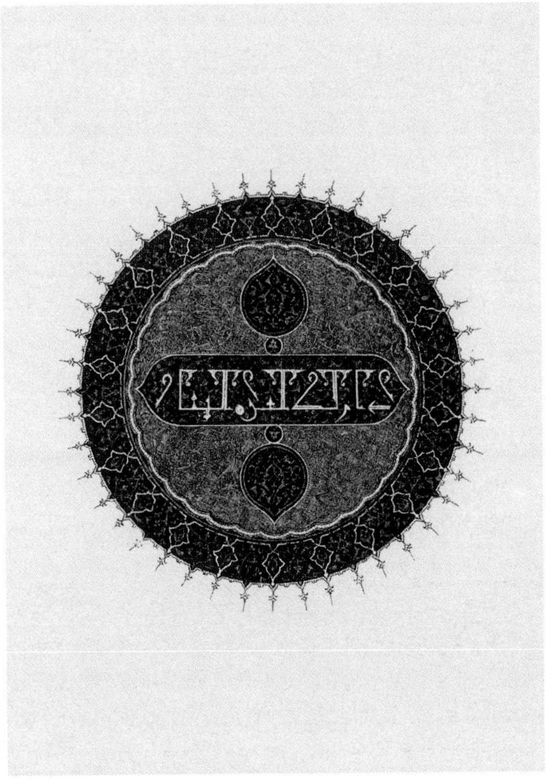

Folio 1r (detail). Cat. no. 28.

Qur'an fragment (detail). Cat. no. 2.

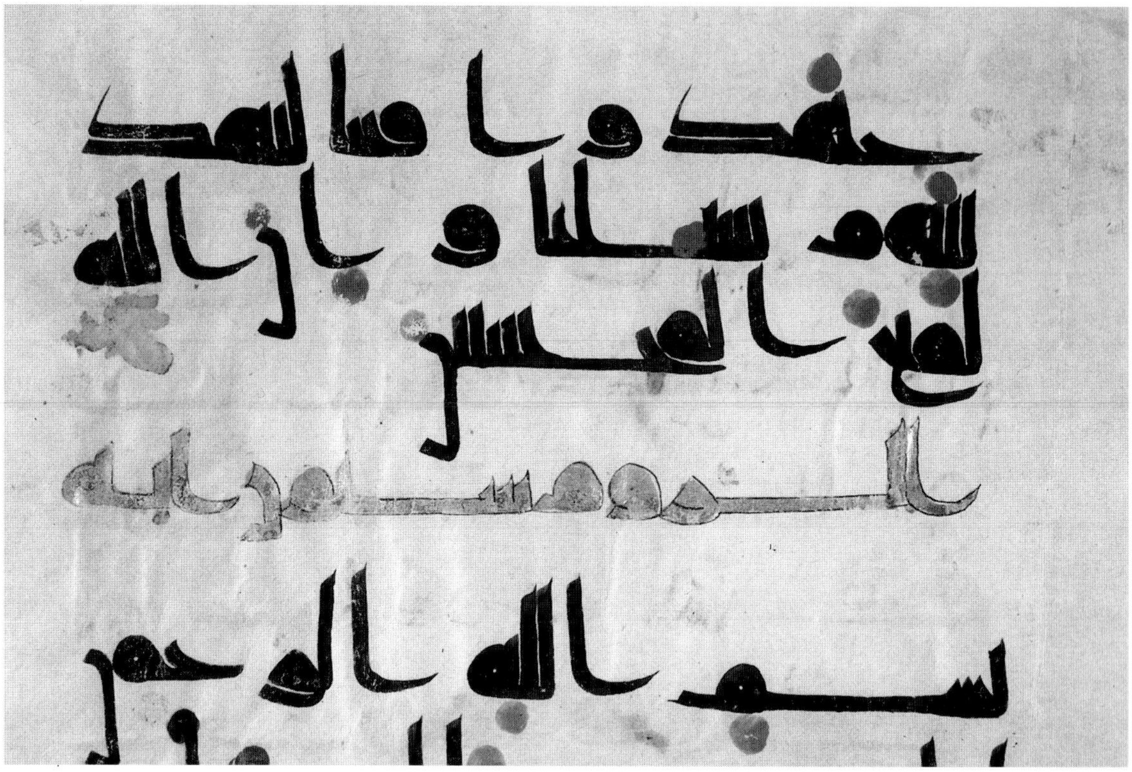

were uttered, according to the tradition set by Muslim science, the suras are divided into suras revealed at Mecca (610–632, 90 suras) and those revealed at Medina (622–632, 24 suras), most of which are longer than the former. On the basis of allusions to historic events, the development of style and vocabulary, as well as ideas developed in Muḥammad's teaching, European scholars proposed far more detailed chronologies, albeit just as hypothetical.

Most suras consist of fragments of various revelations pronounced at different times. This mosaic pattern is primarily the result of the way the text was set.

As the Islamic Arab world expanded as a socio-ideological process, the Qur'an assumed a very high profile in all aspects of social life. It became the main source of religious precepts, social behavior, ethical and cultural standards, and models of human relations. The Qur'an played a major role in all aspects of social life. It became the main source of religious instruction and social behavior as well as ethnic and cultural relations. The sacredness of the Qur'anic language played a significant role in the unification of the territory of the Caliphate, as well as the establishment of new means of communication. The study of the Qur'an by theologians and Muslim linguists, initially determined by the need to provide commentaries, gave birth to a whole range of scientific disciplines.

Practically all publication of Muslim Arab epigraphic materials, studies on calligraphy or Arabic paleography, research into Muslim religious architecture provide a mass of information as to the existence of Qur'anic fragments in stone, wood or metal. Qur'anic calligraphy is the central art of the Islamic world.

One of the main reasons for Islam to reject figurative art was the influence of the stance taken by Islamic authorities and the general social trend prevalent in the 6th century as well as the great disapproval with which Jews and Christians responded. The adoration of the divine via the image wrought by the hand of man was gradually considered as being a concession to paganism and increasingly disapproved of. The identification of God with Logos (the Word) raised the question of its symbolic representation.

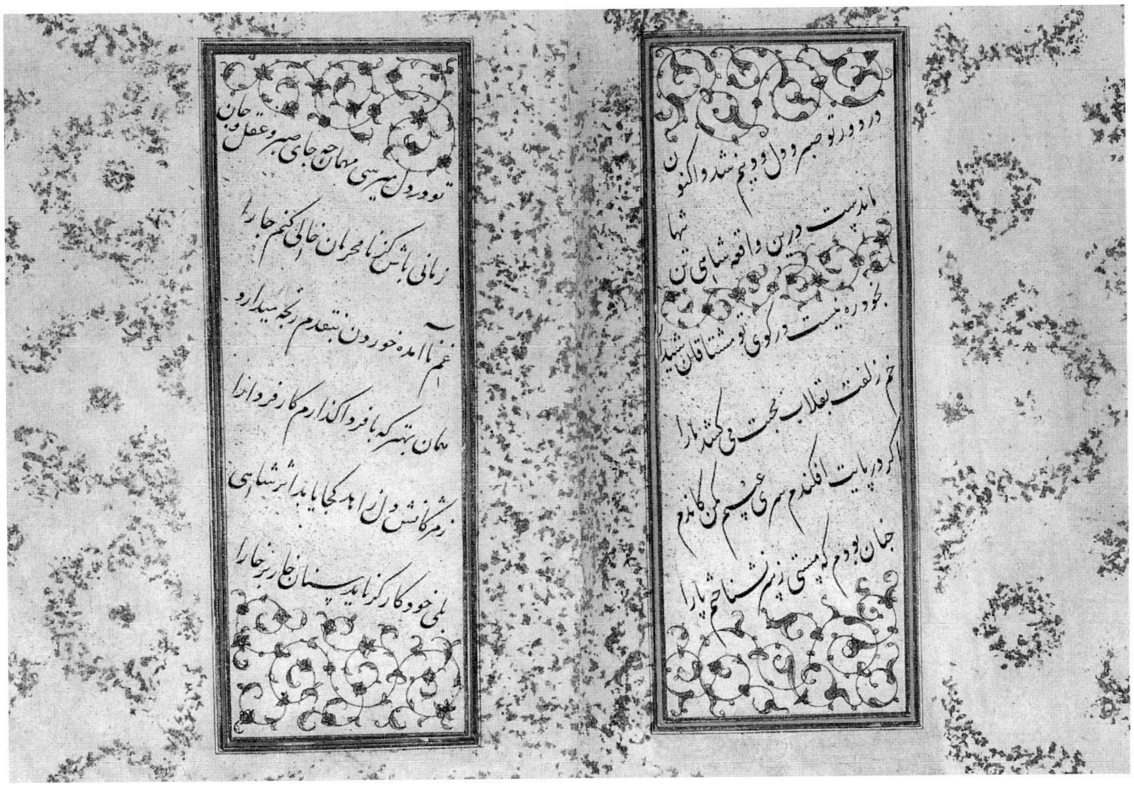

Folios 27r–26v (detail). Cat. no. 41.

Discussions within the Jewish community, the iconoclastic movement in Christianity and, finally, the prohibition of figurative representations at the end of the 8th century, firstly in mosques, then in Islamic art as a whole, are, in the minds of partisans to this viewpoint, signs of the struggle between two long-lasting trends that coexisted in the religious thought and social consciousness of the Mediterranean people (and, in reality, in a much larger temporal and spacial context).

Representations of Qur'anic fragments—sketches of the divine word—progressively started playing the same role in mosques as paintings in Christian churches, making an original system of signs specific to the religious description of the world.

The fragments of the Qur'anic text represented above are of great interest. It is a rare source full of immensely important data on the earliest period of the sacred text's existence, a time that is the subject of dispute among Western Islamic experts. Each of these individually unique fragments rewards the attentive researcher with useful information on the history of how Arabic writing developed, early grammatical theory, certain differences in reading originally permitted in the reading of the sacred text, regional transmission traditions, etc. Today, despite painstaking research of several decades, we still know very little of this period.

1. Qur'an Fragment

Late 8th–early 9th century
Kufic
Parchment
81 folios, 52.5 × 34 cm
Text on both sides, 22 to 26 lines to the page
Accession no. E-20
Provenance: coll. I.G. Nofal; purchased in 1936.
Bibliography: Abbot N., 1939, pl. VIII, IX; Déroche F.,1983, pp. 37, 67, pl. IX; Krachkovskii I.Y.,1955, pp. 116–118; Maṣāḥif Ṣanᶜā, 1985, p. 56.

This Qur'anic fragment is the most important and the oldest in the collection of the Institute. It contains approximately one quarter of the Qur'an's text. The writing is a fine example of the late Hijazi kufic style. The suras are separated by an ornament made up of green and red triangles (in some cases, half circles). The names and number of the verses were inscribed in black ink at a later date inside the pattern. Judging by a number of signs, the ornaments too, were inserted later in the gaps between the suras. The verses are separated by groups of oblique lines in triangular form, cut-off most of the time. Each tenth, hundredth, two hundredth verse is also signaled by special figures (colored rosettes, of variable size, or stars with several points). There are diacritical marks, but no signs of vocalization. The spelling has been corrected with red ink, apparently identical to that used in tracing the ornaments between the suras. There are also instances of the last letter of a word being transferred to the next line (catchword), a characteristic of the archaic period in Arabic writing. This fragment bears the signs of the most important stages in the development of setting the Qur'anic text. Initially, it was inconceivable to add titles of suras to the Qur'an—Divine Utterance—that being the act of a mortal. Nor was it permitted to decorate the spaces between suras, one simply left a blank. The need to read and to clearly understand the Holy Book required an explanation of the bases of Arabic grammar and research for means to mark vowels and distinguish consonants. This document is an example from the time when such a method had still not been devised. The scribe used the archaic form of spelling in conveying the literal "backbone" of the word. This was the cause for the corrections mentioned above. Overall, the practice of copying the Qur'an was a very conservative process. This explains why, by following an old model for reasons of piety, one can copy any ancient manuscript, maintaining all its particularities. But, as is the case here, one could also modify and add finishing touches. For a variety of reasons, this copy can be taken as being one of the oldest copies of the Qur'an, dating from the turn of the 9th century. The way the manuscript was acquired is of interest. In 1936, an elderly lady came to the Institute to sell some odd folios of the Qur'an. All attempts by Krachkovskii to find out from the lady where the manuscript originated from were frustrated by the visitor's blatant reluctance to say anything. In that time of terror, there was nothing unusual in such a reaction. People who offered such manuscripts were frightened of having them confiscated. The woman returned soon after with other folios from the same copy, and some other books. On the back of one of them, Krachkovskii noticed the initials "I.N." which he knew well. He acted as if he had not noticed anything and, continuing to talk, he said to the lady: "So, the Qur'an is also from the library of Ireney Georgevitch Nofal?" "How do you know that?" she asked, turning pale in fright. He explained frankly of how he had guessed, but she would not tell him any more. She almost fled without waiting for the promised sum, and left in great haste as if fearful of pursuit. He wondered whether she was really leaving Leningrad or had his discovery frightened her so much that she would never show up at the Institute again. Ireney Nofal had for many years been professor of Arabic and Islamic law at the School of Oriental Languages of the Ministry of Foreign Affairs during the last half of the 19th century. As a diplomat he was brilliant, often representing the Ministry, and even the government, at international conferences for Orientalists. Born into a well known Christian Arab family from Tripoli, Syria, he had received a Levantine education and spoke fluent French. During his youth, in his country he had, like so many Arabs of his upbringing, practiced many occupations: business, representation of foreign powers and literature, which was going through a minor renaissance in the middle of the century. He even wrote several novels that became very popular. At the ministry, he was a center of attraction, and when the shaykh Ṭanṭāwī, who taught at the school, fell terminally ill, he was invited to take his place. He arrived in Russia around 1860, and integrated so well there that his children never returned to their fatherland and even completely forgot Arabic. He did very well at the ministry, and held high positions, receiving many decorations. But unfortunately his library came to a sad end. His sons, half russified, half gallicized, were educated in private schools and were part of the famous "golden youth" of the time. They were not interested in science or literature. They lived at their father's expense and, profiting from his old age, secretly sold off his library, one book at a time, to bookdealers. After his death, his entire library was disposed of. [E.R.]

End of sura XLVIX, from the incomplete verse 15 to the end, and beginning of sura L, verses 1–18.

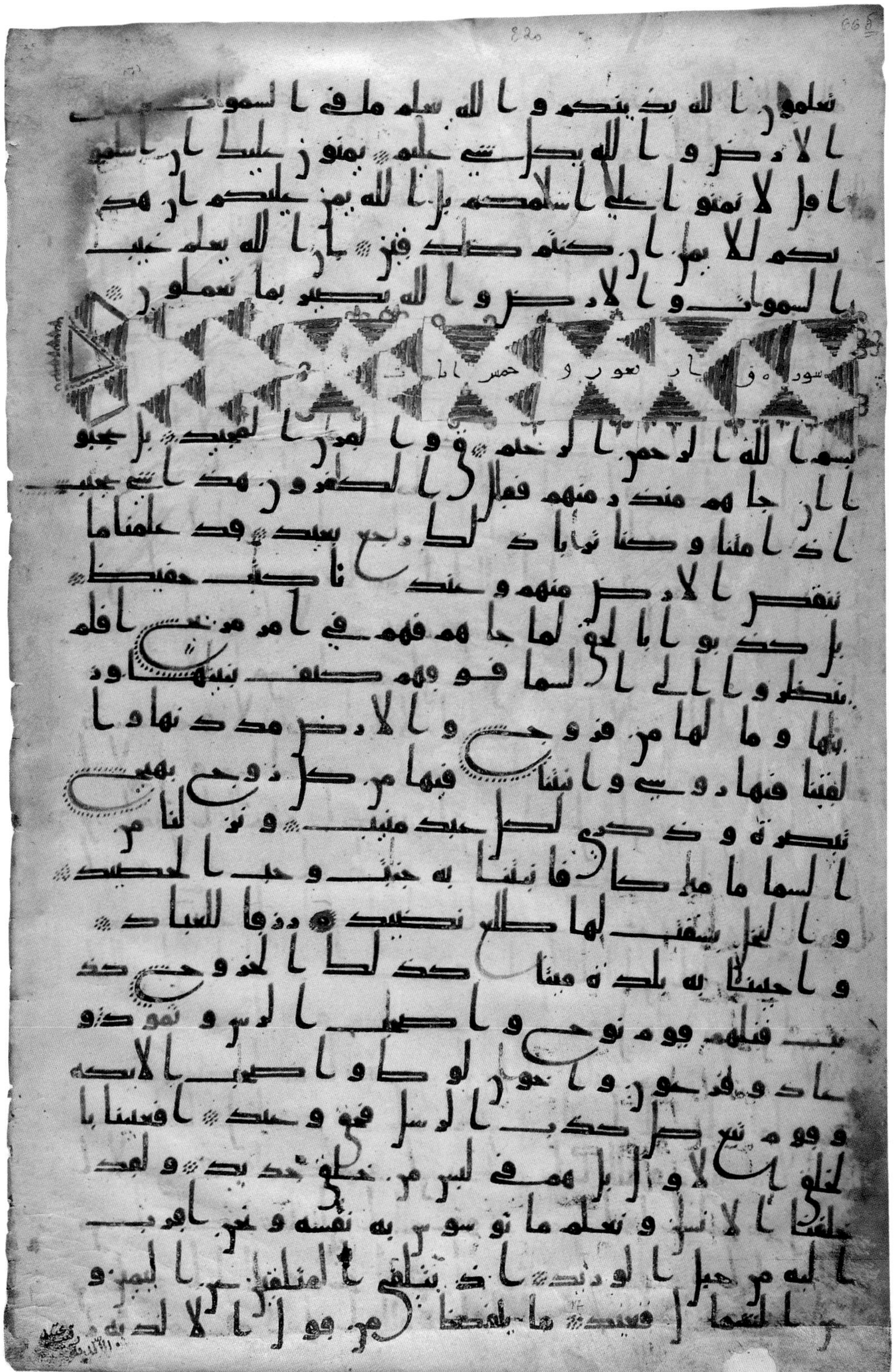

2. Qur'an Fragment

9th century (?)
Kufic
Parchment
2 folios, 28 × 37.5 cm
Text on both sides,
7 lines to the page, dark brown ink
Accession no. E-4/322 a
Provenance: sent by F. di Castiglione in 1826.
Bibliography: Maṣāḥif Ṣanʿā, 1985, pp. 17–40; Rosen, V.R., 1881, no. 14.

This fragment contains a part of sura XXIX, starting with verse 67 (incomplete) to the end, and the beginning of sura XXX. The text of the second passage runs on from verse 1 to verse 6 (the latter is incomplete). There are no diacritical points and vocalization is indicated with red and green marks. A gold and green ornament marks the end of sura XXX:4, whose title is in gold, indicating the number of verses it contains. As with fragment E-20 (cat. no. 1), one can see that the *alif* in one word has been replaced in green ink at a later date. It would appear that the ornament marking the end of the verse, like the vocalization points and corrections were made simultaneously and mark the second stage of the work on the text. There is a break in the words on the change in line, which is characteristic of the archaic period in Arabic writing.

The writing contains elements of the *mashq*—the intentional prolongation of certain letters on a horizontal plane that gives the text a majestic beauty. Recent research has proved that various kufic styles coexisted, which is why analysis of this style alone would not provide sufficient data to establish a given chronological succession. The weight of tradition gives kufic its special character, the Qur'anic script *par excellence*. It would be used to copy the Holy Writings even when cursive script (*naskh*) was commonplace.

The first director of the Asiatic Museum, Ch.D. Fraehn managed to decipher this fragment. [E.R.]

Sura XXIX, from verse 69 to the end, and beginning of sura XXX.

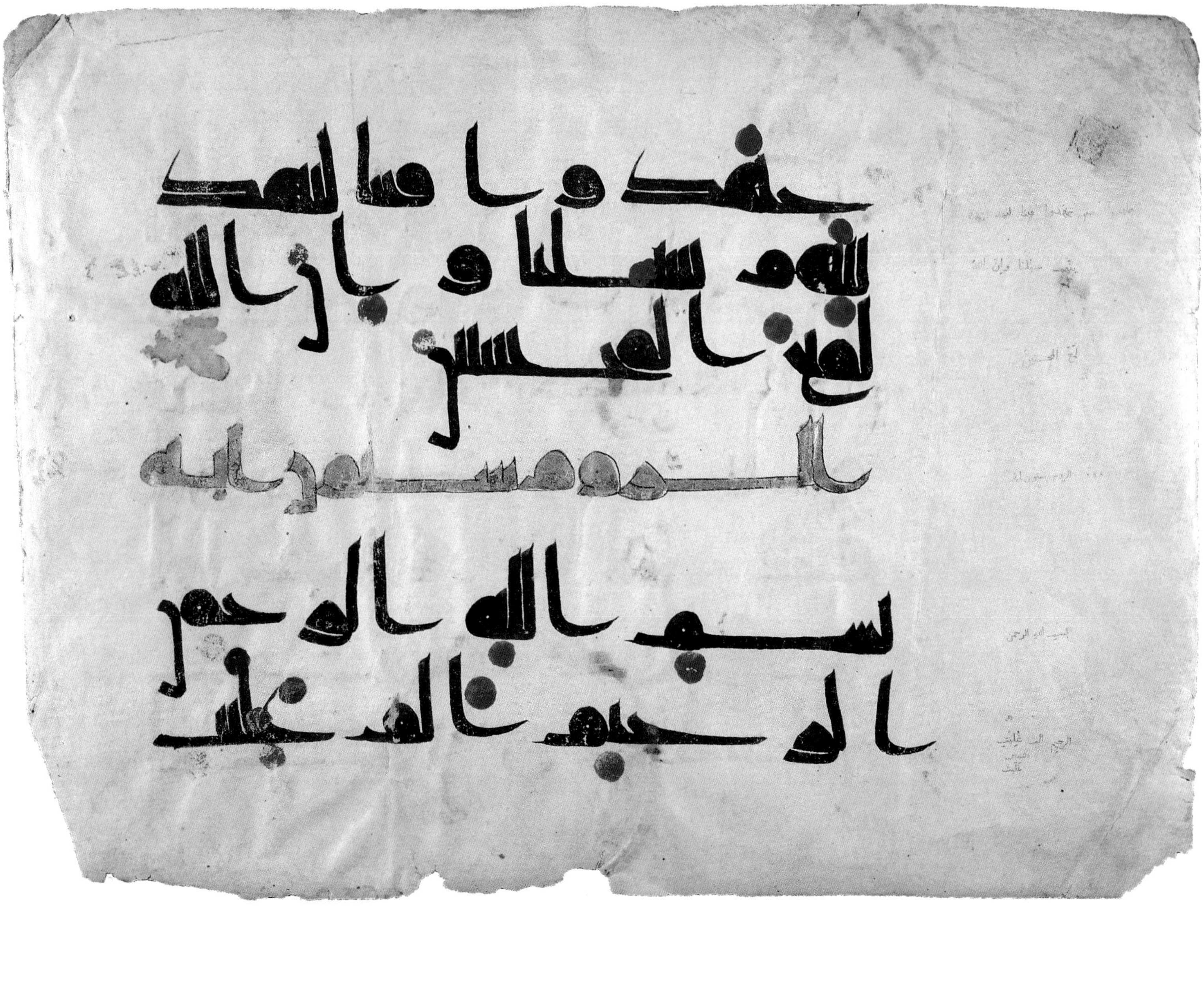

3. Qur'an Fragment

Sura X:100–106.

9th century (?)
Kufic
Parchment
1 folio, 14.5 × 20.5 cm
Text on both sides,
16 lines to the page, dark brown ink
Accession no. E-4/322 h
Provenance: part of a package sent by N.V. Khanykov, from Central Asia and Khurasan, between 1857 and 1860.
Bibliography: Maṣāḥif Ṣanᶜā, 1985, p. 36; Rosen V.R., 1881, no. 21.

This fragment contains a part of sura X, beginning with verse 100 (incomplete) to the end, and a part of sura XI:1–3 (final verse incomplete). The diacritical points are marked in dark brown ink and vocalization signs with red ink. A large golden rosette with ornament marks the end of sura X:100; a smaller golden rosette, slightly damaged by water indicates the end of verse 105. One can see the letters of the same word carried over to the next line, and even from one side to the other of the sheet, which is characteristic of the archaic period in Arabic writing.
The title of sura XI is traced in gold and indicates the number of verses.
The text on this side of the folio is well conserved, while the other side has been washed out by water. One can, however, make out the outlines of the letters. [E.R.]

4. Qur'an Fragment

On the left, sura XXVIII: 21–31;
on the right, sura XXV: 54–72.

10th century (?)
Kufic
Parchment
8 folios, 11 × 8 cm
Text on both sides,
28 lines to the page, dark brown ink
Accession no. E-4/322 1
Provenance: part of a package sent by N.V. Khanykov, from Central Asia and Khurasan, between 1857 and 1860.
Bibliography: Maṣāḥif Ṣanʿā, 1985, pp. 12–15; Rosen V.R., 1881, no. 21.

This fragment contains a part of sura XXV:1–72 (the first and last incomplete), and LXXIV:1–85 (the last being incomplete). The ink has turned light brown with age. The diacritical points are indicated with the same ink as the text and vocalization marks with red and green points. The end of each tenth verse is marked by large gold points. The titles of the suras are traced in gold. In the margins, there are traces of numerous gold and colored rosettes, cut in half by a clumsy binder. At one end, one can see traces of stitching to attach the manuscript to the spine of the binding. The small and tidy writing corresponds to the variety of oriental kufic that developed in Persia and Iraq during the 10th century. In certain respects, it is similar to *naskh*. This is a rare copy of a kufic Qur'an in pocket-book format.
Unfortunately, some passages of the text have been badly damaged by humidity. [E.R.]

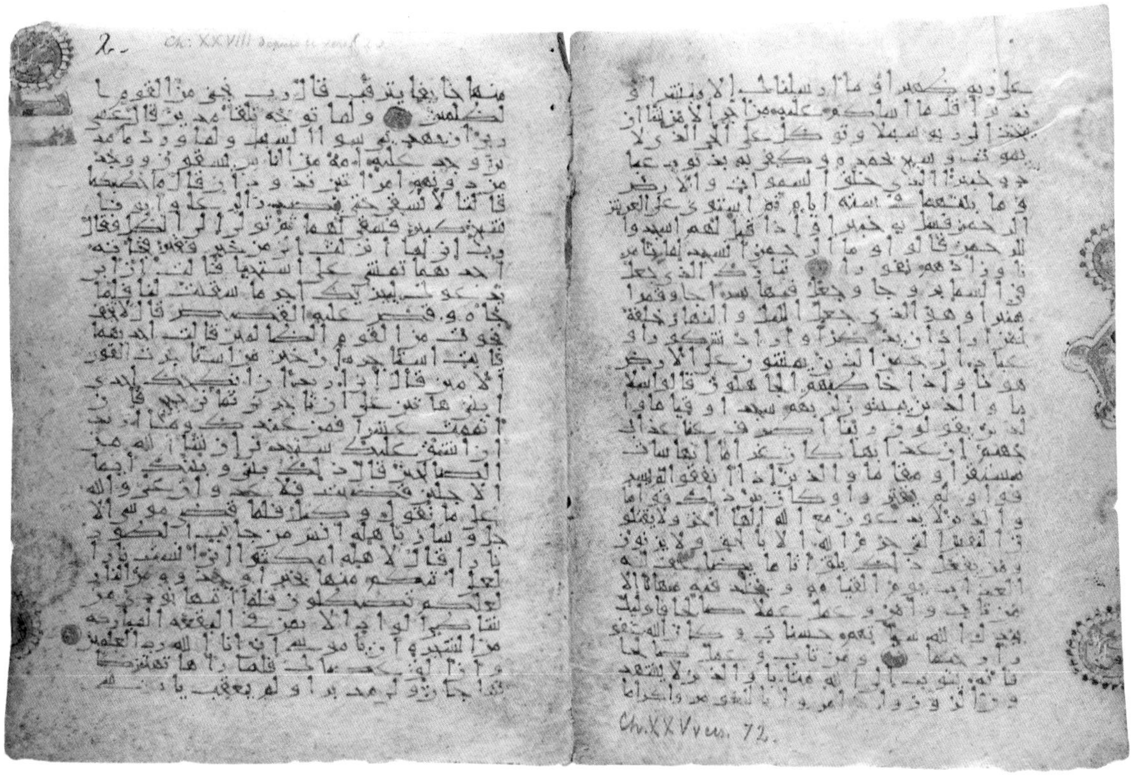

5. Qurra ibn Sharīk, Governor of Egypt
Official Letter to the Sovereign of Asuh

About 709–714
Naskh
Papyrus
1 folio, 15 × 14 cm
Accession no. A-240
Provenance: coll. of N.P. Likhatchev
Bibliography: Becker C.H., II, 1902–1903, pp. 100–102; Becker C.H., III, 1906, pp. 15–19; Bosworth C.T., V, 1986, pp. 500–501; Grohmann A., 1924, p. 46, I/3,; Lammense H., 1930, pp. 305–323; Ragib Y., IV, 1990, pp. 14–28.

This document, like the following, is part of a set from the chancellery of Qurra ibn Sharīk ibn Marthad ibn Ḥāzim al-ᶜAbsī al-Ghaṭafānī and his successors, now kept in numerous depositories for manuscripts around the world. Qurra ibn Sharīk was the governor of Egypt 709–714, on behalf of the Umayyad Caliph al-Walīd ibn ᶜAbd al-Malik. He was from Syria, which since pre-Islamic times had been in contact with the Byzantine administration. As a result, many Syrians had the experience and expertise required for a meteoric career as administrators or soldiers in the young Islamic state.

Documents of this type provide scholars with a unique opportunity for studying the economic, financial and social structures prevalent in Egypt, a key province in the Caliphate, during the radical reorganization of the state. On the eve of the appointment of Qurra ibn Sharīk in 705–706, there was rampant famine in Egypt. The country's finances and agriculture were in ruins. The new governor had the complex task, albeit with full tax-raising powers, to get the country economically and financially back on its feet and to breathe life back into the agricultural structure. In 713–714, Qurra ibn Sharīk launched a reform of his administration which increased the use of Arabic in an official capacity.

Unlike historic Arabic works, the Egyptian papyrus relics of this period cast light on essential details of this complex period and rehabilitated Qurra ibn Sharīk. Like many other servants of the Umayyads, he was accused of immoral and tyrannical management in written works under the ᶜAbbasid dynasty that had overthrown their predecessors after a civil war. Among the accusations was the description of an orgy in a recently restored mosque.

An Egyptian papyrus of this period is also unique material showing how the official language in the province had changed. A little before Qurra's arrival in Egypt, Arabic definitively replaced Coptic and Greek in official documents. The Institute also has bilingual papyri in Arabic-Coptic and Arabic-Greek combinations. [E.R.]

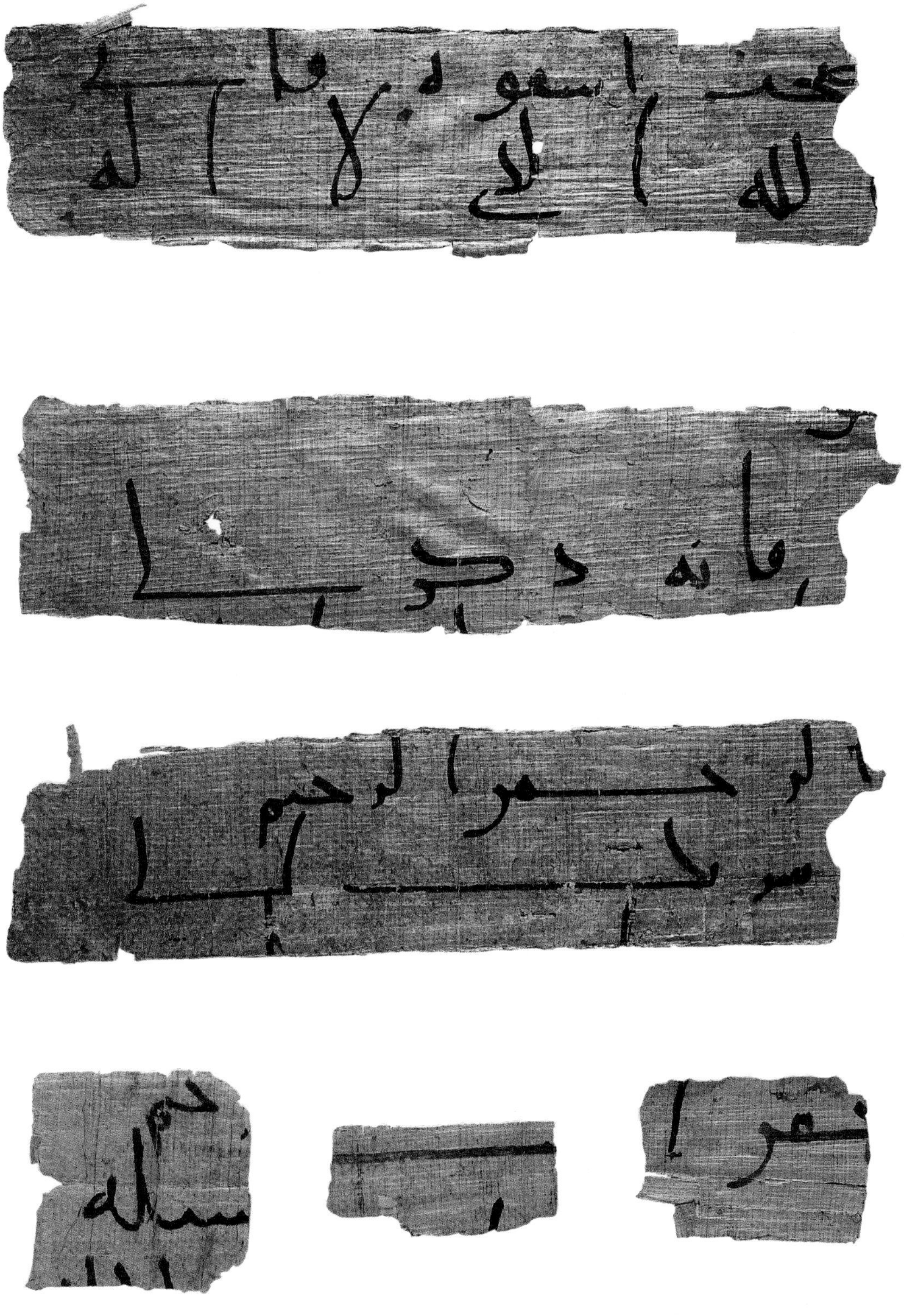

6. Order of the Viceroy of Egypt Concerning the Increase in Property Tax

8th century (?)
Naskh
Papyrus
1 folio, 19 × 13.5 cm
Accession no. A-241
Provenance: coll. of N.P. Likhatchev
Bibliography: Belyaev V.I., 1936; Belyaev V.I., 1941, pp. 71–80; Krachkovskii I.Y., vol. I, 1955, pp. 119–120.

The collection at the Institute has 77 documents on papyrus. For the most part, they are from the collection of the Russian historian and paleographer, N.P. Likhatchev (1862–1935), consisting of acquisitions from Russian and foreign antique dealers, mainly between 1890 and 1917. Five years after the revolution, N.P. Likhatchev donated the collection to the Academy of Sciences. Initially, they went to the Institute of the Book, Document and Writing in the Academy of Sciences, however, when it was abolished, the collection was dispersed among several depositories. This is how the academician I.Y. Krachkovskii described the collection and its owner in *Concerning Arabic Manuscripts*: "At the beginning of the 20th century, there stood a rather gloomy, not very big three-story house in the Petrozavodskaya Street, not being far from the Gesslerovskii Prospect. From the outside it was not prominent in any way, lacking, if one may say so, any architectural style. All the neighbors knew was that the owner and his family lived there. But no one would have guessed, and few in St. Petersburg knew, that apart from a few rooms used for living quarters, the rest was a veritable museum of large and very rare collections. Some people said that the owner had spent two huge inheritances on this museum, in addition to his own modest fortune. It would be difficult to sum up in a word the character of this museum which clearly reflected the tastes, broad interests and the systematic spirit of the collector. A Russian historian by profession, Likhatchev was also an expert in Byzantine art and culture and an absolutely exceptional specialist in the auxiliary disciplines of history. This broad intellectual scope, combined with his refined expertise and great experience as a collector who could see through all the antique dealers of the world can be seen in his collections. When this museum eventually became the property of the Academy of Sciences, it was difficult to find a suitable name. First, it was called the Museum of Paleography, then the Institute of the Book, Document and Writing and finally, the collection was divided among various academic and non-academic collections. The only thing that characterized the items as a whole was the truly original and broad range of documents manifestly assembled by an impressive collector regardless of academic interests. The orientalist, as well as the expert in Occidental history, could find something of interest in the anonymous museum on Petrozavodskaya Street.
Almost every item was unique, ranging from archaic Babylonian tablets, papal bulls, Arabic tombstones from the first centuries of Islam and Byzantine maps, to Acts from Cremona in Italy and Arabic papyrus scripts from Egypt. It was not only the Arabic scholar who could find great pleasure there. The hospitable collector knew how to attract visitors with his treasures, which were really quite extraordinary." We have taken the liberty of citing such a long passage here, devoted to the collection of N.P. Likhatchev, because we think that the words of Krachkovskii form a remarkable epilogue to the life of this eminent man, one among a group of collectors and Russian patrons of the turn of the 19th and 20th centuries. Like the collection of French Impressionist paintings of Stchukin and Morozov, which became the pride of Russia, N.P. Likhatchev's collection that enriched the nation's holdings will forever be the best memorial to this man. [E.R.]

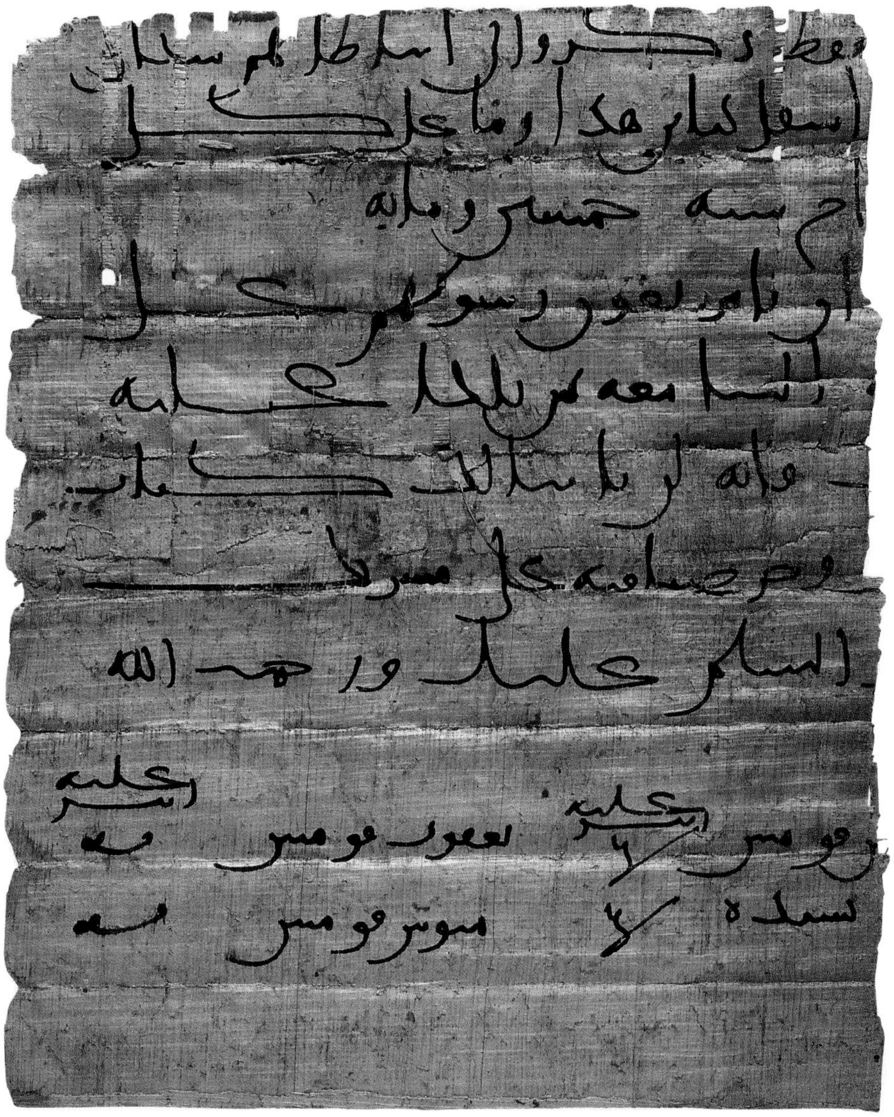

7. A Letter from the Sovereign Dīvāstich to an Arab Commander

718–719
Sogd (Central Asia)
Kufic
Leather, 26 × 18.5 cm
Accession no. B-12
Provenance: excavations of the Russian Academy of Sciences in Tajikistan, 1933.
Bibliography: Krachkovskaya V.A., 1934; Krachkovskii I.Y., 1934, pp. 52–90; Krachkovskii I.Y., vol. I, 1955, pp. 110–115.

The initial period of the history of the Islamic world is quite well explained by contemporary documents of events or by later texts known by way of old or recent copies. Sometimes, there is mention of documents whose authenticity does not hold up to examination. As for documentary sources that are generally recognized as reliable, they are extremely rare. The only exception is Egypt perhaps, with its papyrus manuscripts.

In this regard, it became a great sensation in 1933, when this Arabic document, alongside Sogdian manuscripts, a Chinese document and various other objects, were discovered in the ruins of a castle on mount Mugh, in the valley of Zarafshān. The document dates back to the first decades of the Arab rule in Central Asia. It is a rarity, not only because of its date and ancient origin, but also for the material on which it is written: a piece of almost rectangular inscription has been made on a meticulously clean yellowish leather surface. The leather is not polished, dry, creased and full of minor irregularities.

It has been badly damaged by worms. The inscription consists of 16 lines in a black velvety Indian ink, and is in poor condition. Although some characters and words are barely visible, or have disappeared, the inscription from Arabic has been deciphered almost entirely by Krachkovskii and V.A. Krachkovskaya.

In this short, undated text, the names of four people are mentioned, all of them known from Arabian narrative sources. The activities of these four people can be precisely dated to the brief time span from 718 to April 719 in Central Asia. This document sheds light on the historic climate in Sogd after the Arab invasion, and helps overcome the excessive skepticism of Western researchers as to the authenticity and exactitude of data contained in Muslim literary narrative sources. This document is also important for Arabic paleography because it is from a period when examples of writing that can be located and dated with precision are extremely rare. It is written with a firm hand, and displays good calligraphy of an experienced secretary who also mastered the cursive style. [A.Kh.]

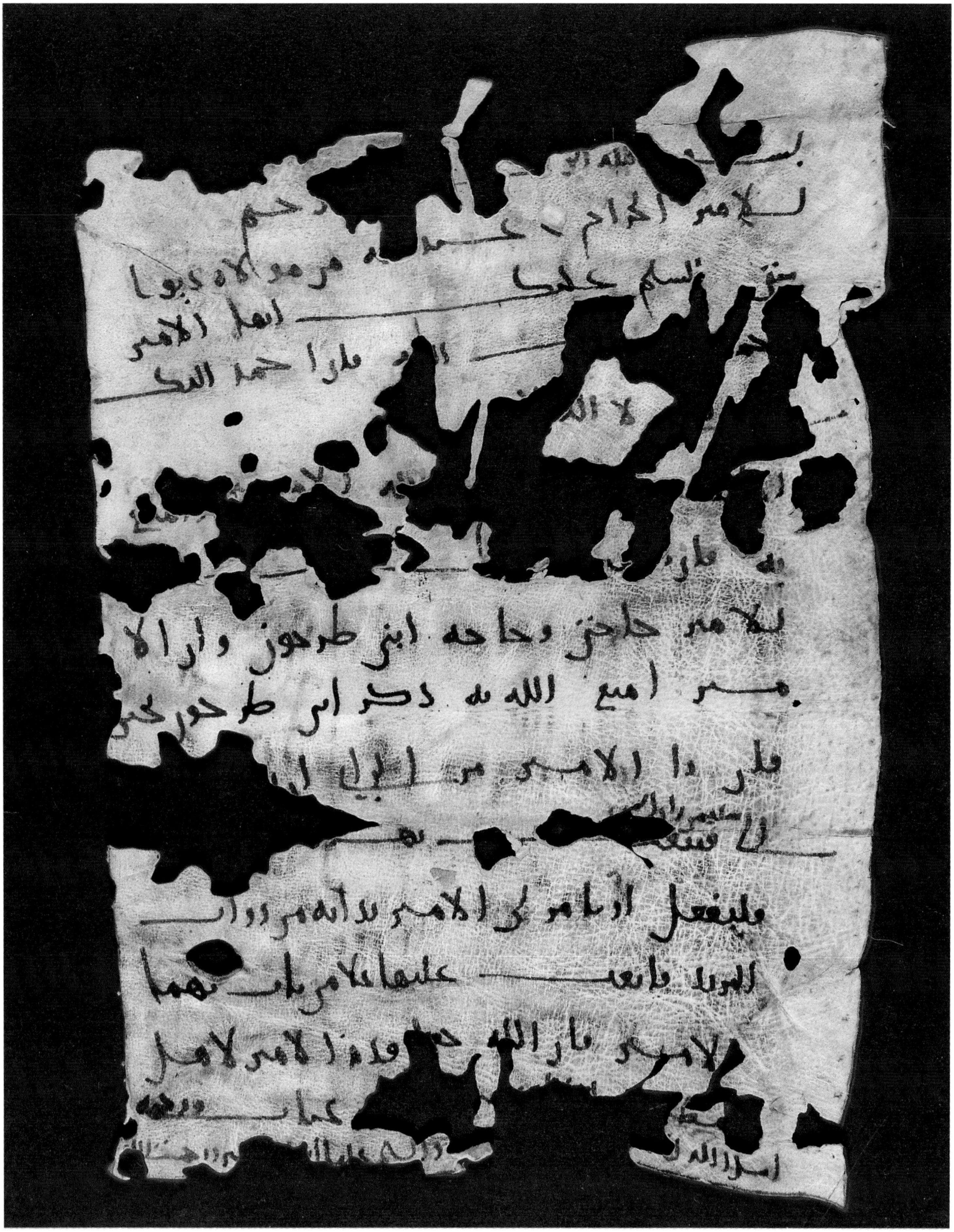

8. Mazāmīr li-dāwūd al-nabī
(Psalms of the Prophet David)

9th century
Naskh
Parchment
171 folios, 21 × 15.5 cm
16 to 17 lines to the page
Accession no. C-868
Provenance: gift of George IV, patriarch of Antioch, to Tsar Nicolas II (1868–1918); transferred in 1919 from the Winter Palace.
Bibliography: Graf G., 1944, p. 115, no. 28; Khalidov A.B., 1986, no. 10376; Krachkovskii I.Y., 1927, pp. 1-20; Krachkovskii I.Y., 1960, p. 430, no. 10.

Folio 95.

Folio 96.

Before definitively switching to the Arabic language, spoken by the Christian community in the Arab world, the Orthodox Christian clergy had been bilingual. From this period date some bilingual Christian manuscripts in Syriac-Arabic, Coptic-Arabic, and Greek-Arabic. This document, called *Mazāmīr li-dāwūd al-nabī* "The Psalms of the Prophet David", is a fine example of that type of literature. It is a Psalter with parallel texts in Arabic and Greek written in separate columns. Parts of the manuscript have disintegrated or disappeared and some pages were put back in the wrong order when the book was rebound at some stage in the past. With many pages now missing there are only 60 psalms left. The document can be tentatively dated to the 9th century. According to an anonymous note (folio 2r), the Greek text goes back to the year 6004 "since Adam," which corresponds to A.D. 496. [A.Kh.]

9. Jarīr ibn ᶜAtiyya Khatafā (650–728) Dīwān (Collected Poems)

Folio 1r.

Binding.

Copy of the 10th–11th century
Paper
203 folios, 23 × 18 cm
12 to 20 lines to the page
Accession no. C-6
Provenance: coll. J.-L. Rousseau; entered the Asiatic Museum in 1819.
Bibliography: Brockelmann C., 1898, pp. 56–58; Khalidov A.B., 1986, no. 8451; Rosen V.R., 1881, no. 262; Sezgin F.,1974, pp. 355–359.

The Arabic poet Jarīr ibn ᶜAtiyya Khatafā (650–728) lived at the time of the Umayyad Caliphs of Iraq, Arabia and Syria. His talents as a poet and writer were employed in the political debates of his time. He became famous as a eulogist of al-Ḥajjāj, the celebrated Umayyad governor of Iraq, then the most prosperous, densely populated and politically unstable province of the Caliphate. But he became particularly well known as the author of some poems directed against fellow poets al-Farazdaq and al-Akhṭal, who represented the interests of rival Arabic tribes and the different political groups backed by them. Jarīr also disputed with many other poets of his time and his audacious satires were feared. It was unusual and with great difficulty, however, that Jarīr managed to gain the favor of the Umayyad court at Damascus. He is considered as a great poet, not just of eulogy (*madīḥ*) and satire (*hijā'*) but also of lyrical poetry (*nasīb*). This manuscript is one of the most precious Arabic books in the Institute's collection, because it is the oldest codex on paper. The few notes in various places allow us to date it either before the month of Shaᶜban 419/1028 when it was read in Basra (folio 37v), or earlier in 384/994–995 or even earlier, to 368/978–979.

The dates 978–979 and 994–995 correspond to the death of the philologists who are known to have participated in the oral transmission and the written recording of Jarīr's poetical works. In fact, the chain of reciters goes back to the 9th-century philologist, Muḥammad ibn Ḥabīb, who in turn referred to Ibn al-Aᶜrābī, great grandson of the poet ᶜUmāra.

Though copied approximately 300 years after the death of the poet Jarīr, this manuscript is extremely valuable and most probably produced by a scholar of poetry. [A.Kh.]

Folio 70r.

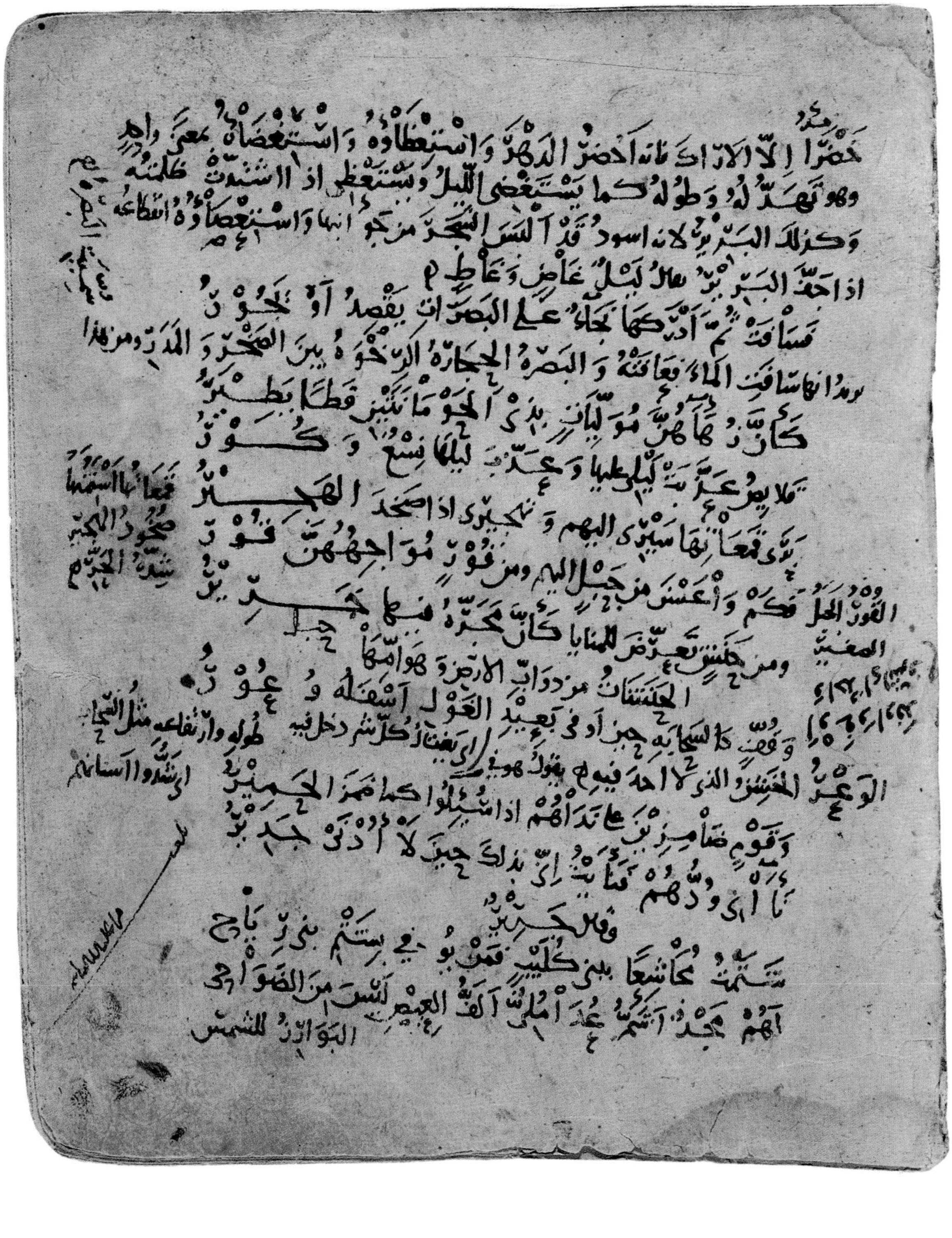

10. Abū al-ᶜAbbās Muḥammad ibn Yazīd al-Mubarrid (al-Mubarrad) (died in 898) al-Kāmil (The Perfect)

Folio 38r.

Copied by an anonymous calligrapher and by Yūsuf ibn Mubārak,
12th century
Maghribi
Thick, glazed paper
309 folios, 26 × 18 cm
Text: 16.5 × 10.5 cm,
14 lines to the page, black ink
Accession no. C-674
Provenance: coll. J.-L. Rousseau; entered the Asiatic Museum in 1819.
Bibliography: Wright W., 1864–1881.

The most important feature of Muslim culture was Arabic philology or, more precisely, a complex of philological disciplines which developed with the written recording of the Qur'an, oral poetry and various legends. The early phases of Arabic philology consisted of teaching various aspects of the pure, that is to say, literary language. This process took place in Iraq, first in Basra and Kufa, then in Baghdad. One of the leading philologists of Baghdad in the 9th century was Abū al-ᶜAbbās Muḥammad ibn Yazīd al-Mubarrid or al-Mubarrad (d. 898). His fundamental work, entitled *al-Kāmil* ("The Complete or The Perfect") became favorite reading among Muslim scholars in Spain and North Africa. It is a complex work, dealing with problems of grammar, lexicology, etymology, semantics, poetry, aesthetics and rhetoric, illustrated by substantial literary material (poetry from pre-Islamic times and later poetry, Qur'anic extracts, etc.).

This document contains the complete text of *al-Kāmil* and is one of the oldest and most reliable of all the *al-Kāmil* manuscripts that have come down to us. It consists of two "books" (*sifr*) in a single volume, each copied by a different scribe. Nothing is known about the first one, but the second was Yūsuf ibn Mubārak and he finished the task during the first ten days of the month of Rabi I 537 (end of September 1142). He copied the text professionally and correctly, using the so-called Western Maghribi style, probably in Spain. A ferrous, walnut-based ink filtered into the paper and spread, giving it a brownish tinge. The leather binding with flap on a cardboard support is very early, but later than the manuscript itself. [A.Kh.]

سلامٌ على الياسين يجمعهم على لفظ الياس ۞ ومن ذا قول العرب المسامعة والمهالبة
والمناذرة يجمعهم على اسم الاب ۞ والأشعرة اسم لقتلى الملوك خاصة كانوا يكرهون
ان يقولوا قتل فلان فيقولون أُشعِر من اشعار البدن ۞ ويروى ان رجلا قال حضرت
الموقف مع عمر بن الخطاب رحمه الله فصاح به صائح يا خليفة رسول الله ثم قال
يا امير المومنين فقال رجل من خلفي دعاه باسم ميت مات والله امير المومنين فالتفت
فاذا رجل من بني لهب وهم من بني نصر بن الازد وهم ازجر قوم قال كثير

سألت اخا لهب ليزجر زجرة وقد صار زجر العالمين الى لهب

قال فلما وقفنا للرمي الجمار اذا حصاة قد صكت صلعة عمر فادمته
فقال قائل أُشعر والله امير المومنين لا يقف هذا الموقف ابدا فالتفت فاذا بذلك
اللهبي بعينه فقتل عمر رحمه الله قبل الحول ۞ **باب**

قال ابو العباس انشدني رجل من اصحابنا من بني سعد قال انشدني اعرابي قصيدة
ذي الرمة   الا يا اسلمي يا دار مي على البلا ولا زال منهلا بجرعائك القطر
بيتين لم تأت بهما الرواة ۞ وهما

رأيت غرابا ساقطا فوق قضبة من القضب لم ينبت لها ورق نضر
فقلت غراب لاغتراب وقضبة لقضب النوى هذي العيافة والزجر
وقدما هاجني فازددت شوقا بكاء حمامتين تجاوبان
تجاوبتا بلحن اعجمي على غصنين من غرب وبان
فكان البان ان بانت سليمى وفي الغرب اغتراب غير دان

وانشدني ابو محلم لرجل من ولد طلبة بن قيس بن عاصم ۞

وكنت اذا خاصمت خصما كببته على الوجه حتى خاصمتني الدراهم
فلما تنازعنا الخصومة غلبت علي وقالوا قم فانك ظالم

وقرأت على ابي الفضل العباس بن الفرج الرياشي عن ابي زيد الانصاري

ولقد بغيت المال من مبتغاته والمال وجه للفتى معروض

صلعة

نضر

وقال آخر [?] قال ابو العميس [?] العقيلي وكان لصا

ساقه [?]

وقدما هاج [?] غراب [?]

طلبة بسكون اللام لا غير

11. Abū al-Fażl Aḥmad ibn Muḥammad al-Maidānī al-Nīshāpūrī (d. 1124)
Kitāb al-sāmī fī al-asāmī
(The Excellent Book of Names)

Folio 80v.

Copied on A.H. Dhu'l-Hijja 6, 573 / A.D. June 22, 1143, by Muḥammad ibn Abī al-Faraj ibn Ādam al-Mutafaqqad al-Davīrī
Naskh
Thick, glazed paper
155 folios, 21 × 15 cm
Text: 16.5 × 10.5 cm,
14 lines to the page, black ink
Accession no. B-523
Provenance: coll. J.-L. Rousseau; entered the Asiatic Museum in 1819.
Bibliography:
Catalogue PTR, 1964;
Miklukho-Maklai N.D., 1960, no. 12.

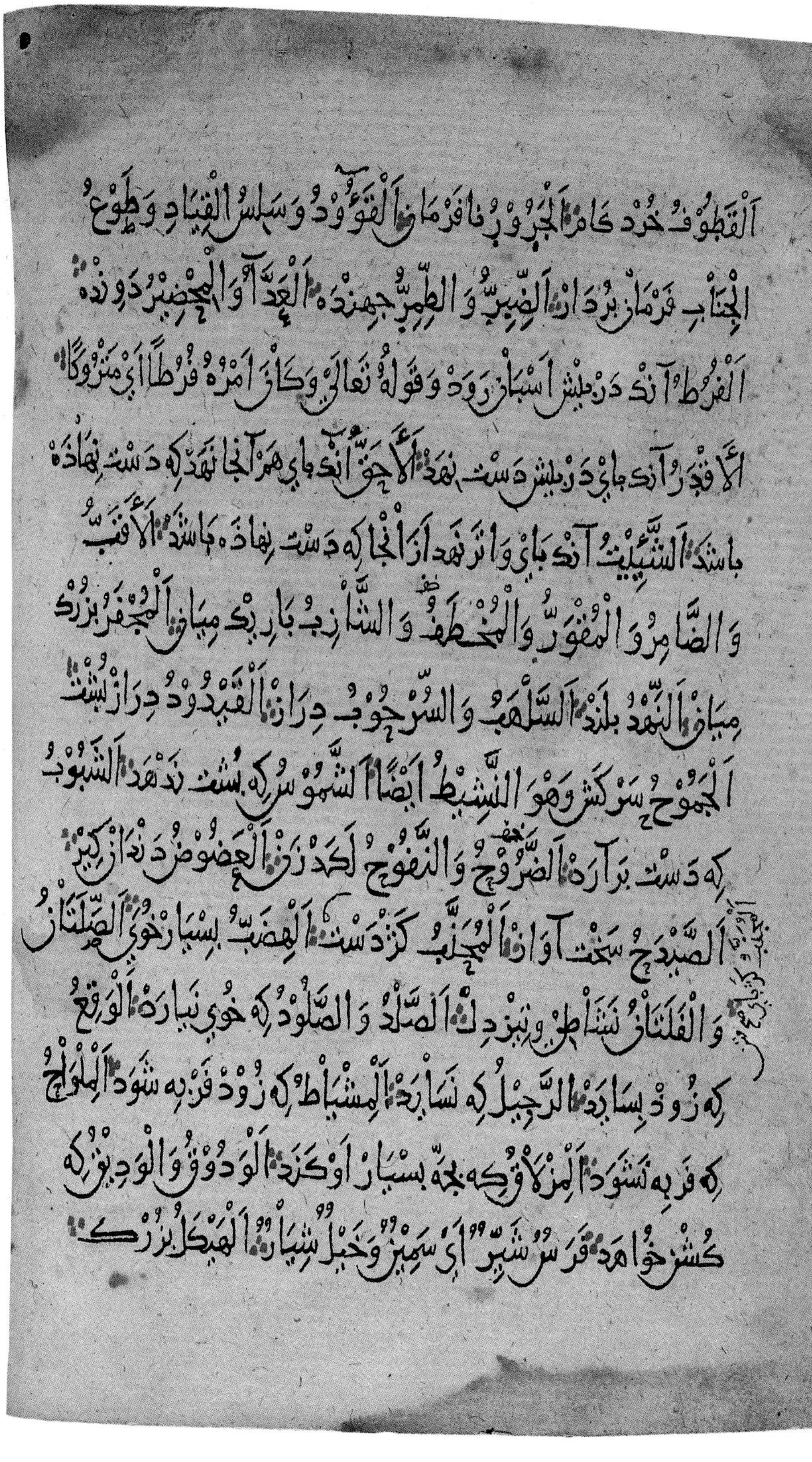

القطوف خرد گام الجرور رفتار فراخ الفؤود وسلس القياد وطوع
الجناب فرمان بردار الضبر والطمر جهنده العدا والمحضير دونده
الفرط آنکه در پیش اسپان رود وقوله تعالى وكان امره فرطا اى متروكا
الاقدر آنکه پای در پیش دست نهد الاحق آنکه پای هم آنجا نهد که دست نهاده
باشد الشئیت آنکه پای وا اثر نهد از آنجا که دست نهاده باشد الاقب
والضامر والمشور والمخطف والشازب باریک میان المجفر بزرگ
میان النهد بلند السلهب والسرحوب دراز القیدود دراز پشت
الجموح سرکش وهو النشیط ایضا الشموس سرکه پشت ندهد الشبوب
که دست بر آرد الضروح والنفوح لگد زن العضوض دندان گیر
الصیدح سخت آواز المجنب کژ دست الهضب بسیار خوی الصلتان
والفلتان نشاط و تیز دل الصلود والصلود که خوی نیارد الوقع
که زود بساید الرجیل که نساید المشیاط که زود فربه شود الملواح
که فربه نشود المزلاق که بچه بسیار افگند الودوق والودیق که
کش خواهد فرس شیر ای سمین وخیل شیار الهیکل بزرگ

Folio 117v.

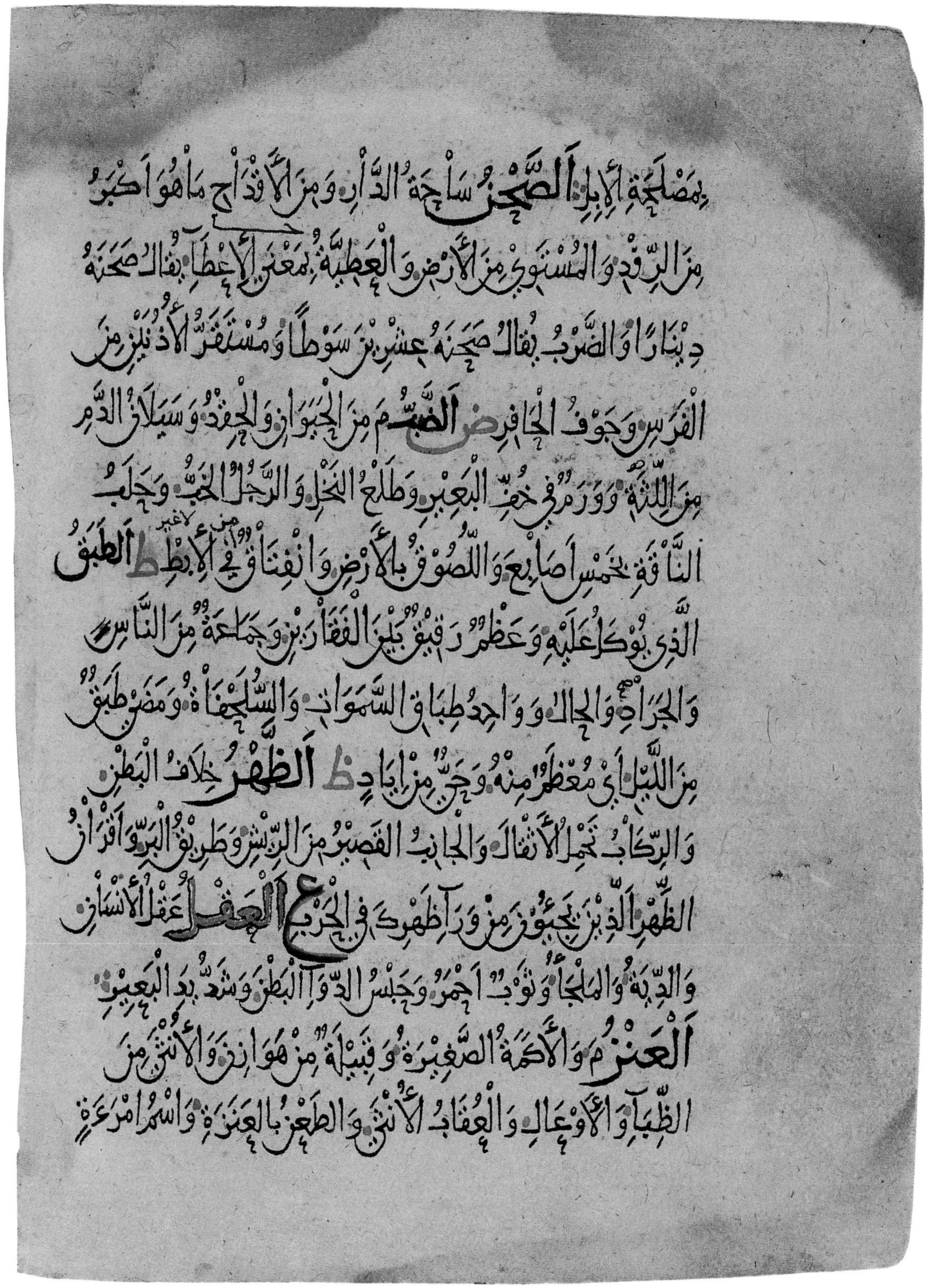

Kitāb al-sāmī fī al-asāmī ("The Excellent Book of Names") is a lexicographic work, an Arabic-Persian dictionary, written in 1104 by the celebrated grammarian and lexicographer from Khurasan, Abū al-Fażl Aḥmad ibn Muḥammad al-Maidānī of Nishapur (died in 1124). It is one of the oldest dated Persian manuscripts in the Institute's collection. There is only one slightly older copy of this text, dated 1133 at the Bibliothèque nationale, Paris.

The manuscript was copied, then carefully checked by an educated person, in a slightly archaic *naskh* with letters which are legible, tall, angular, and firm. Muḥammad ibn Abī al-Faraj ibn Ādam al-Mutafaqqad al-Davīrī produced this copy for his personal needs on A.H. Dhu'l-Hijja 6, 573 / A.D. June 22, 1143 (folios 15v, 1v) in Western Khurasan. The manuscript, on a heavy glossy paper, has no decoration. [O.A.]

12. Muḥammad ibn Muḥammad al-Ghazālī (d. 1111) Tahāfut al-falāsifa (The Incoherence of the Philosophers)

Folio 1v.

Copied by Abū al-Ḥasan ᶜAlī ibn Nāṣir al-Ḥusaynī in 1160
Naskh
Paper
87 folios, 21 × 17 cm
Accession no. B-2167
Provenance: purchased in 1915 in Bukhara by V.A. Ivanov for the Asiatic Museum.
Bibliography: Krachkovskii I.Y., 1925, pp. 47–49, 72–73; Krachkovskii I.Y., vol. VI, 1960, pp. 463–467, 470–471.

The manuscript contains the work of the famous scholar, jurist, theologian and sufi, Muḥammad al- Ghazālī (d. 1111), entitled *Tahāfut al-falāsifa* ("The Incoherence of the Philosophers"). This example of a highly intellectual Middle Eastern production during the Seljuq epoch has a strict and simple appearance. The entire text is copied in "a confident cursive script, generally without principle points and in most cases without diacritical points," as Krachkovskii remarked.

Among the many existing copies of this text, this manuscript is unique because of its age and reasonable fidelity to the original text. The copyist provides detailed and exact information about himself and his job: "This book was completed with Allāh's blessing and divine support, on Tuesday morning of 25 Rabi I of the year five hundred and fifty-five, in the fortress of Sanvājird in the Sarakhs village complex, in the house of the shaykh rais Jamāl al-Dīn ibn Aḥmad ibn Khālid, may Allāh grant him peace! By the hand of Abū al-Ḥasan ᶜAlī ibn Nāṣir al-Ḥusaynī." In all probability, ᶜAlī al-Ḥusaynī copied this philosophical and theological treatise when he was still a pupil. Several decades later, he wrote a work on the history of the Seljuq dynasty that reached us and was recently published.

The imprint of the *waqf* seal of Muḥammad Pārsā on this manuscript indicates that it was once in his possession. He was one of the main disciples of Muḥammad Naqshband and leader of the *ṭarīqa* (sufi order) of the *naqshbandiyya* order of Bukhara, during the Timurid period, from the end of the 14th to the beginning of the 15th century. He died in 1420. One can reasonably assume that the manuscript belonged to one of the libraries in Central Asia, in Merv for example. [A.Kh.]

ولما ثقل ابو بكر رضي الله عنه واستخلف عمر
رضي الله قال الناس استخلفت علينا فظا
غليظا فلماذا تقول لربك قال اقول اني استخلفت
على خلقك خير خلقك ثم ارسل الى عمر رضي الله
عنه فقال اني موصيك بوصية اعلم ان لله تعالى
حقا في النهار لا يقبله بالليل وان له حقا بالليل
لا يقبله بالنهار وانه لا يقبل النافلة حتى تؤدى
الفريضة وانما ثقلت موازين من ثقلت موازينهم
يوم القيامة باتباعهم الحق في الدنيا وثقله عليهم
وخفت موازين من خفت موازينهم باتباعهم
الباطل وخفته عليهم وحق لميزان لا يوضع فيه الا
الباطل ان يخف وان الله تعالى ذكر آية الرحمة وآية
العذاب ليكون المؤمن راغبا راهبا ولا يلقي بنفسه
بيده الى التهلكة ولا يتمنى على الله الا الحق فان حفظت
وصيتي هذه فلا يكون غائب احب اليك من الموت
ولا بد لك منه وان ضيعت وصيتي فلا يكون غائب
ابغض اليك من الموت ولست بمعجزه

قال النبي صلى الله عليه وسلم ما من اله يعبد من دون الله
ابغض الى الله من هوى متبع وقال عليه السلام الهوى
والشهوة يغلبان العلم والعقل والبيان وقال عليه
السلام لو يعلم [illegible] الا اعطاكم ما هو خير منه

اوصى رسول الله عليه الصلوة والسلام ابا ذر
[illegible] در احكم السفينة فان
البحر [illegible] الحمل فان العقبة كؤود
واخلص العمل فان الناقد بصير . قال ابن
عباس رضي الله عنهما ما انتفعت بكلام احد
بعد رسول الله صلى الله عليه وسلم كانتفاعي بكلام
علي ابن ابي طالب رضي الله عنه في كتاب له الي
اما بعد فان المرء يسره درك ما لم يكن ليفوته
ويسوءه فوت ما لم يكن ليدركه فليكن سرورك
بما نلت من آخرتك واسفك على ما فاتك منها
وما نلت من دنياك فلا تكثر به فرحا وما فاتك
فلا تكثر عليها جزعا وليكن همك فيما بعد الموت
وقال رجل لعمر بن عبد العزيز رحمه الله عليه
اوصني فقال لا تكن [illegible] ممن يحب الصالحين
ولا تخالطهم وممن يلوم المذنبين ولا تجتنب
الذنوب ولا تهجرهم وممن يلعن الشيطان
في العلانية ويطيعه في السر . وقال رجل
للفضيل اوصني فقال والداك احياء
قال لا قال قم عني فانك اذا لم تنتفع بالمعاينة
لم تنتفع بالموعظة

13. Usāma ibn Munqidh (12th century)
Kitāb al-manāzil wa al-diyār
(The Book of Halting Places and Encampments)

Folio 1v.

Copied by Abū al-Ghanā'im
at the end of the 12th century
Naskh
Paper
250 folios, 25.5 × 18 cm
13 lines to the page
Accession no. C-35
Provenance: coll. J.-L. Rousseau; entered the Asiatic Museum in 1819.
Bibliography: Khalidov A.B., *Kitāb al-manāzil*, 1961; Krachkovskii I.Y., 1925, pp. 1-18; Krachkovskii I.Y., vol. I, 1955, pp. 71–44; Krachkovskii I.Y., vol. II, 1956, pp. 266–283.

This is a collection of extracts from poems, of various named authors, compiled by the Arab emir Usāma ibn Munqidh, known to oriental scholars as the "Muslim Knight," "the Contemporary of the First Crusade," etc. It contains over 1,000 fragments by more than two hundred different poets. It is a collection of verses entirely devoted to the theme of abandoned houses, nomad campsites and various types of places of human habitation. In Arabic poetry, there were a great many poems on this subject, since this tradition of poetry was Bedouin from the very beginning and remained faithful to its origin. The main lyric hero was a young warrior or shepherd. When setting up camp along the desert trail, he recognized the place where he previously stopped over with his tribe, and where he lived his first love, recollecting happy and sometimes dangerous trysts. He confides his memories and thoughts of the past—generally of a sad disposition—to his traveling companion. This type of lyric introduction (*nasīb*) to a poem (qasida) then became a convention which even became standard in poems written by authors living in large cities. Usāma was very familiar with the creation of poetry and found comfort in the poetry of a dozen authors of the six or seven previous centuries of Arabic poetry. In August 1157, a very violent earthquake destroyed the towns of northern Syria, including Shayzar, where his family had gathered for a celebration in their palace. Almost his entire family perished and it is of this tragedy that he speaks in the first page of this book.
The manuscript is unique and for a long time it was thought that Usāma had written it himself. However, further research has brought to light that it was copied by Abū al-Ghanā'im, a friend of the author and his faithful companion in old age. But there is no reason to doubt what is written in a reader's note which indicates that the collection of poems was completed by Usāma at Ḥiṣn Kayfā in Upper Mesopotamia (not far from the city of Diyarbakir, now in Turkey) in December 1172, and immediately recopied. [A.Kh.]

مصنف هذا الكتاب المسمى بالمنازل والديار هو الامير مجد الدين اسامة بن منقذ
الكناني ولد بشيزر سنة ثمان وثمانين واربعمائة وكانت له اليد البيضاء في الادب
والكتابة والشعر وكان غزير العقل كثير الفضل حسن التدبير كثير التصانيف
مليحها وكان يحفظ من شعر الجاهلية عشرين الف بيت سافر الى بغداد وعاد
الى مصر فاقام بها ثم عاد الى حماة فسكنها ذكره العماد الكاتب في الخريدة فقال
الامير مؤيد الدولة اسامة كاسمه في قوة نثره ونظمه لزم طريق السلامة
وتنكب سبيل الملامة انتقل الى مصر ايام الصالح بن رزيك ثم عاد الى الشام
ثم مضى الى حصن كيفا فاقام به الى ان ملك صلاح الدين دمشق وكان ولده
عضد الدولة مرهف جليس السلطان وخصيصا به فاستدعاه السلطان
الى دمشق واقام عنده ثم انتقل الى حماة فتوفي بها وقد جاوز ستة وتسعين سنه
وله ديوان شعر مشهور وكان صلاح الدين مشغوفا بشعره وكان مما يستحسن من قوله

يا مدعي الصبر عن احبابه وله ، دمع اذا عن ذكراهم يكذبه
خلفت قلبك في ارض الشام وقد ، اصبحت في مصرنا اليوم تطلبه
هلا غداة النوى استصحبته واذا ، اخترت المقام فهلا كنت تصحبه
افردته بالاسى في دار غربته ، وغدت لا غدت تبكيه وتندبه
هيهات قد حالت الايام بينكما ، فعز نفسك عما فات مطلبه

ومن لطيف شعره قوله

قالوا نهته الاربعون عن الصبا ، واخو المشيب يجور ثمت يهتدي
كم حار في ليل الشباب فدله ، صبح المشيب على الطريق الارشد

وله وقد قلع ضرسه وهو معنى بديع

وصاحب لا امل الدهر صحبته ، يشقى لنفعي ويسعى سعي مجتهد
لم القه مذ تصاحبنا فحين بدا ، لناظري افترقنا فرقة الابد

وله في محبوس

حبسوك والطير النواطق انما ، حبست لميزتها عن الاضداد
وتهيبوك وانت مودع سجنهم ، وكذا السيوف تهاب في الاغماد

14. Kitāb uqlīdis fī al-usūl (Euclid's Book of Elements)

Copied by Masᶜūd ibn Muḥammad ibn Saᶜīd in 1188
Naskh
Paper
280 folios, 24 × 17 cm
Accession no. C-2145
Provenance: purchased in 1917 at Bukhara by V.A. Ivanov for the Asiatic Museum.
Bibliography: Khalidov A.B., 1986, no. 9653; Sezgin F., 1974, pp. 83–120.

The origins of scientific Arabic literature go back to the heritage of Iran and Byzantium, a tradition which in turn can be traced to Indian antiquity and ancient Oriental civilizations. The general public, outside the Muslim world—and particularly Europeans—tend to be largely unaware that these are indeed the origins of the Arab cultural heritage. It is often with amazement that foreigners realize that Muslims of the Middle East studied geometry from the work of Euclid, whose influence on school books is prevalent throughout the entire world even today.
This manuscript is an anonymous translation of Euclid's work, and executed prior to the famous 13th-century translation by Nāṣir al-Dīn al-Ṭūsī, that was to become the most widespread. It is called *Kitāb uqlīdis fī al-usūl* ("Euclid's Book of Elements"). The copy was completed on Jumada II 25, 584 / August 21, 1188, and carried out by Masᶜūd ibn Muḥammad ibn Saᶜīd in a large and careful *naskh*, with abundant diacritical punctuation, but no vocalization signs. The text contains a considerable number of drawings. [A.Kh.]

Folio 223v.

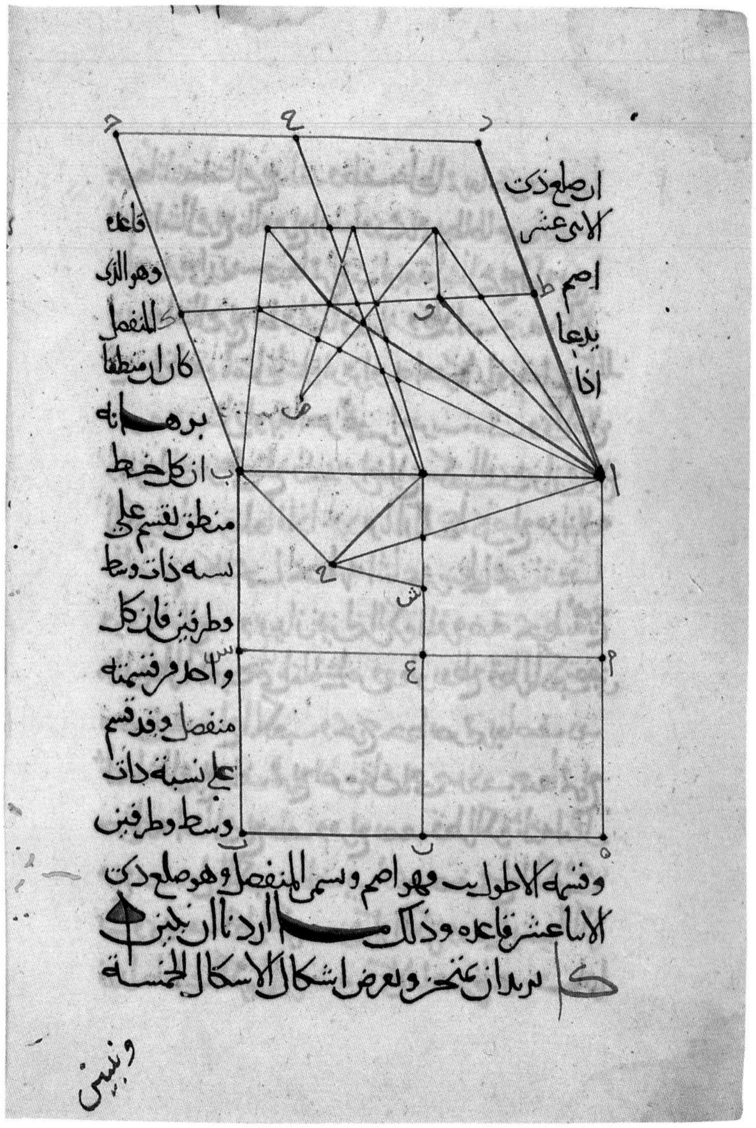

Folios 196r–195v.

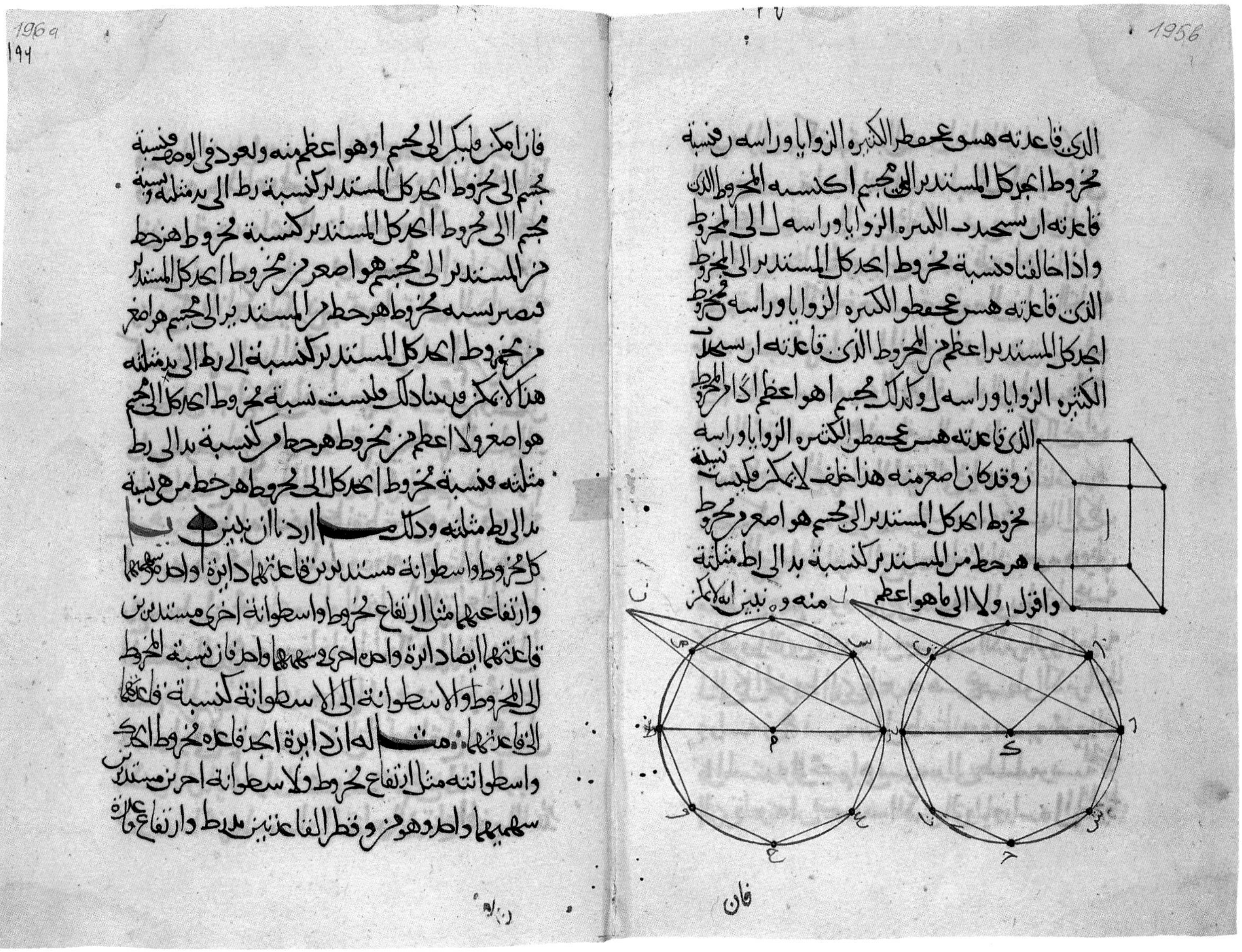

15. Muḥammad ʿImād al-Dīn al-Iṣfahānī (1125–1201) Kitāb al-fatḥ al-qussī fī al-fatḥī al-qudsī (The Book of Revelation Concerning the Capture of Jerusalem)

Folio 308v.

Copied by Muḥammad ibn Muḥammad ibn Aḥmad ibn al-Bazdī ibn ʿIkrima al-Jazīrī al-Kātib in 1199
Naskh
Thick, glossy paper
366 folios, 24 × 16.5 cm
Accession no. C-345
Provenance: coll. J.-L. Rousseau; entered the Asiatic Museum in 1819.
Bibliography: Mikhailova A.I., 1965, no. 19; Rosen V.R., 1881, no. 158.

This manuscript is a magnificent example of Arabic calligraphy at the time of its apogee in the Middle East. It contains the complete text by the historian and man of letters, Muḥammad ʿImād al-Dīn al-Iṣfahānī (1125–1201), entitled *Kitāb al-fatḥ al-qussī fī al-fatḥī al-qudsī* ("The Book of Revelation Concerning the Capture of Jerusalem"). It tells the story of the battles waged and won by Ṣalāḥ al-Dīn (Saladin) al-Ayyūbī in Syria, Lebanon and Palestine in 1187–1193 against local rulers and invading crusaders. The work is written in rhyming prose in a complex style.

This copy on heavy, glossy paper was written by Muḥammad ibn Muḥammad ibn Aḥmad ibn al-Bazdī ibn ʿIkrima al-Jazīrī al-Kātib in the town of Amīd, Northern Mesopotamia. The author was still alive in mid Shaʿban 595 / mid-June 1199. The professional scribe worked very carefully correctly indicating all the diacritical marks and complementary signs. [A.Kh.]

وابهجه وابهاه واضوعه واضواه واوعاه للفضايل واحواه ولقد
فجعت به صديقا صدوقا وشفيقا ورفيقا رفيقا فما لي عليه من شهم
موطن التراب وسهم اصيب بعدما اصاب وجواد بلا حساب
لم يعطر بالبال من رزئه جاب لكل اجل كتاب

وتوفي في هذه السنه

علم الدين سليمن ابن جندر

قد سبق ذكره في غزواته ومواقفه ومقاماته وكان في الخدمة
مقيما والسلطان لاثره مستبنها فعرض له مرض استاذن لاجله في
العود الى وطنه بحلب وسمح له السلطان بجميع ما طلب وتوجه من
القدس سادس عشر ذي الحجه واستقام على المحجه وقضى نحبه عند
قريه من دمشق في قريه غباغب وستر التراب منه المناقب
ووصل الخبر بوفاته الينا يوم الخميس ثامن عشري الشهر

وفي هذه السنه توفي ٥٨٥

مالك مظفر الدين قزل ارسلان بن ايلدكز في
همذان ليله الاحد مستهل شعبان

16. Anonymous Author
The History of the Caliphs

Folios 265r–265v.

Copied at the end of the 12th–beginning of the 13th century
Naskh
Paper
296 folios, 28 × 17 cm
Accession no. C-1911
Provenance: library of Muḥammad Pārsā (died in 1420) in Bukhara; coll. of V.A. Ivanov, 1916.
Bibliography: Belyaev V.I., 1930, pp. 15–37; Gryaznevich P.A., 1960; Gryaznevich P.A.,1967.

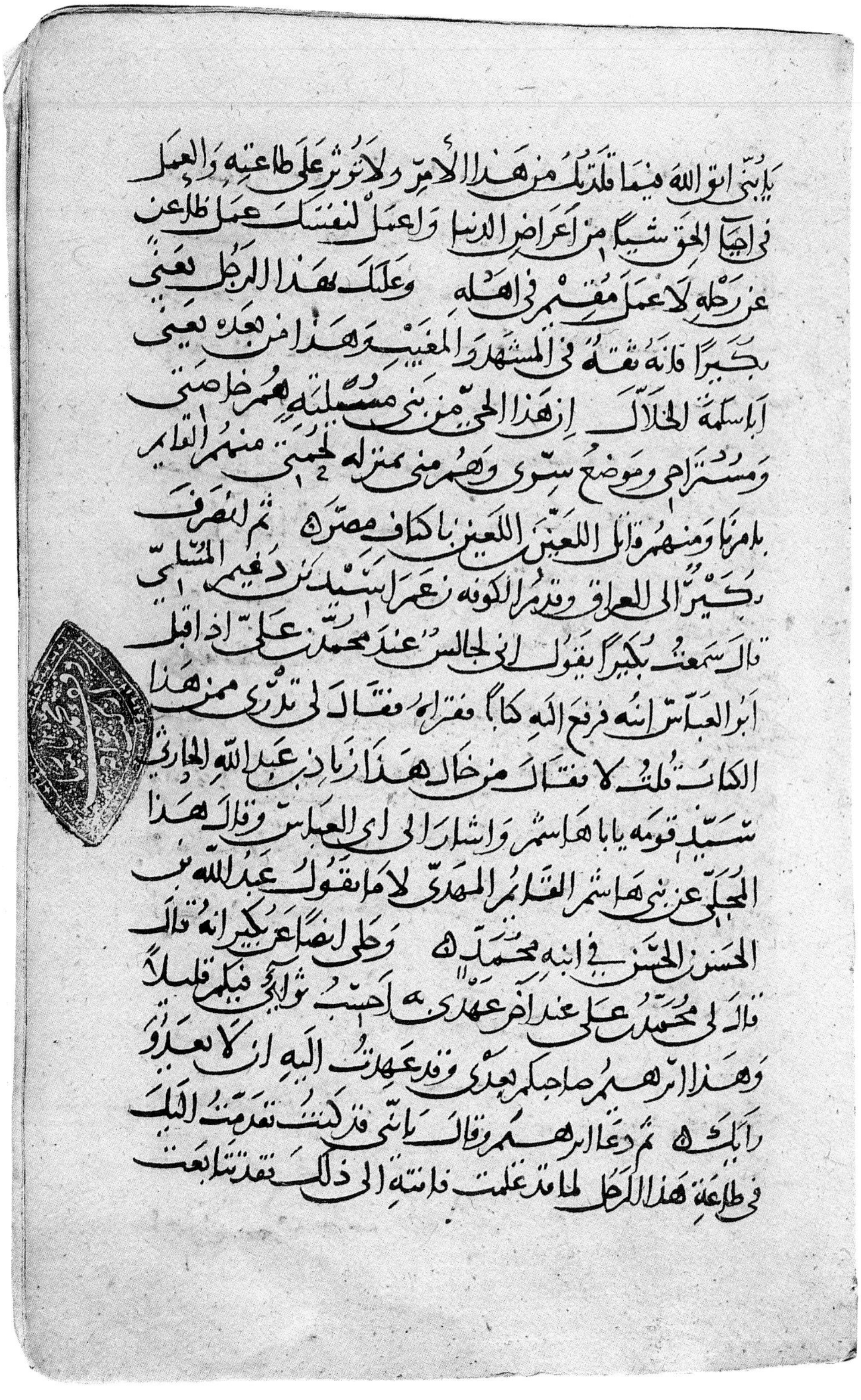
يا بني اتق الله فيما قلدتك من هذا الامر ولا تؤثر على طاعته والعمل
في احيا الحق شيئا من اعراض الدنيا واعمل لنفسك عمل ظاعن
عن رحله لا عمل مقيم في اهله وعليك بهذا الرجل يعني
بكيرا فانه ثقة في المشهد والمغيب وهذا من بعده يعني
ابا سلمة الخلال ان هذا الحي من بني مسلية هم خاصتي
ومستراحي وموضع سري وهم مني منزلة الجبين منهم القائم
بامرنا ومنهم قال اللعين اللعين باكتاف مصره ثم انصرف
بكير الى العراق وقدم الكوفه زعم اسيد بن دعيم المسلي
قال سمعت بكيرا يقول اني لجالس عند محمد بن علي اذ اقبل
ابو العباس ابنه فرفع اليه كتابا فقراه فقال لي تدري من هذا
الكاتب قلت لا فقال من خال هذا زياد بن عبد الله الحارثي
سيد قومه يا ابا هاشم واشار الى ابي العباس وقال هذا
المجلي عن بني هاشم القائم المهدي لا ما تقول عبد الله بن
الحسن الحسن في ابنه محمد وطلى انصاع بكير انه قال
قال لي محمد بن علي عند اخر عهده احسب ثوابي فيكم قليلا
وهذا ابراهيم صاحبكم بعدي وقد عهدت اليه ان لا يعدو
رايك ثم دعا ابراهيم وقال اني قد كنت تقدمت اليك
في طاعة هذا الرجل لما قد علمت فانته الى ذلك تقد تتابعت

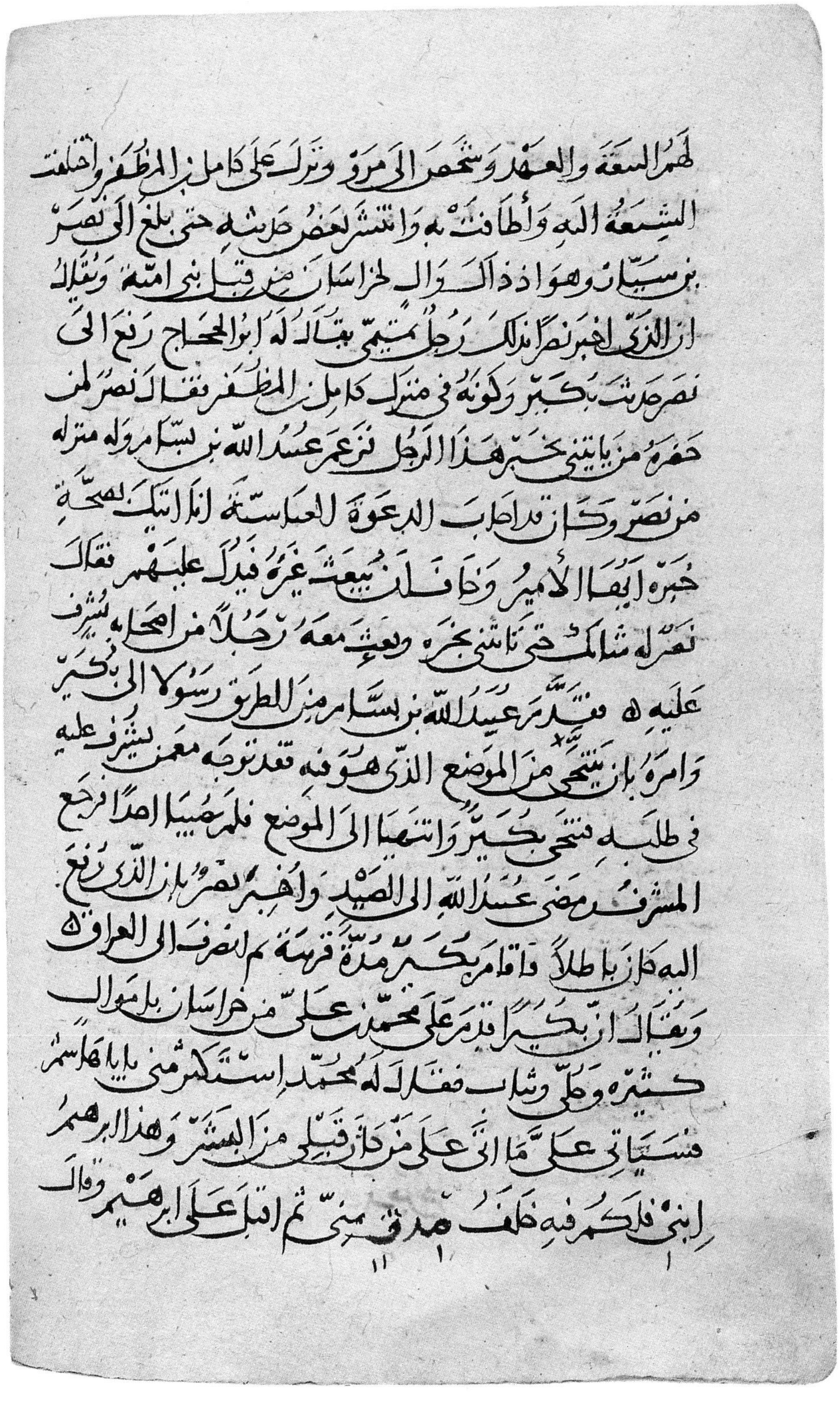

لهم السعة والعهد وشخص الى مرو ونزل على كامل بن المظفر واختلفت
الشيعة اليه واطافت به وانتشر بعض حديثه حتى بلغ الى نصر
بن سيار وهو اذ ذاك وال لخراسان من قبل بني امية ويقال
ان الذي اخبر نصر بذلك رجل تميمي يقال له ابو المحجاج رفع الى
نصر حديث بكير وكونه في منزل كامل بن المظفر فقال نصر لمن
حضره من يأتيني بخبر هذا الرجل فزعم عبد الله بن بسام وله منزلة
من نصر وكان قد اجاب الدعوة العباسية انا اتيك بصحة
خبره ايها الامير وخاف ان يبعث غيره فيدل عليهم فقال
نصر له شأنك حتى تأتيني بخبره وبعث معه رجلا من اصحابه يشرف
عليه فقدم عبد الله بن بسام من الطريق رسولا الى بكير
وامره بان يتنحى من الموضع الذي هو فيه فقد توجه معي من يشرف عليه
في طلبه فتنحى بكير وانتهيا الى الموضع فلم يصيبا احدا فرجع
المشرف ومضى عبد الله الى الصيد واخبر نصر بان الذي رفع
اليه كان باطلا واقام بكير مدة قريبة ثم انصرف الى العراق
ويقال ان بكيرا اقدم على محمد بن علي من خراسان بمال
كثيرة وطي وثياب فقال له محمد استكثر مني يا ابا هاشم
فسيأتي على ما اتى على من دان قبلي من البشر وهذا ابرهيم
ابني فلكم فيه خلف صدق مني ثم اقبل على ابرهيم وقال

Apart from data borrowed from older works that have been passed down to us, this history of the caliphs contains highly original information that probably refers back to works that have been lost. Alas, it is incomplete, and we therefore do not know the title and name of the author. However, on the basis of the remaining fragments of text, the researchers V.I. Belyaev and P.A. Gryaznevich determined that the author lived at the end of the 10th century and the beginning of the 11th, and that he wrote this text between 1017 and 1020. In its complete form, this historical chronicle must have covered a period ranging from the life of the prophet Muḥammad to the beginning of the 10th century and apparently consisted of several volumes. This manuscript describes events dating from the time of the caliph ᶜUmar ibn al-Khaṭṭāb (634–644) until the arrival in power of the ᶜAbbasids in 749. It is copied in a magnificent archaic *naskh*, apparently at the turn of the 13th century. The correct order of the folios was mixed up when the book was bound. [A.Kh.]

17. Mu'īn al-Dīn Abū al-ᶜAlā Muḥammad ibn al-Shaykh al-Ajall Maḥmūd ibn Abī al-Ḥasan al-Nīshāpūrī Tafsīr-i basā'ir-i yamīnī or Basā'ir fī al-tafsīr (1151) (Commentary on the Qur'an)

Folio 104v.

Copied by Muḥammad ibn Muḥammad al- ᶜAmīd al-Imām Awḥad al-Dīn al- Khaṭṭāṭ in 1232–1233
Thuluth and *naskh*
Paper
210 folios
29.7 × 19.4 cm
Text: 22 × 12 cm
7 to 16 lines to the page
Accession no. C-189
Provenance: donation of N. Khanykov, 1854.
Bibliography: Catalogue PTR, 1964, no. 810.

This *Tafsīr* ("Commentary on the Qur'an") was written in the middle of the month of Ramadan 545 (beginning of January 1151) and dedicated to the Ghaznavid Sultan, Yamīn al-Daula Bahrām-shāh (1117–1157). The author, Mu'īn al-Dīn Abū al-ᶜAlā Muḥammad ibn al-Shaykh al-Ajall Maḥmūd ibn Abī al-Ḥasan al-Nīshāpūrī was in the service of Bahrām-shāh's court as poet, man of letters and expert on the Qur'an. The *tafsīr* is copied in two types of script of which the Qur'anic text itself is written in an excellent, large *thuluth* calligraphy, in liquid gold surrounded by a black or red outline; the Persian translation of the Qur'anic verses and commentaries are written in a magnificent, large Persian *naskh*. Diacritical marks, the range of colors decoratively dividing the suras and the verses, as well as the left side of the conserved frontispiece (dark brown watercolor tones, white and gold pigment) would indicate that the manuscript was probably produced in eastern Khurasan. This copy contains commentaries on sura LX: 45–48. The colophon is of great interest. On the last double page (209v–210r), the name of the calligrapher and the date the copy was finished are traced in gold on a white background, surrounded by a black line in four circles (two per page). [O.A.]

بود بیست عیسی علیه السلام مگر بنده کی ما روی
نیکوئی کرده ایم و ورا منصب پیغامبری رسانیده
واورا مثلی کرده ایم برای بنی اسرائیل تا بدو دلیل کیرند
بر قدرت وحکمت کی ادمی زاده بی پدر بیافریدیم
و ورا بدین درجت رسانیدیم واکر ما خواهیم بدل شما
فریشتکان فرستیم کی اندر روی زمین خلیفتان
یکدیکر باشند چنانک بس از نوبت ادم علیه السلام
بودند

وانه لعلم للساعة فلا

تمترن بها واتبعون هذا

صراط مستقيم ولا

18. Abū Muḥammad al-Qāsim ibn ᶜAlī al-Ḥarīrī al-Baṣrī (1054–1122) Maqāmāt (The Assemblies)

Copied in Iraq towards 1240
Naskh
Thick, glossy paper
177 folios
26.5 × 21.5 cm
96 miniatures
Accession no. C-23
Provenance: coll. J.-L. Rousseau; entered the Asiatic Museum in 1819.
Bibliography: Borisov A.Y., 1938, pp. 171–178; Khalidov A.B., 1960, no. 43; Krachkovskaya V.A., 1962, pp. 171–184.

The Arabic manuscripts with colored miniature paintings are of immense appeal to art historians studying Mediaeval Middle Eastern art. The miniatures reproduced on these pages illustrate a text which has become a monument to Arabic literature. Al-Ḥarīrī created its text at the beginning of the 12th century in Iraq. This rare version of the *Maqāmāt* was copied by an unknown calligrapher and painter, most likely one and the same person, probably around 1240. The author, Abū Muḥammad al-Qāsim ibn ᶜAlī al-Ḥarīrī al-Baṣrī (1054–1122) is considered by Arabs as a great storyteller and man of letters. His name is still known to every school child in Iraq. His *Maqāmāt* has been copied and commented upon innumerable times and people often memorized the story.

Al-Ḥarīrī's work consists of fifty *Maqāmāt* episodes which recall the adventures and metamorphoses of a character by the name of Abū Zayd al-Sarūjī. *Maqāmāt*—usually translated as "The Assemblies"—is a form of Arabic literature, which can be compared to the genre of the short, lighthearted novels in European Renaissance literature. The *Maqāmāt* consists of a series of short stories in rhyming prose interspersed with poems. Alongside the main hero of the story, the author comments and constructs events and observations around a fictional observer-narrator. Secondary characters are sometimes introduced. The fifty *Maqāmāt* form a complete cycle, all based on the theme of quarrels and disputes between the two main characters, Abū Zayd and al-Ḥārith.

Emphasis is placed above all on the oratorial skills of the two main characters, the liveliness of their dialogue and epithets, and the elegance and variety of rhyme in both prose and verse.

The *Maqāmāt* of al-Ḥarīrī belonged to a limited group of stories that, during that period, circulated in the form of illustrated manuscripts. However, of the hundreds of surviving copies, there are only a dozen or so illustrated with miniatures. This manuscript is one of the oldest and best among them.

It was copied around 1240, with black ink in a large calligraphic *naskh* with diacritical marks and complete vocalization. The copyist left empty spaces for the artist to place his miniatures. There were presumably originally about one hundred and twenty, of which there remain ninety-six. The numbers of the *Maqāmāt* are written in a stylized kufic script, in rectangular, colored and gilded blocks. Forty of these blocks remain. The manuscript changed hands repeatedly, was badly conserved and has even been intentionally damaged. Thirty-five folios have been lost. There were attempts long ago at restoration and at completing the text, the miniatures and surroundings. [A.Kh.]

Maqāma of Damietta *(no. 4): the camel caravan's stop (p. 22; folio 12r). The narrator, al-Ḥārith ibn Ḥammām, travels with the caravan to the Egyptian town of Damietta. At a halt, he hears two men discussing outside a tent. The youngest, the son of Abū Zayd, talks in refined terms of the duties of friendship and hospitality towards one's neighbor. The older man, Abū Zayd al-Sarūjī, advises him to think only of himself.*

Maqāma of Marāgha *(no. 6): a literary meeting with the person chairing the meeting in the center (p. 35; folio 16v). Al-Ḥārith was in the town of Marāgha (Persia) in the company of erudite* kātibs *who are complaining of the decline in professional skills within the bureaucracy. An unknown modest speaker, whom the narrator recognizes as Abū Zayd, presents a letter that he has just written, in which he praises the emir, and pronounces his own personal request. He subsequently refuses to join the service of the emir declaring that he prefers his freedom and to travel around as he pleases.*

Maqāma of al-Rahba *(no. 10): a man hands a letter to another man, with a third person standing to one side (p. 63; folio 32v). In the town of al-Rahba on the Euphrates, al-Ḥārith meets an old man and a youth in a crowded square and recognizes them to be Abū Zayd and his son. The old man accuses the youth of murder and takes him before the ruler for judgment. But the governor is charmed by the boy and asks the old man, Abū Zayd, how he knows the youth is the culprit. Since no witnesses are to be found, Abū Zayd makes up a frightful oath for the boy to swear which he refuses to do. As the governor becomes more and more fond of the youth, he suggests that for one hundred dinars the old man forget the entire affair. Abū Zayd agrees, but as the governor has only twenty dinars on him, Abū Zayd stays to guard the youth overnight. Al-Ḥārith approaches the two of them, recognizes his friend and the boy, and finds out that the two plan to escape at dawn. They do so, leaving al-Ḥārith with a mocking letter to the governor, which instead he tears up.*

Maqāma of Damascus *(no. 12): an elderly guide at a caravan resting place (p. 72; folio 37r). Al-Ḥārith tells us of his travels from Iraq to Damascus where he experiences all imaginable pleasures; when he is ready to return, he organizes a caravan with his companions, and looks for a guide to help them cross the desert. A man dressed like a holy man offers his services, promising to safeguard their goods and their peace of mind by means of mysterious magic formula. Later, this same man, no other than Abū Zayd, turns out to be a drunkard.*

Opposite:
Maqāma of Mecca *(no. 14): Abū Zayd and his son in front of the tents belonging to wealthy pilgrims (p. 85; folio 43v). From Baghdad, al-Ḥārith leaves for the ḥājj. Once he has carried out the ritual, he starts looking for shelter from the heat. When he is seated in a tent with his friends, an old man accompanied by a youth approaches them. The old man flatters all those present in order to gain their sympathy, while the youth asks them, in verse, for provisions for their journey.
These men are Abū Zayd and his son.*

عرفكم على تبلّج عرفكم وبشّرني تضوّع رندكم بحسن المنقلب من عندكم فاستخبرناه حينئذ

شجر لحظة طيبة

عن لبانته لنكفل باغاثته فقال إنّ لي مآرباً ولفتاي مطلباً فقلنا كلا المرامين سيقضى وكلاكما

سوف يرضى ولكن الكبر الكبر فقال أجل ومن دحا السبع الغبر ثم وثب للمقال

كالمنتشط من العقال وأنشد

ر انقباض القوم واضطرارهم الى الصوم عرّض بالمطارحة واستاذن في المفاتحة فقالوا له

ذا ومن لنا بذا فقال اتعرفون رسالة ارضها سماؤها وصبحها مساؤها وهي نسجت على منوالين

نسجت في لونين وصلت الى جهتين وبرزت ذات وجهين ان بزغت من مشرقها

عشّاك بريق نفثها وان طلعت من مغربها فيا العجبها قال فكان القوم رموا بالصمات او خفت

Opposite:
Maqāma of "the Cantankerous Lily" *(no. 17): a literary meeting p. 105; folio 53v). During one of his journeys, al-Ḥārith finds himself in the company of a quarrelsome crowd, including a shaykh with a remarkable skill with words. He presents his composition, in which the words can be arranged in different ways, each group can be read backwards, thus producing a different meaning. The shaykh in question was Abū Zayd.*

Maqāma of the Euphrates
no. 22): a boat with passengers and rowers (p. 135; folio 68v). While sailing on a boat in the Euphrates one day, al-Ḥārith joins up with a group of civil servants who are off to calculate the tax on the harvest. With them is an old man, poorly dressed, who is excellent at characterizing two categories of civil servant: the accountant and the scribe. We recognize Abū Zayd as the orator.

Maqāma of the Bedouin *(no. 27): the encounter of Abū Zayd and al-Ḥārith under the trees (p. 174; folio 88r). Al-Ḥārith recounts that as a youth he liked to live among the Bedouins, adopting from them their pride of spirit and true Arabic speech. One day he lost his female camel, so he got on his horse and searched a long time. Tired, he rested under a tree, and a traveler, a shaykh from Sarūj, joins him. Of course it is Abū Zayd, who helps him find camel but takes off with his horse.*

Maqāma of Wasit *(no. 29): Abū Zayd leaves with the loot (p. 196; folio 99r). In a caravanserai near the town of Wasit (on the Tigris), al-Ḥārith meets Abū Zayd who suggests arranging a profitable marriage between him and the daughter of a wealthy citizen. He invites many guests to the wedding and spices their food with an intoxicating potion, and then, with the help of his son, robs the guests of their belongings.*

Maqāma of Sur *(no. 30): al-Ḥārith travels from Sur to Cairo. There, he follows a wedding procession that leads to a magnificent house. Once inside, he discovers beggars' rags and sacks (p. 201; folio 101v). He inquires and learns that the house is a refuge for the poor and homeless.*

Opposite:
Maqāma of Sur *(no. 30): at the back of the house, he finds a richly decorated room where the reception is being held (p. 205; folio 103v). A venerable old man, Abū Zayd praises the couple using tricks in order to soften their hearts and obtain alms from the guests.*

البحامد دارا حتى اذا استشرف الدمع استنفضت الجمع وقال لي اسمع
بنفذ

مسقط الراس سروج وبها كنت اموج
بلدة يوجد فيها كل شىء ويروج
وردها من سلسبيل وصحاريها مروج

وبنوها

رجل قد اختطم بلثام وقبض على زند غلام وقال

اشترِ مني غلامًا صنعا   في خَلقه وخُلقه قد برعا

بكل ما نطت به مضطلعا   ينبيك إن قال وإن قلت وعا

وإن تصبه عثرة يقل لعا   وإن تسمه السعي في النار سعا

وإن تحاجه ولو يومًا رعا   وإن تقنعه بلطف قنعا

Opposite:
Maqāma of Zabīd *(no. 34): in the slave market (p. 231; folio 116v), al-Ḥārith tells the story of when he wanted to buy a slave in the town of Zabīd in the Yemen. A man with a covered face sold him a youth; it later turned out that it was Abū Zayd who had sold him his son. The judge declared the sale invalid, and Abū Zayd had to charm the victim of his trickery with clever excuses.*

Maqāma of Saʿda *(no. 37): Abū Zayd complains of his disrespectful son to the judge (p. 256; folio 128r). On arriving at the town of Saʿda in Yemen, al-Ḥārith befriends a judge and regularly goes to see him. One day, an old man comes to the judge with his son complaining about the disrespectful attitude of his son. Aiming accusations at each other, the father and son cleverly flatter the judge, who not only provides them with advice but gives them generous gifts. Once the two men have left, al-Ḥārith follows them and recognizes them to be Abū Zayd and his son.*

Maqāma of Oman or of the Sea *(no. 39): a man on the shore watches a boat full of people on the waves (p. 260; folio 132r). A great traveler, al-Ḥārith decides to visit Oman and loads his goods onto a boat. Just before setting sail, a man asks to be taken aboard as a guide and to dispel the dangers of the sea. It is indeed, Abū Zayd.*

Following page:
Maqāma of Hadramaut *(no. 43): a Bedouin shows Abū Zayd a sandal bought in Hadramaut (p. 288; folio 145r). This story is one of the longest and most profusely illustrated. It begins with al-Ḥārith riding along on a camel. He encounters another camel carrying a sleeping rider who we discover to be Abū Zayd. The two friends ride together throughout the night. As they rest in the morning Abū Zayd tells the story of how he bought a beautiful camel, how he lost it, how someone else found it and refused to give it back, and how a judge returned it to him. Al-Ḥārith is taken by the story and asks his friend whether he has ever met his match. This inspires Abū Zayd to tell another story about a discussion he had with a youth on whether it was preferable to marry a virgin or a matron. Eventually they arrive at a village where they meet a young man. Abū Zayd asks him whether the village would appreciate his literary talents, and the youth wittily answers in the negative. Abū Zayd borrows al-Ḥārith's sword to pawn it and flees.*

Maqāma of Ḥajr al-Yamāma *(no. 47): a doctor, Abū Zayd, bleeds a patient in the midst of a curious crowd (p. 328; folio 165r). One day when in Ḥajr al-Yamāma, al-Ḥārith falls ill and goes to see an old man, who cures people by bleeding them. He finds the doctor in discussion with a young man who had been trying to be treated for free or on credit. It turns out to be Abū Zayd and his son playing to the crowd, in order to collect money and leave.*

288

ولا مساغ غضبي الا ان اتق الحكم ولو لكم فانخرطنا الى شيخ ركين النصبة انيق العصبة يونس
منه سكون الطاير وان لبس ما جاير فاندرأت انظلم واتالم وصاح حرم لا يبرم امرا حتى اذا ثلثت

كنانته وقضبت من القصص لبانته ابرز نعلا رزينة الوزن محذوة لمسلك الحزن وقال هذه التي
عرفت واياها وصفت فان كانت هي التي اعطي بها عشرين وها هو من المبصرين فقد كذب
في دعواه وكبر ما افتراه اللهم الا ان يمد قذاله ويبين مصداق ما قاله فقال الحكم اللهم غفرا
وجعل يقلب النعل بطنا وظهرا ثم قال اما هذه النعل فنعلي واما مطيتك ففي رحلي فانهض

أراك قد أبرزت لي راسك قبل أن تبرز قرطاسك ووليتني قذالك ولم تقل ذالك ولست

ممن يبيع نقدا بدين ولا يطلب اثرا بعد عين فإن انت رضخت بالعين حجمت في

الاخدعين وإن كنت ترى الشح أولى وخزن الفلس في النفس أحلى فاقرأ عبس وتولى

واغرب عني والا فقال الفتى والذي حرم صوغ المين كما حرم صيد الحرمين اني لا فلس

19. Ibn Quzmān (known as Guzman, died around 1160)
Dīwān ibn quzmān al-musammā bi-kitāb iṣābat al-aghrāḍ fī dhikr al- aʿrāḍ
(A Guide to Achieving Goals in Reference to Various Situations)

Folios 55v–56r.

Copied in Syria by ʿAbd al-Raḥmān ibn ʿIsā or Mūsā
13th century
Naskh
Heavy, yellowed paper
74 leaves, 22 × 16.5 cm
23–24 lines to the page, black ink
Accession no. B-86
Provenance: coll. J.-L. Rousseau; entered the Asiatic Museum in 1819.
Bibliography: Corriente F., 1980, 1984 and 1989; de Ginzburg D., 1896; Krachkovskii I.Y., vol. I, 1955, pp. 67–70; Rosen V.R., 1881, no. 296.

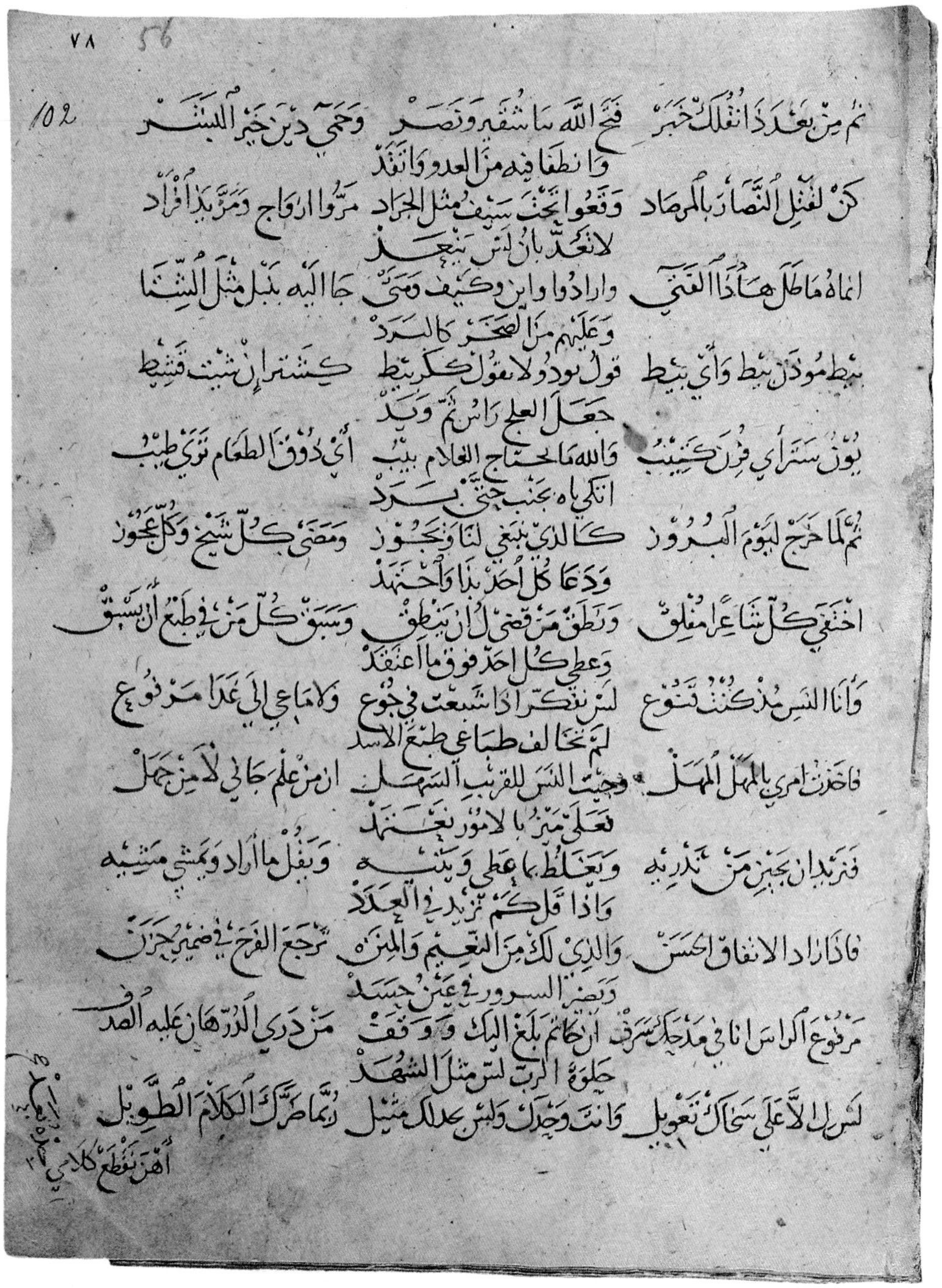

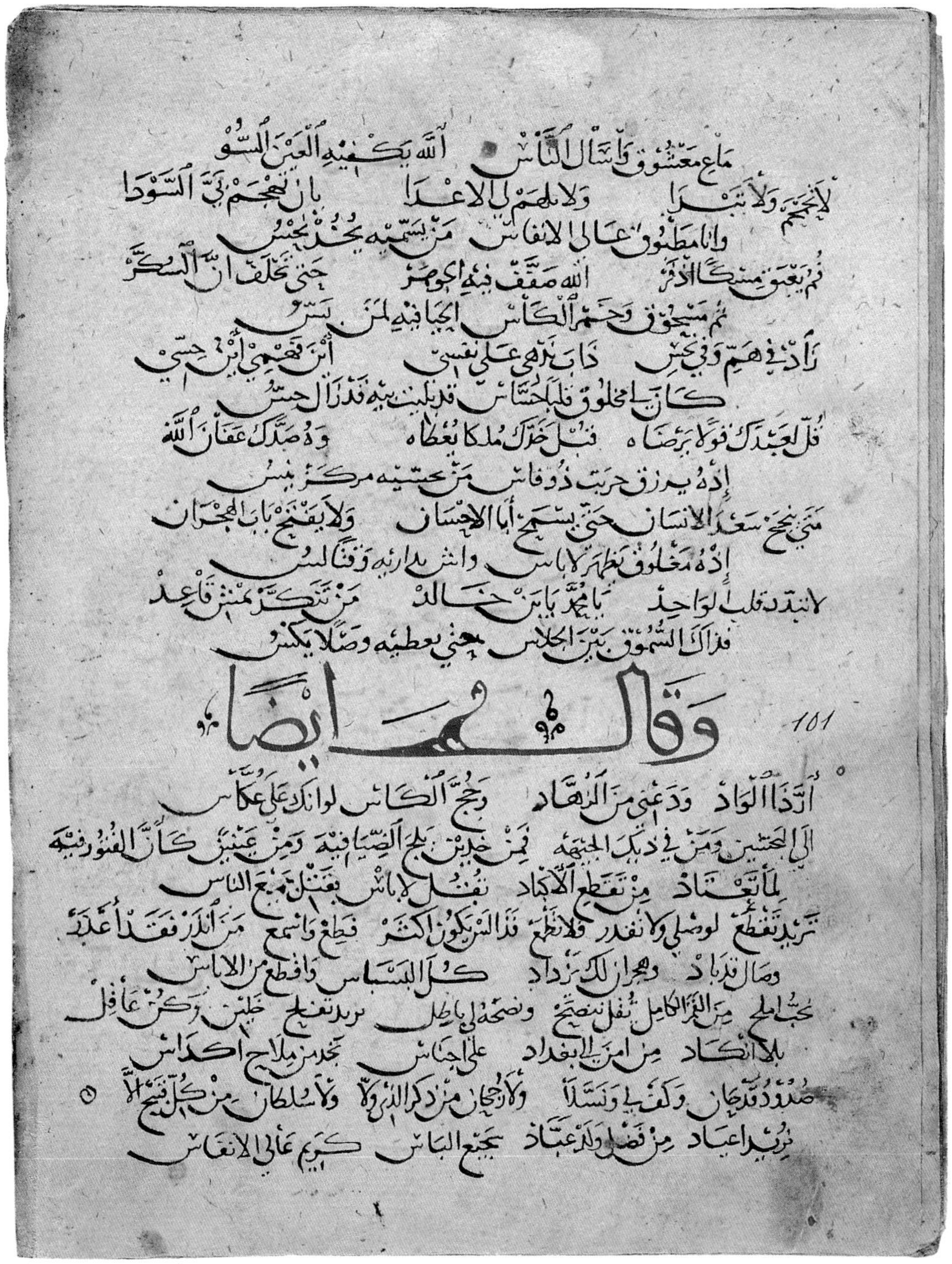

وقال ايضا

This manuscript helps to explain the link that exists between the beginning of Spanish and Provençal romantic poetry on one hand, and Andalusian poetry (especially popular poetry) on the other.

There is nothing exceptional to be observed in its calligraphy, nor in its decoration. Written in a standard *naskh* style, it has plenty of diacritical and vocalization marks, although it contains a number of mistakes. It consists of 149 *zajal*—poems in medieval Andalusian Arabic dialect with the addition of a number of romantic expressions. The author, the Andalusian poet Ibn Quzmān (Guzman), died around 1160. The same name was used by his contemporary, the vizier of the ruler of Badajoz. When referring to literary sources the two are often confused. According to the colophon of folio 73v the copy was completed in the town of Ṣafad on Ramadan, 3 of the year 600 A.H. However, the year was written in a decorative, cursive script, thus making the word "six hundred" easier to guess than to read. Folio 74r has notes by owners and readers, one of which is dated 683. We can therefore confirm that the manuscript dates back to the 7th–8th centuries A.H. It is only just possible to make out the name of the copyist as ʿAbd al-Raḥmān ibn ʿIsā or Mūsā. The name of the person who commissioned the book also appears, a certain *adīb* Muḥammad ibn Abū Zayd al-Qaṭṭān. It is only through this Syrian copy that this very interesting work of al-Andalus has reached us. [A.Kh.]

20. Anonymous Author
Kitāb-i ḥudūd-i ᶜālam min al-mashriq ilā al-maghrib (982)
(The Regions of the World from East to West)

Copied by Abū al-Mu'ayyad ᶜAbd al-Qayyūm ibn al-Ḥusain ibn ᶜAlī al-Fārsī in 1258
Naskh
Paper
Folios 29r-67v
28.5 × 18 cm
Text: 20.5 × 13 cm
23 lines to the page, black and red ink
Accession no. C-612
Provenance: purchased by the USSR Academy of Sciences in 1924 from the widow of A.G. Tumanskii in Paris (he died on December 1, 1920 in Istanbul), he had bought it in Bukhara with the help of V.F. Minorskii.
Bibliography: Barthold V., 1930; Catalogue PTR, 1964, no. 1035; Minorskii V., 1937.

Kitāb-i ḥudūd-i ᶜālam min al-mashriq ilā al-maghrib ("The Regions of the World from East to West"), also known as the "anonymous Tumanskii." This famous geographic work by an anonymous author was written in Persian at Gūzgān or Gūzgānyān in 372/982–983. It is dedicated to the ruler of the province, a member of the Farīghūnid dynasty, Amīr Abū al-Ḥārith Muḥammad ibn Aḥmad. It is the oldest known geographic work in Persian. This is the only example known, copied in 1258 by Abū al-Mu'ayyad ᶜAbd al-Qayyūm ibn al- Ḥusain ibn ᶜAlī al-Fārsī, who apparently lived in Khurasan, for his personal use (folios 29r and 67v). The work is part of a collection of manuscripts made up of works by different authors, from folios 29r to 67v. The same lover of books copied another work in the same manuscript collection on Friday Jumada I 26, 658 / Thursday, June 10, 1259, entitled *Jāmiᶜ al-ᶜulūm* by Fakhr al-Dīn Muḥammad ibn ᶜUmar al-Rāzī (died in 1209) and incorporated it into this volume. The clear and confident *naskh* script belongs to an educated person who was not a professional copyist. He used a particular style incorporating elements of *thuluth and tawqīᶜ*. [O.A.]

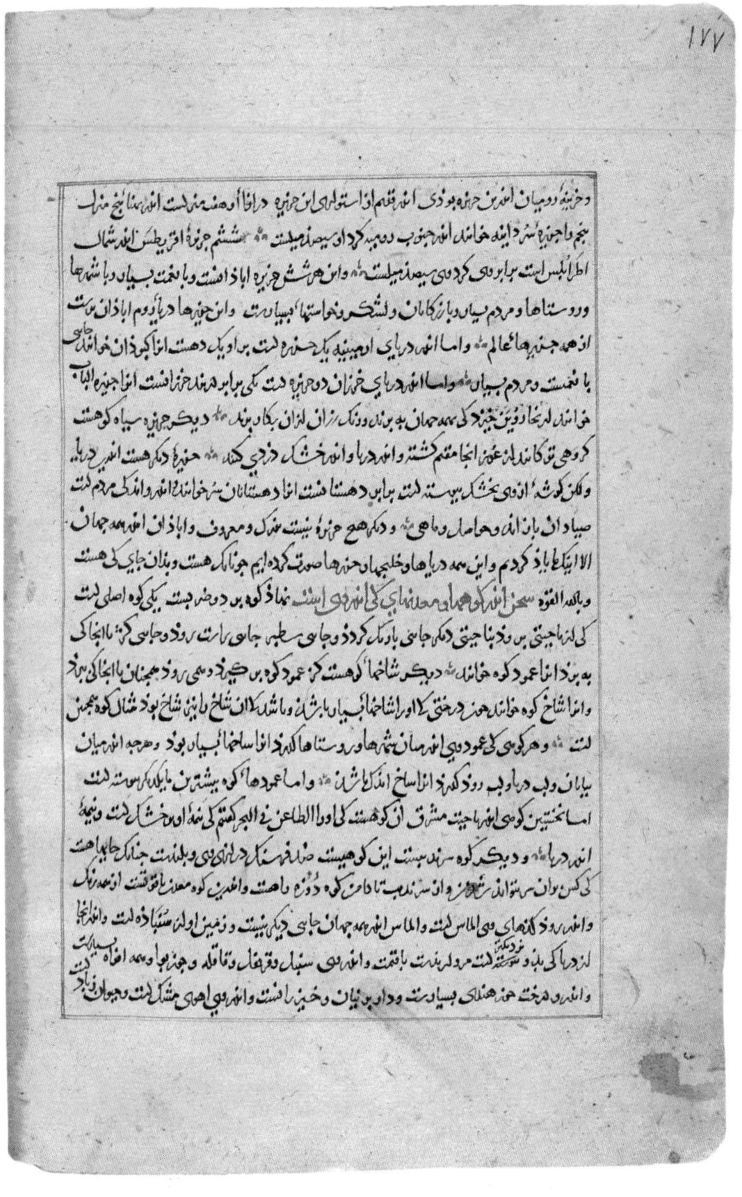

Folio 33v.

21. Abū Muḥammad Ilyās ibn Yūsuf ibn Zakī ibn Mu'ayyad Niẓāmī Ganjavī (died in 1209–1210) Makhzan al-asrār (Treasure of Mysteries)

Copied by Muḥammad ibn al-Quraish ibn Muḥammad al-Ḥasanī al-Ṭabāṭabāyy al-Iṣfahānī of Shiraz in 1310
Naskh
Paper
287 folios (124v–210v),
24 × 13 cm
Text: 18 × 9.2 cm
12–14 lines to the page,
black and glossy ink
Accession no. C-1102
Provenance: library of the celebrated Iranian man of letters, poet and historiograph, Rizā Qulī-Khān Hidāyat (1800–1871) (notes dating from 1843); donated by L. Bogdanov, 1906.
Bibliography: Catalogue PTR, 1964, no. 3987.

Makhzan al-asrār ("Treasure of Mysteries") is an ethical and didactic poem (*masnavī*) written in the sufi spirit in 570/1174–1175 by one of the great mediaeval Persian poets, Abū Muḥammad Ilyās ibn Yūsuf ibn Zakī ibn Mu'ayyad Niẓāmī of Ganja (died in 603/1209–1210). This manuscript in the collection of the Institute of Oriental Studies is the oldest copy known to exist. It contains the complete text and differs from other versions in details relating to structure and composition, and by the large number and variety of *bayts*. It was copied by the same master and to order. It is written in large artistic *naskh* script very similar to *thuluth*. The calligrapher, Muḥammad ibn al-Quraish ibn Muḥammad al-Ḥasanī al-Ṭabāṭabāyy al-Iṣfahānī thus reveals a very personal calligraphic manner. The manuscript bears a seal and notes of the important 19th-century Iranian manuscript collector Riẓā Qulī-Khān Hidāyat. [O.A.]

Folio 127v.

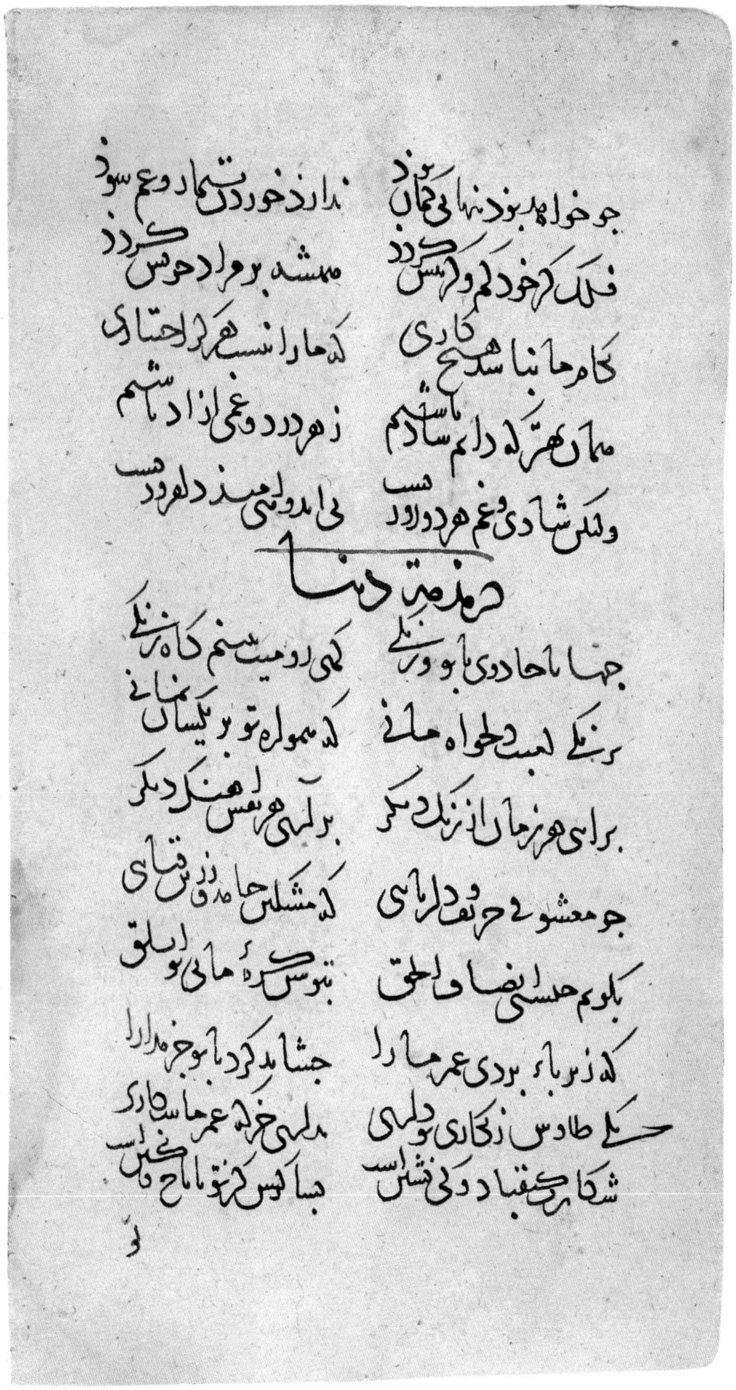

22. Anonymous author (Egypt, 14th century)
al-Rawḍ al-zāhir min sīrat mawlānā al-sultān al-malik al-nāsir (The Blossoming Garden from the Life of Our Lord, the Sultan al-Malik al-Nāsir)

Folios 1v–2r.

Probably written by the author
Naskh
Paper
40 folios, 22 × 15.5 cm
5–7 lines to the page
Accession no. B-623
Provenance: coll. of J.-L. Rousseau; entered the Asiatic Museum in 1819.
Bibliography: Mikhailova A.I., 1965, no. 32; Rosen V.R., 1881, no. 164.

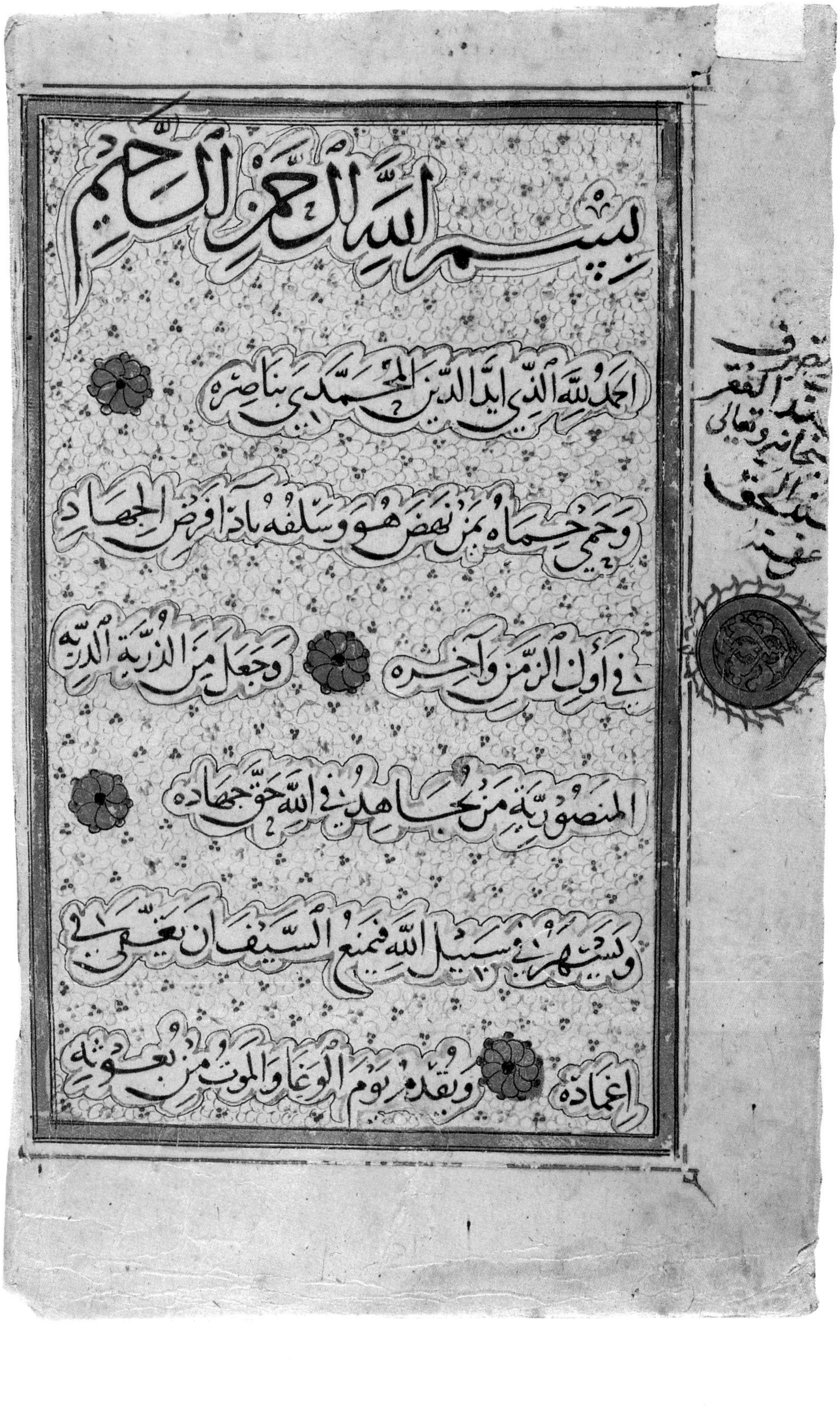

This manuscript was intended as a personal gift to the library of Mūsā ibn al-Malik al-Ṣāliḥ, the nephew of the Mamluk Sultan of Egypt, a circumstance which explains why it has been beautifully decorated. This is rare for a historic document. The reverse side of the first page is entirely taken up by an artistic *'unvān* in gold and light blue pigment, with geometric patterns of stars and polygons whose surfaces are covered with plant motifs. The title of the book is written, word by word, within each of the stars and polygons. In the center is an octagon containing a crowned eagle—a symbol which is rarely seen within the Muslim tradition. The other pages of the manuscript are decorated with a large number of rosettes, some of which are framed in gold. The space between the verses is decorated with a dotted pattern.

The name of the author is unknown, although the text would suggest that he might have been a freed slave who belonged to the inner circle of the Sultan, and therefore witness to many events. The biography first describes the campaign conducted by the Sultan of Egypt against Qutlugh-Shāh Noyan, the head of the Īl-Khānid Sultan Ghāzān's army, and his victory over the Īl-Khānids at Marj al-Ṣuffar in 1302. The second section gives great praise to Mūsā, the Sultan's nephew. It is written in a pompous style, often in rhyming prose.

Experts believe that the manuscript was written by the author himself. It is the only example of this text known to exist. [A.Kh.]

23. Rasā'il al-rusūl wa a'māluhum (The Epistles and Acts of the Apostles)

Folios 1r–1v.

Copied by Thūmā al-mutarahhib, known by the name of Ibn al-Ṣafī, in Damascus in 1341
Naskh
Thick, glazed paper
236 folios, 30 × 21 cm
13 lines to the page, in black, red, green, blue ink and gold
Accession no. D-228
Provenance: gift of George IV, patriarch of Antioch, to Tsar Nicolas II (1868–1918); transferred in 1919 from the Winter Palace library.
Bibliography: Khalidov A.B., 1986, no. 10375; Krachkovskii I.Y., 1927,; Krachkovskii I.Y., VI, 1960, p. 430, no. 9.

The Arabic-speaking Christians of the Middle East, Monophysites, Orthodox, Nestorians, etc., were particularly fond of the Epistles and Acts of the Apostles, as can be seen by the large number of existing copies of this Christian text.

This document is one of the most remarkable works of Christian art from the Middle East during the Middle Ages. It was copied in Damascus in 1341 by Thomas the Monk (Thūmā al-mutarahhib, also known as Ibn al-Ṣafī), upon order of the consul "sire Giacomo al-Sukhaynī" (probably from one of the Italian city republics). The text is written in a large calligraphic *naskh* script. The first four lines of each epistle are traced in inks of different colors: red, blue, green and black. The diacritical marks are painted in large red dots, whilst groups of dots and commas as well as rosettes are painted in gold and blue.

Three pages of this superb manuscript (folios 1v, 141r, 172) are decorated with illumination. There is a circular motif in the center of the pages, painted in gold and blue, and the remaining part of the pages is almost entirely filled with plant ornaments. Along the edges of the page are dozens of alternating salient or concave arches within concentric circles. Above and below the central motif, are horizontal cartouches carrying citations from the Epistles on a gold background. [A.Kh.]

24. Zakariyā ibn Muḥammad ibn Maḥmūd al-Qazvīnī (1203–1282) ᶜAjā'ib al-makhlūqāt wa gharā'ib al-mawjūdāt (The Wonders of Creation and the Oddities of Existence)

Folio 26v. Signs of the Zodiac: Constellations of Canis Minor and Argo Navis.

Copied in the 14th century
in Iraq or Iran
Arabic
Thick, glazed paper
215 folios, 40 × 29 cm
25 lines to the page
Accession no. E-7
Provenance: coll. A. Italinskii (died in 1825); transferred in 1919 from the library of the Teaching Section of the Ministry of Foreign Affairs.
Bibliography: Krachkovskii I.Y., IV, 1957, pp. 358–363; Mikhailova A.I., 1961, no. 13; Rosen V.R., 1877, no. 64.

One of the most cherished and popular books of science in the Islamic world was, until very recently, the cosmography entitled *ᶜAjā'ib al-makhlūqāt wa gharā'ib al-mawjūdāt* ("The Wonders of Creation and the Oddities of Existence"). Its author, Zakariyā ibn Muḥammad ibn Maḥmūd al-Qazvīnī, lived at a time when the Muslim states of the Middle East were torn apart by internal strife but had to defend themselves against invasion by both the Crusaders from the Mediterranean and the Īl-Khānids from Iran. At that time, science and culture in these Middle Eastern countries were well advanced.

Born in Qazvin in 1203, al-Qazvīnī was a judge in Mesopotamia. He dedicated his opus to an eminent dignitary and man of letters, ᶜAṭā Malik Juvainī, who had become the de facto sovereign of Baghdad after the city was taken by the Mongols in 1258. Al-Qazvīnī died in 1283.

His cosmography consists of an introduction followed by two sections. The first describes the celestial world with its stars and inhabitants, the angels. It also explains the measurement of time and discusses chronology, the calendar, and the holidays during the year. The second section is devoted to the earth and its phenomena, the four elements, earth, fire, air and water; they are described together with the division into seven climates, and the main oceans and rivers. Then follows an explanation for earthquakes, the formation of mountains, the origin of springs and an analysis of the three realms of nature: minerals, plants, and animals. In this category we find human beings together with imaginary creatures, the jinns.

The author based his text on, and refers to, the numerous works of his predecessors. Sometimes he quotes them word for word, skilfully blending them together to form a clear and concise account. Two drafts by the same author exist, as well as abridged and expanded versions. While he was alive, and possibly under his supervision, the work was illustrated by diagrams, tables and pictures.

The manuscript contains the full text and is one of the oldest copies in existence (14th century, according to all the indirect data). It is superbly illustrated and comes from Iraq or Iran.

There is no mention of the copyist or the painter.
[A.Kh.]

على برثنه مرزم العبور وتسمى الاربعة التي منها على كتفه وعلى ذنبه وما بينهما وعلى فخذ العذارى والاربعة المصطفة على
الاستقامة التي هي خارج الصورة تسمى القرود والنيرين من خارج الصورة حضار والوزن ومن العرب من يسميها محلفين لانهما
تطلعان قبل سهيل فيقدّر احدهما سهيلا فيحلف عليه

كوكبة الكلب المقدم

هما كوكبان بين النيرين اللذين على راسي التوامين وبين
النير الذي على فم الكلب الاكبر تاخر عنهما الى المشرق احدهما
انور تسميه العرب الشعرى الشامية لانها تغيب في شق الشام
ويقال له الشعرى الغميصاء ايضا لانه عندهم اخت سهيل
وقد عبرت اليمانية المجرة الى ناحية سهيل بقيت هذه
في ناحية الشمالية الشرقية فبكت على سهيل وغمصت
عيناها وتسمى الاثنين ايضا ذراع الاسد المقبوضة سميت مقبوضة لتاخرها عن الذراع الاخرى وهما النيران اللذان على راس التوامين

كوكبة السفينة

كواكبها خمسة واربعون كوكبا من الصورة وليس حواليها شيء من الكواكب المرصودة ذكر بطلميوس ان النير
العظيم الذي على المجداف الجنوبي هو سهيل وهو ابعد كوكب من السفينة في الجنوب برسم على الاسطرلاب
واما العرب فالروايات عنهم في سهيل وفي كواكب السفينة مختلفة ورووا ان النير الذي على طرف المجداف الثاني سهيل على الاطلاق والقطب
الجنوبي تحت السفينة بقرب المجداف الذي عليه سهيل وهذه صورتها

وملائكة السماء السادسة
على صورة الولدان
والملك الموكل بهم اسمه شمخائيل
وملائكة السماء السابعة
على صورة بني آدم
والملك الموكل بهم اسمه دوبائيل

Opposite:
Folio 39v: the Archangel of the sixth heaven, Shamkhā'īl, and the Archangel of the seventh heaven, Rūbā'īl. The Mongolic features of the angels' faces are indirect indicators of the period and the place where the illustration was made.

Folio 63v: diagram of the Surrounding or World Ocean.

Folio 71v: three sea monsters: the Sea-dragon, a "Green fish with a proboscis" and a "circular, shield-like fish" (sting-ray).

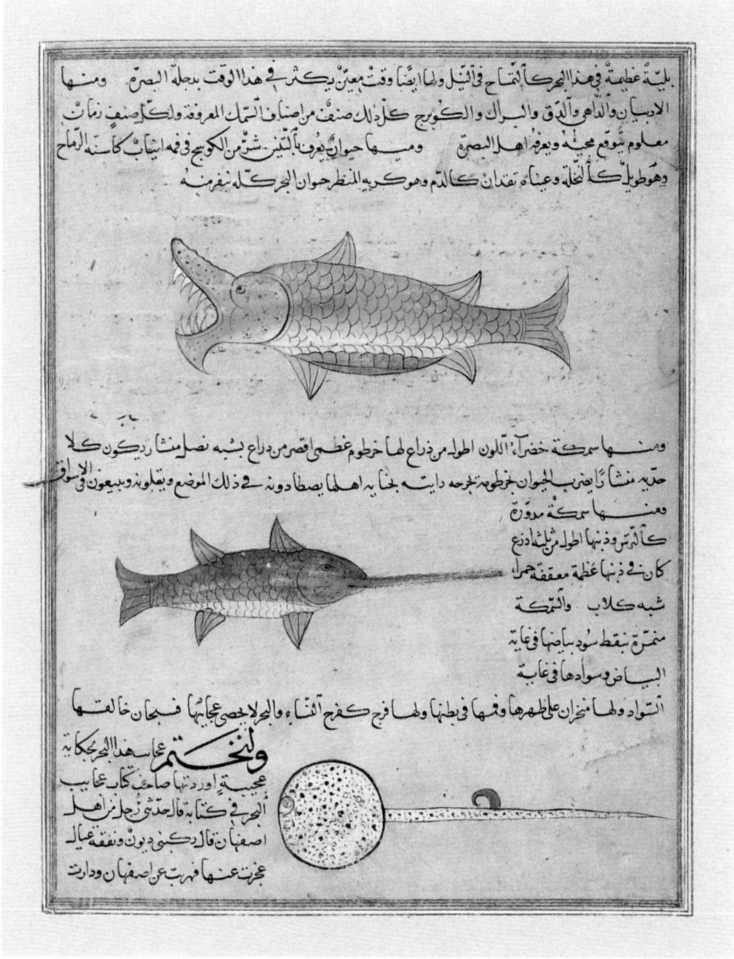

Folio 72r: a merchant from Isfahan flying through the air hanging on to the legs of a fabulous bird, during his travels to the islands of the South Sea.

Folio 135r: a chestnut tree, a sandalwood tree and a Mediterranean pine. Extracts from these trees were used in medicine.

Opposite:
Folio 199v: the magpie, "known for its habit of stealing precious objects"; the fabulous giant double-headed ᶜ*anqā bird.*

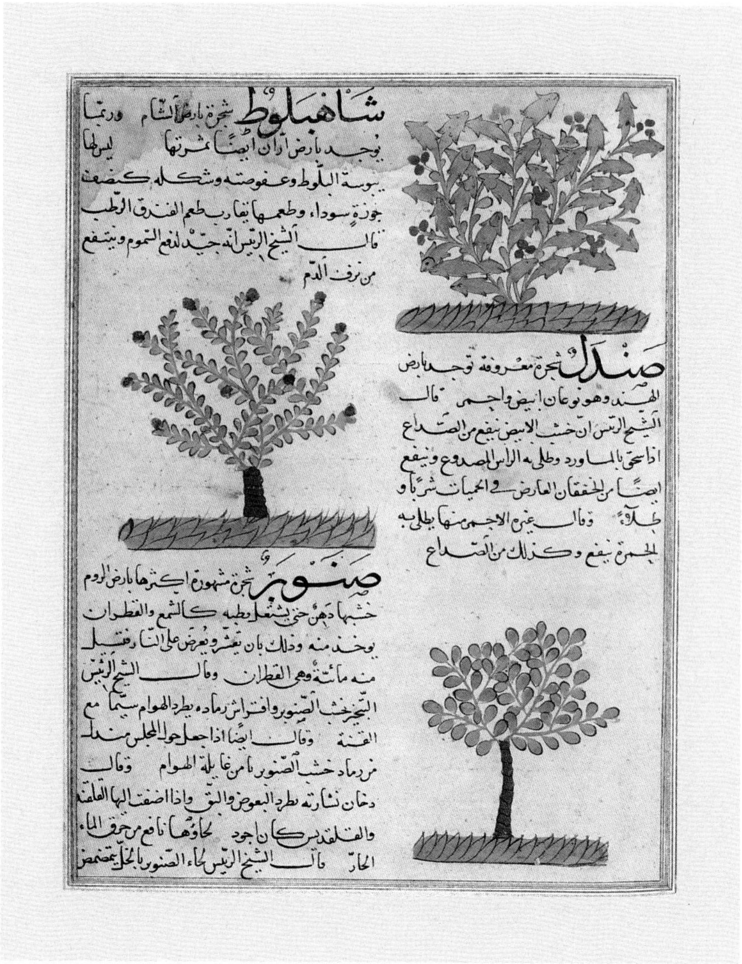

ينفع او تحت سنسن ويأتي بورق الدلب فتتركه حوله لئلا يقصد الخفاش بيضها وفراخها وكثيرا ما ينسى بيضها وافراخها

لها خاصيته اجزائه فالواد دماغه يخالط بالغاليه ويسعط

به للقوة والفالج فانه يعطس ويذهب ما به من الاذى دمه

يجفف في الظل ويخلط بماء الورد ويسقى انسانا يبقى ثرثارا مكثارا

ومرارته يطلى به الموضع الذي فيه شوك او عظم او نصل فانه يخرجها

…تهواه مخه يطعم الصبي يبقى فصيحا حافظا ريشه يحرق ويذر

رماده في جحر النمل تهرب عنها كلها ولا يبقى واحد مخ بيضها ينفع من بياض العين ان اكتحل بها على الريق بعد الخروج من الحمام يفعل ذلك

ثلث مرات يذهب ذلك بالكلية **عنقاء** اعظم الطيور جثة واعظمها خلقة يختطف الفيل والجاموس كما تختطف

الحداة الفارة ذكر انه كان في قديم الزمان بين الناس ويتأذى الناس من جنايته الى ان سلب يوما عروسا محلية فدعا عليه

حنظلة النبي عليه السلم فذهب الله به الى بعض جزائر البحر المحيط تحت خط الاستواء ولا يصل اليها الناس وفيها حيوانات كثيرة كالفيل

والجاموس والكركدن والببر وسباع الجوارح والعنقاء لا يصيد منها لانها تحت طاعته واذا صاد شيئا يأكل منها وترك الباقي

للحيوانات التي تحت طاعته ولا يصيد الا فيلا او سمكا عظيما او تنينا فاذا فرغ من اكله يصعد الى مكانه ويخلي الباقي بين

الحيوانات التي تحت طاعته ويتفرج على اكلها وعند طيرانه يسمع من جناحه صوت الهجوم من السيل او صوت الاشجار عند هبوب الريح العاصف

وذكروا ان عمر العنقاء الف وسبعمائة سنة ويتزاوج اذا اتى عليه خمسمائة سنة فاذا حان وقت بيضها وجد لذلك الما شديدا

Folio 191v: the rhinoceros "with the body of an elephant and the temperament of a bull."

Folio 202v: an ostrich, "the animal that combines the qualities of a bird with those of a camel"; a hoopoe, "a strange bird, with beautiful plumage and unpleasant smell, who led Sulaymān and his army to water."

Opposite:
Folio 213v: the camel is a cross-breed between a dromedary and a mountain camel. The man portrays a figure which is as hairy as a bear but possesses human speech and intelligence. The third illustration depicts an animal which is a cross between a wolf and a hyaena.

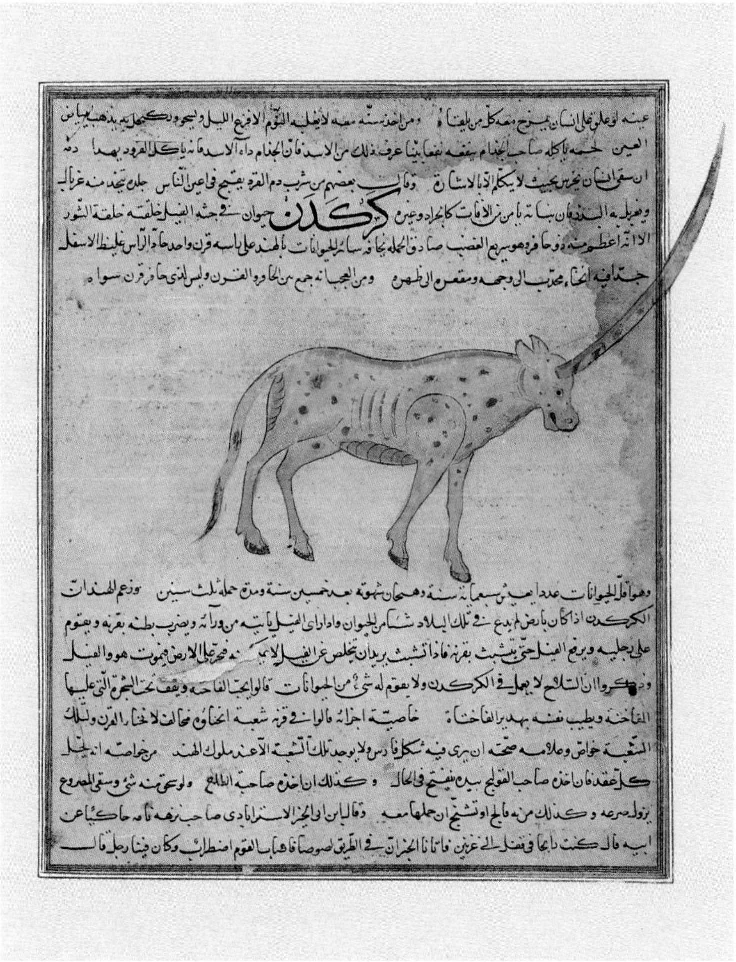

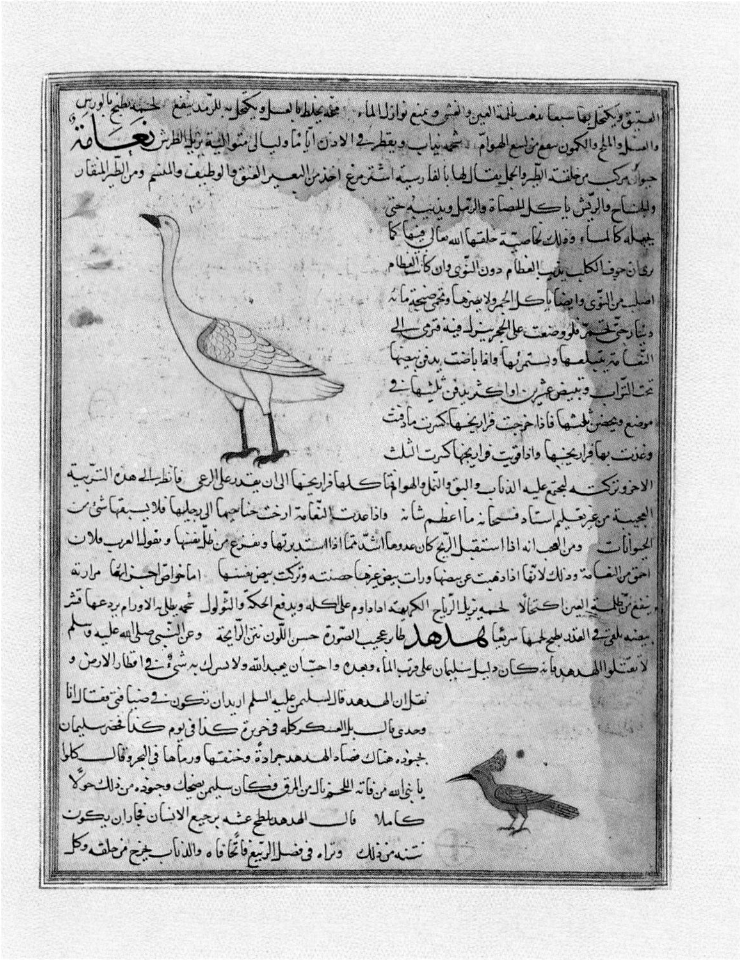

ومنها المتولد من الانسان والذئب حدثني من رآه قال انه على صورة الانسان الا انه كان عليه شعر
كما على الذئب وكان ناطقا يتكلم كالانسان ويفهم كفهمه ومنها المتولد من الذئب والضبع
وهو شكل عجيب جدا ان كان الذكر
ضبعا يقال له السمع وان كان
الذكر ذئبا يقال له العسبار

ومنها المتولد من الذئب والكلب يقال له الديسم قالوا ان الكلاب يسفدها الذئاب بارض سلوقة باليمن فيتولد الكلاب
السلوقية وهي اخبث
الكلاب ومنها
المتولد من الحمام والورشان
وهو ايضا شكل عجيب
يقال لها الراعبي

25. Aḥmad ibn Muḥammad ibn Yaʿqūb ibn Miskawayh (died in 1030) Kitāb ādāb al-ʿarab wa al-furs (Rules for Daily Arab and Persian Life)

Decoration of the front cover of the binding.

Folio 2r.

Persian translation entitled *Jāvidān-i khirad*, by ʿUsmān ibn Abī al-Vafā ibn Muḥammad (13th century)
Copied by Isḥāq ibn Maḥmūd ibn Muḥammad ibn Maḥmūd al-Yamanī, February 8, 1358
Naskh
Paper
205 folios, 29 × 19.1 cm
Text: 19.7 × 12 cm
17 lines to the page, black and red Indian ink
Accession no. C-650
Provenance: unknown.
Bibliography: Catalogue PTR, 1964, no. 912.

Jāvidān-i khirad is an extremely rare Persian translation of an Arabic literary work on ethics by Aḥmad ibn Muḥammad ibn Yaʿqūb ibn Miskawayh (died in 1030), entitled *Kitāb ādāb al-ʿarab wa al-furs*, in which the author includes a translation of *Mirrors* of Central-Persian rules governing daily life at home and in society. The Persian translation was completed in Shiraz by ʿUsmān ibn Abī al-Vafā ibn Muḥammad (folio 26v), during the reign of the Salghurid atabeg Abū Bakr ibn Saʿd Zangī (who reigned between 1226 and 1260) to whom the celebrated Musharrif al-Dīn Saʿdī dedicated his *Bustān*. It is curious that the name of Sharaf al-milla wa al-dīn Muḥammad al-Qazvīnī as translator should be mentioned on the left section of the title page (folio 1r). The very personal manner of the calligrapher, Isḥāq ibn Maḥmūd ibn Muḥammad ibn Maḥmūd al-Yamanī, draws one's attention to the large calligraphic *naskh* that is reminiscent of the medium-size *muḥaqqaq*.
The entire frontispiece (*sarlauḥ, dībācha*, folios 1r–2v) represents a single composition, divided into three sections, both vertically and horizontally. The composition is unified by means of the three golden cartouches situated on the outer margins of folios 1r and 2v. Half a century earlier, integrated compositions of this kind did not exist. The range of colors used to decorate this frontispiece, with rectangular cartouches above and below, and large lateral margins, is dominated by the gold background and decorated with plant motifs finely traced in white pigment and black ink (*islīmī-i bargī*). The central section contains the text, where spaces between the lines are decorated with golden hachures (*tashʿīr*) falling obliquely from right to left and outlined by a fine black line (*taḥrīr*). The overall decoration is characteristic of the southwestern Iranian style from the 14th century. The manuscript is elegantly bound in dark leather with gold motifs stamped on the front cover. There is a cartouche (*turunj*) in its center with fan shapes (*sarturunj*) which run from top to bottom. The corners (*kunj*) are decorated with engraved cartouches. To the front of the binding is an embossed gold fillet (*ṭarīq*). It is believed that the book comes from southwestern Iran (*Fars*). [O.A.]

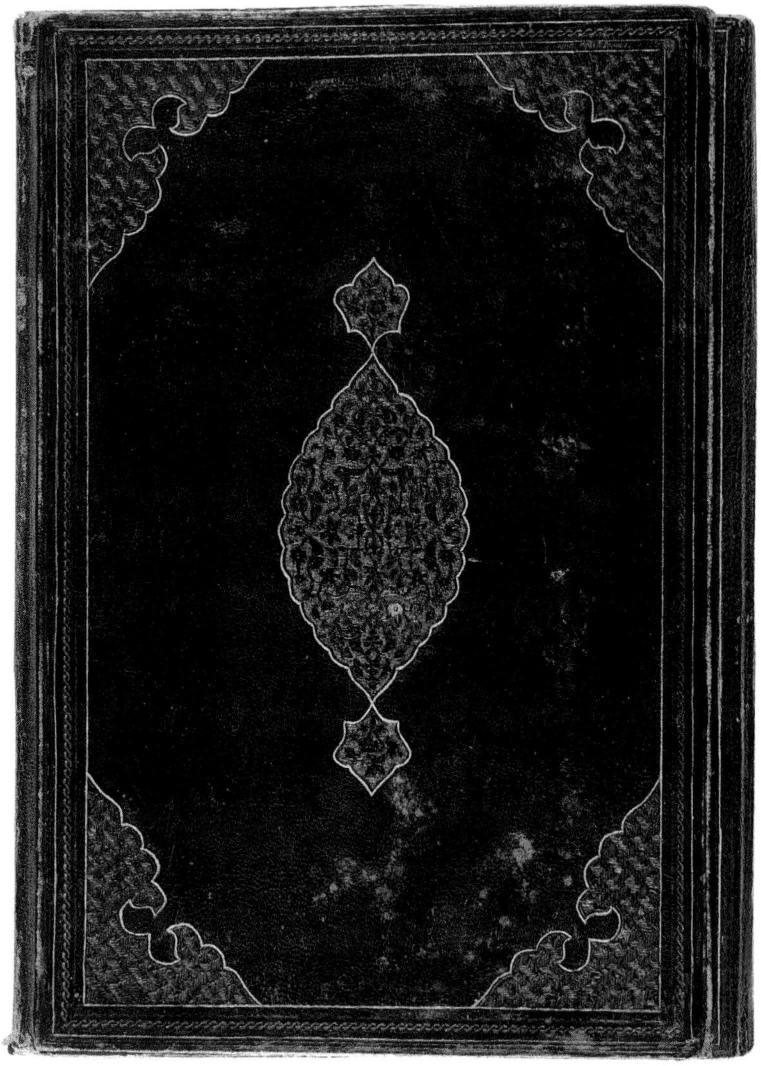

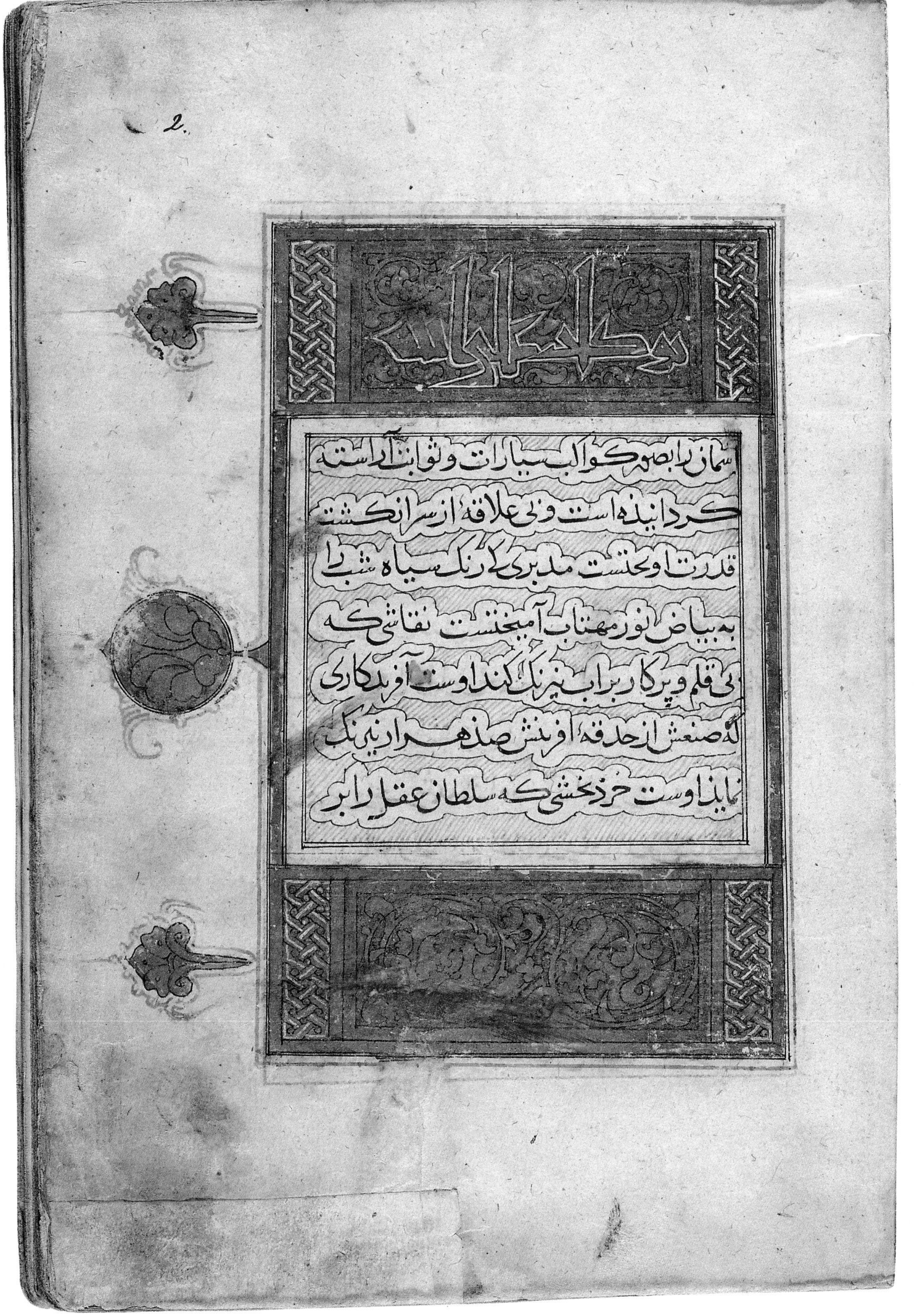
2.
آسمان را بصور کواکب سیارات و ثوابت آراسته
گردانیده است و بی علاقه از سر انگشت
قدرت او بحسنت مدبری که رنگ سیاه شب را
به بیاض نور مهتاب آمیخته است نقاشی که
بی قلم و پرگار بر آب نیرنگ کند اوست آفریدگاری
که صنعش از حدقه او فتش صد هزار نیرنگ
نماید اوست خردبخشی که سلطان عقل را بر

26. Sharaf al-Dīn Muḥammad ibn Saʿīd al-Būṣīrī (died in 1294) Qaṣīdat al-burda (The Cloak)

Folio 1v.

Copied in 1379
Thuluth
Paper
29 folios
39 × 28 cm
Accession no. D-180
Provenance: transferred in 1919 from the library of the Teaching Section of the Ministry of Foreign Affairs.
Bibliography: Brockelmann C., 1898, pp. 264–266, no. 16; Rosen V.R., 1877, no. 96.

Sharaf al-Dīn Muḥammad ibn Saʿīd al-Būṣīrī (died in 1294), who was originally from Egypt, became one of the most widely read poets in the Muslim world thanks to one single ode (qasida) in honor of the Prophet Muḥammad, which he created, as legend would have it, after the Prophet appeared to him in a dream. The ode has the pompous title *al-Kawākib al-durriyya fī madḥh khayr al-baḥriyya* ("Stars of Pearl in Praise of the Best of Mankind"), and it is commonly known as *Qaṣīdat al-burda* ("The Cloak"). The explanation is that, when the Prophet was alive, another poet, Kaʿb ibn Zuhayr, wrote a eulogizing qasida for the Prophet and in appreciation was given a cloak. His qasida was therefore from then onwards called *al-Burda* ("The Cloak"). Almost seven centuries later, al-Būṣīrī followed his example. His work, while respecting the rules governing the composition of this type of poem, inspired prayer devoted to Muḥammad. A traditional poetic form served to combine the worldly Bedouin principles with spiritual mystic contemplation. His qasida gave rise to innumerable imitations, commentaries and variants in the form of *takhmīs*, "multiplying the hemistiches by five." Both *al-Burda* were thought to bring good luck to those who copied them, read or owned them.

The manuscript, dating from 1379, contains both the text of the qasida, written in large *thuluth* characters, only containing three lines per page, plus the *takhmīs* text of a certain Muḥammad ibn Manṣūr ibn ʿUbāda, written in plain *naskh* and positioned under the corresponding verses of the qasida. Here and there, we find written one of the ninety-nine "Most Beautiful Names" of Allāh. Each section of text and the page as a whole are placed within a frame of red lines. At the beginning of folios 1v and 2r there is a short introduction. Both pages have the same layout: the text is enclosed in a frame consisting of ten colored lines that divide it into smaller rectangles; to the right and left of the text are rectangles painted in gold and blue and carrying a floral motif.

At the top of folio 1v, the phrase "In the name of Allāh..." is written in large characters, and below it is the first hemistich. Folio 2v contains the subject matter of the benedictory qasida. [A.Kh.]

بسم الله الرحمن الرحيم

قال الشيخ الإمام العالم العلامة العمدة شرف الدين أبو عبد الله محمد
بن سعيد البوصيري نعمه الله تعالى برحمته سبب إنشائي لهذه القصيدة
المباركة أنه كان أصابني فالج أبطل نصفي ولم أنتفع بنفسي ففكرت
في إنشاء قصيدة في مدح النبي صلى الله عليه وسلم وأستشفع به إلى الله
عز وجل فأنشأت هذه القصيدة المباركة ونمت
فرأيت النبي صلى الله عليه وسلم في المنام فمسح علي بيده المباركة فعوفيت
لوقتي وخرجت من بيتي فلقيني بعض الفقراء فقال لي يا سيدي
أريد أن أسمع منك القصيدة التي مدحت بها النبي صلى الله عليه وسلم
فقلت وأي قصيدة تريد فإني مدحته بقصائد كثيرة قال التي أولها

أمن تذكر جيران بذي سلم

واستقن

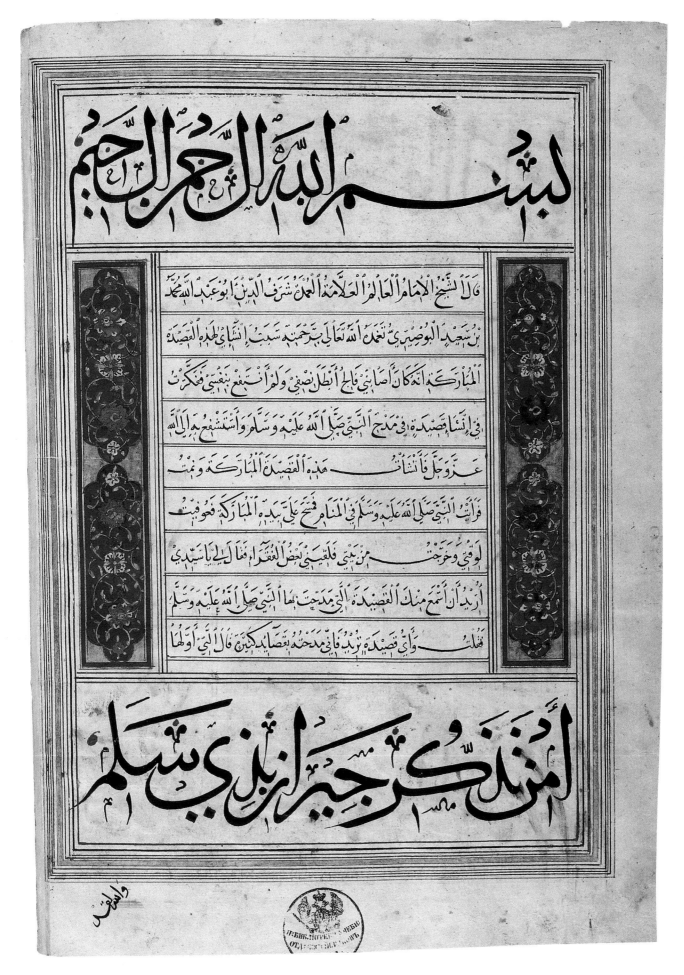

27. Japheth Ben 'Ali ha-Levi (10th century)
Commentary in Hebrew and Arabic of the Book of Genesis (XVIII.2- XXVIII.4)

Folios 4v–5r.

Copied in Bukhara
14th century
Hebrew, Arabic
Paper
205 folios, 17.5 × 13 cm
Accession no. A-140
Provenance: coll. of V.A. Ivanov.
Bibliography: Mann J., 2, 1935, pp. 30–33; Nemoy L., 1952, pp. 83–102.

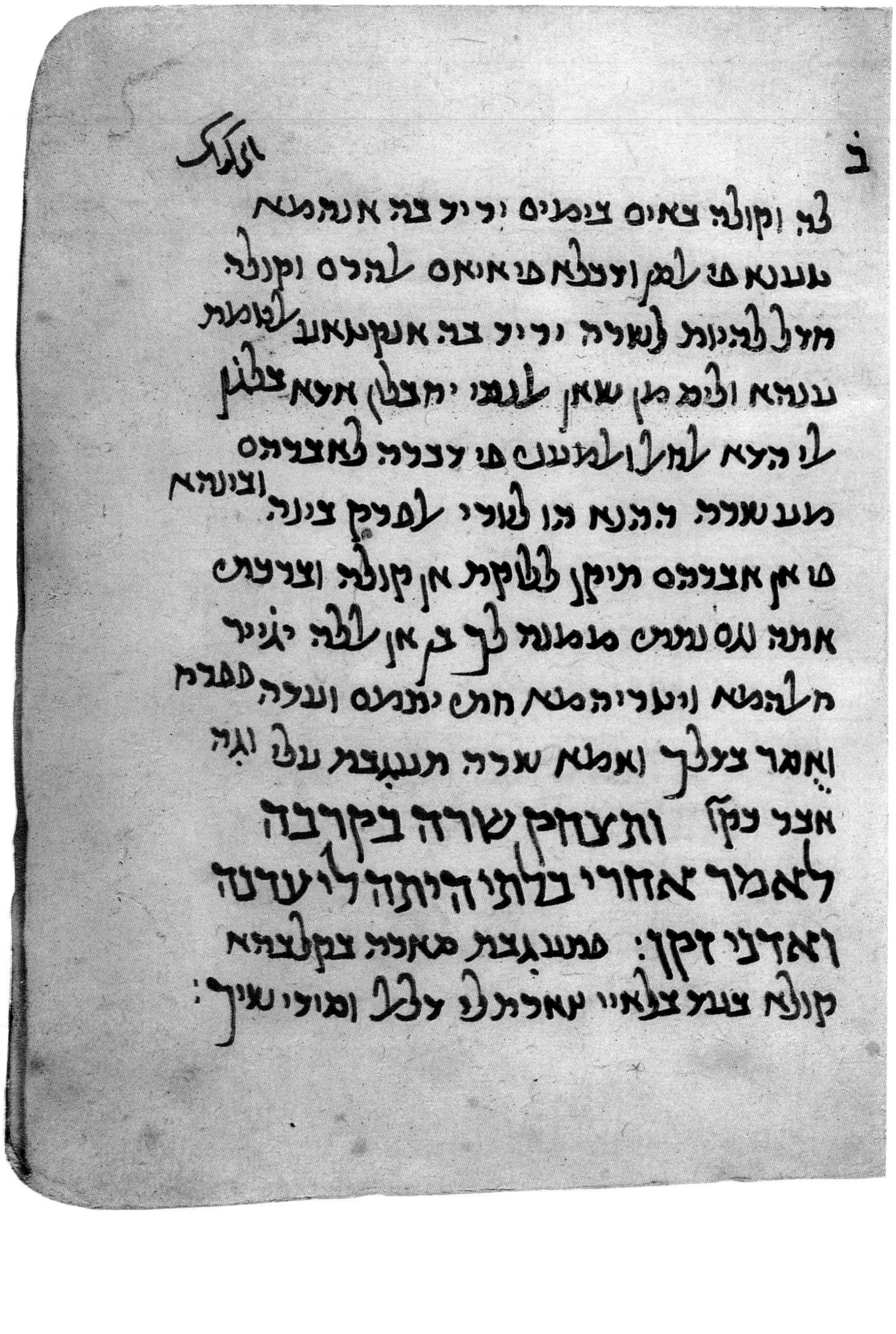

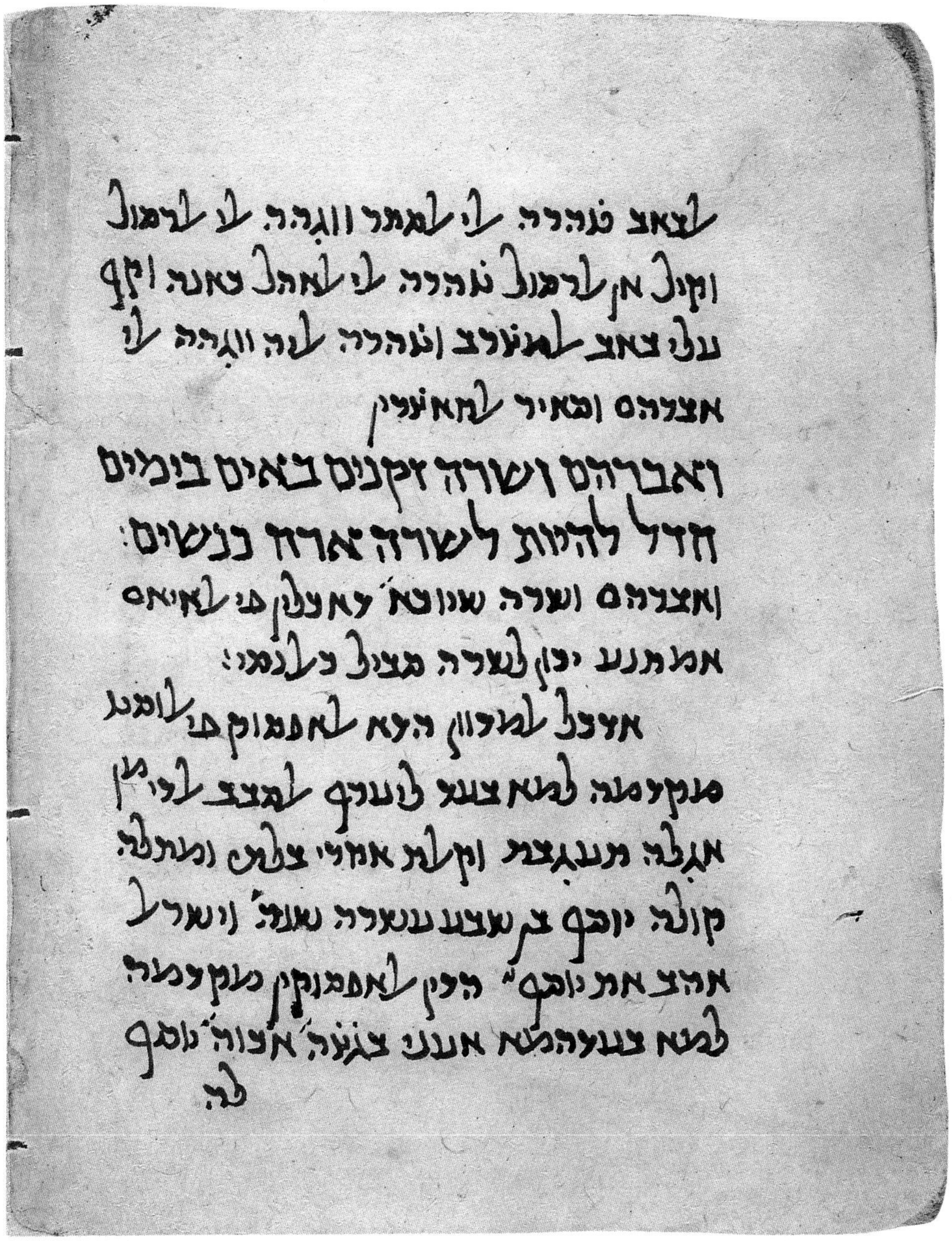
ואברהם ושרה זקנים באים בימים
חדל להיות לשרה ארח כנשים:

This work was created by the famous exegete and grammarian of the 10th century, the karaite Japheth ha-Levi, a native of Jerusalem (also called Yāfith ibn ᶜAlī or Abū ᶜAlī al-Ḥasan ibn ᶜAlī al-Lāwī al-Baṣrī). His commentaries in Arabic of biblical texts, which were very familiar within the karaite community, were later translated into Hebrew, becoming accessible to those karaites in Byzantium who could not read Arabic. The commentaries by this traditionalist author, who extensively referred to the works of his predecessors, are generally of a literal nature, but one sometimes finds allegoric interpretations of the text. Our manuscript, copied four hundred years after the death of the scholar, and a thousand kilometers from his homeland, is proof of how popular his work was. Each verse of the *Book of Existence* is cited with its Arabic translation and followed by the commentary in Arabic. The Arabic text is written without vocalization, in contrast to the verses of the Bible. The manuscript comes from Bukhara. [E.R.]

28. Abū Muḥammad Ilyās ibn Yūsuf ibn Zakī ibn Mu'ayyad Niẓāmī Ganjavī (died in 1209–1210) Khusrau u Shīrīn (Khusrau and Shīrīn)

Folio 1r.

Following pages:
Folios 1v–2r.

Copied in 1421 by Ja^cfar ibn ^cAlī al-Bāisunghurī in Herat
Nasta^clīq
Glazed paper
73 folios
23.7 × 18.5 cm
Text: 18 × 13 cm
4 columns of 17 to 23 lines to the page, black ink, blue, dark brown and orange pigment
Accession no. B-132
Provenance: donation of I.F. Gottwald, 1852.
Bibliography: Catalogue PTR, 1964, no. 1150.

Khusrau u Shīrīn is the second poem (*maṣnavī*) by the famous Persian poet Abū Muḥammad Ilyās ibn Yūsuf ibn Zakī ibn Mu'ayyad Niẓāmī of Ganja (died in 603/1209–1210) in which he recounts the romantic tale of the love and destiny of two historic characters, the Sasanian king, Khusrau Parvīz and the beautiful Armenian queen, Shīrīn. The poem was completed in 576/1180–1181. The text in this manuscript is not the complete text of the original *Khusrau u Shīrīn*. This once again confirms that masters of calligraphy treated the original work with a certain liberty.
The copyist is himself worthy of interest. His full name was Farīd al-Dīn Ja^cfar ibn^c Alī al-Tabrīzī al-Bāisunghurī (died around 1456). Born in Tabriz, he probably studied calligraphic *nasta^clīq* from the two Mīr ^cAlīs: Mīr ^cAlī ibn Ḥasan and Mīr ^cAlī ibn Ilyās.
Stylistically he was very close to the former. He became famous for his mastery of six traditional calligraphic styles: *muḥaqqaq*, *rayḥān*, *tawqī^c*, *riqā^c*, *naskh*, *thuluth*. He signed his first works with the name of Ja^cfar Tabrīzī al-Ḥāfiẓ. Later he left Tabriz for Shiraz. In 1417, he worked in the town of Yazd. Finally, around 1420, he was in Herat, working at the court of Prince Bāisunghur Mīrzā (died in 1433). The latter appointed him chief librarian of the manuscript workshop he had just set up. When in operation, there were twenty-five other masters of the hand-written book (calligraphers, illuminators, miniature painters, designers and binders) working with him. This workshop produced masterpieces, at least eighteen of which have survived.
Traditionally, it is thought that Ja^cfar ibn ^cAlī laid the foundations for the Khurasan school of artistic writing in the *nasta^clīq* style and along with his students gave the six other traditional styles of calligraphy their specific Iranian features.
This manuscript was copied in 1421, without doubt in Herat. Its decoration is beautiful, elegant and refined. Folio 1r has a circular medallion (*shamsa*) painted with a range of colors typical of the period. In the center there is a golden circle containing a blue rectangular panel with the title of the poem in a floral kufic script; surrounded by swirling green ornamental patterns on a gold background (*islīmī-i bargī*). The golden circle is traced by a blue band of 44 scroll-rosettes and their radii. The text on each page is framed in two fine gold and blue lines. The text is written in small, calligraphic *nasta^clīq* not yet perfect and mature. Judging by the decoration and the prestigious identity of the calligrapher, the manuscript was commissioned by an influential citizen of Herat.
The manuscript is bound in superb dark red leather. The center is embossed with a circular medallion (*shamsa*) with two fans (*sarshamsa*). On a gold backdrop are black tooled inlays of leaves and flowers, *islīmī-i bargī* and *band-i rūmī*. It is interesting to note the absence of corner decorations (*kunj*). The central plate is bordered with two fine lines (*ṭarīq*) of *band-i rūmī*, and *gira-i rūmī* motifs. This binding, like the manuscript, is probably from Herat, but judging by the elegance and skill of its decoration, it was most likely the work of an artist from Tabriz. [O.A.]

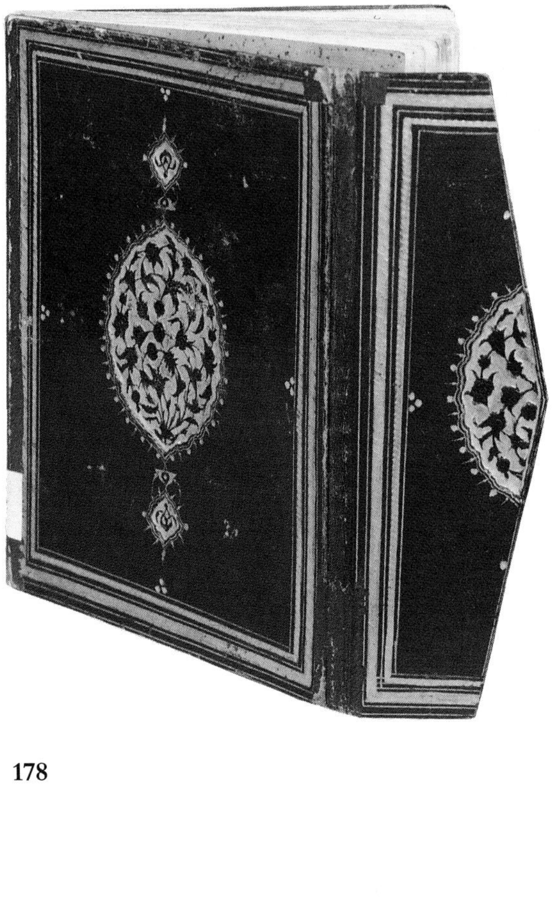

Off side of the binding and its flap.

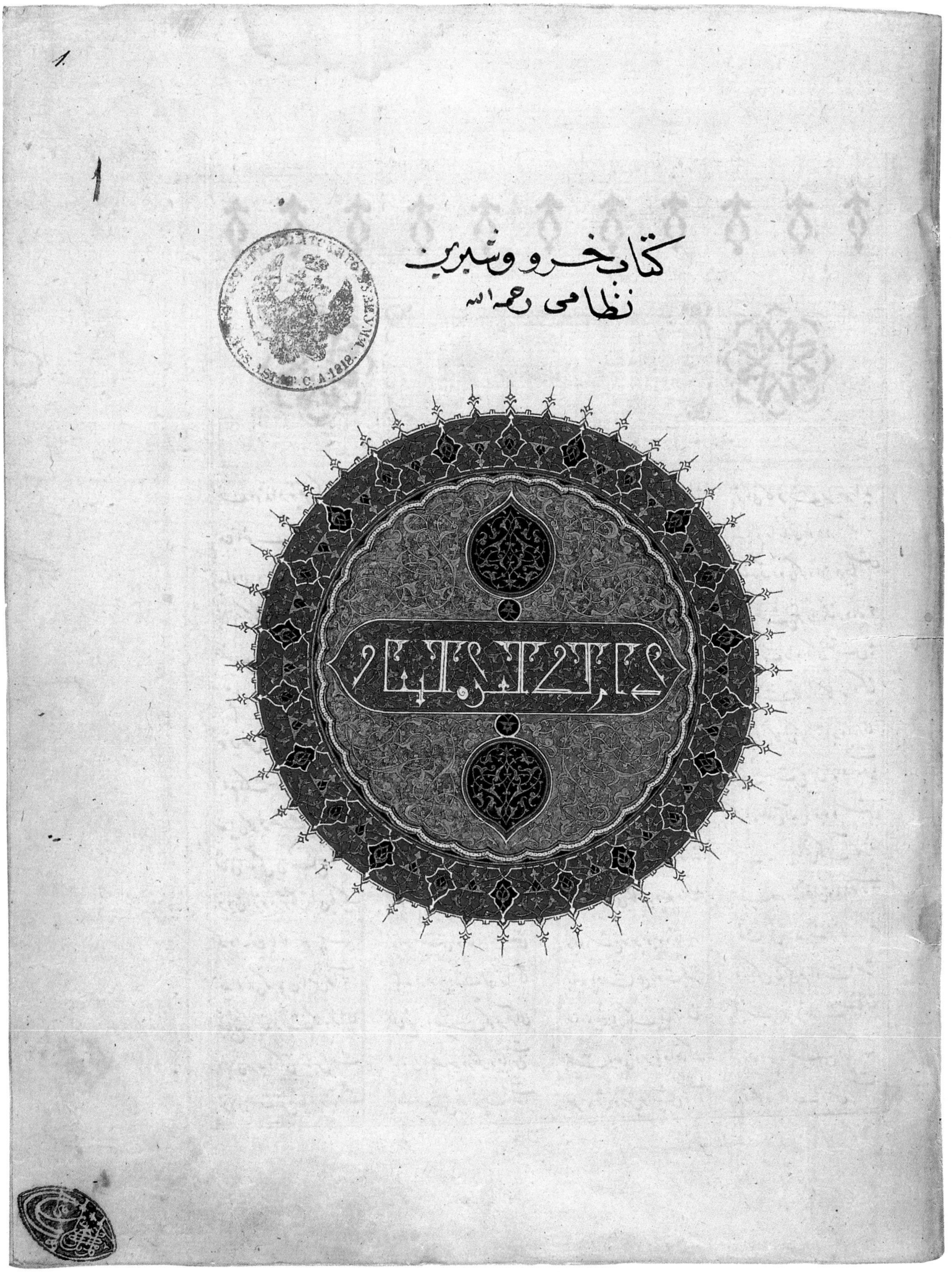
کتاب خسرو وشیرین
نظامی رحمه الله

2

2

سر اگهش از دوری و دری
چو گل صد پاره کن خود را در آن باغ
شناسایی بر کس نیست دشوار
ز هر شمعی که جوئی روشنایی
فکند از هیبت آن بحرف افلاک
جهت را شش گریبان در سر افکند
نفس پاید همه فرسود پنهان
بهر مایه نشانی داد از اخلاص
نه بخشنده خبر دارد ز دادن
خدا را ملک با کس نیست شرکت
گر از مه زحالان را هش
بسنجد خاک و موئی بر ندارد
زهی قدرت که در عبرت فزودن
درین محراب که معبود شان گشت
حران ثابتات این منقلب نام
مرا حیرت بر آن آورد صد بار
شو قتنه برین تنها که هستند
تو نه ز اخر هم از دست بلندی
نظر بر بت نهی صورت پرستی
طلسم بسته را با رنج یابی
مبین در نقش گردون کان خیالست
اگر دانستنی بودی خود این راز
درست آنست کین گردش نگار است

نه زه دانش از بالا و زیری
که نتوان تن درست اندازان داغ
ولیکن هم بحیرت می کشد کار
بوحدانیتش یابی گواهی
رقوم هندسی بر تخته خاک
زمین را چار گوهر در بر افکند
هم او قادر بود بر بود پنها
که او را در عمل کاری بود خاص
نه آنکس کو پذیرفت از نهادن

حروف کاینات ار باز جوئی
تو ز آنجا آمدی کانجا دویدی
که از خاری چو گل زنگی بر آرد
خرد بخشید تا او را شناسیم
نبات و روح را آب از جگر داد
جهان گرد آفرینش را سر آغاز
چو بخشاینده و بخشنده جود
یکی را داد بخشش تا رساند
نه آتش را خبر کوهست سوزان

همه در تست و تو در لوح اوئی
از اینجا در گذر کانجا رسیدی
کر آن آئی چو ما نقشی نگارد
بصارت داد تا زو هم هراسیم
چراغ دیده را پیه از بصر داد
گوی بردن نداند کس بدان راز
نخستین نا بیارا کرد موجود
یکی را کرد ممسک تا ستاند
نه آب اگر گهست او جان ورزان
همه حمال فرمانند شک نیست
که تخلیطی کند در بارگاهش
بیارد باد و موئی بر ندارد

در استدلال نظر در توفیق شناخت خداوند

چنین تر تنها داند نمودن
وزین آمد شدن مقصود شان چیست
که گفت این را و آن را بیارام
که بندم در چنین بتخانه زنار
که این تنها نه خود را می پرستند
چه انجا نه را در در بندی
قدم بر بت نهی زفتی و رستی
چو بشکستی بزیرش گنج یابی
گشادن بند این مشکل محالست
یکی زین پرده ها در دادی آواز
درین گردندگی هم اختیاریست

خبر داری که سیاحان افلاک
چه می خواهند ازین محمل کشیدن
قبا بسته چو گل در تازه روئی
ولی چون کرد حیرت تیز کامی
همه هستند سرگردان چو پرگار
جوابر هیم با بت عشق می باز
نمو داری که از نه تا بنا بیست
طبائع را بکار یک میل در کش
مرا بر سیر گردون رهبری نیست
ازین گردنده گنبدهای پر نور
بلی در طبع هر داننده هست

چرا گردند گرد کعبه خاک
چه می جویند ازین منزل بریدن
پرستش را کمر بستند گوئی
عنایت بانگ بر زد کای نظامی
بدید آرنده خود را طلب کار
ولی بتخانه را از بت بپرداز
طلسمی بر سر گنج الاهیست
بدین خوبی خبر دارائیل در کش
خریدن کین نقش دانم سرسری نیست
بجز گردش چه شاید دیدن از دور
که با گردنده گرداننده هست

1b

بسم الله الرحمن الرحیم

خداوندا در توفیق بگشای / نظامی را ره تحقیق بنمای
دلی ده کو یقینت را بشاید / زبانی کافرینت را سراید
مده ناخوب را بر خاطرم راه / بدار از ناپسندم دست کوتاه
درونم را بنور خود برافروز / زبانم را ثنای خود درآموز
بداودی دلم را تازه گردان / زبورم را بلند آوازه گردان
عروسی را که پروردم بجانش / مبارک روی گردان در جهانش
چنان کز خواندنش فرخ شود رای / ز مشک افشاندنش خلخ شود جای
سوادش دیده را پر نور دارد / سماعش مغز را مخمور دارد
مفرح نامهٔ دلهاش خوانند / کلید بند مشکلهاش دانند
معانی را بدو ده سربلندی / سعادت را بدو کن نقش بندی
بچشم شاه شیرین کن جمالش / که خود بر نام شیرین است فالش
نسیمی از عنایت یار او کن / ز فیضت قطرهٔ در کار او کن
چو فیاض عنایت کرد یاری / بیارای کان گهر تا چه داری

فی توحید باری جل جلاله

بنام آنکه هستی نام ازو یافت / فلک جنبش زمین آرام ازو یافت
خدایی کافرینش در سجودش / گواه مطلق آمد بر وجودش
تعالی الله یکی بی مثل و مانند / که خوانندش خداوندان خداوند
فلک برپای دار و انجم افروز / خرد را بی میانجی حکمت آموز
فزون از وهم و فکرتهای باریک / برون آرندهٔ شبهای تاریک
غم و شادی نگار و بیم و امید / شب و روز آفرین و ماه و خورشید
نگه دارندهٔ بالا و پستی / گواه هستی او جمله هستی
وجودش بر همه موجود قاهر / نشانش بر همه بیننده ظاهر
خداوندی که چون نامش بخوانی / بباید در جوابت لن ترانی
نیاید پادشاهی زوت بهتر / ورا کن بندگی هم اوت بهتر
طبایع را بقدرت کارفرمای / طبایع را بصنعت گوهرآرای
مراد دیدهٔ باریک بینان / انیس خاطر خلوت نشینان
ورای هرچه در گیتی اساس است / برون از هرچه در فکر و قیاس است
بجست و جوی او بر بام افلاک / دریده وهم را نعلین ادراک
خرد در جستنش هشیار برخاست / چو دانستش نبداند چه و راست
نظر مدهوش چون نقش خویش برداشت / بدانگاهی حجاب ازش برداشت

29. Musharrif al-Dīn Saᶜdī of Shiraz (died in 1292)
Kulliyyāt-i Saᶜdī (Collected Works)

Folios 1r, 1v–2r.

Copied by Muḥammad ibn Aḥmad ibn ᶜUmar al-Murshidī on Muharram 30, 829 / December 12, 1425, most probably in Shiraz
Naskh
Fine, well glazed, brownish paper
398 folios
18.7 × 12 cm
Text: 12.8 × 6.5 cm, 25 lines to the page, black ink, gold and watercolors
Accession no. A-31
Provenance: coll. of V.V. Velyaminov-Zernov, 1858.
Bibliography: Catalogue PTR, 1964, no. 3340.

Front cover of the binding.

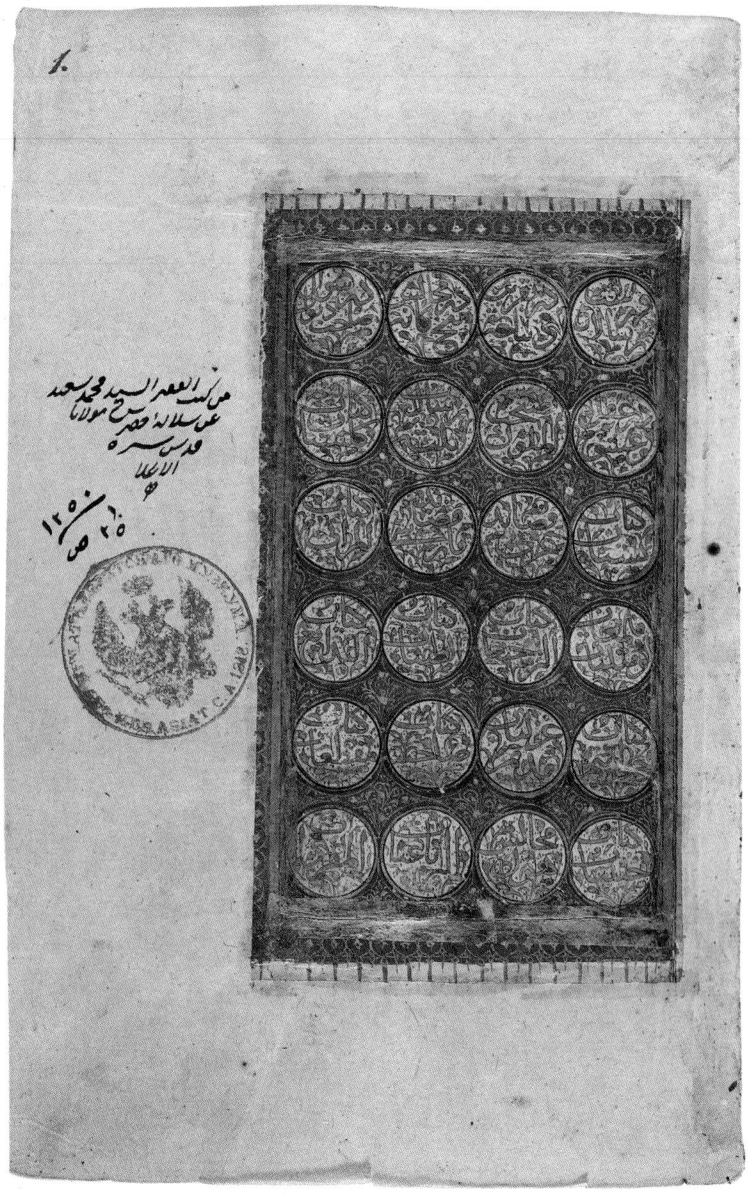

Kulliyyāt-i Saᶜdī ("Collected Works") is a compilation of all the works by an eminent Persian writer of poetry and prose, Musharrif al-Dīn Saᶜdī (died in 1292). This manuscript contains 28 works, with a preface by Bīsutūn, the first editor and compiler of the *Kulliyyāt* (1326). The calligraphic *naskh* is beautiful and small, while the titles of the works and chapters are written in larger *naskh* script and a fine *thuluth* within special cartouches (*ᶜunvān, sarlauḥ*). In the excellent composition and decoration, a faded blue color predominates with the addition of gold and red pigment. The copyist, Muḥammad al-Murshidī (folio 398v) came from a long line of Shirazi copyists, active in this profession as far back as the 12th century.
The manuscript is richly and skilfully decorated. The range of colors (predominantly blue and gold), and the design of the decoration are characteristic of the time and place the manuscript was produced. There is a fine web of pink and gold, outlined in gold between the lines of text (*tashᶜīr*), and golden inscriptions. The frontispiece is divided into three sections over a double page (folios 1v–2r) with rectangular panels (above and below). The title page, at the beginning of the work (folio 1r), containing a detailed summary, is in the tradition of the schools of Syria, Egypt and Western Iran at the end of the 14th century. Twenty-four circles are inserted in a vertical rectangle (13 × 7 cm), in which the titles of the works of Saᶜdī represented in the *Kulliyyāt* are written in golden *thuluth*. Finally, the manuscript has 31 illustrations of varying dimensions in the familiar color scheme. The dark red binding has been tastefully done. The center of the front and back covers shows an oval medallion (*turunj*) embossed in low relief and gilded; the corner decorations (*kunj*) have also been stamped and gilded. The inside of the covers of the binding, in black leather, are decorated with a central medallion of oval-shape and tooled, on a gold background of glued paper, with tooled inlay of black leather (stylized leaves and flowers). [O.A.]

30. Abū al-Qāsim Firdausī al-Ṭūsī (died around 1020–1030)
Shāhnāma (The Book of Kings)

Copied by Muḥammad ibn Jalāl al-Rashīd at the beginning of the month of Ramadan 849 / December 1445
Nastaᶜlīq
Fine, glossy, yellowed paper
410 folios
25.6 × 17 cm
Text: 18.2 × 12 cm
20–25 lines to the page, ink, watercolors, gold, 29 miniatures of the Yazd school
Accession no. C-1654
Provenance: offered on September 24, 1899, by the Qājār Prince ᶜImād al-Daula to the Russian Ambassador Agiropulo (folio 410v); coll. of V.A. Zhukovskii, 1919, no. 57.
Bibliography: Akimushkin O.F., Ivanov A.A., 1968, pp. 10–11; Gyuzal'yan L.T., Dyakonov M.M., 1935, p. 15; Stchoukine I., 1963.

Folio 70r: The fire ordeal of Siyāvush in the presence of Kaikāvūs and Sudāba *(no. 10, 16 × 12 cm); by safely managing to jump through a corridor of flames on his horse, Siyāvush relieves himself of the accusations of immoral behavior with his father's wife.*

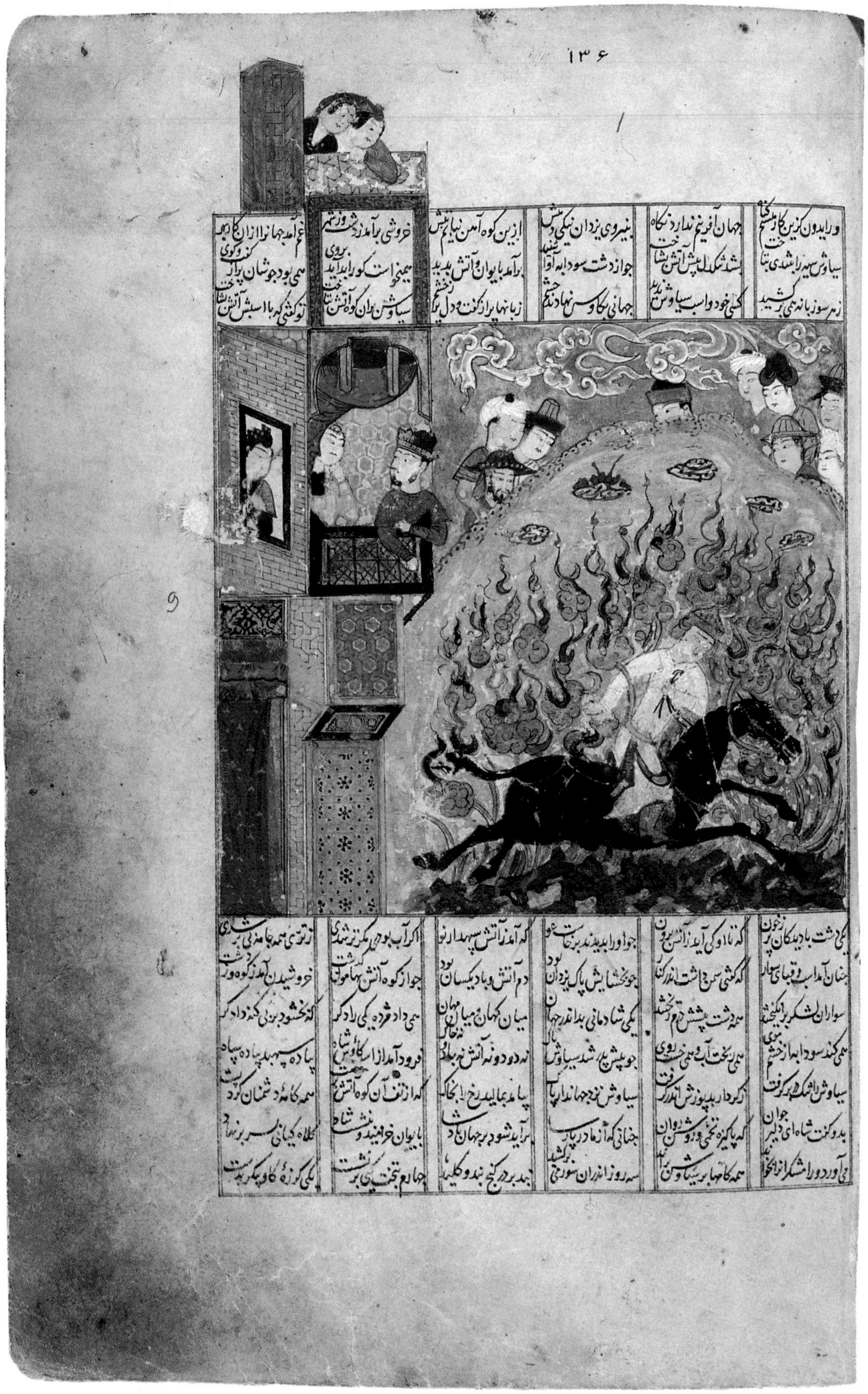

Folio 147v: The battle between Bārzū and Rustam *(no. 17, 11 × 12 cm); after his victory over the Iranian army, the gallant Turanian warrior Bārzū is defeated and slained by Rustam, who fails to recognize his grandson. This is a rare example of its time where the miniature extends beyond the frame of the text and into the margins. Another example of this type of composition in this manuscript is at folio 143r.*

Shāhnāma (*The Book of Kings*), the Persian epic poem, was written by the great Iranian poet Abū al-Qāsim Firdausī al- Ṭūsī (died around 1020–1030). This copy provides the complete text of the second copy by the author, approximately 54,000 couplets, and the "pre-Bāisunghur" preface together with a satire by Firdausī on Maḥmūd Ghaznavī. It was copied by a professional scribe from southwest Iran, Muḥammad ibn Jalāl al-Rashīd. Folios 2v-3r contain a double-page frontispiece (*dībāᶜha, sarlauḥ*), a single composition divided vertically into three sections. Both pages have two rectangular panels (above and below) and in the the central area, the text is outlined with a golden web (*tashᶜīr*) and a golden band (*taḥrīr*). On folio 7v is an introductory illumination (*ᶜunvān, sarlauḥ*) painted in intense blue, light green and gold hues. Chapter titles, in special cartouches, are painted in gold *thuluth* characters surrounded by an orange, pink or gold web (*tashᶜīr*) and a border (*taḥrīr*). The miniatures in this manuscript together with those in six other copies, formerly believed to be of the Shiraz school 1440–1450, are in reality from another school of Southern Iran, Yazd. The Yazd school of miniature painting was first identified and described in 1963 by I.S. Stchoukine. It can be recognized by its archaic style with crude compact figures and a muted color scheme of sandy yellow, pale violet, pink and brown tones. [O.A.]

31. Abū al-Qāsim Firdausī al-Ṭūsī (died around 1020–1030) Shāhnāma (The Book of Kings)

Folio 149r.

Copied around 1440–1450
Nastaᶜlīq
Fine, strong paper
410 folios
25.7 × 17.1 cm
Text: 17.7 × 11.7 cm
4 columns of 24 lines
74 miniatures from Central Asia
Accession no. C-822
Provenance: in 1792, the manuscript was in Constantinople in the possession of a certain Akerbladt; coll. of P. Sukhtelen, 1837; Teaching Section of the Asiatic Department in the Russian Ministry of Foreign Affairs.
Bibliography: Catalogue PTR, 1964, no. 2293; Dyakonova N.V., 1964, pp. 16–17, 21–22, pls. 1–6; Gyuzal'yan L.T., Dyakonov M.M., 1935, p. 15, pl. II, pp. 14–17, 22–26.

This manuscript contains the first authorized version of the *Shāhnāma* with the "pre-Bāisunghur" preface that includes the satire on Maḥmūd Ghaznavī, traditionally attributed to Firdausī. The copyist's name is not mentioned, nor the date when the copy was completed. It was written in Herat or in the north-eastern part of Iran (Khurasan) and decorated in the same region around 1440–1450. The neat and confident *nastaᶜlīq*, a little angular in style, was written by an experienced professional scribe from the school of Jaᶜfar Bāisunghurī (died around 1456).

The manuscript is richly decorated. The double-page frontispiece at folios 9v–10r (*dībācha*) (each page measuring 18 × 12 cm) is unified by a single elegant composition.

Divided into three sections both vertically and horizontally, it is framed by a wide dark blue band decorated with a polychrome band of plant motifs (*islīmī-i bargī* and *gul-i khaṭā'ī*). At the top and bottom of both pages is a blue rectangular cartouche surrounded by a *band-i rūmī* decorative pattern. In the center of each cartouche the basmala is written in white pigment, using a stylized floral kufic script, as well as the poet's name and the title of the book. In the central field, the text is placed in two columns. The design, composition and multicolored decoration of the text are typical of mid-15th-century Central Asian miniature painting.

The first two miniatures make up a double-page frontispiece (folios 1v–2r). Produced in Shiraz around 1460–1470 (the so-called Turkman school), they were glued onto the frontispiece at a later date. Judging by the central scene, they illustrate *The Master Defeats His Boastful Pupil*, taken from Musharrif al-Dīn Saᶜdī's *Gulistān*.

The remaining miniatures illustrating the *Shāhnāma* were painted by a single artist, probably at the beginning of the 16th century in Central Asia (Transoxiana), although they have elements characteristic of the school of Southwestern Iran (Shiraz) of the end of the 15th century. It is quite probable that the artist came from that region. [O.A]

دل گیو شد زین سخن پر ز دود که اندیشه کرد از گشاد فرود
فرستاد و گستهم را پیش خواند بسا داستان جوانی براند
فرستاد ورع سیاوش برش بسان خسروانی یکی مغفرش
بیاورد گستهم درع نبرد بپوشید بیژن بکردار گرد
بسوی سپیدکوه بنهاد روی جهانجوی نو و مرد جنگ جوی
چنین گفت شاه جهان تاجوار که آمد جهانجوی یکی نامدار
نگر کین پیاده را نام چیست بدین مرد جنگی که خواهد گریست
بنخجیر و نخوار سراینده گفت که این را بیاران کسی نیست جفت
که فرزند گیو است مرد دلیر به هر جنگ پیروز باشد چو شیر
تو اکنون سوی بارگی دارد دست دل شاه ایران بباید شکست
و دیگر که دارد همی آن زره نگه کن و دیگر بیابان گره
برو تیر و زوبین بنه بدگذار بنه دیگر پیاده کنند کارزار
تو با او بسنده نباشی بجنگ نگه کن که الماس دارد بچنگ
بزد تیر بر اسب بیژن فرود تو گفتی که اسب اندرو جان نبود
بیفتاد بیژن جدا گشت از وی سوی تیغ با تیغ بنهاد روی
یکی نعره زد کای سوار دلیر بمان تا ببینی کنون رزم شیر
ندانی که اسپان گوان جنگ نیابد زدن گفت بر نیزه چنگ
کسی کش بیفکنده شد اسپ جنگ بیابند با تیغ هندی بچنگ
به بینی مرا گر به بینی بجای به پیکار ازان پس بیاید ت رای
چو بیژن همی برگشت از فرود فرود اندر و تیر هندی نمود
یکی تیر دیگر بینداخت شیر سپر بر سر آورد مرد دلیر
سپر بر درید و زره را بتافت ازو روی بیژن بسستی نتافت
ازان شد بالا چو بر سر کشید بزد دست و تیغ از میان برکشید
فرود گرانمایه زو بازگشت همه باره و در برآوار گشت
دوان بیژن آمد پس پشت اوی یکی تیغ زد بر بر پشت اوی
بنزدیکی در رسید اندر وی برآمد ز باره یکی گفت و گوی

بزد دست و دنبال اسپش گرفت بدیگر یکی تیغ تیز ای شگفت
بر گستوان بر زد و کرد چاک گرانمایه زاسب اندرآمد بخاک
در بند حصن اندرآمد فرود دلیران در دژ ببستند زود
ز باره فراوان بیارید سنگ بدانستند کان نیست جای درنگ
خروشید بیژن که ای نامدار ز مردی پیاده دلیر و سوار
چنین بارگی کشته شهرت نبود دریغا دل و نام جنگی فرود
بیامد بر طوس ازان رزمگاه چنین گفت کای پهلوان سپاه
سر دیگر بر رزم چنین یک دلیر شنو و نام بردار یک مست شیر

Folios 1v–2r.

Folios 9v–10r.

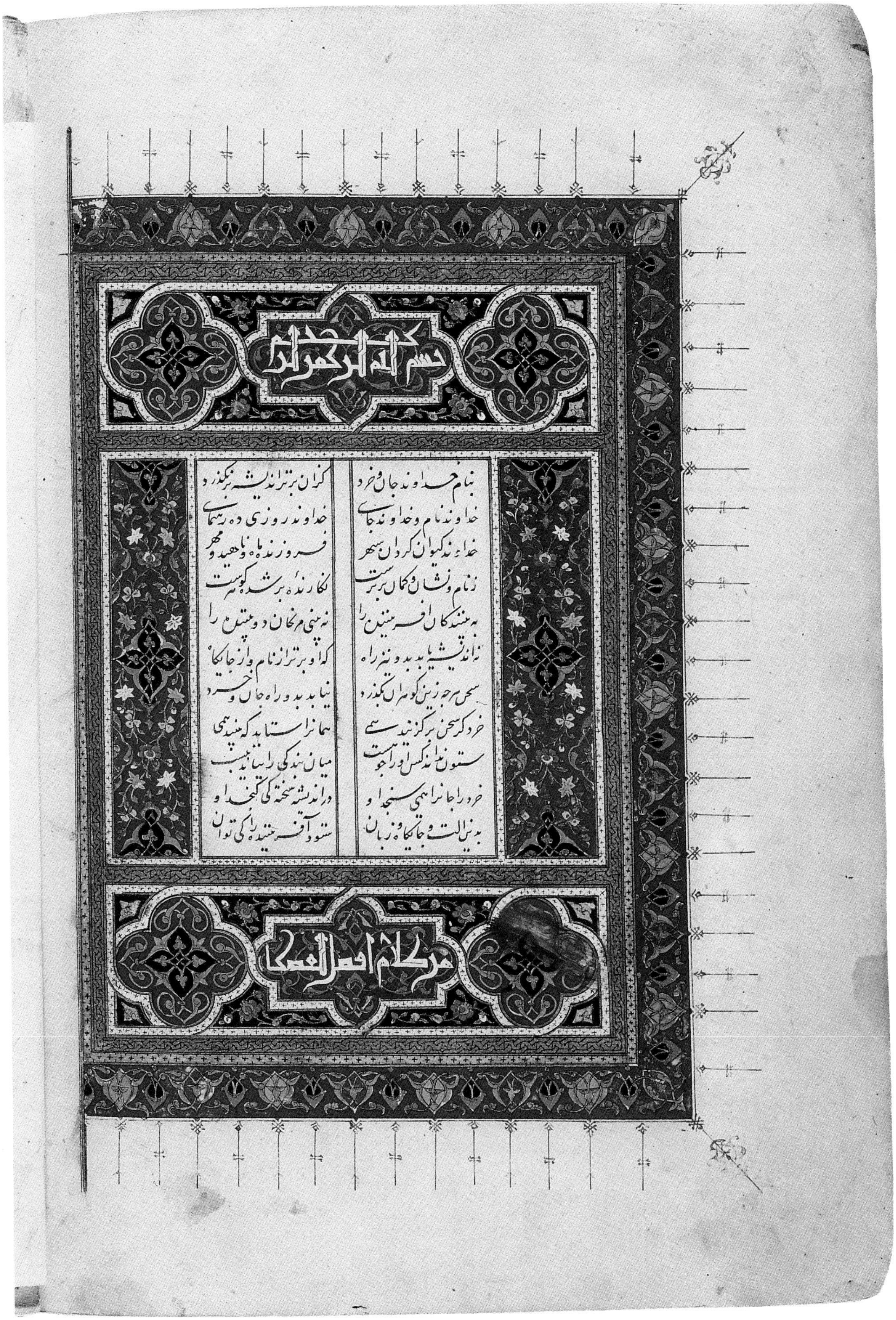
بسم الله الرحمن الرحيم
بنام خداوند جان و خرد
کزان برتر اندیشه برنگذرد
خداوند نام و خداوند جای
خداوند روزی ده رهنمای
خداوند کیوان و گردان سپهر
فروزنده ماه و ناهید و مهر
ز نام و نشان و گمان برترست
نگارنده بر شده گوهرست
به بینندگان آفریننده را
نبینی مرنجان دو بیننده را
نیابد بدو نیز اندیشه راه
که او برتر از نام و از جایگاه
سخن هر چه زین گوهران بگذرد
نیابد بدو راه جان و خرد
خرد گر سخن برگزیند همی
همان را ستاید که بیند همی
ستودن نداند کس او را چو هست
میان بندگی را ببایدت بست
خرد را و جان را همی سنجد او
در اندیشه سخته کی گنجد او
بدین آلت و جایگاه و زبان
ستود آفریننده را کی توان
من کلام افضل الفصحا

32. Abū al-ᶜAbbās Aḥmad ibn Muḥammad ibn ᶜArabshāh (1389–1450) Fākihat al-khulafā' wa mufākahat al-ẓurafā' (The Sweet Fruit for Caliphs and the Joyful Meetings of the Admirers of Elegance)

Folio 1r.

Copied by Ismāᶜīl ibn ᶜAbd al-Raḥmān al-Iṣfahānī, in 1448
Naskh
Paper
272 folios, 20 × 12 cm
Text: 17 lines to the page
Accession no. C-651
Provenance: coll. J.-L. Rousseau; entered the Asiatic Museum in 1819.
Bibliography: Brockelmann C., II, 1902, p. 28, no. 5; Khalidov A.B., 1960, no. 91.

This manuscript entitled *Fākihat al-khulafā' wa mufākahat al-ẓurafā'* ("The Sweet Fruit for Caliphs and the Joyful Meetings of the Admirers of Elegance"), was written in the form of rhyming prose apologues and fables. For example, one of the chapters is called *About Wise Aphorisms of the Pious Lion and the Sayings of a Runaway Camel*. It is, in fact, an Arabic adaptation of *Marzbānnāma* (the Persian *Mirror of Princes* created in the 11th century by the Prince of Ṭabaristān, Marzbān ibn Rustam ibn Sharvīn).

The author, Ibn ᶜArabshāh (his full name is Abū al-ᶜAbbās Aḥmad ibn Muḥammad ibn ᶜArabshāh) was born in Damascus in 1389. As a young man, he was taken prisoner with other Syrians by Tīmūr to his capital Samarqand. His captivity in Central Asia came to an end only after Tīmūr died. After he had returned to his homeland, he continued his literary profession in Damascus and Cairo until his death in 1450. He wrote a history of Tīmūr, *Fākihat al-khulafā' wa mufākahat al-ẓurafā'*, in which he is bitterly critical of him as a tyrannical ruler.

This manuscript is a remarkable example of *naskh* writing, the prevalent calligraphy at the time of the Mamluks. The copyist, Ismāᶜīl ibnᶜ Abd al-Raḥmān al-Iṣfahānī, completed the manuscript on Ramadan 25, 852 / November 22, 1448, several months after the text had been copied (Rabi I 852 / June 1448) while the author was still alive. It was also copied under the supervision of the author himself who wrote the following note on folio 272r: "The author has finished reading this text, all is correct—according to the will of Allāh, the Most High."

The manuscript was commissioned by the vizier Abū al-Khayr Muḥammad al-Ẓāhirī, who probably held this position at the court of the Mamluk Sultan al-Ẓāhir Jaqmaq. The manuscript was most likely written in Cairo.

The title page is decorated with a large *ᶜunvān*, in gold and colors, within which are written the title of the book and the name of the author in white pigment. On the same page, it is mentioned that the manuscript was made for the vizier. The volume has an elegant leather binding, with an embossed ornament on the base of the flap, and is cased in a box. [A.Kh.]

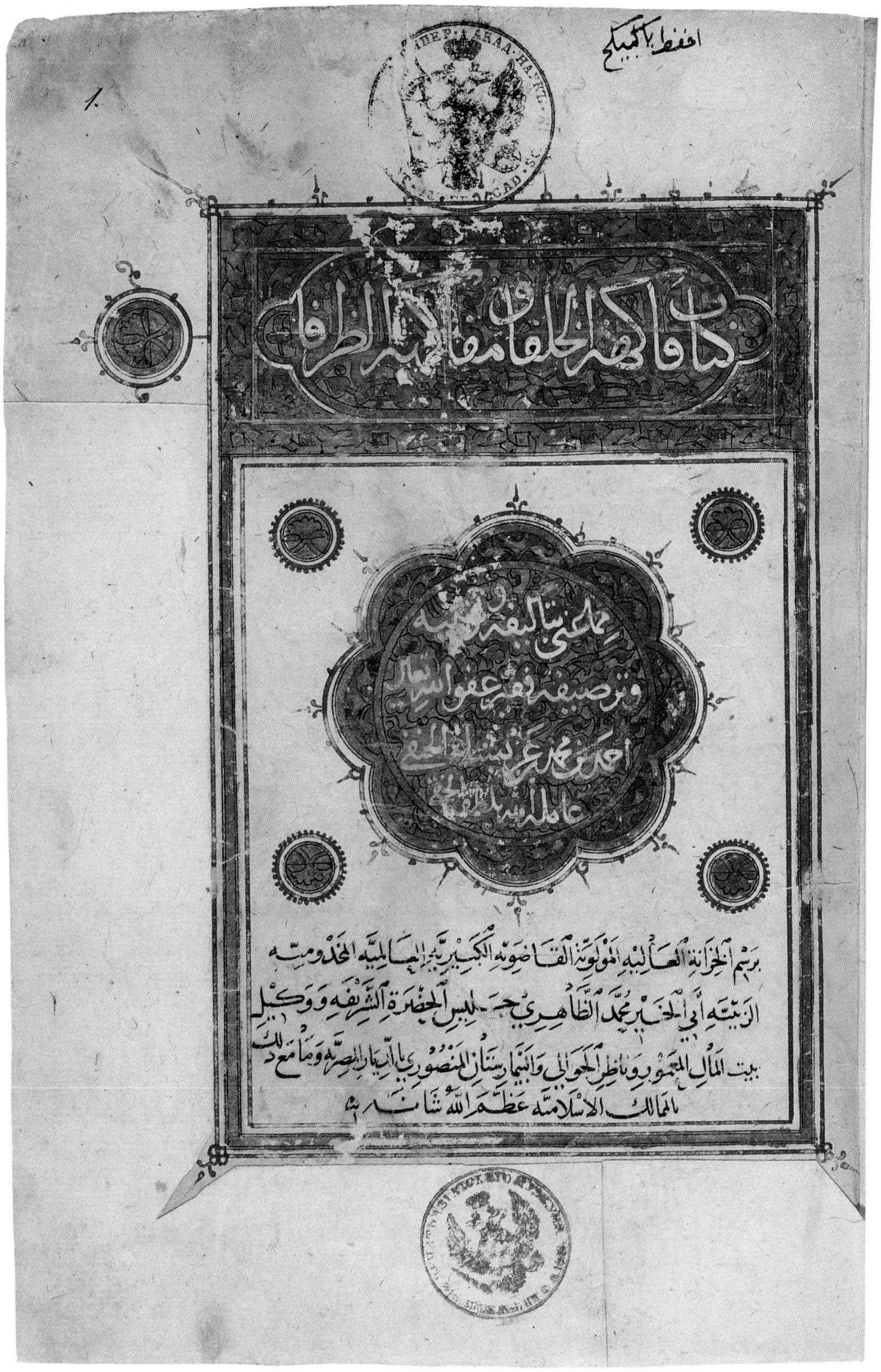
كتاب فاكهة الخلفاء ومفاكهة الظرفاء
برسم الخزانة العالية المولوية القاضوية الكبيرية الجمالية المخدومية
الزينية أبي الخير محمد الظاهري جليس الحضرة الشريفة ووكيل
بيت المال المعمور وناظر الجوالي والبيمارستان المنصوري بالديار المصرية وما مع ذلك
بالممالك الإسلامية عظم الله شأنه

33. Jalāl al-Dīn Muḥammad ibn Muḥammad al-Balkhī Rūmī (1207–1273) Masnavī-i maʿnavī (The Poem of Hidden Sense)

Copied around 1450, no doubt in Herat
Nastaʿlīq
Well glazed paper
435 folios, 24 × 15 cm
Text: 15 × 10 cm, 4 columns of 12 to 17 lines; colors, black ink, gold
Accession no. C-68
Provenance: coll. J.-L. Rousseau, entered in 1819, no. 232.
Bibliography: Catalogue PTR, 1964, no. 3719.

Masnavī-i maʿnavī ("The Poem of Hidden Sense") is a famous poem made up of six books (*daftar*) devoted to various problems of intellectual mysticism in Islam (*taṣavvuf*). It is the work of an eminent Persian poet, Jalāl al-Dīn Muḥammad ibn Muḥammad al-Balkhī Rūmī (1207–1273), written in Konya (Asia Minor). This poem was referred to as the "Persian Qur'an" by contemporaries and followers of its author.

This copy is a perfect example of the production of a workshop belonging to a private individual or attached to a court. It is copied by an anonymous scribe in a magnificent and neat *nastaʿlīq*, following the tradition of the Herat school of Jaʿfar ibn ʿAlī Bāisunghurī, and richly ornate. It has a double-page frontispiece, six rectangular illuminations in the body of the text (*sarlauḥ*, *ʿunvān*) preceding the prefaces to each of the six books and is written in gold in excellent *naskh*. The decorative scheme is a well balanced combination and alternation of the intense blue ground strewn with plant arabesques on the one hand, and golden cartouches and vignettes (*islīmī-i bargī*, *gul-i khaṭā'ī*, *gira-i rūmī*) as well as white pigment, a rose colored web framing the text and fine black lines traced with golden spots (*tarsīʿ*) between the lines on the other, making this manuscript a piece of rare elegance and striking refinement.

The sophisticated binding (24 × 19.1 cm), is delicately worked in dark brown leather, with applications, both gilt and colored, cut in leather, in a pattern of vegetal motifs. The central area of the cover has a large tooled oval medallion (*turunj*), with leather inlays on a blue, pale pistachio background. The main design consists of four stylized lotus flowers (*khaṭā'ī*) in a form reminiscent of an Armenian cross. Each corner is decorated with a cartouche (*kunj*) in the same technique and colors. Golden bands and lines run alongside the edges. The inside of the binding has a large central tooled oval-shaped medallion. The brown background is decorated with black and gold plant pattern inlays on a dark brown leather background. The four corner cartouches (*kunj*) are tooled with leather inlays. Each inlay is glued to a cardboard backing. [O.A.]

Binding (inside and outside).

Folios 2v–3r.

34. Muḥammad ibn Yaᶜqūb ibn Khazzām al-Khuttālī (14th century) Kitāb al-makhzūn fī jāmiᶜ al-funūn (The Book of Sciences)

Copied in 1474
Naskh
Dense and thick glazed paper
108 folios, 30 × 20 cm
Text: 25.5 × 14.8 cm
15 lines to the page
83 illustrations
Accession no. C-686
History: coll. of Count W. de Rzhevusky in Vienna, 1809; purchased in April 1832 in Constantinople by the Russian ambassador to Turkey, A.P. Butenev, and sent by him two years later to the Asiatic Museum.
Bibliography: Arendt V., 1936, pp. 129–203; Ayalon D., 1979; Grube E., 1979, pp. 72–81; Haldane D.,1978; Mostafa M., 1969–1970, pp. 1–13 (in English) and pp. 1–14 (Arabic text).

The identity of the author has been hypothetically established by means of a comparative analysis of a series of manuscripts and fragments in St. Petersburg, Paris, Istanbul, Dublin, Cairo and in a private collection in Great Britain. He was Muḥammad ibn Yaᶜqūb ibn Khazzām al-Khuttālī, who lived in Egypt during the 14th century. *Kitāb al-makhzūn* is in the manner of *ᶜilm alfurūsiyya (funūn al-furūsiyya, anwāᶜ al-furūsiyya)*: the science of the art of chivalry, its forms and divisions. Although it may be traced back to a Persian tradition, it blossomed apparently in Egypt and Syria at the time of the crusades. Works of this kind often became a type of encyclopaedia essential to the "real man" of the time, including subjects such as how to medically treat horses, the principles of trick riding, the rules for games on horseback, combat exercises for cavalry, falconry, archery, fencing, etc.
The Mamluk state united Egypt, Syria and Palestine. The state was founded by former soldier-slaves, guards, military men of the Ayyubid dynasty (1171–1256), and for its ruling class *furūsiyya* was part of their lifestyle. Polo was not just a game, the mallet was almost considered a sign of royal dignity, carried by its owner on official parades. From an early age, the Mamluks started learning the art of cavalry in special schools, inside the citadel of Cairo.
Presumably, the exercises practiced there turned into military games that enjoyed immense popularity. Crowds of spectators came to specially built hippodromes to watch them.
In the 1450–1460s, a prominent Mamluk general, Jarbash al-Silāḥdār al-Malikī al-Ashrafī, responsible for training young slaves recruited for the army, ordered copies of books on the art of war for his library. Destiny had it that two of his manuscripts are now in the Institute's collection: the present one and al-Tadbīrāt al-sulṭāniyya by Muḥammad al-Nāṣirī (Accession no. C-726). The present book is especially interesting as it contains, apart from the traditional disciplines relating to *al-furūsiyya*, the description of firethrowing weapons, portable explosive devices like modern grenades, fire and signal arrows, as well as primitive artillery. The latter represented the first steps towards the use and power of gunpowder. These firearms, made of wood, were made with the same principles as the arquebus that was made in Western Europe during the 14th century.

The book is full of an internationally acknowledged specialized vocabulary belonging to professional soldiers, the result of several hundred years of traditions common to both the Mediterranean and the Near and Middle Eastern regions.
The text is written in large script similar to classical *naskh*, including practically all diacritical and vocalization marks. The copy is richly decorated. The frontispiece is especially noteworthy; with the use of three colors, black, blue and gold, the painter created a perfect composition.
The Mamluk school of miniatures was based on the artistic traditions of the Egyptian school created in the 10th–12th centuries and on works of artists from Iraq and Syria of the 12th–13th centuries. After the conquest of Baghdad by the Mongols in 1258, many artists working in Iraq emigrated to Damascus and Cairo. The Mamluk school could not remain untouched by the influence of Persian and Central Asian painting, that was blossoming in the 14th-15th centuries. The artists of the Mamluk epoch were also familiar with examples of European art that had been brought over to Egypt and Syria. The craftsmen of the Mamluk school, when illustrating manuscripts of zoology, botany and other natural sciences, as well as military art, aimed for exact and detailed representations of reality. The culture, science and art of the Mamluk state were at the crossroads of Arabic, Turkish, Persian and European cultural influences. This is apparent in the content and form of this manuscript. The illustrations are highly descriptive. It is a very traditional painting, with flat images, although the folds in clothing as well as other carefully worked details give an impression of volume. What counts the most for the artist is to show the details of the arms or a certain action. There is no background or landscape.
The miniatures are in saturated opaque colors. When there are two or more figures, they are distinguished by different colored clothing. The same applies to the horses. The favorite colors used are pale green, lilac, orange and brown. The decorative effects are achieved through a harmonious rhythm of colored spots, however, the palette employed is relatively limited.
To begin with, the artist apparently used stencils. Then the contours of the drawing were filled with the main color and certain areas with gold (saddles, the metal parts of arms and armour, the

Fig. 47, page 146: Greek fire or the art of the "flammable mixture" (funūn al-nafṭ). *The Arabic word* al-nafṭ *(literally, oil) is used for a mixture of incendiary properties. Numerous formulae contain the three basic ingredients: white, black or yellow saltpetre, carbon and sulfur, that make up gunpowder. The miniature presents incendiary projectiles in the center and, on the side, explosives or fire-pots loaded with flammable material to be thrown against fortresses and ships by means of catapults. In the upper section, there are spherical or conical containers (prototypes of the modern grenade) with a hole for the detonator.*

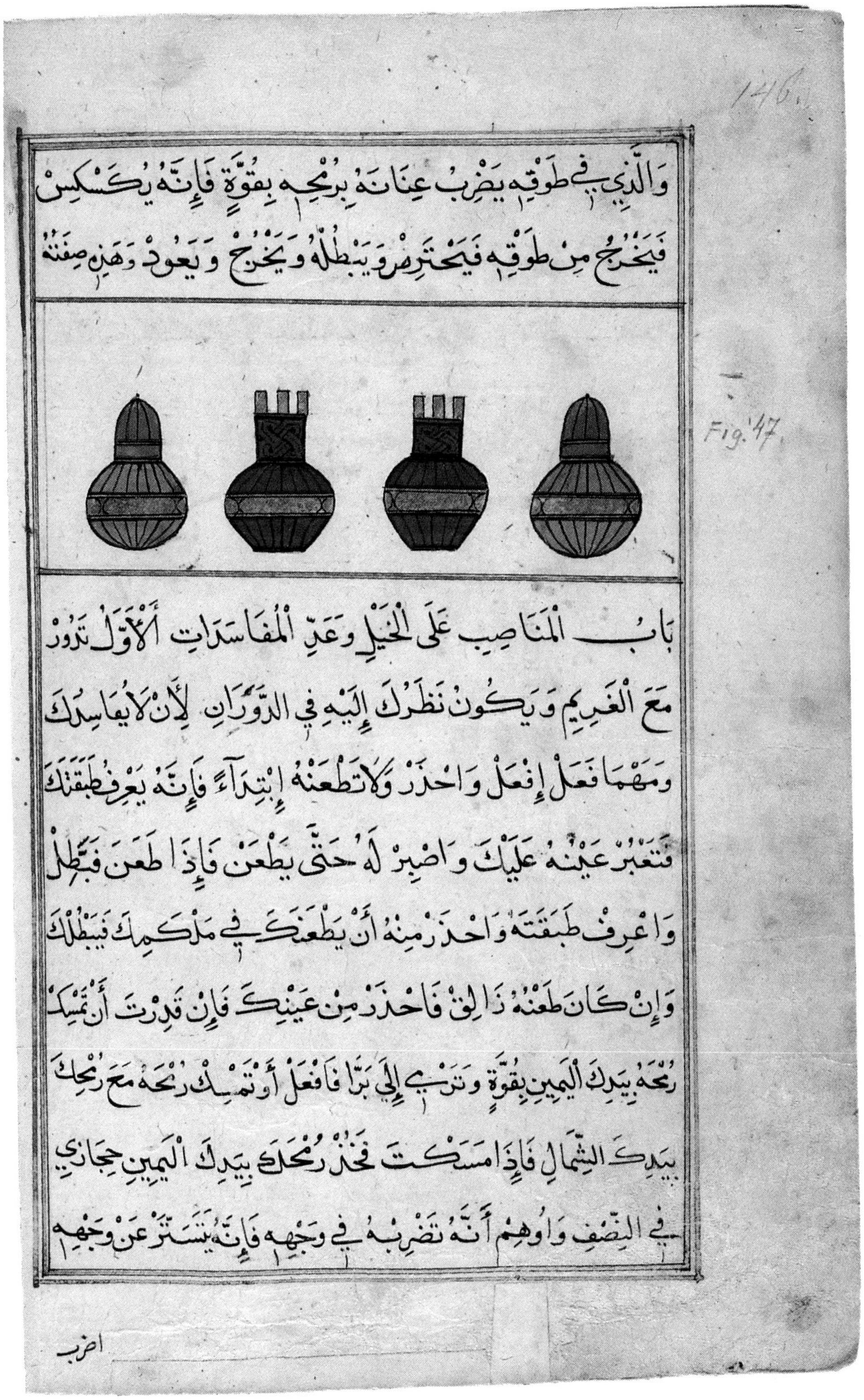

sleeve yokes, or the lower part of the stirrups). Then the artist painted the figures in detail. The binding is contemporary with the manuscript and consists of several sheets of paper firmly glued together and covered with dark brown leather. The flap has been restored. On both sides the binding is decorated with a double recessed frame, outlined by three gold lines. A central almond-shaped field is decorated with appliqué of embossed plant motifs. The gilding has only been conserved on the inside cover. The borders of the petal-shaped inlay are surrounded by a gold line with radii.

A facsimile edition of the manuscript by E. Rezvan and A. Alikberov is under preparation. (Garnet Publishing, Great Britain). [E.R.]

*Fig. 23 to 25: the Indian spiral (*ḥalazūn hindī*); the line formations are in gold, whereas the cavalry positions are marked with small flags in different colors. It was not so much a tactical maneuver but a parade of cavalry formations on a drill field, in front of a large number of spectators, the Sultan and senior officers. The participants in these competitions were meant to move in circles in a given order while performing specific exercises. The Europeans sometimes copied these exercises and performed them in the tournaments.*
*Fig. 23, page 110: the cavalry in two ranks (*al-ṣufūf *means "rows" in Arabic). Fig. 24, page 117: the cavalry deployed in ranks for combat, first forming loops (*dulāb*) then a double hook (*al-kullāb*).*

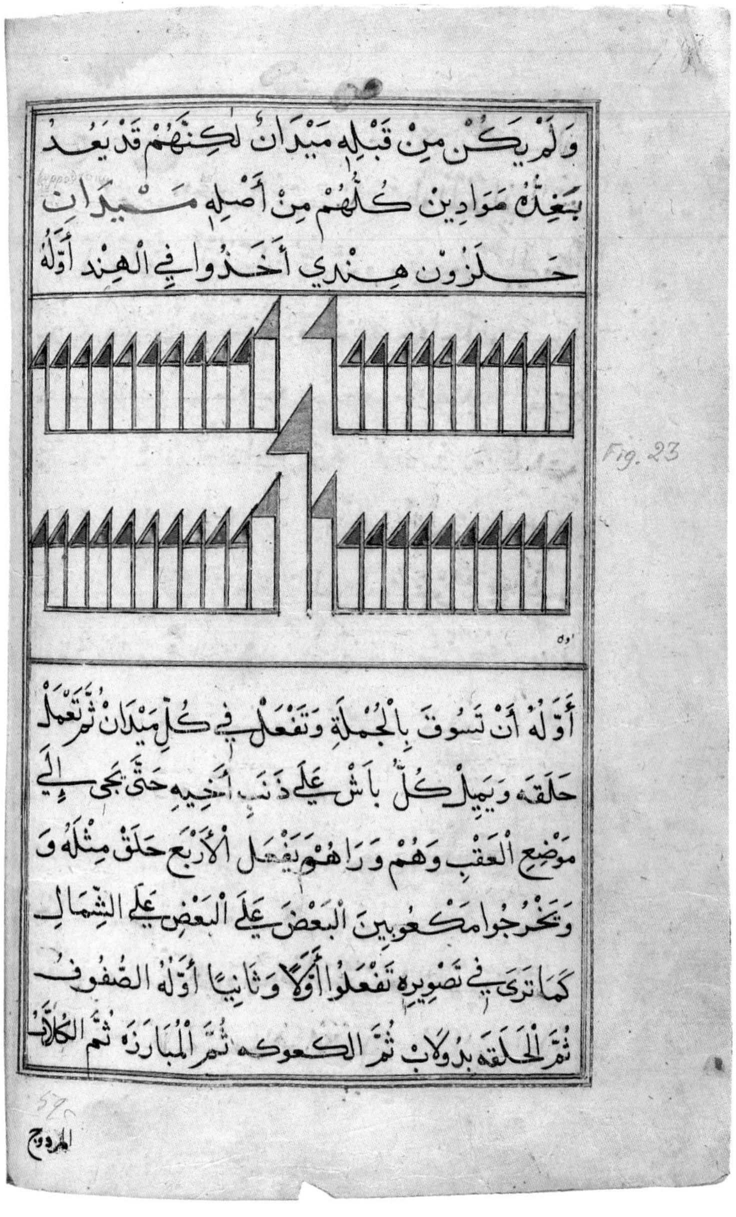

ولم يكن من قبله ميدان لكنهم قد يعد
بعده موادين كلهم من أصله ميدان
حلزون هندي أخذوا في الهند أوله
أوله أن تسوق بالجملة وتفعل في كل ميدان ثم تعمل
حلقه ويميل كل باش على ذنب أخيه حتى يجي إلى
موضع العقب وهم وراهو يفعل الأربع حلق مثله و
يخرجوا مكعوبين البعض على البعض على الشمال
كما ترى في تصويره تفعلوا أولاً وثانياً أوله الصفوف
ثم الحلقه بدولاب ثم الكعوكه ثم المبارزه ثم الكلاب
المزدوج
Fig. 23

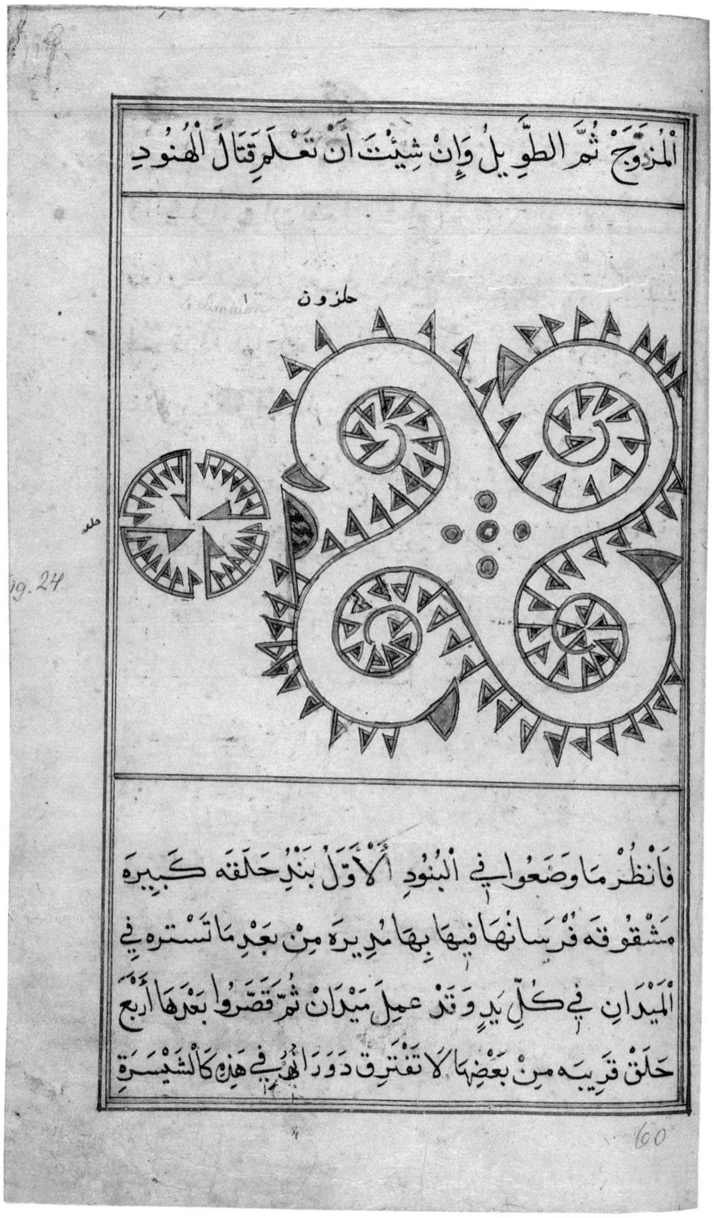

المزدوج ثم الطويل وإن شئت أن تعلم قتال الهنود
حلزون
فانظر ما وضعوا في البنود الأول بند حلقه كبيره
مشقوقه فرسانها فيها بها مديره من بعد ما تستره في
الميدان في كل يد وقد عمل ميدان ثم قصروا بعدها أربع
حلق قريبه من بعضها لا تفترق دورانها في هذه كالشيسره
Fig. 24

Fig. 25 to 26, page 119: variation of the Indian spiral, where the weak points have been removed; the ranks are first deployed in the opposing directions, then the commander closes the left flank rather than the right. The Sultan is at some distance from the fighting formations. This is a variation of the cavalry "ring formation" (al-ḥalaq).
Fig. 28, page 121: the Turkish quadruple spiral (ḥalazūn murabbaᶜ turkī).

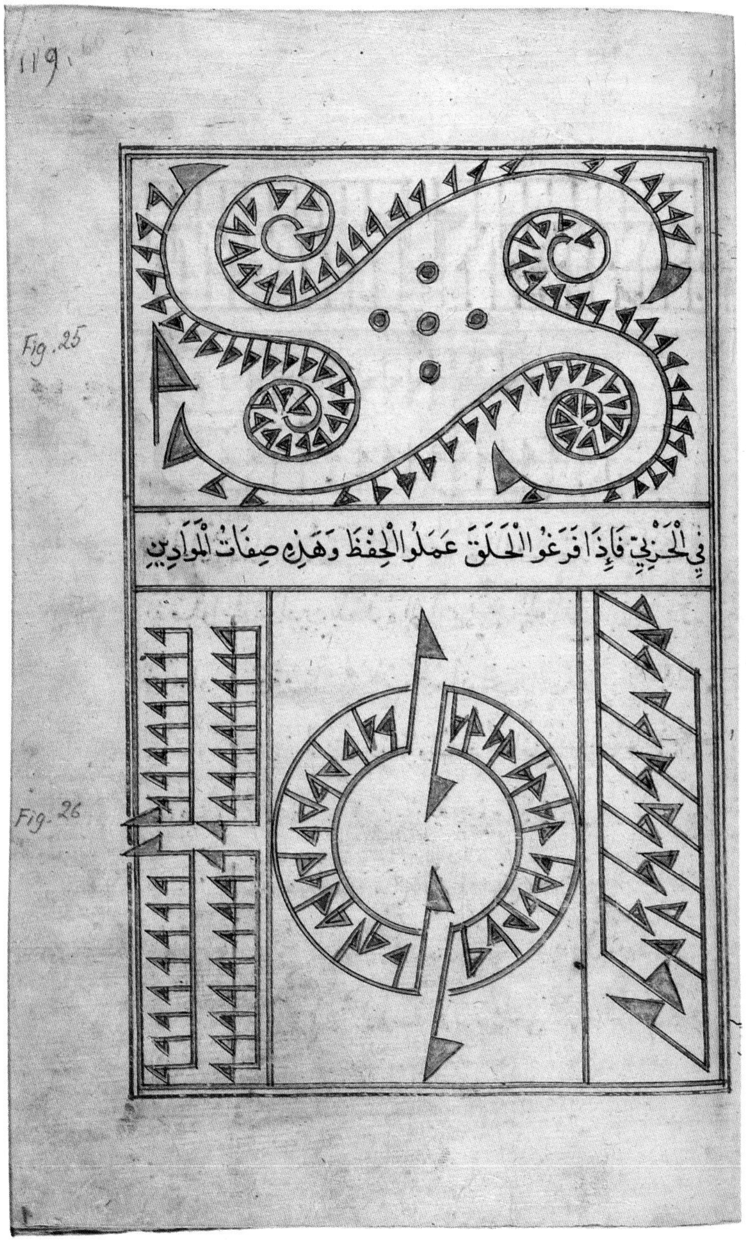

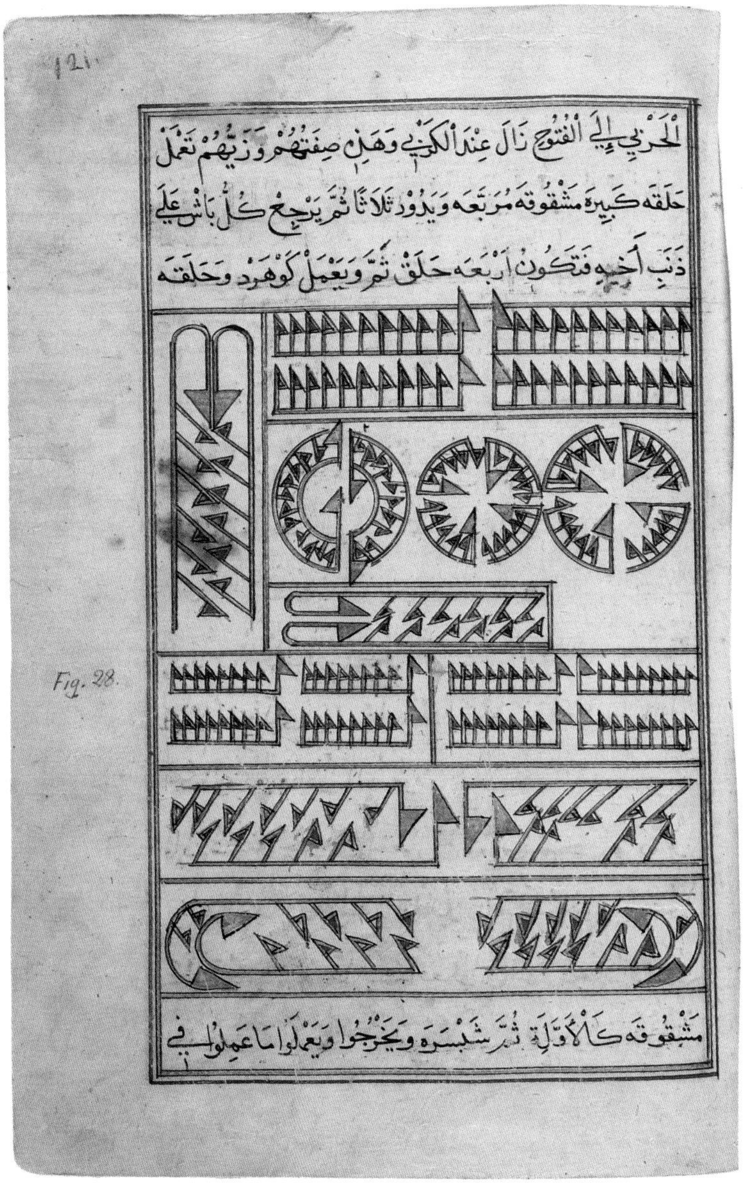

ثم بالراس ثم بالعقب ويدق على رمح الغريم ثم يعطف
على السيف بالرمح ثم يعطف يمينا بالطويل ثم يعطف وينتقل
ويقف ويطاعن ثم يفعل كما فعل من اوله الى آخره
ثم يدمن على ذلك اياما وهذه صفة اللعب على الارض

الطعن في الصدر ودخول الرمح الطوق له تبطيلين
احدهما ان تضرب عنانه مع يده والثاني فبترس الرمح
في صدر فرسه فلا يقدر يتحرك هذه مسئلتين طعن في كمه
والآخر طعن في صدره وكل دخلوا في القماش فالذي طعنه
في كمه يلزق يده الى باطه فاذا احمل عليه انكسر رمحه

Fig. 46, page 145: ground combat with lances (luʿb al-rumḥ ʿalā al-arḍ).

156.

فأينما وقعت النشابه أحرقت ولا يكون رميك عليه إلا في
جهته ويعمل على عجل وتشحطه أي الطنب صفة السهام
الخطائية والطيارات والمدافع الحربيه والسعاة والصوارخ

Fig. 50.

صفة قنديل يعلق في مكان عالي وتشير إليه يوقد وتشير
إليه ينطفي وهو أنك تأخذ صوفان بالميزان وتوقده ويكون
في يدك ساعة رمل وتنظر على كم يفرغ ثم تحطها في القنديل
عند راس الفتيلة وتحط عليها كبريت وتجعله عند راس الفتيلة
فإذا فرغ الرمل من الساعة يكون الرمل قد وصلت إلى
الفتيلة فأشير إليها تنطفي ويكون الزيت الآخر بالميزان فلما

فلما

Fig. 50, page 156.

وصفة الرجاله الذي معه والتراسيم بالدبابيس
كانت الملوك من قديم الزمان ما يدخلوا للحرب إلا
بالحيل لأن النبي صلى الله عليه وسلم قال الحرب خدعة
فاستعملت ذلك إلى زمان قلاون فاستعملت أهل مصر
هذه الحيله فكسروا التتر بذلك لأن الأكاديش
لا يجسروا على النار ويأخذ صاحبه ويهرب والعمل أنه
يستعمل على قدر ما يختار من الفرسان ويرسم رماحهم
بالبارود من الراسين ويكون على الفارس قرقل
وجهه من البلاس الأسود ويغرزه أكثر من مشاق
Fig. 52

Fig. 52, page 159: the naffāṭūn*; a horseman with a double-headed spear and two foot-soldiers with a selection of arms from the fire arsenal. One of them (left) has a* dabbūs *(literally a club), a device made up of a torch to light the fire and a match. The soldier on the right has a torch made from a ball of cloth soaked in a flammable substance in one hand, and in the other an explosive projectile already lit. The burning, sticky substance is to be sprayed at the enemy. Such devices were also used against buildings and warships. The clothes of the* naffāṭūn*, as well as the mantles for the horses and the lances were coated with a fireproof substance. The author of the work said: "ten horsemen like those we have just described would be enough to turn a mighty army to flight."*

Fig. 65, page 177: a real battiyya *stroke. It consists of a piece of wood loosely attached to a mast. The artist has illustrated the correct position in which to hold the lance in order to avoid it breaking in the hands of the lancer.*

Fig. 68, page 184: polo playing.

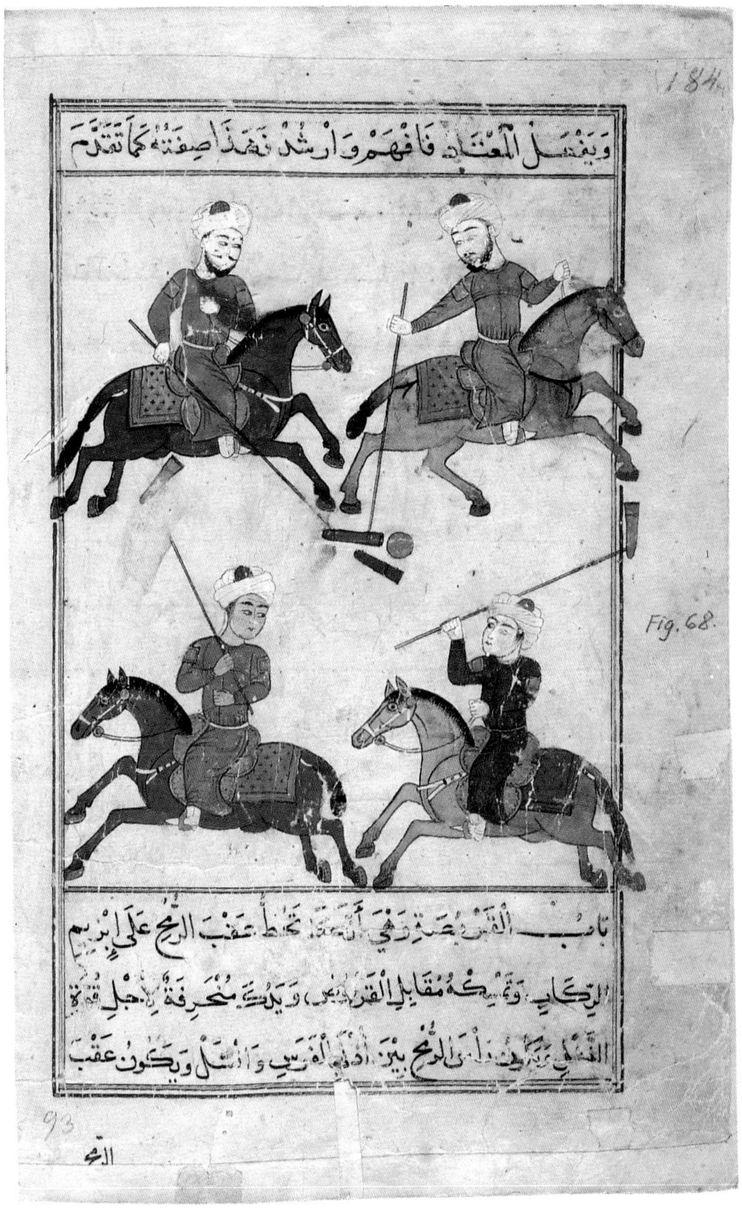

35. Abū al-Faraj ʿAbd al-Raḥmān ibn ʿAlī ibn al-Jawzī (died in 1201)
al-Nuṭq al-mafhūm min ahl al-ṣamt al-maʿlūm
(The Speech Understood by Those Known for Their Silence)

Folios 42v–43r.

Copied by Aḥmad ibn al-Khaṭīb al-Saʿdī in 1476
Naskh
Thick glazed paper
251 folios, 26 × 18 cm
17 lines to the page
Black ink, titles in red ink
Accession no. C-707
Provenance: transferred in 1919 to the Teaching Section of the Asiatic Department in the Russian Ministry of Foreign Affairs.
Bibliography: Brockelmann C., 1898, p. 499, no. 5; Khalidov A.B., 1986, no. 767; Rosen V.R., I, 1877, no. 26.

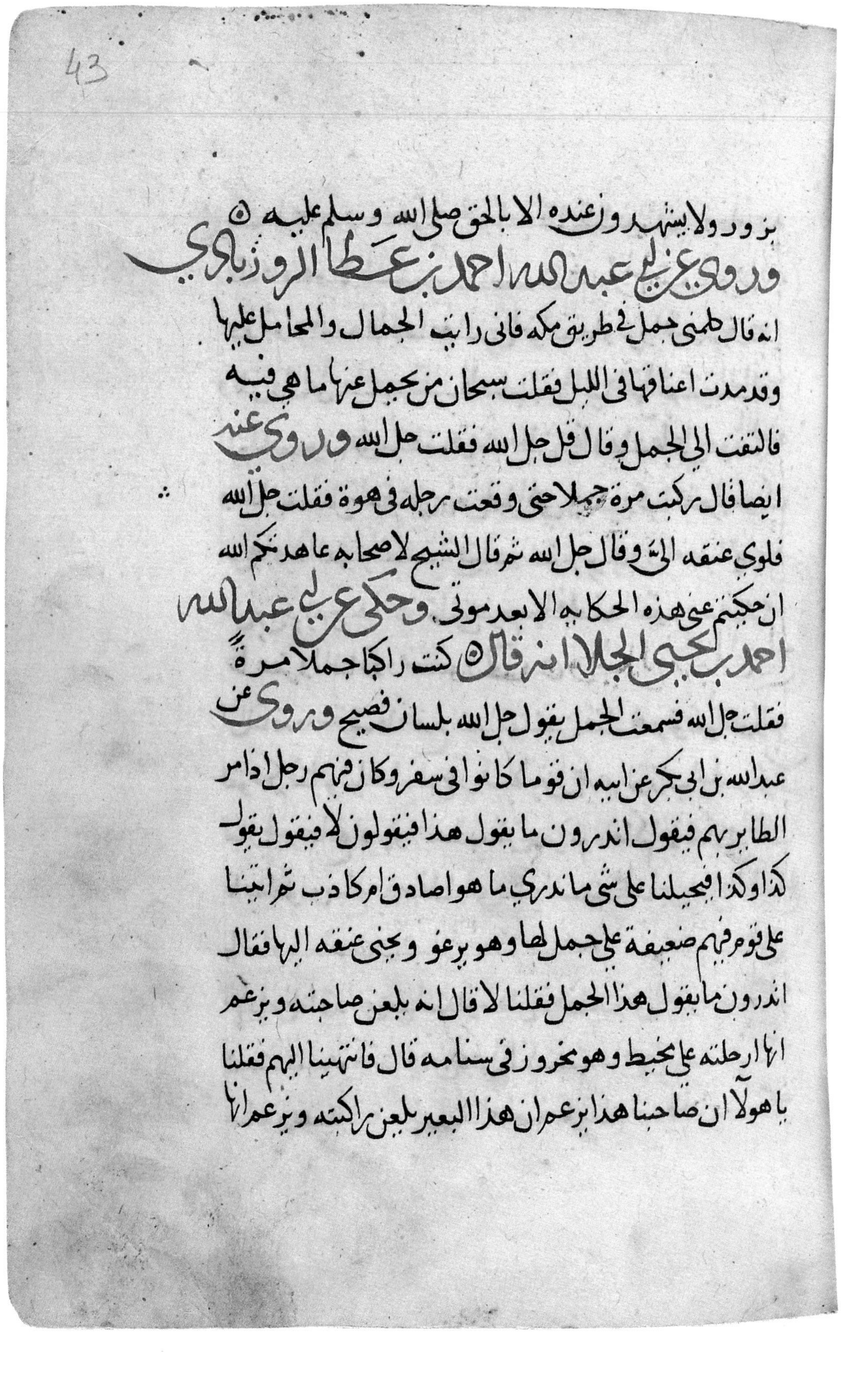
43
بزور ولا يشهدون عنده الا بالحق صلى الله وسلم عليه ٥
وروى عن ابي عبد الله احمد بن عطا الروذباري
انه قال كلمني جمل في طريق مكه فاني رايت الجمال والمحامل عليها
وقد مدت اعناقها في الليل فقلت سبحان من يحمل عنها ما هي فيه
فالتفت الي الجمل وقال قل جل الله فقلت جل الله وروى عنه
ايضا قال ركبت مرة جملا حتى وقعت رجله في هوة فقلت جل الله
فلوى عنقه الي وقال جل الله ثم قال الشيخ لاصحابه عاهدكم الله
ان حكيتم عني هذه الحكايه الا بعد موتي. وحكى عن ابي عبد الله
احمد بن يحيى الجلا انه قال ٥ كنت راكبا جملا مرة
فقلت جل الله فسمعت الجمل يقول جل الله بلسان فصيح وروى عن
عبد الله بن ابي بكر عن ابيه ان قوما كانوا في سفر وكان فيهم رجل اذا مر
الطاير بهم فيقول اتدرون ما يقول هذا فيقولون لا فيقول يقول
كذا وكذا فيحيلنا على شي ما ندري ما هو اصادق ام كاذب ثم اتينا
على قوم فيهم ضعيفة على جمل لها وهو يرغو ويحني عنقه اليها فقال
اتدرون ما يقول هذا الجمل فقلنا لا قال انه يلعن صاحبته ويزعم
انها رحلته على مخيط وهو محزوز في سنامه قال فانتهينا اليهم فقلنا
يا هولا ان صاحبنا هذا يزعم ان هذا البعير يلعن راكبته ويزعم انها

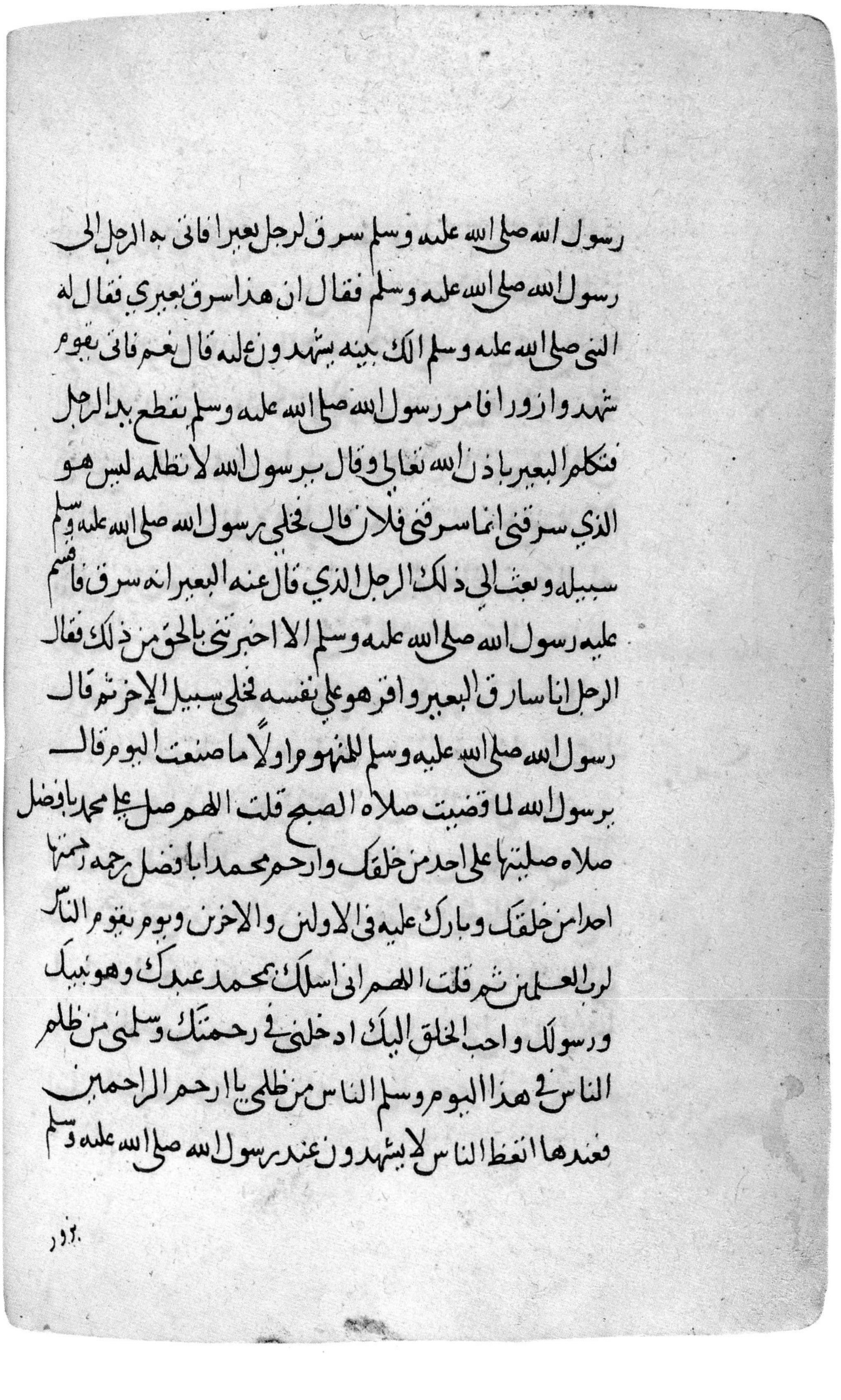
رسول الله صلى الله عليه وسلم سرق لرجل بعير فاتى به الرجل الى
رسول الله صلى الله عليه وسلم فقال ان هذا سرق بعيري فقال له
النبي صلى الله عليه وسلم الك بينة يشهدون لك قال نعم فاتى بقوم
شهدوا زورا فامر رسول الله صلى الله عليه وسلم بقطع يد الرجل
فتكلم البعير باذن الله تعالى وقال يا رسول الله لا تظلمه ليس هو
الذي سرقني انما سرقني فلان قال فخلى رسول الله صلى الله عليه وسلم
سبيله وبعث الى ذلك الرجل الذي قال عنه البعير انه سرق فاقسم
عليه رسول الله صلى الله عليه وسلم الا اخبرتني بالحق من ذلك فقال
الرجل انا سارق البعير واقر هو على نفسه فخلى سبيل الاخر ثم قال
رسول الله صلى الله عليه وسلم [illegible] والا ما صنعت اليوم قال
يا رسول الله لما قضيت صلاة الصبح قلت اللهم صل على محمد بافضل
صلاة صليتها على احد من خلقك وارحم محمدا بافضل رحمة رحمتها
احدا من خلقك وبارك عليه في الاولين والاخرين ويوم يقوم الناس
لرب العلمين ثم قلت اللهم اني اسالك بمحمد عبدك وهو نبيك
ورسولك واحب الخلق اليك ادخلني في رحمتك وسلمني من ظلم
الناس في هذا اليوم وسلم الناس من ظلمي يا ارحم الراحمين
فعندها انطق الناس لا يشهدون عند رسول الله صلى الله عليه وسلم

The manuscript opens with a frontispiece enclosing a circular pattern surrounded by eight arches. The name of the Mamluk emir Tamrāz is inscribed within the book indicating that it was intended for his library. In a rectangular frame above is the book's title: *al-Nuṭq al-mafhūm min ahl al-ṣamt al-maʿlūm* ("The Speech Understood by Those Known for Their Silence"). Below, in the same horizontal frame is the name of the very prolific author, Abū al-Faraj ʿAbd al-Raḥmān ibn ʿAlī ibn al-Jawzī (died in 1201), well-known both in public and religious life in Baghdad.

The text is copied in *naskh* script by Aḥmad ibn al-Khaṭīb al-Saʿdī and completed on Jumada II 15, 881 / October 5, 1476, most probably in Cairo, the capital of the Mamluk state.

The originality of this book lies in the fact that the instructions, the religious traditions, and wise words, transmitted in a sequence of most improbable situations totally divorced from real time and space, are supported by references to accepted literary authorities and the line of oral transmitters, as is the case with the hadith. All the instructions and advice are given by different types of living creatures, such as human beings, as well as by plants, clouds, stones, vases, mountains, etc.

The book enjoyed a certain popularity, and, as can be seen, was sought after by the Egyptian Mamluk elite. [A.Kh.]

36. Shaikhzāda ʿAṭāʾī (end of the 14th century–middle of the 15th century) Dīvān (Collected Poems)

Folio 62v.

Copied in Iran around 1470–1490
Nastaʿlīq
Paper
76 folios, 19.2 × 12.7 cm
Text: 13.2 × 8.6 cm
2 columns of 11–12 lines
3 miniatures of the Shiraz school, around 1490–1510
Accession no. B-2456
Provenance: probable gift from Prince Vassily Bebutov, around 1830.
Bibliography: Dmitrieva L.V., 1980, p. 43, no. 130; Samoilovitch N.A., 1927.

Dīvān-i Shaikhzāda ʿAṭāʾī ("Collection of Shaikhzāda ʿAṭāʾī's Poems") is a compilation of 260 poems (ghazals) by the Turkish poet ʿAṭāʾī, a native of Balkh (end of the 14th century–middle of the 15th century). He spent most of his life in Samarqand. He died and was buried in Balkh (Northern Afghanistan). This manuscript bears no mention in the colophon (folio 76v) of the copyist nor of the date of its completion. It is written in a fine, neat *nastaʿlīq*, somewhat enlarged and angular, according to the tradition of Western Iran (ʿAbd al-Karīm Khwārazmī). The manuscript was decorated in the style characteristic of the south-west in the years 1470–1490. Folio 1v contains the main frontispiece composed of two rectangles of different sizes placed side by side with a central section, framed by a gilded *band-i rūmī* motif. This carries the title and the name of the author traced in gold, in a large *naskh* script on a blue background. The entire frontispiece is embellished by a decorative plant motif (*islīmī-i bargī*). The gold inscription is surrounded by a fine black outline (*taḥrīr*). The poems are separated by scrolls decorated with loops of convolvulus (*islīmī*). The illuminations of folios 46r–46v and 76v (colophon) are decorated with golden hachures (*tashʿīr*) surrounded by a contour. [O.A.]

Folio 25v: The Departure of the King *(7.8 × 8.7 cm). The range of muted colors, the composition and small stocky silhouettes with large turbans suggest that the artist worked in the style of the Shiraz school or Turkman school of Persian painting around 1490–1510.*

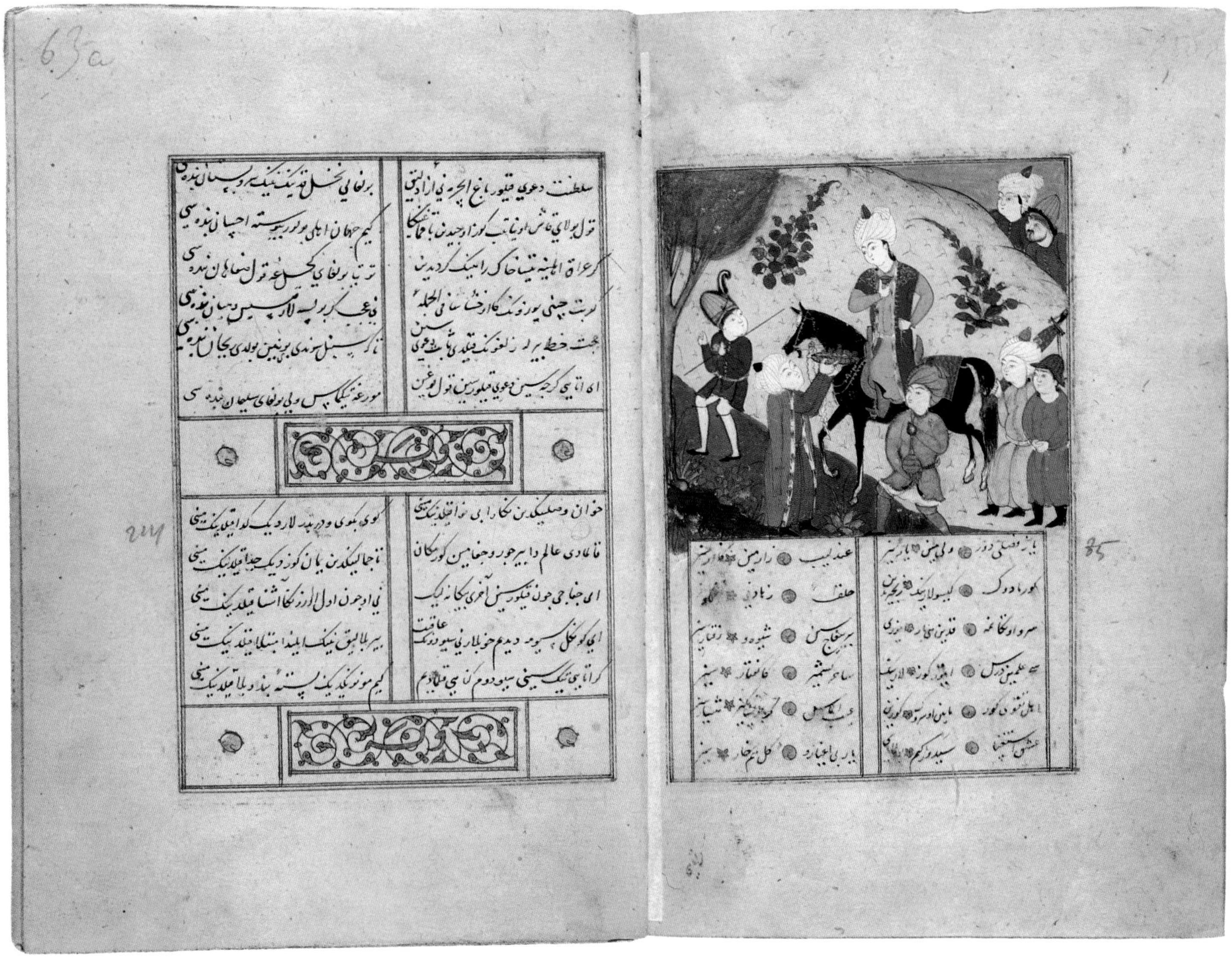

37. Ḥusain Bāiqarā
Dīvān-i Ḥusainī (1491)
(Collection of Ḥusain Bāiqarā's Poems)

Copied by an unknown calligrapher in Herat around 1540
Nastaʿlīq
Paper
54 folios, 25 × 16 cm
Text: 13.5 × 7.8 cm
2 columns of 10–11 lines
4 miniatures probably from Herat, around 1540
Accession no. B-284
Provenance: gift from V.S Golenischchev, 1910.
Bibliography: Dmitrieva L.V., 1980, p. 64, no 237.

Dīvān-i Ḥusainī is a collection of 154 lyric poems (ghazals) compiled in 1491, written by the Timurid Sultan Ḥusain Bāiqarā who reigned from 1469 to 1506.

In the colophon (folio 54v), there is no mention of the calligrapher nor the date of its completion. The manuscript is written in a beautifully neat and confident *nastaʿlīq*, by a professional scribe. The manuscript is richly decorated. Folios 2v–3r have a double-page frontispiece consisting of a single composition divided into sections, both vertically and horizontally: in the center, on a gold background is the text; above and below are rectangular panels with floral decorations in gold and colors on a gold and blue background. The same colors were used for the wide framing band with twenty scrolls in each section. Inserts have been affixed to the margins covered with gold semis. Each ghazal is separated by narrow rectangular scrolls.

The copy contains four miniatures. The double-page miniature frontispiece (folios 1v–2r) represents *The Court of the King* and *The King's Hunt* (16.5 × 9 cm each). The head-dress of the figures (*kulāh-i ḥaidarī*) indicate that the approximate time when the miniatures were painted was during the Safavid dynasty of the 16th century. The delicate and pale decoration, the harmonious contours of the mountains and hills, the style in which the plants are depicted, the simple tones and the many figures crowded neatly into the scene enable us to specify more accurately when it was painted: Herat around 1540. The miniature at folio 50v was painted during the same period by another artist, closer to the style belonging to the Tabriz school of the years 1530–1540. It is quite possible that a painter from Tabriz carried out the miniature in Herat.

The binding is in dark brown leather, embossed with plant motifs (*islīmī-i bargī*) covering the entire surface, deep-relief embossed on the entire surface. The tooled corners (*kunj*) and the central medallion (*turunj*) with two palms (*sarturunj*) are covered in gold and pink lacquer. The central field is painted with gold and transparent lacquer.

The frame consists of two fine ornamental bands (*band-i rūmī*). The binding was probably made in Turkey around 1550, perhaps for another manuscript. [O.A.]

Exterior of binding.

Folio 51r.

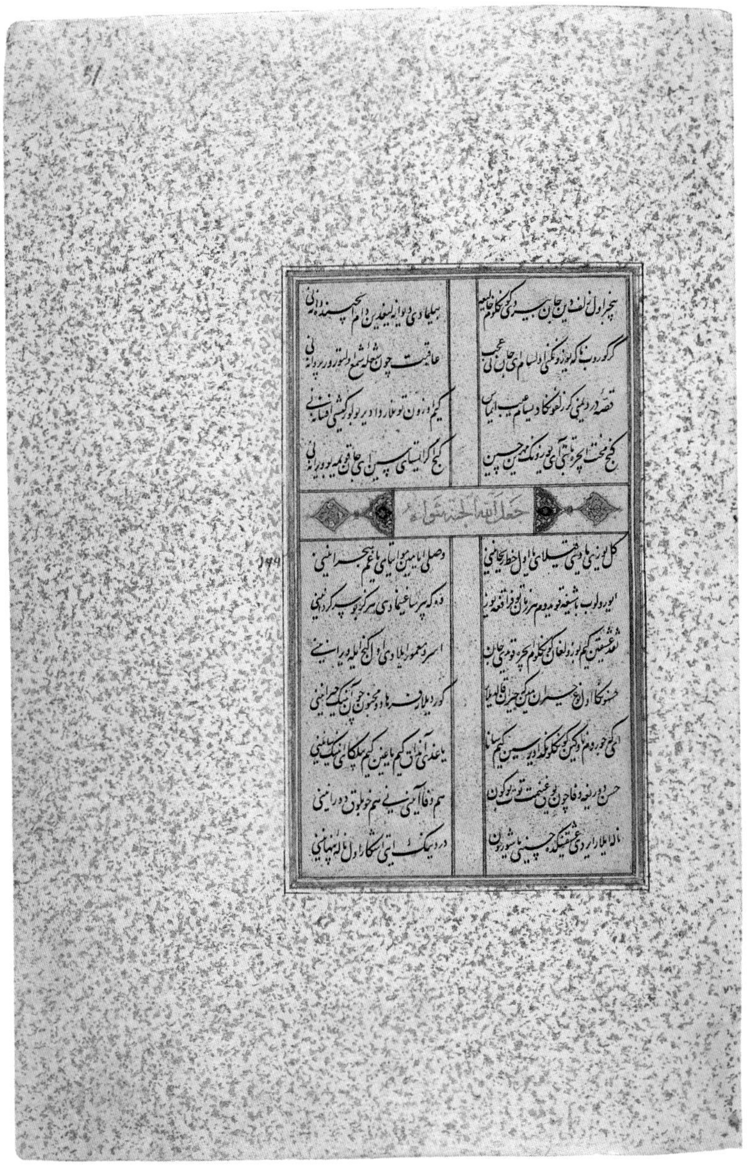

Folios 1v–2r.

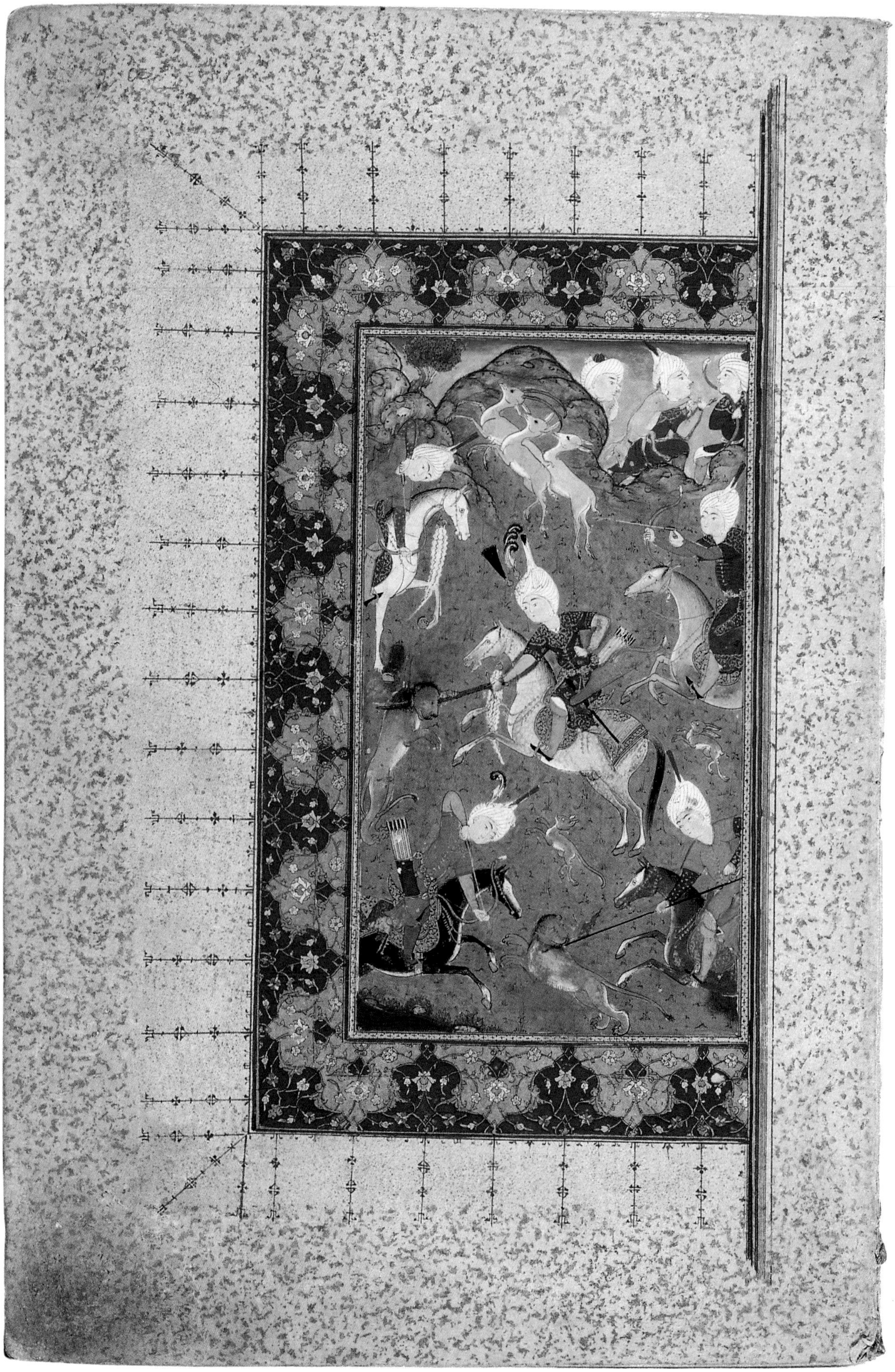

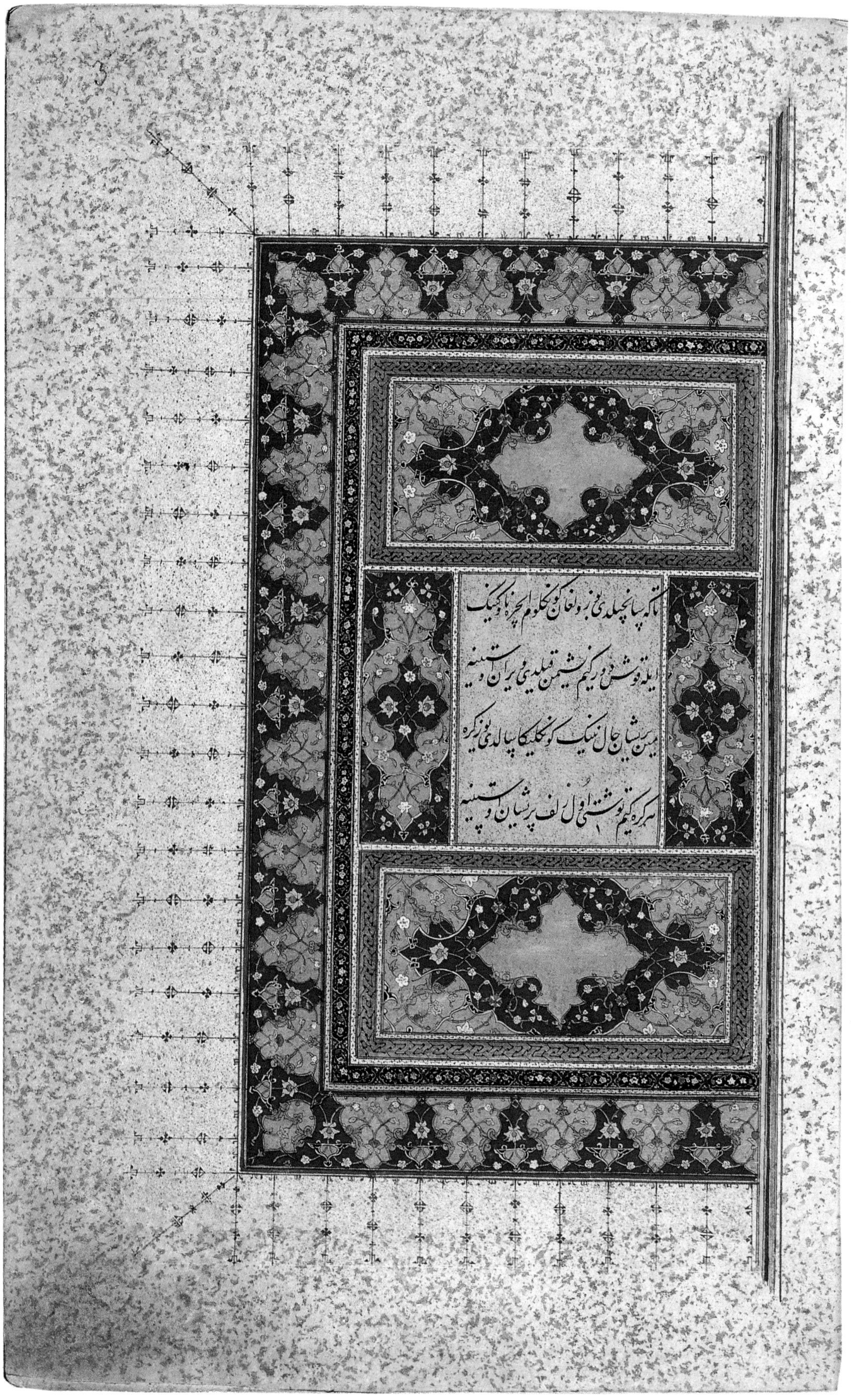

Folios 2v–3r.

Folio 33v.

ساقیا هجران خراب ایتمیش منی تولدور قدح
چون خراب اولماق کیراک باری بولای مست خراب

Folio 50v.

38. Musharrif al-Dīn ibn Muṣliḥ Sa^cdī al-Shīrāzī (died in 1292)
Gulistān (The Rose Garden)

Copied by an unknown calligrapher in Herat around 1520
Nasta^clīq
122 folios, 28.2 × 17.5 cm
Text: 18 × 10.5 cm, 12 lines to the page
4 miniatures of the Bukhara school, around 1540–1550
Accession no. C-777
Provenance: coll. of P.K. Sukhtelen, 1837.
Bibliography: Catalogue PTR, 1964, no. 3584.

Gulistān ("The Rose Garden") is a famous work on ethics, written in prose and verse by one of Persia's most popular poets, Musharrif al-Dīn ibn Muṣliḥ Sa^cdī al-Shīrāzī (died in 1292).
The manuscript is not dated, however the anonymous copyist worked in the style of the Herat tradition. The manuscript using beautiful, large and confident *nasta^clīq* was presumably finished in Herat around 1520. The introductory words, the Arabic citations and contents are in large gold and colored *naskh*. The manuscript is richly decorated: the text is framed with lines of gold and colors with large margins, colored in lemon yellow, rose, olive green, decorated with plant and animal motifs painted in gold, convolvulus loops, trees, shrubs, birds, gazelles, etc. A section of the margins (folios 116r–117v) is covered with gold semis (*zar-afshān*). In the center of folio 1r is a rosette-shaped medallion (*shamsa*) with sixteen radii with a gold and colored motif on a lapis lazuli background. In the center of the medallion is a gilded tooled oval panel. The frontispiece (*^cunvān*), consists of a rectangular panel topped by a cupola, in the same palette of colors and gold (folio 1v). The manuscript is decorated with four miniatures typical of the Transoxiana school in the years 1540–1550, probably in Bukhara. The manuscript was copied in Herat, taken as loot over to Transoxiana after an Uzbek incursion, and only then were the decorations and illustrations completed. [O.A.]

*The binding (28.3 × 17.6 cm) is of dark brown leather embossed and then gilded. There is an oval tooled medallion (*turunj*) in the center front on a gilded cardboard background on which dark pink inlays have been glued forming a plant pattern. The corners (*kunj*) are decorated with a simple incised gold line.*

Folio 27r: An Old Wrestler Defeats His Pupil *(12.3 × 13 cm), a popular tale that became a favorite subject for artists illustrating the Gulistān. A young wrestler, who thought he was invincible, boasted that he could beat his teacher who was much older than him. The latter accepts the challenge and wins by using a hold that he had not taught his presumptuous pupil.*

39. Abū al-Qāsim Firdausī al-Ṭūsī (died around 1020–1030) Shāhnāma (The Book of Kings)

Copied by the famous calligrapher Muḥammad al-Haravī on Muharram, 5 931 / November 2, 1524 in Tabriz
Nastaʿlīq
592 folios, 33.8 × 23.5 cm
Text: 25.4 × 15 cm, 4 columns of 25 lines to the page; ink, colors, gold, paper
27 miniatures most likely painted in Tabriz
Accession no. D-184
Provenance: coll. of Teaching Section of the Asiatic Department of the Russian Ministry of Foreign Affairs, 1919.
Bibliography: Catalogue PTR, 1964, no. 2299; Gyuzal'yan L.T., 1935, pp. 17, 52–57, pl. 18–22; Kerimov K., 1980, pl. 17–22; Stchoukine I., 1963, pp. 52–53, no 1.

*Upper binding cover (34 × 23 cm): dark brown leather, embossed, gilded and decorated with plant motif inlays (stylized lotus and loops of convolvulus). An oval medallion (*turunj*) in the central plate is decorated with two palm trees and the same motif on a gold background. The frame consists of a wide tooled band with four corners, eight oval scrolls and eight rosettes. On the very edge of the binding, there is a small, shallow embossed piping (*ṭarīq*) with a gilded* band-i rūmī *motif. Tabriz school of book binding from the first half of the 16th century.*

This manuscript contains the complete text of the poem, with an abridged version of the "pre-Bāisunghur" preface and the satire against the sultan Maḥmūd Ghaznavī. It was copied by the celebrated Persian calligrapher from Herat, Muḥammad al-Haravī (folio 592v), in a good assured *nastaʿlīq* of medium size. Titles of chapters are traced in *naskh* in gold (sometimes blue pigment).
The manuscript is richly decorated, but not in its entirety.
There are 27 miniatures, painted by at least five artists from the same workshop, representing three schools at the beginning and the first half of the 16th century: two painters from the Shiraz, and two painters from the local Tabriz schools. [O.A.]

Folio 5v: Firdausī Presents His Poem to the Sultan Maḥmūd Ghaznavī, in the Hope of Earning the Remuneration of Sixty Thousand Dinars *(14 × 15 cm). The painter artfully sets off the two main heroes in this scene. They are depicted with clothing and accessories from the Timurid epoch, whereas the courtiers are already dressed according to the Safavid fashion, with a high* kulāh *adorning their turbans and draped in elegant kaftans, that sweep the floor. The decoration, the composition and manner of representing the rich vegetation are very similar in style to the Shiraz school of the end of the 16th century. The miniature was painted in Tabriz by an artist from Shiraz, some time after the text of the manuscript itself was completed.*

Folio 140r: Siyāvush Playing Polo with Afrāsiyāb *(no. 8, 18.4 × 22 cm). The Prince Siyāvush disobeyed his father, Kaikāvūs, the king of the Iranians, and turned to the Turanians. Solemnly welcomed by the Turanian king, Afrāsiyāb, he took part in a polo tournament where he proved his extraordinary skill. The painter worked in the style of the Tabriz school. Certain specialists attribute this miniature to Sulṭān Muḥammad Tabrīzī, the leading painter of the Safavid manuscript workshop in Tabriz around 1510–1540; however, this attribution raises some doubt.*

Folio 251r: Gūdarz Pursuing Pīrān up a Mountain *(no. 15, 15 × 16 cm), the last episode in a series of decisive victories of the Iranians over their eternal enemies, the Turanians. The gallant Prince Pīrān, the Turanian general, preferred death to life without glory. In the middle of a fight, he lost his sword and was chased by Gūdarz up a rock, where he died from a javelin wound inflicted by the Iranian knight. The miniature is painted in two different styles. One of them tends towards the archaic Shirazi style of the 1460–1470s as exemplified in the large figures of Gūdarz, Pīrān, the arms-bearers and their horses, which are painted out of proportion to the scenery. The other manner was used to paint the landscape, the vegetation and rock formations of the mountains, brimming with faces of fantastic creatures. Together with the choice of bright colors these features point to the picture being painted in Tabriz around 1530.*

Folio 370v: The Death of King Dārā *(no. 21, 14.8 × 20 cm). After suffering defeat in his fourth battle against Iskandar, Dārā dies, stabbed by a traitor. This miniature was painted by the same artist as the previous one.*

Opposite:
Folio 388r: Iskandar Leaves in Search of the Water of Life, *detail (24.5 × 21.7 cm). Having decided to find the "Water of Life," Iskandar meets a guide by the name of Khiḍr in a town where he leaves his escort. Together they march for two days and three nights, when two paths open up in the dark. Just then Iskandar disappears, Khiḍr continues on the way and reaches the Water of Life. First he bathes, then drinks and rests. He begins his return journey, singing the praise of God. The miniature is full size and skillfully done, with numerous characters disposed in an arc around the edge of the miniature. It is in the style of the Tabriz school of the 1530s. It is strikingly different from other miniatures in the same manuscript, painted by two other artists working in the archaic style of the Shiraz school in 1460–1470. The detail and purity of line, the intensity of color used in the decoration, the manner of treating the surroundings, the costumes and expressions of the figures, create the impression of refined subtlety typical of the Tabriz court. The miniature was painted by a remarkable artist, perhaps Sulṭān Muḥammad Tabrīzī himself.*

N. 29

چنین داد پاسخ که از ماست گنج | ز شهر شما یارمندی و رنج | به بندم من این راه ایشان برای | به نیروی نیکی ده کدخدای

همه شهر گفتند کای شهریار | ز تو دور باد آز و غم روزگار | زما هر چه خواهی همه بنده‌ایم | پرستنده باشیم تا زنده ایم

سکندر بیامد نگه کرد کوه | بیاورد از آن فیلسوفان گروه

م

بفرمود کاهنگران آورند | مس و روی و سنگ گران آورند

گچ و سنگ و هیزم فزون از شمار | بیارند چندانکه باید بکار | چو اندازه بردند چیزی که خواست | چو شد ساخته کار و اندیشه راست

ز هر کشوری دانشی تند گرد | دو دیوار کرد از دو پهلوی کوه | ز بن تا سر تیغ بالای او | دو صد شاه رش بود پهنای او

40. Mīr ʿAlī al-Ḥusainī al-Kātib al-Haravī (died in 1544) Jung (1529) (Album)

Autograph produced in Bukhara in Dhu'l-Qaʿdah 935 / July 1529
Nastaʿlīq
56 folios, 23 × 13 cm
Text: 14 × 6.2 cm
2 columns per page, 8 lines by column on the right and 6 on the left
2 miniatures of the Transoxiana school around 1540–1550
Accession no. C-860
Provenance: Asiatic Department of the Russian Ministry of Foreign Affairs, 1919.
Bibliography: Akimushkin O.F., 1962; Catalogue PTR, no. 3909; Dyakonova, 1964, pp. 11, 22, pl. 9–10.

The present *Jung* ("Album") contains the lyric poems of eleven poets belonging to the literary circle of ʿAlī Shīr Navā'ī (died in 1501) and other older poets. At the end of the compilation, the author added five of his enigmas (*muʿammā*) and a short poem (*qiṭʿa*). The copyist (who was also the editor of the compilation), was a well-known calligrapher of Herat, whose skill in writing neat *nastaʿlīq* was recognized by all authorities and experts. His name, Mīr ʿAlī al-Ḥusainī al-Kātib al-Haravī (died in 1544) became a household word among calligraphers and he was respectfully called (*laqab*) "Kātib al-Sulṭānī." This manuscript was made in Bukhara in the month of Dhu'l-Qaʿdah 935 / July 1529 (folio 56r). Judging by the poem in the colophon, written by the author of the compilation, the copy was intended for the Uzbek sovereign of Bukhara, the Shaibānid ʿUbaid-Allāh Khān (died in 1533), an avid bibliophile.

Generally, this manuscript is a magnificent example of the production from the Shaibānid court of Bukhara: neat *nastaʿlīq*, elegant and confident, is beautifully written; colored margins are glued down and covered with a fine semis of gold; the text is placed in a frame of gold and colored bands. On each page, the text is decorated with two to five scrolls and decorations in an extremely varied range of colors, representing various plant motifs. The two miniatures (folios 9r, 41v) are typical of the Transoxiana school of the 1530–1540s and skillfully painted.

The binding is beautifully done in dark brown leather. The two covers are both embossed with miniatures containing a tree, animals and birds in the central section. [O.A.]

The binding (23 × 13 cm), in dark brown leather is embossed in deep relief and gilt. The central field of the inside cover depicts a scene with animals, birds and plants, surrounded by a gold band of plant motifs and four scrolls (two below and two above) containing verses. This magnificent work is in the style of the Herat school of the beninning of the 16th century. It is quite probable that it was carried out in Bukhara towards 1530 by a craftsman from Herat.

Folio 41v: Two Lovers in an Orchard in Full Bloom *(11.8 × 7.5 cm). The subject has nothing to do with a specific text in this compilation and could illustrate any ghazal proclaiming friendship, love, spring, joy, etc. The purity of line, the intensity of color and the drawing of the trees indicate a master from the Herat school at the beginning of the 16th century. In addition, the rather crude manner of treating the background and the vegetation would point to Transoxiana, perhaps Bukhara around 1530–1540. It may be suggested that this miniature, like the first (folio 9r) was either by Maḥmūd Muzahhib or by ʿAbd-Allāh, an artist working in the manner of his master.*

Folio 46v.

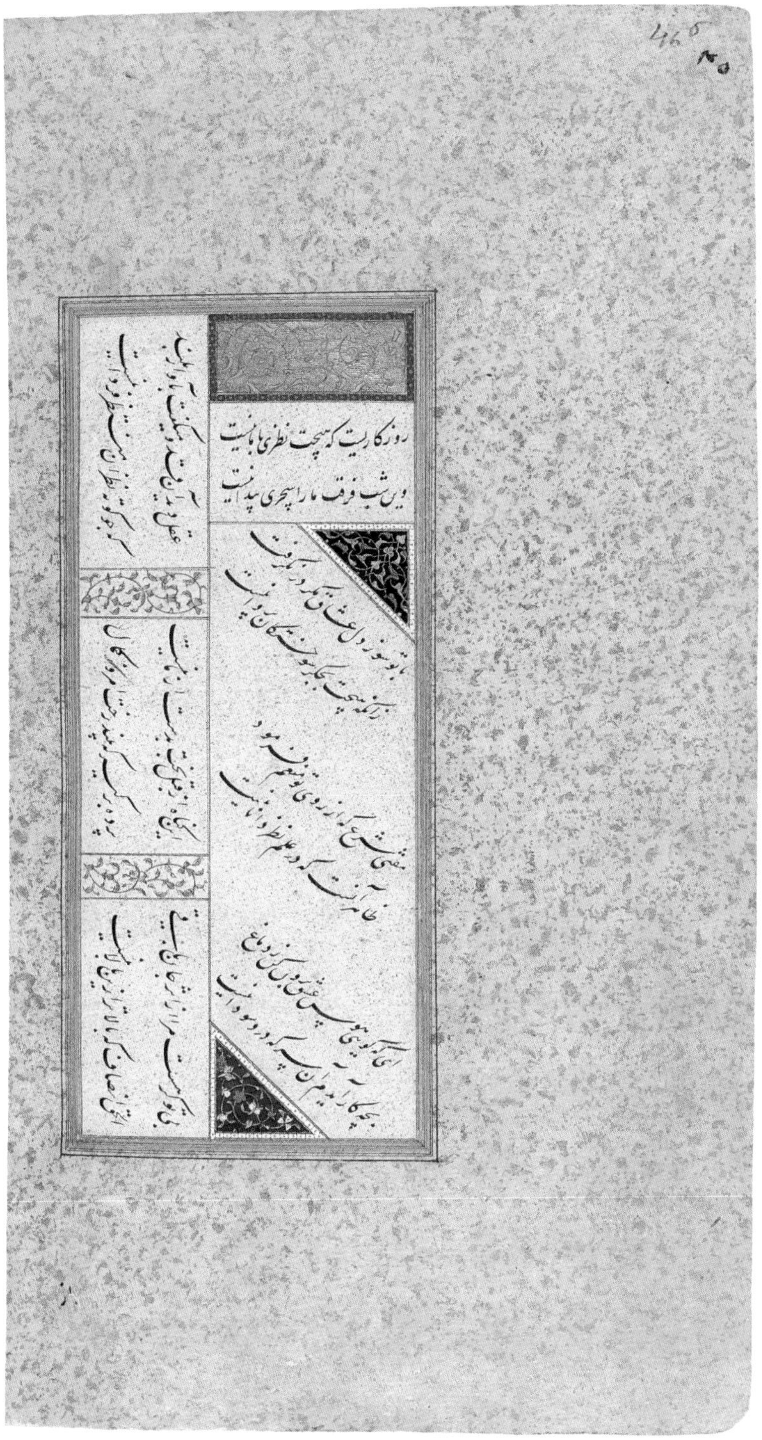

Folio 9r.

41. Amīr Āq Malik ibn Jamāl al-Dīn Shāhī al-Sabzavārī (died in 1453) Dīvān-i Shāhī (Collection of Short Poems by Shāhī)

Folios 26v–27r.

Copied by Ḥasan, court calligrapher in 938/1531–1532, in Constantinople, for the library of Sultan Sulaimān the Magnificent
Nastaʿlīq
115 folios, 16.5 × 8 cm
Text: 9.3 × 3.4 cm
6 lines to the page
Accession no. A-480
Provenance: probably a gift of Rzevuzskii around 1850, transferred from the library of the Ministry of Foreign Affairs, 1919.
Bibliography: Catalogue PTR, 1964, no. 1518.

Dīvān-i Shāhī ("Collection of Short Poems by Shāhī"), is a compilation, along traditional lines (divan), of lyric works by the Persian poet Amīr Āq Malik ibn Jamāl al-Dīn Shāhī al-Sabzavārī, who had the literary pseudonym of Shāhī (died in 1453). Apart from his popularity as a talented lyric poet, he had a very specific reputation in Persian literature because he bore the poetic nickname (*takhalluṣ*) Shāhī, given to him by the all-powerful Bāisunghur Mīrzā (died in 1433) who claimed he served him as court poet.
This manuscript was written by Ḥasan, the "court library calligrapher" (*kātib-i khazīna-i ʿāmira*) for the Ottoman sultan Sulaimān the Magnificent. At folio 1r there is a frontispiece with a gold oval medallion (*turunj*) in *thuluth* script. The copy is not as richly decorated as one might have hoped. The beginning and end of the text on each page are decorated with a gilded loop of convolvulus (*islīmī-i bargī*); the margins are covered with gold spots (*tarṣīʿ*) with a pounced pattern. There are also *taḥrīr*. A neat, enlarged *nastaʿlīq* is the personal touch of the copyist. The frontispiece is written in professional calligraphic *thuluth*.
The binding in brown leather is tastefully done (16.5 × 8 cm). The lower cover has a tooled geometric motif inside which there is an embossed plant motif. [O.A.]

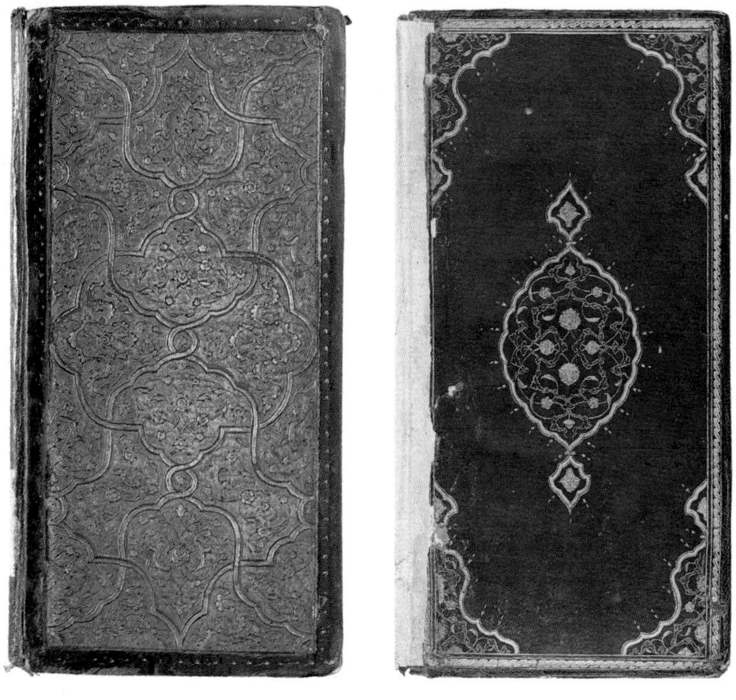

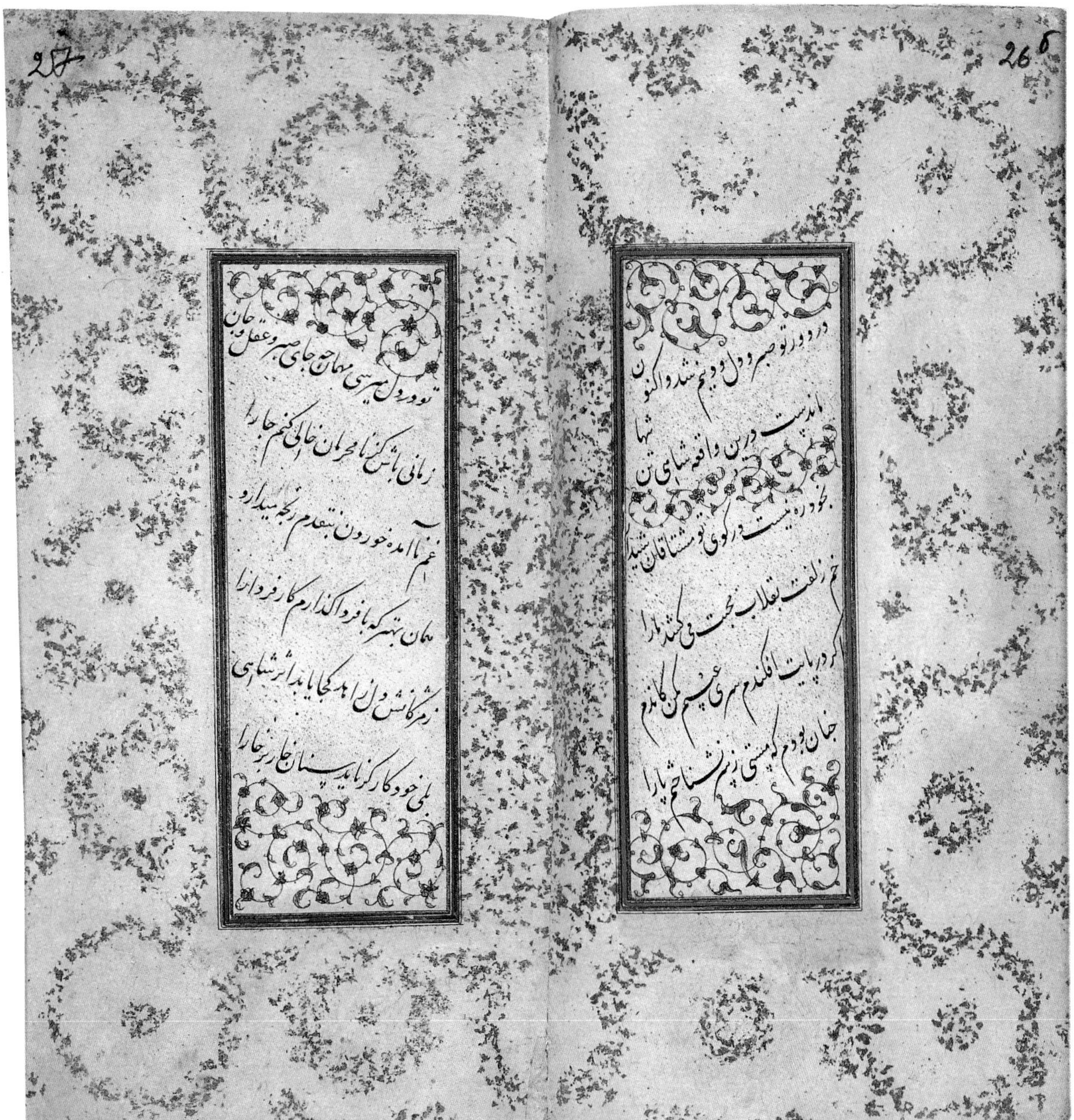

42. Musharrif al-Dīn ibn Muṣliḥ Saᶜdī al-Shīrāzī (died in 1292) Gulistān (1258) (The Rose Garden)

*Folio 12r: this decoration (35 × 23.5 cm) uses the same technique and the same range of colors as folio 1v. The text is framed with a large band made up of a colored background with plant motifs in gold and colors (*islīmī-i khaṭā'ī*). Large glued colored margins with a gilded plant ornament and scrolls in the form of clover (*shurfa*) are painted in gold.*

Unknown calligrapher
(16th century)
Nastaᶜlīq
Dense and thick paper for the margins, fine and glazed for the text
80 folios, 35 × 23.5 cm
Text: 18.3 × 9.5 cm
15 lines to the page
Richly decorated in Transoxiana (probably Bukhara), around 1540
Accession no. D-716
Provenance: a gift from The Asian People's Institute in Moscow, 1962.
Bibliography: Catalogue PTR, 1964, no. 80.

Folio 50r: this decoration (35 × 23.5 cm) uses the same technique, the same design and the same palette of colors as folios 1v and 12r. The only differences are the colored margins, the use of a single sheet of thick paper, and the three clover-scrolls with plant motifs which are not inserted, nor glued (see folios 1v, 12r), but drawn in gold and colors.

This is the famous text written in prose which was completed in 1258 by the great Persian poet Musharrif al-Dīn ibn Muṣliḥ Saʿdī al-Shīrāzī (died in 1292). The name of the calligrapher in the colophon (folio 80v) has been rubbed out. The excellent, slightly enlarged *nastaʿlīq* is by a copyist from the Herat school of Sulṭān ʿAlī al-Mashhadī. The pear-shaped stamp of the Shaibānids, with its curved top in the form of a stylized lotus flower, has also been erased.

The manuscript was very richly decorated in Transoxiana (Bukhara) in the 1540s. [O.A.]

Folio 2r: left section of the frontispiece.

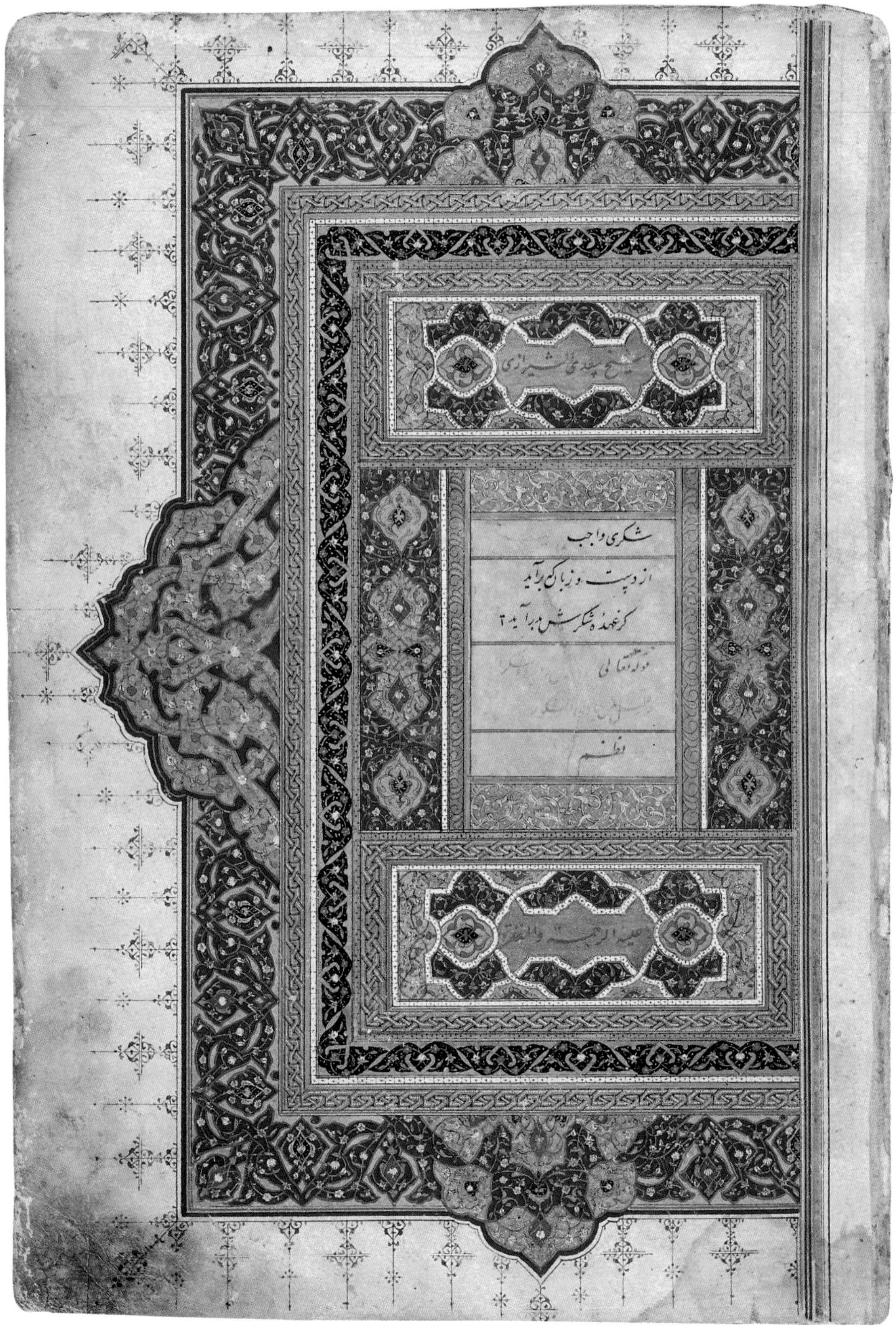

*Folio 1v: right section (35 × 22.5 cm) of this unique frontispiece (*dībācha, sarlauḥ*), a composition divided into three sections, vertically and horizontally; two rectangular panels (above and below) carrying the title of the book and the name of the author. The text is placed in the center. Each margin has a wide blue border and three scroll-indentations (*shurfa*). The main colors used are blue and gold. Ornaments are all inspired by plant motifs (leaves, flowers,* islīmī-i bargī, gul-i khaṭā'ī, band-i rūmī*). The margins are made of two sheets of colored paper glued together with a plant motif in gold, drawn or using a pouncing device on a pink, lemon yellow and light brown background. On the upper, lower and lateral sides of the margins, there are scrolls inserted in colored clover-form with a gilded plant motif (*islīmī-i marī*). The border of the insert is covered with gold. This is a perfect example of work by a decorator from the Herat and Bukhara schools around 1540. The manuscript is decorated in an exceptionally elegant and tasteful manner.*

43. Aḥmad ibn Tāj al-Dīn, literary pseudonym: Aḥmadī (1334–1412) Kitāb-i iskandarnāma (1390) (The Book of Iskandar [Alexander the Great])

Folios 1v–2r.

Copied by Muḥammad Kātib
in Shiraz in 948/1541–1542
Nastaᶜlīq
259 folios, 24 × 15 cm
Text: 15.5 × 7.5 cm
2 columns of 13–15 lines
21 miniatures of the Shiraz
school, around 1550
Accession no. B-277
Provenance: coll. of Kondakov,
1990.
Bibliography: Dmitrieva L.V.,
1980, pp. 35–36, no. 96;
Nuryakhmetov A.H., 1965,
pp. 146–148.

Kitāb-i iskandarnāma ("The Book of Iskandar ([Alexander the Great]") is a poem (*masnavī*) composed in 1390 in Turkish by Aḥmad ibn Tāj al-Dīn (1334–1412), who wrote under the literary pseudonym of Aḥmadī.

This copy is of an abridged version of the poem, copied by Muḥammad Kātib, the famous calligrapher from Shiraz in 948/1541–1542 (folio 259r). It was ordered by the emir of the Dhulqādir tribe, Khāzin Shāh Qulī beg (folio 259r), in a medium-size, clear, confident and compact *nastaʿlīq* script in the tradition of the Shiraz school of the mid-16th century.

The manuscript is well decorated, the frontispiece is on a double page spread (*dībācha*, folios 1v–2r) made up of a single composition, divided into three sections both vertically and horizontally, with the text in the central part. It is decorated with gold dots (*tarṣīʿ*) with a black and gold border (*taḥrīr*), and colored plant motifs on a gold and cobalt blue background. On certain folios, the copyist has written the text in the form of a cross (*ʿhalīpā*). It has twenty one miniatures from the Shiraz school of the mid-16th century. [O.A.]

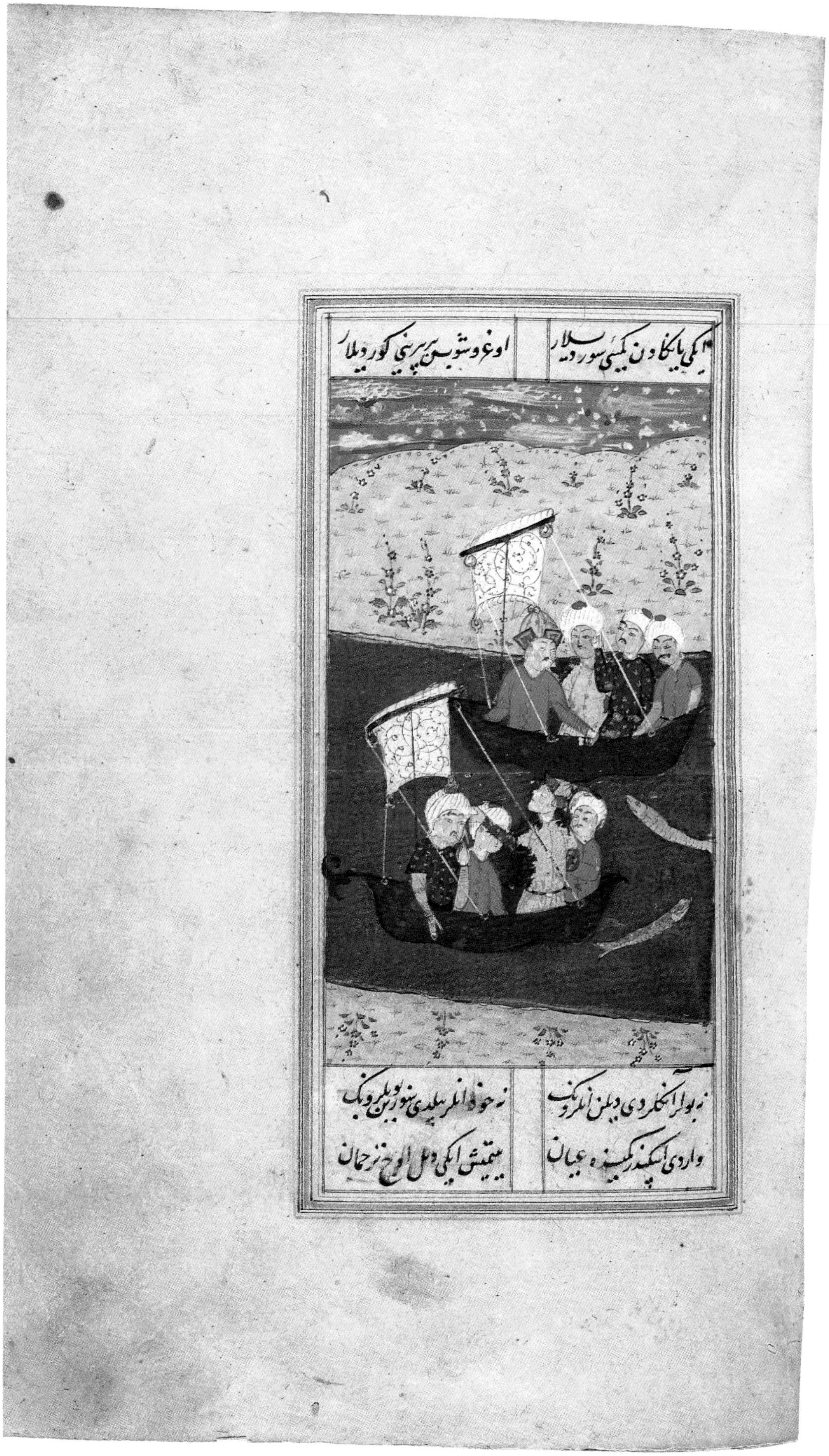

Folio 165r: Iskandar Takes to the Sea to Visit Foreign Lands *(no. 16, 11 × 6.5 cm).*

Folio 248r: Iskandar on a Leopard Hunt *(no. 20, 12.5 × 7.5 cm).*

44. Abū Muḥammad Ilyās ibn Yūsuf ibn Zakī ibn Mu'ayyad Niẓāmī Ganjavī (died in 1209–1210) Khamsa (Quintet)

Copied by Muḥammad ibn Qavām al- Shīrāzī, known as Ḥammāmī, on 29 Jumada II 950 / September 1543, probably in Shiraz
Nasta'līq
365 folios, 32 × 20.5 cm
Text: 19 × 9.5 cm
4 columns of 19–20 lines to the page
24 miniatures of the Shiraz school, around 1550
Accession no. D-212
Provenance: coll. of the Asiatic Department of the Russian Ministry of Foreign Affairs, 1919, no. 306.
Bibliography: Catalogue PTR, 1964, no. 1199; Dodkhudoeva L.N., 1980, p. 150, no. 81:55; p. 159, no. 94:46; p. 191, no. 143:57; p. 219, no. 184:71; p. 279, no. 313:37; p. 285, no. 328:11.

Folios 2r–1v.

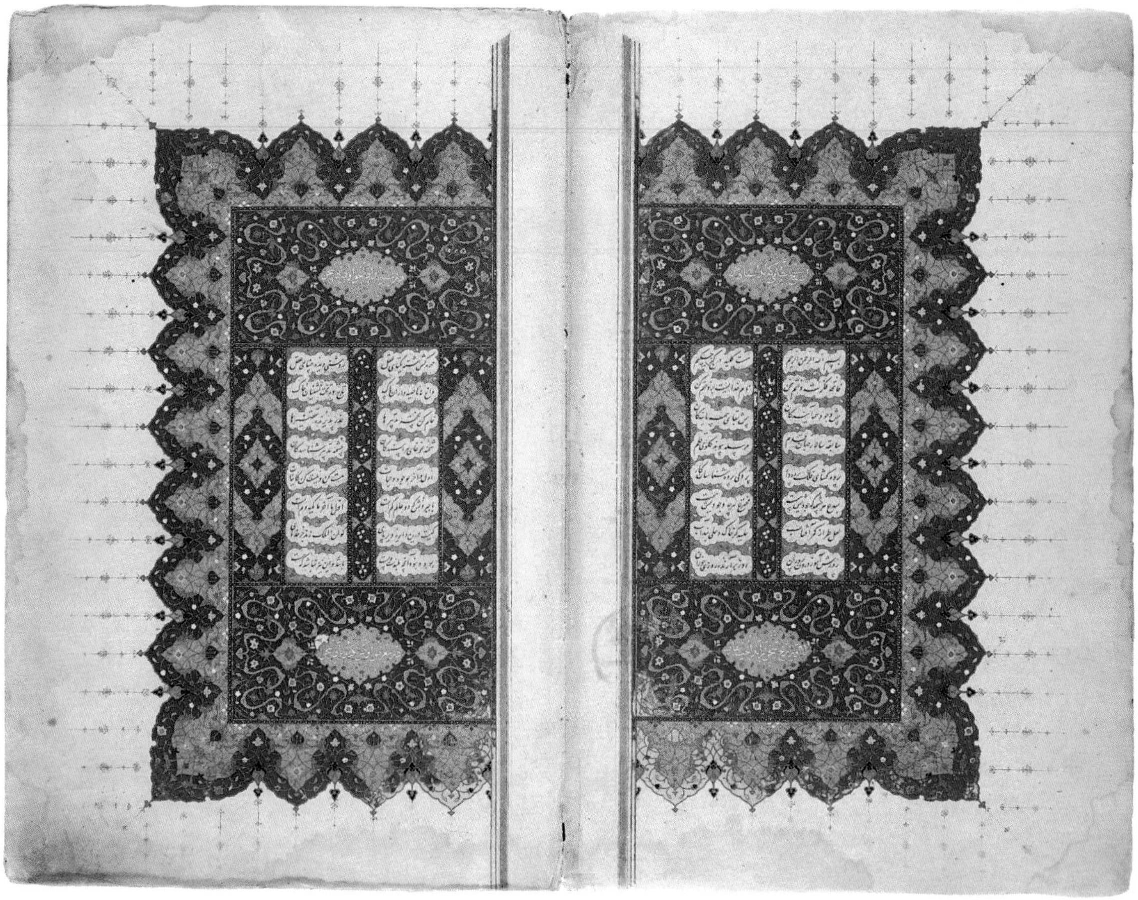

The "Quintet" was written by the illustrious Persian poet Abū Muḥammad Ilyās ibn Yūsuf who went by the name of Niẓāmī, originally from the town of Ganja. This copy was made by the famous Shirazi calligrapher Muḥammad ibn Qavām al-Shīrāzī, known as Ḥammāmī, on 29 Jumada II 950 / September 1543 (folio 365r), probably in Shiraz, in a fine and neat *nasta'līq*, assured and compact, typical of the 16th-century Iranian school from the west and southwest.
This manuscript is richly decorated with a frontispiece on a double page (*dībācha*, folios 1v–2r), five ordinary frontispieces (*'unvān, sarlauḥ*), 24 miniatures from the Shiraz school of the mid-16th century; dark brown leather binding, embossed then gilded, with inlaid plant ornaments. [O.A.]

Folio 79v: Shīrīn Arriving at Mount Bisutūn *(no. 6, 13 × 20 cm), a scene taken from the second poem of Niẓāmī, entitled* Khusrau and Shīrīn, *written in 576/1180–1181. Farhād built a road across mount Bisutūn. When she learnt of the heroic exploits of the mason, Shīrīn came to find him, treated him to milk and spoke to him. The miniature, typical of the traditions of the Shiraz school of the mid-16th century, depicts the meeting of the two in front of Mount Bisutūn.*

Folio 91r: Khusrau in Front of Shīrīn's Castle *(no. 7, 14 × 20 cm), another episode from the same poem; having heard of the charms of a beauty from Isfahan, named Shakar, Khusrau visits her and enjoys her company, then incapable of forgetting Shīrīn, he hurries back to her castle in order to seek her pardon, but in vain.*

Folio 150r: Majnūn in the Desert Amid Ferocious Beasts *(no. 8, 14 × 19.5 cm), scene taken from the third poem of Niẓāmī,* Lailā and Majnūn, *that was completed in 584/1188–1189. Wandering in the desert, Majnūn makes friends with the wild animals and takes care of them. In return, they offer their love and fidelity.*

Folio 212r: Bahrām Gūr Visits the Slav Princess in the Red Pavilion *(no. 15, 14 × 27 cm).*

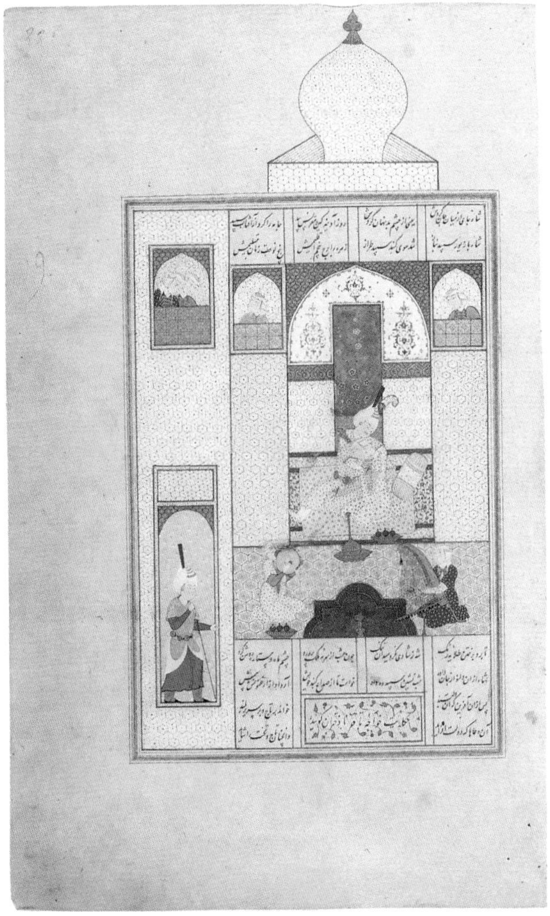

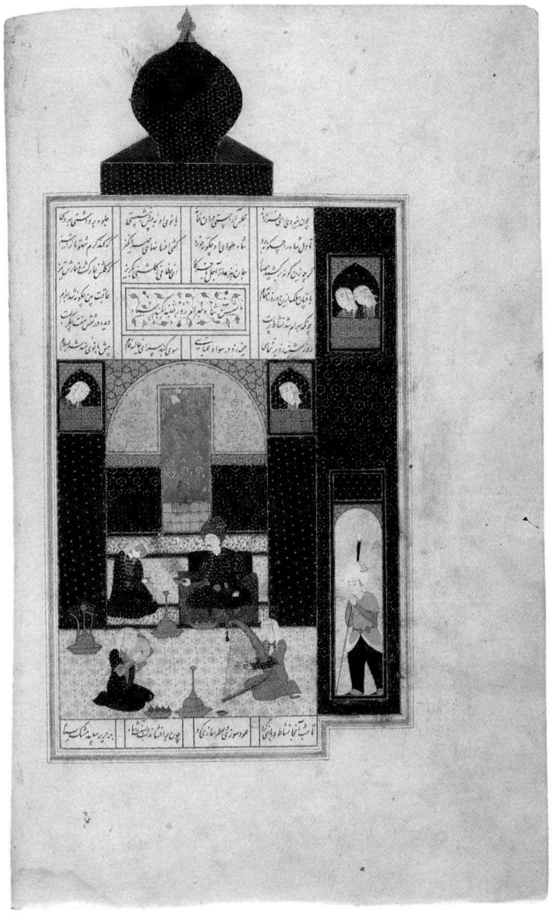

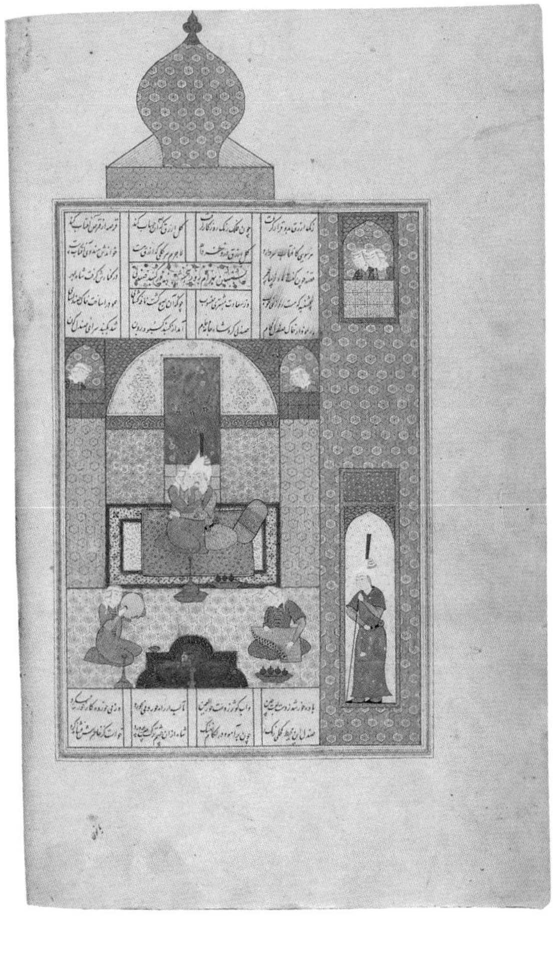

Folio 226r: Bahrām Gūr Visits the Iranian Princess in the White Pavilion *(no. 18, 14 × 26.5 cm).*

Folio 198v: Bahrām Gūr Visits the Indian Princess in the Black Pavilion *(no. 13, 13.5 × 26.5 cm), episode taken from the fourth poem of Niẓāmī,* Haft paikar *("The Seven Portraits"), composed in 593/1196–1197. Bahrām Gūr, the mythicized Sasanian king of Iran Bahram V, knight and bon vivant, married seven beautiful princesses from different countries. For each one, the architect Shīda built a pavilion in the colors of the country. When the king visited them, they told him a story.*

Folio 221v: Bahrām Gūr Visits the Princess of Rūm in the Sandalwood Pavilion *(no. 17, 14 × 26.5 cm).*

Folio 205v: Bahrām Gūr Visits the Princess of Turkestan in the Yellow-Gold Pavilion *(no. 14, 14 × 27 cm).*

Folio 339r: Iskandar with Seven Wisemen Whom He Has Invited to Discuss the Universe and the Laws That Govern It *(no. 23, 10.5 × 13 cm), episode from the fifth poem of Niẓāmī,* Iskandarnāma, *finished in 597/1200–1203.*

Opposite:
Folio 353r: The Voyage of Iskandar Across the Sea of China, *detail (no. 24, 17 × 23 cm).*

45. Abū Ṭāhir Muḥammad ibn Yaᶜqūb al-Fīrūzābādī al-Shīrāzī (died in 1415)
al-Qāmūs al-muḥīṭ wa al-qābūs al-wasīṭ (The Surrounding Ocean and the Middle Spring)

Copied by Sulaymān ibn Yūnus ibn Khaṭṭāb in 1614
Arabic
476 folios, 27.5 × 18 cm
Accession no. C-738
Provenance: Unknown
Bibliography: Brockelmann C., II, 1902, p. 181, 2, no. 1; Rosen V.R., 1877, no. 153.

The lexical wealth of the Arabic language, a subject of surprise to many people, has not yet been satisfactorily interpreted. The compilation of dictionaries, complete and partial, started in the 8th century and became the favorite occupation of many philologists in various regions of the Muslim world. Dictionaries and their creators enjoyed great authority. One of the most reputed dictionaries was *al-Qāmūs al-muḥīṭ wa al-qābūs al-wasīṭ* ("The Surrounding Ocean and the Middle Spring"), by Abū Ṭāhir Muḥammad ibn Yaᶜqūb al-Fīrūzābādī al-Shīrāzī. During his long life, he lived in Iran, Syria, Turkey, Iraq and Arabia. He died in 1415. His literary work is vast, but it is this dictionary that takes pride of place, a dictionary whose title became a common name (*qāmūs*: dictionary). The text, which also contains a wealth of information, became a sort of memory aid for practically all Muslim scholars during the 15th–19th centuries. Obviously, copies were in high demand and very widespread. This manuscript is a spectacular example of the long and applied work of Sulaymān ibn Yūnus ibn Khaṭṭāb who copied the complete text of *al-Qāmūs* in a neat *naskh* script, scrupulously respecting all diacritical and vocalization marks. It is dated 1614. The beginning is decorated with a colored frontispiece and a *ᶜunvān* above folio 1v. The titles of the chapters are enclosed in colored frames, the titles of articles and vocables are written in larger letters. The text of the dictionary itself takes up 471 sheets. Folios 472r–476r consist of a short treatise on Arabic philology by the author. [A.Kh.]

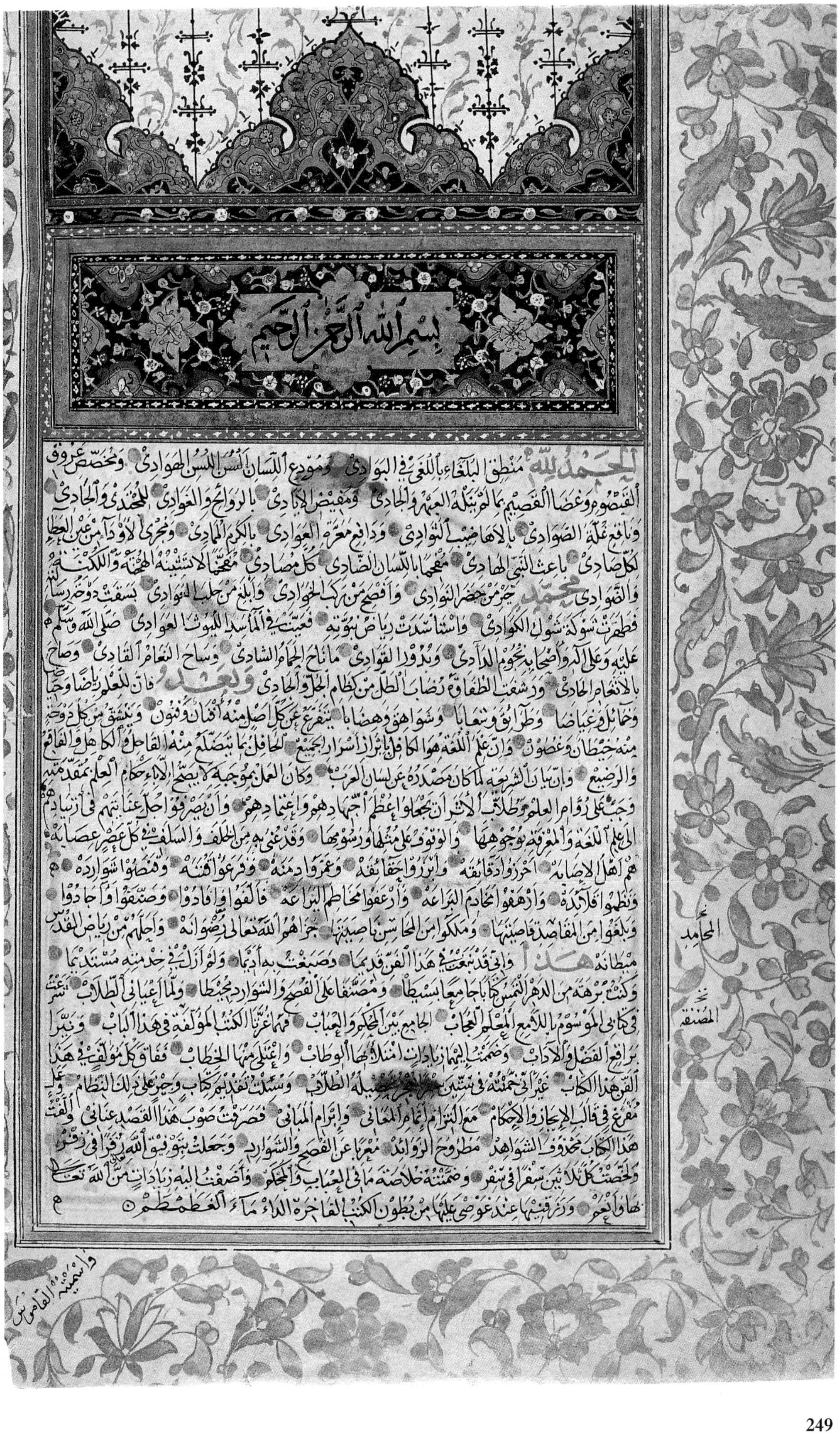
بسم الله الرحمن الرحيم

Folio 1v: the first page of the Arabic vocabulary al-Qāmūs al-muḥīṭ wa al-qābūs al-wasīṭ, *by Abū Ṭāhir al-Fīrūzābādī, crowned by a* ʿunvān. *The text was copied with great care and entirely vocalized.*

Folio 1r: frontispiece of the Arabic vocabulary al-Qāmūs al-muḥīṭ wa al-qābūs al-wasīṭ, *by Abū Ṭāhir al-Fīrūzābādī.*

Folios 2v–3r: pages of the Arabic vocabulary al-Qāmūs al-muḥīṭ wa al-qābūs al-wasīṭ, *by Abū Ṭāhir al-Fīrūzābādī with the chapter title enclosed within a colored frame.*

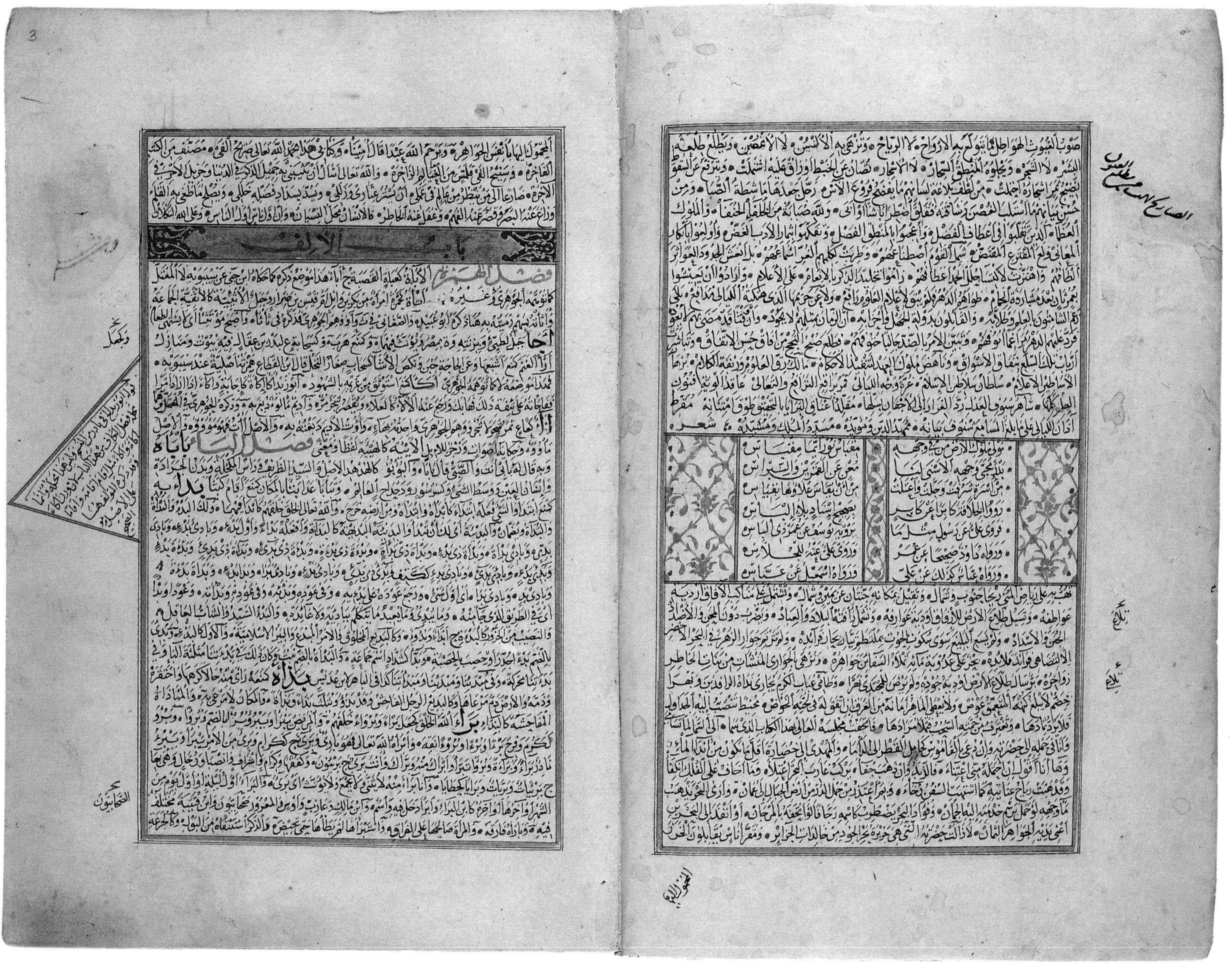

46. Kamāl al-Dīn Ḥusain ibn ᶜAlī Vā'iẓ al-Kāshifī (died in 1504) Akhlāq-i Muḥsinī (The Ethics of Muḥsin)

Copied by ᶜAbd al-ᶜAzīz
around 1640
Nastaᶜlīq
Paper with dense, thick, glossy, cream-tinted margins; dense, fine, glossy and slightly yellowed paper
219 folios, 26.8 × 16 cm
Text: 16.5 × 9.8 cm
12 lines to the page
10 miniatures of the post-Rizā school of Isfahan around 1640
Accession no. C-633
Provenance: coll. of R. Graf, 1867, no. 4
Bibliography: Catalogue PTR, 1964, no. 71.

Folio 97r.

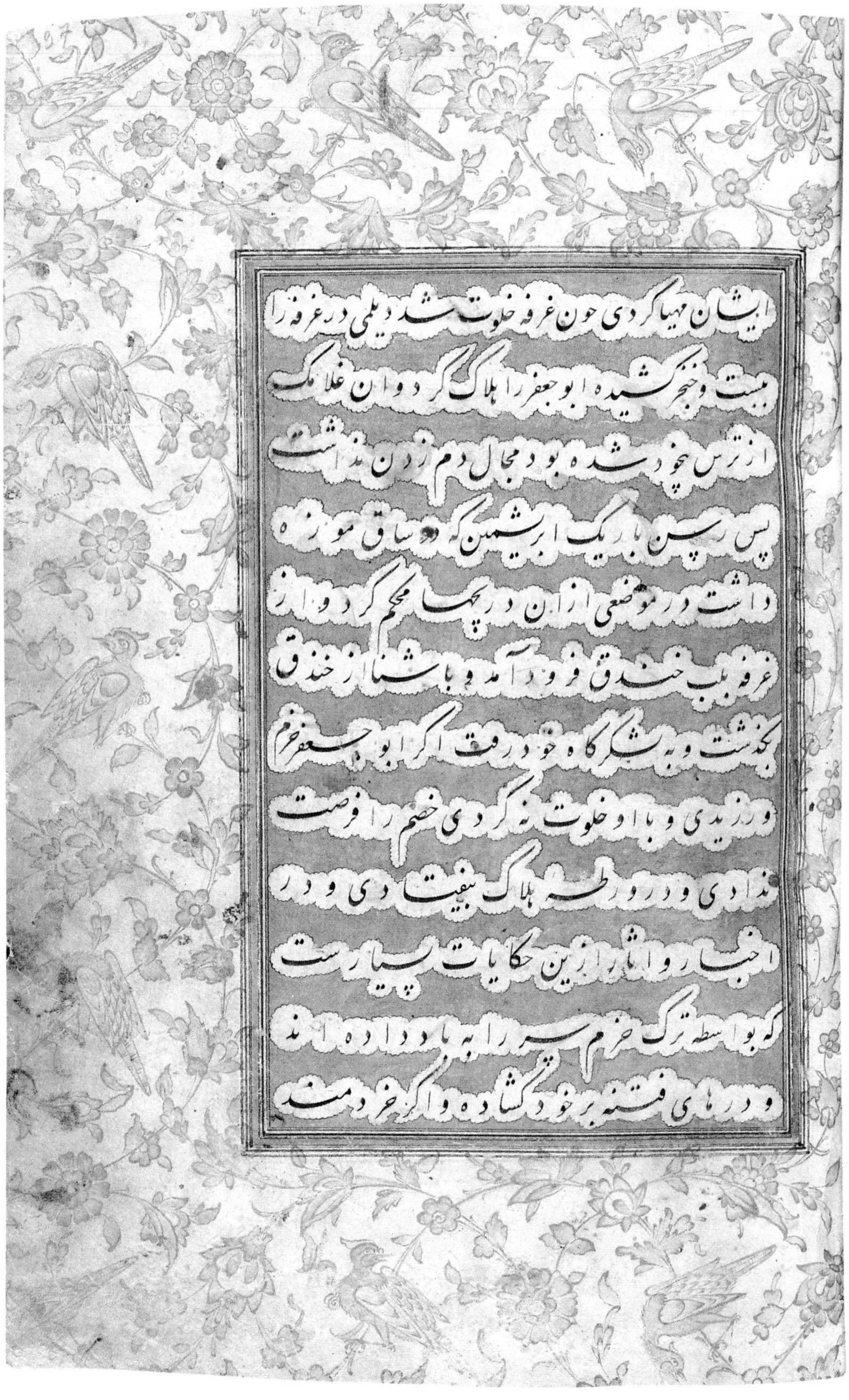

Folio 96r: Crossing a Flooded River.

Akhlāq-i Muḥsinī ("The Ethics of Muḥsin") is a work devoted to Muslim ethics, illustrated by parables and historic anecdotes. The author, a famous Persian man of letters, Kāmal al-Dīn Ḥusain Ibn ʿAlī Vā'iẓ al-Kāshifī (died in 910/1504–1505) composed this opus in 1501–1502.

The copyist, ʿAbd al-ʿAzīz (folio 219r) completed this manuscript in Isfahan around 1640, in a large, confident *nastaʿlīq* script. It is richly decorated and illustrated with ten miniatures belonging to the Isfahan school from the post-Riẓā-i ʿAbbāsī period of the 1640–1650s. Five of them take up the whole page. All the chapter titles, Qur'anic citations, the hadiths and introductory words, are in a gold and painted calligraphic *naskh* script (sometimes *rayḥān*). The text opposite the pages with miniatures is interspersed with golden scrolls (*tarṣī*), surrounded by a fine black line (*taḥrīr*); the margins are decorated with plant or animal motifs (*islīmī-i bargī, gul-i khaṭā'ī*). We believe that the binding in lacquer dates from the 1820–1830s (Iran). [O.A.]

47. Qūja Ḥusain (Būsnalī Ḥusain efendi) (died around 1650) Badā'i^c al-vaqā'i^c (Extraordinary Events)

Folios 224v–225r.

Copied by the author around 1640–1650
Naskh
Thick, fine, white paper of European fabrication
517 folios, 29 × 19 cm
Text: 23 × 12 cm
25 lines to the page; black ink, watercolors, gold
Accession no. C-564
Provenance: coll. of P. Petrovsky, 1862
Bibliography: Tveritinnova A.S. and Petrosyan Y.A. (eds), 1961.

Bada'iʿ al-vaqā'iʿ ("Extraordinary Events") is the second volume of a universal history dating from the time of the *bailak* ʿUthmān in Asia Minor, to the end of the reign of Sultan Selīm I (1512–1530). The author, Qūja Ḥusain, also known as Būsnalī Ḥusain efendi (died around 1649–1650), was head of the chancellory for the divan of Sultan Murād IV (1623–1640). There is no mention in the colophon (folio 517v) either of the copyist's name, or when the copy was completed. The large calligraphic *naskh*, clear and confident, is typically Turkish.
Written by the author, partially corrected by him, and partially under his supervision, this volume was probably carried out in Istanbul around 1640–1650. It is modestly decorated, the text is framed within two bands, one golden, the other blue; the names of Muslim personalities, citations from the Qur'an, hadiths and all titles are in red or white. It has a small, unassuming frontispiece (*ʿunvān*) in gold with a plant motif, crowned with a low cupola.

The binding is of Turkish manufacture, of cardboard covered with dark brown leather, with an embossed central medallion (*turunj*) decorated with plant motifs inlaid on a gold background (*islīmī-i bargī, gul-i khaṭā'ī*). [O.A.]

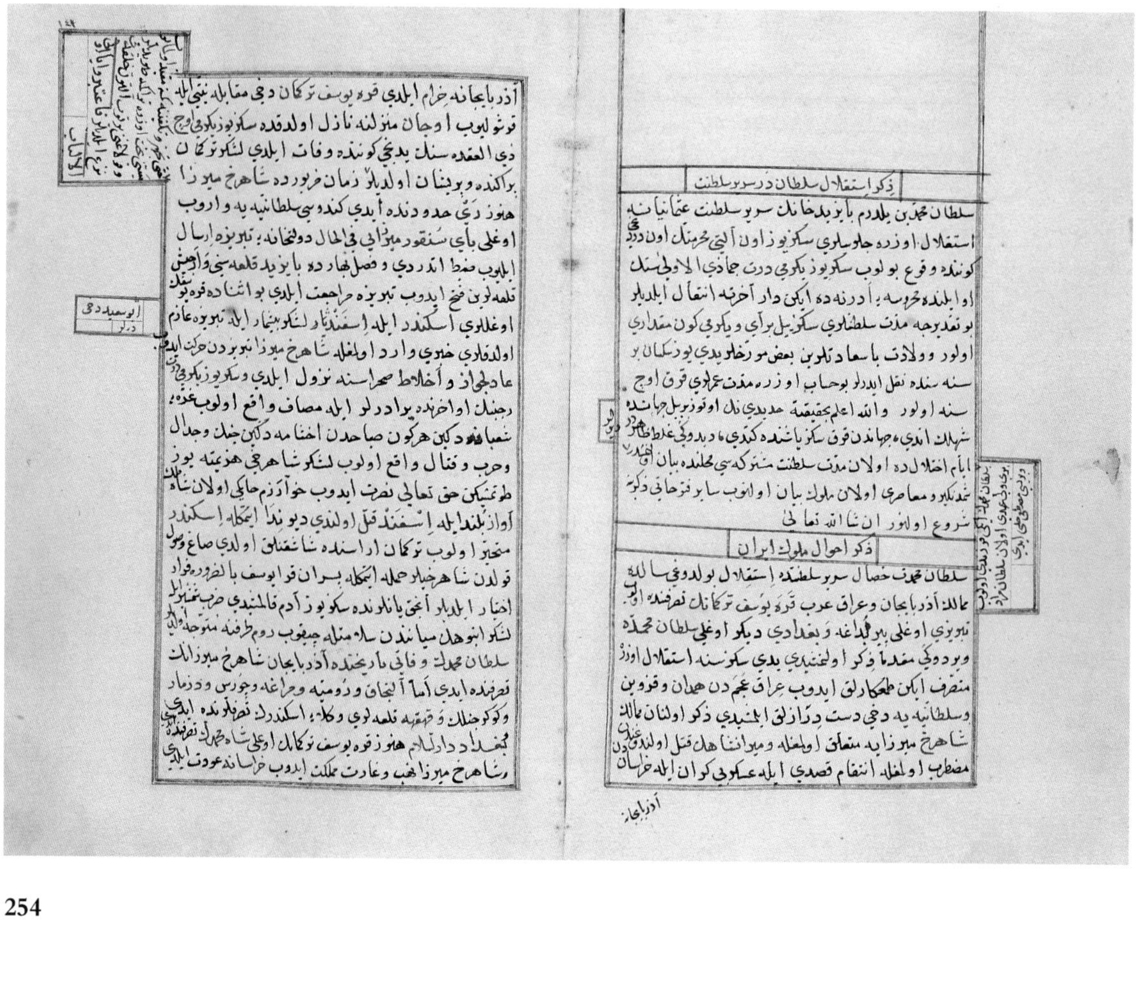

48. The Gospel according to St. Matthew

Copied by Būlus al-Ḥalabī
in 1654 at Kolomna,
near Moscow
Arabic
European paper
150 folios, 18 × 12.5 cm
Black and red ink
Accession no. B-1214
Provenance: gift of George IV, patriarch of Antioch, to Tsar Nicolas II (1868–1918); transferred in 1919 from the Winter Palace.
Bibliography: Graf G., 1944, p. 147, no. 2; Khalidov A.B., 1986, no. 10373; Krachkovskii I.Y., 1927; Krachkovskii I.Y., IV, 1960, p. 429, no. 6.

This manuscript of the Gospel according to St. Matthew is proof of the close ties that existed from time to time between the Orthodox Russian and Arabic churches. There is nothing exceptional about the text, it is an example of traditional canonical text, a preface added by the copyist and a general introduction by Ibn al-ᶜAssāl to accompany his Arabic translation of the Four Gospels. This exerpt, taken from a Coptic-Arabic manuscript dating from 1260, was copied from an autograph manuscript of the translator.

What is extraordinary, however, is that the manuscript was produced near Moscow, in the town of Kolomna. It was copied by the archdeacon Būlus al-Ḥalabī (Pavel Halebskii) when he was in Russia with his father, the patriarch of Antioch Macarius in 1654.

The binding was made at the same time as the manuscript with the assistance of Russian master craftsmen, out of leather of excellent quality, reddish in color, plated with silver on the front cover. In the center is a silver cross with floral decoration, and in the corners, angels with wings and halos, separated by six small decorations. In the middle of the two binding covers, one can see where a lock has been mounted and later broken and lost. [A.Kh.]

Binding.

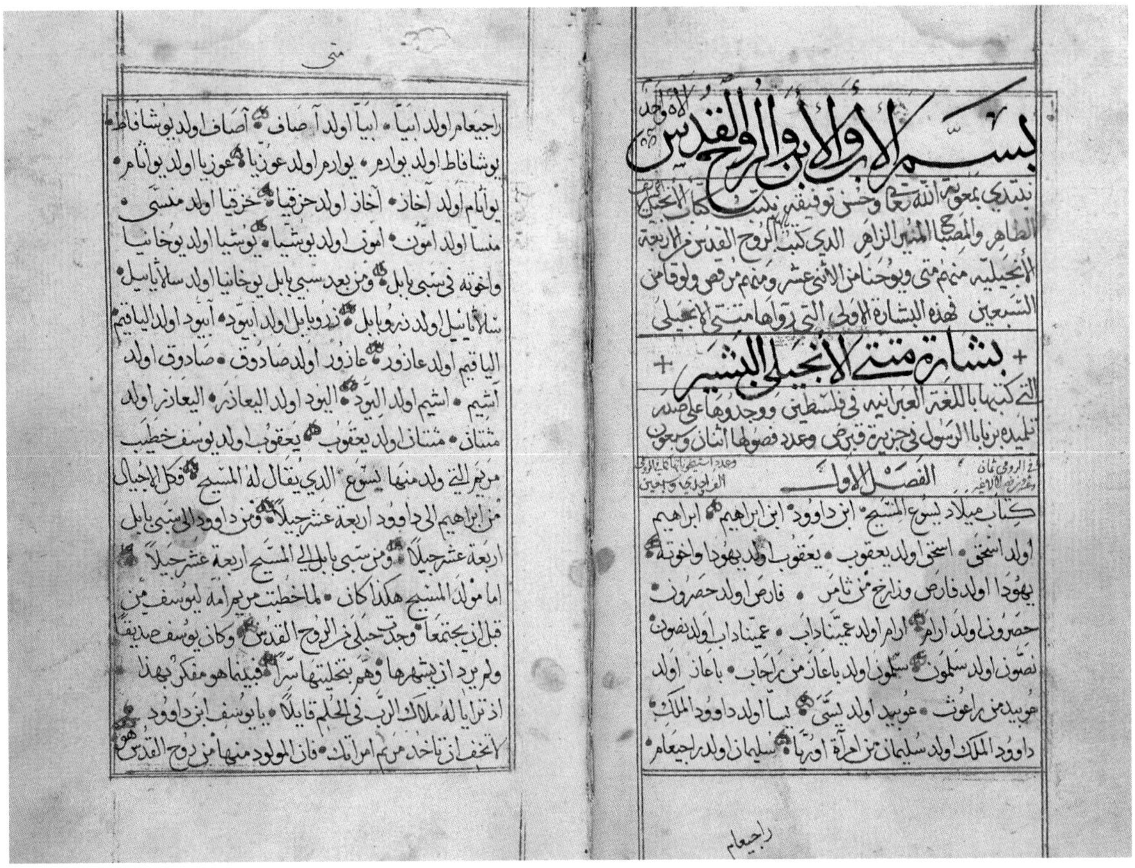

Folios 5v–6r.

49. Dioscorides (1st century) Kitāb-i ḥashā'ish (The Book of Herbs)

*Folio 50v (20 × 10 cm): brown and black bulls (*baqar^{c}*), detail.*

Persian translation by Ghiyās al-Dīn Muḥammad Razvī (or Razavī) from the Arabic translation by Isḥāq ibn Ḥunayn of the Greek text of Dioscorides' *De Materia Medica*, from the Syriac translation. Copied by an unknown scribe in Jumada II 1068 / March 1658, probably in Isfahan
Nasta^{c}līq
Paper
174 folios, 38 × 24.5 cm
Text: 25.5 × 16.5 cm
23 lines to the page; ink, watercolors, and 490 colored drawings
Accession no. D-143
Provenance: coll. of R. Graf, 1867, no. 38.
Bibliography: Catalogue PTR, 1964, no. 3364.

Kitāb-i ḥashā'ish ("The Book of Herbs"), a work on pharmacology, is a Persian translation of the Arabic translation that was from a Syrian translation of Dioscorides' original Greek book written in the 1st century, entitled *De Materia Medica.* The Persian translation was carried out by Ghiyās al-Dīn Muḥammad Razvī (or Razavī); the Arabic translation by Isḥāq ibn Ḥunayn (died in 298/910–911. This manuscript was copied by an unknown calligrapher in Jumada II 1068 / March 1658 (folio 173v), probably in Isfahan, in a large, clear and confident *nasta^{c}līq* script from the Isfahan school of the post-Mīr ^{c}Imād period (died in 1615). It is beautifully decorated and illustrated with 490 colored drawings representing herbs, plants and animals.

They are drawn with remarkable precision by an unknown master. It is possible that the artist drew some subjects from nature, without blindly following the Arabic model. [O.A.]

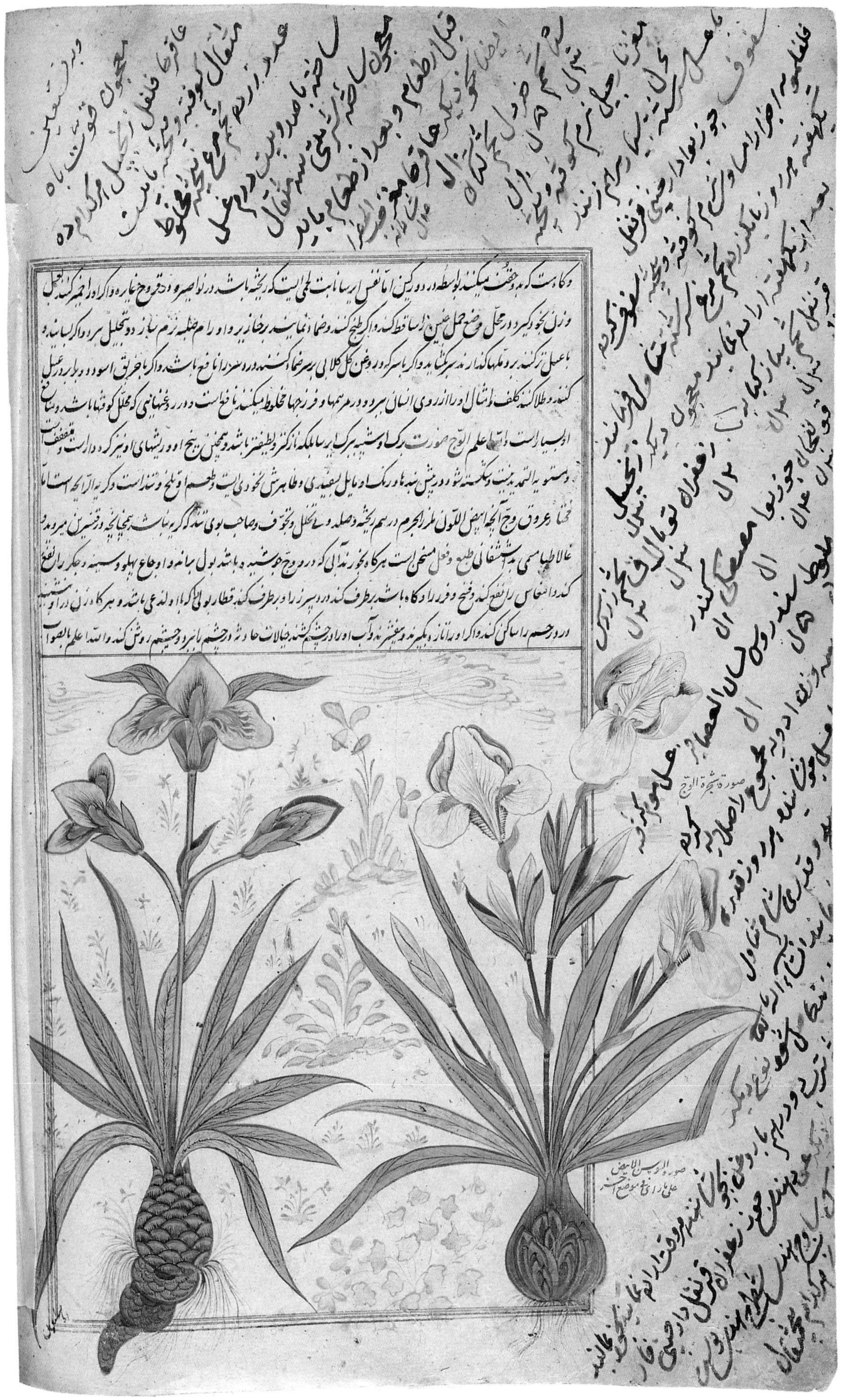

Folio 36v: I
Garden Lily
their roots.

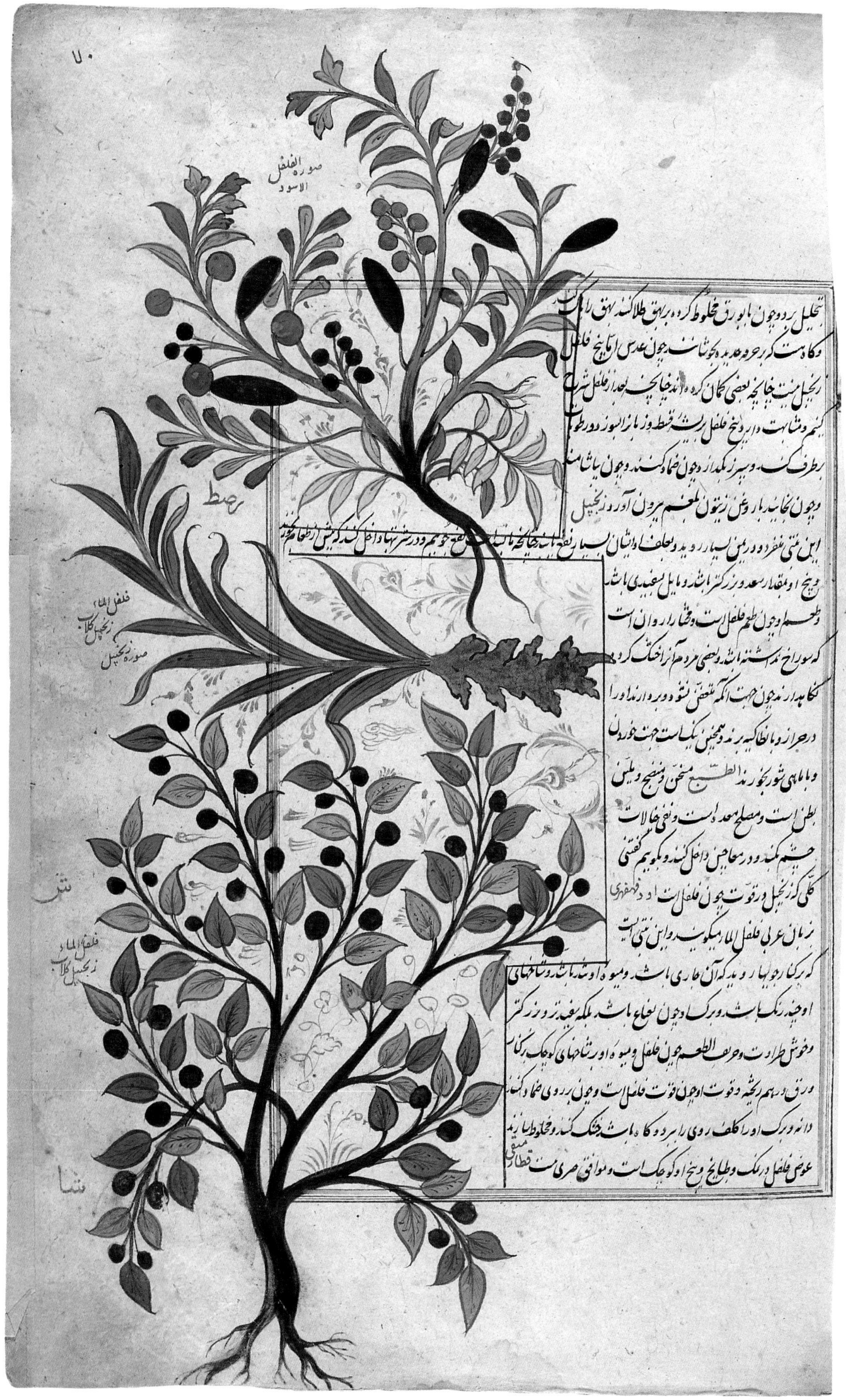

Folio 87r.

Folio 157r (31 × 23.5 cm) and folio 117r (31.5 × 15 cm): the first has a description and drawing of three plants, the second of four.

Folio 36r (20.5 × 21 cm): the Inula (alūj) and the White Garden Lily (sūsan-i abyaẓ) with their roots.

Folio 79r.

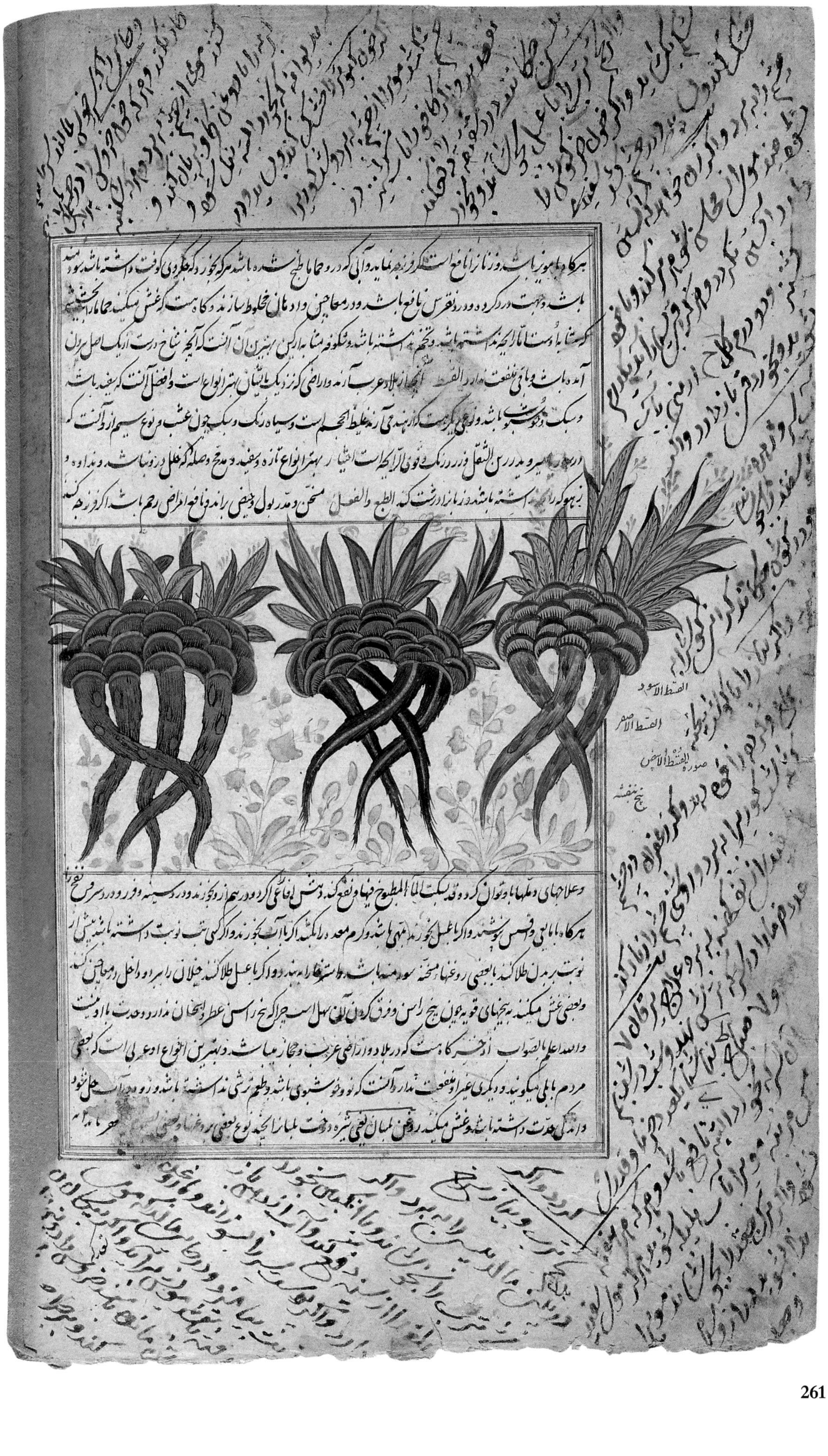

Folio 39v.

Folio 55r.

Folio 80v.

Folio 48r.

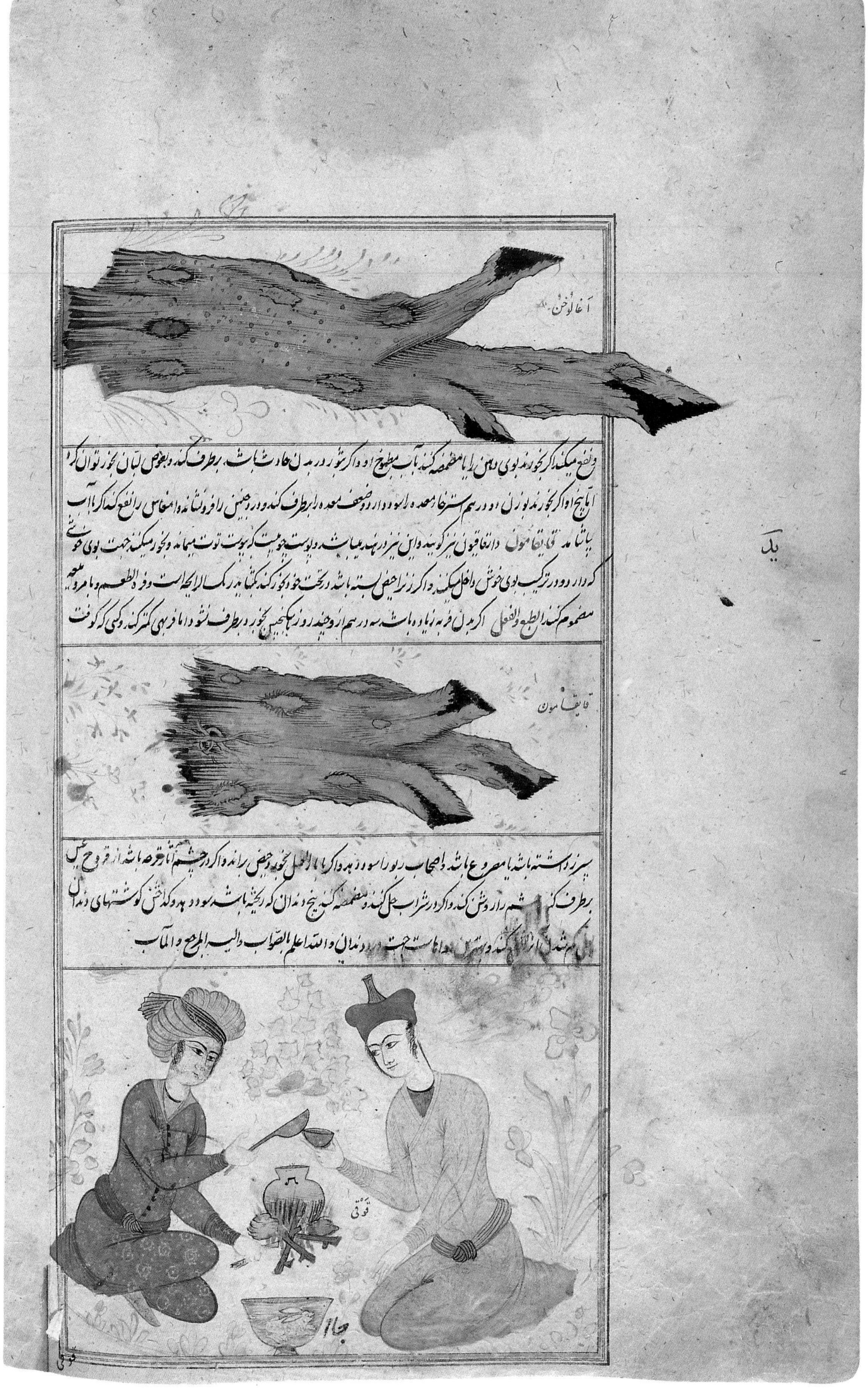

Folio 41v: The Preparation of a Medicament *(16 × 11 cm); the miniature was made according to the traditions of the Isfahan school around 1660, in the style of Riẓā-i ʿAbbāsī (died in 1635) and his closest students, notably Muḥammad Yūsuf, Muḥammad Muṣavvir and Mu'īn Muṣavvir.*

Folio 64v.

50. Matthew Cigala
al-Durr al-manẓūm fī akhbār mulūk al-rūm
(A Threaded Pearl of the History of the Byzantine Kings)

Translated in Arabic, copied and illuminated (94 miniatures) by Yūsuf ibn Anṭūniyūs ibn Sūdān al-Ḥalabī in Aleppo between 1659 and 1667
Arabic
Paper
197 folios (plus 2 blanks at the beginning and 6 at the end), 22 × 12 cm
Accession no. C-358
Provenance: coll. J.L. Rousseau, entered the Asiatic Museum in 1819.
Bibliography: Graf G., III, 1949, pp. 106–107, no. 21; Mikhailova A.I., 1965, no. 90; Mikhailova A.I., 1966.

Access to Greek texts in translation greatly enriched Arabic scientific and philosophical literature during the 8th–9th centuries, and this development continued in later periods especially within the Christian community. An example is this chronicle, in modern Greek, of Matthew Cigala (17th century). One part of the chronicle deals with the history of the Byzantine emperors from Constantine the Great (306–337) to the fall of Constantinople in 1453 to the Turks, and the history of the first Turkish sultans (Ottomans) up until Murād IV (1623–1640). The Arabic translation was done in Aleppo commissioned by the patriarch of Antioch, Macarius, who wrote a preface in which he mentions his crafstmen: the pope Yūsuf (Joseph) al-Muṣawwir and the archdeacon Būlus al-Ḥalabī (Pavel Halebskii). The title of the translation is *al-Durr al-manẓūm fī akhbār mulūk al-rūm* ("A Threaded Pearl of the History of the Byzantine Kings").
Macarius of Antioch was a prominent representative of the Eastern Orthodox Church, famous for his literary works. He traveled to Moscow, and extensively in Georgia. His son, Pavel, was also an author and translator. As for Yūsuf ibn Anṭūniyūs ibn Sūdān al-Ḥalabī (died around 1667), he was renowned for his calligraphy and miniature painting, hence the name al-Muṣawwir.
The chronicle was written by Yūsuf al-Muṣawwir who also decorated the 94 miniatures representing Byzantine emperors and Turkish sultans. The portraits are painted in the post-Byzantine style but with European influence. It is likely that the artist created the portraits from models that have not been conserved, partly by copying, partly by drawing himself. Each miniature is framed by thick lines and inscribed with the name of the emperor or sultan in Greek. [A.Kh.]

Folio 190r: portrait of Sultan Sulaimān Qānūnī.

Folio 116v: effigy of Basil the Macedonian.

51. Muraqqa^c (Album)

Paper
45 folios, 36.5 × 22.5 cm
37 miniatures: 15 Persian (Isfahan school of the 17th century) and 22 Indian (Mughal and Deccan schools, mid-16th–end of 17th centuries) and 8 models of calligraphy from the 16th to the start of the 18th centuries, grouped on one side of the album sheets; the decoration was started but never finished.
Accession no. D-181
Provenance: coll. A. Italinskii, 1827, no. 1.
Bibliography: Akimushkin, Ivanov, 1968, pp. 29, 31–34, 28, 39, 40, ps. 62, 70, 74, 75, 77, 33–34, 40, pl. 75; Catalogue PTR, 1964, no. 4034; Coomaraswamy K., 1929, p. 35, no. 48, pl. XXVI; Gray B., 1977, p. 157; Rosen V.R., 1886, pp. 322–323, no. 131.

The binding in papier mâché (22.5 × 36.7 cm) is decorated, on the top cover, with a watercolor painting coated with lacquer. The central field is decorated with floral (roses, tulips, peonies) and plant (large-leaf branches) motifs, surrounded by a fine frame of gilded lines, against a dark red background sprinkled with gold dust. Around its edge is a large band embellished with a garland of flowers (khaṭā'ī) *on a black background. A fine band similar to the inside frame runs all the way around. The back cover of the binding is made and decorated the same way. In the center of the cover, on a large leaf, is the signature of the master decorator "Made by the very humble Muḥammad Shafī^c ibn Muḥammad Masīḥ, 1144" (1731–1732). The two inside covers are made the same way: a monochrome central field (gold color), framed by a dark gold band decorated with three white lines. It is believed to come from Isfahan.*

Folio 1r: Portrait of Mīrzā Jalālā *(16 × 9.1 cm). Annotated signature: "Him! This is the portrait of Mīrzā Jalālā. The old slave, ʿAlī Qulī." ʿAlī Qulī beg Jabbādār was a painter at the court of Shāh Sulaimān (1666–1694). His work has a European touch. According to the Iranian man of letters and historiography, Luṭf ʿAlī beg Iṣfahānī Āzar (1134–1195/ 1722–1781), he was a European artist who became a Muslim. I.S. Stchoukine questions this, observing that elementary errors of perspective can be found in his work ("Syria," t. 41, fasc. 1–2, Paris, 1964, p. 176). The same Persian source suggests that ʿAlī Qulī beg was the founder of a dynasty of court artists and that his son Abdāl beg, like his grandson Muḥammad ʿAlī beg were the head artists (*naqqāsh bāshī*) of the last Safavids and of Nādir Shāh Afshār (1736–1747).*

Folio 16r: Portrait of Tīmūr Khān Turkmān *(19.3 × 11.6 cm). Annotated signature: "Portrait of Tīmūr Khān Turkmān, painted in 1002 [1593–1594] by the late Ṣādiqī beg Afshār. Completed by Mu'īn Muṣavvir, the miserable slave, in 1095 [1683–1684]. May he be blessed."*
*This portrait of the chief of a large clan of Turkman tribes was painted by a remarkable individual, poet and warrior, scholar and artist, the first director (*kitābdār*) of the library at the court of Shāh ʿAbbās I (1587–1629), Ṣādiqī beg Afshār, known in literary circles as Ṣādiqī (1533–1610). As an artist, he was active from the 1570s to the early 17th century and his work is an example of the transition between the Qazvin style (second half of the 16th century) and the Isfahan school of the 17th century.*
He was a prolific artist. This portrait was finished by a direct pupil of Riẓā-i ʿAbbāsī, Mu'īn Muṣavvir (died after 1697–1698), who rigorously maintained the Isfahan tradition founded by his teacher.

Folio 6r: The Shaykh and the Harlot *(18.2 × 11.3 cm). Annotated signature on the miniature: "He! Painted by the most humble Muḥammad Yūsuf Muṣavvir in the sublime, very pure and holy [city of] Mashhad, 1068" (1658). It illustrates a quatrain (*rubāʿī*) attributed to the famous mathematician and poet ʿUmar Khayyām (1048–1131): "A shaykh says to a harlot, 'You are drunk. At every instant, you are caught up in someone's snare !' She replied, 'O shaykh ! I am what you say, but you, are you sure you are what you make yourself out to be?'" The painter of this miniature, Muḥammad Yūsuf Muṣavvir, clearly followed the style of Riẓā-i ʿAbbāsī. It is the third master that we know with the same double name as two other of his colleagues working in the middle of the 17th century. While following the general trend of the Isfahan school, his work gradually loses clarity of line, becoming more stiff and heavy. It is a provincial variant of Mashhad in the Isfahan style.*

Folio 17r: Portrait of a Man *(11.8 × 8.2 cm). Annotated signature: "Completed on Thursday 6 in the month of Rabi I in the year 1044 [August 30, 1634]. Painted by the most humble Riẓā-i ʿAbbāsī." The painter was a great Persian craftsman, the main founder of the Isfahan school of the 17th century, Āqā Riẓā ibn ʿAlī Asghar Kāshānī, better known first as Āqā Riẓā-i Kāshānī, then as Riẓā-i ʿAbbāsī (died in April-May 1635). The miniature dates from the last years of his life and is among his best works.*

Folio 36r: The Dervishes Picnic in the Mountains *(25.5 × 14.5 cm). Probably painted by Muḫammad in Herat, around 1580–1590. This miniature, expertly painted with great sensitivity, surely illustrates the sufi notion of intoxication by divine love, achieved by means of an ordinary drinking session. Some dervishes are already in trance and perhaps in divine union (*tawḫīd*), others are in ecstasy, yet others are sober or just a bit happy. We know little of the painter who signed in the name of Muḫammad Muṣavvir. He left many single sheets of drawings with scenes of dervishes, nomad campsites, and portraits of various personalities. Many of the signatures however, have raised doubts. He worked in Herat during the years 1560–1590, at the court of the Safavid governors. There is no question as to his influence on the work of Riżā-i ʿAbbāsī. The artist is thought to have sympathized with sufi mysticism.*

Folio 42r: Portrait of a Courtier *(28 × 18.6 cm). Annotated signature: "Painted by Muḥammad Sulṭānī," who worked in Isfahan at the end of the 17th century. We know that one of his miniatures (this album, folio 43r) was signed by him and dated 1109/1697–1698. He was clearly attracted by the European style, but he did not always master the techniques. He continued within the tradition of a famous painter of the second half of the 17th century, Muḥammad Zamān ibn Ḥājjī Yūsuf Qumī. He is known today mainly as a portrait artist, repeatedly using the same composition: the subject is depicted in three-quarter profile, sitting on a carpet, in the open gallery of a palace, against a backdrop of mountains.*

52. Muraqqa[c] (Album)

Cardboard
98 folios, 44.7 × 33 cm
Indian miniatures of the Mughal school of the end of the 16th–beginning of the 17th centuries
Persian miniatures of the Isfahan school, second half of the 17th century, beginning of the 18th century
Persian calligraphy by ᶜImād al-Ḥasanī (1551–1615) on reverse
Accession no. E-14
Provenance: purchased in Tehran in 1909, for Tsar Nicholas II by Ostrogadskii, agent of the Russian Imperial Ministry of Finance in Iran, for the sum of 15,000 silver roubles. It has 100 folios; since the Hermitage Museum refused to keep it, it was transferred to the Russian Museum in St. Petersburg, and kept in the ethnographic section, from where it reached the Asiatic Museum in 1921.
Bibliography: Ivanov A.A., Grek T.V., Akimushkin O.F., (eds), *Album des miniatures indiennes et persanes du XVI au XVIII siècle*, 1962; Ivanov A.A., 1979; Akimushkin O.F., *The St. Petersburg Muraqqaᶜ. Indian and Persian XVI-XVIII Century Miniatures and Specimens of Calligraphy of ᶜImad al-Ḥasanī*, Milan, 1994.

There is no doubt at all that this album is on a par with, if not better than, the famous albums created in India for the Great Mughals Jahāngīr (1605–1627) and Shāh Jahān (1628–1657), known as *Muraqqaᶜ-i Jahāngīr* and *Muraqqaᶜ-i Gulshān*.
The miniatures, like the models of calligraphy, are surrounded by narrow frames (generally two) and large margins decorated with floral and plant motifs in gold and colors. Initially, the folios were bound so that there was a continuous flow of miniatures on one side and text on the other, which was the traditional way of compiling an album. At the same time, miniatures similar in subject or texts in the same calligraphy were placed on adjacent pages. Both sides of each double page spread were decorated in the same manner. The current numbering of the folios does not correspond to the initial order.
The magnificent margins and borders were painted in Iran in the 1750s. At least four decorators took part in this work, and three left their notes on the pages. Muḥammad Hādī started decorating the album at the very beginning, working uniquely on the margins of 95 folios with calligraphic specimens. He signed 82 folios in the margin, with dates ranging from 1747 to 1759. The work progressed slowly, with a seven-year interruption (1749–1756). Muḥammad Bāqir decorated the margins of the pages of miniatures, as well as the borders of both miniatures and text. His signature is found on 24 margins and 12 borders, but only once did he date his work, 1172/1758–1759 (frame of folio 84v). He painted the miniature *Birds and a Flowering Acacia* (folio 77r).
Muḥammad Ṣādiq decorated the least in the album. He left three inscriptions dated 1751.
The last two painters set to the task after Muḥammad Hādī.
The decorative work was not completed and there was no visible effort subsequently to do so. Fourteen margins (11 folios with miniatures and three with models of calligraphy) and 61 borders remain without decoration.
One hundred and twenty miniatures in the album were painted in India between the end of the 16th century and the 1730s. They belong mainly to the Mughal school and give a good general idea as to the standard of painting in India at that time, thanks to the works of eminent or lesser known artists.
Abū al-Ḥasan ibn Āqā Rizā Jahāngīrī (born in 998/1588–1589) worked at the court of Jahāngīr and Shāh Jahān (1628–1657). In 1614, he was given the title Nādir al-Zamān ("The Wonder of the Time"). Of the seven miniatures attributed to him in the album, four are signed.
Vishnū Dās, a major Indian portrait painter, who worked at the court of Jahāngīr, signed two miniatures.
Manūhar Dās, an Indian, who first worked at the court of Akbar I (15561605), and then for Jahāngīr, signed five miniatures.
Manṣūr, a portrait-artist, who worked at the court of Jahāngīr and Shāh Jahān, with the sobriquet Nādir al-ᶜAṣr ("The Wonder of the Epoch"), signed two miniatures.
Nānhā signed one miniature.
Govardhan who was the great master at the beginning of the 17th century, signed two miniatures.
Payāk signed two miniatures.
Mīr Kalān signed one miniature though two can be attributed to him.
Two miniatures are representative of the Deccan school; one has an inscription that has been attributed to Ḥusain Farrukh beg, considered to be one of the best artists of the court of Ibrāhīm ᶜĀdil Shāh II (1580–1627). There are 33 Persian works, mainly painted between 1670 and the beginning of the 18th cen-tury, by artists from the Isfahan school, working towards the development of a second style. This style was developed in the second half of the 17th century by artists who used techniques borrowed from European painting (using light and shadow, perspective), and made copies of European models. The majority of the miniatures representative of this style included in the album are the best examples of the work of two painters: Muḥammad Zamān and ᶜAlī Qulī Jabbādār. Muḥammad Zamān ibn Ḥājjī Yūsuf Qumī, active between 1675 and 1688, worked at the court of Shāh Sulaimān (1666–1694). The assumption that he studied in Italy where he was sent by Shāh ᶜAbbās II (1642–1666) and where he converted to Christianity is, in fact, a colorful legend. He died in 1112/1700–1701. The album has seven miniatures painted and signed by him, and two more can be attributed to him.
ᶜAlī Qulī Jabbādār is traditionally taken to be a European converted to Islam. He was working at the court of Shāh Sulaimān as of 1674. He signed five of the miniatures and three others can be attributed to him.

Ḥājjī Muḥammad, whose full name is Ḥājjī Muḥammad Ibrāhīm ibn Ḥājjī Yūsuf Qumī, was the brother of Muḥammad Zamān, mentioned earlier. He signed three of the miniatures (the signature on the last one, entitled *The Combat of a Knight with a Dragon* raises a few questions). Ḥājjī died some time between 1712 and 1718.

Muḥammad Riżā-i Hindī is the author of twelve small miniatures; with six on each of the two folios, *Flowers and Birds*, produced in the middle of the 18th century.

The decorator of some of the margins and frames in the album, Muḥammad Bāqir, painted and signed a miniature in the middle of the 18th century.

The miniature *The Offering of a Ring by the Grand Vizier Shāh Qulī Khān* can be attributed to the painter Muḥammad Sulṭānī. It is dated 1106/1694–1695.

Models of artistic writing are displayed on one side of the 97 folios, by a great Persian calligrapher of the last quarter of the 16th century and the first decade of the 17th century, ʿImād al-Mulk Muḥammad ibn Ḥusain al-Ḥasanī al-Saifī al-Qazvīnī (1551–1615), known as Mīr ʿImād or ʿImād al-Ḥasanī. According to the tradition that developed among calligraphers in Iran, ʿImād al-Ḥasanī was the third and last great stylist of the *nastaʿlīq* script. Supposedly born in Qazvin in 1551, he worked in many countries. Around 1601–1602, at the request of Shāh ʿAbbās I, he joined his court and became the head calligrapher. He died in 1615, leaving a substantial artistic heritage, currently dispersed around the globe. The album has 198 specimens of writing and 34 exercise samples (*mashq*), produced in Aleppo (Ḥalab), Qazvin, Isfahan, and Tahan (Faraḥābād) between 1595 and 1615.

Based on dated notes in the binding, margins and frames, one can assume the following schedule for the creation of the album. In 1734–1735, a very influential individual named Mīrzā Mahdī ordered a binding in which to insert a selection of miniatures and models of calligraphy that he owned. But more or less at the time that the binding was completed, in 1738–1739, the selection increased considerably.

The troops of Nādir Shāh had just returned from the Indian campaign, bringing the manuscripts looted from the court library. The owner of the album gained possession of some of these treasures. It is tempting to read in the name of Mīrzā Mahdī the famous Mīrzā Muḥammad Mahdī Khān Astarābādī, companion in arms of Nādir Shāh (killed in 1747), as well as his historiographer and secretary. We know that he was a fervent book-lover and that in 1739 in Mashhad he personally purchased from soldiers miniatures and manuscripts they had stolen in India, and in this way built up a fabulous library. Under pressure from Fath. ʿAlī Shāh Qājār (1797–1834), the collection was sold to the Treasury by his heirs. That is, apparently, how in 1739 or shortly after this album was composed in Iran. It took many a long year to assemble, and in 1747 the unifying decorative work was begun so as to give it a homogeneous aspect. Work progressed slowly, with one artist-decorator, then two others with several interruptions. Obviously, the unstable situation in Iran, caused by the struggle of the pretenders to Nādir Shāh's succession, created a handicap. When the situation had calmed down, the work of decoration proceeded faster. The album was practically finished in 1759. We do not know how many folios were in the original album, probably 200 to 216 (100 were in St. Petersburg until 1931, the year that folios 28 and 33 were transferred to the Leningrad Museum of the History of Religion to be put on permanent display). The assumption that the album had over 100 folios is confirmed by the information that eight or ten folios briefly appeared on the European and Iranian antique markets as of 1909. The latest examples are: Sotheby's *Islamic and Indian Art, Oriental Manuscripts and Miniatures*, London, October 22–23, 1992, no. 502; *Abolala Soudavar, Art of the Persian Courts, Selections from the Art and History Trust Collection*, Rizzoli Publishers, New York, 1992, plates 131a-b. [O.A.]

*Binding decorated with floral paintings of papier mâché under pale yellow lacquer (34.5 × 51.5 cm). The paintings decorating the inside covers consist of a compositional scheme of a central field with three medallions, vertically arranged, decorated with flower motifs and silhouettes of birds, surrounded by one large frame and two narrow borders with gilded plant motifs. The central field of both covers is decorated in a similar way: two loops with intertwining leaves and flowers that completely cover the surface with a symmetrical motif on a black background. The central part of the back cover is of a single color, a cherry-red background sprinkled with gold dust, with no ornamentation. The large frame on the covers consist of sixteen scrolls containing verses alternating with floral medallions. In each cartouche is the date 1147/1734, the total of the numeric value in the letters of each hemistich (*miṣrāᶜ*) being 1147. On the inside cover of the binding is a panegyric mentioning the name of the person who ordered the binding. It is Mīrzā Mahdī, who, judging by the praise of his name, was a highly important person. In the center of the right vertical frame on the inside back cover is the date 1151/1738–1739.*

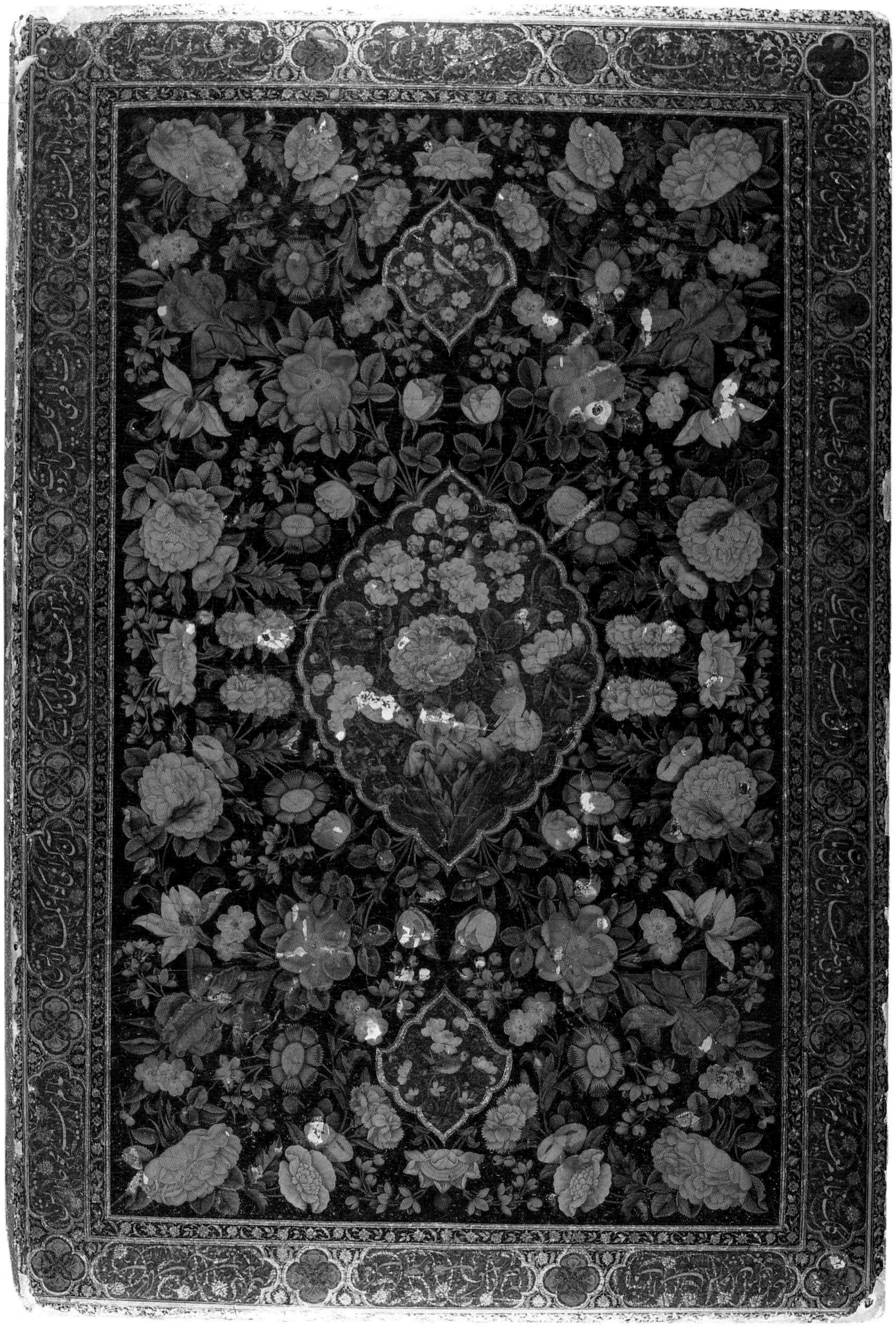

*Folio 40v: Model of calligraphic writing (*qiṭᶜa*) (31 × 16.5 cm). Annotated signature: "The miserable sinner ᶜImād al-Ḥasanī, may [Allāh] pardon him. 1007 [1598–1599]". This example, a quatrain, is written in beautiful large* nastaᶜlīq*. ᶜImād al-Ḥasani had no rivals in his mastery of this style.*

Folio 21r: Celebrations at the Occasion of Jahāngīr's Coronation *(22 × 37.8 cm). Annotated signature: "Painted by the most insignificant of creatures, Abū al-Ḥasan Jahāngīr-shāhī"; dated on the central section of the gate, 1014 (1605–1606). There are also inscriptions in Persian. High on the gate, "God is great, may your conquest of the world be fruitful! May your reign be blessed," and below, "On the throne... noble... Nūr al-Dīn Jahāngīr ibn Akbar Pādshāh." On four small sacks: "Thousand rupees from Ahmedabad," "Thousand rupees," "Thousand," "Five hundred." Finally, in the bottom right hand corner are the verses celebrating the coronation written on a sheet of paper in the hands of the poet. This miniature was painted by one of the most talented Mughal artists of the 17th century, Abū al-Ḥasan ibn Āqā Riẓā, known by the names Jahāngīrshāhī and Nādir al-Zamān ("The Wonder of the Time"). He was born at the court of Agra in 998/1588–1589. His father, a painter who came to India from Iran, went by the name Āqā Riẓā Jahāngīr. Abū al-Ḥasan spent his entire life at the court and in 1614 was given the name Nādir al-Zamān. This miniature, filled with people and details, represents the celebration of Jahāngīr's coronation in Agra in 1605. In the huge crowd in the foreground, each figure has individual features. A series of scenes united within this composition perfectly represent the complexity of Indian society of the period. The painter was very talented, able to skillfully compose and depict a crowd, drawing with a confident line, using a clever and varied combination of colours. Apart from these unquestionable qualities, this miniature is a remarkable historical and ethnographic document.*

Folio 34v: The Court of Shāh Jahān *(20.5 × 32 cm). This miniature from the Mughal school, around 1628–1631 contains an inscription to glorify Shāh Jahān (reigned from 1628–1657), on a narrow architectural band above the canopy: "May those who watch through the night remember the glory of Shāh Jahān. May those who get up in the morning remember to pray for his happiness. Wherever the courageous soldier, similar to the sun, turns his blade, may the hordes of his enemies be strewn like stars." This work reflected a new tendency in Indian miniature painting around 1625; while maintaining faithfulness to individual resemblance in a portrait, the miniature started to become dominated by decorative and elaborate aspects of sumptuous refinement, manifest in the abundance of gold and lively contrasting colors. Rich clothing and sophisticated ornaments are carefully painted in detail. Shāh Jahān is depicted seated on his throne surrounded by his sons and most faithful dignitaries.*

Folio 89r: The Sacrifice of Abraham *(24.9 × 17.8 cm). Annotated signature: "He! Completed by the undersigned for the happy, the most noble, the most holy, the most august, the most high and royal lord who holds fate in his hands. Painted by the most insignificant of slaves, Muḥammad Zamān. 1096 [1684–1685]". The blade of the sword has the inscription "Abraham, the friend of God." This miniature in the new European style of the Isfahan school of the second half of the 17th century is a copy of a Flemish engraving.*

Folio 2r: Ibrāhīm ʿAdil Shāh hunting with a falcon
Supposedly painted by Ḥusain-Farrukh Bek
Deccan school, end of the 16th century (27.1 × 15.8 cm).
Inscription one (annotational): "Portrait of the greatest ruler of peoples, Ibrāhīm ʿAdil Shāh."
Inscription two (attributive) in a special cartouche upon a golden ground close to the frame and above green hills is damaged but can be read as "[Ḥusain Farrukh Bek".
The miniature depicts the ruler of Bijapur at a young age. It is elegantly done and reflects characteristic features of the Deccan school; at the same time, the influence of Muslim painting is noticeable. Farrukh Ḥusain was regarded the best painter at the court of Ibrāhīm ʿAdil Shāh; he was also known as Farrukh Chela.
The margins and the frame (golden vegetal ornament upon a raspberry-red colored ground) are illuminated by the painter Muḥammad Bāqir.

Folio 82r: Hyacinths *(17.5 × 10.2 cm). Annotated signature: "Painted by the most insignificant of slaves, Muḥammad Zamān. 1094 [1682–1683]". It is very difficult to determine whether the style of painting flowers in miniatures came from India or if the painters of the Isfahan school of the 17th century took inspiration from local textile designers. The fact remains that famous painters from this school paid tribute to this fashion during the 17th century by complying with requests by connoisseurs.*

Folio 98r: The King and his Courtiers *(42.1 × 28.2 cm). Annotated signature: "He! The son of an old slave ʿAlī Qulī Jabbādār." In the top left corner, are illegible Georgian inscriptions. The painter mentioned above, was an eminent representative of the European trend in the Isfahan school of the second half of the 17th century (cat. no. 51).*

This miniature is of official and solemn aspect, the young shah (probably Sulaimān, crowned in 1666) is sitting on the terrace of a pavilion in his palace, surrounded by his entourage and musicians. It is a solemn portrait showing numerous individuals, creating a certain tension across the pictorial surface. The fine silhouettes of the young men with deliberately elongated faces and narrow waists are characteristic of the artist, as are the huge, pointed head-dresses (turbans, kulāh*) and gaudy fabrics, the striking individualization of the characters, the special way of painting the foliage and perspective of the landscape. The painter's signature is in the upper right hand corner in a special cartouche.*

53. Arabic Version of Ancient Popular Stories

Copied probably in the first half of the 17th century
Naskh
European paper
17.5 × 12 cm
17 lines to the page
Accession no. A-448
Provenance: coll. of General P.K. Sokhtelen, beginning of the 19th century, library of the Education Section of the Russian Ministry of Foreign Affairs; Asiatic Museum 1919.
Bibliography: Khalidov A.B., 1960, no. 9 and no. 108; Rosen V.R., 1877, no. 123.

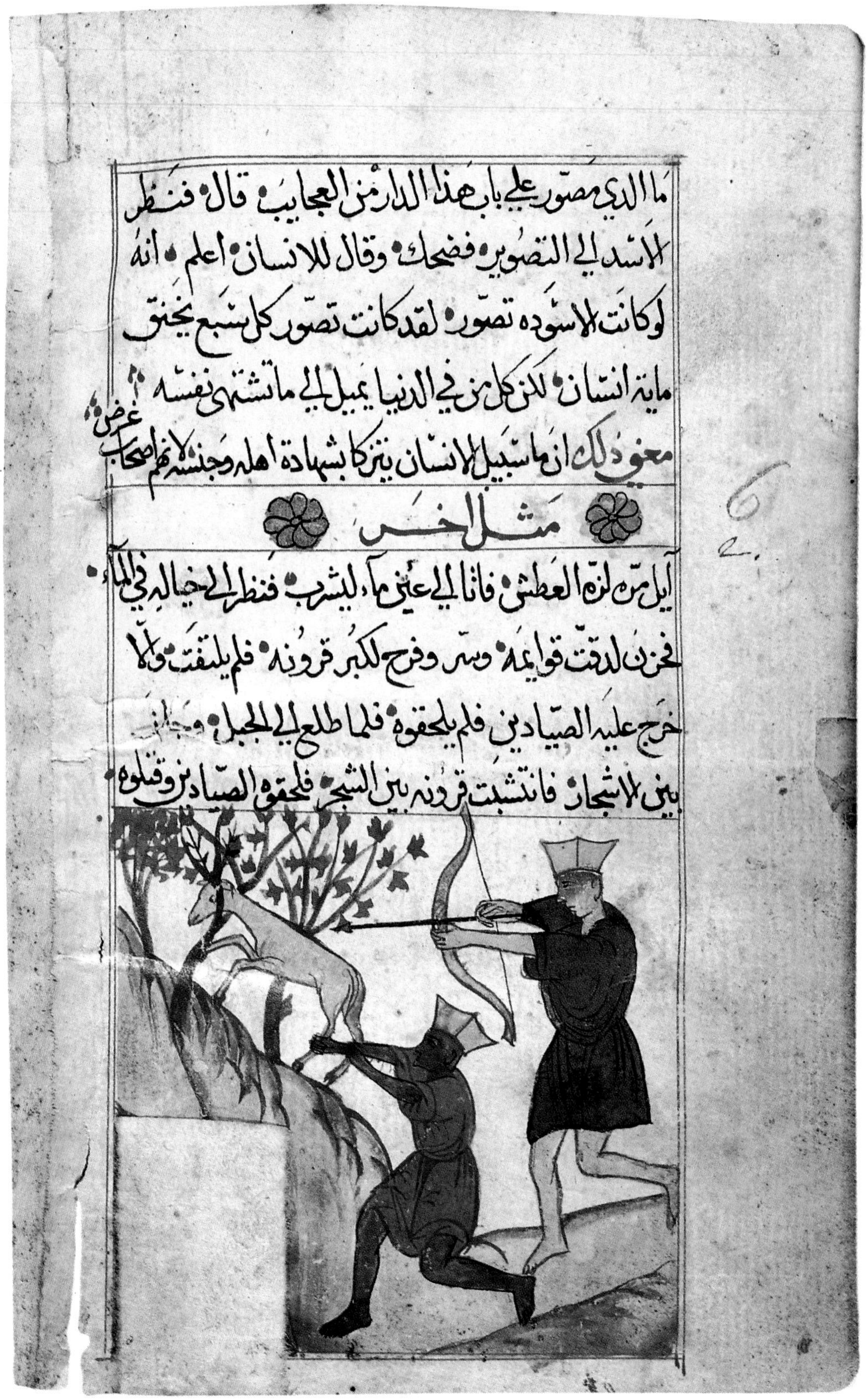
ما الذي مصور على باب هذا الدار من العجايب • قال • فنظر
الاسد الى التصوير • فضحك • وقال للانسان • اعلم • انه
لو كانت الاسوده تصور • لقد كانت تصور كل سبع يخنق
مائة انسان • لكن كل من في الدنيا يميل الى ما تشتهي نفسه
معنى ذلك ان ما سبيل الانسان يتزكا بشهادة اهله وجنسه لانهم اصحاب غرض

مثل اخر

ايل من لزه العطش • فاتا الى عين ماء ليشرب • فنظر الى خياله في الماء
فحزن لدقت قوايمه • وسر وفرح لكبر قرونه • فلم يلتفت ولا
خرج عليه الصيادين فلم يلحقوه • فلما طلع الى الجبل • و[illegible]
بين الاشجار • فانتشبت قرونه بين الشجر • فلحقوه الصيادين وقتلوه

Folio 59v: Seeing his reflection in the water, the stag is distressed at having such thin legs, but delighted at his superb antlers, however the hunters arrive on the scene, and the stag fails to find refuge in the forest because despite the agility of his legs, his antlers catch in the branches.

Opposite: *Folios 81v and 62r: The fable of the hares who ask the foxes for help in their struggle against the falcons. The fable of the race between the hare and the tortoise.*

Folio 5v: The story of King Kal'ād and his Vizier Shīmās. Hunting Scene.

Folio 12v: The story of King Kal'ād and his Vizier Shīmās. A Hermit Complaining to the Sultan of His Poverty.

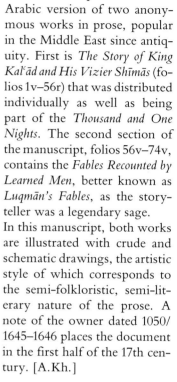

This manuscript contains the Arabic version of two anonymous works in prose, popular in the Middle East since antiquity. First is *The Story of King Kalʿād and His Vizier Shīmās* (folios 1v–56r) that was distributed individually as well as being part of the *Thousand and One Nights*. The second section of the manuscript, folios 56v–74v, contains the *Fables Recounted by Learned Men*, better known as *Luqmān's Fables*, as the storyteller was a legendary sage.

In this manuscript, both works are illustrated with crude and schematic drawings, the artistic style of which corresponds to the semi-folkloristic, semi-literary nature of the prose. A note of the owner dated 1050/1645–1646 places the document in the first half of the 17th century. [A.Kh.]

54. Abū Manṣūr ᶜAbd al-Malik ibn Muḥammad al-Thaᶜālibī (961–1038) Yatīmat al-dahr (The Jewel)

Folio 2v.

Copy dated 1195/1781
Naskh
Paper
378 folios, 30.5 × 21cm
Accession no. D-162
Provenance: transferred in 1919 from the library of the Department of Education in the Ministry of Foreign Affairs.
Bibliography: Brockelmann C., 1898, p. 284, no. 1; Khalidov A.B., 1986, nos. 8947, 8948; Rosen V.R., 1877, no. 86.

Towards the beginning of the 11th century, figures from the Arabic literary world realized that the political unity of the Muslim world was already a thing of the past. It was Abū Manṣūr ᶜAbd al-Malik ibn Muḥammad al-Thaᶜālibī (961–1038) who best expressed this idea when composing his anthology *Yatīmat al-dahr* ("The Jewel"). Unlike other anthologies which gave credit always to the old over the new, this text contains a marked preference for the creations of contemporary poets or those of recent times. The manuscript focuses on the provincial poets, distinguishing them according to their regions. It provides us with unique information surrounding the history and culture of Muslim literature. "The Jewel" was greatly praised and many copies were made.

The author made his career within the court of the rulers of various dynasties (Samanids, Khwārazm-Shāhs, etc.) in the east of the Caliphate. He dedicated "The Jewel" to the sovereign of Gurgan (Hyrcania) Qābūs ibn Vashmgīr and subsequently wrote a supplement (*Tatimmat al-yatīma*).

This copy, written in a mediocre *naskh*, was made for Muḥammad Khalīl ibn ᶜAlī al-Ḥusaynī al-Murādī, the mufti of Damascus in 1781. The beginning of each of the four sections of the anthology and of the supplement is marked with a rectangular, colored *ᶜunvān*.

The first two pages also have decorated margins. On the title page the *ᶜunvān* is triangular, inside which is written both the title of the book and the name of the author. The eight sheets left blank at the beginning were marked with lines for a detailed summary that was never written. [A.Kh.]

كتب هذا الكتاب
برسم العالم الجليل
النسيب السميدع الاديب المولى محمد
خليل بن علي الحسيني الحنفي المعروف
بالمرادي المفتي بدمشق
الشام حماها الله من
بوايق الايام ١١٩٥

55. Elisha ibn Shemu'el (17th century)
Kitāb-i shāhzāda va ṣūfī
(The Prince and the Dervish)

Copied in Bukhara in the 18th century
Hebrew script
68 folios
21 × 16 cm
Accession no. B-157
Provenance: Acquired in 1915 in Bukhara for the Institute of Oriental Studies from the V.A.Ivanov collection
Bibliography: Freimann A., 1918, p. 1282; Gintzburg I.I., 1936; Kuhn E., 1922; Kuhn E.,1893; Nentzer A., 1936, pp. 24–25; Oldenburg, 1889.

This manuscript is a Persian translation from Hebrew of the story of Barlaam and Josaphat. The poetic adaptation of the Hebrew version by Ibn Ḥasdāy entitled "The Prince and the Dervish" has been attributed to Elisha ibn Shem'uel (17th century, apparently a native of Samarqand), who no doubt used the Hebrew translation made in Spain. The text however also illustrates the profound influence of sufi ideas and traditions, characteristic of Central Asia.

The story of the hermit Barlaam and the Indian prince Josaphat is one of the great texts belonging to world literature. It has been translated into dozens of languages from Asia, Europe and Africa. There are known to exist: one version in Pahlavi, five in Arabic, one in Persian, one in Uighur, one in Hebrew, two in Georgian, two in Latin, one in old Slav, one in Armenian, one in Swahili, nine in Italian, eight in old French, five in Spanish, one in Provençal, one in Portuguese, one in German, one in Czech, one in Polish, one in English, one in Irish, one in Hungarian, as well as others.

The text uses lively and passionate language, including numerous engaging parables which are easy to understand and to memorize, it raises and clarifies major issues concerning the conception of the world—all elements which contributed to making this book one of the most popular books during the Middle Ages.

As is true today, readers from that epoch could not remain indifferent to the questions of spirituality, to the role of tradition in society, to the happiness of having a real teacher and the responsibility of the master towards his pupil. These are some of the subjects that the characters in the story consider. Naturally, each nation has highlighted one aspect or another of the book, so that in each case it succeeds in renewing both its form and content. [E.R.]

Folios 54v–55r.

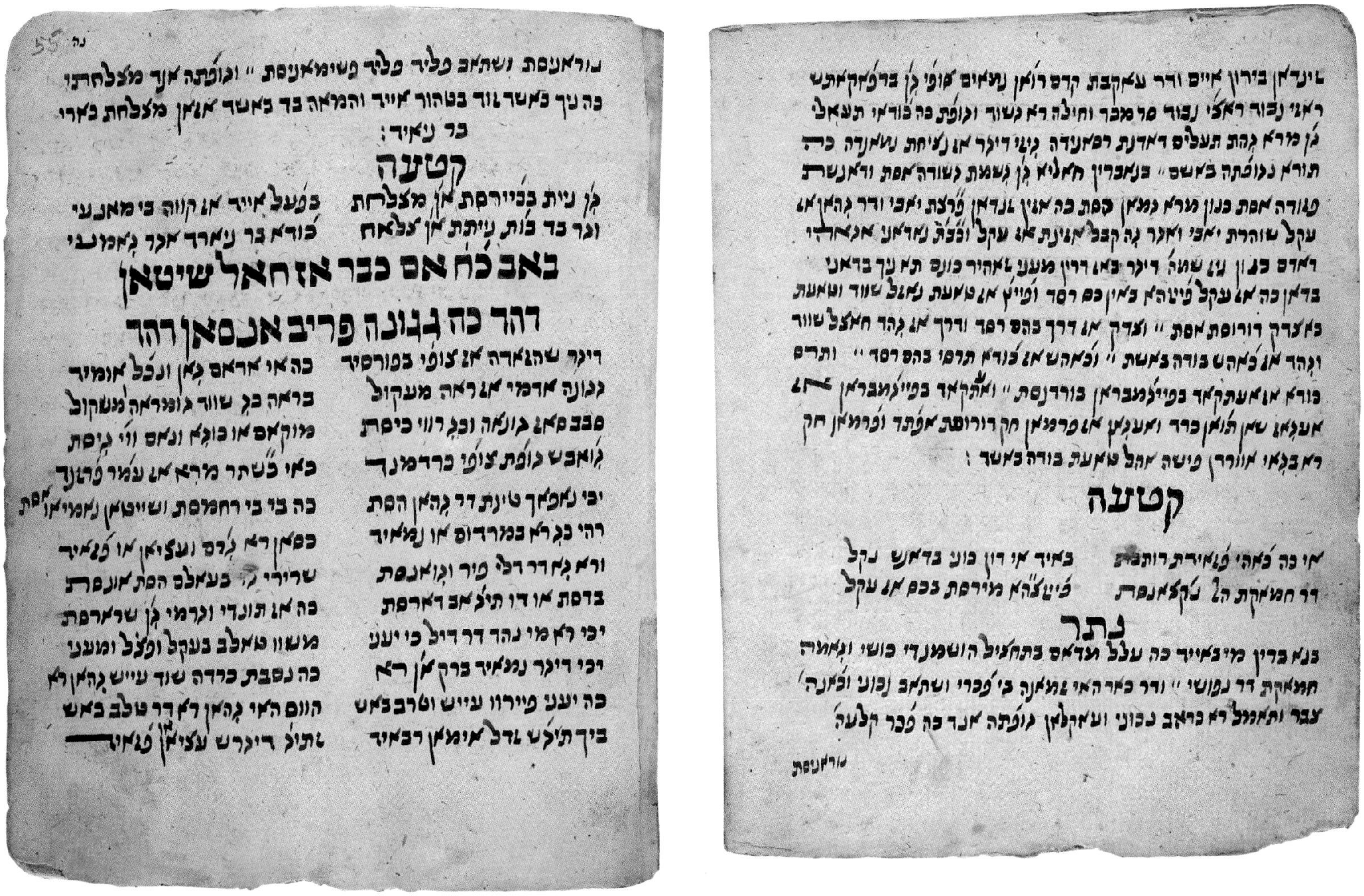

56. Druze sect
Manshūr ilā āl ᶜabd-allāh wa sulaymān
(The Call of the Family of ᶜAbd-Allāh and Sulaymān)
Manshūr abā ᶜalī (The Call of Abā ᶜAlī)

Folio 73r: call to the spiritual leaders of the Druze community. These texts were copied with great care and completely vocalized.

Syria, 18th century
Arabic
105 folios, 18.5 × 14 cm
Accession no. B-1054
Bibliography: Brockelmann C., 1937, pp. 716–718; Khalidov A.B., 1986, no. 2779–2995; Rosen V.R., 1881, no. 96–103.

The Druze sect, from Western Syria and Lebanon, believed in the divinity of the Fatimid Caliph al-Ḥākim (in power from 996–1021) as an incarnation of God. They were so extreme in their belief that there were sometimes doubts as to their Muslim faith. The books detailing their teaching were believed to be accessible only to those initiated into the sect. Copies therefore hardly ever left the hands of a very limited number of the sect's senior members. It was only after Bonaparte's expedition to Egypt that some Druze manuscripts fell into the hands of French scholars, and subsequently found their way to Paris, Berlin and St. Petersburg.
The Druze manuscripts are a series of terse texts, treatises, messages and instructions dating from the time of the founding of the sect during the 11th – 12th centuries. The elements characteristic of the decoration of the manuscripts are the frames consisting of colored lines and geometric patterns.
This manuscript includes the text entitled *Manshūr ilā āl ᶜabd-allāh wa sulaymān* ("The Call of the Family of ᶜAbd-Allāh and Sulaymān") and the beginning of the text entitled *Manshūr abā ᶜalī* ("The Call of Abā ᶜAlī"). It comes from Syria and is believed to date from the 18th century. The use of minute detail follows in the steps of a long-standing independent tradition in which a special role is reserved for the combination of black, green and red inks used to trace words and signs. [A.Kh.]

النَّصِيرُ المُعِينُ عَلَى مَكَايِدِ الأَشْرَارِ وَالكُفَّارِ وَكُتِبَ
فِي شَهْرِ رَبِيعٍ الآخِرِ مِنْ سَنَةِ اثْنَيْنِ وَعِشْرِينَ مِنَ السِّنِينَ
المُبَارَكَةِ إِلَى آلِ عَبْدِ اللهِ وَآلِ سُلَيْمَانَ • فَصْلٌ وَلَمَّا
وَرَدَ الشَّيْخُ أَبُو القَاسِمِ وَالشَّيْخُ أَبُو المَعَالِي إِلَى البُسْتَانِ
وَاجْتَمَعَا مَعَ نَصْرٍ وَقَضَيَا مَعَهُ مَا وَرَدَ مِنْ جِهَتِهِ إِلَيْهِ
وَمَضَيَا وَرَدَ إِلَيْهِ كِتَابٌ شُكْبَنَ خَطَّ بِدَاهُ يُذْكَرُ
فِيهِ وَقَدْ جَعَلْتُ لَكَ النَّظَرَ فِي جَمِيعِ الأَمْلَاكِ وَمُطَالَبَةِ
مَنْ عَلَيْهِ دَيْنٌ وَاقْتِضَاهُ • تَمَّتْ وَالحَمْدُ
لِمَوْلَانَا وَحْدَهُ وَالشُّكْرُ لِوَلِيِّهِ عَبْدِهِ •

مَنْشُورُ أَبَا عَلِيٍّ

وَصَلَ كِتَابُكَ يَا أَخِي وَالعَزِيزُ بَرَّ عَلَيَّ وَعِنْدِي أَطَالَ
اللهُ بَقَاكَ وَأَدَامَ عِزَّكَ وَنَعْمَاكَ • وَوَقَفْتُ عَلَيْهِ
وَشَكَرْتُ مَنْ لَا يَخِيبُ شُكْرُهُ • فَهَذَا يَا أَخِي كُلُّهُ شَيْءٌ

57. Khalīl ibn Isḥāq al-Jundī (died in 1365)
al-Mukhtaṣar fī al-fiqh
(A Short Manual of Fiqh)

Folios 1v–2r.

18th century
Maghribī
163 folios
17.5 × 12 cm
16 lines to the page, black, blue and red inks
Accession no. A-139
Bibliography: Brockelmann C., 1902, pp. 83–84, no. 2; Khalidov A.B., 1986, no. 4665; Rosen V.R., 1881, no. 122.

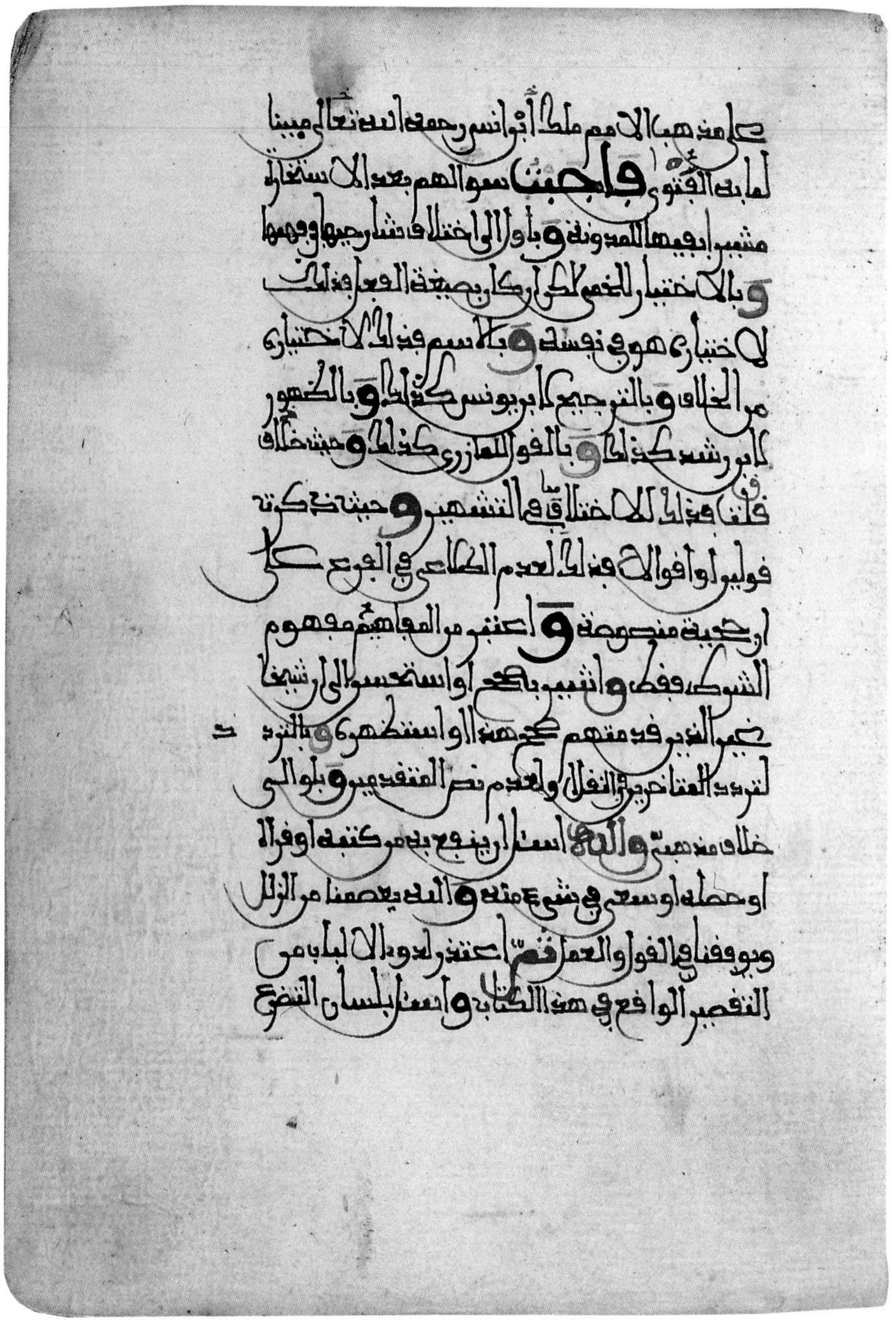

على مذهب الإمام مالك بن أنس رحمه الله تعالى مبينا
لما به الفتوى فأجبت سؤالهم بعد الاستخارة
مشيرا بفيها للمدونة وبأول إلى اختلاف شارحيها في فهمها
وبالاختيار للخمي لكن إن كان بصيغة الفعل فذلك
لاختياره هو في نفسه وبالاسم فذلك لاختياره
من الخلاف وبالترجيح لابن يونس كذلك وبالظهور
لابن رشد كذلك وبالقول للمازري كذلك وحيث قلت خلاف
فذلك للاختلاف في التشهير وحيث ذكرت
قولين أو أقوالا فذلك لعدم اطلاعي في الفرع على
أرجحية منصوصة واعتبر من المفاهيم مفهوم
الشرط فقط وأشير بصحح أو استحسن إلى أن شيخا
غير الذين قدمتهم صحح هذا أو استظهره وبالتردد
لتردد المتأخرين في النقل أو لعدم نص المتقدمين وبلو إلى
خلاف مذهبي والله أسأل أن ينفع به من كتبه أو قرأه
أو حصله أو سعى في شيء منه والله يعصمنا من الزلل
ويوفقنا في القول والعمل ثم أعتذر لذوي الألباب من
التقصير الواقع في هذا الكتاب وأسأل بلسان التضرع

Muslim society is meant to live in strict observance of religious law, the *sharīʿa*, delivered by God to his chosen prophet through the Archangel Jibrīl (Gabriel). The specifics of Islamic law were elaborated by generations of knowledgeable jurists referring to the holy Qur'an, the beliefs and actions of the Prophet and the consensus of the entire community (*ijmāʿ al-umma*). Consequently, works on fiqh, or knowledge of the law, make up the largest section of Muslim literature. A wide range of questions are dealt with, such as ritual and prayer, taxes and alms, fasting and pilgrimage, holy war, justice and oath, praiseworthy and blamable actions, crime and punishment, succession, trade, etc.

Generally speaking, religious and legal manuscripts are devoid of any decoration. However, when preparing this type of manuscript, a few simple decorative elements were included. The document contains *al-Mukhtaṣar fī al-fiqh* ("A Short Manual of Fiqh"), by the Egyptian Khalīl ibn Isḥāq al-Jundī (died in 1365) who was the representative of the most widespread school of law in North Africa, the Maliki. The beginning is decorated with a clumsy, rectangular *ʿunvān* in which the title of the book is written. Similar *ʿunvāns* are to be found in folios 41v, 83v and 123v and mark the start of a chapter. [A.Kh.]

58. Āqā Muḥammad Kāẓim Vālih (died in 1813–1814)
Safīna
(The Ship)

Copied by the poet in person, mid-Dhu'l-Hijjah 1201 / September 1787, no doubt at Isfahan
Shikasta-i nastaʿlīq
Colored paper (lemon yellow, pink and brown)
thin and well-glazed
141 folios, 19 × 10.4 cm
Text: 15 × 8 cm, 2 columns of 10 lines, black ink, watercolors, gold
10 miniatures of the Isfahan school around 1775
Accession no. A-1646
Provenance: sent by the Moscow Library of Oriental Studies in 1962.
Bibliography: Akimushkin O.F., 1993, no. 12; Catalogue PTR, 1964, no. 87.

Safīna ("The Ship, the Ark") is a collection of poems composed by a celebrated man of letters and mystic poet, Āqā Muḥammad Kāẓim Iṣfahānī (died in 1229/1813–1814), known under the literary pseudonym of Vālih, bestowed upon him by an admirer originally from Isfahan, Muḥammad Qulī Āqā. It contains the ghazals of twelve Persian poets, including 61 poems composed by the poet himself.
This manuscript was most probably copied in Isfahan by the author himself, in mid-Dhu'l-Hijjah 1201/September 1787 (folio 141r), in an excellent professional *shikasta-i nastaʿlīq*. It is richly decorated with the text framed within two gilded bands, an ordinary frontispiece crowned by a tent-form cupola (*ʿunvān*) with a colored plant motif (*islīmī-i bargī*) against a blue and gold background; between the lines, the text is decorated with gold dots (*tarṣīʿ*) with a dark contour (*taḥrīr*).
It is illustrated with ten miniatures of the Isfahan school from the last quarter of the 18th century (in folios 89r and 128r, the poet Vālih is pictured). [O.A.]

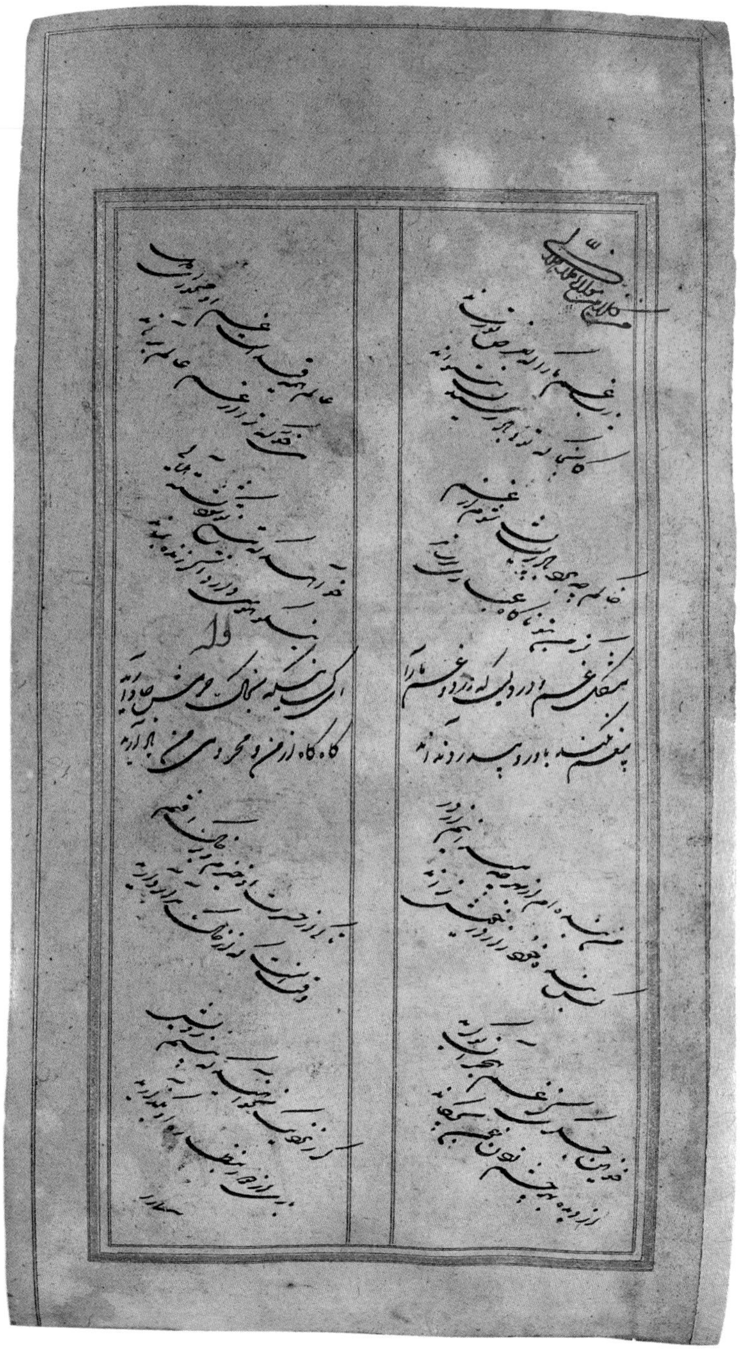

Folio 50v: superb calligraphy.

Folio 89r: An Evening in the Company of the Poet Vālih *(no. 6, 17.3 × 9.4 cm). Vālih, dressed in white, in the company of his friends at his home-retreat, Takiya-i ilāhiyya, specially built for him by the Isfahan authorities.*

59. Abū Muḥammad Ilyās ibn Yūsuf ibn Zakī ibn Mu'ayyad Niẓāmī Ganjavī (died in 1209–1210) Lailā u Majnūn (Lailā and Majnūn) (1188–1189)

Copied in Kashmir around 1810–1820
Nastaʿlīq
265 folios, 15.7 × 9 cm
Text: 13.5 × 7.5 cm
2 columns of 12 lines
42 miniatures of the Kashmir school of the 1810–1820 period
Accession no. A-20
Provenance: J.L. Rousseau collection, bought by the Russian Government for the Asiatic Museum, in 1819.
Bibliography: Adamova A., Grek T., 1976, pp. 76–77, 157, no. 36; Catalogue PTR, 1964, no. 3678.

This poem is the sad love story of Lailā and Majnūn, based on an oral Arabic legend, and was composed in 584/1188–1189 by the famous Persian poet, Abū Muḥammad Ilyās ibn Yūsuf ibn Zakī ibn Mu'ayyad Niẓāmī Ganjavī (died in 606/1209–1210).

In the colophon (folio 265r), no mention is made of the name of the copyist nor the date when this copy, executed in neat, well-proportioned and assured *nastaʿlīq* from the Kashmir school, was completed. It is richly decorated, the text is in a large colored frame decorated with plant motifs (*islīmī-i bargī*). The columns of text are separated by garlands of flowers; on the double-page frontispiece on folios 2v–3r, the composition is enclosed within a multi-colored frame decorated with lotus flowers and buds (*gul-i chīnī, gul-i khaṭā'ī*); folios 85v, 86r and 265r have floral decorations against a gilded background; folios 106r and 114v are entirely decorated. Some of the pages with text have been sprinkled with gold. The 42 miniatures were painted at the time the text was copied and are typical of the Kashmir school of 1810–1820 with regard to the color range, the selection, the composition, the somewhat primitive manner of painting the landscape, and the archaic way of depicting figures, looming large in proportion to background and landscape details. [O.A.]

Folio 11r: The Ascension of the Prophet Muḥammad to Heaven *(8.7 × 6 cm). According to tradition, Muḥammad climbed on a winged human-headed steed named Burāq, and rose up to the heavens.*

60. Kamāl al-Dīn Bāfqī Vaḥshī (died in 1582) and Muḥammad Shafīᶜ al-Shīrāzī Viṣāl (1783–1846) Farhād u Shīrīn (Farhād and Shīrīn)

Copied by Muḥammad Ismāᶜīl al-Anjavī al-Shīrāzī in Rabi I 1284 / July 1867, probably in Shiraz
Shikasta-i nastaᶜlīq
113 folios, 15.7 × 10 cm
Text: 10.7 × 5.6 cm
2 columns of 10–11 lines to the page
3 miniatures in the Qājār style
Accession no. A-910
Bibliography: Catalogue PTR, 1964, no. 3059.

"Farhād and Shīrīn" is a romantic poem (1000 couplets—*bayt*) begun by the poet, Kamāl al-Dīn Bāfqī Vaḥshī (died in 1582), in the Indian style of Persian poetry and completed (1800 further couplets) by a great cultural figure in Iran during the 19th century, Muḥammad Shafīᶜ al-Shīrāzī Viṣāl (1783–1846). The calligrapher, Muḥammad Ismāᶜīl al-Anjavī al-Shīrāzī, from the family of sayyid al-Ḥusain, copied this manuscript probably in Shiraz during Rabi I 1284/July 1867, using calligraphy belonging to the style of *shikasta-i nastaᶜlīq*. Overall, the copy is a perfect example of the handwritten book from Iran in the second half of the 19th century. The text is separated by gold dots (*tarṣī*ᶜ) surrounded by black bands (*taḥrīr*); it contains a frontispiece (*sarlauḥ*, ᶜ*unvān*) in the Qājār style, a delicate and refined design with a predominantly gold and blue background, decorated with numerous interwoven motifs (*islīmī-i bargī, gul-i khaṭā'ī.*); the margins of folios 1v and 2r are decorated with indentations (*shurfa*).
Three miniatures (folios 48r, 51r, 65r) in the Qājār style show obvious signs of European influence, such as light and shade, perspective, and depth of image.
The lacquer binding (16 × 9.2 cm) has a leather spine, and its covers are decorated with loops of convolvulus and a plant motif in gold, as well as flowers (*islīmī-i bargī*), against a dark green background. The decoration of the manuscript would suggest it was made to order. [O.A.]

Folios 1v–2r.

Qur'ans Made on Commission

Efim A. Rezvan

"I said (to the merchant): "And for what purpose is this voyage?" He replied, "I will transport sulfur from Persia to China, where it is apparently in great demand. From there, I will take porcelain to Greece and Greek brocades to India, then Indian steel to Aleppo, Aleppo glass to the Yemen, and Yemeni fabrics to Persia..."
(French translation by Omar Ali Shah; Saᶜdi, *Le Jardin de Roses*, Albin Michel, Paris, 1966, p. 127)

These words describing the activities of an Arab merchant, are quoted from the famous Persian poet, Muṣliḥ al-Dīn Saᶜdī (died in 1292). Muslim merchants traveled throughout China and Indonesia, Central Asia and North Africa, Spain and along the Volga River. Given the danger due to bandits or pirates, wars, epidemics, etc., the merchants carried the Qur'an with them as their most treasured companion. An example of the sacred text in a small format is catalogue no. 4, probably dating from the 10th century. It acted both as a talisman against all possible misfortunes (*āyāt al-ḥafẓ*, verses of protection: 2:225/226; 12:64; 13:11/12; 15:17; 85:20–22), and first aid in case of sickness (*āyāt al-shifā'*, verses of cure: 9:14; 10:57/58; 16:69/71; 26:80, etc.). A Muslim's final journey was also accompanied by the melodious sounds of Qur'anic recitation (suras 1, 2, 18, 36, 44, 97, generally read during the funeral ceremony). Talismans inscribed with single verses were also worn on the body, as well as occasionally a selection of suras (generally seven), but most of the time the entire text of the Qur'an was carried when traveling. Seen in this context, it became customary for wealthy Muslims to commission copies of the sacred text in small format, carefully written and elegantly decorated.

Books were expensive. Despite this, thousands of manuscript copies of the Qur'an have been passed down to us, and through these, it is possible to understand the way various concepts of beauty evolved over time.

One day, impressed by the frescoes in Venetian churches, B.L. Pasternak wrote: "I understand that the Bible is not just a book with a rigid text, but more of a written notebook on humanity and thus eternal. It is valid not when one has decreed that it should be so, but when it is receptive to all assimilation through which it has gone in centuries past." The numerous commentaries on the Qur'an, like the diversity in its presentation, make these words applicable to the Qur'an as well.

Bibliography: 1870, Barsov P., p. 792; 1951, Braginskii I., p. 335; 1985, Pasternak B., p. 252.

61. Qur'an

Folio 222v: end of sura XLVI (end of verse 32 and verses 33–35), beginning of sura XLVII (verse 1 and beginning of verse 2).

Copied in Iran (perhaps Shiraz), first half of the 14th century
Naskh
Excellent quality paper
272 folios
25 × 19 cm
Accession no. C-705
Provenance: coll. of P. Sukhtelen, 1837; Teaching Section of the Asiatic Department in the Russian Ministry of Foreign Affairs, Asiatic Museum in 1919.

The manuscript is richly decorated, but has been partially damaged. The central field in the part of the frontispiece that has been preserved is divided into three vertical sections citing the beginning of sura II using the *tarṣīʿ* and *taḥrīr* decorative features and a convolvulus loop motif. The text made up of six lines is written in golden *riqāʿ* script. The two rectangular cartouches, above and below, are decorated with *band-i rūmī* ornaments. The main colors used are lapis lazuli and gold, as well as carmine and light blue.
A leaf has been stuck in the place of the missing folio 1v, which carries the text of sura I, written in a beautiful and bold *nastaʿlīq* in black ink on coffee-colored paper. The text is interspersed with gold (*abrī*) and an extremely fine plant motif in red and blue pigment.
In folio 1r, there is an annotation in French indicating that the copy of sura I was written by the "famous calligrapher Ebul-Baka" (Abū al-Baqā, the Indian calligrapher of the mid-17th century).
The unusual composition of the main part of the text is interesting. The elegant, assured *naskh*, is in a complex frame (22 × 15.3 cm) divided horizontally into two parts, generally enclosing six lines each. One line in the upper part, one in the central and one in the lower part of the page are written in *riqāʿ* script; and two polychrome pendant-shaped decorations are placed on the left and the right of the text; outside of the frame are two complex polychrome half-rosettes, sometimes indicating the beginning of a *juz'* or a *ḥizb* that follows.
At the beginning of each sura is an elegant rectangle decorated with a gold tooled cartouche, and the title of the sura worked in white painted *thuluth*, in addition to an indication of where it was pronounced and the number of verses it contains. The decorative elements of the cartouches are the same as those used in the frontispiece. The end of each verse is marked with a gold rosette. [O.A., E.R.]

من عذاب اليم ومن لا يجب داعي الله

فليس بمعجز في الارض وليس له من دونه اولياء اولئك في ضلال مبين
اولم يروا ان الله الذي خلق السموات والارض ولم يعي بخلقهن بقادر على
ان يحيي الموتى بلى انه على كل شيء قدير ويوم يعرض الذين
كفروا على النار اليس هذا بالحق قالوا بلى وربنا قال فذوقوا
العذاب بما كنتم تكفرون فاصبر كما صبر اولوا العزم من
الرسل ولا تستعجل لهم كانهم يوم يرون ما يوعدون لم يلبثوا الا ساعة من

نهار بلاغ فهل يهلك الا القوم الفاسقون

سورة محمد صلى الله عليه وآله ثمان وثلثون آية

بسم الله الرحمن الرحيم

الذين كفروا وصدوا عن سبيل الله اضل اعمالهم والذين
امنوا وعملوا الصالحات وامنوا بما نزل على محمد وهو الحق من ربهم

كفر عنهم سيئاتهم واصلح بالهم

62. Qur'an

Copied probably in Khurasan, middle of the 17th century
Naskh
High quality glazed paper
32 folios, 27 × 16 cm
Text: 19.5 × 10.5 cm
49 lines to the page
Accession no. C-184
Provenance: acquired in 1874 from the first governor general of the Turkestan region, K.P. von Kaufman.
Bibliography: Dorn B., p. 397, 1875, no. 1; Rosen V.R., 1881, no. 32.

This copy, in well-proportioned miniature *naskh*, is richly decorated. The composition of the frontispiece is on a double page, divided into three vertical and horizontal sections; two rectangular cartouches, above and below the text on each page, against a light blue background, with gold, black and red pigment; in the upper tooled oval-shaped cartouche, we read the title of the sura. In a similar cartouche below is the indication of where it was pronounced and the number of verses it contains. In the center in *naskh* writing, with elements of *muḥaqqaq* in white pigment on a gold background we read the text of sura I (folio 1v) and the beginning of sura II (folio 2r). To the left and the right of the text, against a pale blue background are two tooled oval cartouches with a flower motif against a gold background. The central composition is framed by a wide border covered with a motif of blue lotus flowers on a gold background. The text is enclosed within two complex frames. The space in-between is taken up with convolvulus loops and division indicators in *juz'* and *ḥizb*, written in simple gilded medallions. The titles of the suras and sometimes the place in which they were pronounced are written in the same writing using white pigment in small gold cartouches. A gilded rosette marks the end of each verse. [O.A., E.R.]

Folio 1r.

Folios 17v–18r.

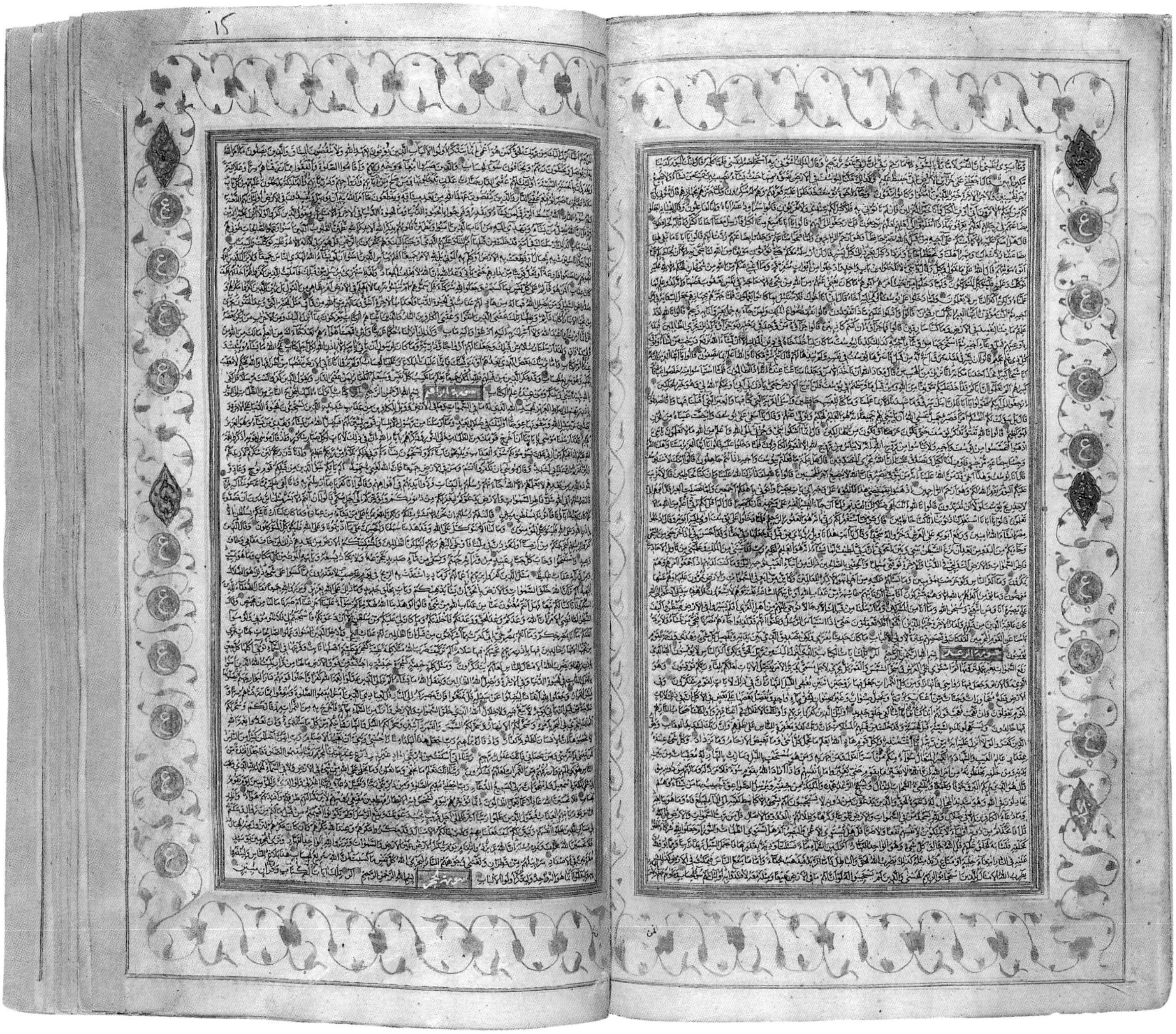

63. Qur'an

Folios *1v–2r.*

Copied by Maḥmūd, known as al-Kāshif, in Iraq, 1778
Naskh
Thick, fine and glossy, pale cream colored paper
310 folios
12 × 18.5 cm
Accession no. A-995

This copy is richly decorated. The frontispiece is decorated on each page by two rectangular cartouches, above and below the text carrying the title of the sura and an indication of where it was pronounced and the number of verses it contains. In the center of the text of sura I and the beginning of sura II the text is separated by a gold area bordered by a fine black line. The background of the frontispiece is mainly gold, with a plant and flower motif also painted in gold. In the center of each page is an oval shaped cartouche running over to the margin. Its edges are decorated with an ornament called *band-i rūmī* in Persian. The text is in a complex polychrome frame. The end of each verse is marked by a rosette decorated with blue and red dots divided into sections by a fine black line. The *juz'* and *ḥizb* are marked with gold cartouches and elements of decoration from the frontispiece. The suras are decorated by fine rectangular cartouches on a gold background, carrying the titles of the suras and the place in which they were pronounced, and the number of verses it contains written in white pigment.

In folio 308v, is a colophon decorated with a tooled semi-circular cartouche. The lines of the colophon, like the lines of the frontispiece are separated by areas of gold surrounded by a fine black line. The edges are decorated with a plant motif in red on a gold background. The text of the colophon states that the copy was made by "Maḥmūd known as al-Kāshif (Maḥmūd al-shāhir bi-al-kāshif) during the first days of Safar 1192" (1778).

The binding is older than the manuscript (beginning of the 18th century). It is made of cardboard covered with dark brown leather and decorated with inlay. In the central area is a geometric pattern covered with transparent lacquer. The frame is formed of two wide borders (*band-i rūmī*). [O.A., E.R.]

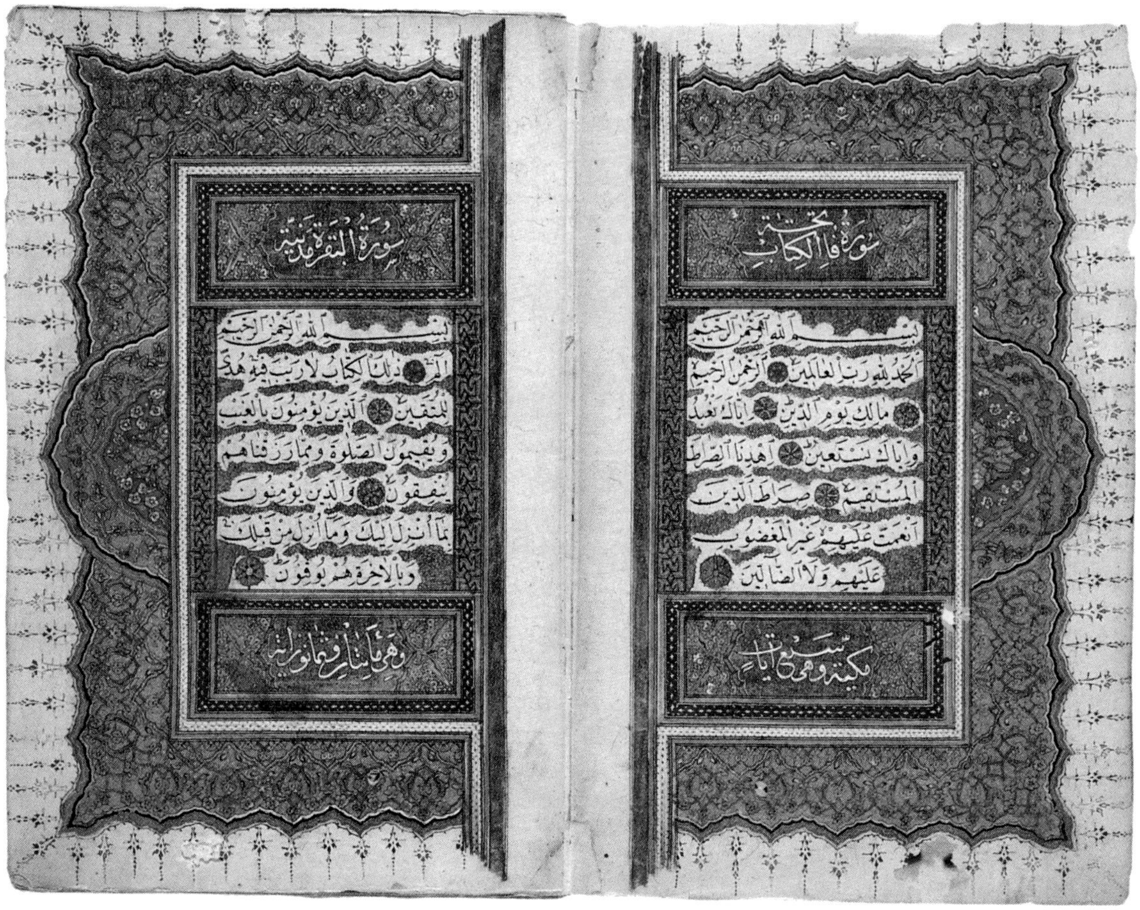

64. Qur'an

Folios 1v–2r.

Copied perhaps in Isfahan, first half of the 19th century
Naskh
High quality strong, fine and well glazed, pale cream colored paper
240 folios
17.8 × 10 cm
Text: 15.5 × 12 cm
19 lines to the page
Accession no. A-939
Provenance: despatched by V.V. Radloff in 1918.

This copy in neat and assured *naskh* calligraphy is richly decorated. The frontispiece on a full double page is a single composition (*dībācha*), in three vertical sections, each page decorated with two rectangular cartouches, above and below the text, carrying the title of the sura and an indication of where it was pronounced and the number of verses as well as two narrow cartouches decorated with plant motifs. In the center of the text of sura I and the beginning of sura II the lines of the text are separated with gold, and surrounded by a fine black serrated line (*tarṣīʿ va taḥrīr*). The same process is used to decorate the entire text of the Qur'an. The edges of the frontispiece are decorated with a wide ornamental band of lapis lazuli blue on a gold backdrop.
In Persia, this type of ornament was given a special name, *khaṭā'ī*. In addition, the text is surrounded by a wide floral ornamental band on a gold background. The suras are preceded by a rectangular decorative panel framed by a complex band decorated mainly by a gilded lily, around the text. In the center of the lapis lazuli blue decoration is an oval cartouche with the title of the sura and indication of where it was pronounced and the number of verses on a gold background. The end of each verse is marked by a gold rosette.
The *juz'* and *ḥizb* are indicated in the margins with cartouches gilded in the form of foliage, and a series of colored cartouches linked together by a fine line. In the top right hand corner of each double page is the number of the *juz'*, and in the left corner, the title of the sura. The *ḥāfiẓ* ("keeper") ensures that the pages are kept in sequential order, thus it is the last word on a page and is written in gold at the foot of each page and corresponds with the first word of the following page which is written in the upper margin; i.e., it is a catchword.
A narrow gold frame surrounds both the text and the various elements in the margins.
The binding is made of lacquered cardboard, with a leather spine, probably originally made for an older manuscript. The surface is decorated with plant and floral motifs, typical of the 18th century. In the upper part of the back plate is a cartouche bearing the name of Faẓl ʿAlī, possibly the owner or binder. [O.A., E.R.]

65. Qur'an

Folios 3v–4r.

Copied probably in Central Asia, Kokand, around 1830
Naskh
High quality glossy paper
259 folios
23.5 × 14 cm
Text: 15 × 8.4 cm
14 lines to the page
Accession no. B-354
Provenance: despatched by A.L. Kuhn in 1890.
Bibliography: Salemann C., X, 275, 1894, no. 26.

This richly decorated copy in large, confident *naskh* calligraphy is the work of a non-Arab professional scribe. The double-page frontispiece is decorated with a single composition in three vertical sections. Each page contains two rectangular cartouches, one above and one below the text. In the upper cartouche is the title of the sura and the indication of where it was pronounced. In the center is the text of sura I and the beginning of sura II; the individual lines of the text are separated by gold bands (using a similar decorative feature as the *tarṣīʿ va taḥrīr* used by the Persians, known under the Ottomans as *abrī*).

The text is enclosed in three complex frames dominated by yellow, gold and red respectively. The suras are preceded by a decorative panel often subdivided into three sections, containing the title of the sura, an indication of where it was pronounced and the number of verses. The end of each verse is marked by a gold rosette. The *juz'* and *ḥizb* are indicated in the margins with blue and gold half-rosettes with decorative ornaments.

Most probably, this manuscript was copied and decorated in Kokand by experts from the Darvaz-Badakhshan school around 1830. [O.A., E.R.]

66. Qur'an

Copied in 1282/1865–1866
by Muḥammad ᶜAlī al-Jumᶜī,
probably in Syria
Naskh
High quality thick, fine
and well-glazed paper
of a pale cream color
306 folios, 19 × 13 cm
Text: 6.7 × 12 cm
15 lines to the page
Accession no. A-1513
Provenance: despatched in 1936
by S.A. Alimov entrusted
by the Institute to gather
manuscripts in the region
of the Lower Volga.

This richly decorated copy is in fine *naskh* calligraphy used extensively throughout Arab provinces in the Ottoman empire. The double-page frontispiece constitutes a single composition in three vertical sections. Each page has two rectangular cartouches, one above and one below the text, containing the title of the sura and the indication of where it was pronounced and the number of verses. On a gold background, a plant and floral decoration with sunrays spread into the margins. In the center is the text of sura I and the beginning of sura II; the lines are separated by areas of gold and colored pigment, a similar process to the *tarṣīʿ va taḥrīr* used by the Persians, sometimes known as *abrī*. The frontispiece is enclosed in a large tooled frame decorated with numerous cartouches in the form of stylized lotus flowers. The suras are preceded by a fine rectangular decoration on a gold background, on which the title of the sura and its *isnād* are written in white pigment. The text is enclosed within a complex gold frame. The *juz'* and *ḥizb* are indicated in the margins interspersed with decorated gold and colored rosettes. The binding, made at the same time as the manuscript, is of cardboard covered by light coffee-colored leather. The outside cover has a geometric embossed design with gilded decoration. The central section consists of a rectangle decorated with gold points and a border of average thickness. [O.A., E.R.]

67. Qur'an

Copied perhaps in Kano, Northern Nigeria, in the middle of the 19th century
Ifrīqī
Thick and rough packing-type paper
206 folios
22.3 × 16.4 cm
Text: 8.5 × 15 cm
15 lines to the page, black and red ink
Accession no. C-1689
Provenance: despatched by V.K. Shileiko of the Academy of the History of Material Culture in 1919.
Bibliography: Brocket A., 1987; Rippin. A., 1988, pp. 31–45.

The copies of the Qur'an presented here represent the most widespread form of reading, that of the *qārī'* ("reciter") from Kufa ᶜĀṣim (died in 744), handed down by the *rāwī* ("transmitter") Ḥafṣ (died in 805). It shows a tradition of textual transmission, common in the western Muslim world, and in Zaidi Yemen. It is the tradition that goes back to the reciter of Medina, Nāfiᶜ (died in 785), handed down by Warsh (died in 812). The appearance of an Egyptian edition, that is now the most widely distributed in the Muslim world, follows the first tradition, although that does not imply that the other versions have disappeared. Today, the Qur'an according to Warsh is published not just in North Africa, but in Cairo and Saudi Arabia, whereas the Qur'an in the Ḥafṣ tradition is published in Tunis. This copy is written in an confident, medium-size *ifrīqī* (the Sudanese call it kufic and the Hausa *ᶜajamī*. This writing derives from the kufic script and is often referred to using the general term *maghribī*. It was widely used in North Africa until the 12th century. This calligraphic tradition was maintained until the beginning of the 20th century in the territory that corresponds to the north of Nigeria.
The diacritical marks are in black ink, as is the text, and the vocalization marks are in red ink. The titles of the suras are in red ink, with diacritical and vocalization marks in black ink. The end of each verse is marked with three yellow points, which presumably goes back to the tradition set by older copies, where the verses were separated by hachures or triangular points.
Typically North African decorative patterns do not require symmetry. On the contrary, this is avoided for fear of the "evil eye." The decoration of this manuscript is an example of such use of an asymmetrical pattern.
The document has a flap binding in dark brown leather, with a geometric decoration embossed on both covers.
It has a leather buckle and strap, another North African characteristic. Most of the folios have the *tre lune* ("three moons") filigrain with a human profile, which helps date the manuscript to the middle or the second half of the 19th century. The comparison made with a manuscript in the collection at the University of Leeds in Great Britain (Leeds Arabic MS.301) has helped to determine locating where it was copied: Kano (Nigeria) where for many years, a local school teaching the study and copying of the Qur'an prospered. It is quite possible that the copyist belonged to the Hausa tribe. [E.R.]

Folios 2r–1v.

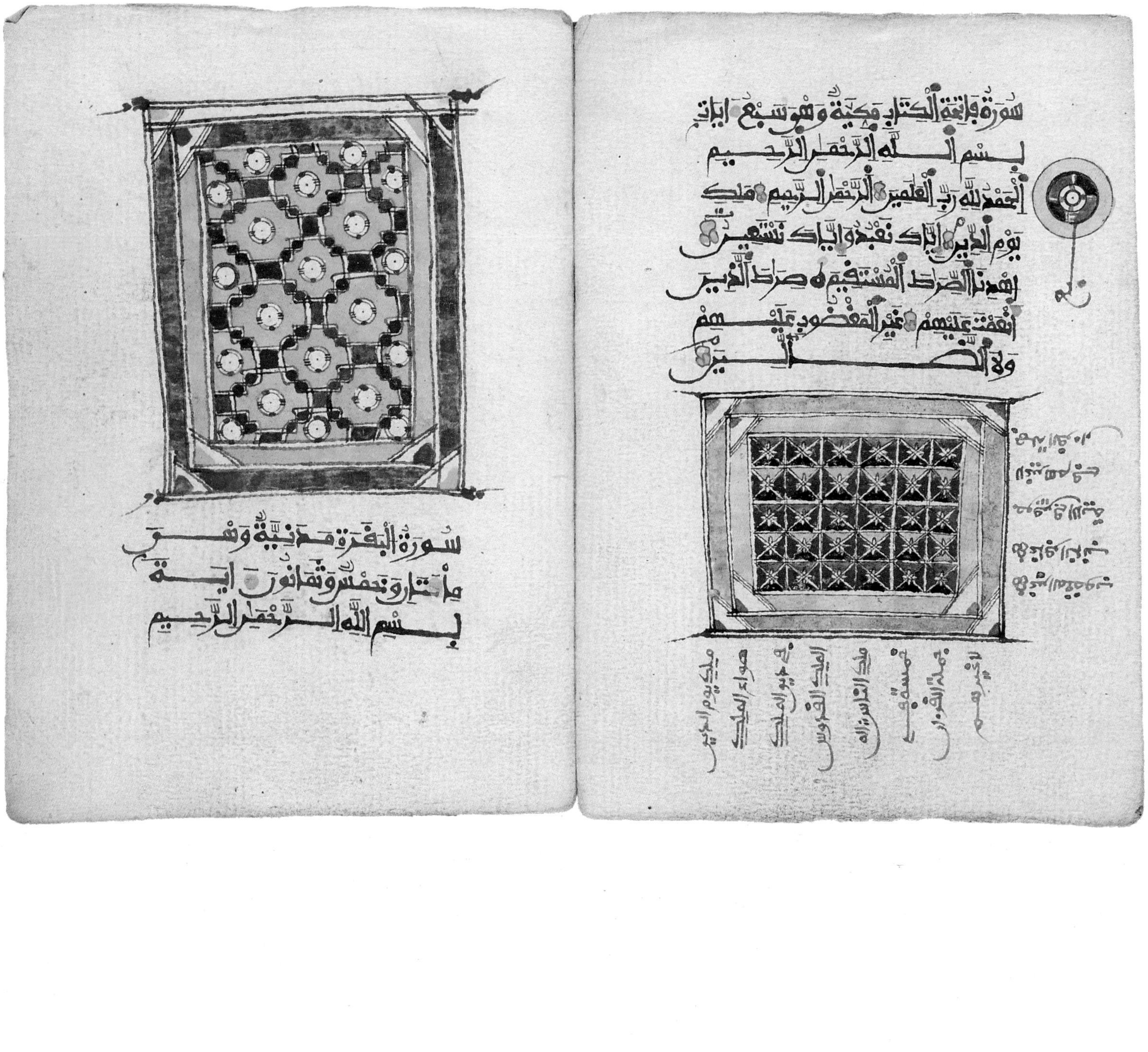

Appendices

ᶜAbbasids
Dynasty named after its ancestor, al-ᶜAbbās ibn ᶜAbd al-Muttalib, the uncle of the Prophet Muḥammad. In 750 it followed the Ummayad dynasty with its capital in Damascus and in 763 it made Baghdad its capital (until the latter was destroyed by the Mongols in 1258).

Akbar
Mughal emperor of India (1542–1605), whose rule (1556–1605) saw a great flowering of art and science and attempts to reconcile the Hindu and Muslim subjects of the Mughal empire.

Allāh
Arabic name for God.

Atabeg
(Turkish *ata bey*, "father + prince"). Term used in the Seljuq period for the tutor of a ruler, later used to indicate an independent prince.

Ayyubids
Dynasty ruling in Egypt, Syria and the Yemen (1171–1220) founded by Saladin (Ṣalāḥ al-Dīn).

Bābur
Descendant of Tīmūr and of Chingīz Khān, from Ferghana. In 1528 Bābur founded the dynasty of the Great Mughals in northern India.

Baghdad
City in Iraq. Capital of the ᶜAbbasid dynasty from 763 to 1258.

Balkh
A city in Northern Afghanistan where are the ruins of Baktra, the capital of ancient Bactria. Balkh was destroyed by Chingīz Khān in 1221.

Basmala
(Arabic). Sacred formula with which Muslims introduce all important actions: *bism allāh al-raḥmān al-raḥīm*, "In the Name of God, the Merciful, the Compassionate."

Bāisunghur
A descendant of the Turkish ruler, Tīmūr-i Lang (Tamerlane or Tamberlain). A great patron of the arts, especially illuminated manuscripts, whose court was at Herat in Persia.

Bedouins
(Arabic *badw*). Pastoral nomads of Arabian blood. The Prophet Muḥammad belonged to the Bedouin tribe of Quraysh.

Byzantium
The Roman Empire in the East which, under the Emperor Justinian (b. 483, ruled 527–565), covered the territory of the modern states of Turkey, Syria, Lebanon, Egypt and parts of Jordan.

Calendar
The Islamic lunar calendar was introduced in 638 and starts with the first month of the year in which Muḥammad moved to Medina in 622 (see Hijra). The lunar year has 354 days; lunar months of 29 days generally alternate with months of 30:
Muharram
Safar
Rabi I
Rabi II
Jumada I
Jumada II
Rajab
Shaᶜban
Ramadan
Shawwal
Dhul-Qaᶜda
Dhu'l-Hijja

Caliph
(Arabic *khalīfat rasūl allāh*, "successor of Allāh's messenger"). Leader of the Muslim community.
The Caliphs possessed temporal as well as spiritual authority.

Caliphate
Office and domain of a Caliph. In the Near East a difference is made between: 1. the Caliphate of the first four Caliphs (632–661: Abū Bakr, ᶜUmar, ᶜUthmān and ᶜAlī) with its capital at Medina; 2. the Caliphate of the Umayyads (661–750, based in Damascus); and 3. that of the ᶜAbbasids (750–1258) with its capital mainly at Baghdad. In addition there were: the Umayyad Caliphate of Cordoba, Spain (929–1031); the Fatimid Caliphate in North Africa and Egypt (910–1171) with its seat first in Kairouan and later in Cairo; and the Ottoman Caliphate (1517–1924), with its capital in Istanbul.

Cartouche
(French). A type of ornament much used in book illumination and later in architecture, consisting of a shield-shaped space for inscriptions and scrolled border decoration.

Central Asia
The area lying to the east of the Caspian Sea, embracing the modern-day states of northern Afghanistan, Kazakhstan, Kyrgyzstan, Tajikistan, Turkmenistan, Uzbekistan and some

western provinces of China (Eastern Turkistan).

Chagatai
All eastern Turkic languages. Also the name of Chingīz Khān's second son, ruler over Turkestan after 1227. The capital of his Khanate was Kashgar, today in the province of Xinjiang in China.

Codex
Precursor of the modern book form; in the 4th–5th centuries the codex supplanted the scroll in many areas. It consisted of numerous leaves of papyrus or parchment enclosed between wooden boards, usually covered with leather.

Colophon
An inscription at the end of a manuscript, or of a section of it, giving details about one or more of the following: author, writer, place, and date of copying.

Ctesiphon
An ancient city on the left bank of the Tigris, principal residence of the Parthians and Sasanians, destroyed by the Arabs in 637.

Dervish
(Pers. *darvīsh*, "poor, beggar"). A Muslim mystic.

Diacritical marks
Visual means (dots and lines above or below letters, etc.) used to distinguish between otherwise identically written characters.

Divan
(Arabic *dīwān*). The collected poems of a single author.

Druze
A sect founded in Egypt in 1017 whose members were forced to flee to Syria on account of their sharp doctrinal differences with Islam and their veneration of the Fatimid Caliph al-Ḥākim (996–1021) as a god.

Faqir
(Arabic *faqīr*). Member of a sufi brotherhood; often a dervish.

Fatiha
(Arabic *al-Fātiḥa*). First sura of the Qur'an. In a sense the Muslim equivalent of the Christian "Lord's Prayer."

Fatimids
North African dynasty that ruled Egypt from 969 to 1171, claiming descent from Muḥmmad's daughter Fāṭima.

Fiqh
(Arabic *fiqh*). The science of Muslim jurisprudence according to the *sharīʿa*, deriving from the Qur'an.

Firdausī
Persian poet (934–1020). Author of the Iranian national epic poem *Shāhnāma* ("The Book of Kings").

Ghazal
(Arabic *ghazal*). A lyric poem. Originally an oriental form of love poetry with usually 3 to 15 couplets, the first of which rhymes while the following even lines repeat this rhyme and the odd lines remain unrhymed (Scheme: aa ba ca da...). The original Arabic form was a feature of the work of the Persian poet Ḥāfiẓ and was used in Germany particularly by Goethe, Platen and Rüchert.

al-Ghazālī
A jurist, theologian and mystic (1058–1111) from Tus in Khurasan. By reconciling ascetic and mystical sufism with the orthodox legal tradition, al-Ghazālī contributed greatly to maintaining religious harmony within Islamic society.

Ghaznavids
Turkic dynasty (998–1186) that ruled what is now Eastern Afghanistan. Its founder, Maḥmūd, came from the Ghaznavid capital of Ghazna. His father was a slave who became a general under the Persian Samanid dynasty.

Hadith
(Arabic *ḥadīth*). The corpus of reports of the words and actions of the Prophet (also denotes any single such report). Together with the Qur'an, the hadiths form the basis of the *sharīʿa*, the Islamic legal code.

Hadramaut
Area in the present-day Yemen with capital Tarim.

Ḥāfiẓ
Persian mystical lyric poet from Shiraz, ca. 1324–1388. His poems, in particular ghazals on nature, wine and love, inspired *inter alia* Goethe's *Westöstlicher Diwan.*

Hajj
(Arabic *ḥājj*). The full pilgrimage to Mecca, which should be undertaken by every mentally and physically fit Muslim adult at least once in his or her lifetime.

Hanafī
(Arabic *ḥanafī*). Member of one of the four Sunnite schools of law, founded by Abū Ḥanīfa (d. 767). The Hanafi school was followed in Central Asia, India and the Ottoman Empire.

Herat
City in what is now Western Afghanistan.
In the 15th century, Herat was the center of the Timurid empire and the center of Persian culture.

Hijaz
The area of Western Arabia containing the holy cities of Mecca and Medina.

Hijra
(Arabic *hijra*). The emigration from Mecca 345 kms northwards to Medina (16 July 622) undertaken by the Prophet Muḥammad and his disciples. From the time of the Caliph ʿUmar, this event was taken as the starting point for the Islamic era.

Ijmāʿ
Consensus of scholars on a particular point of Islamic law.

Imam
(Arabic *imām*). Leader, especially of ritual prayers. For the Shiʿites, the imam is the legitimate spiritual leader.

Imami
Sect of "Twelvers." The doctrine of the Shiʿite "Twelver" sect has been the state religion in Iran since the early 16th century.

Isfahan
Third biggest city of Iran; capital of the Safavid dynasty from ca. 1590 to 1722.

Iskandar
Arabic form of the name Alexander.

Islam
(Arabic *islām*, "submission; devotion to God's will"). This is the term the Prophet Muḥammad used to indicate the form of non-idolatrous monotheism founded by him according to the example of the Prophet Abraham, and destined to become the last of the world religions. A follower of this religion is called Muslim.

Ismaili
A Shiᶜte sect which particularly venerates its seventh imam, Ismāᶜīl, who died in 762.

Jinns
(Arabic *jinn*). Intelligent beings with subtle bodies, composed of fire. The jinns can take on the most diverse forms and are capable of accomplishing arduous or complicated tasks. Like mankind, they have the power to choose between good and evil.

Kaᶜba
(Arabic *al-kaᶜba*). Cube-shaped building inside the Great Mosque of Mecca, an ancient Arab shrine.
According to Islam, this is where Abraham built the first holy place for the worship of the one God. One of the main rites of pilgrimage consists in the sevenfold circumambulation of the Kaᶜba.

Khamsa
(Arabic, "Quintet"). Applied to a collection of five epic or didactic poems by a single author.

Khan
(Chagatai *khān*). Turkic-Mongol title for a ruler or dignitary appended to a name, e.g. Chingīz Khan.

Kokand
City and Khanate in the fertile Ferghana Valley in what is today the Republic of Uzbekistan. From 1700, under the Shaibānid dynasty, Kokand enjoyed relative prosperity.

Khurasan
(Persian *khurāsān*, "[land of the] east"). A large province in Northern and Eastern Iran and Western Afghanistan.

Khusrau
Name of two kings of the Persian Sasanian dynasty: Khusrau I (ruled 531–579), conqueror of Antioch and the Yemen, and Khusrau II (ruled 590–628), who conquered Jerusalem in 614 and captured the "True Cross." Soon after the latter's assassination the Arabs conquered Persia.

Khwarazm
(Persian *khwārazm*). A once fertile and prosperous region west of the river Oxus (Amu-Darya), south of the Aral Sea in modern-day Uzbekistan, Central Asia.
From the 10th to the 13th centuries it was an independent kingdom whose capital was Urgench Khwarazm. It flourished under Shāh ᶜAlā al-Dīn Muḥmmad (ruled 1200–1220) and his predecessors before being destroyed by the Mongols.

Kufic
(Arabic *kūfī*, "from Kufa"). All geometric monumental forms of the old form of Arabic script, named after Kufa in Iraq renowned as a seat of learning. In the 10th century, kufic was supplanted by the more rounded script known as *naskh* or *naskhī*.

Madrasa
(Arabic *madrasa*). School for the teaching of theology, knowledge of law, grammar and literature.

Maghrib
(Arabic *maghrib*, "west"). In the Middle Ages, a term used to designate the entire Islamic World west of Egypt, today rather more narrowly the North African states of Morocco, Algeria, Tunisia and Libya.

Mamluks
(Arabic *mamlūk*, "slave"). Turkish and Circassian hired soldiers who took power after the assassination of the last Ayyubid in Egypt in 1250, where they established the dynasty of the Bahrī Mamluks and thereafter of the Burjī Mamluks. The Mamluks held important posts even after the conquest of Egypt by the Ottomans in 1517, not losing their influence entirely until Napoleon's victory in 1798.

Maqāmāt
(Arabic, "assemblies, sessions"). Short stories or anecdotes narrated purely as entertainment.
A favorite literary genre in the Middle Ages.

Mawarannahr
(Arabic *mā warā' al-nahr*, "what lies beyond the river"). See Transoxiana.

Mecca
(Arabic *Makka*). Before the coming of Islam, Mecca was the commercial center of the Arabian Peninsula, famous for its markets and fairs which took place there in the four months during which all struggles between different clans ceased and general civil peace reigned. Mecca is the first holy city of Islam, containing the sacred mosque in which is the Kaᶜba.

Medina
(Arabic *madīna*). The second holy city of Islam, containing the mosque and tomb of the Prophet Muḥammad. The town is 345 kms north of Mecca and was formerly called Yathrib. Many Jews lived there and Muḥammad hoped to receive support from them for his monotheistic religion. The Prophet emigrated there in 622.

Middle East
A term for the territory that includes the regions from what is now Morocco in the west to Iran in the east.

Mīrzā
(abbreviation of Arabic-Persian *amīr-zāda*, "prince's scion"). A common title of honor in Persia prefixed to the name of a person of distinction.

Mosque
(Arabic *masjid*). Place of collective worship and Friday prayer for the Muslim community. The mosque often serves also as a school, courthouse and community center.

Mughals
Indian Muslim dynasty of Central Asian origin, descended

from Tīmūr and Chingīz Khān. After the conquest of Delhi by Bābur in 1526, Akbar extended the Mughal empire to take in the whole of Northern India. Mughal power reached its apogee under Akbar, Jahāngīr and Shāh Jahān. The last Mughal Emperor was banished to Burma by the British in 1857.

Muḥammad
(ca. 570–632). "The most praised." Also called *rasūl allāh* ("Messenger of God"). Founder of the religion of Islam.

Muraqqa[c]
Album of calligraphic specimens and miniature paintings.

Naskh
(Arabic). Also *naskhī*. Standard script employed by ᶜAbbasid scribes from the first half of the 10th century onward. *Naskh* gradually supplanted the kufic script.

Nastaᶜlīq
(Abbreviation of Arabic-Persian *naskh + taᶜlīq*).
Arabic cursive handwriting style in which the letters slant sharply downwards. It was particularly suited to Persian poetry.

Niẓāmī
A Persian poet (1141–1202) from Ganja in the present day Republic of Azerbaijan. He was the foremost exponent of the romantic epic in Persia.

Olearius, Adam
Real name: Oelschläger (1603–1671). A German writer who accompanied embassies to Russia and Persia as an interpreter. His 1647 account, *Neue Orientalische Reise* ("New Journey to the Orient"), was a pioneering example of scholarly travel reporting. Olearius also published the first anthology of Oriental poetry translated into German.

Omayyads
See Umayyads.

Ottoman Empire
Turkish dominated empire from 1300 to 1923, so named after the founding father of the Ottoman dynasty, Sultan ᶜUs̱mān I (b. 1258, reigned 1288–1326).
The victory of Selīm I (b. 1470, reigned 1512–1520) over the Mamluks in Syria and Egypt confirmed the Ottoman State as the leading power in the Near East.

Pahlavi
An Indo-European, Persian language used between the 3rd and 10th centuries.

Papyrus
Writing material derived from the papyrus plant, a reed growing up to 13 ft. Scrolls were produced by joining together sheets made by sticking thin strips of the pith crosswise over each other.

Parchment
Writing material made of plucked, dried and smoothed animal skin, usually of calf, kid, or lamb, occasionally of gazelle.

Quadi
(Arabic *qāḍi*). Judge in an Islamic court whose task it is to give judgements according to the *shariᶜa*.

Qājārs
The ruling dynasty in Iran from 1797 to 1925 with its capital in Tehran.

Qalam
(Arabic *qalam*, from Greek *kalamos*). A reed pen with a pointed and a flattened end, the preferred writing instrument among Muslims from the 8th century onwards.

Qasida
(Arabic *qaṣīda*, "purpose poem"). A poetic form originally comprising between seven and fifteen couplets. Qasidas were often panegyrics dedicated to a patron.

Qur'an
(Arabic *Qur'ān*). The entirety of the pronouncements given by God through the angel Gabriel to the Prophet Muḥmmad. The Qur'an consists of 114 suras. The definitive edition was compiled by order of the Caliph ᶜUthmān. For the purposes of recitation these are divided into 30 roughly equal parts (*juz'*), each of which is divided into two sections (*ḥizb*).

Ramadan
(Arabic *ramaḍān*). The ninth month of the Islamic lunar year, throughout which Muslims fast between dawn and dusk.

Rūmī, Jalāl al-Dīn
Persian mystic poet (1207–1273). His *Masnavī* is one of the key works of sufism.

Saᶜdī
Persian poet (1213 or 1219–1292) from Shiraz. Famous for his didactic poems *Bustān* ("Orchard") and *Gulistān* ("Rose Garden") as well as his *Divan* (collected qasidas and ghazals).

Safavids
Iranian dynasty, 1501–1722. Under the Safavids Shiᶜism became the state religion of Iran. Art and culture flourished, particularly under Shāh Ṭahmāsp (1524–1576) with its capitals at Tabriz and later at Qazvin. Under Shāh ᶜAbbās I, known as Shāh ᶜAbbās the Great, the capital moved to Isfahan.

Sarlauḥ
(Persian, "ornamental heading"). Ornamental, decorated double-page frontispiece of a manuscript.

Sasanians
Iranian dynasty, 224–651. Their empire expanded in the reign of Khusrau II (590–628) to cover the territory of present-day Iran and Iraq.

Seljuqs
Dynasty descended from the Central Asian Turkic tribe of Oghuz that ruled Iran and Iraq in the 11th and 12th centuries and Anatolia until the 13th century. After the conquest of Baghdad its leader dominated the Caliphs and took the title of Sultan.

Shah
(Persian *shāh*, "king"). Title of ruler in Iran, and other lands.

Shāhnāma
(Persian, "Book of Kings"). The Iranian national epic poem by Firdausī (flourished ca. 1000), which contains the history of Iran from the first king of ancient times, Gayūmars̱ to the

last Sasanian ruler, Yazdgird III (d. 651).

Shari^c^a
(Arabic *shari^c^a*). The legal code of Islam, based on the Qur'an and the hadiths, embracing every aspect of private and public life.

Sharif
(Arabic *sharīf*). A descendant of the Prophet Muḥammad. In Ottoman times, title of the governor of Mecca. Also, the royal house of Morocco, claiming descent from the Prophet Muḥammad, from 1549 until today.

Shaibānids
16th-century Uzbek dynasty in Central Asia whose capital was Bukhara.

Shaykh
(Arabic, "elder"). Title given to a religious leader, learned man, tribal leader, or village elder.

Shi^c^ites
(Arabic *al-shi^c^a*, "the party of ^c^Alī"). One of the two principal denominations of Islam; Shi^c^ites, unlike Sunnites, recognize only ^c^Alī and his descendants (through his marriage to Faṭīma, the Prophet's daughter) as rightful Caliphs. The Shi^c^ites are split into various groups: the Sa^c^idi, the Ismaili, the Imami (since the 16th century the state religion of Iran), etc. Some eight per cent of Muslims are Shi^c^ites, most of whom live in Iran and Iraq.

Shiraz
Capital of Fars Province in Southern Iran; a city of great cultural importance.

Sogd
An ancient term for the area between the upper reaches of the Oxus (Amu-Darya) and the Jaxartes (Syr-Darya), centered on Samarqand, in present-day Uzbekistan.

Sufi
(Arabic *ṣūfi*, "dressed in wool"). Mystic, ascetic.

Sultan
(Arabic *sulṭān*). Turkish and Ottoman ruler; the title was used earlier also by the Mamluks, the Ghaznavids, and the Seljuqs.

Sunna
(Arabic *sunna*). The example of the Prophet Muḥammad as recorded by the hadiths. Also used to refer to orthodox Islam, based on the Qur'an. Sunnites follow one of the four schools of law: Hanafi, Hanbali, Maliki and Shafi^c^i.

Sunnites
Orthodox Muslims, as distinct from the Shi^c^ites.

Sura
(Arabic *sūra*). One of the 114 sections, or chapters, of the Qur'an, written in dynamic rhymed prose. The order is neither chronological nor thematic but generally corresponds to the length of each sura. The shortest is at the end. Since the shortest were also among the first to be revealed, readers are often advised to start reading the book at the end.

Tabriz
The second biggest city in Iran; during the 13th and 14th centuries Tabriz was capital of the empire of the Mongol Īlkhānids, and for the first half of the 16th century of the Safavids.

Tafsīr
(Arabic). The exegesis of the Qur'an.

Thousand and One Nights
(Arabic *Alf layla wa layla*). Also known as *The Arabian Nights*. A collection of over 300 tales, legends, didactic and humorous stories, anecdotes, fables and love stories written in Arabic between 900 and 1500 in different parts of the Muslim world.

Tīmūr
(b. 1336, ruled 1370–1405). A Turkish conqueror who subjected vast areas of Central Asia and, from 1380, Iran and Mesopotamia. In 1402 he defeated a great Ottoman army under Sultan Bāyazīd I outside Ankara. His sumptuous palace was at Samarqand in modern-day Uzbekistan. The rulers from his tribe are called Tīmurī (Timurids).

Transoxiana
An extensive region east of the Oxus River (Amu-Darya). Its main cities were Bukhara and Samarqand in modern-day Uzbekistan.

Thuluth
(Arabic). Also *thulth*. Arabic handwriting style with elongated astae.

Turkmen
Tribal union, today numbering ca. 1.2 million in the republic of Turkmenistan and in Khurasan (Iran) and Iraq. The so-called Turkmen style of art developed in the period of the Qarā-Quyūnlū and Āq-Quyūnlū dynasties in Iran in the 15th century.

Ulama
(Arabic *^c^ulamā'*, sing. *^c^ālim*). Learned men.

^c^Umar
The second Caliph who conquered Persia in 636, Syria in 638 and Egypt in 642.

Umayyads
Damascus-based dynasty founded in 661 by Mu^c^awiyya, under which the empire of the Caliph was extended to Carthage (conquered in 697) and the whole of North Africa, spreading over Spain and into Southern France until the defeat of the Muslim armies at Tours in 732 by Charles Martel. The Umayyad dynasty was supplanted in 750 by the ^c^Abbasids, except in Spain.

^c^Unwān or ^c^Unvān
(Arabic-Persian). A decorative border used in manuscripts to highlight the beginning of a new section of text.

Vizier
(Arabic *wazīr*, "support, carrier"). Official entrusted with the administration of a given sovereign territory. Under the Ottomans, a member of the Council of State.

List of Contributors of Islamic Manuscripts (Individuals and Organizations) to the Asiatic Museum Institute of Oriental Studies of the USSR Academy of Sciences[1]

Abd al-Akhad, emir of Bukhara (1885–1910). *1905 - 1 manuscript (by the agency of Ya.Ya. Lyutsh).

Abd al-Khakim-effendi, mullah. 1842 - 1 manuscript.

Academic bookstore, Leningrad. 9 manuscripts: 1947 - 3 manuscripts; 1954 - 1 manuscript (contributed by Kornilov E.P.); 1955 - 1 manuscript; 1957 - 1 manuscript (contributed by Pomerantsev D.V.); 1958 - 1 manuscript; 1960 - 1 manuscript; 1964 - 1 manuscript.

Academy of Sciences Library. 6 manuscripts: 1931 - 4 manuscripts (3 manuscripts from the library of the former Russian Archaeological Institute in Constantinople); 1938 - 1 manuscript; 1965 - 1 manuscript.

Academy of the History of Material Culture. Leningrad, 1924 - 1 manuscript.

Adamov A.A., consul in Sistan. Iran, *1911 - 4 manuscripts.

Aidarov G.A., Orenburg, 1937 - 3 manuscripts.

Aksakov Z.A. (b. 1905), researcher from the Institute of Oriental Studies (1933–1938), Turkologist. Lower Volga, 1947 - 1 manuscript.

Al'bun V.P., Lomonosov (Leningrad region). 1974 - 1 manuscript.

Alekseev, merchant, Moscow. 1864 - 1 manuscript (from I.M.Tolstoy's collection).

Alikhaev O., Daghestan, 1939 - 1 manuscript.

Alim, emir of Bukhara (1911–1920). 1911 - 1 manuscript (via the agency of Kalmykov A.D.).

Alimov A.A. (1900–1935), researcher from the Institute of Oriental Studies, Turkologist, 1935 - 1 manuscript.

Alimov S.A. (d. 1939), teacher of Arabic in Astrakhan (collected manuscripts on the request from the Institute), Lower Volga, 472 manuscripts: 1936 - 111 manuscripts; 1937 - 34 manuscripts; 1938 - 171 manuscripts; 1939 - 107 manuscripts; 1940 - 21 manuscripts; 1941 - 28 manuscripts (manuscripts deposited in 1940 and 1941 had been sent by S.A. Alimov's widow).

Andreev M.S. (1873–1948), Academy's Corresponding Member, ethnographer and linguist. Central Asia, 1928 - 3 manuscripts.

Anichkov N.A. (1809–1892), Consul General in Tabriz (from 1838), Envoy Plenipotentiary to Persia (from 1856). Tabriz,* 1851 - 1 manuscript.

Anitova Yu.V. Central Asia, 1949 - 1 manuscript.

Anuchin V.I. (1875–1941), professor of Kazan and Uzbek universities, botanist. Volga region. Central Asia, 1928 - 22 manuscripts.

Archaeographic expedition of the Academy of Sciences to the Tatar SSR (consisted of the Institute's employer Zabirov V.A. and the local Tatar researcher and bibliophile Vakhidov S.G.). Volga region, 1934 - 1202 manuscripts.

Archive of the Institute of Oriental Studies, Leningrad Division. 2 manuscripts: 1965 - 1 manuscript; 1981 - 1 manuscript.

Archive of the USSR Academy of Sciences, Leningrad Division, Leningrad. 3 manuscripts: 1938 - 1 manuscript; 1940 - 1 manuscript; 1943 - 1 manuscript (by the agency of the Archive employee Loseva I.S.).

Asadullaev S., Leningrad. 1978 - 1 manuscript.

Ashurov K.M. (b. 1897). The Institute's librarian. 1940 - 1 manuscript.

Asiatic Dept. School at the Ministry of Foreign Affairs. 1919 - 527 manuscripts.

Atyzgil^{c}dina, akhund, Ufa. 1927-1 manuscript.

Azerbaijan Division of the USSR Academy of Sciences. Baku, 1939 - 4 manuscripts.

Babadzhanov Rasikh, mullah. Bukhara. *1852 - 1 manuscript.

Baidzhanov K., Kokand. *1974. - 1 manuscript (by the agency of the Finance Ministry).

Bakh, Central Asia. 1900 - 1 manuscript; 1901 - 1 manuscript.

Bakikhanov A.K. (1794–1847), Azeri public and political figure, historian and teacher. Iran, Azerbaijan. *1852 - 24 manuscripts (by the agency of Sakine-khanym, A.K. Bakikhanov's widow).

Bakulin F.A. (1846–1879), Consul General in Astrabad, Iran. 4 manuscript: *1874 - 1 manuscript; *1875 - 3 manuscripts.

Barabanov A.M. (1906–1941), orientalist specializing in Arabic studies, an employee of the Institute. Makhar-Kala (Daghestan). 1939 - 1 manuscript (bought from Gaziev).

Bartold V.V. (1869–1930), Academician, orientalist, historian specializing in Central Asia and Iran. Central Asia. 24 manuscripts: 1904 - 16 manuscripts (collected in 1902 and 1904); 1915 - 1 manuscript; *1916 - 4 manuscripts; 1921 - 2 manuscripts; 1928 - 1 manuscript.

Bartolomei I.A. (1813–1870), Academy's Corresponding member, Lieutenant-General, specialist in Iranian numismatics, archaeologist, Transcaucasia. *1863 - 2 manuscripts.

Bashkirov S.S., Miyasov. 1934 - 2 manuscripts.

Bat'yanov, inspector of educational institutions in Nikolaev. 1848 - 3 manuscripts (by the agency of the Ministry of Education).

Bauer, 1930 - 1 manuscript.

Bazilevskii A.A. (d. 1918?), Consulate secretary in Tabriz, then mission secretary in Tehran. Iran. *1924 - 7 manuscripts.

Bazlov I.I., second-hand bookseller and book trader in St. Petersburg. 1895 - 1 manuscript.

Belenitskii A.M. (b. 1904), historian and archaeologist specializing in Central Asian studies. Central Asia (Samarqand). 1939 - 1 manuscript.

Belyaev I.A., orientalist, Turkologist, inspector of public schools in the Transcaspian region. 5 manuscripts: *1905 - 1 manuscript (by the Russian Committee for Study of Central and Eastern Asia); 1915 - 4 manuscripts.

Benediktov. Central Asia. 1939 - 5 manuscripts.

Beneshevich V.N. (1874–1943), Academy's Corresponding Member, historian of Byzantium. 1911 - 2 manuscripts.

Berezin I.N. (1818–1896), Turkologist, professor of Kazan and St. Petersburg universities. Daghestan, Iran, Volga region. 19 manuscripts: 1863 - 3 manuscripts; 1896 - 16 manuscripts.

Berezovskii M.M. (1848–1912), zoologist, traveller. Eastern Turkistan. 1908 - 5 manuscripts.

Berg L.S. (1876–1950), Academician, geographer and ichthyologist. Ravenduz (Iraq). 1921 - 1 manuscript (found in 1916 by Tamantsev).

Berget A.P. (1828-1896), archaeographer specializing in Caucasian studies, orientalist. Transcaucasia. Iran, 1863 - 3 manuscripts.

Bernstein G.H. 1861 - 5 manuscripts.

Bertels E.E. (1870–1957), Academy's Corresponding Member, specialist in Iranian studies, philologist and literary critic. 33 manuscripts: Bukhara, 1930 - 17 manuscripts; Dushanbe, 1933 - 16 manuscripts.

Bezmenov. 1856. - 4 manuscripts.

Bikchenteev I.M. Bashkiria. 1936. - 66 manuscripts.

Bode K.K., baron; traveller, mission's first secretary in Tehran. Iran. *1842 - 2 manuscripts.

Bogdanov L.S., orientalist, specialist in Iranian studies, employee of the Russian-Persian bank in Tehran. Iran. 246 manuscripts (Persian mostly): 1904 - 4 manuscripts; 1906 - 8 manuscripts; *1907 - 52 manuscripts; *1910 - 2 manuscripts; 1912 - 39 manuscripts; 1913 - 139 manuscripts; 1914 - 2 manuscripts.

Boraganskii I.M., bookbinding shop owner in St. Petersburg. 1981 - 3 manuscripts.

Borodin A.V., 1st Artillery Corps lieutenant. 1908 - 3 manuscripts.

Brechet V. 1906. - 8 manuscripts.

Brock - 1 manuscript.

Butenev A.P. (1787–1866), diplomat, Ambassador to Turkey 1830–1842, 1856–1858). Turkey. 5 manuscripts: *1834 - 1 manuscript; *1937 - 1 manuscript; *1840 - 3 manuscripts.

di Castiglione F., 1826 - 2 manuscripts.

Censorship Committee in St. Petersburg. 1900 - 3 manuscripts.

Central Geological Library, Leningrad. 1933 - 2 manuscripts.

Charov M.M. 1936 - 4 manuscripts (from the collection of Nofal I.G., 1828–1902, specialist in Arabic studies).

Cherevitskii A.A. 1940 - 4 manuscripts.

Chigogidze I.E. 1915 - 1 manuscript.

Clot-Bey A.V., Surgeon-General of the Egyptian army. Egypt. 1839 - 8 manuscripts.

Cohen D., official of Russia's political agency in Bukhara. Bukhara. 1901 - 2 manuscripts.

Colenati. Transcaucasia. 1844 - 1 manuscript.

Dagdarov. 1847 - 1 manuscript (copy of the manuscript from the St. Petersburg University collection No. 105 commissioned by B.A. Dorn.

Dal' V.I. (1801–1872), writer, physician, ethnographer and lexicologist, Academician Hon. of the Academy of Sciences. Orenburg. 12 manuscripts: *1838 - 1 manuscript; *1840 - 1 manuscript; 1842 - 10 manuscripts.

Davydov. 1912 - 2 manuscripts.

Demezon P.I. (1807–1873), Baron; orientalist-Turkologist, Director of the Oriental Languages School of the Asiatic Dept. at the Ministry of Foreign Affairs (from 1843) - 2 manuscripts.

Denison-Ross E. (1871-1940), British orientalist, Iranologist and Turkologist, professor at London University. Iran, Central Asia. *1897 - 11 manuscripts.

Desnitskii I.I., student of St. Petersburg university Oriental Dept. Central Asia. *1907 - 10 manuscripts.

Dittel V.F. (1816–1848), professor of Turkish at St. Petersburg university Oriental Dept. Turkey. 2 manuscripts: 1854 - 1 manuscript; 1871 - 1 manuscript (by the agency of his son, Dittel V.V.).

Dorn B.A. (1805–1881), Academician, orientalist (Iranologist and Afghanologist), Asiatic Museum director (1842-1881). Iran, Azerbaijan. 1861 - 11 manuscripts.

Dubenetskii N.I. Vernyj (Alma-Ata). *1913. - 1 manuscript.

Dudin S.M. (1893–1929). 1917 - 1 manuscript.

Dudshiraev U. 1857 - 4 manuscripts.

Eberman V.A. (1899–1937), employee at the Institute Arabic studies. 1923 - 2 manuscripts.

Eichwald, von. 1827 - 2 manuscripts.

Faberge K.G., jeweller and collector in St. Petersburg. 1920 - 11 manuscripts and 26 miniatures.

Faizkhanov, mullah Husein (1828–1866), lecturer at the Oriental Languages Dept., St. Petersburg University. 38 manuscripts: 1854 - 22 manuscripts; 1863 - 6 manuscripts; *1866 - 10 manuscripts and 3 firmans (by the agency of H. Faizkhanov's widow).

Fath Allah Abu Hallak. Beirut. 1917 - 1 manuscript.

Filatov P. 1914 - 1 manuscript.

Filonenko V.I., professor of the Kabardino-Balkar Institute, Nal'chik. 13 manuscripts: 1937 - 2 manuscripts; 1947 - 11 manuscripts.

Florenskii A.A., student. 1911. - 1 manuscript.

Fonton G.R. (d. 1864). *1876 - 19 manuscripts (by the agency of the Austrian Consul General in Odessa Blau E.O.).

Fraehn Ch.D. (1782–1851), Academician, orientalist and numismatist, first Director of the Asiatic Museum. 69 manuscripts: 1828 - 30 manuscripts; 1837 - 21 manuscripts; 1842 - 1 manuscript; *1852 - 17 manuscripts.

Fraehn R.Ch. (1817–1882?), second Secretary of the Mission in Tehran, Consul in the Ottoman Empire. 19 manuscripts: Egypt, Iran. 1838 - 4 manuscripts; 1839 - 1 manuscript; *1842 - 13 manuscripts; 1882 - 1 manuscript.

Frank U., former German Consul in the Middle East. 1904 - 18 manuscripts.

Froman-Brun. 1862 - 3 manuscripts.

Gadzhikhalikov A. Kubachi (Daghestan). 1964 - 5 manuscripts.

Gartier E.K., bookseller and antiquarian. St. Petersburg. 1902 - 8 manuscripts.

Golenishchev V.S. (1856–

1947), Egyptologist, Assyriologist and Semitologist, a known collector. 7 manuscripts: 1908 - 6 manuscripts; ★1910 - 1 manuscript.

Gomolitskii D.N. 1928. - 1 manuscript.

Gordeev D.P. 1932. - 1 manuscript.

Gorkii M., see Peshkov A.M.

Gotwald I.F. (1813–1897), Academy's Corresponding Member, specializing in Arabic studies, professor at Kazan University, Kazan. 9 manuscripts: 1851 - 1 manuscript; 1852 - 8 manuscripts.

Graf R. (1819–1867), aid for special missions of the Caucasian Governor General, interpreter of the Embassy in Iran. Iran, Transcaucasia. ★1867 - 39 manuscripts.

Gramenitskii D.M., Justice of the Peace in Osh, Kirghizia. Central Asia. ★1897 - 24 manuscripts.

Gregory IV, Patriarch of Antioch, see Winter Palace Library.

Grigor'ev, Consul in Turkey. 1839 - 1 manuscript.

Gryaznevich P.A. (b. 1929), researcher from the Institute's Leningrad Division, specialist in Arabic studies, Jafar (Yemen). 1979 - 1 manuscript.

Gues G. Athens. 1914 - 2 manuscripts.

Gumilev N.S. (1886–1921), Russian poet. 1917 - 8 manuscripts.

Gusev V. (d. 1869), consul in Astrabad (Iran). Iran. 1860 - 1 manuscript.

Halil Iman Muhammad, Kokand envoy. ★1847 - 2 manuscripts (by the agency of the Ministry Finance).

Hamacher (d. 1837), professor at Leyden University. 1837 - 2 manuscripts.

Harrassowitz O., book trading company in Leipzig. 1900 - 4 manuscripts.

Hartmann, 1899 - 1 manuscript.

Ignatiev V.I., see Mir Salih Mirakbaev.

Il'minskii N.I. (1822–1891), orientalist-philologist, professor at Kazan University. ★1882 - 1 manuscript.

Imperial Archaeological Commission. 1896 - 2 manuscripts.

Imperial Mission in Athens, 1914 - 1 manuscript.

Institute of History, Academy of Sciences, Leningrad Division. 1938 - 16 manuscripts.

Institute of the Book, Documents and Writing, Leningrad. 1938 - 18 manuscripts.

Institute of the History of Material Culture, Leningrad. 2 manuscripts: 1939 - 1 manuscript; 1956 - 1 manuscript.

Institute of the Living Oriental Languages. Leningrad. 7 manuscripts: 1922 - 1 manuscript; 1923 - 1 manuscript; 1928 - 4 manuscripts; 1938 - 1 manuscript.

Institute of World Literature, AS, USSR, Moscow - 7 manuscripts.

Isheev A.I. 1927 - 1 manuscript.

Ivanov P.P. (1893–1942), Soviet historian specializing in Central Asia. Central Asia. 4 manuscripts: 1936 - 1 manuscript; 1939 - 2 manuscripts; 1941 - 1 manuscript.

Ivanov V.A. (1886–1970), Russian scientist, the prominent authority on Muslim sectorianism. 1178 manuscripts: Iran (collected in 1913–1914), Central Asia. 1915 - 41 manuscripts; Central Asia, ★1915 (Bukhara collection) - 1057 manuscripts; Iran (collected in 1912), India (collected in 1913–1914), Central Asia (Bukhara), 1916 - 77 manuscripts; 1966 - 3 manuscripts.

Ivanov, Consul General in Smyrna (Turkey). Turkey. 1836 - 13 manuscripts.

Jaubert R.A. (1779–1847), French orientalist specializing in Arabic, Turkic and Iranian studies. 1847 - 1 manuscript (by the agency of Russia's Consul General in Paris P. Shpiss).

Jouset V.P., professor, son of P.K. Jouset, specialist in Arabic studies (1871–1942). 1961 - 1 manuscript.

Kalmykov A.D., diplomatic officer associated with the Turkistan Governor General. Central Asia. 5 manuscripts: 1891 - 3 manuscripts; 1908 - 1 manuscript; 1917 - 1 manuscript.

Kamalov I.Z. Chistopol, 1932. - 2 manuscripts.

Karaim National Library, Yevpatoria. 1936 - 1 manuscript.

Kartashov, Major-General. Central Asia. 1874 - 1 manuscript.

Kartashova A.L. 1927 - 1 manuscript.

Kartavov P.A. (1873–1914), Russian studies bibliographer, 1926 - 1 manuscript.

Kaufmann K.P., von (1818–1882), first Governor General of Turkistan (from 1867). Central Asia, ★1874 - 38 manuscripts.

Kazembek A.K. (1802–1870), orientalist (Iranologist-Turkologist, Arabic studies), professor and first Dean of the Oriental Languages Dept. at St. Petersburg University. ★1842 - 5 manuscripts.

Kazimirskii. ★1850 - 1 manuscript.

Kel'zi F.I. (1819–1912), teacher of Arabic at the Oriental Languages Dept., St. Petersburg university. 1857 - 1 manuscript.

Kerem (d. 1917), Crimean publicist and poet. Stary Krym. 1916 - 1 manuscript (by the agency of A.N. Samoilovich).

Khalikov I. Bukhara, 1931 - 1 manuscript.

Khan-Iomudskii N.N. Kelyat (Turkmenia). ★1913 - 1 manuscript (by the agency of Samoilovich A.N.).

Khanykov N.V. (1819–1876), Academy's Corresponding Member, orientalist-Iranologist, Consul General in Tabriz. Iran, Afghanistan, Central Asia. 70 manuscripts (including 18 Afghani ones): ★1855 - 2 manuscripts; ★1856 - 6 manuscripts; ★1857 - 2 manuscripts; ★1858 - 32 manuscripts (including 13 Afghani ones); ★1859 - 27 manuscripts (including 5 Afghani ones).

Khilinskii. Mashhad (Iran). 1914 - 1 manuscript.

Khvol'son D.A. (1819–1911), professor at St. Petersburg University, Semitologist. 5 manuscripts: 1909 - 4 manuscripts; 1911 - 1 manuscript.

Klemm V.O., von, Secretary of the diplomatic agency in Bukhara. Central Asia. 1917 - 1 manuscript.

Kohler, Berlin antiquarian. 13 manuscripts: 1866 - 3 manuscripts; ★1867 - 6 manuscripts; 1891 - 4 manuscripts.

Kondakov N.P. (1844–1925), specialist in Byzantine studies and archaeologist, professor at St. Petersburg University.

1900 - 1 manuscript.
Kornilov P.E., see Academic bookstore.
Kostsov M.S. 1920 - 1 manuscript.
Krachkovskii I.Yu. (1883–1951). Academician, Arabic studies. 3 manuscripts: 1914 - 2 manuscripts; 1924 - 1 manuscript.
Kraush O.A. (d. 1942), specialist in Arabic studies, the Institute's staffer. Central Asia. 1936 - 2 manuscripts.
Krotkov N.N. (1869–1919), Consul in Kuldja and Turfan. Eastern Turkistan. 1898 - 1 manuscript.
Kufaev M.N. 1946 - 2 manuscripts.
Kuhn A.L. (1840–1888), orientalist (Iranologist and Turkologist), chief inspector of educational institutions in Turkistan. Central Asia. *1890 - 133 manuscripts.
Kuzuni. 1914 - 1 manuscript.

Lapin S.A. 1894 - 1 manuscript.
Lemm O.E., von (1856–1918), Academy's Corresponding Member, orientalist-Egyptologist, curator of the Asiatic Museum. 1918 - 1 manuscript.
Lerkh P.I. (1828–1884), orientalist (specialist in Kurdish studies, numismatist, archaeologist and historian). Central Asia. *1859 - 46 manuscripts.
Library of the Ministry of Finance Academic Council. *1845 - 17 manuscripts.
Library of the Institute of Oriental Studies, Leningrad Division. 3 manuscripts: 1958 - 1 manuscript; 1967 - 2 manuscripts.
Library of the Institute of Oriental Studies, Moscow. 72 manuscripts: 1949 - 1 manuscript; 1956 - 10 manuscripts; 1958 - 1 manuscript; 1960 - 7 manuscripts (bought from Molchanov A.A.); *1962 - 42 manuscripts; 1963 - 2 manuscripts; 1964 - 3 manuscripts; 1965 - 5 manuscripts; 1971 - 1 manuscript.
Library of the Russian Archaeological Institute in Constantinople, see Academy of Sciences Library.
Lieven Kh.A. (1774–1838), Prince, Ambassador to London, 1819 - 1 manuscript.
Likhachev P.V. 1941 - 6 manuscripts.
Logachev K.I. 1958 - 1 manuscript.
Lorsbach G.V. 1829 - 3 manuscripts.
Luk'yanov V.V., Leningrad. 1964 - 1 manuscript.
Lyntsh Ya.Ya., secretary of Russia's political agency in Bukhara (political agent subsequently). Central Asia, Eastern Turkistan. 28 manuscripts: *1897 - 20 manuscripts; 1901 - 4 manuscripts; 1903 - 1 manuscript; 1908 - 3 manuscripts.

Makis, bookseller in Vienna. 1900 - 1 manuscript.
Makkaveeva. 1944 - 1 manuscript.
Mamedbeili Sh.D., Azerbaijan, 1957 - 3 manuscripts.
Mamedov M.M. Baku, 98 manuscripts: 1937 - 76 manuscripts; 1939 - 22 manuscripts.
Margulan A.Kh. (b. 1904), Academician, Kazakh Academy of Sciences, archaeologist and ethnographer. Central Asia. 30 manuscripts: 1937 - 4 manuscripts; 1940 - 15 manuscripts; 1941 - 11 manuscripts.
Marr N.Ya. (1864–1934), Academician, linguist, philologist, archaeologist. 1916 - 1 manuscript.
Marr Yu.N. (1893–1935), Iranologist-philologist, employee at the Asiatic Museum. Iran, Transcaucasia. 14 manuscripts: 1937 - 2 manuscripts; 1950 - 12 manuscripts (by the agency of Marr S.M.).
Mel'gunov G.V. (1834-1873), Russian orientalist (Iranologist, historian), assistant professor at St. Petersburg University. *1860 - 1 manuscript.
Mel'nikov V. Turkey. 1916 - 27 manuscripts.
Meshcherskii V., prince, Consul General in Algeria. 1835 - 2 manuscripts.
Mezonov. Central Asia. 1891 - 1 manuscript.
Mikhailov. 1892 - 1 manuscript.
Miller A.Ya., Consul in Sistan and Kerman, Iran. 1898 - 1 manuscript.
Miller B.V. (1877–1956), orientalist (Arabic and Iranian studies). *1919 - 1 manuscript.
Miller V.F. (1848–1913), Academician, linguist and specialist in Caucasian studies, 1912 - 1 manuscript.
Ministry of Foreign Affairs of the USSR. 1949 - 1 manuscript. See also People's Commissariat of Foreign Affairs.
Minorskii V.F. (1877–1966), Russian orientalist (historian-Iranologist). 31 manuscripts: 1917 - 1 manuscript; 1958 - 1 manuscript; 1960 - 3 manuscripts; 1966 - 26 manuscripts (by the agency of T.A. Minorskaya).
Mir-Salih Mirakbaev (d. 1901), bookseller in Bukhara. Bukhara. 47 manuscripts: *1900 - 34 manuscripts; *1901 - 13 manuscripts (by the agency of Ignatiev V.I., Russia's political agent in Bukhara).
Mishchenko I.P. 1931 - 7 manuscripts.
Mishutushkin, Captain 2nd grade. 1914 - 6 manuscripts.
Mlokosevich. *1913 - 1 manuscript.
Molchanov A.A., see Library of the Institute of Oriental Studies.
Moskalev A. 1915 - 9 manuscripts.
Muhammad-Ali Mahmud-oglu. *1886 - 1 manuscript.
Muhammedov Yu.D. Kokand. 1914 - 1 manuscript.
Mukhanov. 1913 - 1 manuscript.
Mukhlinskii A.O. (1808–1877), professor at St. Petersburg University, specialist in Arabic and Turkic studies. 1868 - 1 manuscript.
Muller G. 1867 - 18 manuscripts.
Mumtaz S. Derbend. 1935 - 5 manuscripts.
Muraviev-Karskii N.N. (1796–1866), General, viceregent of Caucasia (from 1854). Transcaucasia. 1911 - 23 manuscripts (by the agency of Koznakov A.N.).
Museum of Anthropology and Ethnography of the USSR Academy of Sciences. Leningrad. 41 manuscripts: 1922 - 1 manuscript; Kala-i Khumb (Tajikistan), 1939 - 39 manuscripts: 1951 - 1 manuscript (by the agency of Kononov A.N.).
Museum of the History of Religion of the USSR Academy of Sciences. 1954 - 78 manuscripts.

Nalivkin V.P. (1852–1918), orientalist (historian, ethnographer and local studies expert on Central Asia), Central Asia. *1897 - 1 manuscript.
People's Commissariat of

Foreign Affairs of the USSR. 9 manuscripts: ★1919 - 4 manuscripts; 1923 - 5 manuscripts. See also the Foreign Ministry of the USSR.
North F. 1837 - 1 manuscript.
NS (as in inventory). 1936 - 1 manuscript.
Nuri-bei. 1913 - 1 manuscript.

Obolenskii M.A. (1805–1873), Prince, Director of the Foreign Ministry's Moscow Archive, historian. Turkey. 1839 - 1 manuscript.
Oldenburg S.F. (1863–1934), academician, Indologist and Tibetologist. Eastern Turkistan. ★1910 - 89 manuscripts.
Ostroumov N.P. (1846–1930), Tashkent - 1 manuscript.

Pantusov N.N. (1849–1909), orientalist, explorer of Central Asia - 2 manuscripts.
Panzner. 1821 - 1 manuscript.
Papayan G.K. (1901–1937), employee of the Institute. 1934 - 1 manuscript.
Pashino P.I. (1836–1891), orientalist, traveler and writer. 1856 - 8 manuscripts.
Paskhin N.F., traveler and manuscript collector. Central Asia. 1929–1930 - 171 manuscripts.
Pegushin V.A. 1940 - 1 manuscript.
Peretts V.N. (1870–1857), academician, specialist in Slavic studies. 1928 - 2 manuscripts.
Perovskii L.A. (1794–1857), count, Governor General of the Orenburg province, Minister of Principalities. Central Asia. 1862 - 8 manuscripts.
Peshkov A.M. (Maxim Gorkii, 1868-1936). 1921 - 1 manuscript.
Petrov A.A. Kunya-Urgench (Central Asia). 1938 - 1 manuscript.
Petra N.P., Central Asia. 1905 - 1 manuscript.
Petrovskii N.F. (1837–1909), Russia's Consul General in Kashgar, orientalist. Eastern Turkistan. ★1909 - 131 manuscripts.
Pisarchik A.K. (b. 1907), ethnographer-Iranologist. 1954 - 1 manuscript.
Pokrovskii N.I. (1897–1946), historian of the North Caucasus, Russian and Arabic studies. 1940 - 2 manuscripts (by the agency of I.Yu. Krachkovskii).
Polovtsev A.A. (1832–1910), State Council member, Senator, historian and known collector. 33 manuscripts: 1895 - 2 manuscripts; ★1919 - 31 manuscripts.
Pomerantsev D.V., see Academic bookstore.
Popov V.V. 1928 - 12 manuscripts.
Popova. 1905 - 1 manuscript.
Pospelov F.F. Katta-Kurgan (Central Asia). 22 manuscripts: ★1908 - 3 manuscripts; ★1910 - 16 manuscripts; 1913 - 3 manuscripts.
Purin. 1913 - 1 manuscript.
Pushkin House. Petrograd. 1923 - 1 manuscript.

Quaritch B. (1819–1899), founder and head of the well-known antiquarian firm in London. 18 manuscripts: 1866 - 1 manuscript; 1868 - 1 manuscript; ★1880 - 7 manuscripts; ★1893 - 9 manuscripts.

Radlov V.V. (1837–1918), academician, orientalist linguist-Turkologist, Director of the Museum of Anthropology and Ethnography. Central Asia. 87 manuscripts: ★1890 - 33 manuscripts; 1897 - 11 manuscripts; 1918 - 2 manuscripts; 1961 - 41 manuscripts (by the agency of the Institute's Leningrad Archive).
Raina N.N., General Secretary of the USSR Friends Society in Kashmir. 1949 - 1 manuscript.
Ramazanov S. Kubachi (Daghestan). 1964 - 5 manuscripts.
Rannenkampf, Kazan. 1896 - 1 manuscript.
Rastopchin F.B. (1904-1938?), Iranologist and employee of the Institute, Central Asia. 1934 - 17 manuscripts (15 of these were delivered to the Institute by Yakubovskii A.Yu.).
Razgonova E. ★1910 - 1 manuscript.
Romaskevich A.A. (1885–1942), orientalist-Iranologist, professor of the Oriental Dept., Leningrad university. 1971 - 6 manuscripts (by the agency of the Institute's Leningrad Archive).
Rosen V.R. (1849–1908), Academician, orientalist specializing in Arabic studies, professor at St. Petersburg University. ★1908 - 49 manuscripts.
Rosenberg, sea captain, 1819 - 5 manuscripts (at the request of Admiral Senyavin).
Rousseau J.L. (1780–1831), French Consul General in Baghdad, Aleppo and Tripoli. Iran, Near East. 700 manuscripts: 1819 - 500 manuscripts; 1825 - 200 manuscripts.

Safiev. 1914 - 1 manuscript.
Salemann K.G. (1849–1916), Academician, orientalist-Iranologist; director of the Asiatic Museum (1890–1916). Central Asia. 131 manuscripts: 1891 - 1 manuscript; ★1897 - 96 manuscripts; 1908 - 34 manuscripts.
Samoilovich A.N. (1880–1938), Academician, orientalist-Turkologist. Central Asia. 52 manuscripts; ★1908 - 6 manuscripts; ★1913 - 34 manuscripts; 1916 - 2 manuscripts; 1927 - 1 manuscript; 1942 - 9 manuscripts (by the agency of A.N. Samoilovich's widow).
Saranchin M.M. 1927 - 1 manuscript.
Schilling von Kanstadt P.L. (1786–1837), Academy's Corresponding Member, physicist and orientalist. 1821 - 2 manuscripts.
Schmidt M. - 1 manuscript.
Semyonov A.A. (1873–1958), professor of Central Asian University, orientalist-Iranologist. Pamirs (Vakhan, Shugnan), Tashkent. 43 manuscripts: 1918 - 9 manuscripts; 1920 - 1 manuscript; 1921 - 6 manuscripts; 1925 - 1 manuscript; 1926 - 26 manuscripts.
Semyonova I.V. Leningrad. 1964 - 3 manuscripts.
Sen'kovskii O.I. (1800–1858), writer, orientalist (Turkic and Arabic studies), professor at St. Petersburg University. 1858 - 5 manuscripts (3 of these by the agency of Saveliev P.).
Serafimov. 1915 - 1 manuscript.
Schnyler E. (1840–1890), American diplomat, consul in Moscow and Reval (now Tallinn), explorer of Central and mainland Asia. Bukhara. 1874 - 1 manuscript.
Shamsutdinov Kh.K. Central Asia. 1937 - 1 manuscript.
Shapshal S.M. (1873–1961), orientalist (Turkologist and Iranologist). Vilnius, 1947 34

manuscripts: 1947 - 2 manuscripts; 1962 - 32 manuscripts (by the agency of Lopatto K.P.).

Shegren A.M. (1794–1855), Academician, linguist specializing in the Caucasian languages. 1857 - 6 manuscripts.

Shileiko V.K. (1891–1930), professor at Leningrad University, Assyriologist and Sumerologist. 1919 - 1 manuscript.

Shirvanov. Volga region. 1936 - 1 manuscript.

Smirnov S.M., professor at Kazan University, botanist, geographer. Central Asia. 57 manuscripts: *1880 - 3 manuscripts; 1881 - 14 manuscripts; *1915 - 40 manuscripts.

Smirnov V.D., turkologist, Turkey. 1930 - 1 manuscript; 1934 - 4 manuscripts.

Smirnova N.K. (1846–1922), widow of the prominent Turkologist V.D. Smirnov. 1934 - 3 manuscripts.

Smirnova O.I. (1910–1982), employee of the Institute, Iranologist-Sogdianologist, philologist and numismatist. Leningrad. 1980 - 2 manuscripts.

Sonin N.Ya. 1856 - 2 manuscripts.

Sotnikov S.N. 1959 - 1 manuscript.

Stanishevskii A.V. (b. 1904), head of the special Tajik-Pamirs group of the Academy's expedition. Pamirs, 1934 - 10 manuscripts (by the agency of the Tajik affiliation of the Academy of Sciences).

Starikov A.A. (1892–1962), Iranologist, professor at Moscow University. 1930 - 1 manuscript.

Stark L.S. (d. 1937), plenipotentiary representative of the USSR in Afghanistan. Kabul. 1931 - 1 manuscript.

State Book Collection, Leningrad. 1928 - 8 manuscripts.

State Russian Museum. Petrograd. 1921 - 1 manuscript.

Statkevich T.A., Leningrad. 1987 - 1 manusccript.

Stepanov D.K. 1924 - 1 manuscript.

Stracker, bookseller in London. 1837 - 5 manuscripts (by the agency of Rosen, secretary of Russia's mission in London).

Sukhtelen P.K. (1851-1836), General of Russia's army, Engineering Corps. 1837 - 35 manuscripts.

Suleikin V.D., son of Suleikin D.A., orientalist-Indologist (1900–1948), 1960 - 1 manuscript.

Sveshnikov N.I. *1878 - 15 manuscripts.

Svir'shchevskii. 1913 - 1 manuscript.

Tajik affiliation of the USSR Academy. Stalinabad. 1933 - 10 manuscripts.

Taktarov. 1849 - 1 manuscript.

Tamaev A.I. Daghestan. 49 manuscripts; 1936 - 6 manuscripts; 1938 - 31 manuscripts; 1948 - 12 manuscripts.

Teben'kov M.M. 1912 - 1 manuscript.

Teimuraz Bagrationi (1782–1846), historian of Georgia, son of Georgia's last tzar George XI. Iran. 1847 - 1 manuscript.

Tolstoy I.M. (1806–1867), count, Minister of Post and Telegraph. 5 manuscripts: 1860 - 2 manuscripts; *1864 - 3 manuscripts.

Trifonov V.T. 1932 - 1 manuscript.

Trigulov, dragoman of the Mission in Iran. - 8 manuscripts: 1851 - 3 manuscripts; 1857-1858 - 5 manuscripts.

Troitskaya A.L. (1899–1980), orientalist-Turkologist, historian and ethnographer specializing in Central Asia, employee of the Institute. 1948 - 2 manuscripts.

Tsvetkov P.P. Turkey, Iran. 1924 - 7 manuscripts.

Tumanskii A.G. (1861–1920), Major-General, orientalist (Iranologist and Turkologist). Bukhara. 2 manuscripts: 1924 - 1 manuscript; 1927 - 1 manuscript (both manuscripts received by the agency of A.G. Tumanskii's widow).

Turaev B.A. (1868–1920), academician, orientalist-historian specializing in the ancient East. 1920 - 2 manuscripts.

Udalets K.I. 1948 - 1 manuscript.

Uspenskii F. 1916 - 1 manuscript.

USSR Mission in Iran. Iran. *1926 - 25 manuscripts.

Uvarov S.S. (1986–1855), Count, President of the Academy of Sciences. 1820 - 1 manuscript.

Vakhidov S.G. (1887–1942), Tatar scientist and collector of Volga manuscripts. 1934 - 362 manuscripts.

Valeev K.G. Tataria. 1935 - 10 manuscripts.

Validov A.Z. (Akhmed-Zaki Validi Togan, 1887–1970), orientalist, Turkologist. Central Asia. 26 manuscripts: 1913 - 4 manuscripts; *1914 - 21 manuscripts; 1916 - 1 manuscript.

Valikhanov Ch.Ch. (1835–1865), first Kazakh scientist (ethnographer) and educator. Eastern Turkistan, 1860 - 1 manuscript.

Van collection. Turkish Armenia. *1916–1917 - 1279 manuscripts.

Vasiliev. 1935 - 1 manuscript.

Veidenbaum E.G. (1845–1918), historian and bibliographer of Caucasia. Daghestan. 1908 - 1 manuscript.

Vel'yaminov-Zernov V.V. (1830–1904), academician, historian specializing in Central Asia. Central Asia. 25 manuscripts: 1858 - 8 manuscripts; *1865 - 16 manuscripts; 1872 - 1 manuscript.

Vereshchagin M.S. 1928 - 4 manuscripts.

Verkhovskii Yu.P. (1891–1962), specialist in Iranian studies, employee of the Institute. Iran. 1938 - 1 manuscript.

Veselovskii N.I. (1848–1918), historian and archaeologist specializing in Central Asian studies, professor at St. Petersburg University. Central Asia. 1898 - 3 manuscripts.

Vil'chevskii O.L. (1909–1965), specialist in Kurdish studies, MAE staffer. *1965 - 1 manuscript (by the agency of Chirkaeva V.O., Vil'chevskii's widow).

V.I. Lenin's Library. Moscow. 1966 - 1 manuscript.

Voinova E.N. 1941 - 1 manuscript.

Vullers J.A. (1803–1880). 1880. - 1 manuscript.

Vyatkin V.L. (1869–1932), historian and archaeologist specializing in Central Asian studies. Central Asia. 6 manuscripts: *1897 - 3 manuscripts; 1901 - 3 manuscripts.

Wangg L., von, collector, Moscow. 1820 - 1 manuscript.

Weila G. 1921 - 1 manuscript.
Winter Palace Library (manuscripts of Gregory IV, the Patriarch of Anteochia). Western Asia. ⋆1919 - 41 manuscripts.

Yahuda, bookseller and antiquarian from Darmstadt (Germany). 10 manuscripts: 1904 - 5 manuscripts; 1907 - 5 manuscripts.
Yakhin A.I. Bairaki settlement, Tataria. 1971. - 1 manuscript (by the agency of Faseev F.S., researcher from the Kazan Division of the Academy of Sciences).
Yudakhin K.K. (b. 1890), academician, Kirghiz Academy of Sciences, orientalist (Turkologist). 1928 - 1 manuscript.
Yunusov B.D. Tashkent. 1944 - 17 manuscripts.
Yusupov A.Kh.G. Volga region. 1936 - 18 manuscripts.
Yuvachev V.P. (1850–1936), publicist, participant of the Populist movement of the 1870. 1928 - 1 manuscript.

Zabirov V.A. (1897–1938), Turkologist, employee of the Institute. Volga region. 1939 - 13 manuscripts.
Zarifov (Zaripov) M.S. Bashkiria. 1940 - 29 manuscripts.
Zarubin I.I. (1887–1964), orientalist (Iranian philology) and ethnographer. Pamirs (Rushan, Shugnan). 12 manuscripts: 1916 - 11 manuscripts; 1940 - 1 manuscript.
Zhaba A.D. (1801–1894), Consul General in Smyrna (Turkey) and Tabriz (Iran), orientalist (Kurdish studies). Smyrna. 1837 - 11 manuscripts.
Zhukovskii V.A. (1858–1918), professor at St. Petersburg University, orientalist-Kanologist, Director of dragomans at the Asiatic Dept. of the Ministry of Foreign Affairs. Iran, Central Asia. ⋆1919 - 33 manuscripts.
Zinoviev A.V. 1928 - 1 manuscript.
Zlatogorova T.S. 1949 - 1 manuscript.

[1] In this list references have been organized in order of: name of institution/collection or surname and initials of the founder of the collection (in parenthesis are birth and death dates, if known); brief biographical details; the city or country from where the manuscripts were received/or their provenance; the date of acquisition into the collections (⋆ if a number of manuscripts were acquired the total number of these is indicated before the date of acquisition); the number of manuscripts; an asterisk placed before the date of acquisition (to the Institute of Oriental Studies) indicates that information concerning that particular manuscript (s) is published in the periodicals of the Russian Academy of Sciences. For those periodical refer to: O.F. Akimushkin, Yu.E. Borshchevskii, "Materialy dlya bibliografii rabot o persidskikh rukopisiakh" ("Material for bibliographic works concerning Persian manuscripts"), in *NNA*, 1963, n. 3, pp. 165–174; n. 6, pp. 228–241; L.V. Dmitrieva, S.N. Muratov, "Katalogi, spiski i obzory tyurkskikh rukopisei XVIII–XX vv." ("Catalogues, lists and surveys concerning Turkish manuscripts of the 18th–20th centuries"), in *PPV*, Moscow, 1972, pp. 145–177; *Bibliografia arabskikh rukopisei (A bibliography of Arabic manuscripts)*, Moscow, 1982, pp. 230–241.

Chronological list and number of acquisitions

		Total per year
1819	Lieven Kh.A. (1); Rosenberg (5); Rousseau J.L. (500)	506
1820	Wangg L., von (1); Uvarov S.S. (1)	2
1821	Panzner (1); Schilling von Kanstadt P.L. (2)	3
1825	Rousseau J.L. (200)	
1826	Castiglioni F. di (2)	
1827	Eichwald, von (2)	
1828	Fraehn Ch.D. (30)	
1829	Lorsbach G.V. (3)	
1834	Butenev A.P. (1)	
1835	Meshcherskii V. (2)	
1836	Ivanov (13)	
1837	Butenev A.P. (1); Shaba A.D. (11); North F. (1); Stracker (5); Sukhtelen P.K. (35); Fraehn Ch.D. (21); Hamacher (2)	76
1838	Dal' V.I. (1); Fraehn Ch. (4)	5
1839	Clot-bei (8); Obolenskii M.A. (1); Fraehn P.Ch. (1); Grigor'ev (1)	11
1840	Butenev A.P. (3); Dal' V.I. (1)	4
1842	Mullah Abd al-Hakim-effendi (1); Bode R.K. (2); Dal'V.I. (10); Kazebek A.K. (5); Fraehn P.Ch. (13); Fraehn Ch.D. (1)	32
1844	Colinati (1)	
1845	Library of the Ministry of Finance Academic Council (17)	
1847	Baidzhanov K. (1); Dagdarov (1); Jaubert A.P. (1); Teimuraz Bagrationi (1); Halil Iman-Muhammad (2)	6
1848	Bat'yanov (3)	
1849	Taktarov (1)	
1850	Kazimirskii (1)	
1851	Anichkov N.A. (1); Gotwald N.F. (1); Trigulov (3)	5
1852	Babadzhanov R. (1); Bakhikanov A.K. (24); Gotwald I.F. (8); Fraehn Ch.D. (17)	50
1854	Dittel V.F. (1); Faizkhanov Kh. (22); Khanykov N.V. (1)	24
1855	Khanykov N.V. (2)	
1856	Bezmenov (4); Pashino P.I. (8); Sonin N.Ya. (2); Khanykov N.V. (6)	20
1857	Dudshiraev U. (4); Kel'zi F.N. (1); Khanykov N.V. (2); Shegren A.M. (6)	13
1858	Vel'yaminov-Zernov V.V. (8); Sen'kovskii O.I. (4); Trigulov (5); Khanykov N.V. (32)	49
1859	Lerkh P.I. (46); Khanykov N.V. (27)	73
1860	Valikhanov Ch.Ch. (1); Gusev V. (1); Mel'gunov G.V. (1); Tolstoy I.M. (2)	5
1861	Bernstein G.Kh. (5)	
1862	Perovskii L.A. (8); Froman-Brun (3)	11
1863	Bartolomei N.A. (2); Berezin I.N. (3); Berget A.P. (3); Faizkhanov Kh. (6)	14
1864	Alekseev (1); Tolstoy I.M. (3)	4
1865	Vel'yaminov-Zernov V.V. (16)	
1866	Kohler (3); Quaritch B. (1); Faizkhanov Kh. (10)	14
1867	Graf R. (39); Kohler (6); Muller G. (18)	63
1868	Quaritch B. (1); Mukhlinskii A.O. (1)	2
1871	Dittel V.V. (1)	
1872	Vel'yaminov-Zernov V.V. (1)	
1874	Bakulin F.A. (1); Kartashov (1); von Kaufmann K.P. (38); Schuyler E. (1)	41
1875	Bakulin F.A. (3)	
1876	Fonton G.R. (19)	
1878	Sveshnikov N.I. (15)	
1880	Vullers I.A. (1); Quaritch B. (7); Smirnov S.M. (3)	11
1881	Smirnov S.M. (14)	
1882	Il'minskii N.I. (1); Fraehn P.Ch. (1)	2
1886	Muhammad-Ali Mahmud-oglu (1)	
1890	Kuhn S.L. (133); Radlov V.V. (33)	166
1891	Baraganskii I.M. (1); Salemann K.G. (1); Kalmykov A.D. (1); Kohler (4); Mezonov (1)	8
1892	Mikhaikov (1)	
1893	Quartich B. (9)	
1894	Lapin S.A. (1)	
1895	Bazlov (1); Polovtsev A.A. (2)	3
1896	Berezin I.N. (16); Imperial Archaeological Commission (2); Rannenkaumpf (1)	19

		Total per year
1897	Vyatkin V.L. (3); Gramenistkii D.M. (24); Denison-Ross E. (11); Salemann K.G. (96); Lyutsh Ya.Ya. (20); Nalivkin V.P. (1); Radlov V.V. (11)	166
1898	Veselovskii N.I. (3); Miller A.Ya. (1)	4
1899	Hartmann (1)	
1900	Kondakov N.P. (1); Makis (1); Mir-Salik Mirakbaev (34); Harrasovits O. (4); Censorship Committee (3); Bakh (1)	44
1901	Vyatkin V.L. (3); Cohen D. (2); Luytsh Ya.Ya. (4); Mir-Salih Mirakbaev (13); Bakh (1)	23
1902	Gartier E.K. (8)	
1903	Luntsh Ya.Ya. (1)	
1904	Bartold V.V. (16); Bogdanov L.F. (4); Frank U. (18); Yahuda (5)	43
1905	Abd al-Akhad (1); Belyaev I.A. (1); Popova (1); Petrov N.P. (1)	4
1906	Bogdanov L.F. (8); Brechet V. (8)	16
1907	Bogdanov L.F. (52); Desnitskii I.I. (10); Yahuda (5)	67
1908	Berezovskii M.M. (5); Borodin A.V. (3); Veidenbaum E.G. (1); Golenishchev V.S. (6); Salemann K.G. (34); Kalmykov A.D. (1); Lyntsh Ya.Ya. (3); Pospelov F.F. (3); Rosen V.R. (49); Samoilovich A.P. (6)	111
1909	Petrovskii N.F. (131); Khvol'son D.A. (4)	135
1910	Bogdanov L.F. (2); Golenishchev V.S. (1); Oldenburg S.F. (89); Pospelov F.F. (16); Razgonova E. (1)	109
1911	Adamov A.A. (4); Alim (1); Beneshevich V.N. (2); Muraviev N.N. (23); Florenskii A.A. (1); Khvol'son D.A. (1)	32
1912	Bogdanov L.F. (39); Davydov (2); Miller V.F. (1); Teben'kov M.M. (1)	43
1913	Bogdanov L.F. (139); Validov A.Z. (4); Dubenetskii I.I. (1); Kerem (1); Mlokosevich (1); Mukhanov (1); Nuri-bei (1); Pospelov F.F. (3); Purin (1); Samoilovich A.N. (34); Svir'shchevskii (1)	187
1914	Bogdanov L.F. (2); Validov A.Z. (21); Gues G. (2); Imperial mission in Athens (1); Krachkovskii I.Yu. (2); Kuzuni (1); Mishutuskhin (6); Muhammedov Yu.D. (1); Safiev (1); Filatov P. (1); Khilinskii (1)	39
1915	Bartold V.V. (1); Belyaev I.A. (4); Ivanov V.A. (41 and 1057); Moskalev A. (9); Serafimov (1); Smirnov S.M. (40); Chigogidze I.E. (1)	1154
1916	Bartold V.V. (4); Validov A.Z. (1); Van collection (1279); Zarubin I.I. (11); Ivanov V.A. (77); Melnikov V. (27); Marr N.Ya. (1); Samoilovich A.N. (2); Uspenskii F. (1)	1403
1917	Van collection; Gumilev N.S. (8); Dudin S.M. (1); Kalmykov A.D. (1); von Klemm V.D. (1); Minorskii V.F. (1); Oldenburg S.F. (1); Fath Allah Alu Hallk (1)	14
1918	Lemm O.E., von (1); Radlov V.V. (2); Semyonov A.A. (9)	12
1919	Winter Palace Library (41); Zhukovskii V.A. (33); Miller B.V. (1); People's Commissariat of Foreign Affairs (4); Polovtsev A.A. (31); Foreign Ministry School (527); Shileiko V.K. (1)	638
1920	Kostsov M.F. (1); Semyonov A.A. (1); Turaev B.A. (2); Faberge (11)	15
1921	Bartold V.V. (1); Berg L.S. (1); Weila G. (1); State Russian Museum (1); Peshkov A.M. (1); Semyonov A.A. (6)	11
1922	Institute of Living Oriental Languages (ILOL) (1); Museum of Anthropology and Ethnography (MAE) (1)	2
1923	ILOL (1); Foreign Affairs Commissariat (5); Pushkin House (1); Eberman V.A. (2)	9
1924	Academy of Material Culture (1); Bazilevskii A.A. (7); Krachkovskii I.Yu. (1); Stepanov D.K. (1); Tumanskii A.G. (1); Tsvetkov P.P. (7)	18
1925	Semyonov A.A. (1)	
1926	Kartavov P.A. (1); USSR Mission in Iran (25); Semyonov A.A. (26)	52
1927	Isheev A.I. (1); Kartasheva A.L. (1); Samoilovich A.N. (1); Saranchin M.M. (1); Tumanskii A.G. (1); Atyzgil'dinov (1)	6

		Total per year
1928	Andreev M.S. (3); Anuchin V.I. (22); Bartold V.V. (1); Vereshchagin I.S. (4); Gomolitskii P.N. (1); State Book Collection (8); Zinoviev A.V. (1); ILOL (4); Peretts V.I. (2); Popov V.V. (12); Yuvachev I.P. (1); Yudakhin K.K. (1)	60
1930	Bauer (1); Bertels E.E. (17); Paskhin N.F. (171); Starikov A.A. (1); Smirnov V.D. (1)	191
1931	Academy of Sciences Library (4); Mishchenko M.P. (7); Stark L.S. (1); Khalikov I. (1)	13
1932	Gordeev D.P. (1); Kamalov I.Z. (2); Trifonov V.T. (1)	4
1933	Bertels E.E. (16); Verkhovskii Yu.P. (1); Tajik affiliation of the Academy of Sciences (10); Central Geological Library (2)	29
1934	Archaeographic expedition (1202); Bakhidov S.G. (362); Papayan G.K. (1); Rastopchin F.B. (17); Smirnova N.K. (3); Stanishevskii A.V. (10); Bashkirov S.S. (2); Smirnov V.D. (4)	1601
1935	Alimov A.A. (1); Valeev K.G. (10); Vasiliev (1); Mumtaz S. (5)	17
1936	Alimov A.A. (111); Bikchentaev I.M. (66); Ivanov P.P. (1); Karaim National Library (1); Kraush O.A. (2); Tamaev A.N. (6); Charov M.M. (4); Shirvanov (1); Yusupov A.Kh.G. (18)	210
1937	Aidarov S.A. (3); Alimov S.A. (34); Mamedov I.M. (76); Margulan A.Kh. (4); Marr Yu.N. (2); Filonenko V.N. (2); Shamsutdinov Kh.K. (1)	122
1938	Alimov S.A. (171); Leningrad Archive of the Academy of Sciences (1); Academy of Sciences Library (1); Institute of the History of the Academy of Sciences, Leningrad (16); Institute of the Book, Document and Writing (18); ILOL (1); Petrov A.A. (1); Tamaev A.I. (31)	240
1939	Azerbaijan Division of the Academy of Sciences (4); Alikaev O. (1); Alimov S.A. (107); Barabanov A.M. (1); Belenitskii A.M. (1); Benediktov (5); Zabirov V.A. (13); Ivanov P.P. (2); Institute of the History of Material Culture (1); Mamedov I.M. (22); MAE (39)	196
1940	Alimov S.A. (21); Academy Archive (1); Ashurov K.M. (1); Zarifov M.Z. (29); Zarubin I.I. (1); Margulan A.Kh. (15); Pegushin V.A. (1); Pokrovskii N.I. (2); Cherevitskii A.A. (4)	75
1941	Alimov S.A. (28); Voinova K.N. (1); Ivanov P.P. (1); Likhachev P.V. (6); Margulan A.Kh. (11)	47
1942	Samoilovich A.N. (9)	
1943	Academy Archive, Leningrad (1)	
1944	Makkaveeva (1); Yunusov B.D. (17)	18
1946	Kufaev M.N. (2)	
1947	Academic bookstore in Leningrad (3); Aksakov Z.A. (1); Filonenko V.I. (11)	15
1948	Institute of Oriental Studies Library (1); Tamaev A.I. (12); Troitskaya A.L. (2); Udalets K.I. (1)	16
1949	Anitova Yu.V. (1); Zlatogorova T.S. (1); Foreign Affairs Ministry (1); Raina N.N. (1)	4
1950	Marr Yu.N. (12)	
1951	Museum of Anthropology and Ethnography (MAE) (1)	
1954	Academic bookstore in Leningrad (1); Museum of the History of Religion (78); Pisarchik A.K. (1)	80
1955	Academic bookstore in Leningrad (1)	
1956	Library of the Institute of Oriental Studies (10); Institute of the History of Material Culture (1)	11
1957	Academic bookstore in Leningrad (1); Mamedbeili Sh.D. (3)	4
1958	Academic bookstore in Leningrad (1); Library of the Institute of Oriental Studies (1); Library of the Institute's Leningrad Division (1); Logachev K.I. (1); Menirskii V.F. (1)	5
1959	Sotnikov S.N. (1)	
1960	Academic bookstore in Leningrad (1); Library of the Institute of Oriental Studies (7); Minorskii V.F. (3); Suleikin V.D. (1)	12
1961	Radvol V.V. (by the agency of the Leningrad Archive of the Institute) (41); Jouset V.P. (1)	42
1962	Library of the Institute of Oriental Studies (42); Shapshal S.M. (22)	64

		Total per year
1964	Academic bookstore in Leningrad (1); Library of the Institute of Oriental Studies (3); Gadzhikhalikov A. (5); Luk'yanov V.V. (1); Ramazanov S. (5); Semyonova I.V. (3)	18
1965	Leningrad Archive of the Institute of Oriental Studies (2); Academy of Sciences Library (1); Library of the Institute of Oriental Studies (5); Vil'chevskii O.L. (1)	9
1966	V.I.Lenin Library (1); Ivanov V.A. (3); Minorskii V.F. (26)	30
1967	Library of the Institute of Oriental Studies, Leningrad Division (2)	
1971	Library of the Institute of Oriental Studies (1); Romaskevich A.A. (by the agency of the Leningrad Archive of the Academy of Sciences) (6); Yakhin A.I. (1)	8
1972	Al'bun V.P. (1)	
1978	Asadullaev S. (1)	
1979	Gryaznevich P.A. (1)	
1980	Smirnova O.I. (2)	
1987	Statkevich T.A. (1)	

The most important Russian publications on Islamic manuscripts from the St. Petersburg Branch of the Institute of Oriental Studies, Academy of Sciences

I. Catalogues, surveys and bibliographic works dealing with collections in the ex-Soviet Union.

1931
Chaikin K.I., *Oriental manuscripts: Persian, Arabic, Turkish*, Moscow.

1938
Struve V.V. et al., *Documents relating to the history of the Turkmenians and the Turkmen regions*, vol II, *16th–19th centuries*. Sources from Iran, Bukhara and Khiva, Leningrad.

1939
Volin S.L. et al., *Documents relating to the history of the Turkmenians and the Turkmen regions*, vol. I, 7th–15th century. Arabian and Persian sources, Leningrad.

1941
Romaskevich S.A. et al., *Documents relating to the history of the Golden Horde*, vol. 2: *Extracts from Persian works*, Moscow-Leningrad.

1945
Krachkovskii I.Yu., *Arabic Manuscripts. Memories of Books and People*, Moscow-Leningrad.

1949
Krachkovskii I.Yu., *Bent over Arabic Manuscripts*. German translation by O.P. Trautmann, Leipzig.

1960
Krachkovskii I.Yu., *Selected Works*, Moscow-Leningrad, 6 vols.

1963
Akimushkin O.F., Borshchevskii Y.E., "Bibliography of Publications on Persian Manuscripts," in *People of Asia and Africa*, nos. 3 and 6.
The Collections of Oriental Manuscripts in the More Important Libraries of the USSR, Moscow.

1966
Rosenfel'd V.A., "Arabic and Persian manuscripts on physics and mathematics in Soviet libraries," in *Physics and Mathematics in the Lands of the Orient*, vol. I, Moscow.
Livotova O.W., Portugal' V.B., *Academy of Sciences Publications on Oriental Studies, 1726–1917*, Moscow.

1968
Antonovich A.K., *Byelorussian texts in Arabic script, their graphic and orthographic systems*, Lithuania.

1975
Urunbayev A.U., *The collection of Oriental manuscripts from the Academy of Sciences of the Republic of Uzbekistan*, Tashkent.

1977
Khalidov A.V., "Arabic manuscripts in the USSR and their study," in *Archeograficheski ezhegodnik*, Moscow.

1981
Lebedev V.V., "A description of Near Eastern and Central Asian manuscripts in the USSR," in *Izvestiya na narodnata bliblioteka*, 16/22.

1982
Mikhailova I.B., Khalidov A.B., *Bibliography of Arabic manuscripts*, Moscow.

II. Catalogues, surveys and bibliographical works dealing with collections in St. Petersburg (excl. the Asian Museum and the Institute of Oriental Studies)

1846–1850
Berezin I.N., "A description of Turkish-Tatar manuscripts in the libraries of St. Petersburg," in *Journal ministerstva narodnogo prosveshcheniya*, nos. 50, 54, 59 and 68.

1936
Belyaev V.I., *Arabic manuscripts in the collection of the Institute for Books, Documents and Letters, USSR Academy of Sciences*, Moscow-Leningrad.

1960
Khalidov A.V., *Catalogue of Arabic manuscripts in the Institute of Asian Peoples, USSR Academy of Sciences*, vol. 1: *Literary Prose*, Moscow.

1961
Mikhailova A.I., *Catalogue of Arabic manuscripts in the Institute of Asian Peoples, USSR Academy of Sciences*, vol. 2.: *Geography*, Moscow.
Miklukho-Maklai N.D., *A description of Tajiki and Persian manuscripts in the Institute of Asian Peoples, USSR Academy of Sciences*, vol. 2: *Biographical works*, Moscow.
Rudenko M.V., *A description of Kurdish manuscripts in the Leningrad collection*, Moscow.

1962
Bayevskii S.I., *A description of Tajiki and Persian Manuscripts in the Institute of Asian Peoples, USSR Academy of Sciences*, vol. 4: *Persian Encyclopaedic Dictionary (farkhangi)*, Moscow.
Muginov S.M., *A description of Uighur Manuscripts in the Institute of Asian Peoples, USSR Academy of Sciences*, Moscow.

1963
Akimushkin O.F., Borshchevskii Y.E., "Bibliographic material on Persian manuscripts," in *The peoples of Asia and Africa*, nos. 3 and 6, Moscow.

1964
Akimushkin O.F. et al., *Persian and Tajiki manuscripts in the Institute of Asian Peoples, USSR Academy of Sciences*, vol.2 (Catalogue of 2976 Manuscripts), Moscow (in the exhibition catalogue abbreviated to PTR).

1965
Mikhailova A.I., *Catalogue of Arabic manuscripts in the Institute of Asian Peoples, USSR Academy of Sciences*, vol. 3: *History*, Moscow.
Konov A.N. (ed.), *A description of Turkish manuscripts in the Institute of Asian Peoples*, vol.1: *History*, Moscow.

1968
Bayevskii S.I., *A description of Tajiki and Persian manuscripts in the Institute of Asian Peoples*, vol. 5: *Bilingual Dictionary*, Moscow.

1974
Berthels D.E. et al., "A description of manuscripts in the Asian Department of the Foreign Ministry," in *Pismennye Pamyatniki Vostoka*. Yearbook 1971, Moscow.

III. Catalogues and descriptions of the Asian Museum/Institute of Oriental Studies and its Collections

1817
Rousseau J.L., *Catalogue of a collection of 500 Oriental manuscripts*, Paris.

1846
Dorn B., *The Asian Museum of the Imperial Academy of Sciences in St. Petersburg*, St. Petersburg (in German).

1853
Dorn B., "The Islamic manuscript acquisitions of the Asian

Museum since 1850," in *Bull. Hist.-phil.*, vol. 10, St. Petersburg (in German).

1855
Dorn B., "A Report on the Fraehn Library bought by the Academy for the Asian Museum in 1852," in *Ch. M. Fraehni Opusculorum postumorum, pars prima*, St. Petersburg (in German).

1877
Rosen V.R., *The Arabic manuscripts of the Institute for Oriental Languages*, St. Petersburg; new edition Amsterdam (Celibus), 1971 (in French).

1881
Rosen V.R., *Brief notes on the Arabic manuscripts of the Asian Museum*, no. 1, St. Petersburg (in French).

1886
Rosen V.R., *The Persian manuscripts of the Institute for Oriental Languages*, St. Petersburg; new edition Amsterdam (Celibus), 1971 (in French).

1891
Günzburg D., Rosen V. et al., *Arabic manuscripts; Karshuni, Greek, Coptic, Ethiopian, Armenian, Georgian and Babys manuscripts in the Institute for Oriental Languages* (From the scientific collection of Oriental languages from the Education section of the Asian Department, Ministry of Foreign Affairs), St. Petersburg; new Edition Amsterdam (Celibus), 1971 (in French).

1894
Salemann C., "The Asian Museum in 1890" (with supplements), in *"Bulletin" de l'Academie*, vols. 3 and 10 (in French).

1897
Smirnow W.D., *Turkish manuscripts of the Institute for Oriental Languages*, St. Petersburg; new edition Amsterdam (Celibus), 1971 (in French).

1917
Krachkovskii I.Yu., *1289* "Arabic manuscripts from the Caucasus Front," in *Academy of Sciences Bulletin* Series VI, vol. 11. Idem. in *Selected Works*, vol. 6 1960.

1920
The Asian Museum of the Russian Academy of Sciences, 1818–1918. A brief review, St. Petersburg.

1932
Belyaev V.I., *Arabic manuscripts in the Bukhara Collection in the Institute of Oriental Studies, USSR Academy of Sciences*, vol. 2, Leningrad.

1953
Belyaev V.I., "Arabic manuscripts in the Institute of Oriental Studies," in *Uchonye zapiski Instituta Vostokovedeniya*, 6, Leningrad.
Tikhonov D.I., *Oriental manuscripts in the Institute of Oriental Studies*, idem, 6.

1955
Miklukho-Maklai N.D., *A Description of the Tajiki and Persian manuscripts in the Institute of Oriental Studies, USSR Academy of Sciences*, Moscow-Leningrad.

1956
Livotova O.E., "Principal writings on the Institute of Oriental Studies (1776–1854)," in *OIRV*, vol. 2, Moscow.

1958
Belyaev V.I., "Documents on the history, technology and culture of the peoples of Central Asia in Arabic manuscripts from the Institute of Oriental Studies collection", in *Reports of the 1st USSR Conference of Orientalists in Tashkent*, Tashkent.

1960
Miklukho-Maklai N.D. et al., "Some rare Persian and Tajiki manuscripts in the collection of the Leningrad Branch of the Institute of Oriental Studies," in *The XXV International Congress of Orientalists: papers presented by the USSR delegation*, Moscow (in English).
Muginov A.M. et al., *Turkish manuscripts in the collection of the Institute of Oriental Studies*, Moscow.

1972
Berthels D.E. et al., *The Institute of Oriental Studies of the Academy of Sciences of the USSR*, Moscow.

1974
Ivanov V.A. (ed.), "Lists of the manuscripts in the Bukhara collection of the Asian Museum," in *Pismennye pamyatniki vostoka*, Yearbook 1970 (compiled 1915–1918).

1975
Miklukho-Maklai N.D., *A description of Turkish manuscripts in the Institute of Oriental Studies*, vol. 3: *Historical Works*, Moscow.
Dmitrieva L.V., Muratov S.N., *A description of Turkish manuscripts in the Institute of Oriental Studies*, vol. II: *History, Biographies, Encyclopedia, Geography, Calendars*, Moscow.

1976
Kushev V.V., *A Description of manuscripts in Pashtu in the Institute of Oriental Studies*, vol. 8: *Persian Literature, 10th–13th centuries*, Moscow.

1979
Niyazov N., *A description of Persian and Tajiki manuscripts in the Institute of Oriental Studies*, vol. 8: *Persian Literature, 11th–13th centuries*, Moscow.

1980
Vorozheikina Z.N., *A description of Persian and Tajiki manuscripts in the Institute of Oriental Studies*, vol. 7: *Persian Literature, 10th–13th centuries*, Moscow.
Dmitrieva L.V., *A description of Turkish manuscripts in the Institute of Oriental Studies*, vol. 3: *Poetry and Commentaries on Poetic Works*, Moscow.

1981
Tumanovich N.N., *A description of Persian and Tajiki manuscripts in the Institute of Oriental Studies, USSR Academy of Sciences*, vol. 6: *Folklore (Tales and stories of entertainment)*, Moscow.

1986
Akimushkin O.F., "Collections of Eastern manuscripts of the Institute of Oriental Studies and their research," *in International Association of Oriental Librarians Bulletin*, no. 28-29 (in English).
Khalidov A.V. (ed.), *Arabic manuscripts in the Institute of Oriental Studies: A concise catalogue*, vol. 2, Moscow.

1987
Akimushkin O.F., "A contribution to the history of the development of the Institute of Oriental Studies' collection of Islamic manuscripts," in *Pismennye pamyatniki vostoka*, Yearbook 1978–1979.

1990
Braginskii V.I., Boldyreva M.A., "Les manuscripts malais de Leningrad," in *Archipel* 40.

1992
Rezvan E.A. "The data base on early Qur'an manuscripts: A new approach to the text history reconstruction," in *Proceedings of the 3rd International Conference on Multi-Lingual Computing* (Durham, 10–12 December 1992), Durham.

1994
Rezvan E.A., Polozin V.V., "Asiatic Museum Project: 1. Data base on Muslim seals," *in Proceedings of the 4th International Conference on Multi-Lingual Computing* (London 7–9 April 1994), Cambridge.

In preparation

Akimushkin O.F., *A description of Persian and Tajiki manuscripts in the Institute of Oriental Studies*, vol. 10: *Anthologies*.
Dmitrieva L.V., *Turkish manuscripts in the Institute of Oriental Studies: A concise catalogue* (a brief description of the complete collection of ca. 1,500 manuscripts (ca. 3,500 texts) (in Turkish).
Polozin V.V., *Druze Manuscripts in the Institute of Oriental Studies*.
Polozin V.V. et al., "Ex libris Marks of Islamic Manuscripts in the Institute of Oriental Studies," in *Petersburger Orientalistik*, St. Petersburg.

1994
Rodionov M.A. (ed.), "Epistles of Wisdom (Rasa'il al-hikma)," in *Petersburger Orientalistik*, St. Petersburg.

Unpublished catalogues

Card index of complete collection.
Hand written inventories.
Vakhidov S.G.: Hand written catalogue of Turkish Manuscripts (accession no. D-488).

IV Description of individual manuscripts in the St. Petersburg Branch of the Institute of Oriental Studies, St. Petersburg selection from the detailed bibliography

1864-1881
Wright W., *The Kamil of el-Mubarrad*, ed. for the German Oriental Society from the manuscripts of Leiden, St. Petersburg, Cambridge and Berlin, Leipzig.

1896
Gunztburg D., *The Diwan of ibn Guzman*, Book 1. *The text according to the sole manuscript in the Imperial Asian Museum of St. Petersburg*, Berlin (in French).
Tumanskii A.G., "A newly discovered 10th century Persian geographer and his account of the Slavs and Russians," in *The Academy of Sciences Bulletin*, vol. 10 (Ḥudūd al-ᶜĀlam, accession no. C-612).

1897
Schiaparelli C., *The canto of Ibn Hamdis*, Rom (accession no. C-30).

1898
Brockelmann C. (ed.), *Ibn Qulaiba's 'Ujun al-Akhbar*, vols. 1–5, Weimar-Strasburg 1898–1908 (Semitic Studies, ed. Berzold C., issue 18). (accession no. B-902).

1910
Hirschfeld H. (ed.), *The Diwan of Hassan b. Thabit*, London-Leiden (GMS, XIII) (accession no. B-13).

1913
Krachkovskii I.Yu., "The Egyptian historian Ibn Taghribirdi as a creative writer," in *Selected works*, vol. 2, 1960 (accession no. C-37).

1917
Ivanov V.A., "A biography of Shaykh Ahmad-i-Jam," in *JRAS* (accession no. 1928).

1925
Krachkovskii I.Yu., "The manuscripts of al-Ghazali's 'Destructio philosophorum' in The Asian Museum," in *Selected works*, vol. 6, 1960.
Ditto, "The Original Vatican manuscript of the Arabic translation of the Bible," *ibid.* vol. 6 (accession no. D-226 from the Collection of Gregory IV).

1926
Berthels E.E., *Bahtiar-nameh*. Persian text and glossary, Leningrad (accession no. A-100).
Barthold V., "A Zamahsari Manuscript with old Turkish glossary," in *Islamica*, vol. II, Book 1. (accession no. C-291).

1928
Salier M.A., "The Leningrad manuscripts of One Thousand and One Nights", in *The Academy of Sciences Bulletin*, No. 3 (accession no. B-1114).

1929
Borisov A.Y., "The Arabic original of the Latin version of Aristotle's so-called *Theologia*" (*Kitab Aristatalis al-failasuf*), in *ZKV*, vol. 5.

1930
Barthold V., *Hudud al-Alam. The Tumanskii-Manuscript*, Leningrad (accession no. C-612), english ed. Oxford 1937 (Gibb Memorial Series, vol. XI).

1931
Kahle P. et al., "The chronicle of Ibn Ijas," in *Bibliotheca Islamica* V, c, d, e, 1931–1936 (accession no. C-728).

1934
Gyuzal'yan L.T., D'yakonov M.M., *The "Shah-nameh" Manuscripts in the Leningrad collections*, Leningrad (description of 29 Manuscripts), new Edition on micro-fiche: Inter Documents, Zug, 1976.

1938
Borisov A.Y., "Miniatures from the 'Book of Maqamat' by al-Hariri," in *Milestones from the times of Rustavelli*, Leningrad (accession no. C-23).

1947
Berthels E.E. (ed.), *Nizami Gandjawi: Sharaf-nameh*, XX (2), Baku (accession nos. C-57 and C-1735).
Ditto, *Nizami Gandjawi: Ikbalnameth*, ibid XX (1), Baku.

1957
Shumovskii T.A., "Three unknown seafarers by Ahmad ibn Majid (Vasco da Gama)," in *A Manuscript (Unikat) in the Institute of Oriental Studies*, Mocow - Leningrad (accession no. B-992).

1958
Muginov A.M., *A Unique Persian manuscript by Rashid al-Din* (accession no. C-375).

1959
Berthels E.E., *Wahid Tabrizi: Djam'i muhtasar. Treatise on the art of poetry*, Moscow (accession nos. A-483 and C-857 in the Foreign Office collection).
Boldyrev A.N. (ed.), *Ta'rih-i'*

Badakhshan (The Story of Badakhshan). Photographic reproduction, Leningrad (accession no. B-2311).

1960

Ali-Zade A.A., *Nizami Gandjawi: The treasurehouse of secrets*, Baku (accession nos. C-57 and C-1735).

Berthels E.E. (ed.), *Nizami Gandjawi: Khusrau and Shirin*, ibid.

Borshchevskii Yu.E., *Muhammad ibn Nadjib Bakran: Djahan-nameh (Book about peace)*, facsimile edition, Moscow (accession no. C-612).

Gryaznevich P.A., *An anonymous 11th century Arabic manuscript (History of the Caliphs)*, edited text, translation and commentary. Moscow (accession no. C-1119: Cat. no. 16).

Miklukho-Mackay N.D. (ed.), *Muhammad Qasim: Nameh-yi 'Alamarayi Nadari* (Nadirs book beautifying the world), facsimile edition, *ibid.* XIII (accession no. D-430-I).

Berthels E.E. (ed.), *Firdausi: Shah-nameh.* Text. Idem, II (vol. 1; vol. 2, 1862) (accession nos. C-822 and C-1654 in the Asian Peoples Institute of the Academy of Science collection).

1961

Petrov P.P., *Muhammad-Qasim: Shah Nadir's Indian Campaign*, russian translation, Moscow (accession no. D- 430-11).

1962

Tveritinova A.S., Petrosyan Yu.A. (eds.), *Hasayn: Bada'i al-waqa'i'i* (astonishing events). Parts I, II, Moscow (accession no. C-564: Cat. no. 47).

1967

Grayaznevich P.A., *The History of the Caliphs*, facsimile edition, Moscow (accession no. C-1911; Cat no. 16).

1984

Prozorov S.M., "Al-Fahri's work on the history of religions (11th-15th centuries)," in Prozorov S.M., Gryaznevich P.A. (eds.), *Islam: Religion, Society, State*, Moscow (accession no. B-629).

1988

Prozorov S.M., *'Ali ibn Muhammad ibn 'Aballah al-fahri: Kitab talkhis al-baian fi sikr firak ahl al-adyan*, facsimile edition, Moscow (accession no. B-629).

In Preparation

Rodionov M.A., "The 'Epistles of Wisdom' as a cultural milestone", in Rodionov M.A. (ed.), *The Epistles of Wisdom (Rasa'il al-hikma)*, facsimile edition and translation of epistles nos. 1, 2, 4, 5, *"Petersburger Orientalistik,"* St. Petersburg, 1994 (accession no. A- 173).

Rezvan E.A., Alikberov A., A 15th Century Mamluk manuscript on the *Art of War*, facsimile edition, London, 1995 (accession no. C-686; Cat. no. 34).

Borges H.L., *Various years of prose*, Moscow, 1984.

Bibliography*

Abbot N., "The Kurrah papyri from Aphrodito in the Oriental Institute," in *Studies in Ancient Oriental Civilization*, 15, Chicago, 1938.

Abbot N., *The rise of the North Arabic script and its Kur'anic development, with a full description of the Kur'an manuscripts in the Oriental Institute*, Chicago, 1939.

Adamova A., Grek T., *Miniatures from Kashmiri manuscripts*, Leningrad, 1976.

Akimushkin O. F., Ivanov A. A., *Persidskiye miniyatyury, XIV–XVII vv.*, Moscow, 1968 (*Persian miniatures from the 14th–17th centuries*).

Akimushkin O. F., Kushev V. V., Miklukho-Maklai N. D., Muginov A. M., Salakhetdinova M. A., *Persidskiye i tadzhikskiye rukopisy Instituta Narodov Azii, AN., SSSR (Kratkii Alfavitnyi Katalog)*, Moscow, 1964 (*Persian and Tajiki manuscripts in the Institute of Asian Peoples, the USSR Academy of Sciences. A concise alphabetical catalogue*).

Akimushkin O. F., "Litsevaya rukopis iz sobraniya Instituta Narodov Azii AN, SSSR", *Blizhnii i Srednii Vostok*, Moscow, 1962 ("Illuminated manuscripts in the collections of the Insitute of Asian Peoples, the USSR Academy of Sciences" in *The Near and Middle East*).

Akimushkin O. F., *Opisaniye persidskikh i tadzhikskikh rukopisei Instituta vostokovedeniya, RAN*, vyp. 10, Moscow, 1993 (*A description of the Persian and Tajikistan manuscripts in the Institute of Oriental Studies, Russian Academy of Sciences*, 10th ed.).

Akimushkin O. F., "Zametki o persidskoi rukopisnoi knige i eyo sozdatelyakh." *Ocherki istorii kultury srednevekogo Irana. Pismenost' i literatura*, Moscow, 1984 ("An appraisal of the Persian manuscript and its creators" in *A study of the cultural history of Medieval Iran. Writing and literature*).

Arendt V., "Grecheskii ogon' (tekhnika ognevoi borby do poyavleniya ognestrelnogo oruzhiya)," *Arkhiv istorii nauki i tekhniki*, Moscow, 1936 ("Greek fire [fire battling techniques before the invention of fire-throwing weaponry]", in *An archive concerning the history of science and technology)*, pp. 129–203.

Ashrafi M., *Persian-Tajik Poetry in XIV–XVII centuries, miniatures from USSR collections*, Irfon, Dushanbe, 1974.

Ashtor E., *Histoire des prix et des salaires dans l'Orient médiéval*, Paris, 1969.

Ayalon D., *The Mamluk Military Society*, London, 1979.

Barsev P. (trans), *Podrobnoye opisaniye puteshestviya golshtinskogo posol'stvo v Moskoviyu i Persiyu v 1633, 1636 i 1639 godakh, sostavlennoye sekretarem posol'stva Adamom Oleariem*, Moscow, 1870 (*A detailed account of travels by the Golshtein Delegation to Moscow and Persia in 1633, 1636 and 1639, compiled by the Delegation's Secretary, Adam Oleary*).

Bartold V., *Izdaniye Hudud al-Alam. Rukopis Tumanskogo. S vvedeniem i ukazatel'em V. Bartolda*, Leningrad, 1930 (A publication of *Hudud al-Alam. A Tumanian manuscript*. Forward by V. Bartold).

Becker C. H., *Beitrage zur Geschigte Agyptens unter dem Islam*, Strasburg, 1902–1903.

Belyaev V. I., "Arabskie rukopisi Bukharskoi kolektsii Aziatskogo museya Instituta Vostokovedeniya, AN, SSSR" - *Trudy Instituta Vostokovedeniya, AN, SSSR*, Leningrad, 1932 ("The Arabic manuscripts of the Bukhara collection at the Asiatic Museum, Institute of Oriental Studies, the USSR Academy of Sciences," in *The Works of the Institute of Oriental Studies* AS, USSR), pp. 1–52.

Belyaev V. I.., "Arabskiye rukopisi v sobranii Instituta Vostokovedeniya, AN, SSSR," *Uchonye zapiski Instituta Vostokovedeniya*, Leningrad, 1953 ("Arabic manuscripts in the collections of the Institute of Oriental Studies, the USSR Academy of Sciences," in *Learned notes from the Institute of Oriental Studies*).

Belyaev V.I., "Anonimnaya istoricheskaya rukopis v kolektsii V. A. Ivanova v Aziatskom musee" – *Zapiski kollegii vostokovedov*, 5, Leningrad, 1930 ("Anonymous historical manuscripts in the V. A. Ivanov collection in the Asiatic Museum" in *Notes by the collegium of Orientalists*, 5), pp. 15–37.

Berthels D. E., "Vvediniye" v *knige Aziatskoi musei – Leningradskoe otdel'eniye Instituta Vostokovedeniya, AN; SSSR*, Moscow, 1972 ("Introduction," *The Leningrad Branch of the Institute of Oriental Studies, the USSR Academy of Sciences*).

Berthels D. E., Dmitriev L. V. (eds), and Zhukovski V. A., "Opisaniye rukopisei Uchebnogo Otdeleniya vostochnykh yazykov pri Aziatskom departamente Ministerstva inostrannykh del", *Pis'mennye pamyatniki Vostoka, Ezhegodnik, 1971*, Moscow, 1974 ("A description of manuscripts in the Education Branch of Eastern languages at the Asiatic Department of the Ministry of Foreign Affairs" in *Literary monuments of the East, [annual reports], 1971*), pp. 455–463, 480.

Borges H. L., *Proza rasnykh let*. Moscow, 1984 (*Various years of prose*).

Borisov A.Y., "Miniatyury 'Knigi Makam' al-Hariri," *Pamyatniki epokhi Rustavelli*. Leningrad, 1938 ("Miniatures from the 'Book of Maqamat' by al-Hariri," in *Milestones from the time of Rustavelli*), pp. 171-178.

Borshchevskii I.E., "The Story of the Acquisition of the Ardebil Collection of Manuscripts by Russia," in *Proceedings of the IV Conference of the USSR concerning Iranian Philology (papers)*, Tbilisi, 1970, p. 158.

Bosworth C.T., *Ḳurra b. Sharīk II, Encyclopédie de l'Islam*, V, nouvelle édition, 1986.

Braginskii I., Rakhimi M., Tursunzade M., and Ulug-zade M. (eds), *Antologiya tadzhikskoi poesii s drevneishikh vremyon i do nashikh dnei*, Moscow, 1951 (*An anthology of Tajiki poetry from antiquity to the present time*).

Brockelmann C., *Geschichte der Arabischen Literatur*, Berlin, vol. I, 1898, vol. II, 1902.

Brocket A., "Aspects of the physical transmission of the Qur'an in 19th century Sudan: script, decoration, binding and paper," in *Manuscripts of the Middle East*, vol. 2, Leiden, 1987.

Brocket A., *The Value of the Hafs and Warsh Transmission for the textual history of the Qur'an*, Leiden, 1987.

Coomaraswamy Anand K., *Les minatures orientales de la Collection Goloubew au Museum of Fine Arts de Boston*, Paris and Brussels, 1929.

Corriente F., *Ibn Quzman. Cancionero andalusi*, Madrid, 1989.

De Ginztburg D., *Le divan d'Ibn Guzman... Le texte d'apres le manuscrit unique du Musée Asiatique Imperial de St. Pétersbourg*, Berlin, 1896.

Deroche F., *Catalogue des manuscrits arabes. Deuxième partie. Manuscrits musulmans. Tome 1, Le manuscrits du Coran. Aux origines de la calligraphie coranique*, Paris, 1983.

Dmitrieva L. V., *Opisaniye tyurkskikh rukopisei Instituta Vostokovedeniya AN, SSSR.*, vyp III: *Poeziya i kommentarii k poeticheskim sochineniyam, poetika*, Moscow, 1980 (*A description of the Turkish manuscripts in the Insitute of Oriental Studies, the USSR Academy of Sciences*, 3rd ed.: *Poetry and commentaries for poetic works*).

Dodkhudoeva L. N., *Poemy Nizami v srednevekovoi miniatyurnoi zhivopisi*, Moscow, 1980 (*Poems by Nizami in Medieval miniature paintings*).

Dorn B., *Das Asiatische Museum der Kaiserlichen Akademie der Wissenschaften zu St. Petersburg*, St. Petersburg, 1846.

Dorn B., "Über die vom General-Adjutanten von Kaufmann dem Asiatischen Museum verlehrten morgenlandischen Handschriften," *"Bulletin" de l'Academie Imperial des sciences de St. Petersbourg*, 20, St. Petersburg, 1875.

Eche Y., *Les bibliothèques arabes publiques et semi-publiques en Mésopotamie, en Syrie, et en Egypte au Moyen-Age*, Damascus, 1967.

Endress G., *Handschriftenkunde – Grundriss der Arabischen Philologie 1: Sprachwissenschaft hrsg. von Fisher, W.*, Wiesbaden, 1982.

Ettinghausen R., *Arab Painting*, Geneva, 1962.

Gintzburg I. I., "Kratkii obzor evreiskogo fonda Rukopisnogo otdela Instituta vostokovedeniya, AN SSSR" – *Bibliografia Vostoka*, vyp. 10, 1936 ("A brief review of the Jewish collection in the Manuscript Department at the Institute of Oriental Studies, the USSR Academy of Sciences" in *Bibliography of the East*, 10th ed.).

Grabar O., *The Illustrations of the Maqamat*, Chicago-London, 1984.

Graf G., *Geschichte der christlichen arabischen literatur*, Città del Vaticano, Rome, vol. I, 1944, vol. II, 1949.

Gratzl E., Creswell, K. A. S., and Ettinghausen R., "Bibliographie der islamischen Einbandkunst 1871–1956," in *Ars Orientalis*, II, Ann Arbor, 1957, pp. 519–540.

Gray B., *La Peinture Persane*, Geneva, 1977.

Gray B., "The Fourteenth Century," in Gray B. (ed.) in *The Arts of the Book in Central Asia, 14th–16th Centuries*, London, 1979.

Grohmann A. (ed), "Corpus papyrorum Raineri III," *Series Arabica*, Vienna, 1924.

Grohmann A., *Arabic papyri in the Egyptian Library*, 1. *Protocols and legal texts*, Cairo, 1934.

Grohmann A., *Arabische Paläographie*, vols. 1 and 2, Vienna, 1967, 1971.

Grohmann A. and Arnold Th. W., *Denkmaler Islamischer Buchkunst*, Munich, 1929

Grube E., "Pre-Mongol and Mamluk painting," in Robinson B. W. (ed.) in *Islamic Painting and the Arts of the Book*, London, 1976, pp. 72–81.

Gryaznevich P.A., *Arabskii anonim XI veka*, Moscow, 1960 (*Arabic anonyms of the 11th century*).

Gryaznevich P.A., *Istoriya Khalifov anonimnogo avtora XI v, facsimile rukopisi*, Moscow, 1967 (*History of the Caliphs by an anonymous author of the 11th century*, facsimile ed.).

Gyuzal'yan L. T. and D'yakonov M. M., *Iranskiye miniatyury v rukopisakh Shah-name leningradskikh sobranii*, Moscow-Leningrad, 1935 (*Iranian miniatures in the Shahnama manuscripts in the Leningrad collections*).

Haldane D., *Mamluk painting*, Warminster, 1978.

Indiiskiye miniatyury XVI–XVIII vekov iz sobraniya Instituta Vostokovedeniya AN SSSR. Leningradskoye otdeleniye, Leningrad, 1988 (*Indian miniatures of the 16th–18th centuries from the collections of the Leningrad Branch of the Institute of Oriental Studies, the USSR Academy of Sciences*).

Ivanov V. A., *Spiski rukopisei Bukharskoi kolektsii*, Moscow, 1979 (*Lists of the Bukhara manuscript collection*).

Ivanov V. A., "Spiski rukopisei Bukharskoi kolektsii." Predisloviye i primechaniye Yu. E. Borshchevskogo. *Pis'mennye pamyatniki vostoka*, Moscow, 1974 ("Lists of the Bukhara manuscript collection." Forward and annotations by Yu. E. Borshchevskii, in *Literary monuments of the East*), p. 412.

Ivanow A. A., "The Life of Muhammad Zaman. A reconsideration," in *Iran*, London, 1976.

Juinboll T. G., and Mathes B.F., *Sochineniya Ibn Taghribirdi – po istorii Egipta*, 1852, 1861 (*Ibn Taghribirdi on the history of Egypt)*.

Kerimov K., "Azerbaizhanskiye miniatyury," *Ishyg*, Baku, 1980 ("Azerbaijani miniatures," in *Ishyg*), pp. 17–22.

Khalidov A. B. (ed), and the Authors Collective, *Arabskie rukopisi Instituta Vostokovedeniya: kratkii katalog*, Moscow, 1986 (*Arabic manuscripts in the Institute of Oriental Studies. A concise catalogue*).

Khalidov A.B., *Arabic Manuscripts and the Arab Manuscript Tradition*, Moscow, 1985.

Khalidov A. B., *Katalog arabskikh rukopisei Instituta Narodov Azii Akademii Nauk SSSR.* vyp. 1: *Khudozhestvennaya proza*, Moscow, 1960 (*A catalogue of Arabic manuscripts in the Institute of Asian Peoples, the USSR Academy of Sciences*, 1st ed.: *Literary prose*).

Khalidov A. B., *Kitab al-manazil wa-l-diyar (Kniga stoyanok i zhilishch)*, Moscow, 1961 (*Kitāb al-manāzil wa al-diyār. A book of halting places and encampments*).

Krachkovskaya V. A., "Miniyatyury *Maqam* al-Hariri leninragradskoi rukopisi C-23 Instituta narodov Azii AN SSSR" – *Uchonye zapiski Leningradskogo gosudarstvennogo universiteta. Seriya vostokovecheskikh nauk*, Leningrad, 1962 ("Miniatures from the *Maqamat* by al-Hariri from the Leningrad manuscript

C-23 at the Institute of Asian Peoples, the USSR Academy of Sciences," in *Learned notes from the State University of Leningrad, Oriental studies series*), pp. 171–184.

Krachkovskaya V. A., and Krachkovskii I. Yu., *Drevneishii arabskii dokument iz Srednei Azii – Sogdiiskii sbornik*, Leningrad, 1934 (*An ancient Arabic document from Central Asia, Sogdian collection*).

Krachkovskii I. Yu., *Pissmo iz Sogdiany – Nad arabskimi rukopisyami*, Moscow-Leningrad, 1948 (*Letter from Sogdia. Concerning Arabic manuscripts*).

Krachkovskii I. Yu. (ed), *Trudy vtoroi sessii assosiatsii arabistov, 19–23 oktyabrya, 1937 goda*, Moscow, 1941 (*Proceedings of the second session of the Arabists' Association, 19th–23rd October, 1937*).

Krachkovskii I. Yu., *Arabskaya rukopisnaya kniga v sobranii instituta knigi, dokumenta, pissma Akademii Nauk SSSR*, Moscow-Leningrad, 1936 (*The Arabic manuscript in the collections of the Institute of books, documents and letters, the USSR Academy of Sciences*).

Krachkovskii I. Yu., "Arabskie rukopisi iz sobraniye Grigoriya IV patriarkha Antiokhiiskogo," *Izvestiya Kavkazskogo istoriko-archeologicheskogo instituta v Tiflise*, II, 1927 ("Arabic manuscripts from the collections of Gregory IV, the patriarch of Antioch" in *News from the Caucasian History and Archaelogy Institute in Tiflisi*).

Krachkovskii I. Yu., *Izbrannye sochineniya*, Moscow-Leningrad, 1955 (*Selected works*, vol. 1).

Krachkovskii I. Yu., *Izbrannye sochineniya*, Moscow-Leningrad, 1960 (*Selected Works*, vol. 5).

Krachkovskii I. Yu., *Memories of libraries and people*, Moscow-Leningrad, 1953.

Krachkovskii I. Yu., *Nad arabskimi rukopisyami. Listki vospominanii o knigakh i lyudyah*, Moscow-Leningrad, 1948 (*Concerning Arabic manuscripts. Memories of books and people*).

Krachkovskii I. Yu., *Ocherki po istorii russkoi arabistiki*, Moscow-Leningrad, 1950 (*A study on the history of Russian Arabists*).

Krachkovskii I. Yu., *Pamyati akademika Rozena*, Moscow-Leningrad, 1947 (*In memory of the Academician Rosen*).

Krachkovskii I. Yu., "Perepishchik rukopisi *Tahafut al- Falasif*, al-Ghazali Aziatskogo muzeya" - *Doklady Akademii Nauk, SSSR*, Leningrad, 1925 ("The scribe of the manuscript *Tahafut al-Falasif*, by al-Ghazali in the Asiatic Museum." A paper by the USSR Academy of Sciences).

Krachkovskii I. Yu., "Rukopis *Destructio philosophorum* al-Ghazali v Aziatskom musee" – *Doklady Akademii Nauk SSSR*, Leningrad, 1925 ("The manuscript *Destructio philosophorum* by al-Ghazali in the Asiatic Museum." *A paper by the USSR Academy of Sciences*).

Krachkovskii I. Yu., "Neizvestnoye sochineniye – avtograf siriiskogo emira" – *Zapiski kollegii vostokovedov*, Leningrad, 1925 ("An unknown work—an autograph of a Syrian emir." *Notes by the collegium of Orientalists*).

Kuhn E., *Barlaam und Ioasaph. Eine bibliographische literatur geschichtiliche Studien*, Munich, 1893.

Kuhn E., *Buddha in der abenlandischen Literatur*, Berlin, 1922.

Lammense H., "Un governeur omayyade d'Egypte, Qurra ibn Sarik, d'après les papyrus arabes." *Etude sur le siecle des Ommayyades*, Beirut, 1930.

Lentz T. W., and Lowry G. D., *Timur and the Princely Vision*, Los Angeles, Washington, 1989.

Mann J., *Texts and Studies in Jewish History and Literature*, Cincinnati, 1935.

Masāḥif Ṣanᶜa, *Dār al-Āthār al-Islāmiyya* (catalogue), Kuwait, 1985.

Mikhailova A. I., *Katalog arabskikh rukopisei Instituta Narodov Azii, Akademii Nauk SSSR*, vyp 3: *Istoriya*, Moscow, 1965 (*A catalogue of Arabic manuscripts at the Institute of Asian Peoples, the USSR Academy of Sciences*, 3rd ed.: *History*).

Mikhailova A. I., *Katalog arabskikh rukopisei Instituta Narodov Azii Akademii nauk SSSR*, vyp. 2 . *Geograficheskiye sochineniya*, Moscow, 1961 (*A catalogue of Arabic manuscripts in the Institute of Asian Peoples, the USSR Academy of Sciences*, 2nd ed.: *Geography*).

Mikhailova A. I., "Litsevaya arabskaya rukopis', perevoda grecheskogo khronografa XVII v." – *Palestinskii sbornik*, Moscow-Leningrad, 1966 ("An illuminated Arabic manuscript, translated from the Greek chronology of the 17th century," in *Palestinian collection*).

Minorski V., *Hudud al-'Alam "The Regions of the World," a Persian Geography 372 A.H. – 982 A.D.*, London, 1937.

Mostafa M., "An illustrated manuscript on chivalry from the late Circassian Mamluk period," in *BIE*, No. LI, Cairo, 1969–1970, pp. 1–14.

Nasbradi, Muhammad-Tahir, *Tazkireh*, Teheran, 1937.

Nemoy L. (ed), *Karaite Anthology. Excerpts from the Early Literature. Translated from Arabic, Aramaic and Hebrew Sources*, New Haven, 1952.

Nentzer A., "*Shahzadeve ve Tzusy" mat Elisha b. Shemu'el. – Pe 'Amim (Studies in the cultural heritage of Occidental Jewry)*, Ben Swi Study Institute of the Jewish community in the East, Jerusalem, 1988.

Nuryakhmetov A. H., *"Iskander-name* Ahmadi v rukopisnykh sobraniyakh Leningrada". *Kratkiye soobshcheniya Instituta Narodov Azii*, Moscow, 1965 ("*Iskandernāma* by Aḥmadī, in Leningrad manuscript collections," in *A brief report from the Institute of Asian Peoples*).

Pasternak B., "Okhrannaya gramota – Vozdushnye puti," *Proza rasnykh let*, Moscow, 1983 ("Sacred writing, Spiritual journeys," in *Various years of prose*).

Ragib Y., "L'ecriture des papyrus arabes aux premières siècles de l'Islam. Les premières écutures islamiques." *REMM 58*, Aix-en-Provence, 1990, pp. 14–28.

Rippin A. (ed), *Approaches to the History of the Interpretation of the Qur'an*, Oxford, 1988.

Robinson B. W., "The Turkman School to 1503," in Gray B. (ed.) *The Arts of the Book in Central Asia, 14th–16th centuries*, London, 1979, pp. 215–247.

Rosen V. R., *Notices sommaires du catalogue des manuscrits arabes du Musée Asiatique*, St. Petersburg, 1881.

Salemann C., "Das Asiatische Museum im Jahre 1890. Nebst Nachträgen," *"Bulletin" de l'Academie Imperial des sciences de St. Petersbourg, N. S. 3*, St. Petersburg, 1894.

Samoilovich N. A., "Materialy po sredneaziatskoi-turetskoi literature, XV v *ʿAṭāʿī*" – *Zapiski kollegii vostokovedov*, Leningrad, 1927 ("Material concerning Central Asian-Turkish literature of the 15th century by ʿAṭāʿī," *in Notes by the collegium of Orientalists*).

Sarre F., *Islamische Bucheinbande*, Berlin, 1923.

Sezgin F., *Geschichte des Arabischen Schrifttums*, vol. V, *Mathematik*, Leiden, 1974.

Soudavar A., *Art of the Persian Courts*, New York, 1992.

Stchoukine I., *Safavis 1, Les peintures des manuscrits Safavis de 1502–1587*, Paris, 1959.

Stchoukine I., "La peinture a Yazd au mileu de XVeme siècle" in *Syria*, vol. XI, Paris, 1963, pp. 139–145.

Tveritinnova A. S. and Petrosyan Yu. A., *Hussein. Beda'i ulveka'i*, Moscow, 1961.

Urunbayev A. U., *Sobraniye vostochnykh rukopisei Akademii Nauk, Uzbekskoi SSR*, Tashkent 1975 (*The collection of oriental manuscripts in the Uzbekistan Academy of Sciences, USSR)*.

Urunbayev A. U., "Sobraniye vostochnykh rukopisei Akademii Nauk. Uzbekskoi. SSSR" – *Materialy vsyosoyuznogo soveshchaniya – Printsipy nauchnogo opisaniya arkheograficheskikh pamyatnikov narodov vostoka*, Baku, 1977 ("The collection of Oriental manuscripts in the Uzbekistan Academy of Sciences, USSR," in *Proceedings of the USSR conference. Guidelines for the description of old, written documents of Oriental peoples)*, pp. 84–86.

Wellesz E. "An early al-Sufi manuscript in the Bodleian Library, Oxford," in *Ars Orientalis*, III, Ann Arbor, 1959, pp. 1–26.

Zabirov V. A., *Predvaritelnoye soobshcheniye o rabote arkhigeograficheskoi ekspeditsii Akademii Nauk – Istoricheskii sbornik*, 1935 (*A preliminary report of the work of the archeographic expedition of the Academy of Sciences, a historical account)*.

*Due to technical difficulties the page numbers of the majority of articles mentioned in the bibliographies are missing.

Printed by Fantonigrafica - Elemond Editori Associati